ADA
A Developmental Approach

ADA
A Developmental Approach

Fintan Culwin

PRENTICE HALL

New York London Toronto Sydney Tokyo Singapore

First published 1992 by
Prentice Hall International (UK) Ltd
Campus 400, Maylands Avenue, Hemel Hempstead
Hertfordshire HP2 7EZ
A division of
Simon & Schuster International Group

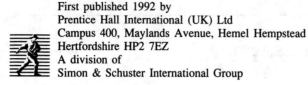

Typeset in 10/12pt Times Roman by
Columns Design and Production Services Ltd
Printed and bound in Great Britain by
Dotesios Limited, Trowbridge, Wiltshire

Library of Congress Cataloging-in-Publication Data

Culwin, Fintan.
    Ada, a developmental approach/Fintan Culwin.
      p. cm.
    Includes index.
    ISBN 0–13–489147–3 (pbk.)
    1. Ada (Computer program language) I. Title.
QA76.73.A35C85 1992
005.13'3--dc20   91–26175
                                                         CIP

British Library Cataloguing in Publication Data

Culwin, Fintan
    ADA: A developmental approach.
    I. Title II. Series
    005.362

    ISBN 0–13–489147–3

1 2 3 4 5 96 95 94 93 92

'For Leah and Seana ...'
... who else??

Contents

Preface

The impetus for this book came from a question asked by a student at the end of an introductory lecture. The lecture had just recommended that the students taking the course would require access to three separate books: one book was a reference manual for the programming language; one was concerned with program design; and one was concerned with software development, including testing. The question asked by the student was reasonable and, given students' incomes, predictable: which of the three books was the most important? The question does not have an easy answer. The title of the course was 'Software Development', a first-year course with no prerequisites.

Software development is concerned with the production of programs. The programs themselves require design and have to be implemented in a particular programming language. The programs which are produced have to be robust; the processes of testing ensure this. Having explained this to the student, there was an obvious supplementary question, why had a book which addresses all three themes not been written?

This book is an attempt to satisfy that student's question. In writing this book, I am aware that I will fail to satisfy many people. Experienced programmers who are unfamiliar with Ada will find the pace of the first part of this book unendurably slow. Experienced Ada programmers will not find this book useful as a program language reference. Those whose primary concern is program design or testing will find many omissions in this book.

Educationally, I have always been concerned with mixed-ability teaching. Many books which purport to introduce programming to beginners seem only concerned with high-ability students. As the needs of the software industry for skilled personnel expand, it is increasingly necessary to develop techniques which increase the proportion of students able to satisfy these needs.

In my experience, many students become disillusioned with software development at a very early stage. For many this is caused by the unreasonable pace of their initial courses. Many lecture courses and books fail to appreciate fully some fundamental educational considerations. The following are the most important of these considerations:

- Abstraction is only possible from concrete foundations.
- Presentation of a construct does not guarantee that it has been cognitively assimilated, merely that it may have been accommodated.

- The development of a new cognitive structure can only be made if prerequisite structures are already present.

Courses which do not take these and other considerations into account rely upon the student's being able to perform cognitive gymnastics, i.e. having a high level of ability. Even for such students their progress can be assisted by well-structured educational techniques. Consequently, the structure of this book is different from existing software development texts.

Block 1 consists of a very gentle introduction. Essential concepts, such as program production, imperatives, sequence, selection, iteration, simple data objects, simple operations, simple designs, procedurization, data flow, testing, project management, debugging and a basic Ada syntax are introduced.

Block 2 is mainly concerned with extending the knowledge of simple data objects and using this to develop concepts of complex objects and structures. The important concept of software modularization, most clearly expressed in Ada by the use of packages, and, via the packages, the concept of information hiding, are also introduced.

Block 3 introduces high-level software abstractions such as dynamic data types, generic modularization, as well as algorithm correctness.

Each block is suitable as a self contained unit. Blocks 1 and 2 together constitute a complete course in 'traditional' programming. The cognitive skills developed are directly transferable to other block-structured language environments such as C or Cobol 85. Block 3 adds to this the additional facilities provided by Ada, which are transferable to other advanced environments such as C++ or Modula 2.

The development of transferable skills is essential for students taking an initial software development course. Although Ada is being used here as an initial language, students should be exposed to other language environments. Consequently, it is not part of the intention of this book to provide a complete introduction to all parts of the Ada language; in particular, the tasking facilities of Ada have not been mentioned.

The design methodology used in Blocks 1 and 2 is an augmented JSP (Jackson Structured Programming), which is suitable for such transfers. Object-orientated design techniques are introduced in Block 3. These two design techniques should be regarded as supportive and complementary. Object-oriented techniques rely upon the implementation of the 'methods' but do not provide a technique by which such methods can be developed. JSP techniques are used in this book to allow the methods to be developed, without which object-orientated design cannot be implemented.

It is anticipated, but not certain, that students taking an initial Software Development course will progress to take a further course in Software Engineering. This book does not attempt to formally introduce software engineering concepts; it provides the cognitive foundations upon which such progression can take place.

Although I have stressed the deliberately slow pace of the book, the reaction of my students who have been suffering draft copies for the last two years has quite surprised me. In writing the book I had to make a choice between being terse and being verbose. My opinion is that I have been verbose; my students believe I have been somewhat terse. Their experience is one of being overwhelmed with a plethora of cognitive hurdles; however, they also report the exuberance of successfully negotiating them.

This book has taken two years to produce during which I have had support, encouragement, criticism and assistance from a large number of people. The greatest in number and perhaps most enthusiastic in support must be the five hundred or so students who have suffered the draft versions. The next in number are the members of the first year programming team, most noticeably my predecessor as team leader Jeff Naylor. The South Bank Polytechnic support staff, particularly Anne Keen of computer services, Eugene Holmes and Alan Lee of rephotographics provided cheerful and excellent service. Helen Martin and Richard Fidczuk from Prentice Hall displayed an exceptional degree of patience and tolerance with the many revisions and errors which seem to be part of the production of a tome of this length. I would also like to thank Richard Leigh, who copy-edited the text with great diligence.

I would like to believe that all errors and inconsistencies have been eliminated, however that would be as naive as claiming that any software I have authored is free of all bugs. Instead I will apologize in advance to any reader who encounters one and ask them to report it to me; in true 'public domain' style all I can promise is that they will at least be read.

Finally I have to thank Leah, Seana and Maria, who put up with less of a father or a lover than they might otherwise have had, particularly during many long weekends when a rational person would have shredded the entire text.

Fintan Culwin
September 1991
FINTAN@UK.AC.SOUTHBANK-POLY.VAX

Block 1

A Gentle Introduction to Software Development

Section 1.1

Programming in context

Programming is a complex activity. It will take the rest of this section to start to explain exactly how complex the activity of programming is, and from these considerations to obtain an understanding of what is required to become an effective programmer. A very simple answer to the question 'What is programming?' is that programming is the activity of designing, producing and maintaining programs. This does not answer the question completely but it gives an easier question to answer: what is a program?

1.1.1 What is a program?

There are many possible answers to this question. The simplest answer is that a program is a set of instructions which cause a computer to perform some specified task. This can be compared with the situation of one person giving a set of instructions to a second person, which if they are followed will allow the second person to perform a specified task. There are several requirements which have to be satisfied before the instructions can be successfully given:

1. The person giving the instructions must know how to perform the task. This may sound obvious, but it is not enough for the person to be merely relaying a set of instructions. Unless the method of performing the task is sufficiently understood by the person giving the instructions, that person will be unable to expand upon the instructions if the second person has difficulty in understanding.
2. The two people must have a common language and some method by which they can communicate.
3. The instructions must be given at a level suitable for the person receiving them. Someone who is inexperienced in performing such tasks will require more detailed instructions than someone who is skilled at performing such tasks.
4. The person giving the instructions will have to spend some time planning what instructions to give, how to phrase the instructions and in what sequence to give the instructions.

In order to give a set of instructions to a computer there are a similar set of considerations:

1. In order for a programmer to produce a set of instructions which will instruct a computer to perform a task, it is essential that the programmer understands the task. In addition the programmer must know a method of performing the task which is appropriate for a computer, methods which are appropriate for humans are not always appropriate for a computer.
2. The instructions have to be expressed in a form which the computer can understand, and entered in this form into a computer system. Computer languages, such as Ada, have been developed which allow instructions to be given to computers.
3. The computer language defines a basic level of instructions which the computer can understand. This basic level of instruction is not appropriate for most tasks and the programmer has to teach the computer a set of higher-level instructions, expressed in terms of the basic-level instructions, and then use these higher-level instructions to tell the computer how to perform the task.
4. As the basic level of the instructions which can be given to the computer is so basic, it is essential that the sequence of instructions is carefully worked out before they are given to the computer.

A computer program may be explained as simply as this, in the context of this book is much more as well. A computer program has some defined requirements which it should satisfy. The statement of what task the program must perform is known as the program's *specification*. One of the most fundamental aspects of developing a program is to ensure that it meets its specification.

A computer program is an economic product. Someone is paying for the development of the program in some way. This implies that development of the program has to meet economic limitations.

A computer program is an engineering product. It has some performance criteria to meet. These criteria might include how robust the program is, how big the program is or how fast the program is.

A computer program is usually a part of a system which includes computers and humans. The program has to be able to cooperate and interact with the other parts of the system.

A computer program is a model of some part of the 'real world' which exists beyond the computer system. It has to model the real world accurately and effectively.

A computer program is a cooperative effort. Most programs are so big that they can only be developed by a team of people working together.

A computer program is a unique product. This implies that the development of the program is not a mechanistic process and requires some degree of creativity.

A computer program has a life span and a life cycle. Programs are initially produced, are used for a period of time, during which they may require maintenance or changes, and at some time stop being used.

Most computer programs have to interact with people in some way. The aspects of the program which are visible to the user have to be designed with human capabilities considered.

When these considerations are added to the simple definition of a program which

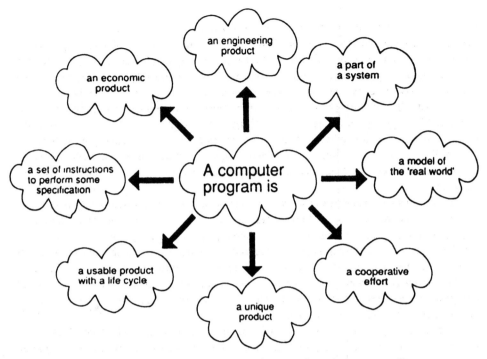

Figure 1.1.1 A computer program is ... and much more as well

was given above, its complexity becomes clear. The activity of programming can now be defined as the process of producing and then maintaining a program. These considerations are summarized in Figure 1.1.1.

1.1.2 The process of producing a program

From the discussion above, programming has been defined as the process of producing computer programs which fulfil given specifications. For any specification there are a large number of different computer programs which could be produced, all of which will fulfil the specification. The task of a programmer is to produce a computer program which not only fulfils the specification but also has the qualities described above.

The initial stage of producing a computer program is for the programmer concerned to ensure that he or she has a complete understanding of the program's specification. If the programmer has any problems with interpreting the specification, these must be resolved before any further progress can take place. The usual method of resolving any problems with interpreting the specification is for the programmer to discuss the problems with the sponsor of the program. The importance of this stage of producing a program cannot be overstated. It is not possible to produce an effective program without first having a complete understanding of the specification. The agreed interpretation of the program's specification constitutes the clearest statement of what the program is required to do. This interpretation will be used at all subsequent stages in the production of the program to guide its development and will also be required after the program has been produced to verify that the program fulfils the requirements of the specification.

Almost all programs have some requirement to interact with people in some manner. Many programs engage in a dialogue with the user, accepting input from the user, usually from a keyboard, and providing output for the user, usually on the terminal screen. Programs of this nature require the dialogue to be designed. The dialogue has to be designed in order to ensure that the user will be able to interact effectively with the program.

This aspect of a program is known as the *user interface* and is the only part of the program which the user is able to perceive directly. The user interface should be designed at this stage in the program's development, possibly overlapping with the previous stage of comprehending the specification. If the programmer designs the user interface at this stage in the program's development, the user interface can be presented to the program's sponsor and used as a vehicle of communication between the programmer and the sponsor when they are ensuring that they have the same understanding of the program's specification.

The next stage in the production of a computer program is to produce a design for the program instructions. The previous stages in program production have concentrated in refining the programmer's understanding of *what* has to be done; at this stage the emphasis changes to *how* the program will accomplish its specification.

Where a large program is being produced by a team of programmers, the initial high-level design will divide the program specification into a number of subprogram specifications. Each of these subprograms will implement a different requirement of the program, subsuming a part of the specification. The program itself will be assembled from these subprograms when they are complete. It is essential that each subprogram is produced according to its assigned subspecification in order to ensure that it will be able to interact correctly with the other subprograms when they are brought together.

The design of the component subprograms can proceed in a similar manner; the subprogram's specification can itself be divided into a number of subspecifications each of which will implement a part of the initial subspecification. This process of refining a specification into several component subspecifications, each of which can then further refined, continues until the resulting specifications are simple enough to be implemented in the programming language being used. This design process is known as *top-down stepwise refinement*.

The design process is not limited to the design of the instructions which comprise a computer program. The instructions which comprise a computer program can be considered as actions which the program will perform when it is used; an action has to have an object upon which it can act. The objects which program actions act upon are expressed in computer programs as data structures. In order for the actions to be fully effective the data structures have to be compatible with the intended actions.

For complex programs the designs of the data structures which will be used in the program are completed before the design of the actions which will be performed upon those data structures. As a computer program is regarded in some senses as a model of some aspect of the real world, the data structures which are implemented in a program are models of the corresponding real-world objects. It is recognized that data objects and actions which are closely modelled upon real-world objects and actions will result in better programs being produced.

This method of developing computer programs is known as *object-orientated* programming and is complementary to stepwise refinement. The elementary actions which can be performed upon program objects will comprise the lowest-level refinements of the stepwise refinement process.

Following the production and verification of the data structure and the program structure designs, they are realized as a computer program listing. This process is known as *coding*; the process of coding is not a complex task given an adequate design and an adequate knowledge of the facilities of the computer language being used.

Once the program has been coded and any coding errors corrected, it has to be tested. Testing is used to establish that the program fulfils its specification and can be designed from two perspectives. The first perspective is to use the specification to design the tests; as this method of testing does not require the code of the program to be available it is known as *black-box testing*. The program is regarded as a black box, a box which has inputs and outputs but whose internal workings are not visible.

An alternative, complementary testing perspective is known as *white-box* (or sometimes *glass-box*) *testing*. Here the internal workings of the program are considered relevant and the program design and code are used as the basis of designing the tests.

The process of designing the tests should commence from a black-box perspective as soon as the programming process is started. As was emphasized above, one of the most fundamental requirements of a program is that it fulfils its specification. Testing is the process by which it can be demonstrated that a program fulfils its specification. Where a large program is being produced by a programming team, one part of the team should be solely concerned with designing and applying the tests.

Where a large program is being produced, the application of the tests to the program should not be left until the complete program has been assembled. Testing is the major process by which the quality of the program is guaranteed The quality of the complete program is dependent upon the quality of its component parts; consequently, the quality of the component parts should be assessed as they are produced. This implies that testing should be applied to the individual parts of the program as they are completed and to the complete program once it has been assembled.

In addition to applying tests to the program components as they are completed, it is also advisable to apply tests to the program designs as they are completed. Unlike a computer program, which can be executed by a computer as it is being tested, it is not possible for a design under test to be executed by a computer. In order to test a design, the design has to be 'executed' by the programmer performing the tests as if the design were a computer program. The best method of doing this is for the designer to present the design and its assumed execution under test to a group of fellow programmers; it is hoped that any faults in the design will be detected as the design is presented. This method of validating a design, which can also be applied to the program listing, is known as a *peer review*.

It is hoped, but it is rarely the case, that a well-designed and well-implemented program will pass all its designed tests on the first attempt. If, or more realistically when, the program fails any of the tests the reasons why have to be investigated and the faults corrected.

This process of investigating, discovering and correcting a detected fault in a program is known as *debugging*. It can be a time-consuming and expensive process. In many programming projects the time spent debugging a program has exceeded the time initially spent developing the program. The nature of the faults and the amount of effort required to detect and correct them cannot be accurately estimated in advance; if testing a program is the last stage in production, then debugging can be disastrous to a production schedule.

The only method by which the amount of debugging required by a program can be reduced is to ensure the quality of all preceding stages in program production. Using the premise that locating and correcting a fault in a small program is easier than locating and correcting a fault in a large program, testing and debugging the component parts of a program as they are produced will cause the overall amount of debugging effort to be reduced and should result in the complete program requiring less debugging.

The initial version of the program which is produced is unlikely to last the entire lifetime of the program without maintenance or changes. A change in the real-world requirements which the program subsumes will require a consequential change in the program. It is also possible that an obscure fault in the program is not detected during program production and only becomes apparent after the program has been in use for some time.

Program maintenance is facilitated by program documentation; the stages and processes which are followed in the production of a program all generate documents of one type or another. These documents will be invaluable to a programmer who is given a task concerned with the maintenance of a program.

The documentation is also useful for the initial production of the program. The user interface design assists in the interpretation of the specification. The finalized design provides the basis for coding. The specification and the design provide the basis for the test plan. All of these documents will be required by the programmers who are producing the program while it is being produced.

The production of a program is illustrated in Figure 1.1.2. This diagram indicates that producing the documentation and designing and applying the tests take place at the same time as the processes of designing and coding the program.

1.1.3 Learning to program

The discussion above has concentrated upon the processes followed by professional programmers. Novice programmers are in a different situation; they cannot be expected

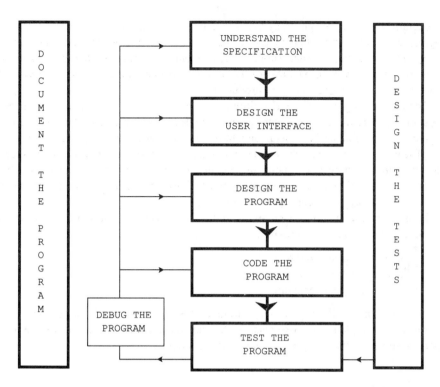

Figure 1.1.2 The production of a program

to have the experiences of producing designs, implementing programs or testing programs which an experienced programmer has assimilated from training and experience.

The contents of this book will provide the training aspects of an initial course in programming for a novice programmer. In order to learn how to program effectively, the experience of producing programs also has to be assimilated.

The production of programs by a novice programmer should follow the developmental process shown in Figure 1.1.2. There is a temptation for novice programmers to become involved with the coding process without first producing an adequate design. The production of undesigned program code, the removal of compilation errors and demonstration that the code fulfils some aspects of the specification produce an illusion of progress. The production and refinement of program designs and test plans do not seem to be as important.

The task of a novice programmer is to learn to produce effective programs which fulfil the specification provided. Like the professional programmer, the novice programmer is working with limited resources, the amount of time that he or she can reasonably allocate to producing programs. This reflects the commercial situation where an amount of resources, including time, has been allocated to the production of a program. The novice must learn to use the time effectively, and, although the production of program and data designs may not seem to be as important as the production of program code, the time taken in producing and debugging the program can only be reduced by producing a tested program design before coding is attempted. Thus the overall time taken in the production of the program will be reduced, although it will take longer before any program code is produced.

The novice programmer, by definition, does not have the assimilated experiences of producing programs and a consequent knowledge of the facilities offered by programming languages in general and those of any particular language. This is one area of learning to program where experimentation with program code is a good idea. If when learning to program a language facility is introduced whose meaning seems unclear, experimenting with a small program which uses the facility is the most effective way of assimilating the meaning of the facility.

Programming is a complex cognitive skill. The process of learning any skill can be summarized in a Confucian proverb:

> You tell me and I forget,
> You show me and I remember,
> I do it and I understand.

The text of this book will do the telling and some aspects of the showing. The experience of completing the exercises at the end of each section and the completion of programming projects will provide the understanding.

EXERCISES

1.1.1 In order to learn to program it will be necessary to write and compile programs on a computer system. To prepare for this make sure you know how to use the computer system. In particular, make sure you can edit text files, print text files and store text files in a directory.

The basic form of an Ada program

Having explained what a program is in some detail in the previous section, this section will concentrate upon the form of a simple Ada program.

In order to write any program a specification for the program must exist. In order to introduce the basic form of an Ada program a very simple specification will be used. A program is required which when executed will produce the following output on the terminal:

```
The answer to life,
the universe and everything is -
forty two.
```

A very useful answer, though not a very useful program. An Ada program which would implement this specification would be as follows:

```
0001    -- Fintan Culwin 7/9/89 v 1.0 b1s2p1 see text
0002    -- a simple Ada demonstration program to display
0003    -- the ultimate answer
0004
0005    with TEXT_IO; use TEXT_IO;
0006
0007    procedure b1s2p1 is
0008
0009       the_answer : constant STRING := "forty two.";
0010
0011    begin -- b1s2p1
0012       PUT_LINE( "The answer to life,   ");
0013       PUT_LINE( "the universe and everything is - ");
0014       PUT_LINE( the_answer );
0015    end b1s2p1;
```

The numbers on the left of the program listing are the *line numbers*; they are not required by the program and are included here in order to allow each line of the program to be easily referred to in the text.

The difference between words in the listing which are shown in **bold**, words which are shown in CAPITALS, and words which are shown in lower case will be explained later in this section. The line numbers and the **bold** effect *must not* be used for program listings which are intended to be used in the production of programs. A version of this program in a suitable format for use would be as follows:

```
-- Fintan Culwin 7/9/89 v 1.0 b1s2p1 see text
-- a simple Ada demonstration program to display
-- the ultimate answer

with TEXT_IO; use TEXT_IO;

procedure b1s2p1 is

   the_answer : constant STRING := "forty two.";

begin -- b1s2p1
   PUT_LINE( "The answer to life,  ");
   PUT_LINE( "the universe and everything is - ");
   PUT_LINE( the_answer );
end b1s2p1;
```

1.2.1 The program heading

The heading of the program is in lines 0001–0007. Lines 0001, 0002 and 0003 are strictly not part of the Ada program, although they are part of the listing. These lines start with the Ada term '--', which is a double hyphen (or minus sign). This term is an instruction to the compiler to ignore the rest of the line. Such lines of text in program listings are known as *comments*. Comments are included in program listings in order that anybody reading the listing can make better sense of it.

The comments in this example program are the minimum comments which should be included in any program. The first identifies the programmer, the date on which the program was written and its version number. The second comment, which will normally be much longer than this, gives some indication of what the program is designed to do and how the program will do it.

Line 0005 is required by this program as the program will be required to produce some text output; text output is composed from a sequence of characters. An Ada program does not know how to produce any output unless it has access to suitable facilities. The line '**with** TEXT_IO; **use** TEXT_IO;' will allow this Ada program access to suitable facilities for the input and output of text information. Including this line in the header of any Ada program will allow all parts of the program to input and output text information. A clause such as this in a program header is known as a *context clause*.

Line 0007 is the final line of the program header; an Ada program is composed of a number of parts which can be of differing types. The simplest of these types is known as a *procedure*, so a simple program such as this is composed of a single procedure. Line 0007 identifies the start of the procedure which in this case is also the program, and gives it a name. The name is 'b1s2p1', and has been invented by the programmer. The rules for inventing names will be given later in this section. This name was chosen to have the meaning 'Block 1 Section 2 Program 1'.

The header also contains lines 0003 and 0006. These lines are very important, although they contain nothing and Ada will do nothing with them. They are included to make the program easier to read, as they indicate where different parts of the program start and finish. The person who reads a program the most is the person who is developing the program; thus it is in the programmer's interest to make the program listing as readable as possible by the use of blank lines and comments where appropriate.

This heading can be used as a template for the heading lines of simple programs. The only parts which will change will be the program name and the comments. More complex programs may input and output information other than text information. Examples of how to include context clauses which will allow the program to access suitable facilities for the input and output of non-text information will be given as they are required in the rest of this block.

1.2.2 The program declarations

The declarations part of this program is between lines 0008 and 0010. In this program there is only one declaration made, the declaration of a *constant*. A constant is an object used within a program whose value will not change as the program executes.

Each constant has to have a name, a data type and a value. The name of the constant is given first, followed by a colon ':'. In this example the name of the constant, which is invented by the programmer, is 'the_answer'. The word '**constant**' follows the colon to indicate that this is a constant declaration and is followed by the data type of the constant, in this example 'STRING'. Objects of the data type STRING can be used to hold information composed of a sequence of characters.

Constants have to be given a value as they are declared. The value is indicated by the symbol ':=', which can be read here as 'has the value of'; and is followed by the actual value. String values are indicated in Ada programs by enclosing them within double quote marks ' " '. This string contains a total of ten characters, the five characters of the word 'forty', the three characters of the word 'two', the single space character which separates them, and the full stop which terminates the string.

This line illustrates the usage of **bold**, CAPITALS and lower case in the program listings presented in this book. The meaning of these different styles will be made clear below in Block 1 Section 2.4.

In a more complex program many constants might be declared, each of which is a separate program object. It is useful to produce a summary table of all the program objects used in a program. The table can then be used as a reference for which objects have been declared, what values they have and what they will be used for within the program. A constant table for this example program would be as follows:

PROGRAM CONSTANTS

NAME	TYPE	VALUE	NOTES
the_answer	STRING	"forty two."	the ultimate answer

The declarations section of the program also includes lines 0008 and 0010, which are blank lines, included to make the program listing more readable.

1.2.3 The program statements

The final part of the program is between lines 0011 and 0015; these are the *statements* which tell the Ada program what actions to perform when it is executed. In this program the executable part consists of a sequence of three 'PUT_LINE' statements.

The three statements are enclosed between a **begin/end** pair on lines 0011 and 0015. A **begin/end** pair in an Ada program listing is used to mark the start and end of a particular part of the program. The **begin/end** pair in this program delineates the start and the end of the procedure b1s2p1. As this is the procedure which identifies the program it is known as the *program procedure*. There can be many **begin/end** pairs in an Ada program; it is important to adopt some convention to indicate what they mark the start and end of.

The **begin** statement on line 0011 has been commented as the start of the procedure b1s2p1, which, being the only procedure of the program, is also the start of the program. The **end** statement on line 0015 could have been expressed simply as '**end**; '. Ada allows an **end** statement which marks the end of a procedure to include the name of the procedure as part of its syntax. Alternatively, the name of the procedure can be included as a comment following the semicolon symbol ';' which marks the end of the procedure, i.e. '**end**; -- b1s2p1'. It is recommended that the name of the procedure be included as a comment accompanying the **begin** statement, and be included within the syntax of the **end** statement, as shown in the example program.

The 'PUT_LINE' statement is one of the methods used by Ada to output text information; it is one of the facilities for output which this program gains access to by using the context clause on line 0005 of the listing. The effect of the PUT_LINE statement, when it is executed, is to output anything within the brackets which form part of the PUT_LINE statement upon the terminal screen and then advance the cursor to the next line of the terminal.

In lines 0012 and 0013 of this program the brackets contain *string literals*. String literals are sequences of characters which are contained between the opening and closing double quote marks, ' " '. A string literal was also used in line 0009 of this program to supply a value for the STRING constant. The effect of these lines when they are executed by the program is to output the sequence of characters between the quote marks but not to output the quote marks themselves.

In line 0014 the PUT_LINE brackets contain the term 'the_answer'. This is not a string literal as it is not included between double quotes; it is the name of the constant declared in line 0009 as having the value 'forty two.'. The PUT_LINE statement will display the value of the constant, in this case 'forty two.'.

If a PUT_LINE statement does not contain a literal then it may contain the name of a program object. What will be printed out is not the name of the program object but the value which it contains. To understand what happens you can think of the program trying to obey the PUT_LINE statements. For the first two statements the opening and closing quotes indicate that the literal contained within the quotes is to be output to the screen.

For the last statement the absence of quotes indicates that a program object is being referred to. Ada can be thought of as taking the name of the object from the statement and looking up in the data table to see if this object is known. In this case the object 'the_answer' is known, and its value can be found in the table. Once its value has been found it is output on the screen. If the object is not known then Ada will report it as an error.

Each of the PUT_LINE statements is a complete Ada statement and is terminated with a semi-colon ';'. The end of the program follows line 0015 of the listing, which includes a semicolon to terminate the procedure. The declaration of a constant on line 0009 requires a semicolon to terminate it. The context clause on line 0005 consists of two declarations, a **with** and a **use**, each of which requires a semicolon to terminate it.

When this program is executed by the computer the sequence of statements which form the executable part of the program are each obeyed, in the sequence specified in the listing. The effect of the execution of the three PUT_LINE statements is to output the three lines of text, as shown in the specification.

1.2.4 Program layout conventions

There are very few rules imposed by Ada upon how an Ada program listing has to be laid out. There are, however, advantages in having conventions which define exactly how a program text should be laid out. For example, within a team of programmers, if all the programmers use the same convention for program layout, it is easier for the programs to be read by all team members. The conventions for program layout in this text will be introduced throughout the text.

In the program listings in this book **bold** lower case text will be used for Ada reserved words; these are words which are reserved by Ada for its own use, and cannot be used for any other purpose within an Ada program. A complete list of Ada reserved words is given in Table 1.2.1. The use of **bold** type to emphasize Ada reserved words is used to make the reserved words easier to recognize in the program listings. Program listings which are intended to be used to produce programs should not reproduce the bold effect.

Table 1.2.1 Ada reserved words

abort	abs	accept	access	all	and
array	at	begin	body	case	constant
declare	delay	delta	digits	else	elsif
end	entry	exception	exit	for	function
generic	goto	if	in	is	limited
loop	mod	new	not	null	of
or	others	out	package	pragma	private
procedure	raise	range	record	rem	renames
return	reverse	select	separate	subtype	task
terminate	then	type	use	when	while
with	xor				

CAPITALIZED text is used for words which have a predefined meaning to Ada. These meanings can be changed by a program, but should not be changed unless it is certain that a change of meaning is required. The most important of these words are given in Table 1.2.2.

Table 1.2.2 Ada words with a predefined meaning

BOOLEAN	CHARACTER	CLOSE	CREATE	DELETE	FALSE
FLOAT	GET	INTEGER	NATURAL	NEW_LINE	OPEN
PUT	PUT_LINE	POSITIVE	READ	RESET	SKIP_LINE
	STRING	TEXT_IO	TRUE	WRITE	

All other words in an Ada program will be in lower case; these are the words which have been invented by the programmer to provide identifiers for various objects in the program. The rules for inventing names will be introduced later in this section.

Although the convention for using upper case and lower case will be followed in this text and recommended as good program layout style, it is not important to Ada. In most circumstances Ada does not regard the case of a character as important, so line 0009 of the program listing could have been typed as follows:

```
The_AnsWer : cOnStAnT strING := "forty two.";
```

although it would not seem sensible to do so. The major exception to this is the content of string literals, where the case of the characters is preserved by Ada when the literal is stored or output.

Program layout conventions will also be used to determine how many statements can be included within one line of text, where on the line the statements should start, where comments should be included within program listings and where blank lines should be left in listings.

These conventions will be introduced in the course of the rest of this book. In general the following conventions are recommended:

1. Only one statement or declaration should be included on a single line of text, but two statements can sometimes be included where they are closely related in their meaning or function. In line 0005 of the program example above, two declarations have been included in one line, as both are required to give access to the facilities for text output.
2. Lines will be *indented* (moved to the right) to show groups of statements which comprise different parts of the program. In the example program above lines 0012, 0013 and 0014 have been indented three characters to the right, to indicate that they comprise the executable statements of the procedure.
3. Comments should be included at the start of programs to identify the programmer and the program. They should also be included to make clear the meaning of any statements or declarations whose meaning is not clear from their position in the listing. There are many other places where comments should be included, which will be introduced as they are met.
4. Blank lines should be used to separate parts of the program, allowing them to be more easily recognized when program listings are being read.

1.2.5 Names in programs

There are many places in a program where the programmer has to invent names for objects. In the example program above a name was required for the program itself and for the constant which was used in the program. These names are known as *identifiers*; there are a number of rules for constructing identifiers. Some of these rules are imposed by Ada, some are suggestions which are included in order to make the program listing more readable.

Identifiers should be as meaningful as possible without being verbose. For example, neither

```
s1 nor the_first_student_on_the_course
```

is regarded as being good identifiers in terms of style. The first, 's1', is too short to be meaningful, and the second is too long. Better identifiers would be

```
student_1 or first_student.
```

This rule is a style requirement, not an Ada requirement, Ada does not impose any restrictions on the minimum length of an identifier; in the example just cited, the identifier could simply be 's'.

Ada does not place any restriction on the maximum length of a name but some compilers, particularly those on microcomputers, do not distinguish different names beyond a certain number of characters.

If a compiler will only distinguish different identifiers on the basis of the first eight characters then it will be unable to distinguish between the following three identifiers:

```
student_1       student_2       student_3
↑↑↑↑↑↑↑↑         ↑↑↑↑↑↑↑↑         ↑↑↑↑↑↑↑↑

12345678        12345678        12345678
```

Ada will regard all these identifiers as being 'student_'. Consequently you should ensure that the identifiers you use in your program can be distinguished by the compiler you are using. A more usual limit is 31 or 32 characters, which is large enough for most people to construct unique meaningful identifiers.

Another style rule is the use of the underscore character '_' to connect two words together to make a single identifier. Spaces are not allowed in identifiers so the following are not valid:

```
student 1        the answer
```

Using more than one word makes identifiers more meaningful so separate words may be connected by an underscore character, as in the following:

```
student_1        the_answer
```

However, take care to use the underscore character rather than the hyphen or minus symbol '-', which has a different meaning. If a minus symbol is used in this identifier

```
tax-rate
```

Ada would interpret this as 'tax' minus 'rate'. If rate and tax are declared identifiers in a program this could have horrendous consequences.

Programmer-defined names are also not allowed to conflict with Ada reserved words, so using the following as identifiers is not allowed:

```
constant              procedure
```

Non-reserved Ada words which have a predefined meaning can be used as identifiers, so the following would be allowed as identifiers:

```
string              put_line
```

Using these as identifiers and giving them a different meaning from their predefined meaning should be avoided unless it is certain that a redefinition is actually required.

1.2.6 Constants in programs

Constants should be used in a program wherever there is a value which is not going to change within the program. The following are examples of numeric constants which might be declared:

NAME	TYPE	VALUE	NOTES
yards_to_miles	INTEGER	1760	conversion factor
weeks_in_year	INTEGER	52	no. of weeks in 1 year
max_no_students	INTEGER	80	max. no. of students on a course
pi	FLOAT	3.142	pi geometric constant
litres_to_pints	FLOAT	0.568	conversion factor

Declared constants have two advantages. The first is that where they are used in calculation, the name of the constant can be used in place of the value allowing the meaning of the program to become clearer:

```
english_drunk := metric_drunk * 0.568;
english_drunk := metric_drunk * litres_to_pints;
```

Without fully understanding the meanings of these statements, it should be clear that the second version of the statement is more meaningful than the first version.

The second advantage of constants is that, should the value of a constant have to be changed, only a single change to the text of the program is needed. In the example above, if the maximum number of students is increased to 100 then only the declaration of the constant will have to be changed. The program should be constructed so that changing the value in the constant declaration will cause other changes in the program, but will ensure that the program still works correctly.

One of the principles which was introduced in Block 1 Section 1.2 to differentiate between well-constructed programs and poorly constructed programs was the ease with which the program could be reconfigured when a change is required. The appropriate use of constants will allow such reconfiguration to be more easily accomplished.

1.2.7 An alternative program listing

Here is an alternative program which will behave in exactly the same way as the first program:

```
0001  -- Fintan Culwin 7/9/89 v 1.0 b1s2p2 see text
0002  -- a simple Ada demonstration program
0003
0004  with TEXT_IO; use TEXT_IO;
0005
0006  procedure b1s2p2 is
0007
```

```
0008    message_1  : constant STRING := "The answer to life, ";
0009    message_2  : constant STRING :=
                                "the universe and everything is :-";
0010    the_answer : constant STRING := "forty two.";
0011
0012 begin -- b1s2p2
0013    PUT_LINE( message_1 );
0014    PUT_LINE( message_2 );
0015    PUT_LINE( the_answer );
0016 end b1s2p2;
```

The difference between the two programs is in the use made of constants. In this implementation the two lines of output which were expressed as string literals have been defined as constants. The PUT_LINE statements which output the messages now do not contain literals but contain the names of the constants, which have been given the values of the first two output lines.

The important point about this alternative implementation is not the differences between it and the first implementation. The point is that alternative implementations are possible. For any program specification there are always more than one possible implementation; for a complex specification there will be a large number of possible implementations. It is not sufficient for a programmer to produce an implementation which merely fulfils the specification; it is also necessary for the programmer to produce a 'good' implementation.

This implies that there must be methods of examining alternative implementations and measuring the 'goodness' of the alternatives. Methods of measuring the goodness of program designs and implementations do exist; the intention in this book is to introduce methods which will ensure that good designs are produced, and consequently that good programs are implemented from them.

1.2.8 Producing a program

The programs above can be regarded as handwritten program listings. In order to execute them on a computer there are a number of stages to go through. These stages depend upon the computer system and the compiler which is being used. The combination of machine and compiler is called the *environment*.

The environment which will be considered here uses VAX Ada on a VAX series computer. The details of the process may change for other environments, but the processes will be largely the same. In order to run this program on the VAX there are various stages to go through, summarized in Figure 1.2.1.

EDIT is an *editor*. It is used to make the source file; in this example the source file will be called 'b1s2p1.ada'. The source file contains the text of the program, that is, a copy of the program instructions given above in a machine-readable format.

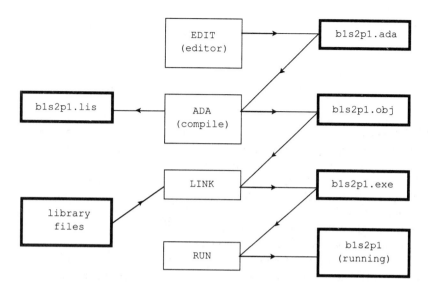

Figure 1.2.1 Stages in the execution of a program

There are other editors which could be used to produce the source file. Which editor is used is not important; what is important is that a text file containing the text of the program is produced from the editor.

The text file 'b2s1p1.ada' is then used by the Ada compiler to produce an *object file* 'b2s1p1.obj'. The object file is a translation of the Ada text program into a form which a particular computer can understand; this process is known as *compilation*.

The file produced by the compiler 'b2s1p1.obj' does not contain all the instructions which are required for the program to run. There are a standard set of computer instructions which have to be added to any program in order that it can run on a particular machine. In the example program above the instructions for the output of text information will have to be added to the object file produced from the compiler.

The addition of these instructions to the program instructions is performed by the *linker*. The linker takes the file 'b2s1p1.obj' as input and links it to the standard set of instructions which can be found in the library files. The product of the linker is an *executable file* called 'b2s1p1.exe'.

Once the executable file is produced it can then be executed by the computer using the RUN command.

The complete sequence of instructions in the VAX environment would be as follows:

```
$ EDT b1s2p1.ada      -- edit the program to produce the text file

      -- editing session here

$ ADA b1s2p1.ada      -- compile the source file to produce the
                                     object file
```

```
$ ACS LINK  b1s2p1.obj    -- link the object file to produce the
                                             executable file

$ RUN   b1s2p1.exe    -- run the executable program

    -- program execution here
```

This listing shows a very unusual situation. It implies that the source file will compile correctly with no errors reported on the first attempt. This is not usually the case; in most cases, the program will not compile correctly on the first attempt.

Assuming the program design and the intended implementation are correct, the commonest reason why a program will not compile correctly are the typing errors made as the source file is typed in. The reasons why the program will not compile correctly will be displayed on the terminal screen as the program fails compilation.

In these cases the errors have to be identified and interpreted. It is useful to have a *listing file* produced by the compiler which contains the program text and the errors which were detected. A listing file called 'b1s2p1.lis' can be produced from the compiler.

Using the listing file, the errors reported can be interpreted and the changes to the source file decided upon. The editor can then be used on the source file to make the changes required. The changed source file can then be submitted to the compiler again.

There is no guarantee that the source file will now be error-free; compilation will probably indicate that there are still errors. This process of attempted compilation, re-editing of the source file and another compilation attempt can (and does) take place indefinitely. It can be a time-consuming and frustrating process. There are methods of reducing the time spent at this stage:

1. The program should not be designed at the terminal. Many novice programmers do not produce adequate designs and attempt to compose the program as they are sitting at the terminal. This is rarely a successful practice; the time spent in perfecting the design on paper will be repaid by an easier production of the program at the terminal.
2. Program listings should initially be produced from the program design in a handwritten form. The handwritten version can then be carefully checked for errors before the program is entered using the editor.
3. If (or, more likely, when) the first compilation attempt fails a hard copy of the listing file should be obtained. The listing file contains a copy of the program and the error messages which were produced by the compiler. The corrections should be made by hand on the listing file, before going back to the editor and re-editing the source file.

This does make it seem as if it would take more time than just sitting at a terminal and entering the program or correcting the errors. However, it is easier to spot and correct errors when the whole program is visible on a listing than when only a small part of the program can be seen on the screen at one time.

EXERCISES

1.2.1 Comment upon the suitability or otherwise of the following constant identifiers. For unsuitable identifiers suggest an alternative:

Constant	Suggested identifier
Conversion factor between pounds and dollars	p_t_d
The speed of light	c
The cost per unit of electricity used	unit-cost
The fastest marathon time	record
The number of smarties in a tube	No_of_smarties_per_tube

1.2.2 This following is the (simulated) output of a VAX Ada compiler including compilation error messages. Identify and correct each error to produce a correct version of the program.

```
      1    -- block 1 section 2 exercise 2 (b1s2e2)
      2    -- program to illustrate (shortened) VAX Ada error messages
      3
      4    with TEXT_IO; use TEXT_IO;
      5
      6    procedure b1s2e2 is ;
.........................1
%ADAC-E-IGNOREUNEXP, (1) Unexpected ";" ignored
      7
      8               msg1 : STRING constant := 'Data design + ';
...........................1..........2............3
%ADAC-E-LEXAPOST, (2) Invalid apostrophe ('); possible unterminated
 character literal or string literal delimited by
 apostrophe (') instead of by quotation marks (")
%ADAC-E-LEXAPOST, (3) Invalid apostrophe ('); possible unterminated
 character literal or string literal delimited by
 apostrophe (') instead of by quotation marks (")
%ADAC-E-FOUNDEXP, (1) Found reserved-word "constant" when expecting one
 of { "delta" "digits" "range" "renames" "'" "(" "." ":=" ";" }
%ADAC-I-IGNOREDECLL, (1) Declaration ignored due to syntactic errors
      9
     10    begin b1s2e2
..................1
%ADAC-E-INSSEMI, (1) Inserted ";" at end of line
     11      PUT( "msg1 ");
     12      PUT( "+ program design ");
     13      PUT( " = programming.");
     14    end b1s2;
...........1
%ADAC-E-PM_NAMDOENOTMAT, (1) Name b1s2 does not match b1s2e2 at line 6
```

1.2.3 This following is the (simulated) output of a Janus Ada compiler including compilation error messages. Identify and correct each error to produce a correct version of the program.

```
-- b1s2e3 exercise question contains deliberate errors
-- with simulated janus compiler error messages
with TEXT_IO; use TEXT_IO;
procedure b1s2e3 is
     msg1 :    constant STRING := "Ada error messages ";
     msg2 :    constant STRING := "are not always very helpful;
------------------------------^
*SYNTAX ERROR* String literal must not cross line boundary (J.3)
     num_err : constant STRING := " five ";
begin -- b1s2e3
     PUT_LINE( msg1 ) PUT_LINE( msg_2 );
----------------------^
*SYNTAX ERROR* Inserted SEMICOLON (J.3)
------------------------------^
*ERROR* identifier is not defined (J.4.8)
     PUT( "This program contains at least );
----------^
*SYNTAX ERROR* String literal must not cross line boundary (J.3)
     PUT_LINE( num_err, " errors.");
-----^
*SYNTAX ERROR* Inserted COMMA (J.3)
----------------------------------^
*SYNTAX ERROR* Inserted RPAREN (J.3)
-----^
*ERROR* unable to resolve expression (J.4.6)
     PUT( "and is only 17 lines long ");
end -- b1s2e3;
---^
*SYNTAX ERROR* Inserted SEMICOLON (J.3)
```

1.2.4 Using the corrected listings from Exercises 1.2.2 and 1.2.3, learn how to use your Ada environment by entering, compiling and running the programs. This will also allow you to find out if you can manage to detect and correct all the errors.

Sequence in programs

The simplest technique available for programming a computer is to produce a source code consisting of a sequence of instructions. It is understood that the computer will obey the instructions in the specified sequence, when the program is executed. In the example program produced in Block 1 Section 2, the statement part of the program consisted of three PUT_LINE statements. It was understood that Ada would obey these three instructions in the sequence in which they appeared in the source file.

1.3.1 A sequence specification

In order to develop the understanding of sequence further, a program will be designed and produced to the following specification:

A program is required which will input two numbers and output the total of the two numbers when added together.

Even an apparently simple specification like this can cause problems in interpretation.

The first rule of programming is to understand the specification. If this specification is read carefully there are a number of questions which might be asked:

1. Where are the numbers to be input from?
2. Are these numbers integers, or do they have any decimal parts?
3. If decimal, how many places after the decimal point?
4. Are negative numbers allowed?
5. What is the largest number which is allowed?
6. Where is the output of the program to be sent to?

None of these questions can be answered from this specification. Before the process of producing a program can proceed to the design stage, these questions will have to be answered.

One way of answering them is to go back to the sponsor of the program and ask for a more detailed specification. A second way is to make assumptions about what the specification might mean. If assumptions are made, then the assumptions should be appended to the specification and included in the program documentation. It is preferable to get the answers from the sponsor of the specification rather than make assumptions which might prove to be invalid. Any design decisions or implementations which are based upon invalid assumptions will then have to be reversed. It is preferable to produce a correct program on the first attempt than to have to rework an incorrect program.

An improved specification for this program would be as follows:

A program is to be written which will input two integer numbers from the keyboard. Either or both of these numbers may be negative. The two numbers will be added together and the result displayed on the terminal screen. The largest number which the program will accommodate is the largest number which the computer system can represent.

User interface design

One way to obtain a fuller understanding of a specification is to design a display of what the screen will look like, when the program is executed:

```
Please enter the first  number     ffffffff
Please enter the second number     ssssssss

The total is    tttttttt
```

In this design the user's input, 'ffffffff' and 'ssssssss', is shown underscored, and 'tttttttt' is the total calculated and displayed by the program.

Producing a representation of what a program will look like as it executes is a part of the design process. Programs which accept input from the keyboard and/or display information on a terminal screen are known as *interactive* programs. For interactive programs producing a tidy and supportive screen display is essential. The design of the screen(s) and the process of interaction which the user will have with the program is known as the *user interface*. As this is the only part of a program which the user will see, it is essential that it is designed to be as tidy and supportive as possible.

Every time the user is asked for an input it should be preceded by a clear and unambiguous prompt. The prompt should inform the user exactly what input is required, and possibly what format it should be supplied in. Likewise, the output from a program should be preceded by an output prompt explaining what the output is.

In the example above an extra space has been included between the words 'first' and 'number' in the first input prompt in order that both input prompts are of the same length.

The output part of the interaction has been separated from the input part of the interaction in order to draw the user's attention to it.

Having interpreted the specification and by designing the user interface become convinced that it is totally understood, production of the program design can proceed.

The program design

For a specification as simple as this there is no need to go through a complete design process; a program could be written from the specification. The detailed processes of producing a design will be used here to illustrate how a design can be produced. This method can be used to produce a design for any program. If a design process is used and understood on small programs, it can later be applied to more complex programs. With complex specifications producing a design is an absolute prerequisite before attempting to produce the program code.

The design process which will be introduced here is known as *top-down stepwise refinement*. It is a suitable design technique for small straightforward specifications. It is not the only design technique which is available; more complex programs may require more complex design techniques. Such techniques will be introduced later in this book.

Top-down design proceeds by dividing the specification into a number of smaller simpler subspecifications, the rationale being that if a specification is too difficult to implement as a design in one stage, then dividing it into a small number of simpler parts will produce a number of simpler smaller design tasks. This process of dividing a specification is known as *refinement*. Each component of the refined specification may itself be too complex to implement directly, and have to be refined further. The process of refinement can continue down many levels, until the design has been refined to the point where it can be implemented in a programming language.

The specification given at the beginning of this section can be refined into three parts. In order to instruct a computer to perform the program add_two_numbers, it will have to be instructed to input the two numbers, then to add the numbers and then to output the answer. The program, refined into three component parts, can be shown on a *program structure chart* as follows:

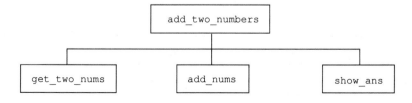

The program structure chart shows that the program called add_two_numbers is a sequence of three components. The components are, from left to right, get_two_nums, add_nums and show_ans. It is understood that the components will be executed in the sequence shown.

Each component part of add_two_numbers is then considered in turn. If any of these parts is too complex to be directly expressed in program code, then it, too, will have to be refined.

The component get_two_nums can be refined into two component parts. In order to get two numbers, the first number has to be input, then the second number. This refinement can be added to the program structure chart as follows:

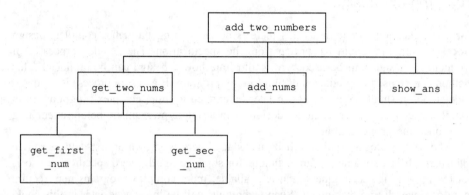

The refinement can be carried a stage further. The component get_first_num can be refined into a sequence of two parts, displaying the prompt for the first number then accepting the first number. Similar considerations can be used to refine the component get_sec_num. When these refinements are added to the program structure chart it becomes as follows:

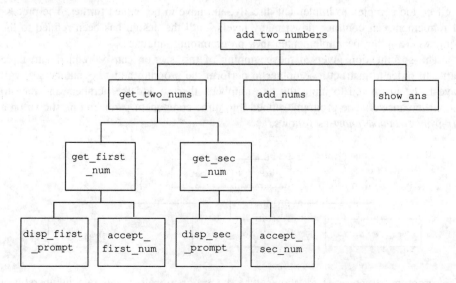

The component add_nums does not need to be refined further as a program statement to add two numbers together can be implemented directly in a programming language.

The component show_ans will need to be refined; in order to show the answer the program has to show the prompt for the answer, and then show the answer itself. The refinement can be added to the structure chart, which is now complete:

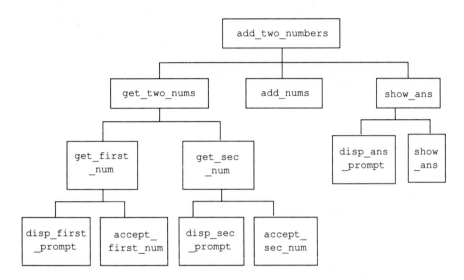

The final program structure chart is read, using the rule 'left-right top-down', as follows: The program add_two_numbers is performed by performing the components get_two_nums, add_nums and show_ans. The component get_two_nums is performed by performing the components get_first_num followed by get_sec_num. The component get_first_num is performed by performing the action display_first_prompt followed by accept_first_num. The component get_sec_num is performed by performing the actions display_sec_prompt followed by accept_sec_num. The component add_nums is performed by the action of adding the numbers together. The component show_ans is performed by performing the actions display_ans_prompt, followed by show_ans.

By following the development of the program structure and considering the final program structure chart it can be seen that the English description in the paragraph above is equivalent to the program structure chart.

It can also be seen that by using the visual technique of a structure chart, the design of the program can be expressed in a more compact and comprehensible form. There is little point, having produced the structure chart, in producing a written form of the design. The meaning of the program as expressed in the written form has to be understood by the programmer from the visual form, in order to use the design to produce the program.

At this stage the structure chart should be checked to make sure the design is correct. The structure chart expresses a design which will be implemented as program code. If the design contains errors then the program produced from it will contain those errors. At some stage while the program is being produced, or after it has been completed, the errors will become apparent. When the errors are discovered, the process of producing the corrected program will have to restart from a corrected design.

The design can be checked using a technique called a *walk-through*. In a walk-through the person checking the design follows the design acting as if he or she were the computer. The person will pretend to perform the actions that the program will perform in the sequence specified by the design. If the walk-through is performed carefully using sample input data, then any errors should be discovered from the behaviour of the design and the output produced.

The written description of the design made a distinction between performing a design component and performing an action. If only the actions of the program are considered they will be performed in the following sequence:

> display first prompt
> accept first number
> display second prompt
> accept second number
> add numbers
> display answer prompt
> show answer

By referring to the specification and the user interface, it can be seen that these actions will fulfil the specification.

Having produced and checked the design, the next stage of producing the program can proceed.

The data design

Data design is as important to programming as program design. At a later stage, these parts of the program design process will be reversed and the data will be designed before the program.

There are three numbers which are required by this program add_two_numbers; the first number input by the user, the second number input by the user, and the sum of the numbers input by the user which will be calculated and output by the program. These three numbers will have to be defined as program objects. In the previous section the only class of program object which was introduced was constants, program objects whose value could be stated at the design stage and whose value would not change as the program executed. The values of the objects in this program are not known at the design stage and will change as the program executes. This class of objects is known as *variable objects* or simply *variables*.

In order to design a variable object, it has to have an identifier by which it can be known and it has to be given a *data type*. A data type defines what values an object can have and what operations can be performed on the object. A table describing the names, types and usage of all data objects used in this program can be produced as follows:

PROGRAM VARIABLES		
NAME	TYPE	NOTES
first_num	INTEGER	first number input by the user
sec_num	INTEGER	second number input by the user
total_num	INTEGER	the result of adding first_num to sec_num

The program listing

The program listing can now be produced from the design. The heading of the program would be as follows:

```
0001    -- Fintan Culwin Sept 1989 v 1.0
0002    -- simple demonstration program illustrating sequence
0003    -- b1s3p1 see text
0004
0005    with TEXT_IO;
0006    package int_io is new TEXT_IO.INTEGER_IO( INTEGER );
0007    with TEXT_IO,int_io; use TEXT_IO,int_io;
0008
0009    procedure b1s3p1 is
```

Once again this listing has included line numbers, used **bold** text and used CAPITALS to make the listing clearer to read. The line numbers and the bold effect should not be reproduced in program listings. The distinction between capitals and lower case for certain words should be retained in listings, as explained in Block 1 Section 2.

The heading is similar to the heading of the program used in Block 1 Section 2. The major difference is that this program will have a requirement to input integer values from the keyboard and output integer values to the terminal, as well as the input and output of text information. This is accomplished by lines 0005–0007 of the heading, which allow this program to access suitable facilities for the input and output of text and INTEGER values. These lines will not be explained in detail in this section. Should a program have a need to input and output INTEGER values as well as text information, then lines 0005–0007 should be included as the context clause of such programs.

Lines 0001–0003 are again comments which are used to identify the program and the programmer. Line 0009 completes the heading of the program by declaring the name of the procedure which comprises the program as b1s3p1.

Blank lines are included in the heading of the program and in the rest of the program as an aid to readability, separating each significant part of the program from other significant parts of the program. What constitutes a significant part of a program will become clear as more programs are introduced. The data table can now be used to produce the variable declarations:

```
0011
0012    first_num,              -- first number from user
0013    sec_num,                -- second number from user
0014    total_num  : INTEGER;   -- result of addition
0015
```

The list of variable identifiers and their data type comprise the declaration part of this program. The members of the list are separated by commas (',') and the last identifier in the list is followed by a colon (':') and then the type name, in this example INTEGER. The end of the list is the end of an Ada declaration and requires a semicolon to terminate it.

The layout convention in use here is that each identifier is on a line by itself and accompanied on the same line by a comment indicating what the variable will be used for within the program.

The executable part of the program can now be produced using the program structure chart as a guide:

```
0016    begin -- of b1s3p1
0017        -- get two numbers
0018        -- get first number
0019        PUT ( "Please enter the first number ");
0020        GET ( first_num ); SKIP_LINE;
0021
0022        -- get second number
0023        PUT ( "Please enter the second number ");
0024        GET ( sec_num   ); SKIP_LINE;
0025
0026        -- add numbers
0027        total_num := first_num + sec_num;
0028
0029        -- show answer
0030        NEW_LINE;
0031        PUT ( "The total is . . . . ");
0032        PUT ( total_num ); NEW_LINE;
0033
0034    end b1s3p1;
```

The statement part of the program is enclosed in a **begin/end** pair. The **begin** is commented as being the start of the procedure add_two_numbers; the **end** has the name of the procedure as a part of its syntax.

The names of the design components have been taken from the program structure chart and included in the program text as comments. Each design component is separated from the other parts of the program by blank lines. This allows someone reading the design and the listing to easily cross reference the design to the listing.

The first part of the program get_two_numbers has been implemented in two parts, get_first_number and get_second_number, as expressed in the structure chart.

Each of these requires two actions, one to display the prompt and one to input the response from the user and store the value in one of the variables. The statement used to display the prompt is the PUT statement. This statement is very similar to the PUT_LINE statement introduced in Block 1 Section 2. The only difference between a PUT and a PUT_LINE statement is that a PUT_LINE statement will advance the cursor onto the next line after it has displayed the information but a PUT statement will leave the cursor on the same line. This can be made clear by considering the screen displays which would be produced by this program, using PUT statements and using PUT_LINE statements:

```
Please enter the first  number ffffffff
Please enter the second number ssssssss
```

and using PUT_LINE statements:

```
Please enter the first  number
ffffffff
Please enter the second number
ssssssss
```

It is clear from these examples and the user guide that the PUT statement is preferable, in this program, to the PUT_LINE statement.

The statement used to input information from the keyboard is the GET statement. The brackets which form part of the GET statement have to contain the name of a variable program object. The effect of the GET statement when it is executed is to input information from the keyboard and to store that information in the variable named in the brackets.

As the variables which are identified in the brackets are INTEGER data objects, it is hoped that the user of the program will type in an integer value. The program would probably stop its execution if the user typed in anything other than an integer; techniques to avoid this behaviour are too complex to be introduced at this stage.

The GET statement will stop accepting input from the keyboard as soon as an integer value has been provided. Although the user will indicate the end of the input by using the enter key, the enter code will not be accepted by the GET statement. This unaccepted enter code has to be taken care of before the next input from the keyboard can be accepted; the SKIP_LINE statement will accomplish this.

Whenever input is being accepted from the keyboard in this manner the GET statement should be followed by a SKIP_LINE statement, to take care of the enter code used to terminate the input. As these statements are so closely related it is acceptable for them to be included on the same line of the listing.

One way of keeping track of what happens during program execution is to visualize the variables of the program as boxes. After the variables have been declared and before the program executes they can be visualized as:

first_num	sec_num	total_num
????????	????????	????????
INTEGER	INTEGER	INTEGER

Each variable has associated with it three parts: the identifier of the variable, which is used by the program to reference the value of the variable; a data type for the variable, which is used to define what information can be stored in the variable; and the value of the contents of the variable. This diagram shows the contents of the variables after they have been declared. It is not true to say that they contain nothing or that they contain the value zero. The value of any Ada variable after it has been declared is undefined, indicated in this diagram as '????????'. A variable in this state is known as an *uninitialized* variable.

If the following inputs are assumed when the program is run:

```
Please enter the first  number 42
Please enter the second number 23
```

then the state of the three variables after execution of the get_two_numbers component would be as follows:

first_num	sec_num	total_num
42	23	????????
INTEGER	INTEGER	INTEGER

The variables referenced in the GET statements have been initialized with values input by the user of the program from the keyboard. The values are stored in the value part of the variable as shown. The value of total_num at this stage is still uninitialized.

The next component of the program structure is add_nums. This is implemented as a single Ada statement in line 0027. The effect of this statement is to add the value of first_num to the value of sec_num and store the result in the variable total_num. The addition is specified by an arithmetic expression using the addition operator ('+'); on the right-hand side of the assignment operator (':='). The assignment operator should be read as 'becomes equal to', it should *not* be confused with the 'is equal to' operator ('=').

Some programming languages do not make a distinction between assignment ('becomes equal to') and equality testing ('is equal to'), using the same symbol ('=') for both. Assignment should be used where the intention is to transfer a value from the right-hand side of the assignment symbol to the variable on the left-hand side of the assignment symbol. The 'is equal to' symbol should be used where the intent is to discover if the values on both sides are or are not equal.

If the example interaction above is considered again, the state of the program variables following the assignment statement is as follows:

first_num		sec_num		total_num
42		23		65
INTEGER		INTEGER		INTEGER

The assignment statement has been used to initialize the value of the variable total_num to the result of the expression which added the values of first_num and sec_num together.

The final component of the design is show_ans. This uses the PUT and the NEW_LINE statements to display the result of the addition stored in total_num together with the output prompt. The NEW_LINE statement on line 0030 is used to produce a spare line on the screen between the input part of the interaction and the output part of the interaction, as shown in the user interface.

The PUT statement is used with a string literal to produce the output prompt and leave the cursor on the same line ready for the result of the addition to be displayed. The result of the addition is displayed using a PUT statement, and the line is completed with a NEW_LINE statement before the program concludes.

It is not possible to use a PUT_LINE statement on line 0032, as the object to be output is an INTEGER not a STRING. It is only possible to output a string value using the PUT_LINE statement. The same effect can be obtained for integer values by using a PUT statement immediately followed by a NEW_LINE statement. As these two statements are so closely connected with each other it is permissible to include them on a single line of the listing.

The program is now complete and can be compiled and run. Testing of this program will be considered in Block 1 Section 7.

EXERCISES

1.3.1   A program is required to input two (integer) numbers from the keyboard, calculate the difference between the first number and the second number and display the difference on the terminal screen. Using the program design, data design and the program listing developed in this section decide what changes will be required to implement this program.

The statement required to subtract the value of a variable called 'little' from the value of a variable called 'big' and put the result into a variable called 'difference' is as follows:

```
difference := big - little;
```

The subtraction operator in Ada is the minus symbol ('-').

Implement this program and use it to discover what happens when the value of 'little' is greater than the value of 'big'.

1.3.2   Modify the design and the program produced in Exercise 1.3.1 to display the results of adding the two numbers together, subtracting the second number from the first number, multiplying the two numbers together and dividing the first number by the second number.

The statement required to multiply the value of a variable called 'first' by the value of a variable called 'second' and store the result in a variable called 'product' is as follows:

```
product := first * second;
```

The multiplication operator in Ada is the asterisk symbol ('*').

The statement required in this instance to divide the value of a variable called 'divisor' by the value of a variable called 'dividend' and store the result in a variable called 'divided' is as follows:

```
divided := divisor / dividend;
```

The integer division operator in Ada is the slash symbol ('/').

1.3.3   The following program has a number of Ada errors. Identify and correct them (ignore any style errors). Assume that the lines required for input and output of STRING and INTEGER values have been included in the listing.

```
0001    demonstration program for b1s3e3
0002
0003    procedure b1s3e3 is
0004
0005        num_1;
0006        num_2  ; INTEGER ;
0007
0008    begin
0009        num_1 = 42;
0010        num_2 = 56;
0011        PUT("The result of multiplying 42 by 56 is ");
```

```
0012      num_1 * num_2;
0013        NEW_LINE;
0014    end b1s3e3;
```

1.3.4 The following program has number of style errors. Identify and correct them. The program is intended to input the length and height of a rectangle and display the area. Assume that the lines required to input and output STRING and INTEGER have been included. There are no Ada errors in the listing.

```
0001    procedure e4 is
0002        l,h,a : integer;
0003    begin
0004      put ("length");get (l);
0005      put (" height");get (h);
0005      a := l*h; put (a);
0006    end;
```

Section 1.4

Selection in programs

The program called add_two_numbers in Block 1 Section 3 was designed as a sequence of actions. This sequence was expressed in the program structure chart and in the program listing. Essentially a sequence of instructions to a computer says 'do this, followed by this, followed by this . . .'.

If this were the only method available to instruct a computer, programming would be impossible. There are two other techniques for instructing a computer to performing actions, *selection* and *iteration* (*repetition*). Selection involves instructing the computer to decide between two (or more) possible courses of action. Iteration involves instructing the computer to repeat a sequence of actions a number of times. This section will deal with selection, the next two sections with iteration.

1.4.1 A selection specification

The following is a simple specification for a demonstration program which involves a selection between two actions only:

> A program is required which will ask the user for the amount of money (positive integers only) in a bank account. It will then ask for the amount of money (integers greater than zero) to be withdrawn from the account. If the amount to be withdrawn is greater than the amount in the account the program is to display a message that the transaction is refused, and the unchanged balance is displayed. If the amount of money to be withdrawn is less than or equal to the amount in the account then the transaction is to be accepted, and the new value of the account's balance displayed.

Although the specification makes it clear that the values of balance and withdrawal have to be between certain specified values, this implementation of the program will not attempt to enforce these restrictions.

User interface design

As the specification involves selection between two different alternatives there are two possible interactions which a user may have with the program:

```
Enter the amount on deposit   100          Enter the amount on deposit   76
Enter the withdrawal           50          Enter the withdrawal         120

Accepted. Balance is           50          Refused! Balance is           76
```

The program design

In the previous section the structure chart representation of a sequence was introduced. There is a convention for representing a two-way selection in a program structure chart:

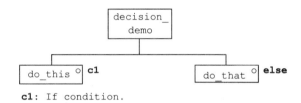

c1: If condition.

This chart indicates that decision_demo is a selection between the components do_this and do_that. The ° symbol in the top right of the components of the decision, indicates that they are selective components. The decision is made on the basis of a condition identified in this diagram as condition 1 (c1). Computer programs are only able to make decisions on the basis of a TRUE/FALSE (or yes/no) decision. Accordingly the condition has to be expressed as a question which can only be answered TRUE or FALSE (or yes or no).

The interpretation of this diagram is that when the component decision_demo is performed by the program, the decision will be evaluated to decide if the do_this or the do_that component will be performed. If the condition evaluates as TRUE then the component do_this will be performed and the component do_that will not be performed. If the decision evaluates as FALSE then the component do_that will be performed and the component do_this will be ignored.

The design for the program can proceed using the method of stepwise refinement starting with the program itself:

```
selection_demo
```

This indicates that the program itself will be known as selection_demo. It is too complex to be implemented in Ada directly so it is refined into subcomponents. In this design there are two major subcomponents:

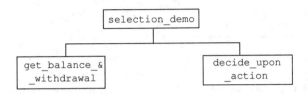

This shows the program selection_demo refined into a sequence of two major components called get_balance_&_withdrawal and decide_upon_action.

The component get_balance_&_withdrawal is itself too complex to be implemented directly so it will have to be refined in turn:

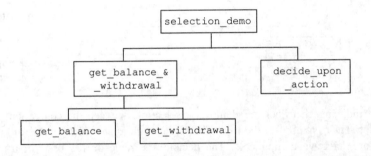

It would be possible to refine each of the components get_balance and get_withdrawal into two further components, one to display the prompt and one to accept the input. This would refine the design to the level where each of the lowest-level components could be implemented directly as an Ada statement; refining a design to this level is not always useful. For a large program this would imply that an unusably large number of components would have to be included in a structure chart.

It is understood that each of the lowest-level components of the design may be implemented in the listing as a short sequence of Ada statements. Such a sequence must implement a single simple functional requirement of the program. Allowing the lowest levels of a design to be implemented as a small number of statements reduces the number of component boxes in a program design, and thus allows the design to be more easily understood.

The component decide_upon_action will have to be refined and, as its name suggests, it will implement the decision:

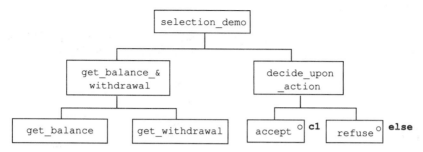

c1: If the withdrawal is less than or equal to the balance.

This shows that the component decide_upon_action is a selection between components refuse and accept with the associated condition **c1**. The condition is keyed and expressed beneath the structure chart.

The expression of the condition is made in the form of an English sentence. There is a temptation at this stage to express the condition as an Ada phrase (if withdrawal <= balance). This temptation should be avoided; a program design should not indicate how a program will be implemented, it should only indicate the logical structure of the program.

Structure charts are read using the rule 'left-right top-down'. This structure chart could be read as follows: The selection_demo program is a sequence of components get_balance_&_withdrawal and decide_upon_action. The component get_balance_&_withdrawal is a sequence of get_balance followed by get_withdrawal. The decision on the action is a decision between accepting the transaction and refusing the transaction. This decision is made by deciding if the withdrawal is less than or equal to the balance.

Once again it should be clear that the visual design of the program and the written design in the paragraph above are equivalent. The visual representation has a number of advantages:

1. When trying to find a part of a design this can quickly be done using the diagram. Trying to find a part of the design in the text can be time-consuming.
2. As designs become larger the visual design is more concise than the written form, allowing the design to be understood and communicated more readily.
3. As designs become more complex the ambiguity of written language will cause an ambiguity in the design. Ambiguity in program structure charts is less likely.

Before proceeding to implement the design, the design has to be verified with a walk-through. This design will require two walk-throughs, one to verify the accept path and one to verify the refuse path.

If the input of balance is assumed to be 100 and the input of withdrawal is assumed to be 50, then get_balance_&_withdrawal can easily be verified. The component decide_upon_action can be walked through. The condition 'if the withdrawal is less than or equal to the balance' will evaluate as TRUE. This will cause the accept component to be performed and the refuse component will be ignored.

By assuming a balance of 76 and a withdrawal of 120, and walking through the design again, the refuse path can be verified. Having successfully verified the design, production can proceed with the next phase.

The data design

The specification and program design indicate that two INTEGER program objects will be required, one for the balance and one for the withdrawal. The data table would be as follows:

PROGRAM VARIABLES

NAME	TYPE	NOTES
balance	INTEGER	balance in the account
withdrawal	INTEGER	withdrawal requested by user

The program listing

In order to implement the program design as an Ada program, a method of implementing a selection in Ada will have to be used. The simplest method of implementing a selection is to use an **if** statement. The general form of an Ada **if** statement is as follows:

```
if test then
    statement(s)_1;
else
    statement(s)_2;
end if;
```

The Ada rules for a general **if** statement are as follows:

1. Test is an expression which will evaluate to TRUE or FALSE; Such expressions are known as BOOLEAN expressions. One form of a BOOLEAN expression is a relational comparison which will be explained below. BOOLEAN expressions in general will be introduced more fully in Block 2 Section 4.
2. Statement(s)_1 and statement(s)_2 can be a single Ada statement, or any sequence of Ada statements.
3. The entire **if** structure is a single Ada statement; consequently it is terminated with a semicolon. Statement(s)_1 and statement(s)_2 are Ada statements and each statement requires a semicolon.

    The **if** part of the **end if** term of the if statement is *not* optional.
    The style rules for a general if statement are as follows:

1. The reserved words **if, then, else** and **end** are shown in bold lower case.
2. Statement(s)_1 and statement(s)_2 are indented to indicate that they are controlled by the **if** statement.

Indentation is used in program listings to show the extent of a program control structure. The style rules in this book recommend consistent indentation by three characters. With a simple statement like this the limits of the **if** are obvious. As programs become more complex the limits of control statements are not always obvious and indentation is essential to make the limits visible.

The simplest form of a test which can be used in an **if** statement is a *relational comparison*. A relational comparison is expressed as a relational expression, which has the following general form:

$$\text{value\_1} \quad \text{relational\_operator} \quad \text{value\_2}$$

where value_1 and value_2 are values of the same type. The only types which have been introduced so far are INTEGER and STRING. It is not sensible to attempt to compare an integer number (such as 42) with a string (such as 'hello'). It is sensible to attempt to compare two integers or two strings. The values on either side of the relational operator can be literals, constants, variables or expressions.

The relational operator is one of the following operators:

is equal to	=
is not equal to	/=
is less than	<
is less than or equal to	<=
is greater than	>
is greater than or equal to	>=

The relational operator will compare the left-hand value with the right-hand value using the relation expressed in the name of the operator. The relation can only evaluate to the value TRUE or the value FALSE, which is used to control the behaviour of the **if** statement. If the test is TRUE then statement(s)_1 will be executed and statement(s)_2 will be ignored; if the test is FALSE statement(s)_1 will be ignored and statement(s)_2 will be executed.

Using the general **if** statement and the program structure chart the program listing can be produced. The heading of this program will be as follows:

```
0001   -- Fintan Culwin Sept '88 v1.0
0002   -- program to illustrate simple selection
0003   -- b1s4 see text
0004
0005   with TEXT_IO;
0006   package int_io is new TEXT_IO.INTEGER_IO( INTEGER );
0007   with TEXT_IO,int_io; use TEXT_IO,int_io;
0008
0009   procedure b1s4p1 is
```

The heading of this program should be understandable from the program headings introduced in previous sections. The data declarations will be as follows:

```
0010
0011    balance,                    -- balance in the account
0012    withdrawal : INTEGER;   -- withdrawal from the account
0013
```

The executable part of the program is between lines 0014 and 0030 and is divided into a sequence of two main parts as shown in the design. The names of the components from the design have been included in the listing; this, together with the use of blank lines, allows the design and the listing to be easily cross-referenced.

```
0014  begin -- of b1s4p1
0015
0016    -- get balance & withdrawal
0017    PUT ( "Enter the amount on deposit   ");
0018    GET ( balance ); SKIP_LINE;
0019    PUT ( "Enter the withdrawal          ");
0020    GET ( withdrawal ); SKIP_LINE;
0021
0022    -- decide upon action
0023    NEW_LINE;    -- separate input from output
0024    if withdrawal <= balance then
0025        PUT ( "Accepted. Balance is ");
0026        PUT ( balance - withdrawal); NEW_LINE;
0027    else
0028        PUT ( "Refused ! Balance is ");
0029        PUT ( balance ); NEW_LINE;
0030    end if;
0031  end b1s4p1;
```

The implementation of get_balance_&_withdrawal is in lines 0016–0020, and is very similar to the component get_two_nums from the program in the previous section.

The implementation of decide_upon_action is in lines 0022–0030. It is implemented using an **if** statement modeled upon the general **if** statement introduced above. The test part of the general **if** statement is implemented as the relational expression 'withdrawal <= balance'. When this statement is executed the values of the two program objects, withdrawal and balance, are compared using the relation 'less than or equal to'. This expression can only evaluate as TRUE or FALSE.

The statement(s)_1 and statement(s)_2 parts of the general **if** statement are implemented as the sequence of statements on lines 0025–0026 and 0028–0029, respectively. These statements are similar to statements used in the program from the previous section to display an output prompt and an integer value, followed by a new line.

The PUT statement in line 0026 contains the expression 'balance - withdrawal'. When Ada executes this statement the values of the two variable objects will be determined. The value of withdrawal will be taken away from the value of balance and the result of the subtraction displayed. In general it is not regarded as good style to include an expression within a PUT statement. A method of avoiding this problem will be introduced in the next program.

1.4.2 A more complex selection specification

Many specifications call for a more complex decision to be made. For example, the specification used for the program above could have been as follows:

A program is required which will ask the user for the amount of money (integer greater than -50) in a bank account. It will then ask for the amount of money (integer greater than 0) to be withdrawn from the account. If the amount to be withdrawn is less than or equal to the balance then the transaction is to be accepted and a suitable message displayed. If the resulting balance after the withdrawal has been processed is greater than or equal to -50 (pounds) then an overdraft is allowed and an overdraft message is to be displayed. If the resulting balance is less than -50, the transaction is to be refused and a suitable message displayed. In all cases the remaining balance in the account is to be displayed.

As with the previous program, the values of balance and withdrawal input by the user will not be checked to make sure they lie within the specified ranges. When specifications involving decisions become complex, one way of resolving the specification and understanding it is to construct a *decision table*. The decision table for this specification would be as follows:

RESULTING BALANCE	ACTION
>= 0	ACCEPT
>= -50 AND < 0	OVERDRAFT
< -50	REFUSED

User interface design

The user interface for this design would require three possible courses of action to be designed:

```
Enter the amount on deposit   100
Enter the withdrawal           50

Accepted. Balance is           50
```

```
Enter the amount on deposit    50
Enter the withdrawal           75

Overdraft! Balance is         -25
```

```
Enter the amount on deposit   120
Enter the withdrawal          200

Refused! Balance is           120
```

The program design

The overall program design will be very similar to the design produced for the simpler specification. A new component, called calc_result_balance, has been introduced. The component decide_upon_action will now have to be refined into three components:

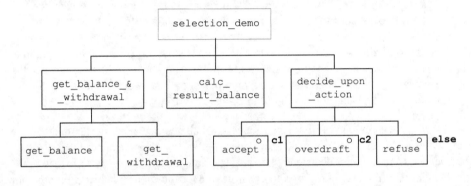

c1: If the resulting balance is greater than or equal to zero.
c2: If the resulting balance is greater than the overdraft limit (and less than zero).

The visual notation used to represent a selection between two alternatives has been extended to allow it to represent a selection between three alternatives.

The interpretation of decide_upon_action is now as follows: If condition c1 evaluates as TRUE then the component called accept will be performed and the other two components ignored. If condition c1 evaluates as FALSE and condition c2 evaluates as TRUE then the component called overdraft will be performed and the other components will be ignored. If neither condition c1 nor condition c2 evaluates as TRUE then the component called refuse will be performed and the other components will be ignored.

The data design

This implementation requires a third variable called resulting_balance to be used. The advantage of using a third variable is to make the program more readable. For example, the phrase 'withdrawal > balance' from the previous program will be replaced with the statement 'resulting_balance > zero' in this program.

The meaning of the decision is clearer in the second form than in the first form. By making the meaning of the program clearer in the text of the program, the program becomes easier to understand and thus to maintain.

The specification is also interpreted so that the £50 limit on overdrafts may at some stage be changed. Consequently it will be implemented in the program as a constant. The data table for this program will be as follows:

PROGRAM CONSTANTS

NAME	TYPE	VALUE	NOTES
overdraft_limit	INTEGER	-50	limit beneath which overdrafts will be refused
zero	INTEGER	0	enough said!

PROGRAM VARIABLES

NAME	TYPE	NOTES
balance	INTEGER	balance in the account
withdrawal	INTEGER	withdrawal requested by user
resulting_balance	INTEGER	resulting balance when withdrawal is taken away from balance.

The program listing

In order to implement this design a method of implementing a three-way decision in Ada will have to be introduced. The general form of the **if** statement was given earlier in this section:

```
if test then
    statement(s)_1;
else
    statement(s)_2;
end if;
```

This version of the simple **if** statement is appropriate for a two-way decision. A three-way decision can be implemented in Ada using the following general form of the **if** statement:

```
if test_1 then
    statement(s)_1;
elsif test_2 then
    statement(s)_2;
else
    statement(s)_3;
end if;
```

The behaviour of this **if** statement can be determined from the consideration of the behaviour of the previous **if** statement. If test_1 evaluates as TRUE then statement(s)_1 will be performed and the rest of the **if** structure ignored; test_2 will not be evaluated and statement(s)_2 and statement(s)_3 will not be executed. If test_1 evaluates as FALSE then test_2 will be evaluated; if it evaluates as TRUE then statement(s)_2 will be performed and statement(s)_3 will be ignored. If test_2 evaluates as FALSE then statement(s)_3 will be performed and statement(s)_2 ignored.

Using this form of the **if** statement the program can be implemented as follows:

```
0001  -- Fintan Culwin Sept '89 v1.0
0002  -- program to illustrate simple selection
0003  -- b1s4p2 see text
0004
0005  with TEXT_IO;
0006  package int_io is new TEXT_IO.INTEGER_IO( integer );
0007  with TEXT_IO,int_io; use TEXT_IO,int_io;
0008
0009  procedure b1s4p2 is
0010
0011     overdraft_limit : constant integer := -50;
0012                                   -- limit for overdraft refusal
0013     zero            : constant integer := 0;
0014
0015     resulting_balance,       -- result of transaction
0016     balance,                 -- balance in the account
0017     withdrawal : integer;    -- withdrawal from the account
0018
0019  begin -- of b1s4p2
0020
0021     -- get balance & withdrawal
0022     PUT ( "Enter the amount on deposit   ");
0023     GET ( balance ); SKIP_LINE;
0024     PUT ( "Enter the withdrawal          ");
0025     GET ( withdrawal ); SKIP_LINE;
0026
0027     -- calculate resulting balance
```

```
0028      resulting_balance := balance - withdrawal;
0029
0030      -- decide upon action
0031      if resulting_balance >=zero  then
0032         PUT ( "Accepted  balance is ");
0033         PUT ( resulting_balance ); NEW_LINE;
0034      elsif resulting_balance >= overdraft_limit then
0035         PUT ( "Overdraft balance is ");
0036         PUT ( resulting_balance ); NEW_LINE;
0037      else
0038         PUT ( "Refused   balance is ");
0039         PUT ( balance ); NEW_LINE;
0040      end if;
0041   end b1s4p2;
```

The validity of this implementation can be easily determined by relating it to the program design produced above.

1.4.3 Other forms of the **if** statement

Before leaving the topic of selection, other forms of the **if** statement will be introduced. The first of these extends the use of the general form of the three-way **if** structure introduced above. It is possible to extend this form of the **if** statement indefinitely. Any number of **elsif** decisions can be introduced into the structure, allowing a multiple-path decision of indeterminate length to be constructed.

The meaning of such a structure would be that the tests are evaluated in the sequence specified by the multiple **elsif** tests until a test evaluates as TRUE. The statements associated with the test which evaluates as TRUE are performed and the rest of the structure is ignored. If none of the tests evaluate as TRUE then the statements associated with the **else** statement are performed. It is not obligatory to include a simple **else** option in the **if** structure but if it is included it must be the last option in the structure.

A second form of the three-way **if** structure could have been used in the example above, with the following general form:

```
if test_1 then
   statement(s)_1;
else
   if test_2 then
      statement(s)_2;
   else
      statement(s)_3;
```

```
        end if;
    end if;
```

In this form statement(s)_2 from the general form of the two-way **if** statement have been replaced with a single simple two-way **if** statement. Such a situation is known as a *nested* **if** statement. The equivalent form of the **if** structure from the program example above, using a nested **if**, would be as follows:

```
0031    if resulting_balance >= zero  then
0032        PUT ( "Accepted balance is ");
0033        PUT ( resulting_balance ); NEW_LINE;
0034    else
0035        if resulting_balance >= overdraft_limit then
0036            PUT ( "Overdraft balance is ");
0037            PUT ( resulting_balance ); NEW_LINE;
0038        else
0039            PUT ( "Refused   balance is ");
0040            PUT ( balance ); NEW_LINE;
0041        end if;
0042    end if;
```

This version of the three-way **if** structure does not differ in its behaviour from the three-way **if** structure introduced above. If the first test is TRUE, statement(s)_1 are executed and the rest of the structure is ignored. If test_1 is FALSE, test_2 is evaluated to determine which of statement(s)_2 or statement(s)_3 should be performed.

Where decisions become more complicated than this, there are differences between the behaviour of the **elsif** and the nested **if** versions of the **if** structure. The general forms of the **elsif** and nested **if** structures for a four-way decision would be as follows:

```
if test_1 then                if test_1 then
    statement(s)_1;               if test_2 then
elsif test_2 then                    statement(s)_1;
    statement(s)_2;              else
elsif test_3 then                    statement(s)_2;
    statement(s)_3;              end if;
else                          else
    statement(s)_4;               if test_3 then
end if;                               statement(s)_3;
                                  else
                                      statement(s)_4;
                                  end if;
                              end if;
```

The behaviour of these two structures is not identical. The differences can be illustrated by a *truth table*. The truth table for the **elsif** structure is given in Table 1.4.1. The truth table for the nested **if** structure is given in Table 1.4.2. These truth tables are obtained from a consideration of the possible flows of control through the structures. Each test can evaluate as TRUE or FALSE and is independent from the other two tests, this gives $2 \times 2 \times 2 = 8$ possible combinations of test results. These eight possible patterns are shown in the tables, and the statement which will be executed is shown with an asterisk in the right-hand half of the table. The differences in the patterns of the asterisks indicate that the behaviour of the two statements will differ.

Table 1.4.1 Truth table for the **elsif** structure for a four-way decision

test_1	test_2	test_3	s_1	s_2	s_3	s_4
F	F	F				*
F	F	T			*	
F	T	F		*		
F	T	T		*		
T	F	F	*			
T	F	T	*			
T	T	F	*			
T	T	T	*			

Table 1.4.2 Truth table for the nested **if** structure for a four-way decision

test_1	test_2	test_3	s_1	s_2	s_3	s_4
F	F	F				*
F	F	T			*	
F	T	F				*
F	T	T			*	
T	F	F		*		
T	F	T		*		
T	T	F	*			
T	T	T	*			

When a complex multi-path **if** structure is being considered then a truth table is essential to design and verify the actions which will be performed under defined conditions. By comparing the truth table with the decision table produced from the analysis of the specification the correctness of the implementation can be demonstrated.

This section ends with a simpler form of the **if** statement. It is sometimes the case that a selection is required to decide if an action should be performed, with no alternative action specified. This can be shown on a program structure chart as follows:

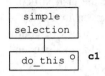

c1: If condition.

This type of selection can be implemented in Ada using the following simpler form of the general **if** statement:

```
if test then
    statement(s);
end if;
```

EXERCISES

1.4.1 Produce a program to the following design. The intent of the program is to convert a number input from the keyboard into its absolute value. (An absolute value is always a positive value. The absolute value of +3 is +3, the absolute value of -3 is +3). The conversion can be performed by multiplying a negative number by -1.

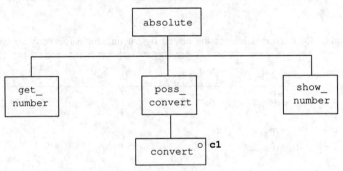

c1: If number is negative.

1.4.2 Design a user interface for the following specification:

A program is required which will estimate the amount of carpet and the cost of the carpet required for a room. The user will input the length and width of the room (in metres, integer values only). The program will then calculate the area of the room and the cost of the carpet.

If the room is 3 metres wide or less the carpet will be supplied from a roll 3 metres wide at a cost of £9 per square metre. If the room is over 3 metres wide the carpet will be supplied from a wider roll at a cost of £7 per square metre.

Produce a complete program design from the following high-level design:

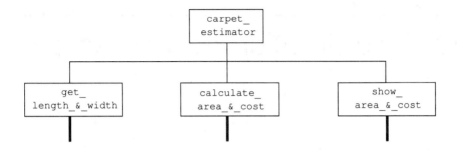

1.4.3 Produce a data design for the program in Exercise 1.4.2.

1.4.4 Implement the program designed in Exercises 1.4.2 and 1.4.3.

1.4.5 Construct a truth table, modelled on the truth tables in this section, for the following **if** structures:

```
if test_1 then                      if test_1 then
   statement(s)_1;                     statement(s)_1;
elsif test_2 then                   elsif test_2 then
   statement(s)_2;                     if test_3 then
else                                      statement(s)_2;
   if test_3 then                     else
      statement(s)_3;                    statement(s)_3;
   else                               end if;
      statement(s)_4;              else
   end if;                            statement(s)_4;
end if;                            end if;
```

Compare these truth tables with those produced in the text. Are any other behaviours of a three-way **if** structure possible?

Definite iteration in programs

The third method available for controlling program execution is iteration (repetition). Iteration is the process of making a computer program repeat a set of actions a number of times.

Definite iteration is where a set of actions has to be performed by the computer a known number of times. If it can be stated in the specification that an action has to take place a given number of times, or if the number of times can be determined as the program executes, then definite iteration is the appropriate program technique.

Where the number of times a set of actions has to be performed cannot be determined from the specification or cannot be determined as the program executes then *indefinite* iteration is the appropriate program technique.

This section will explain the concept and implementation of definite iteration. The next section will introduce the concept and implementation of indefinite iteration.

1.5.1   A definite iteration specification

The following is a simple specification for a program to illustrate definite iteration:

> A program is required to calculate the average number of assignments marked by a lecturer per month over a twelve-month period. The program will ask the user for the number of assignments (positive integer) marked in each month, identifying the month by its number. When all twelve items of data have been input the average number for a single month will be calculated and displayed to an accuracy of two decimal places.

This specification indicates clearly that a set of actions will have to be carried out twelve times. The design process will have to reflect this by performing a part of the program twelve times. Although the specification indicates the number of assignments must be a positive integer, this implementation will not enforce this.

User interface design

A suitable interface for this specification would be as follows:

```
        ASSIGNMENT AVERAGE PROGRAM

No marked in month  1        iiiiiiii
No marked in month  2        iiiiiiii

    ...

No marked in month 12        iiiiiiii

Average per month is         fffff.ff
```

where 'iiiiiiii' indicates an integer value, 'fffff.ff' indicates a floating-point value.

The user interface is divided into three parts: a heading, which indicates the function of the program; a middle part, where twelve similar prompts and inputs are obtained; and a final part, where the average is output. This description of the interaction with the user will be useful as the design of the program is produced.

The program design

The convention for representing iteration in a program design is as follows:

c1: Iteration condition.

The chart indicates that the component iteration_demo is an iteration of the component do_this. The * symbol in the top right-hand corner of the iterated component box indicates that it is an iteration. The name of the component do_this is a reminder that it is a singular component. The iteration is an iteration of a singular component (do_this), which forms an iterative component (iteration_demo).

For a definite loop the condition indicates the number of iterations which are required. For an indefinite loop the condition indicates the condition to be satisfied before the iteration terminates. The interpretation of the above diagram is: when the component iteration_demo is performed the program will perform the component do_this as many times as is specified by the condition.

The final program structure chart for this program is as follows:

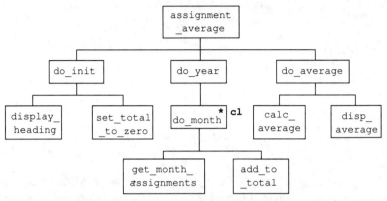

c1: Twelve times.

This structure chart indicates that the program assignment_average is a sequence of three components called do_init(ialization), do_year and do_average. The basis of this high-level design is taken from a consideration of the user interface as a sequence of title, months and average.

In order to do the initialization component the title is displayed and the total is set to zero.

In order to do the component do_year the component do_month has to be performed twelve times. In order to do do_month the number of assignments marked that month has to be input from the keyboard and added to the total.

In order to do the component do_average, the average is first calculated and then displayed.

When iteration is being used the language used in the structure charts should use singular and plural forms very carefully. The design rationale for the component do_year might have been as follows: 'In order to do a year then a component to do a single month has to be done twelve times.' A common mistake is to name the iterative component do_months; this will cause confusion when implementation is attempted. The singular form do_month will remind the programmer that within this component a single month is to be processed. Naming it do_months would indicate that a series of months would have to be implemented. This would cause problems if an attempt was made to produce a design based upon this understanding.

The data design

The data design for this program will be as follows:

PROGRAM CONSTANTS

NAME	TYPE	VALUE	NOTES
max_month	INTEGER	12	No of months in one year

PROGRAM VARIABLES

NAME	TYPE	NOTES
ass_month	INTEGER	No of assignments in any one month
total_ass	INTEGER	Total no of assignments in one year
this_month	INTEGER	Loop parameter for the month number
average_ass	FLOAT	Average assignments per month

The meaning of 'loop parameter' will be made clear below in the description of the general form of the **for** statement.

The variable average_ass has to have the capacity to represent a number which has decimal parts, thus it is not an INTEGER. A data type which has the capacity to include decimal parts is FLOAT. The variable average_ass will be declared to be of this type. The FLOAT data type will be introduced in detail in Block 2 Section 1.

The general form of the **for** statement

The method of implementing a definite loop in an Ada program is to use the **for** statement. The general form of the **for** statement is as follows:

```
for loop_param in index_type range low_value .. high_value loop
   statement(s);
end loop;
```

The Ada rules for this from of the general **for** statement are as follows:

1. Loop_param is a variable object which does not have to be declared; it is implicitly declared in the **for** syntax, with a type indicated by index_type. It is known as the *loop parameter*.
2. Within the statements which form the body of the loop, the loop parameter can only be used as a constant.
3. The low_value and the high_value can be variables, constants, literals or expressions.
4. The value of the expression high_value has to be equal to or greater than the value of low_value for the loop to iterate at least once. If the value of low_value is greater than the value of high_value the loop will not iterate.
5. The statement(s) which form the body of the loop can be any Ada statements.
6. The entire **for** structure is a single Ada statement and is terminated by a semicolon.

The style rules for a general **for** statement are as follows:

1. The reserved words **for, in, range, loop** and **end** are shown in **bold**.
2. The statement(s) controlled by the **for** statement are indented.
3. The **loop** term within **end loop** is *not* optional.

The behaviour of the **for** statement when it is executed is as follows:

1. The loop parameter is created and initialized to the value specified by low_value.
2. The value of the loop parameter is compared with the value specified by high_value. If the value of the loop parameter is greater then the value of high_value, the loop terminates.
3. The statement(s) are performed.
4. The value of the loop parameter is incremented by a single unit value.
5. The value of the loop parameter is compared again and execution of the loop continues as before.

The program listing

As this program uses and outputs objects of type FLOAT, the program will have to have the capability to input and output FLOAT values. This capability can be included within all parts of a program by including the following declarations in the program heading:

```
with TEXT_IO; package float_inout is new TEXT_IO.FLOAT_IO( FLOAT );
with float_inout; use float_inout;
```

Using the **for** statement the program can be implemented as as follows:

```
0001   -- Fintan Culwin Sept '88 v1.0
0002   -- program to illustrate simple definite iteration
0003   -- b1s5p1 see text
0004
0005   with TEXT_IO;
0006   package int_io is new TEXT_IO.INTEGER_IO( INTEGER );
0007   with TEXT_IO;
0008   package float_inout is new TEXT_IO.FLOAT_IO( FLOAT );
0009
0010   with TEXT_IO, int_io, float_inout;
0011   use  TEXT_IO, int_io, float_inout;
0012
0013   procedure b1s5p1 is
0014
0015      max_month : constant INTEGER := 12;
0016                                 -- months in one year
0017
0018      total_ass,                -- total no of assignments
0019      ass_month   : INTEGER;    -- assignments this month
0020
0021      average_ass : FLOAT;      -- average per month
0022
0023   begin -- of b1s5p1
```

```
0024      -- do init
0025      PUT_LINE ("  ASSIGNMENT AVERAGE PROGRAM "); NEW_LINE;
0026      total_ass := 0;
0027
0028      -- do year
0029      for this_month in INTEGER range 1 .. max_month loop
0030         PUT ( "No marked in month");
0031         PUT ( this_month, WIDTH => 3); PUT ( "   ");
0032         GET ( ass_month ); SKIP_LINE;
0033         total_ass := total_ass + ass_month;
0034      end loop;
0035
0036      -- do average
0037      average_ass := FLOAT ( total_ass) / FLOAT ( max_month );
0038      NEW_LINE;
0039      PUT ( "Average per month is ");
0040      PUT ( average_ass, FORE => 6, AFT => 2, EXP => 0 ); NEW_LINE;
0041   end b4s5p1;
```

The program listing commences with the statements necessary for allowing the program access to the facilities required for the input and output of STRING, INTEGER and FLOAT values. The program heading comments completes the heading of the program.

The data declarations are taken from the data design. The only point to make is that the object this_month, which will be used as the loop parameter, is not declared.

The statement part of the program commences with do_init, whose construction from the structure chart should be clear.

The implementation of the component do_year has been made using the general form of the **for** statement introduced above. The **for** statement on line 0029 can be considered as being equivalent to:

```
for this_month in INTEGER range 1 .. 12 loop
```

The effect of this is to execute the body of the loop twelve times. The body of the loop, which comprises the statements on lines 0030–0033, is indented in the listing. The first time the loop is executed the value of the loop parameter (this_month) is 1. The second time the loop is executed the value of the loop parameter is 2. The process continues until the twelfth time the loop is executed, when the value of the loop parameter is 12.

The value of the loop parameter can only be used within the body of the loop as a constant. In this example it is only used to make the input prompt more meaningful. By including the loop parameter in the PUT statement in line 0030, the month number is displayed as part of the input prompt.

The input prompt is improved by the use of a format specifier within the INTEGER PUT statement. The variable reference this_month is followed by the term 'WIDTH =>

3'. This specifies that the output is to be displayed with a field width of three characters. When the value of the output only requires a single digit, it will be padded with two spaces to increase its length to three characters. When the output value requires two digits, they will be preceded by a single space making a total length of three characters.

This improves the user interface by restricting the number of characters output to a sensible value. If the format specifier were not included then the output would be wide enough to contain the largest value which the Ada compiler can represent; this could be as much as twelve characters. This will be explained further in Block 2.

A format specifier is also used in line 0033 where the value being output is of type FLOAT. If no format specifier were included in the term then the value would be output in exponent notation (e.g., 3.142E0). The specification states that the number is to be output with two decimal places of accuracy (e.g., 3.14).

The format specifier for a FLOAT value comprises of three parts, FORE, AFT and EXP. The EXP specifier controls the use of exponent notation; by specifying a value of 0 exponent notation is turned off. The remaining specifiers specify the number of character positions before the decimal point (FORE) and the number of characters after the decimal point (AFT).

The value which is output by this statement is the value of the FLOAT object called average_ass. This object on line 0036 is given the value of the result of the division of the value of total_ass by max_month. Both of these objects are of type INTEGER and consequently the result of 'total_ass/max_month' would be of the type INTEGER. It is not possible in Ada for an INTEGER value to be assigned to a FLOAT object.

To allow the value to be calculated and the result assigned to a FLOAT object the INTEGER values have to be converted into FLOAT values, before the division takes place. This can be achieved by using the *type conversion* facility of Ada. To convert an INTEGER value to a FLOAT value, the term FLOAT(int_obj) is used. To convert a FLOAT value into an INTEGER value, the term INTEGER(float_obj) could be used. Thus the expression

```
FLOAT(total_ass) / FLOAT(max_month)
```

on line 0037 converts the values of the INTEGER objects to FLOAT and then performs a FLOAT division. These facilities will be explained more fully in Block 2 Section 1.

The validity of this implementation can be determined by relating it to the program design given above, by walking through the program listing and by implementing the program listing as a Ada program.

1.5.2 A second definite iteration specification

The number of iterations which were required within the program above could be determined from the specification. A definite loop can also be used where the number of iterations cannot be determined from a consideration of the specification, but can be determined by the program as it executes before the loop is reached: This program will provide an example of such a loop.

> A program is required which will produce a conversion table from mph (miles per hour) to kph (kilometres per hour). The program will ask the user for the lowest value to convert and the highest value to convert (both integer values). The program will then display a conversion table starting with the highest value and ending with the lowest value, the converted values being displayed to an accuracy of one decimal place. (The program will assume that the highest value input by the user is in fact higher than the lowest value and will not attempt to check this.)

This design is appropriate for implementation as a definite loop. It is not possible to state how many times the loop will have to iterate from the specification. The number of times the loop will iterate is dependent upon the actual values input by the user. These values are not available until the program is executing but they will be known by the program before the loop has to commence. The program can at this stage, just before the loop iterates for the first time, determine the number of iterations. If the number of iterations could not be determined by the program until the loop has commenced then an indefinite loop would be appropriate (see Block 1 Section 6).

User interface

A suitable user interface for this design would be:

```
        KPH TABLE

Please enter the lowest value    10
Please enter the highest value   20

20 mph is 32.2 kph
19 mph is 30.6 kph
   ...
10 mph is 16.1 kph
```

The program design

The final program structure chart for this program would be as follows:

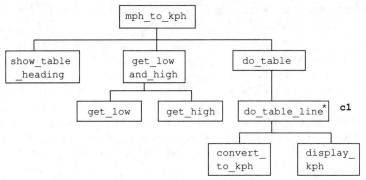

c1: Number of times between high and low.

The data design

PROGRAM CONSTANTS

NAME	TYPE	VALUE	NOTES
mph_to_kph	FLOAT	1.61	Conversion factor

PROGRAM VARIABLES

NAME	TYPE	NOTES
high_value	INTEGER	Highest value in table
low_value	INTEGER	Lowest value in table
mph	INTEGER	Loop parameter
kph	FLOAT	kph equivalent of mph

The program listing

This specification requires the loop to execute 'backwards'. A variation of the general **for** loop will accommodate this:

```
for loop_index in  reverse index_type range low_value .. high_value loop
   statement(s);
end loop;
```

The only difference between this form of the **for** statement and the previous form of the **for** statement is the inclusion of the reserved word **reverse**. This will cause the loop parameter to be initialized to the value of the expression high_value and to decrement the loop parameter by one unit value on each iteration of the loop. It is not necessary to reverse the sequence low_value .. high_value, (as in high_value .. low_value), as this would cause the loop not to iterate at all.

```
0001    -- Fintan Culwin Sept '88 v1.0
0002    -- program to illustrate simple definite iteration.
0003    -- b1s5p2 see text.
0004
0005    with TEXT_IO;
0006    package int_io is new TEXT_IO.INTEGER_IO( INTEGER );
0007    with TEXT_IO;
0008    package float_inout   is new TEXT_IO.FLOAT_IO( FLOAT );
0009
0010    with TEXT_IO, int_io, float_inout;
0011    use  TEXT_IO, int_io, float_inout;
0012
0013    procedure b1s5p2 is
0014
0015       mph_to_kph   : constant FLOAT := 1.61; -- conversion factor
0016
0017       low_value,                       -- low  value of table
0018       high_value  : INTEGER;           -- high value of table
0019
0020       kph          : FLOAT;            -- kph equivalent
0021
0022    begin -- of b1s5p2
0023       -- show table heading
0024       PUT_LINE("          KPH TABLE "); NEW_LINE;
0025
0026       -- get high and low
0027       PUT( "Please enter the lowest value ");
0028       GET( low_value ); SKIP_LINE;
0029
0030       PUT( "Please enter the highest value ");
0031       GET( high_value); SKIP_LINE;
0032       NEW_LINE;
0033
0034       -- do table
0035       for mph in reverse INTEGER range low_value .. high_value loop
0036          kph := FLOAT( mph ) * mph_to_kph;
0037          PUT( mph, WIDTH => 4); PUT(" is   ");
0038          PUT( kph, FORE =>4, AFT =>1, EXP =>0);
0039          PUT( " kph."); NEW_LINE;
```

```
0040        end loop;
0041    end b1s5p2;
```

The implementation of this program from the program design and the data design should largely be obvious. The loop has been implemented using the **reverse for** loop option as explained above. In line 0036 the value of the INTEGER loop parameter 'mph' has been converted into a FLOAT value in order to allow it to be used in the calculation.

The validity of this program can be established by relating it to the design, walking through the listing and by implementing the listing as an Ada program.

EXERCISES

1.5.1 Design and implement a program to the following specification:

A program is required to provide a 'ready reckoner' for the costs of items. The user will be asked to input the cost (minus VAT) of a single item and the program will produce a table giving the costs of up to ten items with and without VAT.

A user interface for this program would be as follows:

```
        READY RECKONER

Please enter the cost of a single item ffff.ff

The VAT rate is 17.5%

        No of items        cost        cost with VAT
             1          fffffff.ff       fffffff.ff
             2          fffffff.ff       fffffff.ff
            ...            ...              ...
            10          fffffff.ff       fffffff.ff
```

where 'fffffff.ff' indicates a FLOAT value.

1.5.2 Amend the design and implementation of the program in Exercise 1.5.1 so that the program will also ask the user what number of items the table is to be centred upon. The ready reckoner will then produce a table which displays a table from five items below to five items above the number of items the table is to be centred upon.

1.5.3 Design and implement a program to output multiplication tables. A user interface design might be as follows:

```
        MULTIPLICATION TABLE

Please enter the table required 6

1 times 6 is    6
2 times 6 is   12

  ...       ...
12 times 6 is   72
```

1.5.4 Design and implement a program which will output a table indicating the value of an investment over a ten-year period assuming a fixed rate of interest. A user interface design (with user input underlined) might be as follows:

```
            INVESTMENT TABLE

Please enter the amount to invest    £1000.00
Please enter the fixed interest rate %5

The value of the investment after  1 years is £1050.00
The value of the investment after  2 years is £1102.50
   ...           ...            ...
The value of the investment after 10 years is £1628.89
```

Section 1.6

Indefinite iteration in programs

Indefinite iteration is an appropriate loop control technique where the number of times the body of the loop has to iterate cannot be determined until the loop has been entered. Indefinite iteration can be performed using the Ada **while** loop construct. This construct can be configured to behave as a true **while** structure or as a *repeat* structure. The difference between the two loop possibilities is that a repeat loop will execute at least once, while a **while** loop may not execute at all.

1.6.1 Specification for a **repeat** iteration

A program fragment which is commonly needed is to ask the user of a program to input 'Y' (or 'y') to indicate yes, or to input 'N' (or 'n') to indicate no. A specification for this program fragment might be as follows:

> The user is to be prompted to enter 'Y' (or 'y') to indicate yes, or to enter 'N' (or 'n') to indicate no. If either of these responses is produced by the user the program will confirm the response and terminate. If the user produces a response which is not one of the responses specified, the prompt and input interaction are to be repeated.

This specification is suitable for an indefinite loop as there is no way of determining if the user has input an acceptable response until the body of the loop is executing. It could be that the user will input one of the correct key presses on the first iteration of the loop, or for a particularly stupid user it might be the 627th iteration before he or she reads the prompt and responds appropriately.

A *repeat* configuration of the **while** loop is suitable for this specification as the user has to respond at least once. A *repeat* loop will iterate at least once, while a true **while** loop may not iterate at all.

User interface design

A user dialogue where an incorrect response is given might be as follows:

```
Please enter 'Y' or 'y' for yes or 'N' or 'n' for no Q
-- any number of incorrect responses
Please enter 'Y' or 'y' for yes or 'N' or 'n' for no n

You entered No.
```

A user dialogue where a correct response is given to the first prompt might be as follows:

```
Please enter 'Y' for yes or 'N' for no Y

You entered Yes.
```

The program design

The final program structure chart for this program would be as follows:

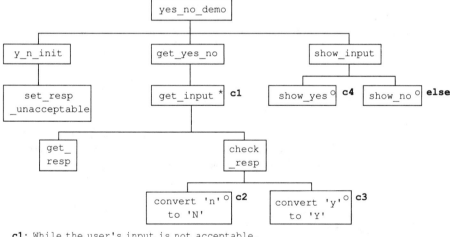

c1: While the user's input is not acceptable.
c2: If the input is 'n'.
c3: If the input is 'y'.
c4: If the input is 'Y'.

This program design involves the use of iteration and the use of selection. The design can be walked through, using the example interactions above, to verify the design.

On the first interaction the program yes_no_demo will commence by performing the component y_n_init (yes_no_initialize); the only action of this component is to set the value of the user's response to an unacceptable value (e.g., 'x'). This is to ensure that the loop control test will fail when it is evaluated for the first time, ensuring that the loop executes at least once.

The program continues by performing the component get_yes_no; this is expressed on the structure chart as an iteration of the component get_input. The behaviour of the iteration is to evaluate the test before deciding if the body of the loop is to be executed. Because of the initialization component, it is guaranteed that the test will fail and the component get_input will be executed.

The get_input component commences by performing the component get_resp, where the input prompt will be displayed and a response accepted from the user. As shown on the user interface design, the user's response on the first iteration of the first walk-through will be assumed to be 'Q'. The check_resp component is then executed and as the input does not satisfy condition c2 or condition c3, neither of the conversion components will be performed.

This point marks the end of the component get_input; the condition c1 is then tested for a second time. As the condition is not satisfied the loop will iterate again. The prompt will be redisplayed and the user's second response accepted. The input from the user will now be assumed to be 'n'. This input will satisfy condition c2 and the input will be converted to 'N'. The value 'N' will satisfy condition c1 and the iteration of get_input will terminate. The end of get_input is also the end of get_yes_no.

The program will continue with the selective component show_input where condition c4 will not be satisfied and the show_no component will be performed. The program will then terminate.

If the design is walked through again with the input from the user assumed to be 'Y' on the first request, the alternative behaviour of the design illustrated in the second user dialogue above can be verified.

The data design

Only a single variable object is required for this program. This object has to be capable of storing a response from the user. A suitable data type is CHARACTER. Objects of type CHARACTER are capable of storing a single character value.

PROGRAM VARIABLES

NAME	TYPE	NOTES
response	CHARACTER	Response from the user

The program listing

The method of implementing an indefinite loop in Ada is to use a **while loop** statement. The general form of this statement is as follows:

```
while test loop
   statement(s);
end loop;
```

The Ada rules for this statement are as follows:

1. The reserved word **while** is used to indicate an indefinite loop.
2. The body of the loop is the statement or statements enclosed between the reserved word **loop** and the corresponding **end loop**.
3. Test is an expression which will evaluate as TRUE or FALSE.
4. The **loop/end loop** statement is a complete statement and is terminated with a semicolon as shown.
5. The term **loop** is the phrase **end loop** is *not* optional.

There is one style rule for the **while** statement: the statement(s) comprising the body of the loop are indented.

The form of the tests which control the behaviour of the loop are identical to the tests which can be used to control an **if** statement. These tests were introduced in Block 1 Section 4 and will be explained in detail in Block 2 Section 4.

The behaviour of the **while** loop is as follows. The test is evaluated. If the test evaluates as FALSE the loop terminates. If the test evaluates as TRUE the loop statements are executed, then the test is evaluated again, and the process is repeated.

The program listing using the **while** loop follows. The only package required is TEXT_IO which contains suitable GET and PUT procedures for the input and output of characters, as well as strings. Consequently a special package for CHARACTER input and output does not need to be instantiated.

```
0001   -- Fintan Culwin Sept '88 v1.0
0002   -- program to illustrate indefinite iteration
0003   -- b1s6p1 see text
0004
0005   with TEXT_IO; use TEXT_IO;
0006
0007   procedure b1b6p1 is
0008
0009          response : CHARACTER;        -- response from user
0010
0011   begin -- of b1s6p1
0012
0013          -- y_n_init
0014          response := 'x';  -- ensure loop iterates at least once
0015          -- get yes no
0016          while ( response /= 'N' ) and ( response /= 'Y') loop
0017             PUT( "Please enter 'y' for yes or 'n' for no ");
```

```
0018            GET( response ); SKIP_LINE;
0019            -- check input
0020            if response = 'n' then response := 'N'; end if;
0021            if response = 'y' then response := 'Y'; end if;
0022        end loop;
0023
0024            -- show input
0025        if response = 'Y' then
0026            PUT_LINE("You entered Yes.");
0027        else
0028            PUT_LINE("You entered No.");
0029        end if;
0030  end b1s6p1;
```

The value of the variable called response which is of the predeclared type CHARACTER has to be tested at various points in the program. These tests compare the variable which is of type CHARACTER with another value of type CHARACTER using the 'is equal to' ('=') and the 'is not equal to' ('/=') relational operators. The values which are used for the relational comparison are expressed as character literals ('Y', 'y', 'N', 'n'). A character literal is a single character contained between single quotes ("'").

The **if** statements on lines 0020, 0021 and 0025 use a simple single relational expression, which, as explained in B1S4, will evaluate to the value TRUE or FALSE and control the behaviour of the **if** statement accordingly. As these **if** statements are so simple and unlikely ever to become more complex, they have been included in the listing on a single line.

The test on line 0016 is expressed on the structure chart as 'while the user's input is not acceptable'. This test is expressed in the program listing by the following:

while (response /= 'N') **and** (response /= 'Y') **loop**

The test now comprises of two simple relational expressions connected by the logical operator **and**. The **and** operator combines two TRUE/FALSE values together to produce a single TRUE/FALSE value; using the rule that the combined expression will only be TRUE if both the left-hand expression and the right-hand expression are TRUE. If either of the two values is FALSE, the **and** expression will evaluate to FALSE.

The loop will iterate for as long as this control expression evaluates TRUE. The expression will be TRUE for as long as both simple expressions are TRUE. As soon as one of the expressions becomes FALSE, which will be when response is equal to 'N' or when response is equal to 'Y', the loop will terminate. The construction and use of expressions involving the **and** operator will be explained more fully in Block 2 Section 4.

At line 0024 following the termination of the loop a statement about the state of the program can be made. The statement would be that the variable response must contain either 'Y' or 'N'. This statement is always TRUE as this point in the program can only be reached by satisfying the condition controlling the loop. A statement about the state of the program made like this is known as an *assertion*. Assertions can be very useful in constructing programs and will be introduced in Block 2.

Using the assertion the decision within the component show_response can be simplified. If the value of response is not 'Y' then its value must be 'N'. This can be taken advantage of in constructing the **if** statement. If the assertion could not be made the implementation of this part of the program would be as follows:

```
0023     value of response is unknown
0024  if response = 'Y' then
0025     PUT_LINE("You entered Yes.")
0026  elsif response = 'N' then
0027     PUT_LINE("You entered No.")
0028  end if;
```

This variation is not only more complex but in this form it does not define what will happen if the value of response is neither 'Y' or 'N'.

1.6.2 Specification for a true **while** iteration

A true **while** specification would include the possibility that the body of a loop may not iterate at all. Let the specification for a true **while** iteration demonstration program be as follows:

A program is required to process a batch of values representing the scores of students on an exam. Valid scores for the exam are integers in the range 0 to 100. The number of students taking the exam is not known in advance and it is possible that no students take the exam. The end of the batch of scores will be indicated by the user of the program inputting a negative value when asked for an exam score.

When all the scores have been processed a summary showing the number of students taking the exam, the highest score, the lowest score and the average score is to be displayed. The average score is to be displayed to an accuracy of one decimal place. The summary information is to be suppressed if no students take the exam.

This specification is suitable for an indefinite loop as there is no way of determining the number of scores until the program is executing. There is also the possibility that no students take the exam, which indicates that a **while** loop is appropriate.

User interface design

A user dialogue for the situation where a number of students take the exam would be as follows:

```
        EXAM ANALYSIS

Enter score (or -1 to finish)   iiiiiiii
Enter score (or -1 to finish)   iiiiiiii
-- any number of valid inputs here
Enter score (or -1 to finish)   -1

No of students is               iiiiiiii
Highest score  is               iiiiiiii
Lowest  score  is               iiiiiiii
Average score  is               ffffff.f
```

A user dialogue for the situation where no students take the exam would be as follows:

```
        EXAM ANALYSIS

Enter score (or -1 to finish)   -1

No of students is               0
```

To simplify the user interface the user is invited to enter -1 to indicate that all exam scores have been entered.

The program design

An initial program structure chart for this program would be as follows:

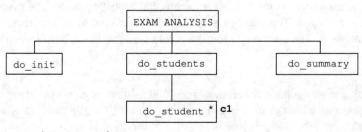

c1: While score is not negative.

This first-level design shows the high-level structure of the program. The main part of the program is called do_students and is an iteration of do_student controlled by condition **c1**. As a **while** loop has the possibility of not executing at all, this condition will have to be evaluated at the start of the loop. If it evaluates as FALSE on the first iteration (if the first and only input is negative) then the body of the loop will never be executed. This requires the first score to be input before this test is evaluated for the first time. Consequently an input from the user is required as part of the component do_init(ialization).

Taking this into account, the structure of the component do_init(ialization) can be refined as follows:

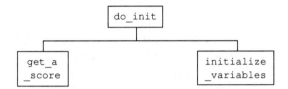

The component do_student can be refined as follows:

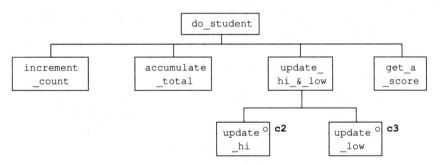

c2: If score is higher than highest recorded so far.
c3: If score is lower than lowest recorded so far.

The actions which have to be performed for each student are shown on the structure chart. Each student has to be counted, his or her score added to the total score in order that an average can be calculated, and a check has to be made if the student's score is high enough to be the highest score so far or low enough to be the lowest score so far.

Following these actions, which are concerned with processing a single student's score, the next possible score is input by the user. As this is the end of the component the next action which will take place is the evaluation of the loop condition. If the score input is a valid score the loop will iterate again processing the valid score. If the score input is a terminating value the loop will terminate without processing that input.

The component do_summary remains to be refined:

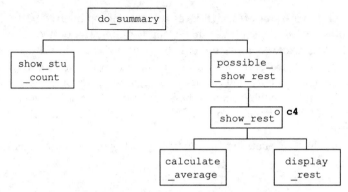

c4: If number of students is greater than zero.

The count of students is to be shown even if the number of students processed is zero. The rest of the summary information is to be shown only if the number of students is greater than zero. This consideration is shown on the structure chart.

It is not necessary to combine the four structure charts which comprise the design into one complete structure chart. When the design is documented each chart will be given a number. The high level structure chart can be cross referenced to each of the lower level structure charts using the chart numbers.

If the charts are numbered from 1 to 4 in the sequence shown, the high-level chart would be presented as follows:

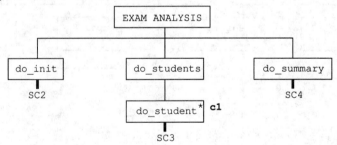

c1: While score is not negative.

The boxes which are refined in separate structure charts are shown as continuing using bold lines and are keyed to the structure chart which defines them by using the number of the structure chart. Each of the three other structure charts would be presented with a structure chart number and title.

With a large design it would be impossible to produce and to maintain one large complete structure chart for the entire design. Even if it were possible it would not be desirable as it would be impossible to comprehend the design of the program. It would also be disadvantageous as a minor amendment may require the entire chart to be redrawn.

As a general rule the number of component boxes in any structure chart should be between 5 and 10. This allows the design to be understood by someone reading the design from the structure charts.

The data design

The data design for this program would be as follows:

PROGRAM VARIABLES

NAME	TYPE	NOTES
num_stu	INTEGER	No. of students
min_so_far	INTEGER	Minimum so far
max_so_far	INTEGER	Maximum so far
this_score	INTEGER	Current student's score
total_scores	INTEGER	Total of all scores
average_score	FLOAT	Average score per student

The program listing

```
0001  -- Fintan Culwin Sept '88 v1.0
0002  -- program to illustrate simple definite iteration
0003  -- b1s6p2 see text
0004  -- assumes int_io and float_inout in library
0005
0006  with TEXT_IO; int_io; float_inout;
0007  use  TEXT_IO; int_io; float_inout;
0008
0009  procedure b1s4p2 is
0010
0011      num_stu,              -- number of students processed
0012      min_so_far,           -- minimum recorded score
0013      max_so_far,           -- maximum recorded score
0014      total_score,          -- total of all scores
0015      this_score   : INTEGER; -- current score
0016      average_score : FLOAT;
0017
0018  begin -- of b1s6p2
0019      -- do init
```

```
0020    PUT( "Enter score (or -1 to finish) ");
0021    GET( this_score); SKIP_LINE;
0022
0023    num_stu      := 0;           -- zero students processed so far
0024    total_score := 0;           -- so total score is zero
0025    min_so_far  := this_score; -- minimum score so far
0026    max_so_far  := this_score; -- maximum score so far
0027
0028    -- do students
0029    while (this_score >=0) loop
0030       num_stu := num_stu + 1;
0031       total_score := total_score + this_score;
0032
0033       if this_score > max_so_far then
0034          max_so_far := this_score;
0035       elsif this_score < min_so_far then
0036          min_so_far := this_score;
0037       end if;
0038
0039       PUT("Enter score (or -1 to finish) ");
0040       GET( this_score); SKIP_LINE;
0041    end loop;
0042
0043    -- do summary
0044    NEW_LINE(2);
0045    PUT("No of students is "); PUT( num_stu, WIDTH => 4);
0046    NEW_LINE;
0047    if (num_stu > 0) then
0048       average_score := FLOAT( total_score) / FLOAT( num_stu);
0049       PUT("Highest score is "); PUT( max_so_far, WIDTH => 8);
0050       NEW_LINE;
0051       PUT("Lowest  score is "); PUT( min_so_far, WIDTH => 8);
0052       NEW_LINE;
0053       PUT("Average score is ");
0054       PUT(-Average_score, FORE => 4, AFT => 2, EXP => 0);
0055       NEW_LINE;
0056    end if;
0057 end b1s6p2;
```

The implementation of this program can be verified by relating it to the program structure charts shown above, by walking through the listing and by implementing the listing as an Ada program.

The only new Ada facility which is introduced is in line 0044 where the statement NEW_LINE(2) occurs. This is the same NEW_LINE statement as has been used previously but uses a variation of syntax to indicate that more than one new line should be output. In this example two new lines are asked for. By including an integer value greater than zero in brackets following NEW_LINE any number of new lines can be requested.

1.6.3 Definite and indefinite loops compared

This section and the last have introduced three possible loop implementations available to the programmer in Ada. Similar constructs are available in most programming languages. The problem for novice programmers is not in recognizing that an iteration is required as a part of the program but in deciding what form of loop to use and then implementing the loop correctly.

The most general form of the loop structure is the **while** loop. By explicitly setting the values of the variables which are used in the test which controls the loop its behaviour can be configured to cause the loop to be executed at least once (a *repeat* loop). Alternatively, the value of control variables can be set from previous actions of the program leading to the possibility of the loop not executing at all (a true **while** loop).

The **while** loop can also be used in situations where a **for** loop would be indicated. Consider the assignment average program from the last section. This could be implemented with a **while** loop as follows:

```
-- do year
this_month := 1; -- prime while loop
while this_month <= 12 loop
   -- body of the loop as before but including
   this_month := this_month + 1;
   -- as the last statement
end loop;
```

As a **while** loop can be made to behave in an equivalent way to a **for** loop, it should be considered first for any program which requires iteration. Some programmers maintain that it is the only loop structure which should be used.

One of the commonest errors in programs, particularly those produced by novice programmers, is to produce a faulty loop control structure. The condition which controls a **while** loop should always be very carefully examined when a design is walked through. In particular the following points should be checked:

1. If the body of the loop has to be executed at least once, have the variables whose values control the loop been set to suitable values to ensure this?
2. For any **while** loop, is it possible for the loop condition to evaluate as FALSE at some stage in the program's execution? If this cannot be guarateed the loop may never terminate.

EXERCISES

1.6.1 Design and implement a program to the following specification:

> The costs of hiring a delivery van are £50 plus £2 per mile travelled. A program is required to produce ready reckoner for the van showing the cost for all mileages travelled between 10 and 200 miles in steps of 10 miles.

The user interface for this program would be as follows:

```
    VAN DELIVERY CHARGES

  miles           cost

   10              60
   20              70
   ...            ...
  200             450
```

1.6.2 Design and implement a program to the following specification:

> A program is required which will ask the user to input the amount of money to be invested, the interest rate offered, and the calendar year it is invested. The program will calculate the value of the investment every year until the value of the investment has more than doubled. The program will then inform the user how long it will take for the investment to double, what the calendar year will be, and exactly what the investment will be worth.

A user interface for this program would be as follows:

```
      INVESTMENT CALCULATOR

  Please enter the amount to invest  fffff.ff
  Please enter the investment rate    fffff.ff
  Please enter the calendar year      iiii

  The investment will double in xx years
  In iiii it will be worth fffff.ff.
```

1.6.3 When a calendar year is being input it is required that it is in the range 1988 to 1999. If a value outside this range is input the program should give an error message and ask for the input again. A user dialogue for this might be as follows:

```
Please enter the calendar year        1987
Valid years are in the range 1988 to 1999.

Please enter the calendar year        2000
Valid years are in the range 1988 to 1999.

-- any number of invalid inputs here

Please enter the calendar year        1989
Thank you, date accepted.
```

Design the program fragment and include it in the program developed in Exercise 1.6.2.

Section 1.7

Procedurized implementation

Compared with realistic programs, all the implementations produced so far have been very small, with less than forty lines of Ada code. All have been easy to understand because of their simplicity, the style of Ada used and the closeness of the design to the implementation. As program specifications become more complex, the designs will consequently become more complex and the listings longer. If the program listings continued to be implemented with the methods that have been used so far they would quickly become too complex to understand.

The method of implementing Ada listings used in the previous sections has been to include all the Ada text within the **begin/end** pair marking the start and end of the program procedure. If this were continued then two things would happen which would make the listings difficult if not impossible to manage. First, the size of the body of text would become impossibly large. The smallest realistic programs are hundreds of lines long; a more usual length for programs would be thousands of lines. If these were implemented as a single block of code it would become impossible for a human to understand the complexity of the listing. A second undesirable effect of this would be in the use of indentation. A single block of code hundreds or thousands of lines long would contain within it many nested levels of structural control statements (**if, for, while**, etc.). If indentation of the structures were maintained an indent of many characters would be required. This would quickly become impractical to use, difficult to maintain and impossible to understand.

A solution to these problems lies in the use of *procedures*. The simplest use of procedures is to collect together a number of Ada statements and give them a (procedure) name. When this body of code is required to be executed, it can be invoked by using the name it has been given.

A procedure in Ada is in three parts, the first of which is the *declaration* of the procedure. A procedure declaration states the name of the procedure, and the names of any data objects it requires. The second part is the procedure *definition*, which states what actions are associated with the procedure. The third part is the procedure *call*, which is the place, or places, in a program where execution of the procedure is requested.

It is usual in simple program implementations for the first two parts of a procedure to be combined; a single set of statements is used as a combined procedure declaration and definition. In more complex program implementations, the declaration and definition of procedures can be made separately.

In this section, procedures will be introduced as a means of partitioning the actions of a program, allowing a program to be considered as a collection of subprograms. The overall complexity of the program is hidden inside a number of simpler subprograms. This is not a complete consideration of procedures; procedures should also partition the data objects used in a program. The use of procedures in this manner will be introduced in Block 1 Section 11.

1.7.1 A first procedure example

The final program design for the program add_two_numbers in Block 1 Section 3 was as follows:

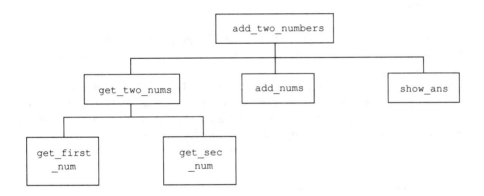

The previous implementation of this program included all the statements required for the program in a single block of code commented as the start and end of the program, which was expressed as the program procedure add_two_numbers.

If this design is to be produced using a procedurized implementation the first stage would be to decide which parts of the program are to be implemented as procedures. From the program structure chart there are three main parts to the program, get_two_nums, add_nums and show_ans; it would seem appropriate to implement these design components as procedures.

The program heading for this program implementation would not change, apart from the program comments:

```
0001    -- Fintan Culwin Sept 1989 v 1.0
0002    -- simple demonstration program illustrating procedures
0003    -- b1s7p1 see text
0004
```

```
0005   with TEXT_IO, int_io; use TEXT_IO, int_io;
0006
0007   procedure b1s7p1 is
0008
0009      first_num,             -- first number from user
0010      sec_num,               -- second number from user
0011      total_num  : INTEGER;  -- result of addition
```

The main part of the program would now be a sequence of calls of procedures which are implemented by stating the names of the procedures:

```
0041  begin -- b1s7p1
0042     get_two_nums;   -- call of procedure get_two_nums
0043     add_numbers;    -- call of procedure add_nums
0044     show_answer;    -- call of procedure show_ans
0045  end b1s7p1;
```

The meaning of this program procedure is that the program add_two_nums is to be performed by performing the procedures get_two_nums, add_nums and show_ans in the sequence specified.

By referring to the program structure chart, it can be verified that this corresponds exactly to the high-level design of the program. In order for this program to be executed the three procedures will have to be defined and declared. The combined declaration and definition of the procedure get_two_nums would be as follows:

```
0012
0013  procedure get_two_nums is
0014  -- procedure to obtain two nums from user
0015  begin -- of get_two_nums
0016     -- get first number
0017     PUT( "Please enter the first number ");
0018     GET( first_num ); SKIP_LINE;
0019
0020     -- get second number
0021     PUT( "Please enter the second number ");
0022     GET( sec_num ); SKIP_LINE;
0023
0024  end get_two_nums;
```

This program fragment starts with the reserved word **procedure**, indicating that a procedure declaration is being made. The line number shows that this declaration is being made following the declaration of data objects in the program heading. The procedure is regarded as an object of the program and consequently has to be declared in the program procedure declarations section, before the **begin** which marks the start of the executable part of the program procedure.

The name of the procedure follows the reserved word **procedure**. The name of the procedure is an identifier, subject to the same rules as other Ada identifiers. This declaration of the procedure is concluded with the reserved word **is**, indicating that the definition of the procedure follows immediately. This is an example of a combined procedure declaration and definition.

Each procedure should commence with a comment indicating what the procedure is intended to do. This is similar to the comment which forms part of the program heading indicating what the program is intended to do. Program comments precede the program procedure declaration so that they can be easily located; procedure comments follow the procedure declaration.

In this procedure the statement part of the procedure follows the procedure's comments, enclosed within a **begin/end** pair. The **begin** has been commented as the start of the procedure by using the procedure name. The **end** marking the end of the procedure indicates the name of the procedure as part of its syntax.

Within the **begin/end** pair are the statements which comprise the body of the procedure. When this procedure is called at line 0042 of this listing, program control is passed to the procedure declaration. The next statement to be executed will be the first executable statement of the procedure, in this example the statement on line 0017.

Program execution will then continue within the procedure. Any sequence of Ada control constructs can be included within the procedure, including calls of other procedures. When all the statements of the procedure have been executed the **end** statement of the procedure will be reached, in this example at line 0024. Execution of the **end** statement causes program control to be passed back to the place in the program from which the procedure was called, in this example the end of line 0042.

In order for this program to be complete, the other two procedures add_nums and show_ans will have to be declared within the program; their declaration would be as follows:

```
0025
0026  procedure add_nums is
0027  -- procedure to add two numbers together
0028  begin    -- add nums
0029     total_num := first_num + sec_num;
0030  end add_nums;
0031
0032
0033  procedure show_ans is
0034  -- procedure to display the answer
0035  begin    -- show answer
0036     NEW_LINE;
0037     PUT ( "The total is . . . . ");
0038     PUT ( total_num ); NEW_LINE;
```

```
0039  end show_answer;
0040
```

Execution of this program commences with the first statement of the program procedure, that is the call of the procedure get_two_nums at line 0042. As explained above, this will eventually cause program control to be returned to the statement following the call of the procedure. The other two procedures will be called in a similar manner, causing the statement parts of them to be executed. When the last procedure is executed the **end** statement which marks the end of the program procedure is reached and program execution terminates.

Using procedures for a program of this size and complexity is not particularly useful. The technique of procedurization becomes useful with complex designs, where a non-procedurized implementation would produce very complex program procedure. The use of procedures within a complex program allows the partition of the design, as expressed in the program design charts, to be reflected in the structure of the code.

1.7.2 Procedurized design

The difficult part of implementing a program design by the use of procedures is in deciding which components of the design will be collected together and implemented as a procedure. It is not as simple as each component box from a design being implemented as a procedure. A number of component boxes from the design are usually collected together to form one procedure.

A general rule is that a procedure should implement one single defined action of the program and that a procedure's length should be less than about 50 lines. The reason for restricting the length of a procedure is, first, to keep the procedure relatively simple in its structure and actions, and second, to allow a single procedure to be produced on one page of a listing. A procedure should only attempt to implement one simple function of the program's requirements. A procedure 'map' of this program implementation can be produced:

```
procedure add_two_numbers is

    procedure get_two_nums is

    begin -- get_two_nums

    end get_two_nums;

    procedure add_nums is

    begin -- add_nums

    end add_nums;

    procedure show_ans is

    begin -- show_ans

    end show_ans;

begin -- add_two_numbers
    get_two_nums;
    add_nums;
    show_ans;
end add_two_numbers;
```

This map of the program code shows, by the use of indentation and boxes, that the three procedures are contained within the program procedure add_two_numbers.

The map also makes clear the difference between the combined declaration and definition of a procedure, and the call of a procedure. A combined procedure declaration and definition is the part of the program where the reserved words **procedure** and **is** enclose the procedure name. The executable part of the procedure follows enclosed between a **begin/end** pair. The call of a procedure is where the name of the procedure is used alone and is interpreted as a request to perform the executable part of the procedure.

If the actions concerned with getting the nums within get_two_nums were more complex, then these parts of the procedure get_two_nums could themselves be procedurized. The design indicates that get_two_nums could be implemented as calls of procedures get_first_num and get_sec_num. If the program were to be implemented using these procedures, there are two possible procedure maps which could be used:

```
procedure add_two_numbers is

    procedure get_first_num is

    begin -- get_first_num

    end get_first_num;

    procedure get_sec_num is

    begin -- get_sec_num

    end get_sec_num;

    procedure get_two_nums is

    begin -- get_two_nums
        get_first_num;
        get_sec_num;
    end get_two_nums;

    procedure add_nums is

    begin -- add_nums

    end add_nums

    procedure show_ans is

    begin -- show_ans

    end show_ans;

begin -- add_two_numbers
    get_two_nums;
    add_nums;
    show_ans;
end add_two_numbers;
```

```
procedure add_two_numbers is

    procedure get_two_nums is

        procedure get_first_num is

        begin -- get_first_num

        end get_first_num;

        procedure get_sec_num is

        begin -- get_sec_num

        end get_sec_num;

    begin -- get_two_nums
        get_first_num;
        get_sec_num;
    end get_two_nums;

    procedure add_nums is

    begin -- add_nums

    end add_nums;

    procedure show_ans is

    begin -- show_ans

    end show_ans;

begin -- add_two_numbers
    get_two_nums;
    add_nums;
    show_ans;
end add_two_numbers;
```

Both of these maps indicate that the procedure get_two_nums would be implemented as a sequence of two procedure calls of the two new procedures, get_first_num and get_sec_num.

When the procedure get_two_nums is invoked from the main body of the program, the first statement of the procedure get_two_nums is executed. This is now a procedure call of the procedure get_first_num; when the procedure terminates, control is passed back to the place in get_two_nums where it was called from. The next statement in get_two_nums is then executed which is the call of the procedure get_sec_num. This procedure is similarly executed and control passed back to get_two_nums. The next statement in get_two_nums is the end of the procedure, which will cause control to be passed back to the place in the body of the program where get_two_nums was called from. Program execution then continues as before.

The only physical difference between the two alternative implementations of the procedures get_first_num and get_sec_num, is the position in the program where they are declared. In the left-hand implementation they are declared as subprocedures of the program procedure. In the right-hand implementation they are declared as subprocedures of the procedure get_two_nums. The map shows that they are fully contained within the procedure get_two_nums, where they are declared following the procedure header before the **begin** statement of the procedure get_two_nums.

This difference in where the procedures are declared has implications concerning where the procedures can be called from within the program. The parts of a program where a program object can be called (for procedures) or referenced (for constants or variables) are known as the *scope* of the object.

In the left-hand implementation the two procedures are program objects and can be invoked from anywhere in the program following their declaration. The procedure get_first_num can be called by any of the four procedures which follows it, and also by the body of the program procedure. The procedure get_sec_num can likewise be called by any of the three procedures which follow it and by the main body of the program.

In the right-hand implementation the procedures are objects of the procedure get_two_nums and are restricted to the scope of that procedure. Procedure get_first_num can only be invoked by the procedure get_sec_num and by the procedure get_two_nums; likewise the procedure get_sec_num can only be invoked by the procedure get_two_nums.

The program structure chart indicates that the components of the design called get_first_num and get_sec_num are component parts of the design get_two_nums. The design also indicates that the only place in the design where these components should be invoked from is the component get_two_nums.

The right-hand implementation reflects the structure of the design more closely and is favoured for this reason. It also has the advantage that a maintenance programmer cannot change the structure of the design by calling a procedure which is a component part of another part of the design.

A general rule which is used in evaluating alternative program designs is to favour those designs which restrict the scope of program objects. By restricting the scope of objects the implementation is always closer to the meaning of the design and the possibility of misusing program objects by referring to them outside their design scope is excluded.

In the introduction to this block it was emphasized that for any program specification there are a large number of possible implementations. The specification for the program get_two_nums has now been demonstrated with four possible implementations. These are the implementation in Block 1 Section 3, the first implementation in this section using three procedures, and the two implementations using five procedures.

Of the four implementations for this particular specification the most favoured would be the first. The specification is so simple that there is no advantage in using the complex procedurized implementations. This is a design principle known as KISS (*k*eep *i*t *s*imple *s*tupid). This principle can be stated as 'the most appropriate design is the one which is sufficiently complex but no more complex than it needs to be'.

If the specification is regarded as being more complex than it actually is, the components get_first_num, get_sec_num, add_nums and show_ans being sufficiently complex to require implementation as procedures, then the most appropriate design would be the right-hand five-procedure design, for the reasons explained above.

One final point needs to be made concerning the scope of procedures. The rules given above are not quite correct: a procedure can invoke itself; it is within its own scope. The situation where a procedure invokes itself is known as *recursion* and will be introduced in Block 3.

The use of procedures as explained in this section is not complete; all that has been considered is the division of the program statements into procedures. The division of data objects within a program design has not been considered. These considerations will be added to the consideration of procedurization in Block 1 Section 11. At this stage all that can be said is that the use of procedures to partition the statement aspects of programs without a similar division of the data aspects of programs is not regarded as producing acceptable implementations.

EXERCISES

1.7.1   Implement the program get_two_nums using the right-hand five-procedure implementation map as given in this section.

1.7.2   Referring to the specification from Exercises 1.6.3 and 1.6.4, implement the program using a procedurized design.

1.7.3   Implement the following specification and design using procedures:

A program is required which will convert (real) input values in Fahrenheit into Celsius values or (real) input values in Celsius into Fahrenheit values.

The program will commence by determining from the user the direction of the conversion. This will be expressed as 'C' (or 'c') for Celsius to Fahrenheit conversions and 'F' (or 'f') for Fahrenheit to Celsius conversions. Any other input will be rejected with an appropriate message.

When the direction has been determined the input value will be requested. The conversion will be performed and the output value will be displayed to an accuracy of two decimal places.

The conversions can be performed using the formulae:

$$f = (c * {}^9\!/_5) + 32$$
$$c = (f - 32) * {}^5\!/_9$$

The high-level design will be as follows:

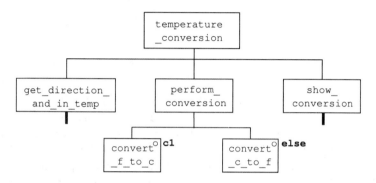

c1: If direction is Fahrenheit to centigrade.

The design of the component get direction can be based upon the design for the program get_yes_no in Block 1 Section 6.

The user interface for this program would be as follows:

```
        TEMPERATURE CONVERSION

  Please enter 'C' for Celsius  to Fahrenheit
  or 'F' for Fahrenheit to Celsius conversion Q

  Enter 'C', 'c', 'F' or 'f' only !
  Please enter 'C' for Celsius  to Fahrenheit
  or 'F' for Fahrenheit to Celsius conversion c

  Enter temperature to be converted cccc.cc
  Converted temperature is          ffff.ff
```

Complete the design of the program and implement it using procedures.

Testing programs

Having designed, implemented and demonstrated a program, it is now necessary to test it. Demonstrating that a program works for some inputs is not the same as testing it. All that is demonstrated by putting some data through a program and obtaining the correct results is that the program will perform correctly for those particular inputs. It does not give any indication that the program will perform correctly for all possible sets of inputs.

Even demonstrating that the output from the program is correct is sometimes difficult. For the simple programs which have been used so far, the correctness of the output can be easily decided. With more complicated programs it is not always as easy to determine the correct output for a given set of inputs.

To test a program it is thus necessary to predict its behaviour, to determine if the outputs provided by it are or are not correct. This is only possible if the person performing the testing has a sufficient understanding of the specification of the program. This again illustrates the need for a complete understanding of the program specification in order to be able to produce an effective program.

1.8.1 Exhaustive testing

One way of proving that a program is totally correct is to run it with all possible sets of inputs which it is designed to accept. If it performs correctly for all these inputs then it has been exhaustively tested, and a proof of its correctness has been obtained.

This is rarely a practical possibility, since virtually all programs are too complex to allow exhaustive testing. A simple program like the first selection demo program from Block 1 Section 4 has only two positive integer inputs. One of these inputs (the balance) has a range of values from 0 to the largest integer value which the Ada compiler can accept. The other input (the withdrawal) has a range of values from 1 to the largest integer value which can be accepted.

The biggest integer value which an Ada compiler can accept is not infinity but a smaller value which varies from compiler to compiler. The actual value for a particular compiler can be determined from the attribute INTEGER'LAST. The Janus Ada compiler has one of the smallest values of INTEGER'LAST with a value of 32767 ($= 2^{15} - 1$); the value for the VAX is 2147483647 ($= 2^{31} - 1$).

To test one of the inputs of the selection demo program exhaustively, all of the values between 0 and INTEGER'LAST will have to be input into the program. To test the program completely every value of the first input will have to be combined with all possible values of the second input.

For the Janus Ada compiler this will involve having to input 32768 * 32767 pairs of values, which will require 1073709056 test runs. Even if these inputs are set up by a computer program and the output is checked by a computer program, this is an unacceptably large number of tests to perform. If it is an impractical proposition to perform an exhaustive test on a simple program like this, it will be equally impractical to perform exhaustive testing on more complicated program designs.

1.8.2 Testing rationale

As exhaustive testing is not feasible, a program can only be demonstrated to be correct for a non-exhaustive set of test inputs. If the program deals with these inputs correctly *and* the inputs are sufficiently representative of all possible sets of input data, then it can be *assumed* that the program will operate correctly for all valid sets of input data.

This does not provide a proof of the correctness of the program; the conclusion that the program will operate correctly for all possible sets of input data is only an assumption. The validity of the assumption depends upon the sets of input data being sufficiently representative of all possible sets of input data. A requirement of test design is to select a set of test data which can be argued to be sufficiently representative.

A second requirement of the program testing process is to test a program adequately with the minimum of effort. Testing can be a time-consuming and thus expensive process. It is a requirement that the tester should design the minimum adequate set of test data which can be used.

The test of the program will be made with respect to the specification of the program. If the specification is incomplete or ambiguous, or the programmer's understanding of the specification incomplete, then adequate testing of the program will not be possible.

Testing can only be used to provide evidence that the program which has been produced will perform according to its specification. However, if the specification is incorrect or inappropriate as part of a system then the program will not fulfil its role within the system. This is a system testing consideration and will not be covered in this book.

1.8.3 The process of testing

Testing a program is an activity which needs to be designed and planned. For a large programming project testing will have to be performed during the production of the program. Parts of the program will have to be tested as they are produced and before other parts of the program can be constructed. These considerations will be introduced in the section on program production (Block 1 Section 10). For the small programs which are being developed at the moment, testing the complete program is an appropriate option.

The process of testing should be planned as a part of the planning of the production of the program. The production of the test rationale and test plans can, and should, take place before, or as, the design of the program is being produced. Documentation of testing is an important part of the program documentation. The testing section of the program documentation can be divided into three parts: the test rationale, the test plan and the test log.

A *test rationale* is a method of determining from the specification, or from the program code produced, the minimum set of test data required to test the program adequately. The black-box considerations which will be introduced in this section are an example of a particular rationale. A rationale is complemented with *methods* which can be used with the basic rationale to implement the tests. The test rationale and method chosen will produce a list of *cases* which have to be tested.

Using the list of cases to be tested a number of test *runs* can be constructed. The test runs should ensure that each case identified by the rationale is tested at least once. The test runs themselves will form the second part of the test report known as the *test plan*. The test plan should list the test runs, giving each test run a test number. The information for each test run should include the cases which will be tested, the input data to be supplied and an indication of how the output from the program can be shown to be correct.

The precise layout of the test plan will depend upon the actual method of testing chosen. The necessary layouts will be explained below as the different test methods are introduced. The test runs should be organized so that the simplest test runs are the first in the test plan and the test runs subsequently increase in complexity.

The third part of the test report is the *test log*. This contains details of how testing was applied to the development of the program. It should consist of a space for the test run number, the date on which this particular test run was performed and a space for a comment on the success or otherwise of the test.

The physical evidence of testing should be included in the program report as an appendix. For simple interactive programs like the ones which have been used so far, the test evidence could consist of a printed log of the final session when all the tests were successfully passed. Most operating systems provide a facility whereby a copy of everything which happens on the screen will also be copied to a text file which can be later printed.

If such a facility is not available, then it is usually possible for screen dumps to be obtained. A screen dump is a facility which will copy the image on the screen to the printer. A series of screen dumps can be used to illustrate the success of each test run.

For more complicated programs involving the use of files, the physical evidence of testing may also consist of printed copies of the contents of the files, indicating how the contents of the files have changed due to the testing process.

Whatever method of producing test evidence is used, the test evidence should be cross-referenced to the test plan in order that a verification of the testing can be shown.

Having produced the test plan as part of the design activity, production of the program code can proceed. When the code has been produced the tests can be performed upon the program.

Testing proceeds by applying each test from the test plan in sequence. If the program passes a test in the test plan, testing can proceed with the next test. If a program fails a test then the reasons why it did so will have to be found. This process of finding and correcting the faults in a partially working program is known as *debugging*.

For simple programs, after a program has been debugged, possibly redesigned and recoded to correct a fault, testing should recommence from the first test in the test plan. It is possible that having introduced a change in the program in order to remove a fault, the program will now fail a test which it has previously passed.

Each test run, successful or unsuccessful, should be recorded in the test log. If the program passes the test, all that is required is the date on which the test was applied and the fact that the program successfully passed the test. If the program fails the test, the date should be recorded, together with an indication of how the output indicates that the test failed. After the fault has been found a note of why the program failed the test should be made on the test log, the test log will then continue starting with the first test run again.

When the last test in the test plan has been successfully completed the testing process is complete and the program can be assumed to be performing according to specification. It may be necessary to repeat the final test runs in order to produce permanent physical evidence that the program has passed all the planned tests.

In the development of a large program by a team of programmers, it is usual and advisable for arrangements to be made for program components to be tested by people other than those who produced them. It is possible for programmers to become 'blind' to the faults in their programs and consequently to fail to design adequate tests. As test plans can proceed from the specification one group of programmers can design the tests, while another group is designing and implementing the program component which will be tested.

The process is summarized in Figure 1.8.1.

The documentation of the testing process is required in order that the program can be maintained; if any changes are subsequently made to the program it will be necessary for all the tests to be performed again. It may also be necessary for new test cases to be added to the test plan in order to test any changes which have been made to the program. These additional tests will then be included in the program's test plan for future maintenance.

The test log is also required for the process of producing the program to be controlled. It will indicate the amount of time which has been spent testing and the number of faults discovered during testing. This may give an indication of the thoroughness of the testing procedures applied to the program and/or the adequacy of the original design. Testing (and debugging) can take a large proportion of the effort involved in a programming project and ideally a program should pass all the tests at the first attempt.

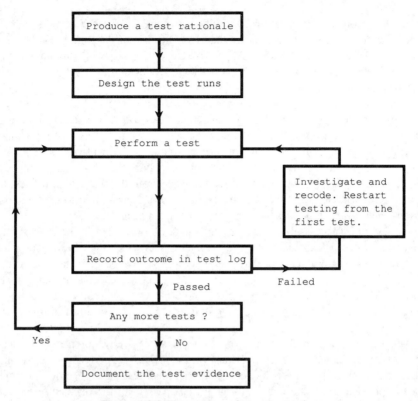

Figure 1.8.1 The process of program testing

Although it is unrealistic to expect a program to pass all tests at the first attempt, the chances of a program doing so can be improved if the program is properly designed at the design stage. A second method of attempting to ensure that a program passes its tests at the first attempt is to design an inadequate set of tests. Although the program will pass these tests, any faults in the program will become apparent at some stage and will then have to be corrected.

It is possible to test a program design with the test cases before the program is produced. This is done by tracing the behaviour of the program when the design is available. This is known as a *desk check* of the program and will be introduced in Block 1 Section 9.

If a program test reveals a fault, the fault has to be investigated and corrected. The fault can be relatively minor, perhaps the consequence of a typing error. In this case the design of the program does not need to be altered and the error can be easily corrected. The test may also reveal a design error which is much more serious. The design of the program will then have to be changed, possibly involving extensive rewriting of the program code.

Thus the sooner in the production process a fault can be found, the easier it is to correct the fault. If an adequate design for a program is produced and tested before being expressed as a program, faults will be revealed at an early stage and will be easier to rectify.

1.8.4 Black-box and white-box testing

Black-box testing is a method of producing a test rationale which can be applied to a program specification before the design has been produced. The phrase 'black box' refers to the need not to know about the internal workings of the program. As black-box testing is designed from a consideration of the specification of the program alone, the internal workings of the program code do not need to be considered in order to produce the test plan.

An alternative method of producing a test rationale is known as *white-box*, or sometimes more accurately *glass-box* testing. A white-box test rationale can only be obtained when the program design is available, as it needs to know about the internal workings of the program in order to produce an adequate set of test data. This book will only introduce black-box testing.

In practice a combination of black-box and white-box rationales is required in order to test a program adequately. Some types of fault which may be missed by black-box testing will be revealed by white-box testing, and vice versa.

In addition to the choice of rationale, there is a further choice to be made concerning the method of determining if the outputs from the program are correct or not. These methods can be applied to both black- and white-box rationales. There are four methods, which will be introduced later in this section.

1.8.5 The black-box rationale in practice

The process of producing a black-box test rationale starts with a black-box diagram. This shows the inputs and outputs from a program. If the second selection demonstration program from Block 1 Section 3 is considered, the black-box diagram would be as follows:

Having identified the inputs and outputs to the program, the possible ranges of the inputs and outputs are established. For this program the possible ranges are as follows:

```
balance        -50 ——— 0 ——————————————— INTEGER'LAST

withdrawal                1——————————————— INTEGER'LAST

resulting
_balance       -50 ——— 0 ——————————————— INTEGER'LAST - 1

response            refuse        overdraft        accept
```

As with the implementation of this program, it will be assumed that the user will never attempt to input a value outside the possible ranges of balance and withdrawal. Techniques for enforcing this aspect of the specification have been introduced in Block 1 Section 6, and testing this requirement will be used as an end-of-section exercise.

The ranges of possible values are then divided into significant subranges. A significant subrange is an area of the possible range where the values can be taken as equivalent; the equivalence can be determined from a consideration of the specification. For the two inputs in this example (balance and withdrawal) the significant subrange is the entire range of the possible input. There is no indication in the specification that any particular input values are to be treated differently from any other values. The range of the output resulting_balance can be divided into two significant subranges. The specification determines that these ranges are the range which will give an acceptance response (>= 0 and <= INTEGER'LAST) and the range which will give an overdraft response (>=-50 and <0). The significant subranges of response are the three possible states, refuse, overdraft and accept.

When the significant subranges have been established they are then indicated on the range diagrams:

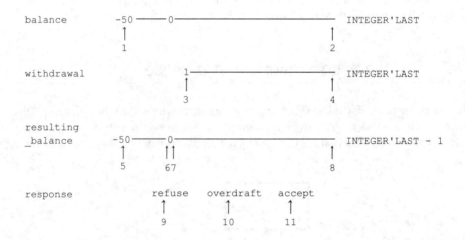

Each arrow on the subrange diagram indicates a point in the range where a subrange starts or ends. For example, in resulting balance the subrange for acceptance is between the points labelled 7 (0) and the point labelled 8 (INTEGER'LAST). Each labelled point becomes a test case, with a test case number as indicated on the diagrams. The basis of the rationale is that as the subranges have been tested at the start and end of the subrange and as the specification indicates that all values in the subrange are to be treated in the same way, then testing at the start and at the end of the subrange is sufficient to test all values in the subrange. If all the subranges on all inputs and all outputs are tested in this way then it can be assumed that all significant parts of the program have been tested. A summary of the test cases can be constructed from the labelled subrange diagrams:

case 1	balance minimum	(-50)
case 2	balance maximum	(INTEGER'LAST)
case 3	withdrawal minimum	(1)
case 4	withdrawal maximum	(INTEGER'LAST)
case 5	result overdraft min	(-50)
case 6	result overdraft max	(-1)
case 7	result accept min	(0)
case 8	result accept max	(INTEGER'LAST -1)
case 9	response refuse	
case 10	response overdraft	
case 11	response accept	

The test runs can now be produced including all test cases and organized according to the complexity of the test being performed. The test runs from these test cases would be as follows:

test number	cases tested	balance	withdrawal	response resulting	balance
1	2, 3, 8, 11	32767	1	accept	32766
2	2, 4, 7, 11	23767	32767	accept	0
3	3, 6, 10	0	1	overdraft	-1
4	5, 10	0	-50	overdraft	-50
5	1, 3, 9	-50	1	refuse	-50

These five test runs will cover all eleven test cases and will test the subranges at the points just before and just after they change. Exhaustive testing of this program, as explained at the start of this section, would have involved 1073709056 test runs. This black-box test plan has reduced the requirement to five test runs. If the program can be shown to operate correctly for these five test runs and the test rationale as outlined above is adequate, then it can be assumed that the program will operate correctly for all other possible sets of inputs.

The test log for this test plan would look like this (assuming that all tests were passed on the first attempt):

test number	date	actual result	balance	comment
1	21/10/90	accept	32766	correct
2	21/10/90	accept	0	correct
3	21/10/90	overdraft	-1	correct
4	21/10/90	overdraft	-50	correct
5	21/10/90	refused	-50	correct

Parallel testing method

A method of testing, as opposed to a test rationale, is a method of establishing that the outputs from a program are correct. The test plan developed above has used a method of testing known as *parallel testing*. Parallel testing involves predicting the actual values of the output and then using the predicted results to verify that the actual results are correct. It is the most obvious method of testing and intuitively satisfying, as a prediction of the results is made before the actual results are obtained.

There are, however, two problems with parallel testing which make it unsuitable in some situations. The first of these is that the method used to obtain the predicted result and the method used by the program to obtain the actual result may both contain the same error and thus produce identical incorrect results. For the parallel method to be relied upon, the way in which the actual and expected results are calculated should be as different as possible.

The other objection to parallel testing is that the calculation of the expected results can be a difficult and time-consuming process. If the calculations are sufficiently complex then the only method of obtaining them may be by using a computer program (which would itself have to be tested). For these reasons there are other methods of testing which can be used which do not rely upon producing an actual expected result in advance.

Inverse testing method

Inverse testing is a method which is applicable if it is possible for a program to be 'driven in reverse'. If the output from a program can be used as the input to another run of the program when the program is reversing the process, then the output from the second run of the program should be equal to the initial input to the program.

The temperature conversion program from Exercise 1.7.3 can be used to illustrate inverse testing. If a value in Celsius is input to the program a Fahrenheit value will be output. This Fahrenheit value can then be reinput to the same program and the output

Celsius value should be (very nearly) equal to the original Celsius value. The black-box diagram for the program would be as follows:

The possible range diagrams for temp_in and temp_out would be as follows:

```
temp_in     lowest ─────────────── 0─────────────── highest
            temp                                     temp


temp_out    lowest ─────────────── 0─────────────── highest
            temp                                     temp
```

temp_in and temp_out are both floating-point values. The possible ranges for these inputs to this program are from the lowest temperature in the physical world (-273.0°C, -459.4°F) to the highest temperature allowed in the specification (+5000.0°C, +9032.0°F). Again, although these ranges are indicated in the specification, the assumption will be made that the user will never attempt to input a value outside these ranges.

The possible range diagram for the direction input is as follows:

```
direction   lowest ───────────────────────────────── highest
            char                                       char
```

The meaning of lowest_char and highest_char will be made clear in Block 2 Section 3.

The possible range diagram for the error message is as follows:

```
                        error_message
```

This indicates that the error message has a single state: the output of a message that only 'F','f','C' or 'c' is acceptable input to the program.

The significant subranges for temp_in and temp_out are the same as the range of possible values. There is no indication from the specification that any temperature value is to be treated any differently from any other temperature value.

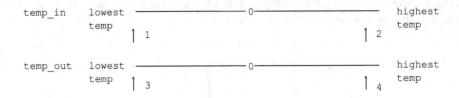

The significant subranges for the direction input are as follows:

```
direction   lowest ──────────────── C─F──────── c─f──────── highest
            char                    ↑ ↑ ↑      ↑ ↑           char
                                    5 6 9      7 8
```

The four characters which will be treated by the program as valid temperature conversion requests have each been identified as a case (5, 6, 7, 8). The remaining case (9) indicates that a character other than the four identified characters will be used.

The significant subrange diagram for the error_message is:

```
                    error_message

                         ↑
                        10
```

The cases to be tested are thus the following:

case 1	lowest temp in
case 2	highest temp in
case 3	lowest temp out
case 4	highest temp out
case 5	C to F request
case 6	F to C request
case 7	C to F request
case 8	F to C request
case 9	invalid request
case 10	error_message output

Using these test cases a test plan can be constructed:

test number	cases tested	direction	temp_in	temp_out	prediction
1	1, 3, 5	'C'	-273	#1	C -> F conversion
2	1, 3, 6	'F'	#1	-273	F -> C conversion
3	2, 4, 7	'c'	5000.0	#2	C -> F conversion
4	2, 4, 8	'f'	#2	5000.0	F -> C conversion
5	9, 10	'?'	--	--	error message

The control over the direction of the conversion is being tested using a parallel testing method, the behaviour of the program being predicted from the input supplied. Test run 5 tests case 9 by using an input of the character '?' to represent a character input other than one of 'C','F','c' or 'f'.

The testing of cases 1–4 is implemented using an inverse testing method. The entries #1 and #2 in the table indicate that whatever output value is produced by test run 1 will be used as input for test run 2; likewise whatever output value is produced by test run 3 will be used as input for test run 4. The prediction made is that the conversion of a temperature value from Celsius to Fahrenheit, followed by the conversion of that Fahrenheit value back to Celsius should result in the same initial value. Due to inaccuracies in the way in which computers store and process floating-point numbers the actual values may not quite agree, but should be very close. This will be explained in detail in Block 2 Section 1.

Exhaustive testing of this program would be impossible, as one of the inputs is a floating-point value. The number of actual input values in the range from the lowest_temp to the highest_temp is in theory infinite and in practice very large indeed.

The test rationale shows that the program could be adequately tested with five test runs. It also indicates that there is no need to calculate the output values to determine the success or otherwise of the program.

For temperature conversions the calculation of the output values would be straightforward, allowing the parallel testing method to be used. The inverse testing method is regarded as being more powerful than the parallel testing method, and can also be used where the calculation of an actual output value is too complex to be attempted by hand. However, programs which can be driven in reverse are very rare.

Relational testing method

The relational testing method can be used where a relationship between the different outputs produced from different inputs can be shown from the specification to have a defined relationship.

The temperature conversion program can be used as an example of relationship testing. The basic formula for converting a temperature from Celsius to Fahrenheit was given in the specification as follows:

$$f = (c * {}^9/_5) + 32$$

If c is set to a known Celsius value called c1, its Fahrenheit equivalent can be expressed as follows:

$$f1 = (c1 * {}^9/_5) + 32$$

If a second value of c is taken having a value one degree higher than c1, that is, c1 + 1, its Fahrenheit equivalent can be expressed as follows:

$$f2 = ((c1 + 1) * {}^9/_5) + 32$$

$$=> f2 = ((c1 * {}^9/_5) + (1 * {}^9/_5)) + 32$$

If the second equation is subtracted from the first equation, the following result is obtained:

$$f2 - f1 = 1 * {}^9/_5$$

This predicts that for a one-degree change in the Celsius input value to the program, the difference between the Fahrenheit output values should be $^9/_5$ (that is, 1.8). A similar argument can be used to predict that the difference in Celsius output values for a one-degree change in Fahrenheit input value would be $^5/_9$ (that is, 0.556).

The black-box considerations will generate the same set of test cases. The test plan using a relational testing method would be as follows:

test number	cases tested	direction	temp_in	temp_out	prediction
1	1, 3, 5	'C'	-273.0	#1	C -> F conversion
2	7	'c'	-272.0	#2	C -> F conversion
3	6	'F'	4999.0	#3	F -> C conversion
4	2, 4, 7	'f'	5000.0	#4	F -> C conversion
5	9, 10	'?'	--	--	error message

The entries #1, #2, #3, #4 in the table indicate that the actual output is not predicted. What is predicted is that the difference between #2 and #1 will be very close to 1.8, as the difference between the two Celsius input values is 1 degree Celsius, which should result in a 1.8 degree difference in the Fahrenheit output value. Likewise, it is predicted that the difference between #3 and #4 will be around 0.556.

Once again this testing method does not require that the actual values produced by the program have to be determined in advance; all that is important is the relationship between pairs of output values. Again the calculation in this instance would be easy enough to perform; however, the method of testing can be applied to situations where the actual values are too complex to be calculated by hand.

Composite testing method

A composite testing method is appropriate where the outputs from the program can be compared or combined with the input in some way to determine the correctness or otherwise of the program.

Composite testing can be applied to the following specification:

Names on a data base are stored as a sequence of three parts, title, firstname and surname. A single colon(':') separates the title from the firstname, a single colon separates the firstname from the secondname, and the end of the name is indicated by a asterisk. A program is required which when provided with a name in this format will divide the name into its three parts.

The black-box diagram for this program would be as follows:

The range diagrams for this program would be as follows:

name_in	sequence of characters + colon
	+ sequence of characters + colon
	+ sequence of characters + asterisk
title	sequence of characters
fname	sequence of characters
sname	sequence of characters

The combination of the outputs from the program when combined together as title + colon + fname + colon + sname + asterisk should be equal to the input to the program.

The significant range of all inputs and outputs to this program is equal to the possible range. This gives four test cases:

case 1	name_in	(as defined above)
case 2	title	(sequence of characters)
case 3	fname	(sequence of characters)
case 4	sname	(sequence of characters)

A test plan for these test cases would be as follows:

test number	cases tested	name_in	title	fname	sname
1	1, 2, 3, 4	Dr.:Fred:Bloggs*	#1	#2	#3

The entries #1, #2 and #3 in the table indicate that the actual output will not be predicted. What is predicted is that the sequence #1 + colon + #2 + colon + #3 + asterisk will be equal to the input 'Dr.:Fred:Bloggs*'.

Again, due to the simplicity of this example, the actual output could be predicted from a consideration of the actual input; this would be an example of parallel testing. The method of testing shown here can be applied to problems which are more complex, and the actual output is more difficult to predict.

1.8.6 Comparison of methods

Of the four methods, inverse, relational and composite testing cannot always be applied. Only the parallel method can be applied to all programs. If there is a choice of methods to be applied then the methods should be considered in the following sequence:

```
most favoured -> inverse
                 composite
                 relational
least favoured -> parallel
```

The consideration should include not only the applicability of the method but also the ease and possibility of performing the composite or relational comparisons which will validate the outputs.

One final consideration to be applied is the possibility of automating the testing. Automated testing involves using a computer program to test a computer program. The advantage of automated testing is that a larger number of tests can be applied in a shorter period of time with greater accuracy. It also allows the tests to be repeated either after the program has been amended when it has failed one of the tests, or when the program has been changed during maintenance.

The disadvantage of automated testing is that a computer program to test the program under test has to be designed and implemented. This program itself will require testing, before its output, which is the verdict on the program under test, can be relied upón. This in itself is not an overwhelming problem as the effort of testing the test harness program will be repaid in the greater number of tests and the greater ease of testing the original program.

EXERCISES

1.8.1 Extend the test plan for the bank balance program to allow it to test for input values which are outside the allowable range.

1.8.2 Produce a test rationale and test plan for the assignment average program from Block 1 Section 5.

1.8.3 Produce a test rationale and a test plan for the investment calculator program from Exercise 1.6.3.

1.8.4 Produce a test rationale and a test plan for the ready reckoner program from Exercise 1.5.2.

Section 1.9

Tracing and debugging

The last section has shown how testing can be used to reveal faults in a program. The action to be taken after discovering a fault is to correct it. The process of locating known faults in a program and correcting them is called *debugging*.

1.9.1 Tracing a program

The method of locating a known fault in a program is called *tracing*. The action of tracing a program is similar to walking through a design or walking through a program listing. The simplest method of tracing a program is to *desk trace* it.

Desk tracing a program (or a section of a program) involves following the path of execution through the program listing by hand, while recording the states of various program objects. At some stage in execution, the path of control will diverge from the expected path of control, and/or the state of some object will diverge from its expected state. This will reveal the fault in the program.

The fault can only be recognized if the expected path of control and the expected states of objects can be predicted by the person tracing the program. This again emphasizes the need to understand the specification and to produce and understand a detailed design before coding a program. Without this knowledge the expected behaviour of a program cannot be predicted and thus the divergent behaviour of a program fault cannot be recognized.

1.9.2 A tracing specification

A program is required which will act as a user menu. The user will be asked to input a single character in the range 'A' to 'E' (or 'a' to 'e'); which will be used to select between four program options ('A', 'B', 'C', 'D') or to exit from the program ('E').

In this version of the program each of the four menu options will simply produce a message that they have been reached and will then return control to the menu.
Option E will produce a 'have a nice day' message before the program terminates.

This specification is in part similar to the specification at the start of Block 1 Section 6 for a yes/no user input. As the problem is similar the solution may also be similar and the design from Block 1 Section 6 can be used as a basis of this design. This may sound like cheating but, having produced and verified a design for one program, there is no reason why a part of that design cannot be included in or adapted for another program.

This idea, of taking verified designs from one program and including them in another program, can be taken a stage further. There are standard designs available for common program operations. These designs can be found in introductory programming texts and in manuals on algorithms (see Block 3). If a design for a program component has been produced, documented and described in a text there is no reason for programmers not to use that design within programs which are being developed.

This is only allowable if the programmer understands the design and implementation of the component he or she is including or reusing. Without such an understanding the component may be used inappropriately.

The design of the program for this specification will be based upon the design of the program yes_no_demo from Block 1 Section 6.

The user interface design

The user interface design for this specification will be as follows:

```
                    MENU DEMONSTRATION
            A . . . option A
            B . . . option B
            C . . . option C
            D . . . option D
            E . . . exit program
            Please enter choice x
            Enter 'A' to 'E' only
         -- any number of invalid choices here

            Please enter choice a
            This is option A
                    MENU DEMONSTRATION
            A . . . option A
            B . . . option B
            C . . . option C
            D . . . option D
            E . . . exit program
            Please enter choice
         -- any number of invalid
         -- or valid choices here
            Please enter choice e
            Have a nice day !
         -- program terminates
```

Program design

A suitable program design for this specification based upon the design from Block 1 Section 6 would be as follows:

S1 MENU DEMONSTRATION – HIGH-LEVEL CONTROL

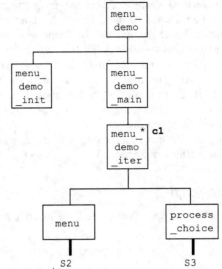

c1: While user input not exit.

S2 MENU DEMONSTRATION – MENU

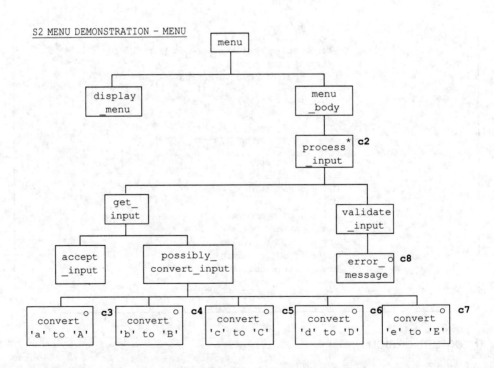

c2: While user's input not acceptable.   **c5:** If input is 'c'.
c3: If input is 'a'.   **c6:** If input is 'd'.
c4: If input is 'b'.   **c7:** If input is 'e'.
                                               c8: If user's input is unacceptable.

S3 MENU DEMONSTRATION – PROCESS CHOICE

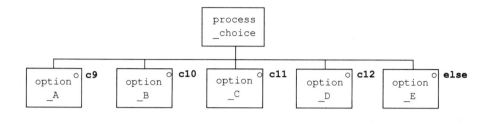

c9: If user chose option A.   **c11:** If user chose option C.
c10: If user chose option B.   **c12:** If user chose option D.

The data design

The only object required is a CHARACTER variable to store the user's input:

PROGRAM VARIABLES

NAME	TYPE	NOTES
choice	CHARACTER	User's choice from the menu

The program implementation

The program will be implemented using procedures. This version of the program contains a deliberate error which will be used to illustrate the processes of debugging. The program header will be as follows:

```
0001  -- menu dispatch demonstration program b1s9p1 see text
0002  -- N.B. contains deliberate error(s)
0003
0004  with TEXT_IO; use TEXT_IO;
0005
0006  procedure b1s9p1 is
0007
```

```
0008        choice : CHARACTER; -- user's choice from the menu
0009
```

The main part of the program procedure will be as follows:

```
0102  begin -- b1s9p1
0103     choice := 'x'; -- prime loop with choice other than 'E'
0104     while (choice /= 'E') loop
0105        menu;
0106        process_choice;
0107     end loop;
0108  end b1s9p1;
```

This implements the two design components menu_demo_init and menu_demo_main directly. Line 0103 sets the variable choice to a value which will cause the test which controls the **while** loop to be FALSE on its first evaluation, thus ensuring that the body of the loop executes at least once. The body of the loop calls the procedure menu followed by the procedure process_choice.

The procedure menu will include a subsidiary procedure called display_menu, as suggested by the design. The call to this procedure is outside the scope of the loop which iterates until an acceptable choice has been input by the user. This will cause the menu to be offered once, following which as many inputs as are required are obtained from the user. Placing the invocation of display_menu outside the body of the loop corresponds with the planned behaviour of the program as shown on the design of the user interface.

```
0010  procedure menu is
0011
0012  -- procedure to offer the user a menu then
0013  -- accept and validate the user's input
0014
0015  procedure display_menu is
0016
0017  -- procedure to display menu to user
0018
0019  begin -- display menu
0020     NEW_LINE;
0021     PUT_LINE( "              MENU DEMONSTRATION ");
0022     NEW_LINE;
0023     PUT_LINE( "A . . . option A");
0024     PUT_LINE( "B . . . option B");
0025     PUT_LINE( "C . . . option C");
0026     PUT_LINE( "D . . . option D");
0027     PUT_LINE( "E . . . option E");
```

```
0028  end display_menu;
0029
0030  begin -- menu
0031     display_menu; -- call display_menu
0032     -- process input
0033     while ((choice < 'A') or (choice > 'E')) loop
0034        PUT( "Please enter choice ");
0035        GET( choice ); SKIP_LINE;
0036        -- possibly convert choice
0037        if    choice = 'a' then choice := 'A';
0038        elsif choice = 'b' then choice := 'B';
0039        elsif choice = 'c' then choice := 'C';
0040        elsif choice = 'd' then choice := 'D';
0041        elsif choice = 'e' then choice := 'E';
0042        end if;
0043
0044        -- validate choice
0045        if ((choice < 'A') or (choice > 'E')) then
0046           PUT_LINE( "Enter 'A' to 'E' only ");
0047        end if;
0048     end loop;
0049  end menu;
0050
```

The sequential **elsif** structure is used to convert responses 'a', 'b', 'c', 'd' or 'e' into 'A', 'B', 'C', 'D' or 'E', respectively, following which an error message is displayed if the response is not acceptable. The test to determine if the response is acceptable is made in two places, once as the loop control test, and once to inform the user of an invalid choice.

The design of the component possibly_convert_input indicates a multiple selection which was implemented with an **if** structure as shown above. The design of the component process_choice also indicates a multiple selection; this multiple selection will be implemented using an alternative to the **if** structure known as a **case** structure. The meaning of this construction and the use of a **case** structure will be made clear later in this section.

```
0051  procedure process_choice is
0052
0053  -- procedure to process a valid user's choice
0054
0055  procedure option_a is
0056  -- dummy option a procedure
0057  begin -- option_a
0058     PUT_LINE( "This is option A");
```

```
0059  end option_a;
0060
0061  procedure option_b is
0062  -- dummy option b procedure
0063  begin -- option_b
0064     PUT_LINE( "This is option B");
0065  end option_b;
0066
0067  procedure option_c is
0068  -- dummy option c procedure
0069  begin -- option_c
0070     PUT_LINE( "This is option C");
0071  end option_c;
0072
0073  procedure option_d is
0074  -- dummy option d procedure
0075  begin -- option_d
0076     PUT_LINE( "This is option D");
0077  end option_d;
0078
0079  procedure option_e is
0000  -- dummy option e procedure
0081  begin -- option_e
0082     PUT_LINE( "Have a nice day !");
0083  end option_e;
0084
0085  begin -- process choice
0086     case choice is
0087        when 'A' =>
0088           option_a;
0089        when 'B' =>
0090           option_b;
0091        when 'C' =>
0092           option_c;
0093        when 'D' =>
0094           option_d;
0095        when 'E' =>
0096           option_e;
0097        when others =>
0098           null;
0099     end case;
0100  end process_choice;
```

A procedure map of this program would be as follows:

```
procedure menu_demonstration is

   procedure menu is

      procedure display_menu is
      begin -- display menu
      end display_menu;

   begin -- menu
      display_menu
   end menu;

   procedure process_choice is

      procedure option_a is
      begin -- option a
      end option_a;

      procedure option_b is
      begin -- option b
      end option_b;

      procedure option_c is
      begin -- option c
      end option_c;

      procedure option_d is
      begin -- option d
      end option_d;

      procedure option_e is
      begin -- option e
      end option_e;

      procedure option_a is
      begin -- option a
      end option_a;

   begin -- process choice
      option_a
      option_b
      option_c
      option_d
      option_e
   end process_choice;

begin -- menu_demonstration
   menu
   process_choice
end menu_demonstration;
```

The procedure map is used to show the layout of the program, illustrating where in the program listing the procedures are declared and where in the listing the procedures are called. The program control structures which may control the calling of the procedures are not shown on the map. The map shows that a procedure is invoked from a certain place in the program, not how it is invoked from that place in the program.

Program testing

A black-box parallel test plan for this program would be as follows:

TEST CASES

case 1	choice = 'x' (not {'a', 'b', 'c', 'd', 'e', 'A', 'B', 'C', 'D', 'E'})
case 2	choice = 'E'
case 3	choice = 'e'
case 4	choice = 'A', 'B', 'C', or 'D'
case 5	choice = 'a', 'b', 'c', or 'd'

TEST PLAN

1	2	'E'	exit message and exit
2	4, 2	'A', 'E'	option a message
			exit message and exit
3	1, 4, 4, 4, 2	'x', 'B', 'C', 'D', 'E'	re-enter message
			option b message
			option c message
			option d message
			exit message and exit
4	3	'e'	exit message and exit
5	5, 5, 5, 5, 3	'a', 'b', 'c', 'd', 'e'	option a message
			option b message
			option c message
			option d message
			exit message and exit

Cases 4 and 5 have been included in the test plan four times in order that all options from the menu can be shown to be working. If the program was subject to this test plan, it would fail on test number 2. The behaviour of the program on this test would be as follows:

```
                MENU DEMONSTRATION

        A...option A
        B...option B
        C...option C
        D...option D
        E...exit program
        Please enter choice A

        This is option A

                MENU DEMONSTRATION

        A...option A
        B...option B
        C...option C
        D...option D
        E...exit program

        This is option A

                MENU DEMONSTRATION

        A...option A
        B...option B
        C...option C
        D...option D
        E...exit program

        This is option A
     -- program output continues indefinitely
```

Following the user's input of a request to perform option A and the subsequent execution of option A, the menu was repeatedly presented to the user, without waiting for a response, and option A executed again. The program had to be interrupted (by using a break key) to halt its execution.

Dealing with errors

Testing has revealed the presence of a error in the program, commonly known as a *bug*. The process of finding and correcting the error is known as *debugging*. The first stage of debugging is to consider the behaviour of the program when it failed during testing. For this program the following observations can be made:

The program exited correctly on test 1.
The program performed option A correctly before failing on test 2.
The program looped indefinitely, indicating that option A was being performed.
The program did not ask the user to input a new menu choice after the first menu choice had been entered.

The evidence suggests that a loop is at fault; the iterative behaviour of the faulty program will most probably be caused by a faulty loop control structure. There are two loops in the program, one in the procedure menu and one in the main program. The procedure menu, which is within the control of the loop in the main program, would seem to be suspect. The program can be traced to determine the nature of the fault.

To trace this program the value of the variable choice will have to be investigated. To do this a trace table will be used to follow the execution of the program. The first line of the trace table would be as follows:

line number	choice	test result	notes and output
0103	x		choice set

This shows that following execution of line 0103, the first executable line of the program, the value of choice is 'x'. As this line did not involve a test the test result column is not completed. The note states that this line has set the value of choice. Program tracing will continue with line 0104, the next executable line:

0104	x	TRUE	loop entered

As this line includes a test, the result of the test is noted as TRUE. The effect of executing this line is to enter the loop, which is noted.

0105	x		procedure called
0031	x		procedure performed
			menu displayed

Line 0105 calls procedure menu, the first executable line of which is line 0031 which calls the procedure display_menu. As this is a very straightforward procedure which does not change the value of any variables, it is not traced. The note indicates that its execution is assumed, the effect of which is to display the menu.

0033	x	TRUE	loop entered

The test in line 0033 involves an **or** operator. An **or** operator combines two TRUE/FALSE values together to a single TRUE/FALSE value, using the rule that the state expression is TRUE if either (or both) of the values being combined are TRUE. The left-hand term (choice < 'A') will evaluate as FALSE, the right-hand term (choice > 'E') will evaluate as TRUE. The **or** rule will evaluate the resulting term (FALSE **or** TRUE) as TRUE.

0034	x		prompt displayed
0035	A		'A' input from user

In line 0035 the value of choice is changed by the user's input; this is shown in the table.

0037	A	FALSE	no conversion performed
0038	A	FALSE	no conversion performed
0039	A	FALSE	no conversion performed
0040	A	FALSE	no conversion performed
0041	A	FALSE	no conversion performed
0045	A	FALSE	no error message

As the test in line 0037 evaluates as FALSE the next line to be executed is line 0038. The **elsif** test on this line and the succeeding **elsif** tests on lines 0039, 0040 and 0041 will also evaluate FALSE. The test on line 0045 which controls the issue of an error message will evaluate FALSE, causing no error message to be output.

The next line following the **end if** on line 0045 is the **end loop** on line 0048; as this is the end of the loop the next executable statement will be the corresponding **while** statement on line 0033 at the start of the loop.

0033	A	FALSE	loop terminates
0049			procedure terminates
0106	A		procedure invoked

The **or** expression which forms the test of the while statement now evaluates as FALSE. The term (choice < 'A') is FALSE, the term (choice > 'E') is FALSE, so the evaluation of the resulting term (FALSE **or** FALSE) is FALSE. A **while** statement evaluating as FALSE has the effect of terminating the loop.

The next statement following the **end loop** is the **end** menu statement on line 0049 which is then end of the procedure. Control returns to the next statement following the statement from which the procedure was called; this is the statement on line 0106 which calls the procedure process_choice.

0086	A		case statement started
0087	A	TRUE	when option satisfied
0088	A		procedure performed
			option A message displayed
			procedure terminates

The first statement of the procedure process_choice is the **case** statement on line 0086. The effect of the **case** statement is to cause the statements which follow the **when** clause which evaluates as TRUE to be executed and all other **when** options to be ignored. In this example the "**when** 'A'" clause will evaluate as TRUE, causing the statement on line 0088 to be executed.

The statement on line 0088 is the call of the procedure option_a. The execution of the procedure option_a is assumed. The value of choice is not changed as option_a executes; the only effect is to display a message. The next statement to be reached following the return of control from procedure option_a is the **end case** statement on line 0099, followed by line 0100 which is the end of the procedure process_choice.

The next statement reached when control is returned from the procedure process_choice, is the **end loop** statement on line 0107, which will cause control to be passed to the evaluation of the loop control test on line 0104.

0104	A	TRUE	loop reiterates
0105	A		procedure invoked
0031	A		procedure performed
			menu displayed
0033	A	FALSE	** wrong **

The test in line 0104 evaluates as TRUE, causing the outer loop to reiterate. The procedure menu is invoked, causing display_menu to be performed and the statement on line 0033 to be reached. This is the start of the inner **while** loop which controls the input and validation of the user's response. If the program is to behave correctly the loop has to be entered; for this to happen the test would have to evaluate as TRUE.

The consequence of this test evaluating as FALSE is that the **while** loop is not entered. The next line to be reached is the **end loop** at line 0048 and the **end** menu at line 0049. As this is the end of the procedure the program would continue as follows:

0106	A		procedure invoked
0087	A	TRUE	
0088	A		procedure performed
			option A message displayed
0104	A	TRUE	loop reiterates
0105	A		procedure invoked
0031	A		procedure performed
0033	A	FALSE	** wrong **

The program has looped; it has returned to line 0033 in exactly the same state as it was in the last time it was at line 0033 It will continue looping indefinitely from this point. The output from the trace will match the output of the program when it failed the test, confirming the location of the fault.

The fault in the program was the failure to ensure that on each execution of the menu procedure the **while** loop was primed to fail, which would cause the body of the loop to be performed at least once. It can be corrected by including a line between lines 0032 and 0033 which will set the value of choice to 'x', causing the **while** test on line 0032 to fail every time the procedure is executed. This correction will ensure that at least one response from the user is solicited.

1.9.3 Debugging

The fault in this program is one of the commonest, a failure to design and implement a loop correctly. Although the fault was simple, tracing the program's execution to discover it consumed a large amount of time and effort. A fault of this nature in a program of this complexity would have been detected by an experienced programmer without having to trace the program. The method of tracing, however, is valid for programs which have a greater degree of complexity.

The person performing the debugging requires two things. First, he or she will have to have a detailed knowledge of the program specification and design in order to be able to determine where the behaviour of the program being debugged deviates from the expected behaviour. Second, he or she will require a detailed knowledge of the programming language in order to determine the effects of the program statements and determine from the code the next statement which would be executed.

The best debugging method is known as *anti-bugging*: attempting to design and implement programs correctly in the first instance. As has already been noted, it is unlikely that this is ever achieved; but on the basis that small programs are easier to debug than large ones, incremental development of programs will make debugging easier. This technique will be fully explained in the next section.

The program above can be considered as the high-level menu driver of a more complex program. By using the dummy procedures (known as *stubs*) at this stage of program development, the menu driver can be implemented, tested and debugged without the options of the menu having to be available.

The program fragments which form the options of the menu can be developed, tested and debugged in a similar manner before being incorporated into the menu driver. As the components of the design have all been tested and debugged in isolation, there will hopefully be fewer bugs in the combined program.

Debugging a program can be made more effective by using debugging techniques very thoughtfully. A debugging trace on a program can generate a vast amount of information, most of which is irrelevant to the fault being sought.

When a program fails a test, the person debugging the program should be able to produce a theory which would explain the fault. The theory can then be confirmed or refuted by using the program design, the program listing and careful reasoning. Only if this approach is impossible should a debugging trace be attempted.

The theory will indicate which parts of the program and which data objects to concentrate upon; this will restrict the amount of information produced from the trace. If the theory is confirmed by either of these methods then the fault has been detected. If the theory is not confirmed then the debugging process has removed one theory from consideration, and the process can continue with a different theory.

Debugging can also be assisted by using an interactive debugger, sometimes known as a *program animator*. This allows the program to be executed from the terminal under the control of the animator. At any point in the program, execution can be interrupted and the contents of any variables examined or changed. Execution can then continue either one line at a time or until a defined point in the program has been reached.

Using an interactive debugger avoids one of the problems with hand tracing. An assumption made about the behaviour of the program by the person performing the debugging may be incorrect, and the faulty behaviour of the program may be missed due to this incorrect assumption. This problem is most likely if the person debugging the program is also the designer and/or the implementor of the program. An interactive debugger will not make the incorrect assumption but will display exactly what has happened during the program's execution.

The only problem with using a program animator to assist in the debugging of a program is ease of use. The debugging process as explained above is most effective if it is performed thoughtfully and a debugging trace is only used as a last resort, to confirm or refute a theory which attempts to explain the program's aberrant behaviour. Many novice programmers use an animator without first attempting to think through the possible causes of the fault. The effect of this is that they are not able to restrict the debugger to a small part of the program and are not always able to recognize the point at which the program's behaviour becomes aberrant. The most effective debugging tool is the intelligence of the person performing the debugging.

1.9.4 The **case** statement

This section has introduced the **case** statement, which is an alternative selection construct to a multiple **if** structure. The **case** structure is preferred to a multiple **if** statement where it is appropriate, as the expression of the multiple selection in the program listing is clearer. The case statement has the following general form:

```
case selector is
    when value_list =>
        statement(s);
    when value_list =>
        statement(s);
    ...
    when others =>
        statement(s);
end case;
```

where the reserved word **case** indicates the start of the **case** structure; selector is an expression of a *discrete type* and is followed by the reserved word **is**. The precise meaning of discrete types will be made clear in Block 2. However, in simple terms, a discrete type is a data type whose values can be easily listed. Of the types which have been introduced so far, INTEGER and CHARACTER are discrete, while FLOAT and STRING are not. The expression can be any Ada statement which evaluates to a value of a discrete type; the simplest form of an expression would be the name of a variable.

The main part of the case statement consists of a indefinite series of **when** alternatives. Each alternative commences with the reserved word **when** and a *value list* followed by the compound symbol '=>'. A value list consists of one or more expressions, each of which defines a range of values of the type of the selector.

The most usual value list is a single constant of the selector type, although it is possible for the value list to be an expression which evaluates to a value of the selector type. There are some restrictions on what types of expression can be included in a value list.

A more complex value list can be constructed by listing a series of expressions of the selector type, each value separated from the next by a '|' symbol. The '|' symbol can be read in this context as 'or'. Where a series of values are contiguous the *range* symbol (..) can be used. The range symbol was introduced in Block 1 Section 5 as part of the **for** syntax. The examples below will clarify the construction and use of value lists.

The following **case** structure is intended to classify a single CHARACTER as either upper case, lower case, digit or punctuation character:

```
-- case structure to classify a single character
case a_char is          -- a_char is of type character
   when 'A' .. 'Z' =>            -- use of range construct
      PUT_LINE( "upper case ");
   when 'a' .. 'z' =>
      PUT_LINE( "lower case ");
   when '0' .. '9' =>
      PUT_LINE( "digit ");
   when '.' | ',' | ';' |':' =>  -- use of 'or' symbol
      PUT_LINE( "punctuation ");
   when others =>
      null;
end case;
```

The statement shows the use of the 'range' construct as in 'A' .. 'Z', 'a' .. 'z' and '0' .. '9'; which define contiguous ranges of character values. It also illustrates the use of the 'or' construct as in '.' | ',' | ';' | ':' which can be read as full stop or comma or semicolon or colon (if this was a realistic example this list would be much longer).

Any number of **when** alternatives can be included in the **case** structure, with two restrictions. The first restriction is that a particular value of the discrete type can only appear once in the value lists. The second restriction is that all possible values of the discrete type of the selector must be included in the value lists. The following example of a **case** structure violates both of these restrictions:

```
-- case structure to classify a single character
case a_char is          -- a_char is of type character
   when 'A' .. 'Z' =>            -- use of range construct
      PUT_LINE( "upper case ");
   when 'a' .. 'z' =>
      PUT_LINE( "lower case ");
   when '0' .. '9' =>
      PUT_LINE( "digit ");
   when '.' | ',' | ';' |':' =>  -- use of 'or' symbol
```

```
        PUT_LINE( "punctuation ");
    when 'a' | 'e' | 'i' | 'o' | 'u' => -- values
                                       -- already used
        PUT_LINE( "vowel ");
  end case;
```

The statement violates the first restriction in the fifth **when** alternative, which includes values which have already been included in the second **when** alternative. It violates the second restriction as not all possible values of the selector's type have been included. The type of the selector in this example is CHARACTER, which implies that the value lists must subsume all possible ·CHARACTER values.

To facilitate the inclusion of all values, Ada allows the last **when** alternative of the **case** statement to have the form **when others**, which implicitly subsumes all values which have not been explicitly expressed in the preceding value lists. If a particular, value of the selector is not matched by any of the preceding lists it will be matched by this **when** alternative.

It is often the case that there is no specific action to be taken for the **others** alternative. Ada provides a statement which specifies that no action is to be taken: the reserved word **null** is interpreted by Ada as a statement which does nothing. In the first example the '**when others => null**' construct was used to comply with the second restriction of the case structure.

The run-time behaviour of the case statement should be obvious from the discussion of its syntax above. When the **case** statement is executed the first action is to determine the value of the selector expression. This value must then match one, and only one, of the **when** value lists; the statement(s) associated with that value list are then executed. Upon completion of the execution of the statement(s) the **case** statement itself terminates.

The recommended style rules for the construction of a **case** statement are illustrated above and in the program listing. The **case** and **end case** statements are indented as appropriate for the **case** statement. Within the **case** statement one level of indent is used for each **when** value list and a second level of indentation is used for the statements which are associated with the **when** alternative.

Any selection which can be implemented as a **case** structure could have been implemented as a multiple **if/elsif** structure. The advantage of the **case** rule can be illustrated if the first **case** structure illustrated above is compared with the equivalent **if** structure:

```
    -- if structure to classify a single character
  if    (( a_char >= 'A') and ( a_char <= 'Z')) then
      PUT_LINE( "upper case ");
  elsif (( a_char >= 'a') and ( a_char <= 'z')) then
      PUT_LINE( "lower case ");
```

```
   elsif (( a_char >= '0') and ( a_char <= '9')) then
      PUT_LINE( "DIGIT ");
   end if;
```

It should be obvious that the **case** structure is a clearer expression of the multiple selection than the multiple **if/elsif** structure; consequently the **case** structure is preferred where it can be used.

EXERCISES

1.9.1 If your environment has an interactive debugger, learn how to use it now, before you need to use it with more complex programs.

1.9.2 The following program is intended to accept a sequence of characters from the keyboard and echo them onto the screen; replacing any space characters in the input with new lines. The program terminates when an asterisk character is input, without displaying the asterisk.

The behaviour is not correct. Determine the fault in the program and perform a debugging trace on the program to confirm the fault.

```
0001  -- program to process keyboard input changing spaces to
0002  -- newlines and terminating when an asterisk is input
0003  -- NB contains deliberate error(s) b1s9e2 see text.
0004
0005  with TEXT_IO; use TEXT_IO;
0006
0007  procedure b1s9e2 is
0008
0009     space    : constant CHARACTER := ' ';
0010     asterisk : constant CHARACTER := '*';
0011     khar     : CHARACTER;
0012
0013  begin -- b1s9e2
0014     khar := space;  -- prime loop
0015     while ( khar /= asterisk) loop
0016        GET( khar );
0017        if ( khar = space ) then
0018           NEW_LINE;
0019        else
0020           PUT( khar );
0021        end if;
0022     end loop;
0023  end b1s9e2;
```

1.9.3 The following program is intended to input a sequence of student scores, terminating when a maximum of five scores or a score of -1 is input. The average score will then be calculated and displayed.

The behaviour is not correct; devise a test plan to determine the fault in the program and perform a debugging trace on the program to confirm the fault.

```
0001  -- program to input series of integer scores, terminating
0002  -- when five scores have been input or when a negative score
0003  -- is input. The average will then be calculated and output.
0004  -- NB contains deliberate error. b1s9e3 see text.
0005
0006  with TEXT_IO, int_io, float_inout;
0007  use  TEXT_IO, int_io, float_inout;
0008
0009  procedure b1s9e3 is
0010
0011     max_stu : constant INTEGER := 5; -- maximum no of students
0012
0013     this_stu,              -- score for this student
0014     total_score,           -- total for all students
0015     num_stu      : INTEGER; -- number of students processed
0016
0017     av_score     : FLOAT;   -- average of all students
0018
0019  begin -- b1s9e3
0020     num_stu := 1;      -- start with first student
0021     total_score := 0; -- no scores at this stage
0022     while (( num_stu < max_stu) and ( this_stu /= -1)) loop
0023        PUT( "Enter score for student number ");
0024        PUT( num_stu ); PUT( " ");
0025        GET( this_stu ); SKIP_LINE;
0026
0027        total_score := total_score + this_stu;
0028        num_stu := num_stu + 1;
0029     end loop;
0030
0031     av_score := FLOAT( total_score) / FLOAT( num_stu );
0032     NEW_LINE;
0033     PUT(" The average score is ");
0034     PUT( av_score, FORE=>4, AFT =>2, EXP =>0);
0035  end b1s9e3;
```

1.9.4 Reimplement the multiple nested **if** structure in the procedure menu of the program used in this section as a **case** structure.

1.9.5 Implement the illegal character classifier **case** structure used in this section so that it functions as intended; that is, it should correctly identify vowels as being both alphabetic and vowels. Hint: it is possible for the statement which forms a **when** alternative to be a second nested **case** statement.

Section 1.10

Production and documentation

1.10.1 Producing a program

The processes of producing even the small programs which have been used in this block are so complex that it is unlikely that they could be completed in a single session. For programs which are of a more realistic length and are divided between a team of programmers it is clear that the production of the program will be a complex task. This production task will have to be planned and managed.

A single programmer working on a small project will have to plan the sequence of tasks which will lead to the completion of the project. For a team of programmers working on a large project, the team leader will have to allocate independent sections of the program among the different members of the team. For a large project subteams may have to be organized and managed. Each team will have to produce a *production plan* for their part of the project. The team leader will have to coordinate the production plans of each team to ensure that the project can be completed effectively.

A production plan lists the stages which are required for the production of a particular program. Each stage in the plan is small enough for an estimate of the amount of time it will take to complete to be made. An estimate of the amount of time required for the complete project can then be obtained by adding together the times estimated for each of the stages.

It is usually essential that certain parts of the project are completed before subsequent parts can be implemented. These implementation considerations are used to help organize the sequence of stages and group a set of tasks together. Completion of such a set of tasks will mark a significant point in the production of the program; such a point is known as a *milestone*.

For a novice programmer the idea of a production plan for a programming project can seem impossible. During the early stages in learning to program it is very difficult to estimate in advance how long to allocate to each task, or even to decide what are appropriate tasks and milestones. For skilled programmers such an estimation is easier to make, but it always has to be kept in mind that unforeseen difficulties may arise, leading to an extension of the actual time taken on a particular stage.

Where a program is being implemented by a team of programmers, the programming team leader has a responsibility to try to make sure that the parts produced by each of the teams are completed on time. As the stages are being completed the programmers involved will maintain a log of the actual time taken to complete each task. This log will be available to the programming team leader and can be used to determine the progress towards the production milestones, towards the production of the independent program parts, and thus towards completion of the whole project.

At any stage in the production of a program it is possible (but unlikely) that all the parts being produced are on or ahead of schedule. It is also possible that all the parts being produced are behind schedule, each to the same. In this case the overall production of the project is delayed but as all parts are equally delayed the implementation considerations will not be affected, beyond extending the completion date.

What is more likely is that some parts of the program are ahead of schedule, some on schedule and some behind schedule. In this situation it may be possible for the programming team leader to reallocate resources from the parts ahead of schedule to those behind schedule. If this is possible the overall production of the project can be better managed, and possibly completed on time. Project control is only possible if an overall production plan has been constructed at the outset of the project.

For a novice programmer working on an individual project these considerations may seem remote. However, most novice programmers will be working to a deadline, a date by which the programming project has to be completed. They are also working with limited resources, the amount of time which they can spend upon the project. These circumstances are similar to those of the professional programmers described above. The novice programmer is in the position of the programming team leader, having to assess the progress being made against the amount of time and resources already used, and the amount of time and resources remaining.

An assessment of how complete a project is can only be made if a production plan is available. For a novice it is probable that the initial allocation of time to the stages was very inaccurate and the actual time taken was greater than that allowed for. It can be assumed that the inaccuracies in the stages of the project which have been completed will be reflected in the stages yet to be completed. A novice programmer can thus only obtain a realistic estimate of the time required to complete a project if a production plan has been constructed.

If the production plan contains implementation considerations and the project starts to run behind schedule, then it may be possible for a restricted but working version of the program to be produced within the limits of the project. Such a submission by a novice programmer is likely to be better received than an incomplete and non-working program which would probably have been produced without a production plan.

A production plan without implementation considerations

In order to illustrate production planning a programming project based upon the specification of the menu example from Block 1 Section 9 will be considered. It is assumed that the overall purpose of the project has been specified and that each of the four menu options (A, B, C and D) has been specified. It is also assumed that the project has a four-week deadline and that about 25 hours per week are available for the project, giving a total of about 100 hours for completion of the project.

This production plan is given as an example only; an actual production plan for a real project would differ significantly in its stages and allocations. In particular, this production plan contains no implementation considerations.

A production plan for the stages to the first milestone of the project might be as follows:

STAGE	ACTIVITY	ALLOCATION		ACTUAL
1	Clarify specification	2	(2)	
2	Produce production and implementation plans	4	(6)	
3	Design user interface	3	(9)	
4	Document user interface	2	(11)	
5	High-level (menu) design	2	(13)	
6	High-level test plan	2	(15)	
	Total to this point	15	(16)	

Each of the six stages in this part of the plan has been given an allocation of hours; the total number of hours to completion of that stage is also shown in brackets. The final line shows that a total allocation of fifteen hours has been made for all these stages. One extra hour, making a total of sixteen hours, has been added to allow for any delays in reaching this milestone.

This first part of the production plan includes within itself an allocation of time for the production of the plan, and for the inclusion of any implementation considerations which would be required for planning the succeeding stages of production.

There is space on the production plan to record the actual number of hours taken to complete the stage. When the milestone is reached the number of hours actually taken can be compared with the number of hours allocated, and progress towards completion of the project can be determined.

The user interfaces for both the high-level menu and the options controlled by the menu are designed and documented completely at this stage. These describe how the program will interact with the user, and, together with the specification, will be required for the design and implementation of the program. They define *what* the program will look like to the user; they do not attempt to define *how* it will be done.

The production of the high-level menu design and the high-level test plan are also completed in this stage and have been given a total allocation of four hours. This may seem a very tight allocation, but a design for this component and a test plan for it are available from Block 1 Section 8. Some modification of the design and/or the test plan may be required but the basis of the design is complete, correct, available, and can be reused here. As a verified design is available there is little point in reinventing it. The use of standard designs for standard activities will allow a program to be completed faster, easier and with fewer errors. The reuse of designs will, however, only be successful if the programmer has an adequate understanding of the program components which are being included.

The plan for production as far as the second milestone might be as follows:

STAGE	ACTIVITY	ALLOCATION	ACTUAL
7	Detailed design of option A	4 (20)	
8	Test plan for option A	2 (22)	
9	Detailed design of option B	4 (26)	
10	Test plan for option B	2 (28)	
11	Detailed design of option C	4 (32)	
12	Test plan for option C	2 (34)	
13	Detailed design of option D	4 (38)	
14	Test plan for option D	2 (40)	
15	Design review	4 (44)	
	Total to this stage	43 (52)	

This shows the second milestone in the project. When this stage is reached the design of the entire project has been completed. It is estimated that about half the time available to the project will be required to reach this point. It has been assumed that all four modules are of equal complexity, and that six hours will be required to design and produce a test plan for each. An overrun of eight hours has been allowed for in the production plan up to this stage.

In a real project it is possible that operations concerned with some or all of the four options are standard and can be incorporated into the designs and test plans directly. This would allow them to be completed faster, thus reducing the time allocation. Other options may be more complex and require more time to be allocated. If this could be determined at the planning stage from the specification, and from the project designer's experience, it would allow a more accurate production plan to be constructed.

This milestone also includes a design review stage (15). The quality of the product and the completion of the remaining production stages are dependent upon the quality of the design. The allocation of time to the preceding design stages (5, 7, 9, 11 and 13) included some time for the designs of the individual components to be reviewed. At this stage the design should be checked in its entirety by the use of walk-throughs and/or peer reviews, to ensure that all the components will operate correctly when brought together.

The plan for the third milestone could be as follows:

STAGE	ACTIVITY	ALLOCATION	ACTUAL
16	Implement high level	3 (55)	
17	Test high level	2 (57)	

18	Implement option A	3 (60)
19	Test option A	6 (66)
20	Implement option B	3 (69)
21	Test option B	6 (75)
22	Implement option C	3 (78)
23	Test option C	6 (84)
24	Implement option D	3 (87)
25	Test option D	6 (93)
	Total to this stage	84 (101)

This milestone implements and tests first the high-level control, and then each of the four options in turn. The allowance of time for testing in this section is deliberately generous; it is unlikely that six hours of testing would be required to test any of the options. The allowance recognizes that testing may fail and that debugging of the option may be required. The overrun allowance of eight hours allocated to the milestone also recognizes this possibility.

These stages are probably the most difficult to control: the testing, debugging, redesigning and reimplementation cycle can consume vast amounts of time. The best way of controlling the amount of time spent at this stage is to ensure that the preceding stages concerned with design are adequately completed. A well-designed component is more likely to complete testing with fewer problems, causing production to be easier, and allowing more control over the processes of production.

The final milestone could be:

STAGE	ACTIVITY	ALLOCATION	ACTUAL
26	Collate documentation	5 (106)	
27	Project review	3 (109)	
	Total to complete project	92 (109)	

This final milestone completes the project. Stage 26 is concerned with the collation of the project documentation; this is not the same as the production of the documentation. Each of the stages in the project would have produced a part of the documentation, which has now to be collected together and indexed. The final stage is an allowance of time to review the project and evaluate the experience.

An estimate of between 92 and 109 hours is required for a project which was originally allocated 100 hours. It would have been more comfortable if the estimated production time including overheads had been less than 100 hours, allowing it to be completed within the initial allocation. However, a requirement of 109 hours is close enough to the limit of 100 hours to be acceptable, as it is likely that not all the overheads will be required.

It should be remembered that at this stage this is only a plan; the actual hours taken to complete each stage will most probably differ from those allocated within the plan. There is little point in reviewing the plan to change an estimated allocation of 109 hours to an estimated allocation of 100. When the project has been completed it is likely that the actual number of hours taken will differ by more than nine hours from the planned allocation.

If the production plan indicates that the estimated allocation of time will overrun the actual allowance by a significant amount, then a review of the plan would be appropriate. If the review does not reduce the estimated requirement significantly, then additional resources will be needed for completion of the project. If this is not possible then the allocation available could be used to complete only a part of the specification. In a real programming project, it would indicate to the project manager that additional resources should be allocated to ensure that this part of the project can be completed on time.

The production plan becomes a production log when the actual times taken for each stage are filled in as the project is completed. An analysis of the production log after the completion of the project will provide feedback concerning how accurate the original estimates of the duration of each stage were. This feedback can be used to plan the allocation of hours to future projects more accurately as well as to measure any increase in efficiency from one project to the next.

A production plan with implementation considerations

To make the idea of implementation considerations clearer, an outline specification expanding the set of menu options will be given.

The program is concerned with weekly diaries. A weekly diary consists of five daily diaries each of which has six appointment slots. An appointment slot is either blank if the appointment is not booked, or contains the name of the person with whom the appointment has been made.
The main menu would now be as follows:

```
        WEEKLY DIARY

    A  Load diary from disk
    B  Make an appointment
    C  Print diary
    D  Save diary to disk
    E  Exit program
```

Each time the program is started the diary is empty and all appointments are blank.

Option A will load a diary which has previously been saved to disk. Option B will allow an appointment in the diary to be booked. It will require the day and the time to be input by the user. If the appointment is not already booked the name of the person making the appointment will be input and stored. If the appointment is already booked a message to this effect will be displayed. Option C will output a copy of the diary to a printer. Option D will save the current diary to disk and clear the diary by setting all appointments blank. An implementation plan is concerned with planning in what sequence the menu options are best implemented; this can be done by establishing dependencies between the options.

In this example it is not possible to load a file from disk until a file exists on the disk which can be loaded. This implies that option D (save) will have to be completed before option A (load) can be implemented. In order to test that option D is working correctly an inverse test using option A would be most appropriate; likewise, in order to test option A an inverse test involving option D would be most appropriate.

The saving and loading of a blank file would not be a convincing or useful test; consequently option B (book) would need to be implemented before options D and A could be tested. This would allow the saving and loading of non-empty data files, which would be a better indication that the save and load options were working correctly.

In order to establish that option B was working correctly option C (print) would be required. A parallel test method would predict that if an appointment was booked for a certain day at a certain time in a certain name, then the print of the diary would confirm it.

This gives the implementation considerations as follows:

high-level control
option B (make appointment)
option C (print diary)
option D (save diary)
option A (load diary)

An implementation plan is concerned with implementing the functions of a program in a manner which allows incremental development and testing to be performed. For this program it would make sense to redesign the production plan to separate menu options B and C from menu options D and A.

The production plan for this project including these implementation considerations would now have seven milestones:

1. High-level design and desk testing, user interface, production plans.
2. Design of options B and C.
3. Design of options D and A.
4. Implementation and testing of high-level control.
5. Implementation and testing of B and C.
6. Implementation and testing of D and A.
7. Documentation and review.

The incorporation of implementation considerations within the production plan will not extend the total allocation of time for the project; it will, however, produce more milestones in the project, which will allow a greater degree of project control.

Although options D and A have been separated from options B and C, the design of the complete program is finalized before the implementation of any parts of it are started. It would not be correct to plan the design, and then implement options B and C, before the designs of options D and A were produced. The reason for this is that it is possible that the designs of options D and A will reveal considerations which have an effect upon the designs of options B and C. If options B and C have already been implemented then they may have to be reimplemented, which is a more time-consuming task than redesigning them before implementation.

The completion of milestone 4 when the high-level menu has been implemented and shown to be working correctly, using program stubs for options A, B, C and D, produces a working but very restricted version of the program.

The completion of milestone 5 when options B and C have been implemented and tested produces a less restricted, working version of the program. At this stage it would be possible to make appointments and to print a diary. The data entered could not, however, be saved and loaded between sessions.

The completion of milestone 6 when options D and A have been implemented and tested completes the implementation of the program, and produces a complete version of the program.

If the production schedule became untenable during the production of options B and C, the production of options D and A could be reviewed. The project could be completed on time but restricted to the implementation of milestone 5. The design of the missing modules and a test plan for the missing modules would have been produced, and could be included in the report.

The production of the program without a production or implementation plan would be much more difficult to control. It is unlikely that a useful working subset of the functions of the program would have been produced, or that the testing of the functions which had been produced could have been completed as easily.

An implementation plan for a more complex specification would itself be more complex. It may involve a first implementation of only a part of each menu option. In the example above, option B may be initially implemented to book an appointment without checking to ensure that an appointment is not already booked. This restricted implementation could then be used to allow implementation and testing of options B, D and A. The implementation plan would allocate time for the implementation of the full specification, checking that an appointment was not already booked at a later stage.

If the production plan was not adhered to and the project ran behind time, the preliminary version of option B would be available. If the production plan was adhered to then it would have been replaced by the fully working version. Thus a restricted but still useful version of the specification would be available on time, which is a better product than a non-working partial version.

The production of these partial versions of the program has other uses. If a program is required urgently then the partial version could be released for use while the final version was being produced. If program is not required urgently then the partial versions could be demonstrated to the sponsor, allowing confirmation from the sponsor that the implementation is congruent with what is expected.

Where production of a project is divided among teams of programmers, the production of an initial version of the part of the project a team is working on can be planned. This restricted version could then be used by the other teams to test their components and would be replaced at a later stage by the fully working version.

This incremental approach to implementation of programs is only possible if the full facilities have been designed at the design stage. The enhancement of the options should not necessitate a redesign of the facility; it should only be the implementation of an already designed facility.

1.10.2 Documentation

The products of a programming project are the program itself and the project documentation which supports it. Of these two products the documentation is the more important; if for any reason the program is lost, it should be possible to recreate it with minimal effort from the documentation. If the program documentation were to be lost it would be much more difficult to recreate it from the program listing.

During the life span of a program maintenance will be required. The maintenance changes will have to be designed; the starting point for designing these changes will be the original designs which will be included in the project documentation. After the changes have been designed and implemented, testing of the changes and retesting of the unchanged components will be required. The original test rationale, test plans and test logs would be available from the original program documentation. Having these available will allow the maintenance changes to be tested with minimal difficulty.

Attempting to make maintenance changes without the documentation, using only the program source code, is a very difficult task. In order to design the changes the original design will have to be recreated from the listing; this reverse engineering of the design is difficult, time-consuming and error-prone. In a commercial environment the time taken will be an unnecessary expense which can be obviated by having available the original program documentation.

When maintenance changes have been made, the program documentation will have to be updated to reflect the changes which have been made. At any stage in the lifetime of a program the program documentation should reflect the state of the program at that point in time. Thus not only will the program itself change over time but the documentation associated with it will also change.

Documentation can be divided into two major parts, the user documentation and the technical documentation. The two parts of the documentation are designed for different types of reader and have to be written accordingly.

The user documentation is intended to be used by the user of the program. It comprises a guide to the functions and operation of the program from a user's point of view; it should not be a technical document. When the program is being produced by a team, the user documentation may be produced by a specialized technical writer. A technical writer is a person who has sufficient technical knowledge to appreciate the complexity of the software task but also has writing skills which allow the complexities of operating the software to be communicated to a non-technical user in a 'friendly' way. The technical documentation is intended to be used by programmers producing the initial version of the program as well as by programmers involved in the maintenance of the program.

For a single-programmer project the production of the user and technical documentation will be the responsibility of the programmer. Novice programmers do not always understand the importance of documentation and neglect this task. If the program being produced by the novice is being produced following the guidelines in this book, most of the documentation will be generated as the stages in producing the program are completed.

For example, the user interface design stages will produce a paper description of the interface, which can be used as the basis of the user documentation. The program design stages will produce program and data structure charts. The test planning stages will produce test rationales and test plans. The production of the documentation at the end of the project will then become a matter of collating together all the documents which have already been used in the production of the program.

Where programs are attempted without planning or design, the production of program documentation is a more difficult task. It is usually omitted until the end of the project and then becomes a description of the program, rather than documents which directly support the project. The difference between the two types of documentation is readily apparent to a reader. It is also a chore to produce the documentation after the project has 'finished' and is usually skimped by novice programmers, leading to poor-quality documentation.

The user documentation

The user documentation is intended as a guide for the user of the program. It must not be assumed that the user has any technical knowledge, so the documentation should introduce the program to the user in terms that the user can understand. These terms should refer to the data objects and the processing of those objects as they are perceived by the user in the real world, rather than how they are perceived by the programmers writing the program.

The user documentation should commence with an overview of what processing the program is intended to do using the terms employed by the user to describe the objects and actions rather than the terms which would be used by a programmer. In the case of interactive programs the main part of the user's documentation should be a tutorial introduction to the operation of the program's user interface.

Where the program is menu-controlled the documentation will take the form of an introduction to the various menus and the options controlled by the menus. The functions of each menu option should be explained, in terms of either what other menus are accessed from that option or what data processing operations are possible from that option.

The visual form of the menus should be included in the user guide. This is very useful for a user who is consulting the guide to solve a problem when operating the program. The terminal screen can be compared with the menus in the user guide to confirm that the correct place in the user guide has been found in order to resolve the problem which the user is experiencing.

Wherever in the explanation of the operation of the menus an input is requested from the user, the precise format of the input expected should be explained. This should include the meaning of the input to the program, the number of characters expected, the range of values allowed and if the enter key is required to terminate the input.

If any error dialogue is produced by the program during input, the possible error messages which could be produced should be listed. The meaning of each error message should be explained, and the action required to correct the error specified. Where a menu option requests the program to provide some output, the format and meaning of the output should also be illustrated in the user guide.

A complex program may generate a large number of error or warning messages. Including an alphabetic list of possible messages and cross-referencing the list to the appropriate point in the user guide can be very useful to the user. Many user guides are only consulted when the program user meets a problem which is made apparent by the output of an error message. As the user guide and the user interface are the two places where the user has most interaction with the program, it is important to make both as supportive as possible.

Most of this documentation will be available from the user interface design which is the first part of the program design phase. If the user guide is also produced at this stage it can be used in two ways. First, as it makes explicit the programmer's interpretation of the specification, the user guide can be shown to the sponsor of the program to confirm that the sponsor's interpretation and the programmer's interpretation are congruent. This will avoid the problem of the programmer's producing a program which differs from the sponsor's requirements.

The other way in which the user guide can be used is during the implementation of the program. As it is an explicit realization of the specification, it and the specification can be used to design the program structure and the user interactions.

The user guide and the program should be congruent. If the user guide is used as the basis of the program design and implementation, then this will not be a problem. If for any reason the program has to be changed at a later stage, then the user guide should be updated to reflect these changes.

The technical documentation

The technical documentation is longer and more complex than the user documentation. It can be divided into five parts: introduction; data design; program design; program testing; and program evaluation. In addition, a number of appendices will be required.

The introduction

The introduction to the project documentation should include a general introduction giving the name of the project, the name of the programmer or programming team which produced the program, the name of the sponsor of the program, when the program was produced, the machine(s) the program is intended to run on, and the language (or languages) the project is written in.

The introduction should also contain a brief summary of the function of the program. Where the program is a part of a system, reference should be made to the system documentation which can be used to establish the context of the program.

The agreed specification and any interpretations, assumptions, extensions to or deletions from the specification will complete the introductory documentation. It would also be useful for a copy of the user guide to be included in the technical documentation introduction.

Data design

The data design for simple programs will be straightforward, consisting of a list of the major data objects which are used by the program. The data tables which have been used as a design tool and produced during the design phase can be used to form this part of the documentation.

A complex program operating on simple data will have a large number of data objects. Only the most important of these need to be described in the documentation. In most cases there is little point in describing the name, type and use of minor variables such as loop parameters. It is more important to describe the name type and use of major variables or constants which represent important objects within the program, such as the user's choice from the main menu.

The complete data tables will also be available in the program listings. The types and names of data objects used by a program are explicitly included in the listing as they are declared; the usage of the objects should be included as a comment accompanying the declaration.

When the data which are being processed by a program become more complex, a more complex description will be required. Blocks 2 and 3 will introduce facilities available in Ada to construct data types which are not predeclared by Ada. The design of these data structures and the reasons for selecting between alternative possible designs should be included in this section of the technical documentation.

Where a program makes use of external files, the types and format of the files should also be described in this section.

Program design

The major part of the program design documentation will be the program structure charts. A set of structure charts describing the program should be included in this section. The charts should be cross-referenced to each other, allowing the complete design to be followed. Each chart should be small, comprising of at most ten or twelve component boxes, and should attempt to describe a single logical facility of the program.

It should not be assumed that the structure chart by itself is always a complete intelligible description of the design. It may be necessary for comments to be included on a chart to explain why a particular design was chosen from alternative possible designs, or to explain the structure of the design if it is not clear from the structure chart.

In most cases these comments should be minimal and straightforward. If they are becoming complex then a commentary on the design of the program may have to be provided separately. This commentary would give an overview of the program design and explain the design decisions which have been taken to choose between alternate designs.

The production plan, together with the implementation considerations, should be included in this section of the documentation. The production log, which is a copy of the production plan with the actual times taken, should be included as an appendix and referenced from this part of the documentation.

Most of this documentation would have been produced as the program was designed in the design stage. Only the commentary may have to be produced at the final stage after the program has been produced.

Program testing

The program testing section of the documentation should contain the test rationale and the test plan only; the test log would be included in the report as an appendix. These documents would have been produced when the testing was designed in the design phase of the project and when the program was tested.

Details of any test files used to test the program, or test harnesses used for automatic testing of the program, should also be included. These files should be preserved when the project is completed as they will be required by programmers involved in the maintenance of the program. They can be used when retesting the program to ensure that the changes made to the program have not affected any existing parts of the program.

Program evaluation

This is an opportunity for novice programmers to include in their project report a critical appraisal of the work they have done. If the project has only been partially completed the reasons for this and the lessons learned from the experience of producing the program can be included here.

If any parts of the program do not perform according to specification the shortcomings can be commented upon. Likewise, if any late changes have had to be made to the specification, or any limitations of the program have been discovered in testing, a report on them can be presented. The adequacy or otherwise of the production plan can be analysed and included in this report.

Program listing

The program listing will be included in the report as a major appendix. A well-produced program listing is to an extent self-documenting. The correct use of comments and the use of sensibly named identifiers in the listing will make it more readable.

Comments should be included in a program listing to delineate explicitly the scope of any control structures used, to explain the usage of all variables declared, and at the start of every procedure or function to explain the purpose of the procedure or function (possibly cross-referenced to the program structure charts). A comment should also be included in the program listing where the meaning of an action performed by the program statements may be unclear to someone reading the program.

The program listing will itself be produced from the implementation phase of the project. The comments should be included within the listing as it is produced; if this is done they can then be used to maintain the listing as it is produced. They should not be added to the program listing after it has been completed in order to satisfy style requirements.

The program listing should be presented in a readable format. It is possible to load the final program listing into a word processor, and include page headers and footers complete with page numbers. An attempt should be made to make sure that page breaks occur at convenient points in the listing. This can be accomplished by including a **pragma** statement in the listing. The statement '**pragma** PAGE;' can appear anywhere in a program listing. The statement has no effect upon the program's execution but will ensure that a new page is started at that point when a program listing is produced. If the compiler can produce a paginated listing file then this should be used for the listing included in the report. The pages should be burst (separated) and bound in sequence to allow them to be easily read.

Other appendices

Other appendices which should be included in the project report are the test logs (cross-referenced to the test plans), the production log (cross-referenced to the production plan), and the files used (the names and functions of all files used in the production, testing or use of the program).

EXERCISES

1.10.1 Using the exam analysis example from Block 1 Section 6 design a production plan using implementation considerations.

1.10.2 For your next programming project be very careful in recording the time taken in the production log. When the project is finished examine the production log to determine where you over- or underestimated the amount of time certain stages would take.

Repeat this exercise in all future projects, until your estimates become sufficiently accurate.

Data flow and scope

The program designs which have been developed so far have concentrated upon designing the flow of control within programs. In addition to designing the flow of control, it is also necessary to design the flow of information within programs. This is only possible for programs which have been implemented using procedures. Without the use of procedures all data objects are declared at the program level and are accessible in all parts of the program. Procedures, which have already been used to divide the program instructions into more manageable blocks, can also be used to divide the data objects into more manageable parts.

When procedures are used it is still possible to declare data objects at the program level, and these objects will still be accessible in all parts of the program. In addition, it is also possible to declare data objects within a procedure. Data objects declared within a procedure are accessible only inside the procedure within which they are declared. Objects declared in one procedure are also accessible in any (sub)procedures which are declared within the procedure. Data objects are not accessible to any procedures which are declared at a higher level than the procedure which declares the objects.

The area of a program within which a program object can be accessed is known as the *scope* of that program object. If at a particular point in a program a data object is in scope but was not declared at that level, then the object is known as a *global* object. If at a particular point in a program a data object is in scope and was also declared at that level the object is known as a *local* object.

1.11.1 Information flow

To introduce information flow in programs the first procedurized implementation of the add_two_numbers program from Block 1 Section 7 will be reimplemented using data flow between the components. The three variables which were required by the program were declared as objects of the program procedure; this made the scope of these variables the entire program.

Variables declared at the program procedure level can be referenced in the program procedure as local variables; they can also be referenced in any of the three procedures get_two_nums, add_nums and show_ans as global variables. They are local to the program procedure, because they are declared objects of the program procedure; they are global in the three subordinate procedures because they are being accessed within the procedures without being declared in the procedures.

The procedure get_two_nums only references the variables first_num and sec_num; procedure add_nums references all three variables; and procedure show_ans only references the variable total_num. Information flow will allow the procedures to access only those variables which are required by a procedure, and ensure that they are referenced as local variables. This restricts access to the variables making the program design more secure.

There are two data flow design rules which should always be applied.

1. The scope of objects should be as restricted as possible.
2. All objects should be local when they are referenced.

There are many reasons for these rules, which are mainly concerned with ensuring the security of the data. If the scope of a data object is restricted to those parts of the program where it needs to be accessed, a greater degree of data integrity is provided. This is because by restricting an object's scope it is not possible for the object to be referenced and its value changed where the design of the program indicates it should not be allowed.

The reason for insisting that all objects are only referenced locally is to ensure that the declarations of the objects are known to the part of the program which is referencing them. If non-local objects are accessed the value of an object can be changed in parts of the program where it is not declared; this can cause problems with program maintenance.

In order to make the variables in this design local to the procedures, it will be necessary to pass them explicitly from the program procedure to each of the subsidiary procedures. As indicated above, the program procedure will pass first_num and second_num to procedure get_two_nums, all three objects to procedure add_nums and only total_num to procedure show_ans.

1.11.2 Data flow

A data object being passed between program components is called a *parameter*. There are three possible ways in which parameters can be passed; they can be passed as *in-only* (**in**), *out-only* (**out**) or as *in-out* (**in out**) data objects. The manner by which the object is passed is known as the parameter's *mode*.

Program structure charts can be used to show data-flow information. The method of showing that an in-only data flow is being used to pass an object from a high-level component to a low-level component is as follows:

This diagram shows the high-level component passing to the low-level component an item of data. The data item would normally be identified either by its name or by its type. The value which is passed in an in-only object is the value which the object has when flow of control is passed from the high-level to the low-level component.

When an object is passed from one part of a program into another part of the program as an in-only object, the part of the program receiving the object can only make use of the value of the object. Within the low-level component the parameter object can only be treated as a constant; it can be used, but its value cannot be changed.

The second possible data flow mode, out-only, is for a lower-level program component to pass information back to a high-level component. This can be shown on a data flow structure diagram as follows:

The diagram shows an out-only parameter being passed from the low-level component to the high-level component. In order to effect this data flow an uninitialized object has to be passed to the low-level procedure. This object has no value on entry to the procedure, and can only be used in the low-level procedure as the left-hand (destination) object of an assignment statement. The value which is passed back is the value of the object when flow of control is returned from the low-level component to the high-level component.

The final mode of data flow between program components, in-out, is for the object to be passed from the high-level component into the low-level component. The value may be changed in the low-level component and returned to the high-level component when control is passed back. This data flow is shown on a structure diagram as follows:

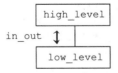

The diagram shows a program object being passed into and out of the low-level component from the high-level component. Within the low-level component the object can be treated as if it were a normal variable; its value can be referenced and changed. The value which is passed back is the value which the object has when flow of control is returned to the high-level component.

In-only example program

The nature of in-only, out-only and in-out data flows can be made clearer by using three small demonstration programs, one for each parameter mode. The following is a demonstration program for in-only data flow:

```
0001   -- program to demonstrate in_only parameters
0002   -- b1s11p1 see text.
0003
0004   with TEXT_IO, int_io; use TEXT_IO, int_io;
0005
0006   procedure b1s11p1 is
0007
0008        in_only : INTEGER := 42; -- object to be passed
0009
0010   procedure in_only_demo (in_param : in INTEGER) is
0011
0012   -- in_param can only be referenced as a constant
0013
0014   begin -- in_demo
0015      PUT( "The value inside the procedure is ");
0016      PUT( in_param ); NEW_LINE;
0017   end in_demo;
0018
0019   begin -- b1s11p1
0020      PUT_LINE ("This is passing as in only ");
0021      PUT ("The value before the procedure is ");
0022      PUT ( in_only ); NEW_LINE;
0023      in_demo( input_only ); -- procedure call
0024      PUT ("The value after  the procedure is ");
0025      PUT ( in_only ); NEW_LINE;
0026   end b1s11p1;
```

The main program declares an INTEGER variable with the name in_only and a procedure called in_demo; the procedure declaration indicates that it requires a single INTEGER parameter with the name in_param. Within the procedure the only action is to display the value of the parameter. The parameter object (in_param) can only be used within the procedure in_demo as a constant.

The declaration of the procedure, which now includes parameters, can be produced from the data-flow information in the design. In this procedure there is one in-only parameter of type INTEGER; the name of this object within the procedure will be in_param. The declaration of the procedure starts as usual with the reserved word **procedure**, followed by the name of the procedure. Any parameters of the procedure are then listed following an opening bracket (( ). Each parameter is identified with the name by which it will be known within the procedure and followed by a colon (:). The type of data flow is then specified; to specify an in-only data flow the reserved word **in** is used. The type of the data object being passed then follows to complete the declaration of the parameter. Where more than one parameter is being passed subsequent parameter declarations would follow separated by semicolons (;). The procedure heading is completed with the closing bracket ( )) and the reserved word **is**.

The parameters specified in the declaration of the procedure are known as the *formal parameters* of the procedure. The parameters specified in the procedure call are known as the *actual parameters*. The formal parameter in this example is named in_param; the actual parameter is named in_only. When control is passed the value of in_only is assigned to the formal parameter in_param before execution of the procedure commences.

The names of the actual and the formal parameters differ; the name of the formal parameter is in_param, the name of the actual parameter is in_only. It is advisable to attempt to ensure that the identifiers used in a program are unique; this can be accomplished by using different names for formal and actual parameters.

For any procedure call the number and types of the actual parameters must correspond with the number and types of the formal parameters. If there is a discrepancy an error will be reported when compilation is attempted.

The main program initializes the value of the variable in_only to 42, displays its value, calls the procedure in_demo passing in_only as the actual parameter, and displays the value of in_only when the procedure returns control. The output produced when this program is executed would be as follows:

```
This is passing as in only.
The value before the procedure is 42
The value inside the procedure is 42
The value after  the procedure is 42
```

Out-only example program

A similar program illustrating out-only parameters would be the following:

```
0001    -- program to demonstrate out_only parameters
0002    -- b1s11p2 see text.
0003    with TEXT_IO, int_io; use TEXT_IO; int_io;
0004    procedure b1s11p2 is
0005
0006         out_only : INTEGER; -- object to be passed
0007
0008    procedure out_only_demo ( out_param : out INTEGER) is
```

```
0009
0010    -- out_param can only be assigned to within procedure
0011
0012    begin -- out_demo
0013        out_param := 42;
0014        PUT( "The value inside the procedure is ");
0015        PUT( 42 ); NEW_LINE;
0016    end out_demo;
0017
0018    begin -- b1s11p2
0019        PUT_LINE ("This is passing as output only ");
0020        PUT ("The value before the procedure is ");
0021        PUT ( "uninitialized."); NEW_LINE;
0022        output_demo( out_only );
0023        PUT ("The value after  the procedure is ");
0024        PUT ( out_only ); NEW_LINE;
0025    end b1s11p2;
```

The structure of this program is identical to the structure of the previous program; it comprises a short program procedure which passes an actual parameter called out_only, to a procedure called out_demo, where it is received as an out-only parameter. The data flow mode of the parameter is identified in the procedure declaration by the use of the reserved word **out**.

An out-only parameter does not have to have a value before the procedure is called, although it is not an error if it does have a value. Any value which the actual parameter has will be lost when the procedure is invoked. Within the procedure the only operation which can be performed on the object is to assign it a value; any other attempted operations will be reported as errors when the program is compiled.

Within this program the value of the actual parameter is uninitialized before the procedure is invoked and a message to this effect is displayed. Within the procedure a value is assigned to the parameter and a message to this effect is displayed. It is not possible in line 0015 of the program to use the term 'PUT(out_param)' to display the value of the object directly, as the only operations which are allowed are those which give it a value. When the procedure terminates, the value of the formal parameter is transferred to the actual parameter. The program procedure terminates by displaying this value.

The output produced when this program is executed would be:

```
This is passing as out only
The value before the procedure is uninitialized
The value inside the procedure is 42
The value after  the procedure is 42
```

In-out example program

The following program illustrates in-out parameters:

```
0001    -- program to demonstrate in_out parameters
0002    -- b1s11p3 see text.
0003    with TEXT_IO, int_io; use TEXT_IO, int_io;
0004    procedure b1s11p3 is
0005
0006         in_out : INTEGER := 42 -- object to be passed
0007
0008    procedure in_out_demo (in_out_param : in out INTEGER) is
0009
0010    -- in_out_param can be used as a local variable
0011
0012    begin -- in_out_demo
0013       in_out_param := in_out_param * 2;
0014       PUT( "The value inside the procedure is ");
0015       PUT( in_out_param ); NEW_LINE;
0016    end in_out_demo;
0017
0018    begin -- b1s11p3
0019       PUT_LINE ("This is passing as in_out");
0020       PUT ("The value before the procedure is ");
0021       PUT ( in_out ); NEW_LINE;
0022       in_out_demo( in_out );
0023       PUT ("The value after  the procedure is ");
0024       PUT ( in_out ); NEW_LINE;
0025    end b1s11p3;
```

The data flow mode of the actual parameter, in_out, into the formal parameter, in_out_param, in the procedure in_out_demo, is defined by the use of the reserved term **in out** in the parameter's declaration. An in-out formal parameter can be used within the procedure as if it were a normal variable. Its value can be referenced in any way and the value can be changed. When the procedure terminates the value of the formal parameter will be exported to the actual parameter.

The output produced when this program is executed would be as follows:

```
This is passing as in_out
The value before the procedure is 42
The value inside the procedure is 84
The value after  the procedure is 84
```

In addition to passing data from program components to program components, it is also possible for data to be passed into a program component from outside the program. The data would be coming from some input device, most commonly the keyboard or a disk file. Likewise, it is possible for data to be passed out from a program component to an output device, most commonly either the screen, a printer or a data file. These data flows can also be shown on data flow structure charts as follows:

The data information being passed into or out of the program would normally be identified on the diagram by its name or by its type.

1.11.3 A realistic example

Data-flow considerations can now be applied to the design of the add_two_numbers program. Each component which forms part of the program design will have to have identified the data objects which it requires together with their modes.

The first procedure, get_two_nums, requires the two variables first_num and sec_num to be passed to it. The objects have no defined values when they are passed into the procedure and are initialized from the keyboard within the procedure. The values are then passed out of the procedure. This identifies the parameters as out-only.

The second procedure, add_nums, requires all three variables to be passed to it. The two variables first_num and sec_num already have values which have been supplied by the procedure get_two_nums. Their values will not be changed by the procedure add_nums. This identifies their mode as in-only. The value of total_num is not defined before it is passed to the procedure but is initialized within the procedure and the new value passed back. This identifies its mode as out_only.

The final procedure, show_ans, requires total_num to be passed to it. It requires, but will not change, its value. This identifies its mode as in-only.

This information can be added to the program structure chart from Block 1 Section 7, to produce a program structure chart which includes data flow information:

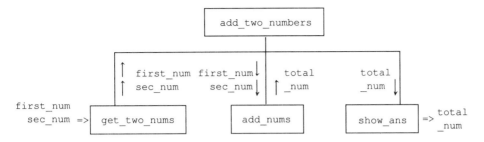

This data-flow structure chart now shows not only the flow of control within the program but also the flow of information within the program. This data-flow design will have to be included in the Ada implementation of the design. This can be done by first producing the procedure declarations using the data-flow information to identify the parameters and their modes.

When program designs using data flow are being implemented using procedures it is advisable to produce a **procedure declaration** from the design before producing the complete procedure. A procedure declaration declares the name of the procedure and the formal names, modes and types of its paramaters only. It does not *define* the actions of the procedure and consequently does not require the **is** reserved word to introduce its definition.

The procedure declaration for get_two_nums will be as follows:

```
procedure get_two_nums ( first_in,
                         sec_in    : out INTEGER );
```

The procedure declaration states the name of the procedure and that it requires two data objects of type INTEGER to be supplied when it is called. The out-only nature of the data flow is indicated by the use of the reserved word **out** in the parameter declarations. The validity of this procedure declaration can be established from the component's data flow in the program structure diagram, which indicates that it requires two out_only INTEGER parameters. The names of the parameters have been chosen as being meaningful to their usage within the procedure and to be distinct from the names of any objects used elsewhere in the program.

A procedure declaration can be transformed into a combined procedure declaration and definition by including the reserved word **is**, the declaration of any local objects required by the procedure and the inclusion of the executable parts enclosed within a **begin/end** pair. The distinction between a procedure declaration and definition becomes relevent when more complex Ada facilities are used. These facilities will be introduced in detail in Blocks 2 and 3.

The procedure declarations of add_nums can also be produced from the data-flow information in the design:

```
procedure add_nums ( an_int,
                     other_int  : in  INTEGER;
                     added      : out INTEGER);
```

The declaration of the two input only parameters as

```
                                        an_int,
                                        other_int   : in INTEGER;
```

is treated by Ada as if it were

```
                                        an_int      : in INTEGER;
                                        other_int   : in INTEGER;
```

The shorter form of the declaration is customarily used where more than one parameter has the same type and mode.

The procedure declaration of add_nums indicates that it requires three data objects of type INTEGER to be passed to it. The first two objects are in-only objects, the third object is an out-only object.

Finally, the declaration of the procedure show_ans can be produced from the program structure chart as follows:

```
    procedure show_ans ( answer    : in INTEGER );
```

The procedure declaration of show_ans indicates that it requires a single in-only INTEGER paramater to be provided.

The calls of the procedures also need to be changed, to reflect the data flow design. The three calls in the main part of the program will now be as follows:

```
    begin  -- add_two_numbers
        get_two_nums( first_num, sec_num );
        add_nums( first_num, sec_num, total_num );
        show_ans( total_num );
    end add_two_numbers;
```

The rest of the implementation of this version of the add_two_numbers program will be left as an end-of-section exercise.

1.11.4 The scope of objects

To introduce the scope of data objects in programs, the assignment_average program from Block 1 Section 5 will be reimplemented. This implementation will incorporate information flow between the components and restricting the scope of data objects where appropriate. The program structure chart from Block 1 Section 5 and the data design tables are reproduced below:

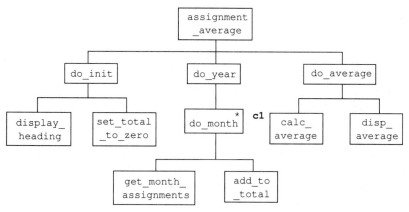

c1: Twelve times.

PROGRAM CONSTANTS

NAME	TYPE	VALUE	NOTES
max_month	INTEGER	12	No of months in one year

PROGRAM VARIABLES

NAME	TYPE	NOTES
ass_month	INTEGER	No of assignments in any one month
total_ass	INTEGER	Total no of assignments in one year
this_month	INTEGER	Loop parameter for the month number
average_ass	FLOAT	Average assignments per month

The first stage in reimplementing this design is to decide upon what parts of the design will be implemented as procedures. From the design it can be decided that the program procedure will be implemented as a sequence of three procedure calls. The subprocedures of the program procedure will be do_init, do_year and do_average. Within the procedure do_year, an iterative procedure called do_month will be called twelve times.

Having decided upon the procedurization of the design, the data flow information can be added. Each data object from the data table will have to be considered in turn, and the places in the design where it has to be accessed decided.

The first object in the data table is the constant max_month; this is required in the procedure do_year, where it is used to define the upper bound of the **for** loop and is also required in the procedure do_average where the average is calculated.

The variable ass_month is only required within the procedure do_month, where it is used as an input variable and added to the variable total_ass. As it is only required within do_month its scope will be restricted to that procedure.

The variable total_ass is required within the procedure do_init, where its value will be set to zero; its value is undefined before the procedure. This indicates that it will have to be implemented as an out-only parameter of the procedure do_init, being passed from the main program where it will have to be declared.

Total_ass will also be required by the procedure do_month, where its value will be changed by the addition of the local variable ass_month. It will thus be an in-out parameter of the procedure do_month. The flow of control within the design indicates that do_month can only be reached from do_year. The variable total_ass will have to be passed from the main program to do_year as an in-out parameter in order that it can be passed onwards to do_month as an in-out parameter.

Only the value of total_ass will be needed by the procedure do_average, where the average will be calculated from it; as its value will not be changed by this procedure it will be passed as an in-only parameter.

The variable this_month will be used as the loop parameter within do_year, where it will be implicitly declared. The value of the variable will be required by the procedure do_month, where it is used as part of the input prompt; thus it will be passed from do_year to do_month as an in-only parameter.

Finally, the variable average_ass is only required by the procedure do_average. It will be declared as a local variable of this procedure.

These scope considerations will have to be added to the data table, which will now indicate not only the name, type and usage of the object but also the component within which it will be declared:

PROGRAM CONSTANTS

NAME	TYPE	VALUE	NOTES
max_month	INTEGER	12	No of months in one year Program level

PROGRAM VARIABLES

NAME	TYPE	NOTES
ass_month	INTEGER	No of assignments in any one month Do_month
total_ass	INTEGER	Total no of assignments in one year Program
this_month	INTEGER	Loop parameter for the month number Do_year
average_ass	FLOAT	Average assignments per month Do_average

This information can be added to the original program structure chart to produce a program structure chart which includes data flow:

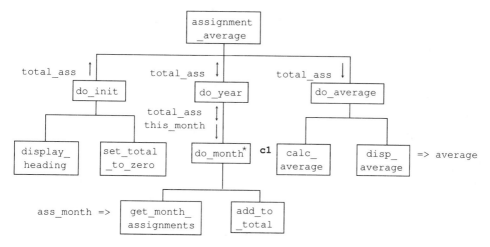

c1: Twelve times.

The data flow information on the structure chart identifies the objects by the name by which they are known at the highest level of the data flow; this will correspond to the actual parameter name when the program is implemented.

The implementation of this design would now be as follows:

```
0001        -- program to demonstrate procedurization, data flow and
0002        -- scope. b1s11p4 see text.
0003        -- Assumes int_io & float_inout in library.
0004
0005        with TEXT_IO, int_io, float_inout;
0006        use  TEXT_IO, int_io, float_inout;
0007
0008        procedure b1s11p4 is
0009
0010           max_month : constant INTEGER := 12;
0011                                     -- No of months in one year
0012           total_ass : INTEGER;        -- total No of assignments
0013
0014        procedure do_init( assignments : out INTEGER) is
0015
0016        -- Display heading & initialize assignments to 0
0017
0018        begin -- do_init
0019           PUT_LINE ("         ASSIGNMENT AVERAGE PROGRAM ");
```

```
0020            NEW_LINE(2);
0021            assignments := 0;
0022         end do_init;
0023
0024      procedure do_year( total_assignments : in out INTEGER ) is
0025
0026      -- procedure to determine total number of assignments by
0027      -- passing object to do_month. Requires global access to
0028      -- max_month for upper bound of loop
0029
0030      procedure do_month ( total_so_far : in out INTEGER;
0031                              month_num : in      INTEGER) is
0032
0033      -- total_so_far is updated from the value input in response
0034      -- to prompt which includes month_num value
0035
0036         ass_month : INTEGER; -- assignments for this month
0037
0038      begin -- do_month
0039         PUT ("No marked in month "); PUT ( month_num );
0040         PUT ( "  ");
0041         GET ( ass_month ); SKIP_LINE;
0042         total_so_far := total_so_far + ass_month;
0043      end do_month;
0044
0045       begin -- do_year
0046          for this_month in INTEGER range 1 .. max_month loop
0047             do_month ( total_assignments, this_month );
0048          end loop;
0049       end do_year;
0050
0051      procedure do_average( ass_total : in INTEGER) is
0052
0053      -- procedure to calc and display average number of assignments
0054      -- requires access to global constant max_month
0055
0056         average_ass : FLOAT; -- average assignments per month
0057
0058      begin -- do_average
0059         average_ass := FLOAT( ass_total ) / FLOAT( max_month );
0060         NEW_LINE(2);
0061         PUT ("Average per month is    ");
0062         PUT ( average_ass, FORE => 8, AFT => 2, EXP => 0);
0063         NEW_LINE(2);
```

```
0064        end do_average;
0065
0066        begin -- b1s11p4
0067            do_init( total_ass );
0068            do_year( total_ass );
0069            do_average( total_ass );
0070        end b1s11p4;
```

The header comments of each procedure now include an explanation of the use to which each parameter will be put, and also identify any global constants required. The variables have been declared at the level which is appropriate, limiting their scope. The only variable which has to be declared at the program level is total_ass. The other variables in the data design have had their scope restricted. The scope of an object is local in the program component where it is declared and global to any component which is declared within the program component in which the object is declared.

The only problem in this implementation is the use of the constant max_month; it is declared at the program level and is referenced globally by the procedures do_year and do_average. One of the design rules given above was that data objects should be referenced locally, either by being declared in the program component they are being referenced within or by being passed into them as a parameter.

There are three possible solutions to this problem. The first is as implemented above. The value of the constant is accessed globally as required and a note to this effect is included in the header comments of the procedures which do so.

The second solution would be to redeclare the constant in each of the procedures where it is required. This should not be done as the value of a constant may have to be changed during the program's life cycle. If the constant is declared more than once then all occurrences of the constant will have to be changed; this can cause maintenance problems. The value of constants such as the number of months in a year is unlikely ever to change, but the value of constants representing, for example, the maximum number of students per course may well change at some time in the life cycle of a program.

One advantage of using a global constant declaration is that, should the value represents ever change, only the declaration of the constant need be changed and all other changes in the program will be made automatically. This is most useful when the constant is declared once. If it is declared more than once then all occurrences of the declaration will have to be found and changed and if one of the declarations were missed the program would no longer be secure. A second reason for using constants is they make the program more readable. The value of the constant max_month in this program, 12, represents something in the real world, not just a value one greater than 11.

The third solution would be to pass the value of the constant as an in-only parameter to the procedures which require it. This would complicate the data-flow design in the program.

Of the three possible solutions, the second solution should not be used; the third solution is the most secure but can become cumbersome. The first solution is less secure as references to global data objects are being made. However, in the case of constants this is allowable as long as a comment is made in the header of the procedure, and a totally secure implementation is not required.

The rest of the implementation of the program should by now be familiar; the program listing is shown with the procedures boxed to make their scope clear. All procedures are declared as procedures of the program procedure, apart from do_month, which is a procedure of the procedure do_year; this is in accordance with the design as shown.

EXERCISES

1.11.1 Produce suitable procedure header declarations from the following data-flow diagrams:

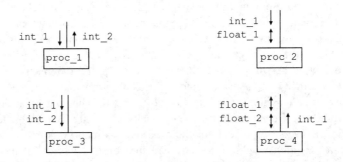

where int_* indicates the name of an parameter of type INTEGER and float_* indicates the name of a parameter of type FLOAT.

1.11.2 Reimplement the add_two_numbers program as discussed in this section.

1.11.3 Redesign the data-flow structure chart from the assignment average program to implement the passing of max_months as a parameter (the third solution as explained in the text).

1.11.4 Reimplement the assignment_average program using the design developed in Exercise 1.11.3.

1.11.5 Using the implementation of the assignment_average program as shown in the text, complete the following table. Each cell in the table represents the accessibility of each data object. Each object can be accessed locally, globally or is inaccessible. For example, the declaration of the variable total_ass can be accessed globally from the procedure do_year. (In the implementation it is actually accessed locally as it is passed to the procedure as a parameter.)

	max_month	total_ass	this_month	average_ass
main program				
do_init				
do_year		global		
do_month				
do_average				

1.11.6 Redesign and reimplement the exam analysis program from Block 1 Section 6 using procedures, parametrization and scope.

Functions

Functions are program objects which have values of some specified type. The objects with values which have been introduced so far are constants, variables and attributes. A reference to a constant or a variable in a program is a reference to the value which is stored as part of the object. A reference to an attribute is a reference to a value which is part of the definition of the data type. The value of a function is not stored or declared, but is evaluated by Ada every time the function is called.

A function, like a procedure, is a named block of code which will be executed when the function is called by name. Unlike a procedure, when a function executes it returns a single value of a specified type. A function call can be used in any place in a program where a value of the function's type is required. Most functions, like procedures, usually require parameters; these are specified much as they are for procedures.

A function can be used in program implementations where the data-flow design indicates that the data flow minimally consists of a single out-only data flow. In addition, a function may have any number of in-only data flows. If a data-flow diagram indicates that a program component has more than one out-only data flow or has any in-out data flow, then it is not suitable for implementation as a function. The following data flows indicate situations where a function may be used:

The following data-flow diagrams indicate situations where a function may not be used:

comp_4 is unsuitable as it has more than one out_only data flow; comp_5 is unsuitable as it has an in_out data flow; comp_6 is unsuitable as it has an input from an external device; a component which had an output to an external device would also be unsuitable.

A data-flow diagram will indicate situations where a function may be used; it would also be possible to implement the component as a procedure using the out-only mechanism as described in the previous section. This decision between a procedure and a function can be regarded as an implementation decision and does not affect the overall design of a program. Wherever it is possible to implement a component as a function, it is usually regarded as good program style to do so.

1.12.1 A first example

To introduce the declaration and use of functions the add_two_numbers program which was first introduced in Block 1 Section 3 and reimplemented in Block 1 Section 7 and in the previous section will be implemented again. The program structure chart, including data-flow information developed in the previous section, was as follows:

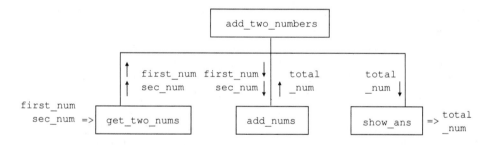

It should be clear from the introduction above that the component add_nums can, and, following the style advice above, should be implemented as a function. The declaration of the function can be derived from the data flow diagram. The two input-only parameters will be specified as formal parameters of the function in a similar manner to the specification of formal parameters for a procedure. The out-only data flow will be declared as being the return type of the function. The declaration of this function would be as follows:

```
function add_nums ( an_int,
                another_int : INTEGER) return INTEGER;
```

The declaration of a function commences with the reserved word **function**; the name of the function, in this case 'add_nums', follows. The list of formal parameters, if any, follows; as the only allowable data-flow method is in-only there is no need to specify the mode of the parameters. The reserved word **return** precedes the declaration of the type of value which will be returned by the function when it executes; this can be any Ada type. A semicolon concludes the declaration of the function.

The definition of the function can now be added to the declaration, producing a combined function declaration and definition:

```
0001   function add_nums ( an_int,
0002                     another_int : INTEGER) return INTEGER is
0003
0004   -- function to add two integers together and return the total
0005   -- bls12p1 see text.
0006
0007      the_total : INTEGER; -- function variable
0008
0009   begin -- add nums
0010      the_total := an_int + another_int;
0011      return the_total;
0012   end add_nums;
```

The function commences with a comment indicating what the function will do when it is executed and what the meaning of the returned value is. Local data objects which are required can then be declared. Among these a function variable of the same type as the function itself should be declared; it is the value of this variable which will be returned as the value of the function when its execution terminates. The executable part of the function follows. Within this part of the function, the function variable should be set to the value which is to be returned from the function.

The final statement of the function should be a **return** statement followed by an expression of the required type of the function. In this example the expression is a reference to the function variable. An **end** statement including the name of the function concludes the body of the function.

Having declared the function as a function object of the program add_two_numbers, the call of the function in the body of the program add_two_numbers has to be changed. The call of the procedure add_nums from the previous section was as follows:

```
add_nums( first_num, sec_num, total_num );
```

In this call the value of total_num was set to the sum of first_num and sec_num and returned to the main program using the out-only data-flow mode of the parameter. Using the function implementation of add_nums this will become

```
total_num := add_num( first_num, sec_num );
```

The value of total_num is now set to the value which is returned from the function add_num as it executes. When this line of the program is executed the sequence of events will commence with the initialization of the formal parameters an_int and another_int to the respective values of the actual parameters first_num and sec_num. The executable part of the function will then commence. The value of the local function variable the_total will be initialized to the sum of an_int and another_int on line 0010 of the function. Line 0011 of the function is the **return** statement, where execution of the function terminates, returning the value of the expression on line 0011 as the value of the function. The **return** expression in this example is a reference to the function variable, whose value will be returned. Program control returns to the point where the function was called, with the function's returned value assigned to the program variable total_num.

A similar example of a suitable place for the use of a function can be found in the assignment_average program as implemented in the previous section. The design component do_average can be refined as follows:

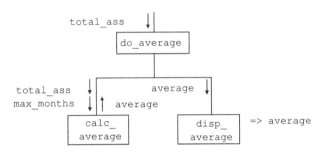

This data-flow diagram indicates that it is possible to calculate the average by implementing the calculation as a function, which would take as in-only parameters the total number of assignments and the number of months, returning as the value of the function the average number of assignments per month. Using the data-flow diagram the function declaration can be produced as follows:

```
function calc_av( total,
            months : INTEGER ) return FLOAT;
```

The name of the function is calc_av. It requires two INTEGER parameters, whose names are chosen to be distinct from the other names in the program; it returns a value of type FLOAT. The data-flow diagram indicates that the function calc_av belongs to the procedure do_average, so the implementation of do_average using the function calc_av would declare the function as one of its objects. The reimplementation of this procedure would be as follows:

```
0001    procedure do_average( ass_total : in INTEGER) is
0002
0003  -- procedure to calculate and display average number of
0004  -- assignments requires access to global constant max_month
0005
```

```
0006        average_ass : FLOAT; -- average assignments per month
0007
0008        function calc_av( total,
0009                          months : INTEGER ) return FLOAT is
0010
0011        -- function to calc and return average score as total
0012        -- divided by months.
0013
0014          the_av   : FLOAT; -- function variable
0015
0016        begin -- calc_av
0017           the_av := FLOAT( total ) / FLOAT( months );
0018           return the_av;
0019        end calc_av;
0020
0021    begin -- do_average
0022        average_ass := calc_av( ass_total, max_month );
0023        NEW_LINE(2);
0024        PUT ("Average per month is   ");
0025        PUT ( average_ass, FORE => 8, AFT => 2, EXP => 0);
0026        NEW_LINE(2);
0027    end do_average;
```

The function is a declared object of the procedure, which initializes a function variable to the value of the average calculated from the in-only parameters and returns this value as the value of the function.

The call of the function calc_av in line 0022 passes to it the two actual parameters ass_total and max_month; the returned value of the function is assigned to the variable average_ass. The sequence of events which will take place when the call of the function is executed by Ada is comparable with the sequence of events which was described above for the call of the function add_nums.

In both of these examples the use of a function to implement the calculations is not strictly necessary. The adding of two integer values together, or the calculation of a float average from two integers, is not complex enough to require implementation as a function. The method of passing parameters into a function and the use made of the returned value of the function can be comprehended from these simple examples. These methods can be used where implementation of a function would be more appropriate.

1.12.2 A second example

To complete the consideration of functions and to conclude this section a new specification will be introduced and a program developed from scratch.

A program is required which will calculate payments for salespersons. A salesperson is paid a basic salary based upon the number of hours that he or she works. The rate of pay is £10.00 per hour for the first 40 hours and £15.00 per hour for any hours over the first 40. Salespersons are also paid a bonus based upon the value of sales they have made. A bonus of 5% is paid on the first £1000 of sales and 7.5% on all sales over £1000. In addition, they are to be paid car expenses of £0.50 per mile for the first 500 miles and £0.40 per mile for all miles over the first 500.

The program, when run, will ask the user to input the information required, calculate the amounts to be paid to the salesperson and then display the payment details.

User interface

The user interface for this program will be as follows:

```
SALES PERSON PAYMENTS

Please enter hours worked      50.0
Please enter value of sales  £1200.00
Please enter mileage          600.0

Salary      £ 550.00
Commission £  65.00
Mileage     £ 290.00

Total       £ 905.00
```

Data design

The data design for the global program objects required will be as follows:

PROGRAM CONSTANTS

NAME	TYPE	VALUE	NOTES
basic_pay	FLOAT	10.0	rate of pay for basic hours
overtime_pay	FLOAT	15.0	rate of pay for overtime hours
basic_pay_limit	FLOAT	40.0	limit of hours for basic pay
basic_commission	FLOAT	0.05	commission factor for basic sales
excess_commission	FLOAT	0.075	commission factor for excess sales
basic_sales_limit	FLOAT	1000.0	sales limit for basic sales

basic_miles	FLOAT	0.50	rate per mile for basic miles
excess_miles	FLOAT	0.40	rate per mile for excess miles
basic_miles_limit	FLOAT	500.0	limit of miles for basic miles

All of these values will be implemented as constants, as it is expected that during the life cycle of the program they may have to be changed. The global variable objects required by this program will be as follows:

PROGRAM VARIABLES

NAME	TYPE	NOTES
hours_worked	FLOAT	hours worked by salesperson
sales_made	FLOAT	sales made by salesperson
miles_travelled	FLOAT	miles travelled by salesperson
pay_due	FLOAT	basic pay for the salesperson
commission	FLOAT	commission due to the salesperson
car_expenses	FLOAT	car expenses due to salesperson

Program design and implementation

The first-level design for this program will be as follows:

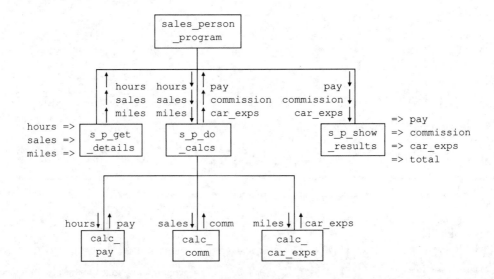

The design indicates that s_p_get_details will be implemented as a procedure which will input information from the keyboard and use it to initialize the three out-only parameters hours, sales and miles.

The component s_p_do_calcs will require the three variables initialized by the component s_p_get_details as in-only parameters and will export as out-only parameters the three variables containing the corresponding payments. These three values will be passed as in-only parameters to s_p_show_results, where they will be used to calculate the total; and all four values will be output to the screen.

Within s_p_do_calcs this design will require three subsidiary components calc_pay, calc_comm and calc_car_exps. All three of these components have a single out_only parameter and a single in_only parameter. This indicates that they are suitable for implementation as functions. The detailed design for the first of these functions (calc_pay) would be as follows:

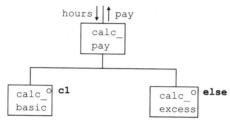

c1: If hours less than or equal to basic.

This design can be implemented directly. The function declaration can be produced from the data flow diagram as follows:

```
function calc_pay( hours_worked : FLOAT ) return FLOAT;
```

This names the function calc_pay and states that it requires a single in-only parameter of type FLOAT. The function itself will return a value of type FLOAT, as indicated by the function's type declaration.

The complete function will be as follows:

```
function calc_pay( calc_hours : FLOAT ) return FLOAT is

-- function to calculate pay due from hours worked.
-- requires access to global constants basic_pay,
-- basic_pay_limit & overtime_pay

   pay_due  : FLOAT; -- function variable

begin -- calc_pay
   if ( calc_hours <= basic_pay_limit ) then
      pay_due := calc_hours * basic_pay;
   else
      pay_due := (( basic_pay_limit * basic_pay )
```

```
                    + (( calc_hours - basic_pay_limit) * overtime_pay));
    end if;
    return pay_due;
end calc_pay;
```

The implementation of the procedure from the design is straightforward, using an **if** structure to implement the selection. In the calculation which forms the **else** part of the **if** statement brackets have been used to make the priority of the individual operations explicit.

The priority of an operator defines the sequence in which the terms which form the expression will be evaluated. In Ada the multiplication operator has a higher priority than the minus and addition operators. Thus the expression:

```
        calc_hours - basic_pay_limit * overtime_pay
```

would be interpreted by Ada as multiply basic_pay_limit by overtime_pay and subtract the result from calc_hours. This has a different meaning to the expression:

```
        ( calc_hours - basic_pay_limit ) * overtime_pay
```

which would be interpreted as perform the subtraction first and multiply the result by overtime_pay (which is the correct sequence of actions for this situation). Where operators of an equal priority are included within an expression, they will be evaluated in a left-to-right manner.

The only brackets which are strictly required in this example are those surrounding the term '(calc_hours – basic_pay_limit)'. The explicit use of non-required brackets is advised to make the meaning of the calculation more obvious, and also to avoid any misunderstanding concerning the priority of the operators. It also allows easy translation of programs from one language to another where the priority rules may differ.

The design for the other two functions required by the program will be identical to the design of calc_pay. Each will have exactly the same structure, a simple decision between two courses of action. The decision in each case will be based upon a comparison between the value of the in-only parameter and a specified limit. Assuming that two suitable functions called calc_comm and calc_car_exps have been implemented as function objects of the procedure s_p_do_calcs, the body of the procedure s_p_do_calcs would be:

```
begin -- s_p_do_calcs
    pay_due      := calc_pay ( hours_worked );
    commission   := calc_comm( sales_made );
    car_expenses := calc_car_exps( miles_travelled );
end do_calcs;
```

The implementation of the procedure s_p_do_calcs as sequence of three function calls is directly comparable with the program design chart.

Within each of these functions the calculation of the out-only parameter for in-only parameters which are below or equal to the basic limit will be a simple multiplication of the value of the in-only parameter by the basic factor for that parameter.

The calculation of the out-only parameter for in-only parameters which are above the basic limit will be to calculate the basic by multiplying the basic factor rate by the basic limit and then adding the excess. The excess can be calculated by subtracting the basic limit from the in-only parameter value and multiplying the result of this calculation by the excess factor.

A second implementation

The three functions above are identical in the number modes and types of the parameters and the type of the result. They are also identical in the internal structure of the function and the method of calculating the result.

They differ in the in-only parameter, the basic limit the basic rate and the excess rate. If all of these are passed into the function as parameters, then one function in the program can be used for all three calculations. A function or procedure like this, which can be used in a more general manner, should always be favoured in program implementations.

The data flow diagram for this general function will be as follows:

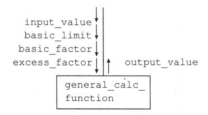

A second advantage of implementing the function in this more general way is that the constants which were accessed globally by the previous versions of the functions are now passed explicitly to the general function. As explained in the previous section, a design which maximizes the use of local data objects should be favoured. The function declaration for this function can be produced from the data-flow diagram as follows:

```
function general_calc( input_value,
                       basic_limit,
                       basic_factor,
                       excess_factor : FLOAT ) return FLOAT is

-- function to calculate general expenses using rule that if input_
-- value is less than or equal to basic_limit, value is input_value
-- times basic_factor. Otherwise value is basic_limit times basic_
-- factor plus amount of input_value over basic_limit times
```

```
-- excess_factor.

        out_value : FLOAT; -- function variable
```

The body of the function would be as follows:

```
begin -- general_calc
   if ( input_value <= basic_limit ) then
      out_value := input_value * basic_factor;
   else
      out_value := (( input_limit * basic_factor )
               + (( input_value - basic_limit) * excess_factor));
   end if;
   return out_value;
end general_calc;
```

The call of this general function to calculate pay within the procedure s_p_do_calcs would be as follows:

```
pay_due := general_calc ( hours_worked, basic_pay_limit,
                       basic_pay, overtime_pay);
```

The actual parameters basic_pay_limit, basic_pay and overtime_pay are being referenced in procedure s_p_do_calcs as global constants. They are being passed to the general function as in-only parameters, which is allowable, as only the value of the object is required for an in-only parameter.

The formal in-only parameters of the general function basic_limit, basic_factor and excess_factor will receive the corresponding values. The calculations which are performed upon these values are identical to the calculations which were performed upon the values in the function calc_pay above. When the general function is used to calculate the commission the function call will be as follows:

```
commission := general_calc ( sales_made, basic_sales_limit,
                          basic_commission, excess_commission );
```

The call of the general function to calculate the car expenses would be as follows:

```
car_expenses := general_calc ( miles, basic_miles_limit,
                            basic_miles, excess_miles );
```

The use of a general function to perform these calculations has several advantages. The number of functions in the program has been reduced. Three functions have been replaced with one; this will make testing and maintenance of the program easier. The reduction in the complexity of the program structure has, however, been achieved with an increase in the complexity of the data flow within the program.

It is possible that during the life cycle of the program the rules for the calculation of salary, commission and car expenses, which in this version are congruent enough to allow a general function to be used, may not remain congruent. In this case the general function will either have to become more complex, or the original design, using different functions to calculate the different values, will have to be implemented.

The use of general functions and procedures contributes to good program design and implementation. It is often the case that a program contains several requirements which, although they appear different at first, are congruent enough to be implemented using a generalized component. It is also the case that a generalized component from one program can be more easily reused in a different program.

The rest of the implementation of this program will be left as an exercise.

1.12.3 An alternative implementation style

An alternative implementation of the general function would be the following:

```
function general_calc( input_value,
                       basic_limit,
                       basic_factor,
                       excess_factor : FLOAT ) return FLOAT is

-- function to calculate general expenses using rule that if input_
-- value is less than or equal to basic_limit, value is input_value
-- times basic_factor. Otherwise value is basic_limit times basic_
-- factor plus amount of input_value over basic_limit times
-- excess_factor.

begin -- general_calc
  if ( input_value <= basic_limit ) then
    return  input_value * basic_factor;
  else
    return (basic_limit * basic_factor )
          + (( input_value - basic_limit) * excess_factor));
  end if;
end general_calc;
```

This implementation of the function is apparently less complex than the previous implementation; both implementations have the same functional behaviour. The difference between the two implementations lies in the use of a function variable. The second implementation avoids the use of a function variable by having two **return** statements, each of which is followed by an expression.

This version of the function has two points within itself where flow of control can be returned from the function to the place in the program from where the function was called. This increases the complexity of the run-time flow of control of the function and can lead to problems when the function requires maintenance. The initial favoured version of the function has one place where flow of control can enter the function, the **begin** statement, and one place where flow of control can exit the function, the **return** statement, which immediately precedes the **end** of the function. By simplifying the flow of control considerations the overall complexity of the function, and thus of the program, has been reduced.

The general advice is to use function variables within a function and avoid multiple exit points by having only one **return** statement immediately preceding the **end** function statement. This advice can be ignored in situations like the function above where the overall structure of the function is so simple that a minimal inspection of the code reveals its entire complexity.

EXERCISES

1.12.1 Implement the salesperson program as described in the text.

1.12.2 Devise a test plan for the salesperson program as described in the text.

Block 2
Data Structures and Simple Packages

Section 2.1

Ada numeric types: INTEGER and FLOAT

2.1.1 Data types

In Block 1 several predeclared Ada data types were informally introduced and used. The following are the major data types which are predeclared in the Ada environment:

```
INTEGER      FLOAT      FIXED

CHARACTER    STRING     BOOLEAN
```

This section will introduce the predeclared numeric types concerned with representing integer and floating point values; Section 3 will introduce the predefined text-orientated types, CHARACTER and STRING; and Section 4 will introduce the BOOLEAN type.

The data types which are available within an Ada program are not limited to the predeclared types listed above. It is possible, and for almost every program advisable, for additional data types different from those which are predefined to be declared and used. Such types are known as *user-declared* types. The methods by which user types can be declared and subsequently used will be the major theme of this block.

The intent of any program is to model within a computer some aspect of the real world. The program statements represent processes which can be applied to objects in the real world; correspondingly, the data objects which the program statements manipulate represent objects in the real world. If data types are declared and used whose structure and operations are more congruent with the objects which exist in the real world, the program becomes a better model of the real world and thus a better program.

The full definition of any predeclared or user-declared data type can be expressed by declaring the range of values which an object of that type can take and by declaring the operations which can be performed upon objects of that data type.

The declaration of the range of values which a data object can take is expressed in an Ada program by declaring a name for the type and by listing, or implicitly listing, the values which an object of the type can take. The expression of the range of values can be done by explicitly listing (enumerating) the values, or by referring to a previously declared or predeclared type.

The declaration of the operations which can be performed upon a data object of a particular type is expressed in an Ada program by declaring functions and/or procedures which require parameters or return a value of the type concerned.

It is also possible for a user-declared data type to inherit properties from a predeclared data type or from a data type previously declared by the user. These inherited properties have to be taken into account when the complete specification of the data type is being considered.

2.1.2 INTEGER data types

In common terms an integer is a positive or negative value within the range minus to plus infinity, which does not have any decimal part. However, Ada data objects of the predeclared type INTEGER can only take a finite range of integer values. The actual range of values which objects of type INTEGER can take is dependent upon the compiler being used.

The actual value of the lowest and highest integer value which can be represented by the Ada compiler being used can be determined by using an *attribute*. For any data type there are a number of different attributes which can be used to determine particular properties of that type. For the predeclared type INTEGER the attribute FIRST will evaluate to the lowest value which the Ada compiler can represent, and the attribute LAST will evaluate to the highest value which it can represent.

The use of attributes can be deduced from the following program fragment:

```
PUT ("The lowest  integer value is ");
PUT ( INTEGER'FIRST ); NEW_LINE;

PUT ("The highest integer value is ");
PUT ( INTEGER'LAST ); NEW_LINE;
```

The name of the type which the attribute qualifies is the first term of the attribute expression, this is followed by a single quote character ("'") and then the name of the attribute required. The attribute expression will itself evaluate to a particular type, in this example the type of the attribute expression is INTEGER.

Input and output of integers

Ada does not provide the facilities for the input and output of integer values directly; the reason for this is that there is the possibility of additional user-declared integer types being used in a program. As these user-declared integer types will also require input and output facilities, Ada provides a general facility for the input and output of integer types. The general facility can be 'tailored' for use with any particular integer type. The facility for declaring new integer types will be introduced in the next section.

The use of this facility has already been introduced in Block 1; the inclusion of the statements

```
with TEXT_IO;
package int_io is new TEXT_IO.INTEGER_IO( INTEGER );
```

in a program will create a new package called int_io, suitable for the input and output of values of type INTEGER. The 'tailoring' of a package for use with a particular data type is known as *instantiation*.

The general facility is supplied by a package called INTEGER_IO which is itself contained within a package called TEXT_IO. The phrase '**with** TEXT_IO' establishes the use of the TEXT_IO package, the phrase 'TEXT_IO.INTEGER_IO' references the integer input/output package contained within TEXT_IO. The specification of the type INTEGER as a parameter to this package instantiates it for a particular integer type, in this example the predeclared INTEGER type. The phrase '**package** int_io **is new**' establishes a user-supplied name for the newly created package by which it can be referenced.

The inclusion of the phrase

```
use int_io;
```

at the start of a program before the declaration of the main program procedure brings the int_io package into the scope of the entire program. This allows the procedures and functions contained within the package to be referenced directly, without having to specify the name of the package within which they are contained {e.g., int_io.PUT()}. This global scope may not be appropriate for all programs; it is only valid if the input and output of integers is being extensively used within all or most parts of the program. If the input and output of integers is not being extensively used, then the scope of the **use** should be restricted to those parts of the program which require the facilities provided.

The precise meaning of and the use of package facilities will be introduced in Block 2 Section 7 and subsequent sections. Up to that point the use of packages will be limited to the use of predeclared input and output facilities contained within TEXT_IO.

Before the input and output of integer objects can be introduced in detail, the way in which integers values can be expressed in Ada will have to be explained. A simple integer literal expression consists of a sequence of digit characters {0,1,2,3,4,5,6,7,8,9} possibly preceded by a positive or negative symbol {+,-}. It is not possible to include commas within an integer literal (e.g., 2,000,000) but it is possible to include an underscore character (e.g., 2_000_000) if this form of notation is desired.

The package INTEGER_IO provides a procedure for the input of integer values into a program by use of the GET procedure, and for the output of integer values by the use of the PUT procedure.

The GET procedure can be used to input an integer value from the terminal, by using it in the form

```
GET( int_var );
```

where int_var is a variable of a suitable integer type. The effect of the procedure is to suspend program execution and accept characters from the terminal until a suitable sequence of characters has been provided. The sequence of characters will be converted into its integer representation and the value of int_var set to this integer representation.

The behaviour of the procedure when an unsuitable sequence of characters is provided by the user will be considered in the next section. The only point to note here is that the character which terminates the integer character sequence is not accepted from the terminal. In simple programs the sequence provided by the user is usually made available to the program by the use of a return key press. This return character is still left unprocessed by the GET procedure. This return can be taken care of by including a call to the procedure SKIP_LINE. SKIP_LINE is a procedure provided by the package TEXT_IO whose effect is to accept and throw away characters from the terminal, up to and including the 'return' character. Thus the use of the GET procedure for input from the terminal is usually but not always followed by a call of the SKIP_LINE procedure as in

```
GET( int_var ); SKIP_LINE;
```

The integer GET procedure can also be used to input integer values from an external file; this use of the GET procedure will be considered in Block 2 Section 11.

The PUT procedure can be used to output integer values from the program to the terminal. The simplest form of the PUT procedure is

```
PUT( int_obj );
```

where int_obj is an object of a suitable integer type. It can be an integer variable, an integer constant, an integer named number, an integer literal or any expression of type INTEGER. The effect of the procedure, when it is executed, is to evaluate the integer object and output the value as a sequence of digit characters, preceded by a minus symbol if the value is negative. In this form the integer value may be preceded by a number of spaces as all integer outputs are forced to the same width. This default width, which differs from compiler to compiler, is large enough to output all possible integer values. For more precise control of the output format, the PUT procedure can be used in the form

```
PUT( int_obj, WIDTH => pos_int );
```

where pos_int is a positive integer expression. The effect of this form of the procedure is to attempt to output as many characters as are specified by the WIDTH parameter. If the number of characters required to express the int_obj is less than the number specified by WIDTH, then the output is preceded by as many space characters as are required to pad the output to WIDTH characters. If the number of characters required to express the int_obj is equal to or greater than the number specified by WIDTH, then as many characters as are required are used, overriding the WIDTH specifier.

For example, if the value of int_obj is assumed to be 123456 the following calls of the integer PUT procedure will have the output shown (assuming a default width of twelve characters):

int_obj := 123456	
PUT (int_obj)	∇∇∇∇∇∇123456
PUT(int_obj, WIDTH => 10)	∇∇∇∇123456
PUT(int_obj, WIDTH => 12)	∇∇∇∇∇∇123456
PUT(int_obj, WIDTH => 6)	123456
PUT(int_obj, WIDTH => 1)	123456

where a ∇ character indicates a space.

The integer PUT procedure can also be used to output integer values to an external file. This use of the PUT procedure will be considered in Block 2 Section 11.

Arithmetic operations on integers

The negation operator '-' (minus), often referred to as 'unary minus', negates an integer to which it is applied. The only other unary operator is **abs**, which evaluates to the absolute positive value of the integer object it is applied to (**abs** 64 is 64, **abs**-64 is 64).

The binary integer arithmetic operators are '+', '-', '*', '/', **mod**, **rem**, '**'. All of these operators take two integers as operands, and evaluate to a result of the type INTEGER. If a general statement of the form

```
result := first op second
```

where result, first and second are objects of type INTEGER and op is one of the operators above. The results of applying the operator with the following values will be as follows:

first	second	op	result	notes
42	84	+	126	addition
126	84	-	42	subtraction
7	6	*	42	multiplication
23	4	/	5	integer division (4 goes into 23 5 times)
23	4	**rem**	3	integer division (4 goes into 23 5 times **rem**ainder 3)
2	4	**	16	exponentiation: 2 to the power of 4

When these operators are used the three objects referenced all have to be of the type INTEGER; the use of these operators with objects of differing numeric types will be considered below in mixed arithmetic operations.

Relational operations on integers

The relational operators ('=', '<', '>', '<=', '>=', '<>') can be applied to INTEGER values; these are considered further in Block 2 Section 4.

2.1.3 Floating-point data types

In common terms a floating-point number is a positive or negative number in the range minus to plus infinity which has decimal parts. Ada data objects of the real types can take a restricted range of values which again depend on the compiler.

Ada, and other computer environments, are able to represent and manipulate integer values within a specified range exactly. When floating-point values are represented within computer environments they may not be represented exactly. In the normal usage of floating-point numbers there are some values ($1/3$, π, etc.) which cannot be represented exactly; these values are usually expressed to a required degree of accuracy.

There are two different methods provided by Ada for the representation of real values; these methods are known as *floating-point types* and *fixed-point types*. Floating-point types are declared by specifying the number of significant digits to be used to represent the value. Fixed-point types are declared by specifying the accuracy required in the representation of the value. Floating-point types allow a larger range of values to be represented with a lower degree of accuracy than fixed-point types. For reasons of space only floating-point types will be considered as they tend to have greater applicability, although in some situations fixed-point types would be more appropriate.

Floating-point values are represented in one of two ways. The most obvious is by representing the value in the form 'integer literal decimal_point positive integer literal' (e.g., 123.456). An alternative way of representing the value of a real value is in the form 'mantissa E exponent', where mantissa is a real (positive or negative) number, as expressed above, with a single non-zero digit before the decimal point, and exponent is an integer in a defined range. The number of digits in the mantissa is the number of significant digits in the value, and the exponent indicates the number of positions by which the decimal point has to be shifted in the mantissa to obtain the value expressed in the conventional notation. Mantissa-exponent notation is also known as *standard* notation or *scientific* notation, and is more convenient for expressing very large or very small numbers. Some examples of values in conventional and standard notation should make this clear:

conventional	standard
123.456	1.23456E2
3.1418	3.1418E0
0.0001234	1.234E-4
-456.789	-4.56789E2

Ada compilers provide a predeclared floating-point type called FLOAT, the precise declaration of which differs from compiler to compiler. The actual declaration of this type for a particular compiler can be deduced from the use of attributes. Attributes available for floating-point types include the following:

```
FLOAT'DIGITS      the number of significant digits

FLOAT'SMALL       the smallest representable positive float value

FLOAT'LARGE       the largest representable positive float value
```

Input and output of floating-point numbers

In order for an Ada program to have the capability to input and output floating-point values, a predeclared package similar to the integer predeclared package introduced above has to be instantiated. An appropriate instantiation for use with the predeclared type FLOAT would be as follows:

```
with TEXT_IO;
package float_inout is new TEXT_IO.FLOAT_IO( FLOAT );
```

As with integer input and output, the use of a global

```
use float_inout;
```

may be appropriate for some programs.

The instantiation of the package provides access to suitable GET and PUT procedures for the input and output of the FLOAT values specified. In a program requiring input and/or output of both INTEGER and FLOAT types, this implies that there are at least two versions of the GET procedure and two versions of the PUT procedure. This is an example of *overloading*; the procedures GET and PUT have more than one possible meaning in an Ada program.

Ada is able to determine which meaning is intended from the context in which the GET or PUT is found. If the object being referenced by the GET is an INTEGER or the object being output is an INTEGER, then the reference can be determined by Ada to be a reference to the INTEGER versions of GET and PUT. If the referenced objects are of type FLOAT, then the FLOAT versions of GET and PUT are being referenced. Ada allows overloading of procedure and function names, including user-declared procedures and functions, as long as there is some way by which the ambiguity can be resolved. If the ambiguity cannot be resolved by any other way, the package name has to be used to qualify the procedure name (as in int_io.PUT(), float_inout.GET(), etc.).

The FLOAT version of the GET procedure can be used in the form

```
GET( float_var ); SKIP_LINE;
```

with the same considerations as were expressed for the integer version of the GET procedure as explained above. The input provided by the user can be expressed in conventional or standard notation. The behaviour of the GET procedure when an input is not in suitable form will be considered in the next section. The FLOAT GET procedure can also be used to input floating-point values from an external file; this use of the procedure will be introduced in Block 2 Section 11.

The FLOAT PUT procedure differs from the integer procedure as there are more options available to express the format in which the output is to be shown. The simplest version of the PUT statement when a float value is to be output is:

```
PUT( float_obj );
```

where the float_obj can be a FLOAT literal, a FLOAT constant, a FLOAT named number, a FLOAT variable or any expression of type FLOAT. If it is assumed that the FLOAT object is a FLOAT variable called a_float with seven significant figures and the value 123.4567, the output of the statement above would be as follows:

```
∇1.234567E+02
```

The effect of the PUT procedure for FLOAT values when used in this simple form is to output values in standard notation, using as many characters as are required. For precise control of the output format, three parameters can be specified:

```
FORE   specifies the number of characters before the decimal point.
AFT    specifies the number of characters after  the decimal point.
EXP    specifies the number of characters for    the exponent part.
```

In standard notation there is always only a single digit before the decimal point; the default value for this parameter is two, allowing a space or a minus symbol to appear before the digit if the value is negative. The number of digits following the decimal points has a default value of one less than the number of significant digits declared for the type. The default value of the EXP field is three characters, allowing one position for the sign character which is always shown, and two for the value of the exponent.

To display the number in conventional form, the number of characters in the exponent part can be set to zero. The number of character positions used for the FORE and AFT parts of the display is then equal to the value specified, if any, or the number required to express the value if none are specified. If the number of characters required for the FORE part is larger than the value specified then as many characters as are required are used. If the number of characters specified for the AFT part is less than the number of characters required then the number is rounded. Some examples will make this clear:

---

a_float := 1.234567

PUT(a_float);	∇1.234567E+00
PUT(a_float, EXP => 0);	∇1.234567
PUT (a_float, AFT => 3, EXP => 0);	∇1.235
PUT(a_float, FORE => 5, AFT => 3, EXP => 0);	∇∇∇∇1.235

Arithmetic operations on floats

The unary negation operator, the unary **abs** operator and the binary arithmetic operators '+', '-' , '*', '/' and '**' which were introduced above for use with integer objects can also be used with FLOAT objects, with the same meanings and restrictions. The only exception is the exponentiation operator, where the exponent has to be INTEGER.

Relational operations on floats

The relational operators (=, <, >, <=, >=, < >) can be applied to FLOAT arguments; these are considered further in Block 2 Section 4.

Accuracy of float variables

As mentioned earlier, FLOAT values represented in computers are subject to rounding errors. In common use is not possible to represent the 'floating-point' value of fraction such as $1/3$ in decimal notation (0.33333 . . .). When floating-point values are stored in a computer, they are subject to a similar problem which means that some values cannot be represented exactly. This includes some values which can be represented exactly in decimal notation, but are subject to rounding error when processed by computer. The following program provides an example:

```
-- program to demonstrate rounding errors by adding 1/10000
-- to itself ten thousand times and then comparing the result
-- with 1.00. b2s1p1 see text.

with TEXT_IO;
package float_inout is new TEXT_IO.FLOAT_IO( FLOAT );

with TEXT_IO, float_inout; use TEXT_IO, float_inout;

procedure b2s1p1 is

                   zero : constant := 0.0;           -- named real number
           ten_thousand : constant := 10_000;        -- named int  number
                    one : constant FLOAT := 1.0;     -- FLOAT constant
    one_ten_thousandth : constant FLOAT := one / FLOAT( ten_thousand )
                                                     -- FLOAT constant

           the_result : FLOAT := zero;       -- variable declaration and
                                                     initialization
begin -- b2s1p1
    -- the_result is equal to zero
    for counter in INTEGER range 1 .. ten_thousand loop
       the_result := the_result + one_ten_thousandth;
    end loop;
    -- the_result is mathematically equal to 1/10_000 * 10_000 = 1.0

    if ( the_result = one ) then
       PUT_LINE("Isn't this what you expected!");
    else
       PUT_LINE("Isn't this a surprise!");
       PUT("One  is "); PUT( one,   EXP => 0); NEW_LINE;
       PUT("The result is "); PUT( the_result, EXP => 0); NEW_LINE;
    end if;
end b2s1p1;
```

This program introduces a number of new facilities concerned with the declaration of constants and variables which will be explained shortly. The intent of the program is to add the floating-point number one_ten_thousandth (1/10000) to itself ten thousand times. Mathematically this should be equal to the number one (1.0), when this program was executed on a VAX computer the output obtained was as follows:

```
Isn't this a surprise!
One is        1.00000
The result is  0.99973
```

The output shows that the result of adding the computer representation of 1/10_000 to itself ten thousand times is not 1.00000 but 0.99973. This difference in values is small and is caused by rounding errors occasioned by the precise manner in which the computer stores FLOAT values. The following version of the program gets around the problem.

```
-- program to avoid rounding errors by using a minimal
-- difference to determine equality rather than strict
-- equality. b2s1p2 see text.
-- assumes float_inout is in the library.

with TEXT_IO, float_inout; use TEXT_IO, float_inout;

procedure b2s1p2 is

                zero : constant := 0.0;                -- named real number
        ten_thousand : constant := 10_000;             -- named int  number
                 one : constant FLOAT := 1.0;          -- FLOAT constant
  one_ten_thousandth : constant FLOAT := one / FLOAT( ten_thousand);
                                                       -- FLOAT constant
        close_enough : constant FLOAT := 0.001;        -- float constant

          the_answer : FLOAT := zero;         -- initialized    variable
          difference : FLOAT;                 -- uninitialized  variable

begin -- b2s1p2
    -- the_answer is equal to zero
    for counter in INTEGER range 1 .. ten_thousand loop
        the_answer := the_answer + one_ten_thousandth;
    end loop;
    -- the_answer is mathematically equal to 1/10_000 * 10_000 = 1.0
    -- but actually different due to rounding errors

    difference := one - the_answer;   -- difference between one and unity
    difference := abs difference;     -- ensure difference positive

    if ( difference < close_enough ) then
        PUT_LINE("Isn't this what you expected!");
    else
        PUT_LINE("Isn't this a surprise!");
        PUT("One  is "); PUT( one,   EXP => 0); NEW_LINE;
        PUT("The Answer is "); PUT( unity, EXP => 0); NEW_LINE;
```

```
    end if;
end b2s1p2;
```

In this version of the program the values of the FLOAT objects one and the_answer are not tested for strict equality. Instead the absolute difference between the two values is obtained and tested as being close enough to zero, to be treated as indicating that the two values are equal. The output when this version was executed was as follows:

```
Isn't this what you expected!
```

When FLOAT values are being tested for equality the approach used in the second program should always be used. If the approach used in the first program is used it is unlikely that two FLOAT values will ever be found to be exactly equal.

The two programs also introduce some new facilities concerned with the declaration of constants and variables. The two lines

```
        zero : constant := 0.0;    -- named real number
ten_thousand : constant := 10_000; -- named integer number
```

are different from the constant declarations which were introduced in Block 1. These constant declarations do not have a data type explicitly stated; they are examples of a type of constant known as a *named number*. They have the implicit type 'universal real' and 'universal integer' respectively. The universal numeric types are compatible with corresponding explicit numeric types but are not genuine Ada types; this point will be expanded upon in the next section.

The constant declaration

```
one_ten_thousandth : constant FLOAT := one / FLOAT( ten_thousand);
```

introduces the setting of a constant object's value using an expression. The examples of setting constant values used in Block 1 used numeric literals to express the value. This example of specifying a constant value uses the value which is obtained when an expression is evaluated. In order for the evaluation to be possible all the objects in the expression have to have values.

The variable declaration

```
the_result   : FLOAT := zero;
```

introduces the setting of the value of a variable object as it is declared. This declaration not only declares a variable object of type FLOAT with the name 'the_answer', but also sets the value of the object to the value of the named number 'zero' (0.0). As was mentioned above, the implicit type of the object 'zero' is universal real, which is compatible with the type FLOAT.

The second version of the program included the phrase '**with** float_inout; **use** float_inout;' without first including the phrase which instantiates the package float_inout. This is permissible within an Ada environment. When the first program is compiled the new package float_inout is not only created but also stored in an Ada library. Programs which are compiled subsequently can use this package directly from the library without having to re-create it.

Storing standard packages of programs such as int_io or float_inout in a library aids program development, as they can simply be used by a program which has a requirement for the facilities they contain, without having to be explicitly created by every program which has such a requirement. The header comment in the program should indicate that this program is *dependent* upon named packages being available in the library. It is the programmer's responsibility to ensure that a package used in this way is present in a library which is in use. Packages and the detailed rules for the use of packages from libraries will be covered in detail in the latter half of this block and in Block 3.

2.1.4 Mixed arithmetic operations

The arithmetic operators '+', '-', '*', '/' are overloaded; they can either be used with operands both of which are of type INTEGER and evaluate to a value of type INTEGER; or they can be used with operands both of which are of type FLOAT and evaluate to a value of type FLOAT. It is not possible to mix operands within an expression; for example, to multiply an INTEGER operand by a FLOAT operand to obtain a result of type FLOAT. The missing operator '**' is also overloaded; its right-hand value is always INTEGER, the left-hand value can be INTEGER or FLOAT, and the result is of the same type as the left-hand value.

Mixed arithmetic operations are often a program requirement. In the program examples used in this section the instantiation of the FLOAT constant one_ten_ thousandth was accomplished by the result of evaluating the expression 'one / ten_thousand'. In this expression 'one' is an object of type FLOAT, and 'ten_thousand' is an object of implicit type universal integer.

The expression 'one / ten_thousand' attempts to divide a FLOAT object by an INTEGER object and return a result of type FLOAT. The Ada compiler would not accept this expression, as the objects are of different types. The expression as shown in the program text uses the term 'FLOAT(ten_thousand)', which is an example of *type conversion*. In this example it converts the type of the object ten_thousand from INTEGER to FLOAT, allowing it to be correctly used in the expression. Using the two numeric data types introduced in this section, it is possible to convert between the two types using expressions which have the general form

```
FLOAT( int_value )
INTEGER( float_value )
```

The conversion of an INTEGER to a FLOAT will always be successful, although some degree of accuracy may be lost. The conversion of a FLOAT to an INTEGER will only be successful if the value of the FLOAT object is within the range INTEGER'FIRST to INTEGER'LAST. If the value is outside this range a run-time exception will be generated when the conversion is attempted.

EXERCISES

2.1.1 Write a very short program which will display on the terminal the values of INTEGER'FIRST, INTEGER'LAST, FLOAT'DIGITS, FLOAT'FIRST and FLOAT'LAST.

2.1.2 If a, b, d, e and f are integer variables with the values a = 15, b = 3, d = 5 and e = -4, what is the value of f after these statements have been evaluated?

(a) f := b + d;   (h) f := -d;
(b) f := b * d;   (i) f := -e;
(c) f := a **rem** b;   (j) f := +d;
(d) f := c **rem** b;   (k) f := +e;
(e) f := a **rem** c;   (l) f := a + b * d;
(f) f := **abs**(e);   (m) f := (a + b) * d;
(g) f := **abs**(a);   (n) f := a ** b.

2.1.3 If pi, e and c are float variables with the values pi = 3.142, e = 2.718 and c = 456.789, what is output when the following PUT statements are executed? (Assume FLOAT'DIGITS is equal to 8.)

(a) PUT(pi);
(b) PUT(pi, EXP => 0);
(c) PUT(e, EXP => 0, AFT => 1);
(d) PUT(e, EXP => 0, AFT => 3, FORE => 5);
(e) PUT(c, AFT => 4);
(f) PUT(c, FORE => 1, AFT => 3, EXP => 0).

2.1.4 Using the variables from Exercises 2.1.2 and 2.1.3 write expressions for the following:

(a) Multiply pi by a and put the result in f.
(b) Multiply pi by a and put the result in c.
(c) Add pi to e and put the result in f.
(d) Add a to b and put the result in c.

2.1.5 Check your answers to Exercises 2.1.2, 2.1.3 and 2.1.4 by writing small programs to perform the operations and/or display the results.

Types and subtypes

This section will introduce the facilities available in Ada to declare and use user-declared numeric data types and subtypes. Predeclared Ada types are not always suitable for effectively representing the variety of objects which exist in the real world and which may have to be represented in a program. The predeclared types can be used as the basis upon which some user-declared types are based. The intent of user-declared data types is to create types whose values and operations are more congruent to the real world objects which they are representing.

This section will provide an introduction to the declaration and use of numeric types and subtypes whose declaration and use are related to the predeclared numeric types. The full definition of any type declares the values which objects of that type can take, and the operations which can be performed upon those objects. For user-declared numeric types the operations are mostly inherited from the numeric types on which they are based and with reference to which they are declared.

2.2.1 Numeric types and subtypes

It is often the case that the values of numeric data objects in the real world take a more restricted range of values than the range of values which are available for the predeclared Ada data types. Using the predeclared numeric data types INTEGER and FLOAT introduced in the previous section as an example, it would be possible to define the following variables:

```
person_age    : INTEGER; -- age of a person
no_on_bus     : INTEGER; -- number of people on a bus
person_weight : FLOAT;   -- weight of a person in kilos
```

Within an Ada program which declared these variables it would be possible for the variables to be assigned values which could produce the following outputs:

> This person is 345 years old.
> There are -5 people on the bus.
> Freda's weight is 556.56 kilos.

A well-implemented program should not produce nonsensical output like this; one of the methods available in Ada to avoid this, is to declare specific numeric types whose highest and lowest values are explicitly declared in the program listing. For example, the no_on_bus variable could be declared to be of a type which can only take integer values between 0 and 80. The variable person_age could be declared to be of a type which can only take integer values between 0 and 110. The variable weight could be of a type which can only take floating-point values between 0.00 and 150.00, to two decimal places (10 grams) of accuracy.

If the variables are declared to be of the types suggested above, then any attempt to assign a value to the variable which is outside the allowable range will result in a compilation error or a run-time exception.

It can be argued that it is perhaps better for a program to produce nonsensical results and to continue processing, than to stop processing with a run-time error. However, the intent is to implement a program design which does not produce nonsensical results and thus will not cause exceptions as it executes.

As a part of the development process, a run-time exception generated when a variable is assigned an out-of-range value is preferable to allowing processing to continue. This is particularly so if the value is used as a part of intermediate processing and is not subsequently displayed as part of the program's output. A run-time exception in a program will halt execution of the program and indicate to the programmer the position in the program where the error occurred. This will allow debugging to be more accurately targeted. If the run-time error did not occur then the result output by the program might be seen to be meaningless but there would be no indication of where the error originated.

To generalize this argument, the use of a restricted numeric type when appropriate will produce a more congruent model of the real-world situation which the program is representing. The more congruent the model expressed within the program, the more robust, effective and elegant the program will be.

There are other reasons why specific numeric types should be used. The first of these is as an aid to portability. As was mentioned in the previous section, the range of values which the predeclared numeric types can represent differs from compiler to compiler. By explicitly stating the minimum and maximum values required for a type, it can be guaranteed that the compiler being used will be able adequately to represent the values required.

For example, the value of INTEGER'LAST on the Janus compiler is +32767, but a program specification may have a requirement to represent integer objects as large as 40000. Such a program could not run effectively on the Janus compiler. By declaring a specific integer type whose largest value is 40000 explicitly in the program listing, the restriction would become obvious when an attempt was made to compile the program using the Janus compiler. If the predeclared integer type was used for these objects, then the limitation may not become obvious until the program had apparently been running adequately for some time, and a value greater than 32767 was generated.

A related reason for explicitly declaring numeric types applies only to floating-point types. With these types, in addition to declaring the minimum and maximum value of the type, the number of significant digits required can also be stated. As with integer types, this will ensure that the compiler being used has the capability adequately to represent the objects which it will be required to manipulate.

The final reason for the explicit use of numeric types is to enforce the distinct nature of the objects which are being represented. Using the simple integer variables whose declaration was given at the start of this section, the following Ada statement would be permissible:

```
no_on_bus := person_age * 2;
```

The real-world meaning of the number of people on a bus being twice a person's age is difficult to imagine. Ada has no objection to this statement as the two objects are of the same type (INTEGER). If they were declared to be of two distinct types (but not subtypes) then meaningless statements like this would be detected when compilation is attempted.

A new Ada data type may be declared with reference to some pre-existing predeclared or user-declared data type; the type which is used when a new type is declared is known as the new type's *base type*.

2.2.2 Declaring and using integer numeric types

The general form of an Ada integer type declaration is

```
type typename is new INTEGER range min_value .. max_value;
```

where the reserved word **type** indicates that the declaration of a type follows and typename is the name by which the type will be known. The reserved word **is** is optionally followed by '**new** INTEGER' to indicate explicitly that this is the declaration of a type whose base type is INTEGER. The reserved word **range** is followed by a range construct which specifies the minimum and maximum values which objects of the type can take. The range construct uses the range term ('..') separating min_value and max_value; these are usually integer constants or integer named numbers, although they can in some situations be simple expressions.

Some examples will make this clearer. The following lines

```
min_age : constant INTEGER := 0;
max_age : constant INTEGER := 110;
type person_ages is new INTEGER range min_age .. max_age;
```

declare a new integer data type with the typename 'person_ages'; objects of type person_ages can have values in the range 0 to 110 inclusive. In the following declaration of a new integer type no_on_buses,

```
min_on_bus : constant := 0;
max_on_bus : constant := 80;
type no_on_buses is range min_on_bus .. max_on_bus;
```

the optional declaration of the base type 'INTEGER' has been omitted. Ada is able to determine that this is the declaration of an integer type by referring to the implicit type of the named numbers which are used to delineate the range. The named numbers 'min_on_bus' and 'max_on_bus' have the implicit type universal integer, as explained in the previous section. This is the customary way of declaring a new INTEGER type.

User-declared data types can be used in the same way as predeclared data types. Constants and variables of the new types can be declared:

```
min_adult   : constant person_ages := 18;     -- constant declaration
person_age : person_ages;                      -- variable declaration

seating_limit : constant no_on_buses := 50; -- constant declaration
no_on_bus     : no_on_buses := 0;              -- initialized variable
```

The convention of using a plural noun for data types is advocated as it reminds anyone reading the program that it is a type which will allow a number of different individual objects to be declared of that type. It also allows the singular version of the type name to be used for variable declarations, as illustrated above. The declaration of the variable object num_on_bus can be read as ' the variable no_on_bus is of type no_on_buses and has an initial value of zero'.

User-declared data types can also be used as the types of formal parameters of subprograms or as the return type of functions, as in the following:

```
procedure get_age( this_age : out person_ages);

function average_on_buses ( total_on_buses : INTEGER;
                            buses_counted  : INTEGER;
                          ) return no_on_buses;
```

The attributes which are appropriate for the predeclared INTEGER data type can be applied to types whose base type is INTEGER:

```
person_ages'FIRST is    0  and is of type universal integer
person_ages'LAST  is  110  and is of type universal integer
no_on_buses'FIRST is    0  and is of type universal integer
no_on_buses'LAST  is   80  and is of type universal integer
```

All the arithmetic and relational operations which were appropriate for INTEGER objects will be inherited by the predeclared types whose base type is INTEGER. The arguments on both sides of the operator must, however, be of the same type, so the following is not allowed:

```
no_on_bus := no_on_bus + person_age; -- not allowed !
```

This is invalid as it is an attempt to add the value of an object of type person_ages to an object of type no_on_buses to give a value of type no_on_buses. The reasons why this should be a valid operation are difficult to understand; this emphasizes the advantages of declaring and using user-declared numeric data types rather than just using the predeclared type INTEGER. If the operation were valid then the type conversion facility can be used to convert the data type of person_ages to type no_on_buses, before the operation is performed:

```
no_on_bus := no_on_bus + no_on_buses( person_age );
```

This conversion will only be valid if the value of the object person_age when the conversion is performed is appropriate for conversion to type no_on_buses. That is, the value of person_age should be in the range 0 to 80 inclusive.

The concept of the type universal integer should now become clearer. The following Ada statement is valid:

```
-- birthday so increment age
person_age := person_age + 1;
```

If the integer numeric literal '1' were of the explicit type INTEGER then the statement would not be allowed, as it an attempt to add an INTEGER object to an object of type person_ages. The integer numeric literal is, however, of universal integer type, and is assignment compatible with any integer type provided that the value of the literal is within the declared range of the integer type. Similar considerations apply to the use of named numbers.

If there is a requirement for the input and output of user-declared numeric types then a new package suitable for the type will have to be instantiated, as in the following:

```
with TEXT_IO;
package age_inout is new TEXT_IO.INTEGER_IO( person_ages );

with TEXT_IO;
```

```
package bus_inout is new TEXT_IO.INTEGER_IO( no_on_buses );
use age_inout, bus_inout;
```

The scope of usage of these packages, and the scope of usage of the data type itself, conforms to the same rules as were expressed for scope expressed in Block 1 Section 11. Briefly, the scope of the objects exists from the point in the program where the object is declared up to the end of the block (procedure or function) within which the object is declared. This scope includes any subsidiary subprograms which are declared. If the declarations are made outside the body of the program procedure then the scope of the object is the entire program.

2.2.3 Declaring and using floating-point numeric types

The general form of an Ada floating-point type declaration is

```
type typename is digits num_digits range min_val .. max_val;
```

where the reserved word **type** indicates that the declaration of a type follows and typename is the name by which the type will be known. The reserved word **is**, is followed by the reserved word **digits**, which indicates that this is the declaration of a floating-point type. The term num_digits is a positive integer value, usually an integer literal, which expresses the number of significant figures required by the type. This is optionally followed by a **range** term which delineates the smallest and largest value which objects of the type can take. The expressions min_val and max_val are usually named numbers or literals of type universal real, although a limited range of expressions are also allowed. If the range term is omitted then Ada will decide upon the range which it can represent for the requested type based upon the range of the predeclared type FLOAT.

The following is an example of a floating-point type declaration:

```
min_weight : constant := 0.00;
max_weight : constant := 150.00;
type person_weights is digits 6 range min_weight .. max_weight;
```

This declares a new type with the type name person_weights, which can take values in the range 0.00 to 150.00 using six significant figures. Six significant figures are required in the declaration in order to ensure that five-significant-figure accuracy is maintained. As with the user-declared integer numeric types above, user-declared floating-point types inherit all the possibilities of the predeclared type FLOAT.

Variable and constant declarations can be made in the same way as with predeclared data types:

```
standard_male  : constant person_weights := 56.00;
person_weight  : person_weights;
```

Formal parameter types and function types can be a user-declared floating-point type:

```
procedure get_weight ( this_weight : out person_weights);

function  standard_weight ( sex      : sexes;
                            height   : person_heights;
                          ) return person_weights;
```

The attributes which are appropriate for the predeclared FLOAT type can also be used with user-declared floating-point types:

```
person_weights'DIGITS   is 6      and is of type universal integer
person_weights'SMALL    is 0.00   and is of type universal real
person_weights'LARGE    is 150.00 and is of type universal real
```

Arithmetic and relational operations are inherited by user-declared types from the FLOAT type:

```
weight_loss,                         -- amount of weight lost
old_weight,                          -- person's previous weight
new_weight    : person_weights;      -- person's current weight

weight_loss := old_weight - new_weight; -- dangerous !!
if weight_loss > 5.00 then
   -- congratulate
end if;
```

This is a dangerous program fragment, as there is no guarantee that the value of weight_loss will always be positive: it is possible for a person to put on weight. The variable weight_loss is of type person_weights, which does not allow negative values. This problem can be solved by the use of type conversion:

```
weight_loss   : FLOAT;               -- amount of weight loss

target_weight,                       -- weight to reach
old_weight,                          -- person's previous weight
new_weight    : person_weights;      -- person's current weight
```

```
weight_loss    := FLOAT( old_weight - new_weight ); -- safe !!

if weight_loss < 0.0 then
   -- person has put weight on, set hard target weight
   target_weight := person_weights( FLOAT( new_weight )
                                     - ( weight_loss * 2.0));
else
   -- person has lost weight, set easy target weight
   target_weight := person_weights( FLOAT( new_weight )
                                     - ( weight_loss * 0.5));
end if;
```

Instantiation of a suitable package for input and output of person_weights is as might be expected:

```
with TEXT_IO;
package weight_inout is new TEXT_IO.FLOAT_IO( person_weights );

use weight_inout;
```

2.2.4 Types and subtypes compared

The declarations of numeric types above have used the facility of declaring a new numeric type whose base type is a predeclared numeric type; types declared in this manner inherit the operations which can be performed upon the base type. However, such types are distinct from each other and as such are not compatible; thus they cannot be used in arithmetic or relational operations without type conversion and cannot share common input and output packages.

A second possibility exists in Ada, the declaration of *subtypes*. A subtype declaration differs from a type declaration in that no new type is created, but a subtypename is given to a range of values within the base type. The base type can be a predeclared or user-declared type. As subtypes are not distinct types they can be used in arithmetic and relational operations without type conversion and can share input and output facilities.

The declaration of a subtype has the general form

```
subtype subtypename is typename range min_value .. max_value;
```

where the reserved word **subtype** indicates that this is the declaration of a subtype with the name subtypename specified. The term '**is** typename' is optional and declares the base type of which this is a subtype. The base type can be predeclared type or a user-declared type or an existing subtype. The **range** term expresses the range of values which objects of this subtype can take. For example:

```
min_on_bus : constant := 0;
max_on_bus : constant := 80;
type no_on_buses is range min_on_bus .. max_on_bus;

max_seated : constant no_on_buses := `50;
subtype seated_on_buses   is no_on_buses
        range min_on_bus .. max_seated;

subtype standing_on_buses is
        range min_on_bus .. (max_on_bus - max_seated);
```

The first subtype declaration declares a subtype with the subtype name seated_on_buses as a subtype of the user-declared type no_on_buses, with the effective range 0 to 50. The second subtype declaration declares a subtype of no_on_buses with the subtype name standing_on_buses and a range of 0 to 30. Ada is able to determine the intended base type from the explicit type of the object max_seated. Although the intended type is unambiguous to Ada, it is not clear to anyone reading the program; consequently, the first form of such declarations where the base type is explicitly stated is advocated.

Having declared the types and subtypes, variables of these types can be declared:

```
no_on_bus       : no_on_buses;
seated_on_bus   : seated_on_buses;
standing_on_bus : standing_on_buses;
```

The variable objects seated_on_bus and standing_on_bus are of the subtypes seated_on_buses and standing_on_buses, respectively. Both of these subtypes are subtypes of the type no_on_bus, and remain assignment-compatible with it and each other; consequently, the following statements are allowed:

```
no_on_bus := seated_on_bus + standing_on_bus;

if no_on_bus > max_seated then
    standing_on_bus := no_on_bus - max_seated;
else
    standing_on_bus := 0;
end if
```

The values of the subtype can also be input and output from the program using the same facilities as were created for the input and output of the type of which they are a subtype. So if the package bus_inout as created above is in use, then the following statements are allowed:

```
GET( standing_on_bus);
PUT( sitting_on_bus );
```

Subtype declarations should be used in preference to type declarations where the objects of the type and subtype are closely related in the real world. In the example above, the real-world concepts of the number of people sitting on a bus and the number of people standing on a bus are closely related and are both subsets of the total number of people on the bus. The conceptual idea of adding the number of people sitting to the number of people standing to obtain the total number of people on the bus makes sense, which indicates that the use of subtypes is appropriate.

There are two INTEGER subtypes which are predeclared in the Ada environment whose names are NATURAL and POSITIVE. The effective declaration of these subtypes is as follows:

```
subtype NATURAL  is INTEGER range 0 .. INTEGER'LAST;
subtype POSITIVE is INTEGER range 1 .. INTEGER'LAST;
```

These subtypes declare the set of NATURAL integers which contains all integers greater than or equal to zero and the set of POSITIVE integers which contains all integers greater than zero. As they are both subtypes of the type INTEGER they are compatible with each other and with the predeclared type INTEGER. The subtypes can be input and output by using the facilities of the int_io package previously created for the input and output of integer values. These subtypes should be used in preference to the INTEGER type where the object being represented in the real world is better described by a natural or a positive integer.

2.2.5 Safe input of numeric values

In the program specifications given in Block 1 there was often a requirement for a numeric value to be input within a certain range. For example, the assignment_average program from Block 1 Section 11 required an assignment score in the range 0 to 100 be input. It was noted that although this was a requirement of the specification it would not be enforced by the program designs or implementations in Block 1.

The input of values into a program from the terminal is one of the most difficult and yet most important aspects of the user interface design. The program will be judged by the user largely on the support which is given as data are input to the system and on the format in which data are output from the system. The difficulty arises because it is not possible to rely upon the user's supplying input as requested.

For example, let the input of a value for an object of type person_heights, which is a floating-point subtype, be declared as follows:

```
subtype person_heights is FLOAT digits 4 range 0.00 .. 2.50;

person_height   : person_heights;
```

Using the float_io GET procedure in the form

```
PUT( "Please enter the person's height ( 0.00 to 2.50 ) ");
GET( person_weight ); SKIP_LINE;
```

the response from the user may typically be as follows:

```
(a)   Please enter the person's height ( 0.00 to 2.50 )   2.51
(b)   Please enter the person's height ( 0.00 to 2.50 )   -0.1
(c)   Please enter the person's height ( 0.00 to 2.50 )   2
(d)   Please enter the person's height ( 0.00 to 2.50 )   help
(e)   Please enter the person's height ( 0.00 to 2.50 )   1.84
```

Of these possible interactions only interaction (e) is valid. Interactions (a) and (b) supply a value in the correct format but outside the allowed range. Interaction (c) provides a value within the specified range but in the format of an integer not a floating-point value. Interaction (d) illustrates the user responding with an alphabetic string.

The behaviour of the program fragment for interactions (a) to (d) would be for a run-time *exception* (known in other programming environments as a run-time *error*) to be generated. There are various conditions which can give rise to exceptions in an Ada program; each condition has associated with it a name for the exception generated. The name of the exception which would be generated in interactions (c) and (d) would be DATA_ERROR, indicating that the input supplied is in an incorrect format. The name of the exception which would be raised by interactions (a) and (b) would be CONSTRAINT_ERROR, indicating that the input is in the correct format, but the value is outside the declared range of values of type person_weights. For all four interactions an error message should be displayed and the input prompt redisplayed, this process continuing until the user supplies an acceptable input.

A general-purpose procedure can be designed which could be used for the input of floating-point values within specified limits. The procedure would need to be supplied with the minimum value and maximum value to be accepted by the routine and would export a floating-point value within those limits. The data flow diagram of the procedure would be as follows:

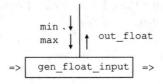

This diagram describes a procedure called gen_float_input, which requires two input-only parameters called min and max which delineate the range of values which will be accepted; and requires an output-only parameter called out_float which contains the value input. It is not advisable to implement this data flow as a function as it has input and output to the terminal as part of its behaviour. The following procedure declaration can be produced from the data-flow diagram:

```
procedure gen_float_input( min, max  : in  FLOAT;
                           out_float : out FLOAT);
```

Using the procedure heading a test harness for the program can be implemented. This test harness can be used to test the procedure interactively once it has been implemented. The text of a possible test harness is as follows:

```
-- test harness for general input of floats program
-- assumes float_inout in library
-- b2s2p1 see text

with TEXT_IO, float_inout; use TEXT_IO, float_inout;

procedure b2s2p1 is

   min_height : constant FLOAT := 0.00;
   max_height : constant FLOAT := 2.50;

   subtype person_heights is FLOAT digits 4
           range min_height .. max_height;

   person_height : person_heights;

   -- procedure gen_float_input here

begin -- b2s2p1
   gen_float_input( min_height, max_height, person_height);
end b2s2p1;
```

The harness declares a floating-point subtype person_heights as discussed above and then defines the procedure gen_float_input which will be implemented below. The executable part of the program procedure consists of the line

```
gen_float_input( min_height, max_height, person_height)
```

which calls the procedure with the input parameters having values which delineate the range of the subtype person_heights. The output parameter is the variable person_height, which is of type person_heights. As person_height is variable of subtype person_heights whose base type is FLOAT, the actual parameter person_height is compatible with the formal parameter out_float which is specified as FLOAT.

The design for the procedure gen_float_input is as follows:

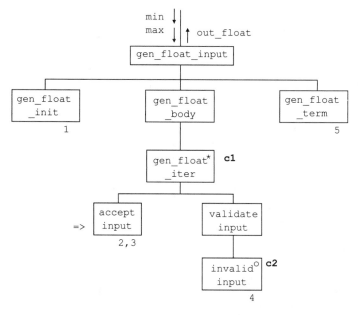

c1: While input is invalid.
c2: If input is invalid.

1. Ensure input value invalid.
2. Display input prompt.
3. Accept user's input.
4. Display error message.
5. Export input value.

This program structure chart extends the program structure chart notation introduced in Block 1. Every operation which is required by the subprogram is identified and listed with an operation number. These numbers are then allocated to the structure chart to indicate precisely what operations will be performed by the design component when it is executed.

Thus the component of the design identified as accept_input has operations 2 and 3 allocated to it. This indicates that when this design component is executed the input prompt will be displayed and the user's input accepted.

This extension to the format of program structure charts allows designs to be expressed in a more compact form. The simpler format used in Block 1 would have required each component which has an operation list associated with it to be refined into a sequence, with each component of the sequence being one of the operations listed.

A first implementation of this design would be as follows:

```
0001   procedure gen_float_input( min, max   : in  FLOAT;
0002                                 out_float  : out FLOAT) is
0003
0004   -- procedure to input float value within limits specified
0005   -- b2s2p1 initial version see text.
0006
0007          local_float : FLOAT := max + 0.1; -- local input var
0008
0009
0010   begin -- gen_float_input
0011      while (( local_float < min ) or ( local_float > max )) loop
0012         PUT("Enter a value in the range ");
0013         PUT( min, AFT=>2, EXP =>0 ); PUT( " to ");
0014         PUT( max, AFT=>2, EXP =>0 ); PUT( " ");
0015         GET( local_float ); SKIP_LINE;
0016
0017         if (( local_float < min ) or ( local_float > max )) then
0018             PUT_LINE("Invalid input, please try again ");
0019         end if;
0020      end loop;
0021
0022      -- this point can only be reached when valid value input
0023      out_float := local_float;  -- export input value
0024   end gen_float_input;
```

In this implementation operation 1 from the design, 'ensure input value valid', has been implemented as the setting of the value of the object local_float when it is declared. This operation will be performed by Ada when the procedure is called, before the executable statements following **begin** are performed. This is in accordance with the design, and consequently the statements between the **begin/end** pair only implement the body and termination components of the design.

When executed from the test harness as shown above, the input parameters min and max will be set to 0.00 and 2.50, respectively. The object local_float is set to max + 0.1 (2.51); this ensures that the loop control test on line 0011 will evaluate as TRUE on its first evaluation, ensuring that the loop is iterated at least once.

Within the loop the prompt is displayed and an input accepted from the user. Assuming for a moment that this input is in the correct format, the next statement to be executed is the **if** statement on line 0017. The **if** structure will output an error message if the value input is lower than min or higher than max.

An invalid input will ensure that the loop reiterates when the end of the loop is encountered at line 0020 following the **if** structure. When a valid input is obtained the loop will terminate and the value will be exported from the procedure in line 0023.

This version of the procedure will deal correctly with interactions (a) and (b) where the input value is in the correct format but outside the allowed range. Interactions (c) and (d) where the input is an incorrect format, will still result in an exception being generated.

To extend this implementation to cope with interactions (c) and (d), an *exception handler* will have to be declared. An exception handler is a body of code which will be executed only if an exception occurs within its scope. When an exception occurs in a program the scope within which the exception is generated is checked for the occurrence of a suitable exception handler. If a suitable handler exists then the executable statements of the exception handler will be executed, following which the block will terminate.

A suitable implementation of the procedure which will cope correctly with interactions (c) and (d) is the following:

```
0001   procedure gen_float_input ( min, max   : in  FLOAT;
0002                               out_float : out FLOAT) is
0003
0004   -- procedure to input float value within limits specified
0005   -- b2s2p1 final version see text
0006
0007            local_float : FLOAT := max + 0.1; -- local input var
0008
0009
0010   begin -- gen_float_input
0011      while (( local_float < min ) or (local_float > max )) loop
0012      begin -- while block
0013         PUT("Enter a float in range ");
0014         PUT( min, AFT => 2, EXP => 0 ); PUT( " to ");
0015         PUT( max, AFT => 2, EXP => 0 ); PUT( " ");
0016         GET( local_float );
0017         -- this point can only be reached if the GET
0018         -- did not raise DATA_ERROR exception
0019         if (( local_float < min) or (local_float > max)) then
0020            raise DATA_ERROR;
0021         end if;
0022         -- this point can only be reached if the input was in the
0023         -- correct format and in the correct range
0024
0025      exception -- start of the exception handler
0026         when DATA_ERROR =>
0027            PUT_LINE("Invalid input, please try again ");
0028            SKIP_LINE; -- tidy up terminal input before retrying
```

```
0029              local_float := max + 0.1;
0030        end; -- while block
0031        end loop;
0032
0033        -- this point can only be reached when valid value input
0034        SKIP_LINE;                    -- tidy up terminal before end
0035        out_float := local_float;  -- export value input
0036
0037  end gen_float_input;
```

The explanation of an exception handler given above emphasized that an exception handler has a specific scope which is that of the block within which it is contained. The only program components which can be considered as blocks which have been introduced so far are the bodies of procedures and functions, the scope of the block is the executable statements enclosed within their **begin/end** pairs. If the scope of the exception handler in this example were the entire procedure then upon the occurrence of an exception, and after the handling of it by the handler, the procedure would terminate.

The design indicates that the scope of the exception handler has to be limited to the iterative loop contained within the procedure. To accommodate this, Ada provides the facility for a block to be explicitly declared; this is done by enclosing a sequence of statements within a **begin/end** pair. In the example above, the statements which comprise the body of the while loop have been made into a block by enclosing them in a **begin/end** pair (lines 0010 and 0030). The **begin** and the **end** have been commented to make the scope of the block explicit.

The easiest way to explain the behaviour of the procedure is to trace it with the same invocation as was used in the trace presented above. The input parameters min and max will be set to 0.00 and 2.50 as before, local_float will be set to 2.51, the **loop** control will be TRUE, the prompt will be displayed, and the input from the user accepted.

Let us assume that the input from the user on this first iteration is the input (c) (2) or (d) (help). Either of these will cause a DATA_ERROR exception to be raised and control is consequently passed from the point where the exception was generated (line 0014) to the exception handler which is identified by the reserved word **exception** (line 0025). The **when** clauses of the exception handler are then examined to determine if an exception for this particular type of **exception** has been declared. In this example only one handler has been declared, for the DATA_ERROR **exception**. The statements associated with this exception handler are executed, which will display the error message, take care of any remaining input from the terminal and ensure the **loop** reiterates.

Control is now passed out of the scope of the exception handler; in this case the scope is the explicit block. The statement immediately following the explicit block is the **end loop** statement on line 0031, which will cause the loop control condition to be re-evaluated, and as it is still TRUE the loop will reiterate.

Assuming the input from the user on this second iteration is 2.51, the GET statement will not raise an exception as the object being given a value by the GET statement is a FLOAT variable and 2.51 is an appropriate FLOAT value. Execution will continue with the statement following the GET statement which is the **if** structure on line 0019. The condition controlling the **if** structure will evaluate as TRUE, as the value of local_float is 2.51 which is greater than the value of max (2.50). The statement on line 0020, '**raise** DATA_ERROR', will be executed causing the DATA_ERROR **exception** to be explicitly generated. The loop will continue with the same behaviour as was experienced when the DATA_ERROR was raised implicitly in the previous iteration.

Assuming that on the third iteration a valid value is input by the user, for example 1.84, the **if** condition will evaluate as FALSE and the body of the **if** statement will not be executed. As an **exception** was not raised, the exception-handler actions will not be activated. The loop control condition will evaluate as FALSE on its next evaluation and the loop will terminate.

The procedure itself will terminate following the statements which take care of any remaining input from the terminal and set the value to the output parameter to the validated value input by the user.

The use of exceptions and the precise syntax and restrictions will be elaborated further in Block 3. A second test harness for this procedure, illustrating its generality, might be as follows:

```
-- test harness for the general input of floats program
-- assumes float_inout in library
-- b2s2p2 see text

with TEXT_IO, float_inout; use TEXT_IO, float_inout;

procedure b2s2p2 is

    min_height : constant := 0.00;
    max_height : constant := 2.50;
    min_weight : constant := 0.00;
    max_weight : constant := 250.00;

    subtype  person_heights is FLOAT digits 4
            range min_height .. max_height;

    type person_weights is digits 6
            range min_weight .. max_weight;

    a_float       : FLOAT;
    person_height : person_heights;
    person_weight : person_weights;

-- procedure gen_float_input here

begin -- b2s2p2
    -- use of the procedure with a FLOAT subtype
    gen_float_input( min_height, max_height, person_height);
```

```
-- use of the procedure with type FLOAT
gen_float_input( 100.0, 200.0, a_float);
-- use of the procedure with new float type
gen_float_input( min_weight, max_weight, FLOAT( person_weight));
end b2s2p2;
```

This test harness differs from the previous harness, which could have been used, in that it exercises the procedure under test three times. The first call of the procedure uses an actual out-only parameter of type person_heights which, as before, is a subtype of FLOAT. The second call of the procedure uses an actual parameter of type FLOAT. The third invocation of the procedure uses an actual parameter of type person_weights which is a new FLOAT type. As this type is incompatible with the formal parameter which is of type FLOAT, the actual parameter is converted into an object of type FLOAT using the type-conversion facility. All three invocations of this procedure are acceptable to Ada, although there are reasons why the third invocation is not completely acceptable.

Although it may seem tedious to have to produce a thirty-five-line procedure for the input of a simple FLOAT value, it is worthwhile. It is an almost totally secure procedure, trapping the user's input errors as soon as they are detected and issuing a suitable error message. As has been emphasized, the user interface design and implementation should be given as much attention as program design and implementation. It is also worthwhile to spend so much effort producing this procedure since, once produced, it can be stored in a library and used in any program which requires secure input of FLOAT values.

EXERCISES

2.2.1 Declare suitable types or subtypes for the following requirements:

(a) Examination scores which are whole numbers in the range 0 to 100.
(b) A proportional probability measure to six significant digits in the range 0.0 to 1.0.
(c) An integer percentage probability measure in the range 0 to 100.
(d) A correlation coefficient to four significant digits in the range -1.0 to +1.0.
(e) Total course scores which are whole numbers in the range 0 to 500 and have examination components in the range 0 to 100 and assignment components in the range 0 to 400.

2.2.2 Amend and test the second version of the procedure gen_float_input in order that the number of decimal places displayed in the output prompt is a parameter of the procedure.

2.2.3 Extend the procedure developed in Exercise 2.2.2 so that a part of the input prompt is supplied as a STRING parameter. For example, the procedure should be capable of producing the following prompts:

```
Please enter the person's height ( 0.50 to 2.50 )
Please enter the person's weight ( 0.00 to 250.00 )
```

where the underlined part of the prompt has been provided as a parameter.

2.2.4 Implement and test a procedure called gen_int_input for the input of integers. Model the procedure upon the second version of the gen_float_input procedure presented in this section.

2.2.5 The probability of an event can be expressed using one of the representations from Exercise 2.2.1 (b) or 2.2.1 (c). For example, the probability of obtaining a head when tossing a 'fair' coin can be expressed as the proportion 0.50000 or the percentage 50.

Implement a pair of functions which will convert a proportional probability measure to a percentage probability measure and vice versa.

Mount these two functions, together with the procedures from Exercises 2.2.4 and 2.2.5, within an interactive test harness.

Section 2.3

Characters and strings

This section will introduce the character-orientated predeclared data types CHARAC-TER and STRING. The manipulation of text information, which is represented within Ada programs as objects of the type CHARACTER and STRING, is more important than the manipulation of numeric information in the majority of commercial computer programs. Consequently, the facilities available for the representation and manipulation of text information in a programming environment are at least as important as those for the representation and manipulation of numeric information.

2.3.1 Characters

Ada data objects of the type CHARACTER can take a range of *single* character values. The range of characters from which this value can be selected is dependent upon the *collating sequence* which is used by the compiler.

Computers represent characters internally by using an integer numeric code, where each character is individually represented by a unique code. There are a number of coding conventions which computers can use, the commonest being American Standard Code for Information Interchange (ASCII); this coding convention is used by all Ada compilers.

One source of confusion for novice programmers is the relationship between the character '1' and the integer value 1. The character '1' is a mathematical symbol for the value 1. Different cultures have different symbols for '1'; however, all these different symbols represent the same mathematical concept of 1.

A computer system needs to be able to represent both the character symbol for '1' and the integer value 1 (and also the real value 1.00). One of the ASCII codes is used to represent the character symbol '1', and this has the type CHARACTER; this is distinct from the integer value 1, which has the type universal integer; and both of these are distinct from the real value 1.00, which has the type universal real. There are ASCII character codes for all the digit symbols ('0', '1', '2', '3', '4', '5', '6', '7', '8', '9').

In addition to the symbols for '0'–'9', 'A'–'Z' and 'a'–'z', the ASCII convention has a large number of other codes for other types of symbol. This book was prepared on a computer system using an ASCII coding system; every symbol used in this text is available in the ASCII coding sequence, although not all possible ASCII codes are available to Ada compilers. An ASCII code table is included as Appendix D.

Individual characters are represented in an Ada program by enclosing the character between single quote marks (e.g., 'A', which represents the character upper-case A); these are known as character literals.

CHARACTER types and objects

The options which were explained in the previous section for the declaration of new numeric types and subtypes are applicable for the declaration of new CHARACTER types and subtypes. For example:

```
type    digit_chars is new CHARACTER range '0' .. '9';

subtype upper_case  is CHARACTER range 'A' .. 'Z';

subtype lower_case  is CHARACTER range 'a' .. 'z';
```

The declaration of a distinct character type differs from the declaration of INTEGER and FLOAT types introduced in the previous section by the inclusion of the reserved word **new**; character types declared in this way do not inherit all the possibilities of the predeclared CHARACTER type. Although it is possible to declare a new character type, the reasons why this might be done are obscure, and the declaration of CHARACTER subtypes is favoured.

Variable and constant objects of these types can be declared in the usual way:

```
zero   : constant := '0'; -- compatible with predeclared CHARACTER
                          -- type, character subtypes and type digit_chars

comma  : constant CHARACTER := ','; -- compatible with predeclared
                                    -- CHARACTER type, character
                                    -- subtypes but not digit_chars

       digit : digit_char;
       char  : CHARACTER;
       upper : upper_case;
       lower : lower_case;
```

The restrictions of the type compatibility of types and subtypes which were explained in the previous section for numeric types can be effectively applied to these types.

```
char  := upper;              -- allowable
char  := lower;              -- allowable
upper := char;               -- allowable if char is in specified range
upper := lower;              -- not allowable as ranges do not overlap
char  := digit;              -- not allowable as distinct types;
char  := CHARACTER( digit ); -- allowable type conversion
digit := digit_char( char ); -- allowable type conversion if char is
                             -- within specified range
```

Character types and subtypes can be used as the types of formal parameters to procedures and functions, or to be the return type of functions; as in:

```
procedure do_something( a_char : in out upper_case );

function calc_something( a_char : CHARACTER ) return upper_case;
```

Attributes which are appropriate for character objects include FIRST, LAST, PRED, SUCC, VAL and POS; each of these will be explained in turn.

FIRST is an attribute which can be applied to a type or subtype and will evaluate as the first (lowest) value of that type. LAST is the complimentary attribute which will evaluate as the last (highest) value of the type. For example:

```
upper_case'FIRST  is 'A' and is of type CHARACTER
upper_case'LAST   is 'Z' and is of type CHARACTER
lower_case'FIRST  is 'a' and is of type CHARACTER
lower_case'LAST   is 'z' and is of type CHARACTER
digit_char'FIRST  is 'Ø' and is of type digit_char
digit_char'LAST   is '9' and is of type digit_char
```

CHARACTER'FIRST and CHARACTER'LAST evaluate to the first and last ASCII characters, respectively. The first value of the type CHARACTER is the character whose ASCII code is 0; the last value of the type CHARACTER is the character whose ASCII code is 127. Both of these are non-printable characters and cannot be shown in the example above.

PRED is an attribute function which requires a single parameter of the specified type and evaluates as the previous value in the sequence. SUCC is the complementary attribute function which evaluates as the next value in the sequence. The type of these attributes when a subtype is specified is the subtype's base type, not the subtype itself. For example:

```
upper_case'SUCC('A') is 'B' and is of type CHARACTER
upper_case'PRED('Z') is 'Y' and is of type CHARACTER
lower_case'SUCC('m') is 'n' and is of type CHARACTER
lower_case'PRED('o') is 'n' and is of type CHARACTER
CHARACTER'SUCC('Z') is '[' and is of type CHARACTER
CHARACTER'PRED('A') is '@' and is of type CHARACTER
```

If an attempt is made to evaluate the SUCCessor of the last CHARACTER value, or to evaluate the PREDecessor of the first CHARACTER value, a CONSTRAINT_ERROR exception will be raised. This implies that it is possible to obtain the SUCCessor of the last value of a subtype, or the PREDecessor of the first value of a subtype:

```
upper_case'SUCC('Z') is '[' and is of type CHARACTER
upper_case'PRED('a') is ''' and is of type CHARACTER
```

POS is an attribute function which requires a single parameter of the specified type and evaluates to an integer value which for any CHARACTER type is equal to the ASCII code of the parameter. VAL is the complementary function which requires an INTEGER parameter and evaluates to the CHARACTER whose ASCII number is equal to the value of the parameter. For example:

```
upper_case'POS('A')   is 65  and is of type universal integer
upper_case'VAL( 66 )  is 'B' and is of type CHARACTER
lower_case'POS('z')   is 122 and is of type universal integer
lower_case'VAL( 121 ) is 'y' and is of type CHARACTER
digit_char'POS('0' )  is 48  and is of type universal_integer
digit_char'VAL( 49 )  is '1' and is of type digit_char
CHARACTER'POS('@' )   is 64  and is of type universal integer
CHARACTER'VAL( 91 )   is '[' and is of type CHARACTER
```

If an attempt is made to evaluate the VAL of an integer which is outside the appropriate range of a type, a CONSTRAINT_ERROR exception will be raised. As illustrated above, the POS and VAL attributes are applicable to a new CHARACTER type such as the type digit_char declared above.

Procedures for the input and output character values are contained within the package TEXT_IO. If a new CHARACTER type is used in a program then input and output of these values can be achieved by the use of the CHARACTER input and output facilities with appropriate type conversion' (e.g., PUT(CHARACTER(digit));).

The relational operators can be applied to data objects of type CHARACTER. The relationship which is applied is implemented by the compiler as a comparison between the integer codes which underlie the symbols. Thus the following can always be assumed to be TRUE:

```
'A' = 'A',  'o' = 'o'  'M' > 'N'  'k' <= 'k'
'a' /= 'A'  'g' /= 'h'  '1' /= '0'  '4' <  '5'
       'a' > 'A'  'A' > '0'  'Z' < 'z'
```

As mentioned above, the ASCII coding system is based upon a mapping between the character symbols and integer codes. The relational operators make use of these underlying codes to implement the relational comparisons. In most cases programmers are only concerned with the character symbols themselves and take no account of the underlying integer values. What has been done is to take a set of integer values and map these values onto a set of character symbols, with some constraints. The symbols are then used as characters and the underlying integer values for the most part can be ignored. This is an example of *data abstraction*. The integer values are no longer relevant and in most cases can, and should, be forgotten by the programmer. All that is important is the concept of a character and the relationship between characters, which is expressed in terms of character relationships. These relationships are compatible with the understanding of characters in everyday life. Data abstraction is a very valuable programming technique which will be used extensively in Block 3.

Other operators which can be applied to CHARACTER (and to numeric) objects are the **in** and the **not in** operators. The format of these operators is:

```
object in     range
object not in range
```

where the object and the range have to be of compatible types. The **in** and **not in** operators evaluate to a BOOLEAN value. For the **in** operator, the expression is TRUE if the value of the object is within the range specified and FALSE otherwise. For the **not in** operator, the expression is TRUE if the value of the object is outside the range specified and FALSE otherwise. It is possible to use the name of a subtype as a range expression with the **in** operators; an example of this is given in the function below.

Example CHARACTER function

A common requirement in many text programs is to ensure that an alphabetic character is, say, upper case. This requirement is suitable for implementation as a function, whose data flow diagram is as follows:

```
char_in  ↓ ↑  char_out
        ┌─────────┐
        │ to_upper │
        └─────────┘
```

The diagram indicates that the name of the function is to_upper and that it requires a single input-only parameter of type CHARACTER and will return as the result of the function a CHARACTER value. The effect of the function, if the input character is a lower-case character, will be to convert the input character from lower-case to the corresponding upper-case character. If the input character is not a lower-case character then it will be returned unchanged. The declaration of the function from the data flow diagram would be as follows:

```
function to_upper( char_in : CHARACTER ) return CHARACTER;
```

A suitable design for this function would be the following:

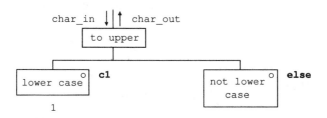

c1: If character is lower case.   1. Convert to upper case.

This function could be defined as follows:

```
function to_upper( char_in : CHARACTER ) return CHARACTER is

-- function to convert characters to upper case
-- b2s3p1 see text

    difference : constant := CHARACTER'POS('a') - CHARACTER'POS('A');
                -- integer difference between ASCII 'a' & 'A'

    subtype lower_case is CHARACTER range 'a' .. 'z';

    char_out : CHARACTER := char_in;   -- function variable

  begin -- to_upper
    if ( char_in in lower_case ) then
        char_out := CHARACTER'VAL( CHARACTER'POS( char_in )
                                        - difference );
    end if;
    return char_out;
  end to_upper;
```

The basis of this function is to return unchanged characters which are not lower-case and to convert upper-case characters. This decision is implemented using an **if** structure, the decision being made by use of the **in** operator, as explained above. The conversion is performed using the expression:

```
CHARACTER'VAL( CHARACTER'POS( char_in ) - difference );
```

where difference is an integer constant whose value has been set to the difference in values between the POS value of lower-case 'a' and upper-case 'A'. This difference between the ASCII codes for 'a' and 'A' has the value 32, and is identical to the difference between any alphabetic lower- and upper-case character, as can be verified from an ASCII table. The difference is subtracted from the ASCII value of the lower-case character, which is obtained using the POS attribute; the result of this subtraction is an integer value which is used to produce the upper-case character using the VAL attribute.

2.3.2 Strings

Single characters are not used extensively in the real world, and consequently are not common in computer programs; it is much more common for an iteration of characters to be used. The programming term for an iteration of characters is a *string*. As strings are used so extensively in computer programs Ada provides a predeclared data type called STRING to implement them. A *data structure diagram* of an object of the STRING data type would be as follows:

This data structure diagram indicates that a STRING object is an indefinite iteration of CHARACTER objects. A data structure diagram, unlike a program structure diagram, does not have to include the condition which constrains the iteration. This implies that a STRING can contain a minimum of zero characters and an unspecified maximum number of characters. Data structure diagrams are used to describe data structures (objects) as opposed to program structures which are used to describe programs (actions). The production and use of data structure diagrams will be introduced and used extensively in the remainder of this book.

Declaring STRING data types

The Ada predeclared type STRING is capable of implementing string objects of differing lengths; it is said to be *unconstrained*. It is not possible to declare an object of the type STRING without also declaring how many characters the STRING is to contain; this is called a *constrained string declaration*. The best way of declaring a constrained STRING object is to declare an explicit constrained subtype for the constrained range and then declare the object to be of that subtype. For example:

```
big_string_length    : constant = 26;
small_string_length  : constant = 4;

subtype string_26s is STRING( 1 .. big_string_length );
subtype string_4s  is STRING( 1 .. small_string_length );
```

The effect of these subtype declarations is to make available structures which are composed of a defined number of characters. This can be shown in data structure diagrams for the subtypes as follows:

The string_26s data type can be more conveniently visualized by considering it as a sequence of 26 characters:

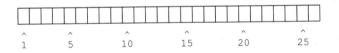

Each box in this structure is a place where a character can be stored. Any individual character can be identified by its position within the structure, indicated by the numbers below the structure.

The declaration above defines the structure of the data type string_26s; it does not declare any data objects of this type. To declare a data object of this type a variable declaration has to be made. Declaring variables of a userdeclared data type is no different from declaring variables of the predeclared data types. If two variables of the type string_26s called 'alphabet' and 'response' were required, the declarations would be as follows:

```
alphabet,
response                 : string_26s;
```

It is also possible for string variables to be given a default assignment as they are declared; so if it were required for a variable of subtype string_4 called 'left_name' to be declared and given the value "FRED", and for a variable of string_4 called 'right_name' to be declared and set to spaces; the declarations might be as follows:

```
left_name            : string_4s := "FRED";
right_name           : string_4s := "    ";
```

The STRING constants which are used to set the values of the variables have to be compatible with the objects which they are initializing. This means that the constants have to contain exactly as many characters as the string is capable of containing. String constants are represented in Ada programs enclosed between double quotes ("), unlike character constants which are enclosed between single quotes (').

It is sometimes desirable to set the values of all the characters which comprise a STRING variable object to a specified character, usually a space. This can be accomplished with declarations of the following form:

```
space              : constant CHARACTER  := ' '; -- ASCII space

twenty_six_spaces : constant string_26s := ( others => space );

right_name         : constant string_4s  := ( others => space );
```

The details of this method of giving a string a value are made clear in Block 1 Section 7.

Using STRING variables: assignment and slices

Having declared STRING variables, there are a number of operations which can be performed upon them. They can be the subject of an assignment statement:

```
alphabet := "abcdefghijklmnopqrstuvwxyz";
```

If this assignment statement were executed by an Ada program, the state of the string_26 variable alphabet after the assignment would be as follows:

a	b	c	d	e	f	g	h	i	j	k	l	m	n	o	p	q	r	s	t	u	v	w	x	y	z

```
  ^         ^          ^          ^          ^          ^
  1         5          10         15         20         25
```

The contents of a STRING variable can also be the source of an assignment statement. For example:

```
response := alphabet;
```

The effect of this statement would be to copy the values of all 26 of the characters in alphabet into all 26 characters in response. If alphabet had the value shown in the diagram above, response would have the same value. As mentioned above, STRING assignments are only possible if the strings are of the same length; consequently, the following assignments are not allowed:

```
left_name    := response;   -- not allowed, strings are of differing lengths
alphabet     := right_name; -- not allowed, strings are of differing lengths
```

It is possible to access an individual character from a STRING by specifying the position within the STRING where the character is located. So if the string alphabet is set as shown above, then:

```
alphabet(10)  has the value 'j' and is of type CHARACTER
alphabet(17)  has the value 'q' and is of type CHARACTER
```

It is also possible to access a sequence of characters from a string by using a range construct, for example:

```
alphabet( 20 .. 23 ) has the value 'tuvw'   and has the implicit type of
                                            a four-character string
alphabet( 4  .. 9  ) has the value 'defghi' and has the implicit type of
                                            a six-character string
```

Accessing a part of a string by using a range construct as shown is known as accessing a *slice* of a string. The slices have implicit types as shown; the types are said to be *implicit* as the subtypes do not have to be formally declared before the reference becomes valid. Using slices the following assignments are valid:

```
-- assuming left_name contains "FRED"
-- and right_name contains "    "

left_name := alphabet( 20 .. 23 );
-- left_name now contains "tuwv"

right_name( 3 .. 4 ) := alphabet( 11 .. 12 );
-- right_name now contains "  kl"

left_name( 2 .. 4 )  := left_name( 1 .. 3 );
-- left_name now contains "ttuw"
```

Accessing a character from a string or accessing a slice from a string can only be successfully performed where the integer expressions used to specify the position of the character or to specify the limits of the slice are within the specified bounds of the string's declaration. If this is not the case then a CONSTRAINT_ERROR will be raised.

Where the values which specify the bounds of the range of the slice are equal, as in alphabet(10 .. 10), the slice is of the implicit type string of one character. A STRING of one character is not compatible with a CHARACTER object. It can be made compatible by use of type conversion. For example alphabet(10 .. 10) is of implicit type one-character STRING and has the value "J".

It is possible for a slice expression to reference an *empty string*. An empty string is a string containing zero characters and can be obtained when the value of the second index is less than the value of the first index. When an empty string is being referenced it is possible for the index values to lie outside the specified bounds of the strings declaration and not cause a CONSTRAINT_ERROR to be raised.

STRING attributes

Attributes which can be applied to strings include FIRST, LAST, LENGTH and RANGE; each of these will be explained below.

The attribute FIRST, when applied to a STRING object or STRING subtype, evaluates to the value of the lower bound of the range expression which was used to declare or implicitly declare the subtype. LAST is the complementary attribute which evaluates to the upper bound. For example:

```
string_26s'FIRST is   1 and has the type universal integer
   alphabet'LAST   is  26 and has the type universal integer
 string_4s'FIRST is   1 and has the type universal integer
 left_name'LAST   is   4 and has the type universal integer
```

It may seem that the attribute FIRST is unnecessary as all strings should have a lower range bound of 1, however it is possible (though strange) to declare a STRING subtype in the form STRING(12 ..16). It is also required as the lower bound of a slice of a string may not be 1.

The attribute LENGTH, when applied to a STRING object or subtype, evaluates to the number of characters contained in the string, for example:

```
string_26s'LENGTH is  26 and has the type universal integer
string_4s'LENGTH is   4 and has the type universal integer
```

The attribute RANGE, when applied to a STRING object or subtype, evaluates to a range expression with the effective declaration string_ref'FIRST .. string_ref'LAST, where string_ref can be a string object or a string type.

The *catenation* operator ('&') can be used to combine two strings together; the result of the operation is a string whose total length is equal to the length of the two strings combined. For example:

```
-- alphabet initialized as above
left_name := alphabet( 1 .. 3 ) & alphabet( 26 .. 26 )
-- left_name is "abcz"
```

The catenation operator can be used to make text output more convenient. For example:

```
PUT( "The alphabet is " & alphabet & '.');
```

when executed, will output:

```
The alphabet is abcdefghijklmnopqrstuvwxyz.
```

This example of the use of the catenation operator indicates that it can be used to catenate a STRING with a CHARACTER; it can also be used to catenate a CHARACTER with a STRING. Two CHARACTER values can be catenated together to produce a STRING of length 2. For example, catenating the two characters 'a' & 'b' results in the two-character string "ab".

Input and output of STRING values

Procedures for the input and output of STRING values are contained within the package TEXT_IO. STRING output procedures have been used extensively in Block 1 using STRING literals. They can also be used with STRING expressions. For example:

```
    PUT( a_string );
PUT_LINE( a_string( low_slice_index .. high_slice_index ));
```

The effect of these procedures is to output all the characters of the string specified, which could be a string slice. PUT will leave the cursor on the same line following the last character, PUT_LINE will effectively call NEW_LINE after the string has been output advancing the cursor to the next line.

The following procedures available for the input of strings:

```
    GET( a_string );
GET_LINE( a_string, num_char );
```

When the procedure GET is executed with a STRING parameter it will input from the terminal sufficient characters to initialize all the characters in the string; any enter codes within the sequence input from the terminal will be ignored. The GET procedure is not very useful for input from the terminal and should only be used for getting strings from an external file (see Block 2 Section 9).

The GET_LINE procedure is more useful for obtaining STRING values from the terminal. When executed it will input characters from the terminal, giving the character's value to successive characters in the string. The procedure will terminate when an enter code is input or when sufficient characters to fill the string have been input. The second output-only parameter num_char is of the INTEGER subtype NATURAL and will effectively be set to the number of characters input.

If fewer characters are input than the string is capable of containing, then the characters in the string which have not been set from the terminal are left unchanged. If more characters are input than the string is capable of containing, the overflow characters are lost. If no characters are input then the value of num_char is effectively zero.

The value of num_char after the procedure call in the explanations above was said to be effectively the number of characters input or effectively zero; however, its value is set with respect to the lower bound of the string. As explained above, this lower bound is not necessarily 1. Some examples should make the behaviour of this procedure clear.

Using the variable left_name as declared above, with the initial value 'FRED' in the statement GET_LINE(left_name, num_char), where num_char is a variable of subtype NATURAL, the state of left_name and num_char with the following successive inputs would be:

input	left_name	num_char
BETH	'BETH'	4
alberta	'albe'	4
SUE	'SUEe'	3
<ENTER>	'SUEe'	0

In the third example only three characters were input before the enter key was pressed, consequently only the first three characters of left_name were initialized and num_char was set to 3; the fourth character of the string was left unchanged. In the last example the enter key was pressed without entering any characters, consequently none of the characters in the string were changed and num_char was set to 0.

If the same inputs are repeated with the following use of the GET_LINE procedure the effects would be, as tabulated below:

```
GET_LINE( alphabet( 10 .. 13 ), num_char );
```

input	alphabet(10 .. 13)	num_char
BETH	'BETH'	13
alberta	'albe'	13
SUE	'SUEe'	12
<ENTER>	'SUEe'	9

The interpretation of the returned value in the num_char parameter from the GET_LINE procedure should always be made with respect to the actual bounds of the string provided as the STRING parameter.

The four procedures PUT, PUT_LINE, GET and GET_LINE can also be used to output STRING values to an external file or to input strings from an external file; this use of these procedures will be considered in Block 2 Section 11.

STRING relational operations

Relational operators can be applied to STRING values; it is possible for strings of differing lengths to be compared. The interpretation of the relations between the strings is made on the basis of the following rules.

For the 'is equal to' operator corresponding characters from each string are compared using the character 'is equal to' operation. If the strings are of identical lengths and all corresponding comparisons indicate that the strings contain the same characters in the same sequence then the operation evaluates as TRUE.

If the left string is shorter than the right string and all corresponding characters are shown to be equal then it becomes a relation between an empty and a non-empty string; likewise, if the right string is shorter than the left string the comparison becomes a comparison between a non-empty string and an empty string. Both of these 'is equal to' comparisons involving empty strings will evaluate as FALSE, causing the entire expression to evaluate as FALSE.

The 'is not equal to' operator has the reverse logic to the 'is equal to' operator. Some examples will clarify this:

```
"Freda" = "Freda"   is TRUE       "Freda" /= "Freda" is FALSE

"Fred"  = "Freda"   is FALSE      "Fred"  /= "Freda" is TRUE

"Freda" = "Fred"    is FALSE      "Freda" /= "Fred"  is TRUE

"Fred " = "Freda"   is FALSE      "Fred " /= "Freda" is TRUE
```

For the 'is less than' operator, corresponding characters from each string are compared until one character from the left-hand string is shown to be less than the corresponding character from the right-hand string, or one of the strings terminates. If any character from the left string can be shown to be lower than the corresponding right string character the expression evaluates as TRUE.

If the left string is shorter than the right string and corresponding characters do not prove the less-than relationship, then the comparison becomes a comparison between an empty string and a non-empty string; such a comparison is always TRUE. Likewise, if the right string is shorter than the left string, the relation can become a comparison between a non-empty string and an empty string; such a comparison is always FALSE.

The logic of the 'greater than or equal to operator' is the inverse of that of the 'is less than' operator. Some examples will clarify this:

```
"Freda" < "Freda"   is FALSE      "Freda" >= "Freda" is TRUE

"Fred"  < "Freda"   is TRUE       "Fred"  >= "Freda" is FALSE

"Freda" < "Fred"    is FALSE      "Freda" >= "Fred"  is TRUE
```

```
"Fred " < "Freda"   is TRUE        "Fred " >= "Freda" is FALSE
```

The remaining relational operators, 'is greater than' and 'is less than or equal to', can be deduced from the explanation of the 'is less than' operator above. The empty string comparisons which may be required for strings of differing lengths are defined as follows:

```
empty_string     > non_empty_string   is  FALSE

non_empty_string > empty_string       is  TRUE

empty_string     < non_empty_string   is  TRUE

non_empty_string < empty_string       is  FALSE
```

STRING functions and procedures

It is possible for STRING subtypes to be the declared formal types of parameters to functions or procedures, or to the returned type of functions, as in the following:

```
procedure something( a_string : in string_26 );

function to_upper( a_string : in string_4 ) return string_4;
```

The problem with these declarations is that the actual parameters have to match the formal parameters exactly. Thus the function to_upper will require an actual parameter consisting of a string of four characters and will return a string of four characters.

This is not as useful as declaring procedures or functions which will take parameters of the unconstrained type STRING; such procedures can use the STRING attributes to determine the exact nature of the string. The procedure example which follows will provide an example of using parameters of the type STRING.

Corresponding to the to_upper character requirement, many programs have a requirement to ensure that all alphabetic characters within a string are upper-case. The data flow diagram of this requirement would be as follows:

This diagram indicates that the name of the function is to_upper and that it requires a single parameter which can be a STRING of any length, with any bounds. The effect of the function is to return a STRING with the same length and bounds; with all alphabetic lower-case characters in the string converted to upper case. Any non-alphabetic or upper-case alphabetic characters in the string will be returned unchanged. The header declaration for this function can be derived from the data flow diagram:

```
function to_upper( str_in : STRING ) return STRING;
```

The design of this function would be as follows:

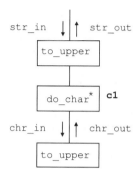

c1: For each character in the string.

This design indicates that the STRING to_upper function will be implemented by using the CHARACTER to_upper function developed earlier in this section. It is possible to have two functions within an Ada program which have the same name, so long as it is possible for Ada to distinguish between them in some way. In this example the type of the parameter can be used by Ada to determine which function is being referenced. If the actual parameter to the function is a CHARACTER then the CHARACTER to_upper function is used. If the actual parameter is a STRING then the STRING to_upper function is used. This is another example of overloading, where one name in an Ada program has more than one possible meaning.

The implementation of this function would be as follows:

```
function to_upper( str_in : STRING ) return STRING is

-- function to convert all lower case characters in the
-- string to upper case. Requires to_upper character
-- function. b2s3p1 see text.

    str_out : STRING( str_in'RANGE );    -- function variable
    -- str_out has same bounds as str_in

begin -- to upper
    for this_char in str_in'RANGE loop
        -- this_char will index all characters in strings
        str_out( this_char ) := to_upper( str_in( this_char ));
        -- pass each character to character to_upper function
```

```
      end loop;
      return str_out;
   end to_upper;
```

The function uses the STRING attribute RANGE and applies it to the input string to declare the bounds of the function variable str_out. This ensures that the length and bounds of str_out are identical to those of str_in. As explained above, it not possible to declare a STRING variable without stating the bounds of the string. The RANGE attribute of the actual input string is then used to provide the range construct of the **for** loop which will allow each character of the string to be accessed.

Within the **for** loop the loop parameter this_char is used to access a character from the input string, which is passed as an actual parameter to the CHARACTER to_upper function. The returned character from this function is then placed into the corresponding position of the output string. When all characters have been processed the loop terminates and the output string is returned as the result of the function.

These two functions can be placed within an interactive test harness in order that they can be tested:

```
with TEXT_IO; use TEXT_IO;

-- test harness for to_upper CHARACTER and STRING functions employing
-- string attributes and slices. b2s3p1 see text

procedure b2s3p1 is

   max_str_bound : constant := 10;

   subtype string_10s is STRING( 1 .. max_str_bound );

   s_lenf      : NATURAL;
   -- effective length of string input by user

   unconverted,
   converted   : string_10s;

function to_upper( chr_in : CHARACTER ) return CHARACTER is
-- text of the CHARACTER to_upper function here

function to_upper( str_in : STRING ) return STRING is
-- text of the STRING to_upper function here

begin -- b2s3p1
   PUT("Enter a string for conversion ");
   GET_LINE( unconverted, s_lenf );

   converted( 1 .. s_lenf) := to_upper( unconverted( 1 .. s_lenf));
   -- process only the characters input by the user

   PUT("The converted string is       ");
```

```
    PUT_LINE( converted( 1 .. s_lenf) ); NEW_LINE;
    -- display only the slice converted
end b2s3p1;
```

The test harness illustrates the use of the GET_LINE procedure for the input of strings from the terminal and the subsequent extraction of a slice from the string which contains only the characters which have been input by the user. The integer value returned in the second parameter of the GET_LINE procedure is used to indicate the number of characters to be extracted from the string in the slice. The slice from the unconverted string is passed to the to_upper STRING function, and the string returned is assigned to a corresponding slice of the converted string which is then displayed.

This implementation places the text of the CHARACTER to_upper function outside the scope of the STRING to_upper function, although the program design indicates that it is contained within it. This implementation decision was made because the to_upper character function in a real program is likely to have a wider applicability than its invocation in the to_upper string function. Placing it outside the scope of the to_upper string function allows it to be called from other places in the program.

EXERCISES

2.3.1 Use the ASCII table (Appendix D) to find the ASCII code for the following characters:

(a) 'A'   (b) 'Z'   (c) 'a'

(d) 'z'   (e) '0'   (f) '9'

2.3.2 Use the ASCII table to find the symbol for the following ASCII codes:

(a) 61   (b) 123

(c) 94   (d) 32

2.3.3 Write a short program using the CHARACTER attribute functions to check your answers to Exercises 2.3.1. and 2.3.2.

2.3.4 Design and implement a CHARACTER function called to_lower which will implement a function which will accept a CHARACTER and, if it is an upper-case alphabetic character, convert it to the corresponding lower-case character; other characters are to be returned unchanged.

2.3.5 Produce the declaration part of an Ada program to define three string variables called 'fruit', 'meat' and 'drink'. Each of these should be capable of holding up to five characters.

2.3.6 If the three variables declared in Exercise 2.3.5 have values as follows:

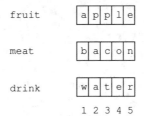

fruit

meat

drink

1 2 3 4 5

what is the result of the following expressions?

(a) fruit = meat; (b) meat /= drink; (c) fruit > meat;
(d) drink < meat; (e) fruit >= "apple"; (f) meat <= "BACON";
(g) drink > "watch"; (h) meat < "backs"; (i) drink > "waters";
(j) "bacons" > meat; (k) "ape" <= apple; (l) "" < drink.

2.3.7 Design and implement a STRING function called to_lower which will ensure that all the alphabetic characters in a string are converted to lower case. Implement the function within an interactive test harness.

2.3.8 Devise a test plan for the program from Exercise 2.3.7.

2.3.9 A simple encryption can be implemented by 'shifting' each character up the ASCII table. For example, the character 'a' can be shifted up the ASCII table by two characters and be encrypted as the character 'c'. Design and implement a function called encrypt with the following function header:

```
function encrypt( str_in : STRING;
                  shift   : INTEGER) return STRING is
```

The first parameter is the string to be encrypted; the second parameter is the number of places to shift the character up the ASCII table; and the returned value of the function is the encrypted string. The second parameter is declared as INTEGER rather than NATURAL in order that the same function can be used to encrypt a string by using a positive value, or to decrypt by passing a negative value.

The user interface showing two runs of the program might be as follows:

```
Please enter string to be encrypted this is a test
Please enter the shift value        3

The converted string is wklv#lv#d#whvw
```

```
Please enter string to be encrypted wklv#lv#d#whvw
Please enter the shift value        -3

The converted string is this is a test
```

Section 2.4

Relational expressions and BOOLEAN data types

2.4.1 BOOLEAN data types

The remaining major predeclared Ada data type is the type BOOLEAN. Objects of type BOOLEAN can take one of two values, TRUE or FALSE. Ada provides two predefined BOOLEAN constants which have these values (TRUE and FALSE). When BOOLEAN objects are first met they seem to have very few uses, and although they are rarely used explicitly as variables they are used implicitly in almost all programs to control program execution. In Block 1 two major program control statements were introduced:

```
if test then ...

while test loop ...
```

The test in these statements is a BOOLEAN expression, a program object of type BOOLEAN which can have the value TRUE or FALSE. The test is usually a relational or BOOLEAN expression which will evaluate to a BOOLEAN value, but it can also be a BOOLEAN variable or a function of type BOOLEAN. The BOOLEAN value is used to determine the behaviour of the **if** or **while** statement and thus controls the behaviour of the program.

2.4.2 Relational operators

The relational operators have already been introduced:

> is greater than
< is less than
= is equal to
>= is greater than or equal to

<= is less than or equal to
/= is not equal to

The operands of relational operators are values which are compatible with each other; the simplest way of determining if two values are compatible is to make sure that the two values are of identical types. Thus two INTEGERS, two FLOATS, two CHARACTERS or two STRINGS can be used in a relational expression. Two values of different types cannot be used in a relational expression unless type conversion is used to convert one of the values into a type compatible with the other. Subtypes can, however, be compared with their base type in a relational comparison.

When a relational expression is evaluated during program execution, it evaluates to a value of type BOOLEAN. Its value when evaluated will be either TRUE or FALSE. Relational expressions can thus be treated as BOOLEAN objects; therefore, a relational expression can be used as the test in the program control statements expressed above.

It is often required that more than one relational comparison have to be combined to implement a test for a control structure; relational expressions can be combined as BOOLEAN objects using the BOOLEAN logical operators.

2.4.3 BOOLEAN logical operators

There are four BOOLEAN logical operators **not, and, or** and **xor**. All of these operators take BOOLEAN values as their operand or operands and evaluate to BOOLEAN values.

The **not** operator is a unary operator, which means that it takes a single BOOLEAN value. When it is evaluated it negates the value of the operand, evaluating to a BOOLEAN value; thus:

```
not( TRUE )    evaluates as FALSE

not( FALSE )   evaluates as TRUE
```

The **not** operator can be used to make the expression of a condition within a program read more naturally. Almost any BOOLEAN expression can be rewritten to avoid using the **not** operator and almost any BOOLEAN expression can be rewritten to include its use. The six relational operators can be considered as a set of three operators with their associated BOOLEAN negations:

```
'is equal to'      is equivalent to   not('is not equal to')

'is greater than'  is equivalent to   not('is less than or equal to')

'is less than'     is equivalent to   not('is greater than or equal to')
```

Using these equivalences any of the relational operators can translated into a form which uses or avoids the use of the **not** operator; this facility can be used to make the relational expression read more naturally in the program text. For example:

```
not( age <= 21 )       is the same as        age > 21
not( sex /= 'f' )      is the same as        sex = 'f'
not( income >= 10000) is the same as    income < 10000
```

In these examples, the right-hand expression would in most cases seem to be a simpler and thus more comprehensible form of the relation in the left-hand expression. Simpler expressions are always to be favoured in programs, as a simpler program is one which is easier to maintain.

The **and, or** and **xor** BOOLEAN operators are binary, taking as operands two BOOLEAN values and evaluating to a single BOOLEAN value. The precise way in which the BOOLEAN values are combined to produce a resulting BOOLEAN value can be expressed in truth tables (see Tables 2.4.1–2.4.3). These tables can be expressed colloquially as follows. For the **and** rule, the expression is TRUE if both the operands are TRUE, otherwise it is FALSE. For the **or** rule, the expression is TRUE if either or both of the operands are TRUE, otherwise it is FALSE. For the **xor** rule, the expression is TRUE if either but not both operands are TRUE, otherwise it is FALSE.

Table 2.4.1 and TRUTH TABLE

FALSE	**and**	FALSE	evaluates as FALSE
TRUE	**and**	FALSE	evaluates as FALSE
FALSE	**and**	TRUE	evaluates as FALSE
TRUE	**and**	TRUE	evaluates as TRUE

Table 2.4.2 or TRUTH TABLE

FALSE	**or**	FALSE	evaluates as FALSE
TRUE	**or**	FALSE	evaluates as TRUE
FALSE	**or**	TRUE	evaluates as TRUE
TRUE	**or**	TRUE	evaluates as TRUE

Table 2.4.3 xor TRUTH TABLE

FALSE	**xor**	FALSE	evaluates as FALSE
TRUE	**xor**	FALSE	evaluates as TRUE
FALSE	**xor**	TRUE	evaluates as TRUE
TRUE	**xor**	TRUE	evaluates as FALSE

The BOOLEAN operators can be used in programs to combine several relational expressions or BOOLEAN values, allowing a more complex rule to be expressed. For example, the following declarations:

```
   sex  : CHARACTER; -- sex code 'm' for male, 'f' for female
   age  : ages;      -- integer subtype, age in years
income  : incomes;   -- integer subtype, income in pounds
```

may be used to store information about the same person. A program commissioned by an advertising company may have a requirement to identify the following groups of people:

(a) anybody between 20 and 35 inclusive;
(b) females aged 21 or older;
(c) females over 60 and males over 65 (pensioners).

The most natural way of expressing (a) would be as follows:

1. (age >= 20) **and** (age <= 35)

although there are other equivalent ways of expressing the same relation, for example:

2. (age > 19) **and** (age < 36)
3. **not**((age < 20) **or** (age > 35))

Likewise, (b) can be expressed in a number of ways:

1. (sex = 'f') **and** (age >= 21)
2. (sex = 'f') **and** (age > 20)
3. (sex /= 'm') **and** (**not**(age < 21))

Requirement (c) will require a more complex expression,

1. ((sex = 'f') **and** (age >= 60)) **or** ((sex = 'm') **and** (age >= 65))
2. ((sex = 'f') **and** (age > 59)) **or** ((sex = 'm') **and** (age > 64))
3. **not**(((age < 60) **and** (sex = 'f')) **or** ((age < 65) **and** **not**(sex = 'f')))

In all three examples the clearest expression of the required relation is given in expression (1); the most convoluted expression of the required relation is given in expression (3). Expression (2) seems almost as acceptable as expression (1); but these forms of the expression should be avoided, as the INTEGER literals used '19', '36', '59' and '64' are not stated in the specifications. It could be argued that expressions such as 'age > 20' are easier to comprehend than expressions such as 'age >= 21'; however, the form which is closest to the most natural English statement of the specification 'aged 21 or older' should always be used.

The **not** operator has the highest precedence, meaning that in the absence of brackets it will be evaluated first. The other BOOLEAN operators are of equal precedence, meaning that in the absence of brackets they will be evaluated from left to right. As with other expressions, the explicit use of brackets to make the order of execution clear is advocated as good programming style.

2.4.4 Validating a BOOLEAN expression

The validity and equivalence of the above expressions can be demonstrated by subjecting them to simulated testing. The expression can be validated by regarding it as a black box with several inputs and a single BOOLEAN outcome. Suitable values for input can be derived from a consideration of the specification, and parallel testing can be used to predict the required outcome of the expression.

Using requirement (b) as an example, the black-box diagram is as follows:

```
sex  ->   ┌─────────────────┐
          │                 │
          │   expression    │   -> BOOLEAN
          │                 │
age  ->   └─────────────────┘
```

This diagram indicates that the expression requires a sex and an age value and evaluates to a BOOLEAN value. The range diagrams with subrange indications and cases, assuming that the character sex will only contain 'f' or 'm', are as follows:

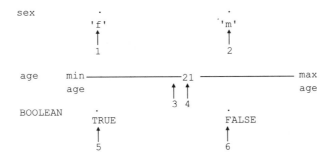

Using the specification, a test plan can produced from the following cases:

test no	cases	sex	age	outcome
1	1, 3, 6	'f'	20	FALSE
2	1, 4, 5	'f'	21	TRUE
3	2, 3, 6	'm'	20	FALSE
4	2, 4, 6	'm'	21	FALSE

This test plan has to include the consideration that all possible combinations of input have to be tested against each other; thus it is not enough just to test inputs 1, 2, 3 and 4 but to test the two possible age cases against each of the possible sex cases, giving a total of four test runs.

When this test analysis is used with expression (b) (1), a simulated test log can be derived from a consideration of the BOOLEAN rules given above:

Simulated test log for '(sex = 'f') **and** (age >= 21)'

test no	sex	age	sex = 'f'	age >= 21	outcome
1	'f'	20	T	F	FALSE
2	'f'	21	T	T	TRUE
3	'm'	20	F	F	FALSE
4	'm'	21	F	T	FALSE

The values of the two subexpressions 'sex = 'f'' and 'age >= 21' are combined using the **and** rule to produce the outcome. This trace of the BOOLEAN expression has validated the expression, by proving that the behaviour of the expression under this simulated test is identical to the behaviour predicted from the black-box test plan, which was in turn derived from the specification.

The alternative expression (b) (3) can be shown to be equivalent by subjecting it to the same test plan:

Simulated test log for '(sex /= 'm') **and not** (age < 21)'

test no	sex	age	sex /= 'm'	**not**(age < 21)	outcome
1	'f'	20	T	F	FALSE
2	'f'	21	T	T	TRUE
3	'm'	20	F	F	FALSE
4	'm'	21	F	T	FALSE

This test log indicates the equivalence of expressions (b) (1) and (b) (3), as both expressions produce identical behaviour when subjected to the same formal testing.

When relational expressions are being constructed during the design and coding of a program, it is required that the expressions produced are valid and are as simple as possible. The validity of a BOOLEAN expression can be determined from a formal black-box investigation of the expression which is derived from the specification. The construction of a test plan at this stage will also allow the completeness of the specification to be determined. For example, using the scenario above the specification may require:

> people over 35 whose income is greater than 10000 or females less than 30 whose income is greater than 8000

This specification does not explicitly make clear what is to happen to females between 30 and 35 of whatever income. By constructing a test plan for this requirement the action to be taken in these cases will have to be made explicit, possibly by determining the correct action from the program's sponsor.

Having produced and validated an appropriate BOOLEAN expression the expression should be investigated to determine if a simpler expression can be constructed. It is possible for a relational expression to be initially constructed in a piecemeal fashion; this can lead to a complicated, convoluted expression. The expression, once constructed, should be examined in an attempt to produce a simpler equivalent expression whose equivalence can be demonstrated by using the test plan. The production of the simplest, most congruent form of a relational expression will enhance program maintainability and thus reliability.

The expressions which are used to control selections and iterations are among the most crucial parts of programs. It is the evaluation of these expressions which controls the behaviour of the program; consequently, erroneous behaviour of a program is often caused by an erroneous control expression. By taking care with the initial construction of such expressions, the production and the maintenance of programs can be made easier.

2.4.5 BOOLEAN variables

BOOLEAN variables can be used to represent the state of some object in the real world. For example, an insurance company may only accept drivers who are older than 25. This can be represented in a **data structure diagram** as follows:

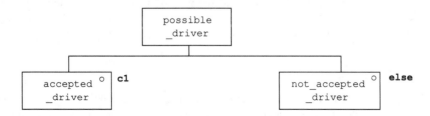

c1: If driver is over 25 years.

The concept of a selection and the diagram for a selection are being used here to represent the structure of a data object, not the processing of the data. The same notation for sequence, selection and iteration, which was introduced in Block 1 to describe program processes, can also be used to describe data structures. Care should be taken when producing or reading structure charts to clarify whether the chart is a *program* structure chart or a *data* structure chart.

Where an item of data has two distinct and mutually exclusive states, a BOOLEAN variable can be used to record this information. BOOLEAN variables should only be used to represent data objects which are TRUE/FALSE or yes/no in their meaning. A data object to represent a person's sex can have one of two values, male or female; it would be possible to use a BOOLEAN variable to represent this information (after deciding the difficult question of which of the real-world values, male or female, will be mapped onto the BOOLEAN value TRUE). A better, more congruent solution would be to declare an enumeration type with two values, male and female, and declare the variable to be of this type (enumeration types will be introduced in the next section).

```
POOR STYLE

sex: BOOLEAN;

...

if sex
then

...
```

```
GOOD STYLE

type sexes = (male, female);
sex      :sexes;

...

if sex = male
then

...
```

Without having a full understanding of the declaration and use of enumeration types it can be seen from the program fragments above that the use of the enumeration type is more congruent with the real world than the use of a BOOLEAN variable. The reason why male is represented in the program as the BOOLEAN value TRUE and female as FALSE is not at all clear from our real-world understanding of male and female. As was emphasized in Block 2 Section 2, the more congruent the data modelling in a program is compared with the real world, the better the program produced using the models will be.

A suitable BOOLEAN variable declaration for the possible driver data object introduced above would be as follows:

```
is_accepted    : BOOLEAN := FALSE;
```

This declares a BOOLEAN variable called is_accepted with the default value FALSE. The value TRUE would indicate that the driver is acceptable to the insurance company, the value FALSE would indicate that the driver is unacceptable. The BOOLEAN variable could be set to an appropriate value from an integer variable called applicants_age and an INTEGER constant called minimum_age using the following statement:

```
if applicants_age >= minimum_age then
   is_accepted := TRUE;
else
   is_accepted := FALSE;
end if;
```

An alterative, more elegant statement which has the same meaning is as follows:

```
is_accepted := applicants_age >= minimum_age;
```

The left-hand side of this assignment statement is a BOOLEAN variable, therefore the right-hand side must be a BOOLEAN value. The right-hand side is a relational expression involving two INTEGER objects: the first INTEGER object is applicants_age, which is an INTEGER variable; the second is the INTEGER constant minimum_age. Both sides of the expression are INTEGER values and are thus compatible and can be used in a relational comparison.

The result of the relational operation when it is evaluated as the program executes is a BOOLEAN value which is stored in the BOOLEAN variable is_accepted. So if the applicant's age is 25 or greater, then the relational expression will evaluate as TRUE and this value will be stored in the BOOLEAN variable. If the applicant's age is less than 25 then the relational expression will evaluate as FALSE and this value will be stored in the BOOLEAN variable.

Thus the BOOLEAN variable has been set to its correct logical condition by using a relational comparison of the integer variable containing the applicant's age and the INTEGER constant containing the minimum acceptable age.

A BOOLEAN variable can be used to support or simplify program control decisions. For example, in the menu choice procedure introduced in Block 1, two identical comparisons were made:

```
choice := 'x'; -- ensure loop iterates at least
while ((choice <= 'A') and (choice >= 'E')) loop
   PUT("Enter your choice  ");
   GET( choice ); SKIP_LINE;
   if ((choice <= 'A') and (choice >= 'E')) then
      PUT_LINE("Enter 'A','B','C','D' or 'E' only  ");
   end if;
end loop;
```

This has involved the expression ((choice <= 'A') **and** (choice >= 'E')), being used twice in this part of the program, once as the BOOLEAN test in the **loop** statement and again as the BOOLEAN test in the **if** statement. Repeating an expression can be avoided by assigning the result of the expression to a BOOLEAN variable and using the variable in place of the BOOLEAN expression in the **if** and **loop** statements. If a BOOLEAN variable called is_bad_choice is declared, this program fragment can be rewritten as follows:

```
is_bad_choice := TRUE; -- ensure loop iterates once
while is_bad_choice loop
   PUT("Enter your choice  ");
   GET( choice ); SKIP_LINE;
   is_bad_choice := ((choice <= 'A') and (choice >= 'E'));
   if is_bad_choice then
      PUT_LINE("Enter 'A','B','C','D' or 'E' only  ");
   end if;
end loop;
```

The vital part of this fragment is the assignment statement

```
is_bad_choice := ((choice <= 'A') and (choice >= 'E'));
```

The left-hand side of this assignment is a BOOLEAN variable; it can only be assigned one of the BOOLEAN values TRUE or FALSE. The right-hand side of the assignment statement is a BOOLEAN expression involving the **and** operator; as explained above, BOOLEAN operators evaluate to a BOOLEAN value. In this case the value returned is not used in the BOOLEAN test of the **while** statement or the **if** statement, but is stored in the BOOLEAN variable is_bad_choice. The value of this variable is_bad_choice is used as the BOOLEAN test in the **if** statement and the **while** statement in place of the complete BOOLEAN expression.

In a program fragment of this complexity the effect is marginal. In the first version of the program the expression is evaluated twice. In the second version of the program the result of the expression is used twice but the expression is only evaluated once. Evaluating an expression can be far more expensive in terms of computer time than examining the state of a BOOLEAN variable. If a condition has to be established by evaluating an expression more than once in a program design, then the use of a BOOLEAN variable to store the result of the evaluation will optimize the implementation of the design.

More importantly than optimization, the use of a BOOLEAN variable will make the program more readable. The meaning of a BOOLEAN expression is not always clear; the meaning of a BOOLEAN variable should always be clear if the name of the variable has been chosen carefully.

In a large or complex program, a condition may have to be established several times in several different parts of the program. Using a BOOLEAN variable simplifies the program in both of the ways explained above. The effect in a large program is to make the implementation more robust.

A common program style error is to include phrases such as the following:

```
if is_bad_choice = TRUE then . . .
```

This phrase is not wrong, but it is very inelegant. The BOOLEAN variable is_bad_choice can only have the value TRUE or the value FALSE. The 'is equal to' relational operator can be used on two BOOLEAN objects; if the two possible values of is_bad_choice are considered then the relational expression will be one of two possibilities:

```
TRUE  = TRUE    which is TRUE
FALSE = TRUE    which is FALSE
```

Thus the result of the relational expression is equal to the state of the BOOLEAN variable; which implies that the BOOLEAN variable itself could simply have been used, instead of the relational comparison, as follows:

```
if is_bad_choice then . . .
```

The BOOLEAN type can be the declared type of formal parameters to functions and procedures, or can be the returned type of functions, as follows:

```
procedure write_policy( driver      : in drivers;
                        is_accepted : in BOOLEAN);
function is_upper_case( a_char : CHARACTER ) return BOOLEAN;
```

The input and output of BOOLEAN values is not a very common requirement and will be considered in the next section.

2.4.6 Other BOOLEAN operators

The two BOOLEAN operators **and** and **or** have another optional form: **and then** and **or else**, respectively. The difference between the two forms of the operator is in the evaluation of the two BOOLEAN expressions which they combine.

In the case of the **and** operator, if the first value is FALSE then the second value is irrelevant to the outcome of the expression, as FALSE **and** *anything* will always be FALSE. Likewise with the **or** operator; the second value is irrelevant if the first value is TRUE as TRUE **or** *anything* will always be TRUE.

With the simple **and** and **or** operators the two values are always combined to determine the outcome of the relational expression. With the **and then** and **or else** operators the second value is only used if it is required.

The appropriate use of these operators can be determined from the following example:

```
-- dangerous as num_students could be 0 causing NUMERIC_ERROR
if (( total_score / num_students ) > pass_mark ) then
    -- Statements
end if;

-- safe as division will only be evaluated if num_students not zero
if (( num_students /= 0 ) and then
    (( total_score / num_students ) > pass_mark )) then
    -- Statements
end if;
```

In this example the use of the **and then** operator prevents the right-hand expression from being evaluated if the value of the left-hand expression is FALSE. This avoids the problem of division by zero, in a more elegant manner than the equivalent

```
if ( num_students /= 0 ) then
    if ( total_score / num_students ) > pass_mark then
        -- Statements
    end if;
end if;
```

EXERCISES

2.2.1   Rewrite the following expressions to avoid using the **not** operator.

(a)   **not**(height > 176);
(b)   **not**(mass <= 325);
(c)   (sex = 'm') **and not**(age <= 15);
(d)   (insurance_group >5) **or not** (engine_size >= 2500);

2.2.2   If the following definitions are assumed:

```
            sex : CHARACTER; -- sex of person coded 'f' or 'm'
         height : INTEGER;   -- height of person in cm
            age : INTEGER;   -- age of person in years
    engine_size : INTEGER;   -- car engine size in cc
        car_age : INTEGER;   -- age of car in years
insurance_group : CHARACTER; -- car insurance group coded '1'. . .'6'
   energy_value : INTEGER;   -- energy value of a food
    fat_content : INTEGER;   -- fat content of a food
```

write expressions to implement the following conditions:

(a)   TRUE for females over 170 cm high.
(b)   TRUE for cars whose engine size is smaller than 2000 cc and which are less than 10 years old.

(c) TRUE for cars whose engine size is 3500 cc or higher or are in insurance group 4 or higher.

(d) TRUE for males who are over 40 or older and below 175 cm tall.

(e) TRUE for foods whose energy value is 1000 or higher or whose fat content is 100 or higher.

(f) TRUE for cars less than 5 years old which are in insurance group 1 or 2, or whose engine size is 1200 cc or less.

2.2.3 Simplify the following expressions:

(a) **not**(age > 21) **or** (sex = 'f');

(b) **not**((engine_size > 2000) **and** (insurance_group >= '4'));

(c) **not**((sex = 'm') **and** (energy_value > 800) **and** (fat_content >= 60));

2.2.4 Devise a test plan for the following expression:

(sex = 'f') **and** ((car_age <5) **or** (insurance_group <= '3'));

2.2.5 Produce an expression equivalent to that in Exercise 2.2.4 and demonstrate its equivalence.

Section 2.5

Enumerated types

There are many real-world data objects whose values do not fit into the ranges or subranges of Ada's predeclared types. A common example of such a requirement is the representation of days of the week; this requirement can be expressed in a data structure diagram as follows:

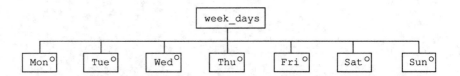

What is required is a data type called week_days whose objects could take one of the values Mon, Tue, Wed, Thu, Fri, Sat or Sun as shown in the data structure diagram. Ada provides a facility for declaring an *enumerated data type*. An enumerated data type is one where all the possible values which objects of the data type can take are listed (enumerated) in its declaration.

2.5.1 Declaring enumerated types and subtypes

To declare an enumerated type, each of the values which an object of the type can take is represented by a symbolic name in an enumeration list. A data type called week_days could be declared as follows:

```
type week_days is ( Mon, Tue, Wed, Thu, Fri, Sat, Sun );
```

Data objects of type week_days can take one of the values listed, mapping them explicitly onto the possible values of the data objects in the real world. In the declaration of an enumerated type, the reserved word **type** indicates that the declaration of a type is being made and the typename follows. The reserved word **is** is then used before the list of **enumeration literals** which will be used to represent the values of the type. The list is enclosed within brackets and each literal is separated from the next with a comma.

236

Having declared an enumerated type within a program it is possible to declare subtypes of the enumerated type, for example:

```
type    week_days    is ( Mon, Tue, Wed, Thu, Fri, Sat, Sun );

subtype work_days    is week_days range Mon .. Fri;

subtype weekend_days is week_days range Sat .. Sun;

a_day    : week_days;
work_day : work_days;
rest_day : weekend_days := Sat;
```

This program fragment declares the enumeration type week_days as explained above, and, having declared it, uses it as the base type for the declaration of subtypes, using the subtype declaration format introduced in Block 2 Section 2.

The variable a_day is of type week_days and can take any of the values expressed in the declaration of week_days. The variable work_day is of the subtype work_days and can take a restricted range of week_day values as expressed in its declaration. Likewise, the variable rest_day is of the subtype weekend_days and can only take one of the week_day values Sat or Sun.

As work_day and rest_day are variables of a subtype of the base type week_days they are compatible with the object a_day which is of the type week_day, without type conversion being necessary. For example:

```
    a_day := work_day; -- always valid
    a_day := rest_day; -- always valid
work_day := a_day;     -- valid if value of a_day is within Mon .. Fri
rest_day := a_day;     -- valid if value of a_day is Sat or Sun
work_day := rest_day;  -- logically invalid as ranges do not overlap
```

The last example is always logically invalid but might not be spotted by all compilers.

It is possible to declare new types whose base type is an enumerated type. For example:

```
type colours        is (red, orange, yellow, green,
                        blue, indigo, violet);
type rainbow_colours is new colours;
type sky_colours     is new colours range blue .. violet;
```

The first of these declarations declares an enumerated type called colours with the enumeration list shown. The second declares a new enumerated type called rainbow_colours, whose base type is colours and whose range of values is identical to that of colours. The third declares a new enumerated type called sky_colours whose base type is colours and whose range of values is the contiguous range of colours as shown. Objects of type colours, rainbow_colours and sky_colours are not compatible with each other without explicit type conversion, even though they share the same values:

```
colour  : colours;
rainbow : rainbow_colours;
sky     : sky_colours;

colour  := rainbow;       -- invalid as distinct types
colour  := sky;           -- invalid as distinct types
rainbow := sky;           -- invalid as distinct types

rainbow := rainbow_colours(colour); -- valid type conversion
sky     := sky_colours(rainbow);    -- valid if rainbow is
                                    -- blue, indigo or violet
```

If the following two declarations exist in the same program and both are in scope:

```
type colours    is ( red,   orange, yellow, green,
                     blue, indigo, violet );
type judo_belts is ( white, yellow, orange,
                     green, blue,   black );
```

then several of the enumeration literals are overloaded. The meaning of the enumeration literals yellow, orange, green, and blue could be of the type colours or of the type judo_belts. An overloaded term in Ada is allowed, providing there is some way by which Ada can determine which meaning of the term is intended. For example:

```
sky := blue;
```

is unambiguous as in this context blue must be of type colours. However, in the following:

```
for something in yellow .. blue loop
```

the intended meaning is unclear. This could be interpreted as an attempt to construct a loop whose loop parameter is of type colours or whose type is judo_belts. The meaning should be made clear to Ada and to the reader by explicitly stating the base type, as in the following:

```
for this_belt in judo_belts range yellow .. blue loop
```

A better expression of this requirement may be to declare an explicit subtype and use the subtype name to define the limits of the loop:

```
subtype novices is judo_belts range yellow .. blue;
for this_belt in novices loop
```

2.5.2 Attributes of enumerated types

The attributes which can be applied to enumerated types include FIRST, LAST, SUCC, PRED, VAL and POS; each of these will be explained in turn, assuming that the enumerated type and subtype declarations above are in use.

FIRST is an attribute which can be applied to types or subtypes and evaluates to the first enumeration value of that type or subtype. LAST is a complementary attribute which evaluates to the last enumeration value. For example:

```
  week_days'FIRST  is  Mon     and is of type week_days
  week_days'LAST   is  Sun     and is of type week_days
` novices'FIRST  is  yellow  and is of type judo_belts
    novices'LAST   is  blue    and is of type judo_belts
```

As is shown in the table above, the type of the attribute for subtypes is the type of the subtype's base type not the subtype itself.

SUCC is an attribute function which requires a single parameter of the specified type or subtype and evaluates to the next enumeration value in the sequence, as specified in the base type's declaration. PRED is the complementary attribute function which evaluates to the preceding enumeration value in the sequence specified in the base type's declaration:

```
week_days'SUCC( Wed )  is Thu  and is of type week_days
week_days'PRED( Fri )  is Thu  and is of type week_days
rest_days'SUCC( Sat )  is Sun  and is of type week_days
rest_days'PRED( Sun )  is Sat  and is of type week_days
```

An attempt to determine the SUCCessor of the last enumeration value of a type, or to determine the PREDecessor of the first enumeration value of a type will raise a CONSTRAINT_ERROR exception. For example:

```
novices'SUCC( blue  ) is black and is of type judo_belts
novices'PRED( yellow) is white and is of type judo_belts
colours'PRED( red   ) will raise a CONSTRAINT ERROR
rest_days'SUCC( Sun ) will raise a CONSTRAINT ERROR
```

POS is an attribute function which requires a single parameter of the type specified and evaluates to a general integer, whose value is equal to the *ordinal position* of the parameter's value in the enumeration list. The ordinal position of an enumeration value is the position of the enumeration literal in the list which declared the base type. When the POS attribute is applied to a subtype the value returned is the ordinal position of the literal in the base type's declaration. For example:

```
week_days'POS( Mon )    is 0    and is of type universal integer
week_days'POS( Sun )    is 6    and is of type universal integer
rest_days'POS( Sat )    is 5    and is of type universal integer
  novices'POS( yellow )  is 1    and is of type universal integer
  novices'POS( black  )  is 5    and is of type universal integer
```

VAL is an attribute function which is the inverse of POS. It requires a single parameter of any integer type and evaluates to the value of the enumeration literal whose ordinal position is specified by the parameter. When a subtype is specified, the ordinal position is the ordinal position in the base type declaration. If the integer value is outside the appropriate range of ordinal values for the base type a CONSTRAINT_ERROR will be raised. For example:

```
rainbow_colours'VAL(2)  is yellow  and is of type rainbow_colours
    judo_belts'VAL(5)  is black   and is of type judo_belts
       novices'VAL(1)  is yellow  and is of type judo_belts
rainbow_colours'VAL(7)  will raise a CONSTRAINT_ERROR
       novices'VAL(0)  is white and is of type judo_belts
```

2.5.3 Input and output of enumeration values

As with the INTEGER and FLOAT data types, Ada provides a general facility for the creation of a suitable package of subprograms tailored for the input and output of particular enumeration types. The name of the general package is ENUMERATION_IO and it is contained within the package TEXT_IO. Using the types declared earlier in this section the creation of suitable enumeration input and output packages can be accomplished with the following statements:

```
with TEXT_IO; use TEXT_IO;
package days_io is new ENUMERATION_IO( week_days );
-- package is suitable for use with week_days, work_days and rest_days

with TEXT_IO;
package colours_io is new TEXT_IO.ENUMERATION_IO( colours );
-- package is suitable for use with colours but not
-- rainbow_colours or sky_colours
```

The creation of such packages is not possible in a program until the enumerated types for which they are to be tailored have been declared. Having declared the package, a suitable scope for a **use** statement has to be found. If extensive use is being made of the input and output of the enumeration values then an appropriate scope might be the entire scope of the enumerated type itself. If only local use is being made of the input and output of the enumeration values then the scope of the use of the package should be restricted.

Having created a suitable package for the input and output, the two procedures GET and PUT configured for use with the enumerated type are accessible. The simplest form of the PUT procedure for enumeration types is

```
PUT( enum_val );
```

where enum_val is an expression of the appropriate enumerated type. This statement, when executed, will output the appropriate enumeration literal as a sequence of upper-case characters, using as many characters are required for the output of the literal. There are two optional parameters to the procedure.

The first optional parameter is WIDTH, which can be used to specify the number of characters to be used. If the value of WIDTH specified is less than the number of characters required it will be ignored and the number of characters required for the literal will be output. If the value specified for WIDTH is greater than the number of characters required the output will be followed by sufficient spaces to make the total width of the output equal to that specified.

The second optional parameter is SET, which requires a value, which is itself an enumeration literal, to be specified. Possible values for this parameter are LOWER_CASE and UPPER_CASE. The default effect of this parameter if no value is explicitly specified is to output enumeration literals with alphabetic characters in upper case. If the value of SET is specified as LOWER_CASE then alphabetic characters will be output in lower case.

Some examples will make the effects of the procedure and its optional parameters clearer:

a_day := Wed;

PUT(a_day)	WED
PUT(a_day, WIDTH => 2);	WED -- width overridden
PUT(a_day, WIDTH => 5);	WED∇∇
PUT(a_day, SET => LOWER_CASE);	wed
PUT(a_day, WIDTH => 5, SET => LOWER_CASE);	wed∇∇

---

where ∇ indicates a space.

The GET procedure can be used to input enumeration values from the terminal; it can be used in the form

```
GET( enum_var );
```

where enum_var is an enumeration variable of some type whose input package is in use. The effect of this procedure, when it is executed, is to accept characters from the terminal. Characters will be accepted, ignoring leading spaces, until it can be determined by Ada that the sequence input is or is not a valid enumeration literal of the base type of the parameter. If the sequence input is a valid enumeration literal, irrespective of the case of the characters, the variable specified will be set to the value represented by the input. If the sequence of characters input is not a valid enumeration literal then a DATA_ERROR exception will be raised. Where enum_var is a subtype variable then if the sequence is a valid enumeration literal of the base type of enum_var's base type but is outside its declared range a CONSTRAINT_ERROR will be raised. This makes the input of enumeration literals rather dangerous. A safe method for the input of enumeration literals will be developed in the program example at the end of this section.

The BOOLEAN type introduced in the last section is implemented in Ada programs as an enumerated type. Should a program have a requirement for the input and output of BOOLEAN literals (TRUE and FALSE) then the ENUMERATION_IO package can be configured for use with BOOLEAN values.

```
with TEXT_IO; use TEXT_IO;
package boolean_io is new TEXT_IO.ENUMERATION_IO( BOOLEAN );
```

The enumeration versions of the procedures GET and PUT can also be used to input values from or output values to an external file; this use of the procedures will be considered in Block 2 Section 11.

2.5.4 Relational operators and enumerated types

The relational operators can be applied to objects of enumeration types. The comparison is implemented as a comparison based upon the objects' ordinal values. Consequently, all the following comparisons can be assumed to be true:

```
Wed = Wed      black = black      Sun /= Sat        black /= white

Tue > Mon      violet > indigo    orange >= orange   white <= yellow

Thu < Sun      Fri <= Fri         white < black      indigo <= violet
```

The case of enumeration literals is not significant, so the following expressions are also all TRUE:

```
blue = BLUE          THU = thu          OrAnGe = oRaNgE
```

The value of the expression 'orange < yellow' is dependent upon what type the values orange and yellow are; Ada must be able to decide this from the context. It is possible to use type conversion to declare explicitly the type intended:

```
judo_belts( orange ) < judo_belts( yellow ) is FALSE
colours(     orange ) < colours(     yellow ) is TRUE
```

2.5.5 Using enumerated types

An enumerated type can be used as a loop parameter. For example, the following fragment of code will have the intended effect:

```
-- assuming TEXT_IO and days_io is in use
PUT("The colours of the rainbow are ");
for this_colour in rainbow_colours loop
   PUT( this_day, SET => LOWER_CASE); PUT(" ");
end loop;
PUT_LINE(".");
```

The output from this code fragment when executed would be as follows:

```
The colours of the rainbow are red orange yellow green blue indigo violet
```

An enumeration object can be used as the selector in a **case** statement. For example:

```
-- novice is variable of type novices

case novice is
   when  yellow          => PUT("beginner ");
   when  orange | green  => PUT("improving ");
   when  blue            => PUT("expert novice ");
end case;
```

will categorize the novice according to the colour of his or her belt.

The membership operator can be used with enumerated types. For example:

```
if today in weekend_days then
   PUT("holiday");
end if;
```

2.5.6 Enumeration functions

A common operation required for some enumeration types is to increment the enumeration value, with the value which follows the last value in the enumeration list being the first value of the enumeration list. For example, the value which follows Sun in the real world is Mon. The attribute function SUCC will implement most of this requirement, but, as noted above, will raise a CONSTRAINT_ERROR if the SUCCessor of the last element in the enumeration list is requested.

To implement this requirement a user-declared enumeration function called next_day would be required; which can be based on the following design:

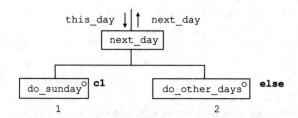

```
c1: If in_day is sunday.  1. return monday
                          2. return successor of in_day
```

This function can be implemented as follows:

```
function next_day( this_day : week_days ) return week_days is

-- function to return the day value following this_day
-- with next day of Sun being Mon. b2s5 see text

begin -- next day
    if this_day = week_days'LAST then
        return week_days'FIRST;
    else
        return week_days'SUCC( this_day );
```

```
    end if;
end next_day;
```

The implementation of this function has employed the use of the enumeration attributes FIRST and LAST to implement the 'wrap-around' decision. This makes the function more robust and more general. It is more robust as a change to the enumeration declaration, perhaps by declaring Sun as the first day and Sat as the last day, will not require any changes to be made to the function. It is more general as the implementation of the function can be used as the basis for any enumeration type which requires the 'wrap-around' successor to be produced.

The function also differs from the functions previously produced as it does not employ a function variable; consequently, it has two **return** statements and thus two places where flow of control can leave the function. For a function of this size and complexity not using a function variable makes the implementation of the function more understandable. When functions become larger or more complex then the use of a function variable is advocated as good style.

Where an enumeration type is declared which requires this 'wrap-around' behaviour, two functions, one to return the next value in sequence, and one to return the previous value in the sequence should be implemented for use with values of the type. As has been mentioned, the full definition of a data type includes not only the values of the type but also the operations which can be performed upon the type. In later sections of this block a method of encapsulating such user-declared values and operations within an Ada program unit called a *package* will be introduced.

2.5.7 Safe terminal input of enumeration values

In the discussion of the use of the enumeration GET procedure to input enumeration values from the terminal, it was pointed out that the procedure is dangerous as any invalid inputs will raise a DATA_ERROR or CONSTRAINT_ERROR exception. This is a similar consideration to the safe input of numeric values which was considered in Block 2 Section 1, where a safe input procedure was implemented. A similar design can be used for the safe input of enumeration values:

```
procedure safe_get_day ( out_day : out week_days;
                         min     : in  week_days := week_days'FIRST;
                         max     : in  week_days := week_days'LAST ) is

-- procedure for the safe input of enumeration values. Design based on
-- b1s2p2, see text. This procedure b1s5p1, see text.
-- assumes package days_io is in use

        local_day : week_days;          -- local input var
```

```
                good_day : BOOLEAN := FALSE; -- loop control

begin -- safe_get_day
   while not good_day loop
   begin -- while block
      PUT("Enter an day between ");
      PUT( min, SET => LOWER_CASE);
      PUT(" and "); PUT( max, SET => LOWER_CASE  ); PUT(" ");
      GET( local_day );
      -- this point can only be reached when input is a valid weekday
      -- enumeration literal
      if (local_day < min) or else (local_day > max) then
         raise DATA_ERROR;
      else
         good_day := TRUE;
      end if;
      -- this point can only be reached if input is a valid weekday
      -- enumeration literal between min and max

   exception
      when DATA_ERROR =>
         PUT_LINE("Invalid day !. Good days are ");
         for this_day in week_days range min .. max loop
            PUT( this_day, SET => LOWER_CASE ); PUT(" ");
         end loop;
         NEW_LINE; -- terminate error dialogue
         SKIP_LINE; -- tidy up terminal
   end; -- while block
   end loop;
   -- this point can only be reached when valid value input
   SKIP_LINE;                 -- tidy up terminal handling
   out_day := local_day;    -- export input value
end safe_get_day;
```

The implementation of this procedure is very similar to the procedure implemented in b2s2p1, where the design of the procedure can be found. Details of how the exception handler mechanism operates are explained there. The only design change is in the use of a BOOLEAN variable to control the operation of the loop, as explained in the previous section.

The implementation of this procedure also makes use of the **or else** relational operator, introduced in the previous section, to optimize the decision which is made when an input enumeration value is tested against the limits supplied to the procedure.

The user interface differs from the procedure in Block 2 Section 1. In this procedure the possible enumeration literals which are allowed by the invocation of the procedure are displayed as part of the error dialogue. This facility is included within the

DATA_ERROR part of the exception handler and is implemented using a definite loop whose loop parameter is of the enumerated type.

A major difference in the implementation of this procedure is the provision of default values for the parameters. The two parameters (max) and (min) which are used to specify the allowable limits of the input are not only declared but also set to a particular value. In this example they are set to the first and last values of the enumerated type being input.

The declaration of default values for formal parameters in this way allows the actual parameters to be omitted from the procedure's invocation. Thus it is possible for the procedure to be called with only the first actual parameter specified. For example:

```
safe_get_day( a_day );
```

With this call, the second and third parameters are not specified and are set to the default values specified in the procedure declaration. Thus this procedure call will accept enumeration values of the type week_days in the full range Mon to Sun. It is possible to override the default values of the formal parameters by providing actual parameters. For example:

```
safe_get_day( a_day, Tue, Sat );
```

With this call, the value of min upon invocation of the procedure is set to Tue and the value of max to Sat. This call will now only allow an enumeration value of type week_days in the range Tue to Sat to be input.

It is possible to invoke this procedure to input values of a subtype of the enumerated type specified as the type of the first formal parameter. For example, a variable of subtype weekend_days can be input with the following procedure call:

```
safe_get_day( rest_day, weekend_days'FIRST, weekend_days'LAST );
```

The values specified for the formal parameters min and max are now the limits used in the declaration of the enumerated subtype weekend_days (Sat and Sun). These values have been obtained by using the attributes FIRST and LAST rather than by specifying them explicitly, in order to allow the limits to be changed without disturbing this part of the program. For example, it is possible that at some time a four-day working week will become the norm and a three-day weekend from Fri to Sun will be expected. If this is the case then only the declaration of the weekend_days subtype will have to be changed and this call of the procedure will conform with the new declaration. Although it seems unlikely that the real world concept of a weekend will change in this manner, this example does illustrate the way in which maintainability can be built into a program.

When default values for a subprogram parameter are specified it is possible to invoke procedures using *named parameter association*. The procedure calls which have been used so far in this book (apart from GET() and PUT()) have used *positional parameter association*. With positional association it is understood that the formal and actual parameters are matched according to their position in the parameter list; the first actual parameter is associated with the first formal parameter, the second with the second, etc. This positional notation can become untenable when default values are provided. For example, the default value of the second parameter may be required, but an actual value has to be specified for the third.

Named parameter association allows parameters to be specified in any order and uses the formal name of the parameter to indicate which parameter is being specified. Using the procedure declared above, the following are examples of named invocations:

```
safe_get_day( out_day => a_day );
-- min and max have default values (Mon & Sun)

safe_get_day( out_day => a_day,
              max      => Thu);
-- min has default value (Sun)

safe_get_day( out_day => rest_day,
              min      => weekend_days'FIRST,
              max      => weekend_days'LAST);
```

It is possible for positional and named association to be mixed in a single subprogram call. When this facility is used any number of actual parameters can be specified in a positional manner. As soon as a named association is made all remaining associations must be named. This should be taken into account when subprogram interfaces are being designed. Any parameters which have default values specified should be positioned after those which have no default values.

2.5.8 A common misconception

An assumption which is often made when enumerated types are met for the first time is that the values declared are strings and can be treated as such. Each of the values within the declaration list is an enumeration literal of the type being declared, not a string. Consequently, statements which assume them to be strings are not allowed, for example:

```
red_letter_day : week_days;
PUT_LINE( red_letter_day );
```

The parameter for the TEXT_IO procedure PUT_LINE has to be STRING. The argument supplied in this example is a variable object of type week_days. As the types are not compatible an error will be reported when compilation of this statement is attempted. Likewise, the enumeration values can only be relationally tested against enumeration literals, not strings:

```
if red_letter_day = "Tue" then . . .      -- wrong
if red_letter_day =  Tue  then . . .      -- correct
```

EXERCISES

2.5.1 Implement the safe_get_day procedure within a test harness and investigate its behaviour. Is it totally secure?

2.5.2 Reimplement the 'colours of the rainbow are ...' program fragment used in the section, to produce the output:

```
The colours of the rainbow are red, orange, yellow,
green, blue, indigo, violet.
```

that is, where each enumeration literal is separated from the next by a comma and the list is terminated with a full stop. A general not a particular solution should be provided.

2.5.3 Using the program fragment from Exercise 2.5.2, reimplement the safe_get_day procedure from Exercise 2.5.1 to improve the quality of the user interface.

2.5.4 If Sunday is 'a day of rest'; Monday, Tuesday, Wednesday and Friday are 'work days'; Thursday is 'a day off' and Saturday is 'shopping day'. Implement a procedure called show_day_activity which will have an input parameter of type week_days and output onto the terminal an appropriate message.

The implementation of the procedure should make use of the **case** statement.

2.5.5 A London fire brigade station has four watches known as red, blue, green and white. Each watch works a pattern of shifts which comprises two day shifts (known as day1 and day2), two night shifts (known as night1 and night2) followed by four rest days (known as rest1, rest2, rest3 and rest4).

(a) Produce suitable enumerated type declarations for watches and shifts.
(b) Using the declarations from (a), instantiate suitable packages for the input and output of the enumeration values.
(c) The watches work a shift pattern which follows the enumeration listing given above, with the shift following rest4 being day1. Implement a function called next_shift which will determine and return the next shift. Implement this in an interactive test harness which might produce the following output:

```
'blue watch is on shift night 1, its next shift will be night 2.'
```

Sequence in structures: records

The data types which have been introduced so far have been used to represent objects which have a single logical component. Many real-world objects which have to be represented in computer programs comprise more than one logical component. For example, a specification for a slimming club may require details of a person's name, phone number, sex, age (in years) and weight (in kilos) to be stored. It would be possible to store this information in five separate variables:

```
name      : names;    -- string subtype
phone     : phones;   -- string subtype
sex       : sexes;    -- enumerated type
age       : ages;     -- integer subtype
weight    : weights;  -- float subtype
```

This declares five separate variables which are all used to represent details of a single person within the program. There would be no indication, apart from comments, that they were in any way connected with each other.

The five pieces of information which have been specified to represent the details of a person are not a complete real-world definition of a person. In the real world any person would have a large number of other pieces of information associated with him or her, ranging from shoe size to music preference. The pieces of information which have been declared in the program are those which are relevant to the specification. This set of information would be appropriate for a slimming club but would probably not be appropriate for a shoe shop or a compact disc club.

When any information about any real-world object is represented in the computer it is always a subset of all possible real-world information concerning that object. This is inevitable and necessary; the information stored in a computer is a partial abstract definition of a real-world object. In order for the definition to be appropriate for the purpose of the program a suitable subset of the real-world data would have to be selected. The decision of what information to store about an object is a systems design consideration; the method of representing the selected information within the program is a programming consideration.

In order to write an effective program, the data structures which are used inside the program should be as close as possible to the perception of the data structure as used outside the program. With the five discrete variables declared above, the perception inside the program is of five separate unrelated things. What is required is a method of declaring a single structure for a person which contains the five distinct components.

This is achieved in Ada by declaring a *record* data structure. A record data structure is a user-defined data structure which contains a sequence of individual data components. The individual data items which make up a record are known as *fields* of the record.

There is another, more pragmatic, reason for using record data structures. It may be required to pass to a procedure or function details of an individual person. With the declaration above it would be necessary to pass each individual field as a separate object, but this would require five separate parameters. If a record structure were used then all five fields could be passed as a single record parameter. This will cause the data flow within program structure charts to become less complex, making the structure chart easier to understand.

2.6.1 Designing and declaring records

A data structure diagram for a person record as described above might be as follows:

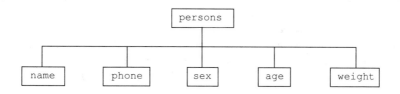

This data structure diagram indicates that a person record is a sequence of five components called name, phone, sex, age and weight. A declaration for this record type could be expressed in Ada in the following manner:

```
-- various constants for declaration of types
space          : constant := ' ';      -- ascii space
max_name_lenf  : constant := 25;       -- maximum no of char in name
max_phone_lenf : constant := 10;       -- maximum no of char in phone
min_age        : constant := 16;       -- minimum age of person
max_age        : constant := 80;       -- maximum age of person
min_weight     : constant := 0.00;     -- minimum person weight
max_weight     : constant := 250.00;   -- maximum person weight

-- various types and subtypes for record declaration
subtype names   is STRING( 1 .. max_name_lenf );
subtype phones  is STRING( 1 .. max_phone_lenf );
```

```
type    sexes   is ( male, female );
subtype ages    is INTEGER range min_age    .. max_age;
subtype weights is FLOAT   range min_weight .. max_weight;

-- input and output of enumerated type sexes see block 2 section 5
package sex_io is new ENUMERATION_IO( sexes );

-- declaration of record data type
type person is
record
   name   : names   := ( others => space); -- name of person
   phone  : phones := ( others => space); -- phone number
   sex    : sexes;     -- sex of person
   age    : ages;      -- age of person
   weight : weights;   -- weight of person
end record;

person,
this_person,
that_person    : persons;                    -- variable declarations
```

Most of these declarations should be understandable from the declaration of data types which have been introduced earlier in this block. Suitable types and subtypes are declared to represent a person's name, phone number, sex, age and weight.

The new part of these declarations is the declaration of a record data type which is capable of containing within itself the five separate pieces of information required. The general form of a record type declaration in Ada is as follows:

```
type record_type_name is
record
   -- fields of the record
end record;
```

In the example above the record_type_name is 'persons'. The fact that this is a record declaration is indicated by the reserved word **record** following the **is**. The list of fields contained in the record follows, each with its data type specified, the end of the list being indicated by the **end record** statement.

Each element of the list of fields in the record defines a single field component of the record. It is declared in the following form:

```
field_name  : field_type;
```

The field_name declares a name for each field in the record; the declaration of the field type is identical to the declaration of any other type in an Ada program. The style which is suggested for laying out field declarations is shown above. The field declarations are indented between the **record** and **end record** markers. Each field of the record is followed by a comment to indicate its usage within the record.

It is also suggested that type declaration names of the types which will be used as the fields of the record are expressed as plurals, allowing the singular form to be used to name the field of the record. Thus the declaration of the string type to contain a person's name is called names, but when it is used in the record declaration the singular form, name, is used. Likewise the STRING type declaration for phone numbers is called phones, which is used in its singular form, phone, when it is used within the record. The record type itself has the type name persons, allowing the variable name person to be used when a variable of this record type is declared.

It is possible, when declaring a record type, for a default value to be specified for any field in the record. When a record type is declared with default values then any variables of that type which are declared will have the fields set to the value specified. In the example above, it would probably be sensible to set the fields 'name' and 'phone' to spaces. This is accomplished with the clause ' := (**others** => space) ', which has the effect of setting all the characters which comprise the string to spaces. There does not seem to be any sensible value to set the other fields of the record to.

The effect of these default values is to ensure that the name and phone fields of any records of type persons which are declared have the name and phone fields filled with spaces. The absence of a default value for the other fields of the record means that the value of these fields is undefined for any records which are declared.

Variables of type persons can be declared, once the declaration of the record persons has been completed. The simple variable declaration shown above takes the form

```
     person,
  this_person,
  that_person : persons;
```

where person, this_person and that_person are variable objects of the type persons. This form of the declaration will create records with values specified by the default (if any).

A more complex form of record object declaration can be used which will declare a single object of type persons and set the fields of the record to specified values. One form of this declaration takes the following form:

```
average_male : constant persons :=  ( "Mr. A Average        ",
                                      "                    ",
                                      male, 34, 65.5);
```

This declares a constant of type persons and sets the fields of the record to the values in the list which follows the assignment operator. The values in this list are associated with the fields of the record in a *positional* manner. The first value in the list is used for the first field of the record, the second value in the list is used for the second field of the record, and so on. Such a list of values is know in Ada as an *aggregate*.

The values in the aggregate list have to correspond in type with the fields of the record which they are associated. In the above, the values in the list have to be a twenty-five-character STRING, a ten-character STRING, a sex enumeration literal, an INTEGER in the range 16–80 and a FLOAT in the range 0.0–250.0. These values are used to set the corresponding fields of the record and will override any default values specified in the record's declaration.

Using this form of aggregate it is not possible to skip the values of any fields, although it is possible to omit any number of fields starting at the end of the record. Thus it is not possible to set only the name, sex, age and weight fields, as the phone field has been skipped. It is possible to set only the name, phone and sex fields by omitting the age and weight fields, which would remain unset (or retain their default values).

A second form of aggregate uses *named* as opposed to *positional* instantiation. The equivalent named aggregate of the example above would be as follows:

```
average_female : persons := ( name   => "Ms. A Average      ",
                              phone  => "                  ",
                              sex    => female,
                              age    => 32,
                              weight => 52.0 );
```

It would probably be sensible for this object to be declared as a constant, not a variable; it has been declared as a variable to emphasize that a variable object can have values specified as it is declared. This form of aggregate has the advantage that fields of the record can be skipped from the list. There is in fact no requirement that the named associations occur in any particular sequence, or that all fields of the record are specified. It is also clearer from the listing which fields have values specified in the aggregate. For these reasons it is recommended that named aggregates are used when records are declared in this way.

It is possible for positional and named association to be mixed in the same declaration. This facility has similar considerations to those which were expressed for positional and named parameter association in the last section. Briefly, any positional associations have to precede named associations, and as soon as a named association is made all remaining associations have to be named.

The values which are used to set the fields of the record do not have to be literals. Any expression which evaluates to an appropriate type and is capable of being evaluated when the object is declared can be used.

2.6.2 Using record objects

The record type declared above has five different component fields. Some uses of the record object may require the entire record to be referenced; this can be accomplished in the usual way by using the identifier of the record object. Some uses of the record object may require the individual fields of the record to be referenced; this is achieved with the dot ('.') operator. The dot operator can be thought of as 'record component of', so the term person.name can be read as 'the name component of the record variable person'. This term is of type names. The rest of the component fields of the record can be accessed in the same way:

```
person.name      is of type      names
person.phone     is of type      phones
person.sex       is of type      sexes
person.age       is of type      ages
person.weight    is of type      weights

person           is of type      persons
```

To set the values of a record object of type persons from the keyboard a procedure called get_person_record could be used. The data flow diagram for this procedure would be as follows:

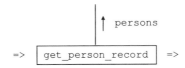

This indicates that the procedure get_person_record exports an output-only object of type persons whose value is set from the terminal. The diagram indicates terminal output of a prompt for each field. It would be possible to name this procedure 'GET'; this is an allowable overloading of the procedure GET as the declaration of this version of the GET procedure would indicate that it will input an object of type persons. However, this would probably not be a good name for this procedure as, because of the prompts, it does not operate in quite the same manner as the other GET procedures. The design for this procedure would be as follows:

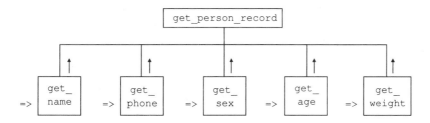

The design indicates that to give values to a record of type persons from the terminal, it is necessary to input sequentially a value for each field of the record. The two string fields (name, phone) can be safely set·using the TEXT_IO procedure GET_LINE. The remaining fields are an enumerated type, an INTEGER subtype and a FLOAT subtype. These fields can be best given a value from the terminal by use of the gen_float_input and gen_int_input procedures developed in Block 2 Section 2, and a version of the safe enumeration input procedure called safe_get_sex developed from the safe_get_day procedure given in the previous section. Using these procedures the get_person_record procedure can be implemented as follows:

```
procedure get_person_record( a_person : out person_records) is

-- procedure for interactive input of person record from terminal.
-- requires access to procedures for safe input of integers, floats
-- and enumerated type sexes developed in b2s2 & b2s5. b2s6 see text.

    space  : constant CHARACTER := ' '; -- ASCII space
    nchar  : NATURAL; -- required for GET_LINE, but not used!

begin -- get person record
    a_person.name  := (others => space);
    PUT("Enter name  "); GET_LINE( a_person.name,  nchar );

    a_person.phone := (others => space);
    PUT("Enter phone "); GET_LINE( a_person.phone, nchar );

    PUT("Enter sex    ");
        safe_get_sex( a_person.sex );

    PUT("Enter age. ");
    gen_int_input( a_person.age, min_age, max_age );

    PUT("Enter weight. ");
    gen_float_input( a_person.weight, min_weight, max_weight );

end get_person_record;
```

If this procedure were invoked with the actual parameter this_person, the following interaction may be obtained:

```
Enter name  Fred Bloggs
Enter phone 123-4567
Enter sex either male or female male
Enter age in range 16 to 80 21
Enter weight in range 0.0 to 250.0 123.45
```

which would set the value of the record this_person to the following:

this_person	
name	Fred Bloggs
phone	123-4567
sex	male
age	21
weight	123.45

Having given a value to the record it would then be possible for the record to be the object of an assignment statement, so the following Ada fragment is allowable:

```
get_person_record( this_person ); -- initialize record
that_person := this_person;       -- assignment of records
```

The assignment operation is allowable as the two records are compatible; they are compatible because they are of identical types. The effect of the assignment can be confirmed if a procedure called show_person_record is available. The implementation of such a procedure might be as follows:

```
procedure show_person_record( a_person : in person_records ) is

-- procedure to display contents of a record. Requires access to
-- i/o for text, INTEGER, FLOAT and enumerated type sexes

begin -- show person record
    PUT("Name   "); PUT_LINE( a_person.name );
    PUT("Phone  "); PUT_LINE( a_person.phone );
    PUT("Sex    "); PUT( a_person.sex, SET => LOWER_CASE); NEW_LINE;
    PUT("Age    "); PUT( a_person.age, WIDTH => 3); NEW_LINE;
    PUT("Weight "); PUT( a_person.weight, EXP => 0, AFT =>2); NEW_LINE;
end show_person_record;
```

2.6.3 Relational operators and records

The only relational operators which can be applied to record data objects are the 'is equal to' and 'is not equal to' operators. These operate in the expected manner; if the two records being compared are identical then the 'is equal to' operator will evaluate as TRUE, and FALSE otherwise. The 'is not equal to' operator will operate in the same manner, evaluating as FALSE and TRUE, respectively.

Although versions of the other relational operators can be declared by the programmer for use with records, in general this is not a good idea. The meaning of statements such as:

```
if this_person > that_person then
```

is not clear. The intention could be to compare the ages of the persons, the weights of the persons, or any other field of the records. If such comparisons are required by the program then specific BOOLEAN functions to perform the comparisons should be declared with meaningful names. For example, a BOOLEAN function to compare the weights of two persons called 'is_heavier_than' could be implemented as follows:

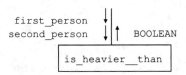

```
function is_heavier_than( a_person,
                another_person : person_records ) return BOOLEAN is

-- function to return TRUE if a_person is heavier than
-- another_person and FALSE otherwise. b2s6 see text

begin -- is heavier than
   return a_person.weight > another_person.weight;
end is_heavier_than;
```

With this function the comparison intended in the statement above could be implemented as follows:

```
if is_heavier_than( this_person, that_person) then . . .
```

assuming that the intended comparison above was on the basis of a person's weights. It may seem a little long-winded to implement this as a function, rather than to implement the comparison directly as in the following:

```
if this_person.weight > that_person.weight then
```

There are, however, good reasons for implementing such decisions as functions. These reasons will be made clear when packages are introduced in Block 2 Section 7.

2.6.4 Records within records

The component fields of a record can be of any valid type. This implies that a component field of a record can itself be a record. For example, the data structure diagram used above could be expanded to make the name field more realistic:

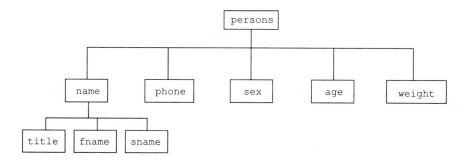

The component field name of the record type persons is now itself a record which consists of three fields: title, first name (fname) and second name (sname). A declaration for this expanded record structure could be expressed in Ada as follows:

```
space              : constant CHARACTER := ' ';
max_title_size  : constant INTEGER := 4;
max_fname_size  : constant INTEGER := 15;
max_sname_size  : constant INTEGER := 20;
-- other constants as before

subtype titles is STRING( 1 .. max_title_size );
subtype fnames is STRING( 1 .. max_fname_size );
subtype snames is STRING( 1 .. max_sname_size );
-- other types and subtypes as before

type names is
record
  title : titles := ( others => space);
  fname : fnames := ( others => space);
  sname : snames := ( others => space);
end record;

type persons is
record
  name   : names;
  phone  : phones := (others => space );
  sex    : sexes;
  age    : ages;
  weight : weights;
end record;
```

This declaration of the record type persons contains a field called name, of type names; names is itself a user-declared record data type which contains three fields, each of which is a STRING type.

In Ada, before an object can be referenced it has to be declared. This applies to data types as well as to subprograms. In the example above, the record type names could not have been declared in the program listing following the declaration of the record type persons which contains a reference to it.

Declaring records within records makes referencing the component fields of the record more complex. If a reference is required for the title field of the name field of the person record, then two dot operators are required:

```
person.name.title
```

This can be read as 'the title field of the name field of the person record'. This term is of the STRING subtype titles. Other references in this expanded structure are as follows:

```
person.name          is of type     names
person.name.title    is of type     titles
person.name.fname    is of type     fnames
person.name.sname    is of type     snames
```

It is possible for this nesting of a record within a record to continue. Referencing a field of a record within a record within a record would, of course, require three dot operators.

EXERCISES

2.6.1 Rewrite the procedure get_person_record in order to input the expanded record structure. The title field should be validated to contain only 'Dr. ','Ms. ','Mr. '.

2.6.2 Design and implement a procedure to display the contents of an expanded persons record structure. Assume that suitable output procedures for all data types are available within scope. Implement and informally test this procedure within a harness, together with the procedure from Exercise 2.6.1.

2.6.3 Produce a record declaration for the following data structure:

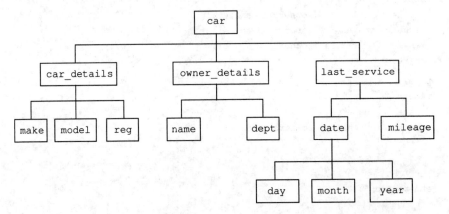

where make, model, reg and name are of suitable STRING subtypes; dept and month are suitable enumerated types; and day, year and mileage are of suitable INTEGER subtypes. Declare two such record variables called MDs_car and demo_car, with suitable specific named aggregates.

2.6.4 In the following partial record declaration:

```
type dates is
record
   day   : days;
   month : months;
   year  : years;
end record;

type patients is
record
   name    : names;
   doa     : dates;
   dor     : dates;
   illness : illnesses;
   doctor  : names;
end record;

deaths_door : patients;
```

doa is the date of admission and dor is the date of release. The type names is as declared in the expanded persons record in this section.

What is the data type of the following references?

(a) deaths_door.illness
(b) deaths_door.doctor
(c) deaths_door.doctor.sname
(d) deaths_door.doa.month
(e) deaths_door.dor.year

What reference is required for the following?

(f) the surname of the patient.
(g) the first name of the doctor.
(h) the month of the patient's dor.
(i) the day of the patient's doa.

Section 2.7

Packages

The facilities available within Ada for the creation of new data types or subtypes are used to create models of real-world objects. These models comprise the declarations of the data structures which are to be used to represent the objects and subprograms which will be used to implement actions which can be performed upon those objects.

It is possible for the declarations of the objects and the associated actions to be included in the same text file as the text of a program which has a requirement to manipulate such objects. Although such an implementation is possible it has many disadvantages, the most obvious of which is the effect upon the size of the program text.

An alternative possibility is for the declarations associated with an object to be implemented in a separate file (or files) which will form an Ada *package*. This package can then be used by a program which has a requirement to manipulate such objects. The effect of this upon the program using the objects is to remove from it the declarations associated with the object; this will make the size of the program which uses the objects smaller and consequently easier to understand.

One way of understanding this effect is to consider the form of Ada programs if they had to declare explicitly the nature and usage of the defined type INTEGER. Before any INTEGER objects could be declared or used in the program, the nature of an INTEGER object would have to be expressed. This expression would require a large amount of program text, following which would be the parts of the program which actually used objects of the type INTEGER. If the INTEGER type were implemented as a package then after the package had been brought into use, the parts of the program which actually declared and manipulated INTEGER objects would become much clearer.

There are other reasons for the use of packages, some of which will be introduced at the end of this section after an example of the design, implementation and use of a package has been given.

2.7.1 An example package

Many programs have a requirement to represent and manipulate times of day in the twenty-four-hour clock format. This format is conventionally expressed as 'hh:mm', where hh is an integer in the range 00 to 23 representing the time of day in hours and mm is an integer in the range 00 to 59 representing the number of minutes past the hour. This requirement can be met by providing a package which implements a type which can be used to store twenty-four-hour clock values. The package will also implement actions which can be performed upon these objects. The name of this package will be 'day_pack', the name of the type will be 'day_times'.

The first stage in designing this package is to produce a list of actions which might have to be performed upon objects of type day_times. One such list might be the following:

1. Display the value of a day_times object on the terminal in the form 'hh:mm'.
2. Set the value of a day_times object from keyboard input in the form 'hh:mm'.
3. Set the value of a day_times object from within the program by specifying the hh and mm parts.
4. Add two day_time values together to produce a resulting day_times value.
5. Subtract one day_times value from another day_times value to produce a resulting day_times value.
6. Apply relational operators to day_times objects producing the expected BOOLEAN results.

This list is not exhaustive; for example, a particular application may have a requirement to multiply a day_times value by an INTEGER (or a FLOATing-point) value to produce a day_times value. The list should, however, be sufficient for most requirements; a program which required additional actions could implement them using these actions as primitives.

Each of these actions will be implemented in the package as a function or a procedure, whose return type or formal parameters are of type day_times. The next stage in producing the package is to consider each action in turn and produce a fuller specification, including a data-flow diagram.

(1) Display the value of a day_times object on the terminal in the form 'hh:mm'. This action requires but does not change the value of a day_times object. The value will be displayed in the format 'hh:mm'. A suitable name for this component would be 'put'. The data-flow diagram for this component would be as follows:

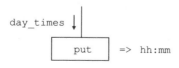

The data-flow diagram indicates implementation as a procedure whose declaration would be the following:

```
procedure put ( a_time : in day_times );

-- procedure to display the valuè of a_time on the
-- terminal in the format 'hh:mm'.
```

The procedure declaration includes a comment which summarizes the actions of the procedure.

The use of put as a procedure name is acceptable as this is the only put procedure which will require an object of type day_times as an actual parameter. Ada will be able to determine which version of the PUT procedure is intended from the type of the actual parameter.

(2)   Set the value of a day_times object from keyboard input in the form 'hh:mm'. This action requires a day_times object which will be given a value from keyboard input. It is expected that the user will respond with an input in the form 'hh:mm'. If input in any other format is supplied, or the hh part or the mm part is outside the appropriate range, the component will raise an exception. A suitable name for this component would be 'get'. The data-flow diagram for this component would be as follows:

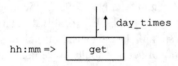

The diagram indicates implementation as a procedure declared as follows:

```
procedure get ( a_time : out day_times );

-- procedure to accept input from the terminal in the
-- format 'hh:mm' and export a_time set
-- to value specified by the input. If input is in
-- incorrect format, or hh out of range, or mm out of
-- range a CONSTRAINT_ERROR exception will be raised.
```

As with the put procedure, the overloading of the get procedure is acceptable as this is the only procedure which will 'get' an object of type day_times.

(3)   Set the value of a day_times object from within the program by specifying the hh and mm parts. This action requires but will not change the hour and the minute parts of a day_times object. It will return an object of type day_times whose value will be set from the inputs. A suitable name for this component would be set_time. The data-flow diagram for this component would be as follows:

The data-flow diagram indicates that the requirement is best implemented as a function of type day_times. The input parameters to the function are of the suggested types hours and mins, which could be implemented as INTEGER subtypes. The header of the function would be as follows:

```
function set_time( hh : hours;
                   mm : mins ) return day_times;

-- function to return a day_times object set
-- to the time expressed in the input parameters
```

(4)   Add two day_times values together to produce a resulting day_times value. This action will require as input two day_times objects whose values it will not change. It will return a day_times object whose value is equal to the sum of the two input objects. Appropriate mapping onto a twenty-four-hour clock will be performed by the procedure; for example, 23:35 + 00:30 will equal 00:05 not 24:05. A suitable name for this component would be "+", which Ada will allow. The data flow diagram for this component would be as follows:

The data-flow diagram indicates that the requirement can best be implemented as a function declared in the following manner:

```
function "+" ( time_1,
               time_2 : day_times ) return day_times;

-- function to add time_1 to time_2 and return the sum
-- taking account of 24 hour clock requirements
-- i.e. 23:35 + 00:30 = 00:05 (not 24:05) etc
```

Ada will allow the name "+" to be used as the name of a function which has two parameters. This causes the "+" operator to become overloaded with another possible meaning. When "+" is used as the name of a user-defined function it is possible to call the function in one of two ways:

```
-- prefix function call
big_time := "+"( this_time, that_time );

-- infix  function call
big_time := this_time + that_time;
```

Of these two methods it is clearly preferable to use the infix notation which is a more natural way of expressing the addition operation.

(5)   Subtract one day_times value from another day_times value to produce a resulting day_times value. This action is clearly comparable with action (4). The function header would be as follows:

```
function "-" ( time_1,
               time_2 : day_times ) return day_times;

-- function to subtract time_1 from time_2 and return
-- the difference taking account of 24 hour clock
-- requirements i.e. 00:05 - 00:30 = 23:35 etc
```

The name of this function is "-", allowing it to be called with infix notation.

(6)   Apply relational operators to day_times values producing the expected BOOLEAN results. These actions will require as input two day_times objects whose values will be compared but not changed. The comparison will result in a BOOLEAN value which will be set TRUE or FALSE according to the expected criteria. Only the ">", ">=", "<" and "<=" operators need to be provided by the package. Ada will provide the "=" and "/=" operations implicitly. The data-flow diagram for these operations, using ">" as an example, would be as follows:

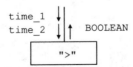

The data-flow diagram indicates implementation as function with the name ">", allowing it to be called with infix notation. The function header would be as follows:

```
function ">" ( time_1,
                time_2  : day_times ) return BOOLEAN;

-- function to compare time_1 with time_2 and return TRUE
-- if time_1 is greater than time_2, and FALSE otherwise
```

The identification of the actions which are required to be performed upon an object and their specification in the form of subprogram declarations have used an object whose type name is day_times. At this stage the way in which this object will be implemented has not been decided. This is deliberate; the actions which are designed for an object should be related to the actions which can be performed upon that object in the real world and not be restricted by the actions which can be performed upon a particular Ada data type. The decision on the representation of the objects should only be made after the actions which are to be performed upon the objects have been defined.

Likewise, the comments which accompany the subprogram declarations have expressed *what* the subprograms will do; they have made no attempt to express *how* the actions will be implemented.

2.7.2 The package specification

The implementation of an Ada package is in two parts, the *package specification* and the *package body*. The specification is the only part of the package whose contents are visible to programs which will use the package. It will contain the declarations of any data types which can be used as objects by a program using the package and the subprogram declarations which implement the actions which can be performed upon those objects.

The package body, which can be a separate file, contains the parts of the package which are not visible to programs which use the package. It contains the definitions of the subprograms declared in the package specification, as well as any subsidiary subprograms required. The package body may also contain any type or object declarations whose use is restricted to the package body.

The package specification cannot be completed until the decision has been made as to how to represent the objects supplied by the package. In this example the package supplies an object called day_times, a data-structure diagram for which is the following:

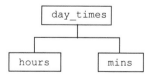

This data-structure diagram shows that the object day_times is a sequence of an hours component followed by a mins component. This diagram indicates that the object can best be implemented as a record declared as follows:

```
type day_times is
record
  hh : hours; -- hours part of day times
  mm : mins;  -- minutes part of day times
end record;
```

The hh and mm parts of the record are shown as being of type hours and mins, respectively; these will be implemented as subtypes which are visible outside the package. The contents of the daypack specification file (omitting the comments associated with the subprogram declarations for the sake of brevity) would be as follows:

```
package day_pack is
-- package declaration file for day_pack
-- b2s7 see text.

   -- various useful constants
   max_min_in_hour  : constant := 59;
   max_hours_in_day : constant := 23; -- max time is 23:59!

   -- subtypes for hh and mm fields
   subtype hours is INTEGER range 0 .. max_hours_in_day;
   subtype mins  is INTEGER range 0 .. max_min_in_hour;

   type day_times is private;
   -- day_times is visible outside the package but the
   -- nature of its representation is invisible

   procedure put( a_time : in day_times );

   procedure get( a_time : out day_times );

   function set_time( hh : hours;
                      mm : mins ) return day_times;

   function "+" ( time_1,
                  time_2  : day_times ) return day_times;

   function "-" ( time_1,
                  time_2  : day_times ) return day_times;

   function ">" ( time_1,
                  time_2  : day_times ) return BOOLEAN;

   function "<" ( time_1,
                  time_2  : day_times ) return BOOLEAN;
```

```
function ">=" ( time_1,
                time_2  : day_times ) return BOOLEAN;

function "<=" ( time_1,
                time_2  : day_times ) return BOOLEAN;

-- functions "=" and "/=" will be supplied by Ada

private -- this part of the package is invisible
        -- outside of the package

type day_times is
record
  hh : hours; -- hours part of day times
  mm : mins;  -- minutes part of day times
  end record;

end day_times;
```

The package specification commences with the reserved word **package** followed by the name of the package and the reserved word **is**. This identifies this as the package specification. The contents of the file are in two parts, the first of which is a visible part which will contain the declarations of constants, types, subtypes and subprograms, which are to be visible from outside the package. It is possible for data types which are declared in this part of the package specification to be declared as **private** or **limited private**, in which case a second part of the declaration file preceded by the reserved word **private** has to be included. This part of the file will elaborate the exact nature of the types declared as private in the visible part of the package specification.

In the example above, the subtypes hours and mins are totally visible outside the package, while the type day_times has only restricted visibility outside the package. The nature of the representation of objects of type day_times is not known to a program which uses this package, thus attempts to reference the components of day_times are not valid. For example:

```
-- assuming an object called day_time of type day_times
-- has been declared by a program using the package daypack

day_time.hh := 12; -- invalid as day_times is a private type
```

The only operations available for a private type outside a package, which are not supplied by the package, are assignment of the value of one such object to another and the equality and inequality relational operators. If the type day_times were not declared as private then any operations which are valid for objects of record types could be employed. It is also possible for a type to be declared **limited private**, in which case even the operations which are available for non-**limited private** types, assignment and equality testing, are disallowed.

Any types which are declared **private** or **limited private** in the visible part of a package specification have to have their exact representation elaborated in the **private** part of the package specification. If no private or limited private types are declared then the private part does not have to be included in the package specification.

One of the purposes of the package facilities in Ada is to assist in data modelling. The package should not only supply appropriate actions which can be performed upon the objects, but also disallow any inappropriate actions which are implicit in the nature of the representation chosen. In this example the declaration of the type day_times as **private** has prevented the referencing of the hours and minutes parts of the day_times record. This prevents a program using the package treating the object day_times as anything other than an elementary object. A program using the package is unaware that day_times is implemented as a record. There are other advantages in declaring types private which will be introduced at the end of this section.

2.7.3 The package body

The second part of the package consists of the package body. This contains the definitions of the subprograms whose declarations are given in the package specification. It may also be necessary for supporting subprograms to be declared here; these functions and procedures are limited in scope to the package body. Likewise, it may be necessary to declare other objects such as constants, types, subtypes or variables whose scope will be limited to the package body.

The implementation of the subprograms for this example package will convert the day_times object into an INTEGER subrange object, whose value is equal to the number of minutes past 00:00. This decision was taken to simplify the implementation of the required actions. For example, without translating the day_times record object into an INTEGER subtype object the ">" function could be declared as follows:

```
function ">" ( time_1,
               time_2 : day_times ) return BOOLEAN is

begin -- ">"
   -- if both hours are equal then decide by using mins parts
   if ( time_1.hh = time_2.hh ) then
      return (time_1.mm > time_2.mm);
   else -- decide by using hours
      return ( time_1.hh > time_2.hh );
   end if
end ">";
```

If the existence of a function called 'convert_to_mins' which will convert a day_times object into an integer subrange object whose value is equal to the number of minutes past 00:00 is assumed. The function can be implemented as:

```
function ">" ( time_1,
               time_2 : day_times ) return BOOLEAN is
begin -- ">""
   return convert_to_mins( time_1)
          > convert_to_mins( time_2);
end ">";
```

This second implementation of the function is simpler and more transparent than the first implementation of the function. There are corresponding versions of the other functions and procedures which could be implemented, where again the equivalent second version is simpler than the equivalent first version. In order for the second method to be employed the package body will have to declare a subtype called day_mins to represent the number of mins past '00:00'. To support this subtype two functions, one called convert_to_mins which will convert day_times to day_mins and the other called convert_to_times which will perform the opposite transformation, will be required. The first part of the procedure body would be as follows:

```
-- package body file for daypack. b2s7 see text

with TEXT_IO, int_io; use  TEXT_IO, int_io;
-- ensure i/o packages are in use, do not assume they will be

package body day_pack is
-- various useful constants
   min_in_hour  : constant := 60;
   hours_in_day : constant := 24;
   min_in_day   : constant := min_in_hour * hours_in_day;

-- local subtype for representing mins past 00:00
subtype day_mins is INTEGER range 0 .. max_min_in_day;

function convert_to_mins( a_time : day_times ) return day_mins is

-- utility function to convert from day_times to day_mins

begin
   return (a_time.hh * min_in_hour) + a_time.mm;
end convert_to_mins;

function convert_to_time( some_mins : day_mins ) return day_times is

-- utility function to convert from day_mins to day_times

   local_time : day_times; -- function variable

begin
```

```
    local_time.hh := some_mins div min_in_hour;
    local_time.mm := some_mins rem min_in_hour;
    return local_time;
end convert_to_time;
```

The method of operation of these functions should be obvious.

Once these utility functions have been declared they can be used to assist the implementation of the functions and procedures declared in the package specification. First, the "+" function:

```
function "+" ( first, second : day_times ) return day_times is

    first_mins,              -- first  day_times as day_mins
    sec_mins,                -- second day_times as day_mins
    total_time   : day_mins; -- sum of first_mins + sec_mins
    out_time     : day_times; -- function variable

begin -- "+"
    first_mins := convert_to_mins( first );
    sec_mins   := convert_to_mins( second );

    total_time := ( first_mins + sec_mins ) rem  max_min_in_day;

    out_time   := convert_to_time( total_time );

    return out_time;
end "+";
```

This function operates by converting the values of the day_times parameters into day_mins values and then adding the two values together to produce a total day_mins value. This value is **rem**med with the number of mins in a day to keep the value in range. The resulting day_mins value is converted back into day_times and returned as the result of the function. The "-" function can be implemented in a similar manner and is left as an end-of-section exercise.

The implementation of the ">" function has already been given. It can be used to implement the "<=" which is the logical opposite of the ">" function (see Block 2 Section 4):

```
function "<=" ( time_1,
                time_2 : day_times ) return BOOLEAN is

begin -- "<="
    return ( not( time_1 > time_2 ));
end "<=";
```

The "<" and ">=" functions can be implemented in a similar manner, and will be left as an end-of-section exercise.

The set_time function and get procedure can be implemented as follows:

```
function set_time( hh    : in   hours;
                   mm    : in   mins ) return day_times is

-- function to return day_times value from values supplied

    local_time : day_times; -- function variable

begin
    local_time.hh := hh;
    local_time.mm := mm;
    return local_time;
end set_time;



procedure get( time : out day_times ) is

-- procedure to input day_time from terminal in form 00:00
-- no format or range checks - invalid input will raise exception

    subtype time_strings is STRING( 1 .. 5 );

    time_string  : time_strings;

begin
    GET( time_string ); -- string GET
    time.hh := hours'VALUE( time_string( 1 .. 2));
    time.mm :=  mins'VALUE( time_string( 4 .. 5));
end get;
```

The day_times get procedure declares a five-character string type and then accepts the input from the user into a string of this type. If the user has input values in the correct format then the hh part will be in positions 1 and 2 of the string, and the mm part will be in positions 4 and 5 of the string. These slices are converted into integer values using the INTEGER'VALUE attribute function. The VALUE attribute function will convert a string into its corresponding integer value if the contents of the string are a valid integer literal. If the string does not contain a valid integer literal a CONSTRAINT_ERROR exception will be raised. A CONSTRAINT_ERROR will also be raised if the string does contain a valid integer literal but the value of the literal is outside the declared range of the subtype.

Finally, the put procedure, whose simplest implementation would be the following:

```
procedure put( time : in day_times ) is

begin -- put
    PUT( time.hh, WIDTH => 2);
    PUT(':');
```

```
        PUT( time.mm, WIDTH => 2 );
   end put;
```

This implementation of the procedure is not quite correct according to the specification, as hours and minute values in the range 0 to 9 will be output in the form '5', instead of '05'. The implementation of a totally correct version is left as an end-of-section exercise.

2.7.4 A test harness

In order to validate the package all the actions which have been designed will have to be tested. This can best be accomplished by the use of a test harness. A suitable test harness, presented with minimal comment, is as follows:

```
-- test harness for day_pack package. b2s7p1 see text
-- note day_pack is withed & used as are other io packages

with TEXT_IO, int_io, day_pack;
use  TEXT_IO, int_io, day_pack;

procedure b2s7p1 is

    time_diff,
    time_now,
    time_then  : day_times;   -- objects provided by day_pack

begin -- time_dem

   -- set time to 14:30 - test set_time
   set_time( time => time_now, hh => 14, mm => 30 );

   -- output a time to terminal - test put
   PUT("the time now is "); put( time_now ); NEW_LINE;

   -- input a time from terminal - test get
   PUT("Please enter a time "); get( time_diff ); NEW_LINE(2);

   -- add two times together - test "+"
   time_then := time_now + time_diff;
   PUT("The time will be "); put( time_then ); NEW_LINE;

   -- relational comparison test
   PUT("The bigger of "); put( time_diff );
   PUT(" and "); put( time_then ); PUT(" is ");

   if time_diff > time_then then
      put( time_diff ); NEW_LINE(2);
   else
```

```
        put ( time_then ); NEW_LINE(2);
    end if;
end b2s7p1;
```

This test harness can be suitably expanded to provide facilities for the interactive testing of the other package facilties. It can then be used in conjunction with a fully developed test plan to test the package formally.

2.7.5 Implementation considerations

It is possible for the text of the package specification and the text of the package body to be included in the same source file. This facility should not, however, be used as during development of the package the specification will be fixed at an early stage but the implementation of the body may require considerable work and incremental development. By maintaining separate files the body can be compiled separately from the specification. Maintaining separate specification and body files also reinforces the conceptual distinction between the package specification, which declares *what* a package will do, and the package body, which defines *how* it will be done.

The construction and development of this package requires three files: the package specification file; the package body file; and the test harness program file. In the example used in this section, the harness represents the class of programs which will make use of the object provided by the package. There are considerations relating to the management of these files in the Ada environment. The files should be named according to a convention which will remind the programmer of the contents of the files. The following convention is suggested, although it may not be appropriate for all compilers:

The harness test file should be named with the extension **.ada** using the name of its program procedure as the filename. In our example the full filename would be 'b2s7p1.ada'.

The package specification should be named with the extension **.pkg** and the name of the package followed by an underscore as the filename. In this example the full filename would be 'daypack_.pkg'.

The package body should be named with the extension **.pkb** using the name of the package as the filename. In this example the full filename would be 'daypack.pkb'.

The reason for not keeping package and body filenames identical is to allow derived files (such as *.lis files) to be distinct.

Before a program which uses the package can be successfully compiled the package specification has to be compiled. The compiler can only determine if the references to objects inside the package are or are not valid, if it has knowledge of the package specification. The '**with** daypack' clause in the harness file establishes that the daypack package will be required and the compiler can extract the appropriate specification from the Ada library in order to check the use of the facilities provided by the package. These considerations are summarized by saying that the harness program is *dependent* upon the package specification.

The body of the package can be compiled before or after a program which uses the package is compiled. The only parts of the package which a program using the package is allowed to know about are those parts which are declared in the package specification. The contents of the package body are hidden from the application program and consequently need not be compiled when it is compiled.

The package body is obviously dependent upon the package declaration; the completeness of the body cannot be determined by the compiler unless the specification has already been compiled. If the package body is not compiled before the program using the package then it has to be compiled before the program is linked.

These dependencies between the various files are enforced by the Ada environment. If any recompilation of any of the files is required then the Ada compiler or the Ada linker will terminate with a suitable message. The dependencies for the example used in this section are shown in the following diagram, where an arrow indicates that the file at the head of the arrow is dependent upon the package at the tail of the arrow.

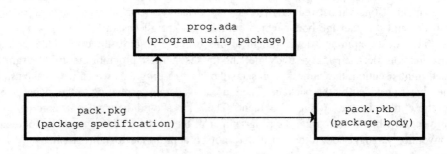

2.7.6 The uses of packages

The example of a package used in this section has implemented a data type whose nature was derived from real-world considerations; it has provided an abstract model of this real-world object. The object implemented within the package is known as an *abstract data type*. This type can be used, by programs which require the type, in a similar manner to the predeclared types.

The package facility can also be used in other ways. It can be used to supply a set of constants and types which can be used by a program without having to be declared explicitly. For example, a scientific program may require many explicit constants (c (the speed of light), e (the mass of an electron), etc.). A single package, possibly called scientific_constants, can be made available which would contain these values. A program requiring scientific constants could bring this package into use and avoid having to declare the constants explicitly. Such a package specification would only contain declarations of constants and types and, as it does not declare subprograms, it need not have a body.

Packages can also be used to supply models of processes, which contain within them models of the process which they implement. For example, a program controlling a petrol filling station will have a requirement to represent the amount of petrol in each tank and the state of each pump. This could not be effectively implemented by use of simple subprograms as the local variables of subprograms cannot retain their values between successive calls of the subprogram. A package can be configured to have a 'memory' which allows the state of the objects modelled by the package to be retained within the package between successive calls to the package's subprograms.

Packages can also be used to provide a collection of related general-purpose functions and procedures, without modelling a particular abstract object or process. For example, most Ada environments will provide a standard package of mathematical functions which can be used to calculate values such as cos, sin, etc. Examples of these alternative uses of the package facility will be introduced in Block 3.

The implementation of packages should attempt to make private as many of the objects used within the package as possible. A package should only make visible *what* it does; it should attempt to hide *how* it is done. In the example package in this section the exact nature of the representation of the object day_times was hidden from the environment which uses the package. It would be possible for the exact implementation of the object day_times to be changed and for a program which uses the package to be unaware of it. For example, the object day_times could be implemented in the package specification as an integer subrange type of the following form:

```
package daypack is

-- alternative implementation of day_times

    mins_in_day : constant := 1439; -- mins in one day

    type day_times is private

-- other declarations as before

private

    type day_times is INTEGER range 0 .. mins_in_day;
```

If this package implementation were used the implementations of the subprograms in the package body would have to be changed. As these aspects are hidden from programs using the package no changes to those programs would have to be made.

This is an aspect of the modularization of program design, which makes modules expressed as packages as independent as possible. It is recognized that groups of modules which interact sensibly with each other (known as high *cohesion*) but are as independent from each other as possible (known as low *coupling*) lead to better program implementations.

EXERCISES

2.7.1 Implement the missing functions ("-", "<", ">=") from the daypack package body and include tests for them within the test harness.

2.7.2 Reimplement the day_times put procedure to allow it to output values in the range 0 to 9 in the format '05'. Hint, the value which can be output is now a selection between a value in the range 0 to 9 and values outside this range.

2.7.3 Reimplement the package daypack using the alternative representation of the object day_times as introduced at the end of this section. Use the test harness to confirm that the two implementations are functionally identical.

2.7.4 It is a common requirement of many programs to represent dates in the form dd/mm/yyyy. Design a suitable package specification for objects of this type.

2.7.5 Implement the package body for the package declaration designed in Exercise 2.7.4, and then test the implementation using a suitable test harness.

Section 2.8

Iteration in structures: arrays

The data objects which have been introduced so far have been treated as single objects. Even records, which may consist of a number of components, were treated for most purposes as single objects. Most programs have requirements which can best be met by using a collection of objects all of the same type. *Iterative data structures* are capable of holding a number of objects, all of which are of the same type. The term *array* is the name given to a data structure capable of containing an iteration of data objects. The data-structure diagram of an array has the following general form:

This diagram indicates that an array is an iteration of single items; each item is known as a component *element* of the array. Simple arrays of this form are sometimes known as *vectors*. Within the array an individual element can be identified by its position. The data type which is used to determine the position of elements within the array is known as the array's *index* type. Each element in the array can be referred by using the element's index value.

When designing arrays for particular requirements the nature of the elements which comprise the arrays must always be known. The data type which will be used to index the array must also be known. The number of items which will comprise the array may or may not be known. If the number of items which will comprise the array can be decided in advance then a *constrained* array type can be declared. The alternative possibility is to declare an array type without explicitly declaring the number of items which will comprise the array until an object of the array type is declared; such an array is known as an *unconstrained* array.

2.8.1 Constrained arrays

In order to declare a constrained array the type of the items which comprise the elements of the array has first to be decided. Elements of an array can be of any Ada data type, including user-declared types. Having decided upon the types of the elements of the array, the type and the range of the index which will determine the number of elements in the array has to be decided. The index type of an array must be a *discrete* type; a discrete type is an Ada data type where each value of the type can be listed. Discrete types include the predeclared types INTEGER, BOOLEAN, CHARACTER and any user-declared enumerated type.

Having defined the two data types which are required to declare the array, the array can then be declared as an Ada type. For example, a program may require an array of eight INTEGERS. This identifies the type of the elements of the array as INTEGER and the index type of the array as INTEGER with the range 1 to 8. The declaration of this structure is best expressed as follows:

```
max_arr_size : constant = 8;
-- largest index value of the array

subtype index_8_range is INTEGER range 1 .. max_arr_size;
-- explicit index range for the array

type int_8_arrays is array( index_8_range ) of INTEGER;

int_8_array : int_8_arrays;
```

The declaration of an array type is indicated by the reserved word **array** following the type name for the array enclosed between the reserved words **type** and **is**. The type and range of the array index then has to be expressed, followed by the reserved word **of**. The type of the elements of the array completes the array declaration. It is recommended practice that the range expression of the array declaration is implemented by an explicit type or subtype, as shown above. The structure of the object int_8_array can be visualized as follows:

VISUALIZATION

int_8_array

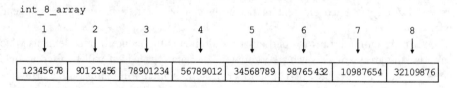

STRUCTURE CHART

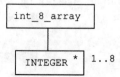

The array itself is of type int_8_arrays; each component element of the array is of type INTEGER and is shown in the visualization as having a random integer value. The index to the array is of the INTEGER subtype index_8_range with values from 1 to 8. When the array object is declared the elements of the array have no particular value, unless an explicit set of values has been supplied. It is not possible to specify a default value for an array type.

When an INTEGER range is used to index an array, the lower bound of the index does not have to be 1; both of the following are valid array declarations:

```
f_array_min : constant :=  0;
f_array_max : constant :=  7;
i_array_min : constant := 25;
i_array_max : constant := 32;

subtype f_array_range is INTEGER range f_array_min .. f_array_max;
subtype i_array_range is INTEGER range i_array_min .. i_array_max;

type float_arrays is array ( f_array_range ) of FLOAT;
type   int_arrays is array ( i_array_range ) of INTEGER;

float_array : float_arrays;
int_array   : int_arrays;
```

The variable objects float_array and int_array can be visualized as follows:

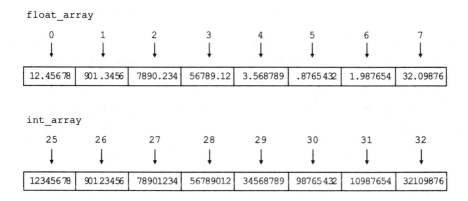

Each element of float_array is of type FLOAT and is shown in the diagram as having a random floating point value. Each element of int_array is of type INTEGER and is shown in the diagram as having a random integer value. The indices to both arrays are of type INTEGER. In the case of float_array the range of the index is from 0 to 7, giving eight elements in total. In the case of int_array the range of the index is from 25 to 32, giving eight elements in total. There is no indication here of why the indices should have such bounds.

The index to an array need not be of type INTEGER, nor need the components of the array be simple numeric objects:

```
max_string_size : constant := 8;
min_str_array   : constant := 'a';
max_str_array   : constant := 'e';

subtype string_8s    is STRING( 1 .. max_string_size );

subtype str_arr_index is CHARACTER range ( min_str_array
                                    .. max_str_array );

type string_arrays is array ( str_arr_index ) of string_8s;

string_array : string_arrays;
```

The array string_array can be visualized as follows:

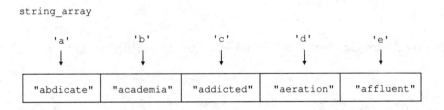

This array is of type string_arrays; each element of the array is of type string_8s and shown in this diagram as containing a random word. The index type of this array is the CHARACTER subtype str_arr_index with a range from 'a' to 'e', giving a total of five elements.

The final example is an array whose index type is an enumeration range and whose element type is a record:

```
with daypack; use daypack; -- see b2s7

max_app_str_size : constant := 12;

subtype app_strings is STRING( 1 .. max_app_str_size );

type appointment_range is ( early, morning, lunch,
                        afternoon, tea, evening );
                        -- enumerated type see b2s5

type appointment is
record
```

```
     appointee : app_strings;
     -- name of person for appointment
     start     : day_times;
     finish    : day_times;
     -- start and finish times from daypack
end record;

type day_appoint_array is array  (appointment_range)
                         of       appointment;

day_appointments : day_appoint_array;
```

The data-structure diagram for the type day_appoint_array is as follows:

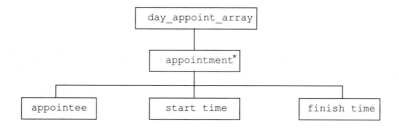

This data-structure diagram combines the iteration notation of the array with the sequence notation of the record. This is congruent with the declaration of the type day_appoint_array as an iteration of records. A visualization of the array day_appointments, with illustrative values, would be as follows:

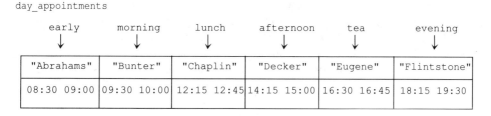

Notice that the naming convention used in this example has used the singular name 'appointment' for the record name of an appointment record. Although the general advice is to use plural nouns for data types, the overriding consideration is to make names as meaningful as possible in the context in which they are used. This use of singular and plural names indicates that the object day_appointments holds details of a number of appointments, and that an object of type appointment holds details of a single appointment.

2.8.2 Array aggregates

It is not possible to specify a default value for objects of array types or subtypes. It is, however, possible for instances of an array to be explicitly given a value expressed in an *array aggregate* as they are declared. As with record aggregates or subprogram calls, an array aggregate can use named or positional notation to specify which components of the array are being given which values. The following array declaration illustrates the form and use of array aggregates:

```
small_array_min : constant := 3;
small_array_max : constant := 5;

subtype small_array_range is INTEGER range small_array_min
                                   .. small_array_max;

type small_arrays is array ( small_array_range ) of FLOAT;
```

It is not possible for an array aggregate value to be specified in the declaration of the array type. It is optional for array variables to be given an initial value using an array aggregate. It is required that array constants be given a value using an aggregate when they are declared.

```
small_array_1 : small_arrays := ( 1.2, 2.4, 3.6 );
-- explicit initialization of a variable array using
-- a positional notation array aggregate

small_array_2 : small_arrays
             := ( 4 => 2.4, 5 => 3.6, 3 => 1.2 );
-- explicit initialization of variable array using
-- a named notation array aggregate
```

The positional notation supplies a list of values which are associated with elements in the array, starting with the first element of the array; not all values need to be specified. Named notation uses the index value of the element to be initialized to associate an element of the array with a value. Named array aggregates can use the **range**, selector and **other** constructs to specify which values are to be associated with which elements:

```
small_array_3 : small_arrays := ( 3 | 5  => 1.0,
                                  others => 0.0 );
                -- explicit named variable initialization

small_array_4 : constant small_arrays := ( 3 .. 4 => 0.0,
                                           others => 1.5 );
                -- explicit named constant initialization
```

These examples indicate that the ' | ' symbol can be used to indicate disjoint elements which are to have the same value, and that the range construct (value .. value) can be used to specify a range of elements to be given a value. Any elements which are not explicitly identified can be identified using the **others** phrase. The effect of using these aggregates is as follows:

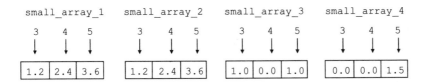

2.8.3 Unconstrained arrays

When the declaration of a constrained array type is made, the type of the index and the bounds of the index have to be declared. There are some applications where this is not desirable; for example, in some situations the required bounds of an array cannot be ascertained until the program is executing. Ada allows for these situations by the provision of unconstrained array type declarations. With an unconstrained array type declaration only the type of the array index has to be declared; the actual bounds of the array for a particular object are deferred until an array object is declared. The type of the elements of the array cannot be deferred and has to be declared when the constrained array type is declared.

Examples of unconstrained array type declarations, which are comparable with the array declarations which have been used so far, are as follows:

```
type int_u_arrays   is array ( INTEGER range < > )   of INTEGER;
type float_u_arrays is array ( INTEGER range < > )   of FLOAT;
type str_u_arrays   is array ( CHARACTER range < > ) of string_8s;
type day_u_arrays   is array ( appointment_range range < > )
                              of appointment;
```

These declarations declare the type of the elements of the array and the type of the index, but do not specify a particular range. The term '< >' which is used to indicate that the array is unconstrained, is known as a *box*. When an object of an unconstrained array type is declared the actual bounds have to be specified. For example:

```
small_int_array : int_u_arrays( 10 .. 17 );      -- 8   elements
large_int_array : int_u_arrays( 1 .. 99 );       -- 100 elements
c_float_array   : float_u_arrays( 0 .. 5 );      -- 6   elements
c_str_array     : str_u_arrays( 'A' .. 'Z' );    -- 26  elements
```

```
c_day_array    : day_u_arrays( morning .. tea ); -- 4   elements
```

It is also possible for a constrained array subtype of an unconstrained array type to be declared. For example:

```
subtype small_int_arrays is int_u_arrays( 1 .. 7 );
       -- constrained array subtype
a_small_array : small_int_arrays;
```

Unconstrained arrays are most useful for producing procedures and functions which have a greater generality. This use of unconstrained arrays will be explained later in this section.

2.8.4 Attributes of arrays

Attributes which can be used with arrays can be applied to an array type or can be applied to an array object. When applied to an array type, the attribute determines the nature of all objects of that type. When applied to an array object, the attribute determines the nature of the object only.

The attributes which can be applied to arrays include FIRST, LAST, RANGE and LENGTH. The attribute FIRST will evaluate to the value of the lower bound of the array's index range and will be of the base type of the type of the array's index. Likewise, LAST will evaluate to the value of the upper bound of the array's index range and will be of the base type of the array's index. The attribute RANGE, when applied to an array, will evaluate to a range expression whose effective declaration is a_type'FIRST .. a_type'LAST. The final attribute LENGTH, will evaluate to an integer value equal to the number of elements in the array. The following are examples of the use of these attributes, using array types and array objects which have been declared in this section:

```
int_8_arrays'FIRST   is    1    and is of type INTEGER
int_8_arrays'LAST    is    7    and is of type INTEGER
 int_8_array'RANGE   is   1..7   and is implicit INTEGER subrange
 int_8_array'LENGTH  is    8    and is of type universal_integer

string_arrays'FIRST  is   'a'   and is of type CHARACTER
string_arrays'LAST   is   'e'   and is of type CHARACTER
string_arrays'RANGE  is 'a'..'e' and is implicit CHARACTER subrange
string_arrays'LENGTH is    5    and is of type universal integer

 c_str_array'FIRST   is   'A'   and has the type CHARACTER
 c_str_array'LAST    is   'Z'   and has the type CHARACTER
```

```
c_str_array'RANGE    is 'A'..'Z' and is implicit CHARACTER subrange
c_str_array'LENGTH   is   26     and is of type universal integer

day_appoint_array'FIRST   is  early   and is of type appointment_range
c_day_array'LAST    is  tea     and is of type appointment_range
day_appoint_array'RANGE   is early ..    and is of an implicit
                          evening        appointment_range subtype
c_day_array'LENGTH   is   4      and is of type universal integer

int_u_arrays'FIRST   is   not allowed
float_u_arrays'LAST  is   not allowed
str_u_arrays'RANGE   is   not allowed
day_u_arrays'LENGTH  is   not allowed
```

Some RANGE attributes, when applied to unconstrained array types, are meaningless, and will be detected by the Ada compiler as an error. For example, the attribute determining the number of elements in an array cannot be applied to an unconstrained array type as the number of elements is indeterminate. The attribute can, however, be applied to an array object declared from an unconstrained array type as the declaration of the object requires the number of elements to be specified.

2.8.5 Using arrays

The commonest requirement when using an array is to reference an element at a particular position in the array. This is done by using an index expression of the appropriate type and within the appropriate range. The value of the index identifies which of the elements in the array is being referenced. For example, using the arrays shown in the visualizations at the start of this section, the following references can be made:

```
int_8_array( 4 )  is of type INTEGER     and has the value 56789012
float_array( 0 )  is of type FLOAT       and has the value 12.45678
int_array( 32 )  is of type INTEGER     and has the value 32109876
str_array('a' )  is of type  string_8s  and has the value "addicted"

          day_appointments( tea) is of type day_appointment
          and has the aggregate value ("E Eugene ", 16:30, 16:45)
```

If an attempt is made to access an element using an index whose type is incorrect, or whose type is correct but whose value is outside the appropriate range, a CONSTRAINT_ERROR exception will be raised.

It is possible to access each element of an array sequentially, from the lower to the upper bound, by iterating through the range of the array's index. For example, to print out the contents of stringπ_array the following program fragment could be used:

```
for this_name in string_array'RANGE loop
    PUT_LINE ( string_array( this_name ) );
end loop;
```

The RANGE attribute of the string_array variable is used to control the bounds of the definite iteration, ensuring that all valid indices of the array from FIRST to LAST are generated. On each iteration, the array element indexed by the loop parameter is displayed on the terminal using the PUT_LINE procedure. When an array object declared from an unconstrained array is used with this facility, the bounds of the iteration will be automatically matched to the bounds of the array object.

```
for this_name in c_str_array'RANGE loop
    PUT_LINE ( c_str_array( this_name ));
end loop;
```

This part of the program does not need to know of the actual declared bounds of the array c_str_array; whatever actual bounds were specified when the object was declared will be determined by use of the array RANGE attribute.

Two complete arrays can be assigned to each other. This can most easily be accomplished if the arrays are of identical constrained types. If the arrays are of different types but are compatible in the type of their elements and the types of their indices, then the assignment can be accomplished by the use of type conversion. Thus the arrays int_8_array, whose index range was effectively 1 .. 7, and int_array, whose index range was effectively 25 .. 32, are assignment-compatible. They are compatible as they are both arrays whose element type is INTEGER, whose index type is INTEGER, and which contain eight elements. The effect of the statement

```
int_8_array := int_8_arrays( int_array );
-- assignment of two constrained arrays using type conversion
```

is to assign the value of int_array(25) to int_8_array(1), int_array(26) to int_8_array (2), and int_array(32) to int_array(7). Type conversion is necessary as the two arrays are of different explicit types.

Slices of arrays can be assigned to each other in a similar manner:

```
small_array_1 := small_arrays( c_float_array( 2 .. 4));
```

The right-hand side of this assignment statement is a three-element slice of the array c_float_array declared from the unconstrained type float_u_arrays. The slice is converted to the constrained type small_arrays by the use of type conversion. This type conversion is possible as the elements of small_array_1 and c_float_array are both FLOAT, the indices are both INTEGER, and the length of both arrays is 3. The effect of the statement is to transfer the value of c_float_array(2) to small_array_1(3), and correspondingly (3) to (4), and (5) to (6).

Two arrays can be *catenated* together to provide a single array. For example:

```
small_array_2( 4 .. 5 ) := small_arrays( c_float_array(5) & c_float_array(1))
```

The effect of this statement is to catenate together elements 5 and 1 of the array c_float_array and then assign this, via type conversion, to a two-element slice of the array small_array_2.

The relational operators can be applied to arrays if the arrays are compatible, or can be made compatible with slicing and/or type conversion and a suitable relational operator exists for the elements of the array. Thus the expression

```
int_8_array < int_8_arrays( int_array )
```

will be TRUE if every INTEGER element of int_8_array is less than the corresponding INTEGER element of int_array.

It is possible for entire arrays or slices of arrays to be passed as the actual parameters of subprograms or to be the return type of functions. It is in these situations where unconstrained arrays can be the most valuable. For example, a function may be required which calculates the sum of the integers contained within an integer array; the data-flow diagram for this function would be as follows:

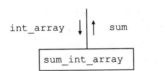

Using a constrained array type as the type of the formal parameter of this function, the declaration would be the following:

```
function sum_int_array( an_int_array : int_8_arrays ) return INTEGER;
```

This declaration declares the type of the array which can be used as the formal parameter of the function to be of the constrained array type int_8_arrays. The only array objects which can be made compatible with this declaration are arrays whose element type is INTEGER, whose index type is INTEGER, and whose length is 8. The alternative declaration of the function using the unconstrained array type as the formal parameter would be as follows:

```
function sum_int_array( an_int_array : int_u_arrays ) return INTEGER;
```

The arrays which can be made compatible with this formal parameter are those whose element type is INTEGER, whose index type is INTEGER, and whose length is indeterminate. This class of arrays includes arrays of the unconstrained array type int_u_arrays which is the type of the formal parameter. The constrained array object int_8_array of the type int_8_arrays has the correct structure but is of the wrong type; it can be converted to the appropriate type by using the type conversion facility (as in int_u_arrays(int_8_array)). Suitable calls of this function would therefore include the following statements:

```
the_total := sum_int_array( small_int_array );
-- small_int_array is of type int_u_arrays, length 8

the_total := sum_int_array( large_int_array );
-- large_int_array is of type int_u_arrays, length 100

the_total := sum_int_array( int_u_arrays( int_8_array ));
-- int_8_array is of type int_8_arrays, it is converted to type
-- int_u_arrays by type conversion to make it compatible with
-- the formal parameter of the function sum_int_array
```

The declaration of the formal parameter as an unconstrained array type allows the function to take as an actual parameter either an unconstrained array or a constrained array. The declaration of the formal parameter as a constrained type only allows it to take as actual parameters arrays of the constrained type or restricted slices of unconstrained arrays.

The second declaration of the function is able to accommodate all the possible actual parameters which the first declaration can take, plus other actual parameters which the first declaration cannot accept. The second declaration is thus more general in its possible application. It is regarded as better design to make functions and procedures as general as possible; consequently, the second declaration is regarded as a 'better' implementation of the requirement. The definition of the function sum_int_array, taking an unconstrained formal argument, would be as follows:

```
function sum_int_array( an_int_array : int_u_arrays ) return INTEGER is

-- function to sum the total of all elements of the array and
-- return the sum.

   the_total : INTEGER := 0; -- function variable

begin -- sum_int_array
   for this_elem in an_int_array'RANGE loop
      the_total := the_total + an_int_array( this_elem );
   end loop;
   return the_total;
end sum_int_array;
```

The use of the RANGE attribute allows the function to deal with arrays of an indeterminate length, implementing the generality commented upon above.

2.8.6 Example array program specification

A newsagent stocks the following newspapers:

```
Sun, Star, Mirror, Express, Mail, Times, Observer
```

Of these the Sun and the Star are not published on Sunday and the Observer is only published on Sunday. The newsagent requires a system which will record details of the number of papers required on a particular day. Initially the system is to deal with Sunday papers only, but is to be designed to be easily expanded to deal with the daily papers. The following functions are required of the system:

To input the number of copies of each type of paper required.
To display a table of all papers and copies required.

The data will be stored in an array of integers indexed by an enumerated type called newspapers. The data-structure diagram of the array is as follows:

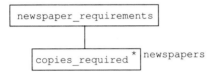

As the number of copies required is an integer value with a minimum of zero, the copies_required will be implemented as the integer subtype NATURAL. The array newspaper_requirements will be implemented as an unconstrained array, of index type newspapers, whose bounds are the entire range of newspapers specified.

The Sunday newspapers will be a constrained instance of this array whose bounds are those newspapers which are printed on a Sunday only. This allows a second instance of the array daily_newspapers to be implemented whose bounds are those newspapers which are printed on a weekday.

The specification indicates that there are only two actions which are to be performed upon an instance of this array: to set the value of all elements of the array from the terminal; and to display the contents of the array on the terminal. The data-flow diagrams of these two actions would be as follows:

The diagrams indicate that these actions are best implemented as procedures declared as follows:

```
procedure set_all_requirements ( requirements : out
                                  newspaper_requirements );
-- procedure to set the value of all elements of the array by
-- user input from the terminal.

procedure show_all_requirements ( requirements : in
                                  newspaper_requirements );
-- procedure to display all elements of the array on the terminal
```

The data structures required for this application and the procedure declarations would be best implemented as a package, with the following specification:

```
-- package declaration for type newspapers
-- b2s8 see text

package newspack is

  type newspapers is ( Sun, Star, Mirror, Express, Times, Observer );
               -- enumerated type for newspapers

  subtype sunday_newspapers is newspapers range Mirror .. Observer ;
               -- enumerated subtype for Sundays
  subtype daily_newspapers  is newspapers range Sun .. Times ;
               -- enumerated subtype for weekdays

  type newspaper_requirements is array (newspapers range < > ) of NATURAL;
               -- unconstrained array type for requirements

  procedure set_all_requirements  ( requirements : out
                                    newspaper_requirements );

  -- procedure to set the value of all elements of the array by
  -- user input from the keyboard.

  procedure show_all_requirements ( requirements : in
                                    newspaper_requirements );
  -- procedure to display all elements of the array on the terminal

end newspack;
```

The body of this package would implement the two procedures; the design of these procedures would be as follows:

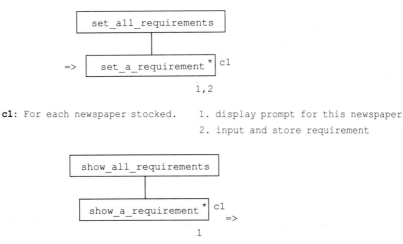

c1: For each newspaper stocked. 1. display prompt for this newspaper
2. input and store requirement

c1: For each newspaper stocked. 1. display requirement for
this newspaper

The program-structure diagrams for these procedures are very similar to the data-structure diagrams which describe the structure. This is not a coincidence; if a procedure has to set or show all the elements which are contained in the array then it will have to iterate through each element of the array to do so. Thus the design of a procedure to process a data object has to reflect the structure of the data object. The newspack package body would be as follows:

```
with TEXT_IO, int_io, news_io;
use  TEXT_IO, int_io, news_io;

package body newspack is

  procedure set_all_requirements ( requirements :  out
                                     newspaper_requirements ) is

  begin -- set_all_requirements
    for this_paper in requirements'RANGE loop
      -- iterate through all newspapers in the array
      PUT("Please enter requirements for the ");
      PUT( this_paper, SET => LOWER_CASE, WIDTH => 10);
      -- display prompt using name of newspaper
      GET( requirements( this_paper )); SKIP_LINE;
      -- safe integer io procedure from b2s2 better
    end loop;
    NEW_LINE(2);
  end set_all_requirements;

  procedure show_all_requirements ( requirements : in
                                     newspaper_requirements ) is
```

```
begin -- show_all_requirements
    for this_paper in requirements'RANGE loop
        PUT("Requirements for the ");
        PUT( this_paper, SET => LOWER_CASE, WIDTH => 10);
        PUT(" are "); PUT( requirements( this_paper )); NEW_LINE;
    end loop;
    NEW_LINE(2);
end show_all_requirements;

end newspack;
```

These two procedures would be required to be called from a program procedure which would offer a menu to the newsagent offering the choice of setting or displaying the Sunday newspaper requirements. For the purpose of testing the procedures they can be called from a test harness which will first call the set_all_requirements procedure and then call the show_all_requirements procedure. A suitable test harness would be as follows:

```
-- test harness for newspaper package b2s8 see text

with TEXT_IO, newspack;
package news_io is new TEXT_IO.ENUMERATION_IO( newspack.newspapers);

with TEXT_IO, newspack, news_io;
use  TEXT_IO, newspack, news_io;

procedure b2s8p1 is

    subtype sunday_requirements_arrays is
                        newspaper_requirements( sunday_newspapers )
    -- constrained subtype of unconstrained array type, index range
    -- limited to those titles published on a Sunday

    sunday_requirements : sunday_requirements_arrays:= ( others => 0)
    -- variable declaration of constrained array with elements
    -- of the array set to 0
begin -- b2s8p1
    set_all_requirements( sunday_requirements );
    -- set all elements of the array from the terminal
    show_all_requirements( sunday_requirements );
    -- display all elements of the array on the terminal
end b2s8p1;
```

The effect of the harness is to create a constrained array subtype and a variable object of that type which is indexed by only those newspapers which are published on a Sunday. This object is then passed to the two procedures, first to have all its values set from the terminal and then to have its contents displayed on the terminal. The inclusion of a menu procedure to call either of the two procedures as indicated by the user of the program would complete the specification.

The program can be adapted for a single weekday operation by the declaration of a constrained array subtype whose index range would be of the enumerated subtype daily_newspapers. The expansion of this specification to accommodate weekly newspaper requirements will be presented in the next section.

EXERCISES

2.8.1 Adapt the newspaper example program from the text to make it capable of storing a single weekday's requirements. Expand the harness program to offer the user a menu to chose which activity to perform.

2.8.2 Reimplement the assignments average program from Block 1 Section 5. The new version should store the number of assignments marked each month in an array, and display the contents of the array as a table, before displaying the average.

2.8.3 Design an appropriate Ada structure which is capable of holding details of monthly rainfall totals for one year. The index type of the array should be a user-declared enumerated type.

2.8.4 Using the data structure developed in Exercise 2.8.3, design and implement:

(a) a procedure to set the values of the array from the terminal;
(b) a procedure to display the contents of the array on the terminal;
(c) a function to calculate the average rainfall;
(d) a function to determine the wettest month;
(e) a function to determine the driest month.

2.8.5 Implement the data structures and subprograms from Exercises 2.8.3 and 2.8.4 within a package and produce a test harness to test the implementation.

Two- (and higher-)dimensional arrays

When the array declaration was formally defined in the previous section, it was stated that the elements of an array can be of any Ada data type. This includes the possibility of an array being declared whose component elements are themselves an array. A general data-structure diagram for an array of this form is as follows:

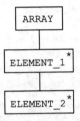

This diagram indicates that a two-dimensional array consists of an iteration of element_1; each of these elements is itself an iteration of element_2. Many of the operations which can be applied to one-dimensional arrays are inherited by two-dimensional arrays, or have corresponding operations which can be applied to two-dimensional arrays.

2.9.1 Two-dimensional constrained arrays

To introduce the declaration of two-dimensional arrays, a two-dimensional array of FLOATing-point values, indexed by an INTEGER in the range 1 to 5 and by a CHARACTER in the range 'a' to 'e', will be used. There are two possible methods which can be used to declare two-dimensional arrays.

The first form of the declaration declares a one-dimensional array type which is then used as the element type of a second one-dimensional array; this second array is thus an array of arrays. The declaration of the type float_2_array in the following declarations is an example of this form of declaration. The alternative method is to declare a two-dimensional array directly, by using two index ranges in the array's declaration; this is shown in the following example as the type float_3_array:

```
min_int_index  : constant := 1;
max_int_index  : constant := 5;
min_char_index : constant := 'a';
max_char_index : constant := 'e';

subtype int_range  is INTEGER   range min_int_index  .. max_int_index;
subtype char_range is CHARACTER range min_char_index .. max_char_index;

type float_1_arrays is array ( int_range ) of FLOAT;
-- declaration of a one dimensional array of float

type float_2_arrays is array ( char_range ) of float_1_arrays;
-- declaration of a two dimensional array as a one dimensional
-- array of one dimensional arrays

type float_3_arrays is array ( char_range, int_range ) of FLOAT;
-- direct declaration of a two dimensional array using two ranges
-- in the declaration
-- declaration of array variables
float_2_array : float_2_arrays;
float-3-array : float_3_arrays;
```

The structure of the variable object float_2_array can be visualized, with random values, as follows:

float_3_array

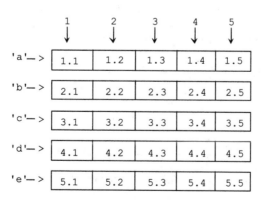

The object float_2_array is of type float_2_arrays; each element of this array is referenced by a single character subscript (e.g., float_2_array('c')). The object referred to in this expression is of type float_1_array. A second subscript can be added to this expression (e.g., float_2_array('c')(4)) and identifies a particular floating-point value.

In the visualization above, the floating-point element referenced by the subscript values ('c')(4) has the value 3.4.

The structure of the variable object float_3_array can be visualized as:

```
float_3_array
```

	1	2	3	4	5
'a' =>	1.1	1.2	1.3	1.4	1.5
'b' =>	2.1	2.2	2.3	2.4	2.5
'c' =>	3.1	3.2	3.3	3.4	3.5
'd' =>	4.1	4.2	4.3	4.4	4.5
'e' =>	5.1	5.2	5.3	5.4	5.5

This structure is more restricted in its possibilities when compared with the structure of float_2_array. It is possible to refer to the entire structure as float_3_array, which would be a reference to an object of type float_3_arrays. It is also possible to reference an individual floating-point value within the structure by using two subscripts in the format float_3_array('c' , 4), which would reference the element with the value 3.4 in the visualization above. It is not possible to reference a row of the array by using a single subscript (e.g., float_3_array('c')) due to the manner in which the array was declared.

As the first way of declaring a two-dimensional array is more congruent with the concept of a two-dimensional array and is more versatile, it should be favoured. The second way of declaring a two-dimensional array should only be used if it is certain that it will never be necessary or advantageous to reference a component array of a two-dimensional array.

The one-dimensional array of appointments which was introduced in the previous section to hold details of a day's appointments can be expanded to a two-dimensional array of appointments which can be used to hold details of a week's appointments. The declaration of a suitable structure would be as follows:

```
with daypack; use daypack; -- see b2s7

max_app_str_size : constant := 12;

subtype app_strings is STRING( 1 .. max_app_str_size );

type appointment_range is ( early, morning, lunch,
                            afternoon, tea, evening );

type day_range        is ( mon, tue, wed, thu, fri );

type appointment
is record
     appointee : app_strings;
     -- name of person for appointment
     start     : day_times;
     finish    : day_times;
```

```
        -- start and end times
end record;

type day_appoint_arrays  is array ( appointment_range )
                            of appointment;

type week_appoint_arrays is array ( day_range )
                            of day_appoint_array;

week_appointments : week_appoint_arrays;
```

The data-structure diagram of the type week_appointments is as follows:

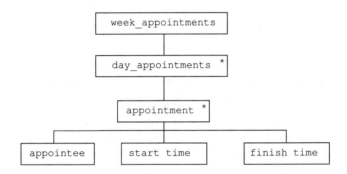

A partial visualization of the variable object week_appointments is as follows:

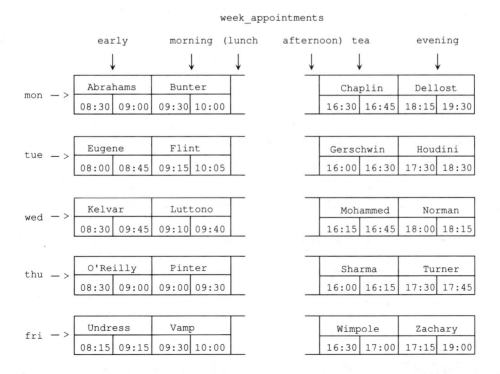

The entire object week_appointments is of type week_appoint_arrays; each element of this array can be referenced with a single subscript of type day_range, for example, week_appointments(fri); the type of such a reference is day_appoint_arrays. As this is itself an array type, an individual element of this array can be referenced by using a second subscript of type appointment_range. This two-subscript reference can be expressed as week_appointments(fri)(tea) which is of type appointment and identifies the appointment with Wimpole from 16:30 to 17:00.

The type appointment is a record type; consequently, a dot selector can be used to reference one of the components of the record. Thus week_appointments(fri)(tea).appointee is of type app_strings and has the value "Wimpole"; week_appointments (fri)(tea).start is of type day_times and has the value 16:30 and week_appointments (fri)(tea).finish is of type day_times and has the value 17:00.

2.9.2 Two-dimensional unconstrained arrays

The advantages of declaring unconstrained two-dimensional arrays are comparable with those which exist for the declaration of one-dimensional unconstrained arrays. Unfortunately, it is only possible to declare a two-dimensional unconstrained array directly by specifying that both subscripts are unconstrained. It is not possible to declare a two-dimensional array as an unconstrained array of unconstrained arrays. Examples based upon a comparable array of FLOAT values to that used to introduce the declaration of two-dimensional constrained arrays should make this point clear:

```
min_int_index  : constant := 1;
max_int_index  : constant := 5;
min_char_index : constant := 'a';
max_char_index : constant := 'e';

subtype int_range  is INTEGER   range min_int_index  .. max_int_index;
subtype char_range is CHARACTER range min_char_index .. max_char_index;

type float_1u_arrays is array (INTEGER range < > ) of FLOAT;
-- declaration of an unconstrained one dimensional array of float

type float_2u_arrays is array ( CHARACTER range < >) of float_1u_arrays;
-- not allowed attempted declaration of an array whose elements
-- are an unconstrained array

type float_3u_array is array ( CHARACTER range < >,
                               INTEGER   range < > ) of FLOAT;
```

```
-- allowed declaration of a two dimensional array, each dimension
-- is unconstrained

subtype float_4_arrays is float_3u_arrays( char_range, int_range );
-- declaration of a two dimensional constrained array subtype from a
-- two dimensional unconstrained array type. This type is congruent
-- with the type float_3_arrays introduced earlier.
```

2.9.3 Two-dimensional array aggregates

Instances of two-dimensional arrays can be given values using named or positional array aggregates, whose forms are expressed in a comparable manner to those used for one-dimensional arrays as introduced in the last section. For example:

```
small_1st_min : constant := 3;    -- min subscript of 1st dimension
small_1st_max : constant := 5;    -- max subscript of 1st dimension
small_2nd_min : constant := 'd'; -- min subscript of 2nd dimension
small_2nd_max : constant := 'e'; -- max subscript of 2nd dimension

subtype small_1st_range is INTEGER range small_1st_min
                                      .. small_1st_max;
-- integer subrange type to declare bounds of 1st dimension

subtype small_2nd_range is CHARACTER range small_2nd_min
                                       .. small_2nd_max;
-- character subrange type to declare bounds of 2nd dimension

type small_1d_array is array ( small_1st_range ) of FLOAT;

type small_2d_array is array ( small_2nd_range ) of small_1d_array
```

An array aggregate to initialize objects of this type can be expressed using positional or named notation:

```
two_dee_var2 : small_2d_array
            := ( ( 1.1, 1.2, 1.3 )
                 ( 2.1, 2.2, 2.3 ));
-- aggregate with positional notation
two_dee_var1 : small_2d_array
            := ( 'e' => ( 3 => 4.3, 2 => 4.2, 1 => 4.1 )
                 'd' => ( 2 => 3.2, 1 => 3.1, 3 => 3.3 ));
-- aggregate with named notation
```

The visualization of these objects is as follows:

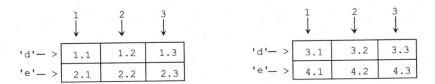

The other aggregate possibilities, using the range construct (value .. value), the selector construct (value | value) and the **others** reserved word can also be used. For example:

```
zero_small_array : constant small_2d_array := ( others => ( others =>0.0));
          -- all elements of the array are set to zero
```

2.9.4 Two-dimensional array attributes

The attributes which are applicable to one-dimensional arrays are also applicable in a modified form to two-dimensional arrays. Each attribute has to be indexed with an integer value to indicate which dimension of the array is being referenced. Attribute expressions with an index value of 1 are used to ascertain the attribute value of the first dimension; attribute expressions with an index value of 2 are used to ascertain the attribute value of the second dimension. Some examples using the array types and objects which have been declared in this section will make this clear:

attribute expression	value	type
float_2_arrays'FIRST(1)	'a'	CHARACTER
float_2_arrays'LAST(1)	'e'	CHARACTER
float_2_arrays'RANGE(1)	'a' .. 'e'	implicit CHARACTER subtype
float_2_arrays'LENGTH(1)	5	universal INTEGER
float_2_arrays'FIRST(2)	1	INTEGER
float_2_arrays'LAST(2)	5	INTEGER
float_2_arrays'RANGE(2)	1 .. 5	universal INTEGER
float_2_arrays'LENGTH(2)	5	universal INTEGER
week_appointments'FIRST(1)	mon	day_range
week_appointments'LAST(1)	fri	day_range
week_appointments'RANGE(1)	mon .. fri	implicit day_range subtype
week_appointments'LENGTH(1)	5	universal INTEGER
week_appointments'FIRST(2)	early	appointment_range
week_appointments'LAST(2)	evening	appointment_range
week_appointments'RANGE(2)	early .. evening	implicit appointment_range subtype
week_appointments'LENGTH(2)	5	universal INTEGER

2.9.5 Higher-dimensional arrays

The concept of an array of arrays can be taken a stage further to the concept of an array of arrays of arrays. This structure is known as a three-dimensional array. For example, the two-dimensional appointments structure introduced earlier in this section could be used as the basis of a yearly diary by using it as the element type of an array type called year_appoint_array; the additional parts of the declaration to accommodate this would be as follows:

```
-- additional declarations to declaration of week_appoint_array
-- to extend to three dimensions for 1 year's appointments

    weeks_in_year : constant := 52; -- no of weeks in a year

    subtype weeks_per_year is INTEGER range 1 .. weeks_in_year;

    type year_appoint_arrays is array ( weeks_per_year )
                        of week_apoint_arrays;

    yearly_appointments : year_appoint_arrays;
```

The references which can be made with this structure are the following:

```
    yearly_appointments                 is of type year_appoint_arrays

    yearly_appointments(week)           is of type week_appoint_arrays

    yearly_appointments(week)(day)      is of type day_appoint_arrays

    yearly_appointments(week)(day)(appoint)
                                        is of type appointment

    yearly_appointments(week)(day)(appoint).appointee
                                        is of type app_strings
    yearly_appointments(week)(day)(appoint).start
                                        is of type day_times

    yearly_appointments(week)(day)(appoint).finish
                                        is of type day_times
```

As the declaration of year_appoint_arrays requires three indices to be specified, the referencing of a single appointment requires the value of three indices to be expressed. A visualization of a three-dimensional array is possible as an iteration of two-dimensional arrays:

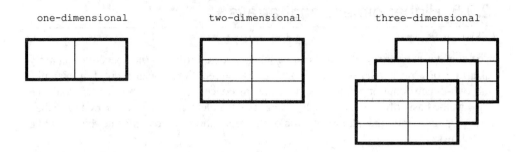

one-dimensional   two-dimensional   three-dimensional

It is possible to declare arrays of more than three dimensions; Ada does not place any restrictions upon the number of dimensions which can be used in the declaration of an array data type. There are, however, reasons for never going beyond three or at most four dimensions. The first reason is cognitive: human brains are capable of holding a mental image of a three-dimensional structure as we live in a three-dimensional world. Producing a mental image of a structure having four or more dimensions is beyond most people's capacity; without a clear cognitive image, the meaning of each dimension becomes unclear.

The remaining reasons are more practical. As the number of dimensions in a structure increases the number of subscripts required to reference a fundamental element increases and the chances of an error creeping in increase. The other practical reason is the usage of space: as the number of dimensions increases the chance of a fundamental element being actually used decreases. In the case of the example above, the chances of having an appointment booked today are very high; the chances of having an appointment booked in the next week are high; but the chances of having an appointment booked in a year's time are low. A different method of representing the information which is not as wasteful of storage space would be a better solution.

2.9.6 Using two-dimensional arrays

To illustrate the use of two-dimensional arrays the newsagent specification from the previous section will be expanded.

The newsagent, having approved the Sunday newspaper implementation, commissions an expansion of the system to deal with weekday (Monday to Saturday) requirements. The program is to be menu-driven and is to offer the following menu options:

(a) to input from the terminal all requirements for all papers on all weekdays;
(b) to input from the terminal all requirements for all papers on a particular day, including Sundays;
(c) to input from the terminal the requirement for a particular paper on a particular day, including Sunday;

(d) to output on the terminal all requirements for all papers on all weekdays;

(e) to output all requirements for a particular day, including Sunday;

(f) to output requirements for a particular paper on all weekdays.

These options will be offered to the user in the form of a menu, which will include an option to exit from the system. As with the newspaper example from the previous section, the newspaper data structure and the operations which can be performed upon it will be encapsulated within a package, which will be made use of by the program which implements the system.

The data structure required by the system will be an unconstrained two-dimensional array of NATURAL integers, with indices of the enumerated types days and newspapers. The name of this type will be weekly_requirements, its data-structure diagram as follows:

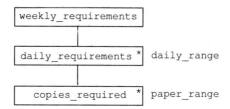

Two instances of this array will be required, one with a daily range from mon to sat and a newspaper range encompassing all newspapers published on a weekday. The other instance of the array will have a daily range from sun to sun (i.e., a range of one day); its newspaper range will encompass all newspapers published on a Sunday.

The data-structure part of the package specification which implements the general array and suitable subtypes would be the following:

```
-- package specification file for type newspapers V 2.0
-- b2s9 see text


package newspack is

    type newspapers is ( sun, star, mirror, express, times, observer );
    -- enumerated type representing newspaper titles

    type days      is ( mon, tue, wed, thu, fri, sat, sun);
    -- enumerated type representing days of the week

    subtype weekday_newspapers is newspapers range sun .. times;
    -- newspapers published on a weekday only

    subtype sunday_newspapers  is newspapers range mirror .. observer;
    -- newspapers published on a Sunday only
```

```
subtype week_days          is days       range mon .. sat;
-- range expressing weekdays only

subtype sun_days           is days       range sun .. sun;
-- range of length 1 expressing sunday !

type weekly_requirements is array ( days range < >,
                                    newspapers range < > ) of
                                    NATURAL;
-- two dimensional unconstrained array type
```

Notice that these declarations overload the enumeration literal sun, which is used once as the name of a newspaper and once as the name of a day. In the use of this package it must be clear from the context which meaning of sun is intended. If the meaning is not clear from the context then the type has to be explicitly stated with a type mark, as in newspapers(sun) or days(sun). With these declarations in use, a particular instance of the array suitable for the storage of weekday requirements would be the following:

```
subtype weekday_requirements_arrays is
        weekly_requirements( week_days, weekday_newspapers );

weekday_requirements : weekday_requirements_arrays;
```

A visualization of the structure of the array variable weekday_requirements is:

	sun ↓	star ↓	mirror ↓	express ↓	times ↓
mon —>					
tue —>					
wed —>					
thu —>					
fri —>					
sat —>					

where each element of the two-dimensional array is a NATURAL integer. The second instance of the array can be declared as follows:

```
subtype sunday_requirement_arrays is
       weekly_requirements( sun_days, sunday_newspapers );

sunday_requirements : sunday_requirement_arrays;
```

The structure of the array variable sunday_requirements can be visualized as follows:

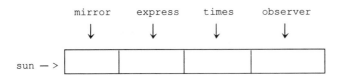

The first option from the menu can be satisfied by a procedure called get_all_requirements, with the following data-flow diagram:

The data-flow diagram indicates that the procedure requires a single out-only parameter of type weekly_requirements. The effect of the procedure will be to set all elements of the array from the terminal.

The second option from the menu can be satisfied by a procedure called get_day_requirements, with the following data-flow diagram:

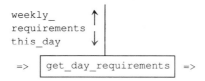

This diagram indicates that this procedure requires an out-only parameter of type weekly_requirements and an in-only parameter of type days. The effect of the procedure is to set all newspaper requirements indicated by the value of this_day. The procedure can be called with the actual parameter weekday_requirements and a day value of the subtype weekdays, when it is required to get a weekday newspaper requirement. Alternatively, the procedure can be called with the actual parameter sunday_requirement and the value sun for this_day, when it is required to get Sunday's newspaper requirements.

The third option from the menu can be satisfied by a procedure called get_a_requirement, with the following data-flow diagram:

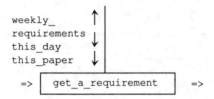

The interpretation of this diagram is similar to the interpretation of get_day_requirement above. By varying the actual parameters which are supplied to the procedure it can be used to obtain a weekday or a Sunday newspaper requirement.

The three remaining options from the menu can be implemented from three corresponding procedures with the following data-flow diagrams:

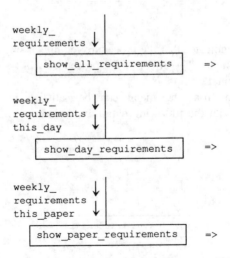

As with the procedures get_day_requirements and get_a_requirement, the procedure show_day_requirement can be used to show a weekday or a Sunday requirement by appropriate use of different actual parameters.

The procedure declarations can be derived from the data-flow diagrams, and the package specification can be completed as follows:

```
-- completion of newspack package specification file

procedure get_all_requirements( requirements :
                                    out weekly_requirements );
-- procedure to set all paper requirements for
-- all days specified in parameter, from the terminal

procedure get_day_requirements( requirements :
                                    out weekly_requirements;
                                    this_day    : in days );
-- procedure to set requirements for all papers
-- for day specified only, from the terminal

procedure get_a_requirement( requirements :
                                    out weekly_requirements;
                                    this_day    : in days;
                                    this_paper  : in newspapers );
-- procedure to set requirements for paper specified
-- for day specified, from the terminal


procedure show_all_requirements( requirements :
                                    in  weekly_requirements );
-- procedure to display all requirements in the array
-- specified, upon the terminal

procedure show_day_requirements( requirements :
                                    in weekly_requirements;
                                    this_day    : in days );
-- procedure to display a particular day's paper
-- requirements upon the terminal

procedure show_paper_requirements( requirements :
                                    in weekly_requirements;
                                    this_paper : in newspapers);
-- procedure to display a particular paper's requirements
-- over all days, on the terminal

end newspack;
```

Once the package declaration has been finalized, the design of the procedures which are required by the package can commence. The processes which were used to design the procedure headings were based upon the newsagent's requirements; they are an expression of *what* is to be done. The completion of the package in the package body expresses *how* these actions are to be done, and should not be influenced by considerations of what has to be done. The package specification should be designed before the package body as what is to be done should not influence how it is to be done.

The design for the procedure get_all_requirements has the following rationale. In order to get all requirements, each day's requirements have to be got; this can best be accomplished by repeatedly using the procedure get_day_requirements. In order to get a day's requirements, each paper's requirement has to be got; this can be best accomplished by repeatedly using the procedure get_a_requirement. These considerations produce the following design:

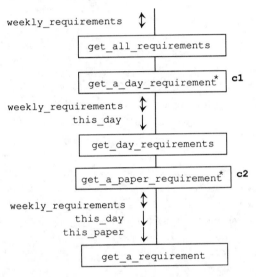

c1: For each day in structure.
c2: For each paper in day.

The design of this procedure, which has to process the entire two-dimensional array, is similar to the data-structure diagram which describes the array. Once again this is not a coincidence; the nature of the data object dictates the design of a process which has to manipulate that data object. The implementation of these procedures would be as follows:

```
-- package declaration file for newspack, b2s9 see text

with TEXT_IO, int_io, news_io, days_io;
use  TEXT_IO, int_io, news_io, days_io;

package body newspack is

    procedure get_all_requirements( requirements :
                                  out  weekly_requirements ) is
    begin -- get all requirements
    -- get all requirements by repeatedly getting a day's requirements
```

```
      for this_day in requirements'RANGE(1) loop
         get_day_requirements( requirements, this_day );
      end loop;
      NEW_LINE(2);
   end get_all_requirements;


   procedure get_day_requirements( requirements :
                                   out weekly_requirements;
                                   this_day : in days ) is

   begin -- get day requirements
   -- get day requirements by repeatedly getting a requirement
      for this_paper in requirements'RANGE(2) loop
         get_a_requirement( requirements, this_day, this_paper );
      end loop;
   end get_day_requirements;

   procedure get_a_requirement( requirements :
                                out weekly_requirements;
                                this_day   : in days;
                                this_paper : in newspapers) is
   begin -- get a requirement
      PUT("Enter requirements for the ");
      PUT( this_paper, SET => LOWER_CASE, WIDTH => 10);
      PUT( " on ");
      PUT( this_day, set => LOWER_CASE, WIDTH => 5);
      GET( requirements( this_day, this_paper ));
      SKIP_LINE;
   end get_a_requirement;
```

The design for the procedure show_all_requirements is more complex as the output is to be in the form of a table. The user interface design of the weekday table which has to be produced by the program, with illustrative data, might be as follows:

```
               newsagents weekday paper requirements

           sun        star       mirror      express     times

   mon     1111       1112        1113        1114        1115

   tue     1121       1122        1123        1124        1125

   wed     1131       1132        1133        1134        1135

   thu     1141       1142        1143        1144        1145

   fri     1151       1152        1153        1154        1155

   sat     1161       1162        1163        1164        1165
```

A data-structure diagram of this table might be as follows:

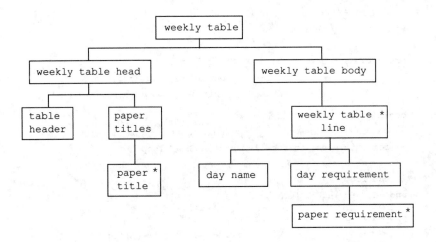

The design of a procedure which will produce this table will have to take account of the structure of the table which has to be produced and the structure of the two-dimensional array from which the data in the table will be obtained. The design of the procedure show_all_requirements is based upon the data structure of the table shown above. The essence of the description of the table body is an iteration of paper requirements, within an iteration of daily requirements. This description of the essence of the production of the table is congruent with the description of the two-dimensional array which contains the information from which the table is composed, allowing both requirements to be met with a relatively simple procedure:

```
procedure show_all_requirements( requirements :
                              in  weekly_requirements ) is

begin
    -- do the table header
    PUT(" ", WIDTH => 20); PUT("Newsagents paper requirements );
    NEW_LINE;
    -- do the paper titles
    PUT("            "); -- twelve space margin
    for this_paper in requirements'range(2) loop
        -- display name of each paper
        PUT( this_paper, SET => LOWER_CASE, WIDTH => 10 );
    end loop;
```

```
      NEW_LINE(2);
      -- do the body of table
      for this_day in requirements'RANGE(1) loop
         -- do day name
         PUT( this_day, SET => LOWER_CASE, WIDTH => 12);
         for this_paper in requirements'RANGE(2) loop
            -- do each paper requirement
            PUT( requirements( this_day, this_paper), WIDTH => 10 );
         end loop;
         NEW_LINE;
      end loop;
   end show_all_requirements;
```

The remaining procedures, show_day_requirements and show_paper_requirements, can be implemented as follows:

```
procedure show_a_requirement( requirement : in NATURAL;
                              a_day       : in days;
                              a_paper     : in newspapers ) is
-- subsidiary procedure to output a single requirement
-- used by both show_day_ and show_paper_requirements

begin
   PUT( "Requirements for the ");
   PUT( a_paper, SET => LOWER_CASE, WIDTH => 10);
   PUT( " on ");
   PUT( a_day, SET => LOWER_CASE, WIDTH => 4 );
   PUT( " are ");
   PUT( requirement, WIDTH => 10 ); NEW_LINE;
end show_a_requirement;

procedure show_day_requirements( requirements :
                                    in weekly_requirements;
                                 this_day : in days ) is

begin -- show day requirements
-- show day requirement by repeatedly showing a paper requirement
   for this_paper in requirements'RANGE(2) loop
      show_a_requirement( requirements( this_day, this_paper ),
                                    this_day, this_paper );
   end loop;
end show_day_requirements;

procedure show_paper_requirements( requirements :
                                    in weekly_requirements;
```

```
                                     this_paper : in newspapers ) is

begin -- show paper requirements
-- show paper requirement by repeatedly showing a day requirement
   for this_day in requirements'RANGE(1) loop
      show_a_requirement( requirements( this_day, this_paper ),
                                  this_day, this_paper );

   end loop;
end show_paper_requirements;
```

The implementation of these procedures employs a subsidiary procedure called show_a_requirement which will display an individual requirement from the array. As this is a common operation of both procedures it has been factored out into a separate procedure. This procedure is then called from each of the two procedures when it is required.

Finally, the package has to be contained within a harness program which will call the appropriate procedures from the package with the appropriate actual parameters to implement the action requested by the user. A possible harness program follows:

```
-- harness program to implement the weekly newsagent package
-- b2s9p1 see text.
with TEXT_IO, newspack, news_io, days_io;
use  TEXT_IO, newspack, news_io, days_io;

procedure b2s9p1 is

   subtype weekday_requirements_arrays is
           weekly_requirements( week_days, weekday_newspapers);
   -- constrained 2d array effectively indexed by mon .. sat
   -- & sun .. times
   subtype sunday_requirements_arrays is
           weekly_requirements( sun_days, sunday_newspapers);
   -- constrained 2d array effectively indexed by sun .. sun
   -- & mirror .. observer

   weekday_requirements : weekday_requirements_arrays;
   sunday_requirements  : sunday_requirements_arrays;
   -- arrays to hold requirements

   choice     : CHARACTER;  -- user's choice from menu
   this_day   : days;       -- day specified by user
   this_paper : newspapers; -- newspaper specified by user

   procedure get_day( a_day : out days ) is
   -- input of enumerated value assumed present
   procedure get_paper( a_paper : out newspapers ) is
   -- input of enumerated value assumed present
```

```
   procedure menu( menu_choice : out CHARACTER ) is
   -- procedure to offer a menu to the user then accept and
   -- validate user's reply. Returns validated character assumed present
begin -- b2s9p1
   menu( choice ); -- obtain user's choice
   while (choice /= 'x') loop
      case choice is
         when 'a' => get_all_requirements( weekday_requirements );

         when 'b' => get_day( this_day );
                     if ( this_day /= sun) then
                        get_day_requirements( weekday_requirements,
                                              this_day );
                     else
                        get_day_requirements( sunday_requirements,
                                              this_day );
                     end if;

         when 'c => get_day( this_day );
                    get_paper( this_paper );
                    if ( this_day /= sun ) then
                       get_a_requirement( weekday_requirements,
                                          this_day, this_paper );
                    else
                       get_a_requirement( sunday_requirements,
                                          this_day, this_paper );
                    end if;

         when 'd' => show_all_requirements( weekday_requirements );

         when 'e' => get_day( this_day );
                     if ( this_day /= sun ) then
                        show_day_requirements( weekday_requirements,
                                               this_day );
                     else
                        show_day_requirements( sunday_requirements,
                                               this_day );
                     end if;

         when 'f' => get_paper( this_paper );
                     show_paper_requirements( weekday_requirements,
                                              this_paper );

         when others => null;

      end case;
      menu( choice );
```

```
  end loop;
end b2s9p1;
```

This listing commences by declaring suitable subtypes of the unconstrained array weekly_requirements which are suitable for holding the weekday and the sunday requirements. Two utility procedures for the input of enumerated values of types days and newspapers are then declared. The details of these procedures have been omitted from the listing for the sake of clarity; a suitable design for these procedures can be found in Block 2 Section 5. The menu procedure has also been omitted from the listing for the sake of clarity; a suitable design can be found in Block 1 Section 9.

The program procedure obtains a menu choice from the user by calling the menu procedure and, within a loop which iterates until the user indicates the wish to exit the program, dispatches control to a suitable routine using a **case** statement. Each branch of the **case** statement calls a suitable procedure from the package with suitable parameters. For some options it is necessary to obtain a day or a newspaper value from the user before the package procedure is called; these requirements are implemented by the utility input procedures defined at the start of the program. For options (b), (c) and (e) a selection is made on the basis of the day specified by the user's input between a call of a procedure with parameters suitable for a weekday, or parameters suitable for a Sunday.

EXERCISES

2.9.1   What changes would be required to the newsagents system if a new Sunday newspaper called the Sport were published?

2.9.2   Expand the program developed in Exercises 2.8.4 to 2.8.5 to cope with a decade's rainfall rather than a year's rainfall.

2.9.3   Design and implement an Ada package suitable for theatre bookings. The theatre has 26 rows of seats labelled 'A' to 'Z', each row having 30 seats. Devise suitable requirements, implement these requirements in a package, and provide a menu harness program to allow these facilities to be used for booking a single performance. Expand the system to be able to cope with a week's bookings.

External iterative structures: the structured file

All the data structures introduced so far have been internal structures; the structure and the information it contains have been stored inside the program and lost when the program terminates. It is a requirement of many specifications that information, once collected, is not lost when a program terminates. The information should be held and made available to the same program when it is executed again, or made available to another program in a data-processing system. This is possible by storing the information in an external structure called a *file*. Ada provides three types of external file: *structured files*, with sequential organization, will be introduced in this section; text files, which also have sequential organization, will be introduced in the next section; structured files, which have direct organization, will be introduced in Block 2 Section 12, where the term 'direct organization' will be explained.

The general structure diagram of a file is as follows:

This shows that a file is an iteration of a file *record*. The record can be of any Ada data type with the exception of the file type itself. This data-structure diagram is identical with the data-structure diagram presented in Block 2 Section 8 as the general data structure diagram of a one-dimensional array. Both arrays and files are iterative structures; both can be iterations of any Ada data type (with the exception of files of files, as mentioned above). So in one sense files and one-dimensional arrays are comparable structures. There are, however, four major differences between files and arrays:

1. An array object has a defined size expressed in the declaration of its index range. Files have no such defined size and can contain an indefinite number of records.
2. Information can be stored in or retrieved from an array at any time. A record in a sequential file can only be read from, or written to, at a particular stage in the processing of the file.

3. The elements in an array can be accessed in any sequence; all elements are immediately available by the use of an index. Records in a sequential file can only be accessed one at a time in the sequence in which they exist in the file.
4. The information stored in an array is volatile, existing only during the execution of the program. The information in a file is permanent and can exist between different executions of the same program, or used to transfer information between two programs.

2.10.1 Instantiation of a file package

Files can be perceived as places where information is transferred out of a program, or places from which information is transferred into the program; thus they are concerned with input and output operations. As with input and output from the terminal, Ada does not supply any particular facilities for input and output to files but supplies a general facility which can be configured for the input and output of a particular data type.

The name of the general package for structured sequential input and output is SEQUENTIAL_IO; and is used to instantiate a new package configured for use with a particular data type in a comparable manner to the instantiation of the packages contained within TEXT_IO. Examples of the creation of suitable packages would include the following:

```
with SEQUENTIAL_IO;
package integer_fio is new SEQUENTIAL_IO( INTEGER );
-- creation of package called integer_fio suitable for use
-- with integer values

with SEQUENTIAL_IO;
package float_fio  is new SEQUENTIAL_IO( FLOAT );
-- creation of package called float_fio suitable for use
-- with float values

with SEQUENTIAL_IO;
package appoint_fio is new SEQUENTIAL_IO( appointment );
-- creation of package called appoint_fio suitable for use
-- with appointment values  - see b2s9 & b2s8

with SEQUENTIAL_IO, day_pack;
package day_times_fio is new SEQUENTIAL_IO( day_times );
-- creation of package called day_times_fio suitable for use
-- with day_times values  - see b2s7
```

Each of the packages created by each of these declarations is capable of being used for the creation and use of files which are suitable for the input and output of the types specified. Thus the facilities of the package integer_fio can only be used for the input and output of INTEGER values and for no other types.

The individual packages provide a file data type whose name is 'FILE_TYPE', which can be used to declare file objects. The package also provides a set of subprograms which are appropriate for use on these file objects. The package need only be created once and the Ada environment will maintain it in the programmer's library, from where it can be **with**ed and **use**d in a comparable manner to the way in which other packages can be **with**ed and **use**d.

2.10.2 Declaring files

Before a file can be used within a program it has to be declared; the declaration of a file object is no different from the declaration of objects of other types. As the file object is provided by a separate package, the package has to be in use for the declaration to be allowed. Examples of the declaration of file objects using the file packages created above follow:

```
with integer_fio, float_fio, appoint_fio, day_times_fio;
use  integer_fio, float_fio, appoint_fio, day_times_fio;

    integer_file          : integer_fio.FILE_TYPE;
    float_file            : float_fio.FILE_TYPE;
    times_file            : day_times_fio.FILE_TYPE;
    lawyers_appoint_file,
    doctors_appoint_file  : appoint_fio.FILE_TYPE;
```

These declarations declare file objects of the types indicated. The file declarations have included the package name, as in the context above the term 'FILE_TYPE' is overloaded. In this example the term 'FILE_TYPE' could be the file type made available by any of the four file packages in use. The term 'integer_fio.FILE_TYPE', which can be read as 'the file type which is contained within the package integer_fio', makes explicit what type of file is being declared. Without this explicit inclusion of the package name Ada has no way of determining which of the four possible file types is intended.

Even in situations where there is only one file package in use, the name of the package should always be specified to make the type of file being declared absolutely explicit in the program listing.

2.10.3 Using files: creating and opening

Having declared a file of a particular type, there are two sets of operations which could be performed upon the file, depending on whether the file is to be used to input information into the program or to output information from the program into a file. The direction of information transfer (input or output) is always expressed with reference to the program not the file.

It is not possible to use a sequential file for input and for output, at a particular point in the program. It is possible to use a file for input (or output), and then, having finished these operations, to use the same file for output (or input). At any instant during execution of a program the file can only be in a state to be used for input or for output; this state is known as the file's *mode*.

Before information can be transferred to or from a file, the file has to be prepared for use by being opened (for input) or by being created (for output), and by being associated with an external file name. A file has an internal existence inside a program and also has an external existence on the computer system's backing storage. The name by which the file is known outside the program is not usually the same name by which the file is known within the program. The name by which the file is known inside the program is the *internal name* of the file and is the identifier which was used to declare the file object. The name by which the file is known outside the program is known as the *external name*. For example, the file declared above with the internal name 'integer_file' may have an external existence on a disk with the name 'stu_mark.dat', indicating that it is a data file which contains student marks.

A new file can be created for output by use of the CREATE procedure. The effective declaration of this procedure in **SEQUENTIAL_IO** is as follows:

```
procedure CREATE( FILE  : in out FILE_TYPE;
                  MODE  : in FILE_MODE := OUT_FILE;
                  NAME  : in STRING;
                  FORM  : in STRING := "");
```

When this procedure is called the parameter FILE is the internal name of the file to be created. MODE is an enumerated type declared within the file input and output package and has the values IN_FILE or OUT_FILE. As a newly created file can only be sensibly used for output the mode should be set to OUT_FILE. NAME is the external name of the file, and FORM (format) is available for implementation-specific uses.

The formal parameters MODE and FORM have default parameters as shown above; this implies that actual parameters do not have to be specified when the procedure is called. The values used by the FORM parameter are environment-specific and will not be considered further. The effect of executing this procedure is to create a new empty output file with the external filename specified. The following are examples of the use of the procedure:

```
CREATE( integer_file, MODE => OUT_FILE, NAME => "stu_mark.dat");

CREATE( lawyers_file, NAME => "lapoint.dat");
```

The style recommended is illustrated above; the first parameter, the file to be created, is specified using positional notation. The other parameters are specified using named notation.

There are a number of problems which may occur, preventing the procedure from successfully creating the file; these will raise the following exceptions:

```
STATUS_ERROR will be raised if the file is already open
NAME_ERROR   will be raised if the NAME parameter is not appropriate
USE_ERROR    will be raised if the MODE is inappropriate for the device
```

An existing file can be opened for input by use of the OPEN procedure. The effective declaration of this procedure in SEQUENTIAL_IO is as follows:

```
procedure OPEN( FILE  : in out FILE_TYPE;
                MODE  : in FILE_MODE := IN_FILE ;
                NAME  : in STRING;
                FORM  : in STRING := "" );
```

When this procedure is called the parameter FILE is the internal name of the file which is to be opened. As this file is being used for input the mode parameter should be set to IN_FILE, which is the default. NAME is the external name of the file and FORM (format) is as above.

The effect of executing this procedure is to attempt to open an existing file with the filename specified and prepare for the first record to be input from the file. The following are examples of the use of the procedure:

```
OPEN( integer_file, MODE => IN_FILE, NAME => "stu_mark.dat");

OPEN( lawyers_file, NAME => "lapoint.dat");
```

There are a number of problems which may occur, preventing the procedure from successfully opening the file; these will raise the following exceptions:

```
STATUS_ERROR will be raised if the file is already open
NAME_ERROR   will be raised if the NAME parameter is not appropriate
                     or if a file with the name specified does not exist
USE_ERROR    will be raised if the MODE is inappropriate for the device
```

2.10.4 Using files: reading and writing

Information can be transferred from the program to the file by use of the WRITE procedure. The effective declaration of this procedure in SEQUENTIAL_IO is as follows:

```
procedure WRITE( FILE : in FILE_TYPE;
                 ITEM : in ELEMENT_TYPE);
```

where FILE is the internal name of the file being written to and ITEM is an object of the declared type of the file. When it is executed, the effect of the procedure is to transfer the contents of ITEM to a new record, which is appended to the end of the file. The effect of this procedure will be explained more fully in the example program at the end of this section.

There are a number of problems which may occur, preventing the procedure from executing successfully; these will raise the following exceptions:

```
MODE_ERROR   will be raised if the file is not in OUT_FILE mode
USE_ERROR    will be raised if the capacity of the file is exceeded
```

Information can be transferred from the file to the program by use of the READ procedure. The effective declaration of this procedure in SEQUENTIAL_IO is as follows:

```
procedure READ( FILE : in  FILE_TYPE;
                ITEM : out ELEMENT_TYPE);
```

where FILE is the internal name of the file being read from and ITEM is an object of the declared type of the file. The effect of the procedure when it is executed is to transfer the contents of the next record in the file, if any, into ITEM. The effect of this procedure will be explained more fully in the example program at the end of this section.

There are a number of problems which may occur, preventing the procedure from executing successfully; these will raise the following exceptions:

```
MODE_ERROR   will be raised if the file is not in IN_FILE mode
END_ERROR    will be raised if no more elements can be read from
             the file
DATA_ERROR   will be raised if the information read is not a value
             of type ITEM
```

2.10.5 Using files: other operations

Other operations are available for use with sequential files. The CLOSE procedure can be used to close an open file. The effective declaration of this procedure in SEQUENTIAL_IO is as follows:

```
procedure CLOSE( FILE : in out FILE_TYPE);
```

The file has to be open when the procedure is executed; the effect of the procedure is to close the file, terminating the connection between the internal file object and the external file. The exceptions which could be generated include the following:

```
STATUS_ERROR will be raised if the file is not open
```

Files should always be closed within a program immediately after they have been used. The use of this procedure will be elaborated in the example program at the end of the section.

The DELETE procedure can be used to delete a file on the computer's backing store. The declaration of this procedure in SEQUENTIAL_IO is as follows:

```
procedure DELETE( FILE : in out FILE_TYPE);
```

The file has to be open when the procedure is executed. The effect of the procedure is to close the file and then to remove it from the computer's backing store, if file deletion is allowed by the environment. The exceptions which could be generated include the following:

```
STATUS_ERROR will be raised if the file is not open
USE_ERROR    will be raised if the file cannot be deleted
```

The RESET procedure can be used to restart a file, and possibly change the mode. The effective declaration of this procedure in SEQUENTIAL_IO is as follows:

```
procedure RESET( FILE : in out FILE_TYPE;
                 MODE : in      FILE_MODE);
```

The effect of the procedure is equivalent to closing the file and then opening it again at the start of the file. If MODE is not specified the mode in use is not changed, otherwise this parameter can be used to change the file's mode. The exceptions which could be generated include the following:

```
STATUS_ERROR will be raised if the file is not open
USE_ERROR    will be raised if the mode is inappropriate to the device
```

The MODE function can be used to determine the mode of an open file. The declaration of this function in SEQUENTIAL_IO is as follows:

```
function MODE( FILE : in FILE_TYPE) return FILE_MODE;
```

The effect is to return the current mode of the file. The exceptions which could be generated include the following:

```
STATUS_ERROR will be raised if the file is not open
```

The NAME function can be used to determine the external name of an open file. The declaration of this function in SEQUENTIAL_IO is as follows:

```
function NAME( FILE : in FILE_TYPE) return STRING;
```

The effect of the function is to return the external name of the file. The exceptions which could be generated include the following:

`STATUS_ERROR` will be raised if the file is not open

The IS_OPEN function can be used to determine if a file is or is not open. The declaration of this function in SEQUENTIAL_IO is follows:

function IS_OPEN(FILE : **in** FILE_TYPE) **return** BOOLEAN;

The effect of the function is to return TRUE if the file is open and FALSE otherwise. No exceptions are associated with this function.

The END_OF_FILE function can be used to determine if an open file of mode IN_FILE is at an end. The declaration of this function in SEQUENTIAL_IO is as follows:

function END_OF_FILE(FILE : **in** FILE_TYPE) **return** BOOLEAN;

The effect of the function is to return TRUE if no more records can be read from the file and FALSE otherwise. The exceptions which could be generated include following:

`MODE_ERROR`   will be raised if the file is not in mode IN_FILE

This function is used extensively to control the input of information from a file to a program, terminating a loop when the function indicates that all information in the file has already been processed. The use of this function will be elaborated in the example program at the end of this section.

2.10.6 Example program specification

To illustrate the use of structured files a program which will accept a series of records from the terminal and write them to an external file will be developed, implemented and traced. The program will then read the records back from the file, displaying them upon the terminal.

The records which are to be used in this example are of a type which will be known as address records, whose structure follows:

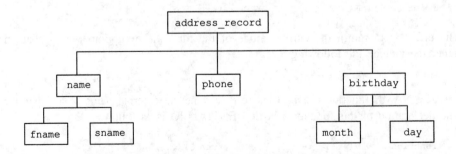

The structure of a file composed of address records would be expressed in the following manner:

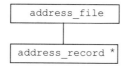

The address_record type will be encapsulated within a package which will only make the address record visible; the implementation of the underlying structure will be hidden in the package declaration's private part. The package will also make available two procedures: one called get_address, which will input an address record from the terminal and export it; and one called show_address, which will require an address record which it will display on the terminal:

The procedure declarations can be derived from these diagrams:

```
procedure get_address( address : out addresses );

procedure show_address( address : in  addresses );
```

The address package (addpack) specification file will be as follows:

```
-- address record declaration file b2s10p1 see text

package addpack is

    type months is ( jan,  feb, mar,  apr, may, june,
                     july, aug, sept, oct, nov, dec );
    -- has to be public as input and output facilities required

    type addresses is private;
    -- nature of the structure is not known outside package

    procedure get_address(  address : out addresses );
    -- procedure to get a record from the terminal

    procedure show_address( address : in  addresses );
    -- procedure to show a record on the terminal

private

    max_fname_size : constant := 15;
    max_sname_size : constant := 20;
    max_phone_size : constant := 10;
```

```
  max_month_size : constant := 3;   -- month string size
  max_day         : constant := 31; -- days in month

  subtype days is INTEGER range  1 .. max_day ;

  subtype fnames is STRING( 1 .. max_fname_size );
  subtype snames is STRING( 1 .. max_sname_size );
  subtype phones is STRING( 1 .. max_phone_size );

  type names is
  record
     fname : fnames;
     sname : snames;
  end record;

  type dates is
  record
     day   : days;
     month : months;
  end record;

  type addresses is
  record
     name  : names;
     phone : phones;
     date  : dates;
  end record;
end addpack;
```

The design of the two procedures declared in the package is straightforward and has been omitted from the text. The package specification file for this package would be as follows:

```
-- address record specification file b2s10p1 see text

with TEXT_IO, int_io, months_io;
use  TEXT_IO, int_io, months_io;

package body addpack is

  procedure get_address( address : out addresses ) is
  -- procedure to get a record from the terminal

     dummy : NATURAL; -- dummy parameter for GET_LINE

  begin -- get address
     -- ensure name and phone contain spaces
     address.name.fname := ( others => ' ');
     address.name.sname := ( others => ' ');
```

```
      address.phone       := ( others => ' ');

      PUT("Enter first name    ");
      GET_LINE( address.name.fname, LAST => dummy );

      PUT("Enter second name   ");
      GET_LINE( address.name.sname, LAST => dummy );

      PUT("Enter phone number ");
      GET_LINE( address.phone, LAST => dummy );

      PUT("Enter month ");
      GET( address.date.month ); SKIP_LINE;

      PUT("Enter day    ");
      GET( address.date.day ); SKIP_LINE;
      NEW_LINE(2);
   end get_address;

   procedure show_address( address : in addresses ) is
   -- procedure to show a record on the terminal

   begin -- show address
      PUT( address.name.fname & ' ');
      PUT( address.name.sname & ' ');
      PUT( address.phone & ' ');
      PUT( address.date.month, SET => LOWER_CASE,
                               WIDTH => 6);
      PUT( address.date.day, WIDTH => 4);
      NEW_LINE;
   end show_address;

end addpack;
```

This package declaration file makes use of a package called months_io for the input and output of month enumeration literals. The demonstration program which will be introduced shortly makes use of a package called address_fio (address file input output). These packages can be created and placed in the Ada library by use of a dummy program, which will ensure that the packages are available when they are required. The dummy program to accomplish this would be as follows:

```
-- filename addelab.ada used to create packages required
-- for address file demonstration program b2s10 see text

with addpack, TEXT_IO;
   package months_io is new TEXT_IO ENUMERATION_IO( addpack.months );

with addpack, SEQUENTIAL_IO;
   package address_fio is new
```

```
SEQUENTIAL_IO( addpack.addresses );
procedure addelab is
begin
   null;
end;
```

This dummy program is dependent only upon the addpack package declaration file. When the dummy program is compiled the input and ouput packages will be created and placed in the library ready for use by the package definition file and the main program file. Creation of packages in this way avoids having to create the packages in the definition or main program files. The dummy file need only be compiled once; a package definition file or a main program file may have to be compiled many times during a program's development. The creation of a package is a time-consuming activity which can slow compilation down noticeably; consequently, the use of a dummy program file to create the required packages can assist in program development.

The design for the main program, based on the specification would be as follows:

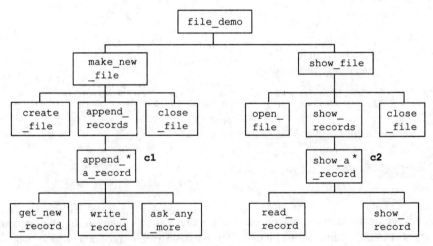

c1: While user indicates more records to write.
c2: While records remain on the file.

The implementation of these designs in the main program follows:

```
-- address demonstration program b2s10 see text
with TEXT_IO, addpack, address_fio;
use  TEXT_IO, addpack, address_fio;
procedure b2s10p1 is

     addfile     : address_fio.FILE_TYPE;

     procedure make_new_file( a_file : in out
                        address_fio.FILE_TYPE) is
```

```
        an_address : addresses;
        any_more   : CHARACTER := 'Y';

    begin -- make new file
        CREATE( a_file, MODE => OUT_FILE,
                        NAME => "address.dat");

        while((any_more = 'Y') or (any_more = 'y' )) loop
            get_address( an_address );
            WRITE( a_file, an_address);

            PUT("any more (y/n) ");
            GET( any_more ); SKIP_LINE;
        end loop;
        CLOSE( a_file );
    end make_new_file;

    procedure show_file ( a_file : in out
                          address_fio.FILE_TYPE ) is

        an_address : addresses;

    begin -- show file
        OPEN( a_file, MODE => IN_FILE,
                      NAME => "address.dat");

        while ( not (END_OF_FILE( a_file))) loop
            READ( a_file, an_address );
            show_address( an_address );
        end loop;

        CLOSE( a_file );
    end show_file;
begin -- b2s10p1
    make_new_file( addfile );
    show_file(  addfile );
end b2s10p1;
```

The effect of this program when it is executed will be considered in the following trace.

2.10.7 Example program trace

The program commences with the call of the procedure make_new_file. The state of the system at the point in procedure make_file when the address_fio.CREATE procedure has just been executed can be visualized as follows:

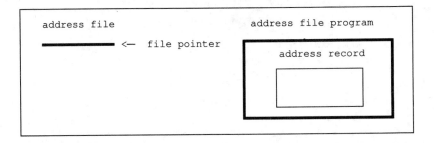

This diagram shows an empty address file with its file pointer pointing to the start of the file. A file pointer is the place in a file to which the next record will be written if the file is being used for output, or read from if the file is being used for input. The diagram also shows the address file program which contains an address record, which at this point in the program has no value. The effect of the execution of procedure get_address is to initialize the address record from the terminal. If it is assumed that the user will input details of a person called Adam, the state of the system following execution of the get_address procedure can be visualized as follows:

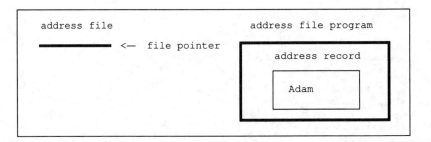

The next statement to be executed is the call of address.fio.WRITE procedure, which will append a new record to the end of the file and set its value to the contents of the address record in the program. The state of the system following the execution of the WRITE procedure can be visualized as follows:

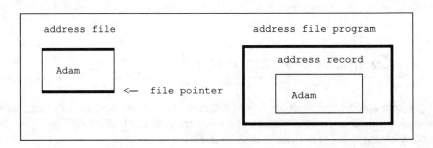

The file now contains a single record containing Adam's details; the file pointer is shown at the end of the file ready for another record to be appended. If it is assumed that the user indicates that another record is to be entered, and that the get_record procedure is executed for a second time, with an input of Beth's details, the state of the system can now be visualized as follows:

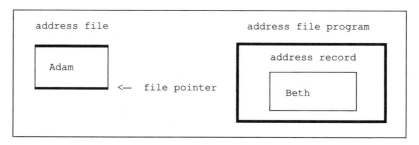

which, after the second execution of the WRITE procedure, becomes:

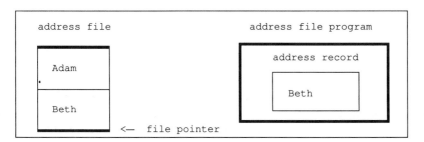

This process will continue, within the iterative program structure, transferring a sequence of records from the terminal to the file via the address record. The only limit to the number of records which can be stored in the file is the amount of backing storage space available. For the purposes of this trace, the process will be assumed to continue with an indefinite number of records, finishing with Zack's record. The state of the system when the file is closed is shown in the following:

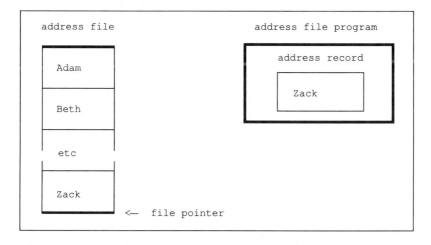

Closing the file terminates the procedure make_new file, and program execution continues with the call of the show_file procedure; show_file commences by opening the address file for input. The state of the system immediately after the file has been opened can be visualized as follows:

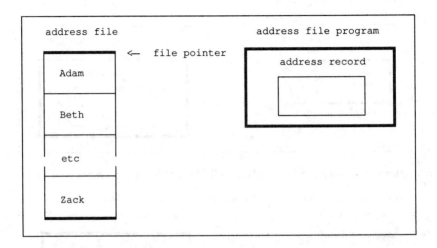

The diagram shows that the file pointer is at the start of the file ready to access the first record of the file, while the address record variable has no particular value. The condition controlling entry to the while loop **not**(end_of_file) is TRUE. The file pointer is not at the end of file, causing the end of file function to return FALSE, which is **not**ted to TRUE. The effect of the call of the address.fio.READ procedure is to transfer the contents of the file record pointed to by the file pointer, into the address record within the program, and to advance the file pointer. The state of the system at this point is as follows:

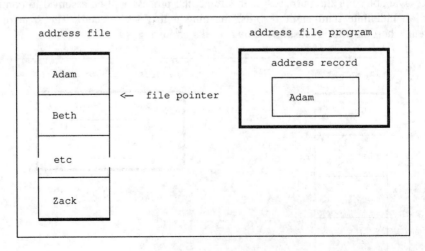

The show_address procedure is then executed, which will have the effect of displaying the contents of the address record on the terminal. The loop control condition is then evaluated again and, as the end of file condition is still not TRUE, the loop will iterate again, reading the next record from the file into the address record and advancing the file pointer by one record. The state of the system can now be visualized as:

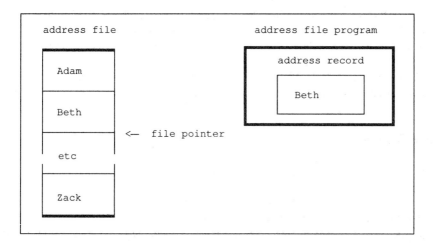

The contents of the address record variable within the program have been overwritten with the contents of the record which has just been input from the file (Beth). The first record (Adam) which was accessible has been lost and is no longer available to the program, although it still exists on the file.

The rest of the file can be processed iteratively, with each record being read from the file into the address record variable and then displayed on the terminal. After the last record (Zack) has been displayed, the system is in the state shown below:

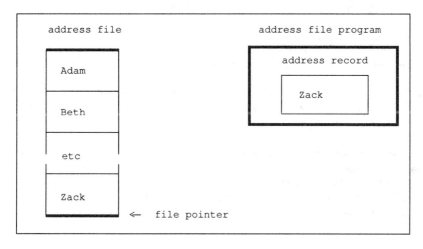

The last record of the file (Zack) has already been transferred from the file to the file buffer variable and subsequently displayed. The file pointer is now at the end-of-file position. If the READ procedure were attempted at this stage an exception would be raised as there is no next record to transfer. This will not happen as the END_OF_FILE function controlling the loop will now evaluate as TRUE, preventing another iteration of the loop.

The termination of the loop after all records have been read from the file and displayed on the terminal causes the CLOSE procedure to be executed, closing the file. Following this action the show_file procedure terminates and then the program itself will terminate.

The designs and implementations which have been presented here can be used as the basis for other designs which have a requirement to create or process sequential files.

EXERCISES

2.10.1 You are given the following specification:

> A warehouse consists of a number of storage locations called *bins*. Each bin is identified by a letter in the range 'A' to 'Z' and a number in the range 1 to 120. Each bin has to have a description of at most 25 characters to describe its contents and an integer value in the range 0 to 500 for the number of units it contains.

Produce a package specification which will make available a bin record which can contain all the information required to describe an individual bin and two procedures. The first procedure is to be called get_bin_details, and will input details of a bin record from the terminal. The second procedure is to be called show_bin_details, and will display the contents of a bin record on the terminal.

2.10.2 Produce a package definition file for the package specification from Exercise 2.10.1.

2.10.3 Assuming that the package from Exercises 2.10.1 and 2.10.2 exists, write a program which will create a suitable SEQUENTIAL_IO package for bin records. The program should then create a bin file and write twenty bin records to it.

2.10.4 Adapt the program from Exercise 2.10.3 to produce a second program which will open the file created and display the bin records on the terminal. Do not assume that the file contains only 20 records.

2.10.5 A common program requirement is to ask the user to input a filename and then attempt to open the file specified. A common problem is that the file specified by the user cannot be opened. Using the NAME_ERROR exception, design and implement a procedure called open_user_file which will repeatedly prompt the user for a filename, until a suitable filename has been specified and the file has been opened. Test this procedure by including it in the program developed in Exercise 2.10.4.

External iterative structures: the text file

Earlier in this block the STRING data type, which is effectively a one-dimensional array of CHARACTER, was introduced. Ada provides operations on strings which have no comparable operations which can be applied to other one-dimensional array data types. Ada provides these operations, which make the STRING data type a special data type, different from other one-dimensional array types, because of the wide applicability of strings in many programs.

Ada also treats the external iterative structure sequential file of CHARACTER differently from other sequential files. Again it does this because of the wide applicability of this type of file. This type of file is commonly known as a *text file* and is predeclared by Ada in the package TEXT_IO.

This file type has two main applications, both of which are external to Ada programs. The first of these is that when a file of characters is sent to a printer or to a VDU it can be easily read and understood by humans. Many applications call for a report to be produced, which will be destined for the printer or screen; the appropriate type for this output is file of CHARACTER.

Program output which is intended for this use can be written from the Ada program to a text file. When the program terminates, this file can be sent to a printer to obtain a permanent (hard) copy of the report; alternatively the file can then be sent to a VDU so that the program output can be read on the screen.

This is not the case for structured files. When information is sent from an Ada program to a structured file there is no requirement that the information is stored in a human-readable format. The information will be stored in the file in a manner which is efficient for the compiler; this format is not defined by Ada and may differ from compiler to compiler.

The other applicability of the text file is to facilitate communication between two or more programs in a system. As mentioned above, the output from a structured file will be in a condensed undefined format which may differ from compiler to compiler. Thus it cannot be guaranteed that a structured file produced as output from one program can be easily used as input by another program.

The text file is a format which can be used by different programs produced by different Ada compilers or even written in different programming languages, to allow information to be interchanged between them. This is a consequence of the standardization of the text file which uses the ASCII coding system. Information stored in a file in this format can be used and understood by a wide range of computer systems.

Two special text files have already been used extensively in this book. Input from the terminal is assumed by Ada to come from a text file known as standard_input; output from an Ada program to the terminal is assumed to be written to a file known as standard_output. These files are special as they do not have to be opened or created and cannot be closed or deleted. The facilities which have been described for the input and output of text information to and from the terminal, primarily the overloaded GET and PUT procedures, have additional overloadings which allow them to be used with external text files.

2.11.1 The general format of a text file

The general format of an Ada text file is as follows:

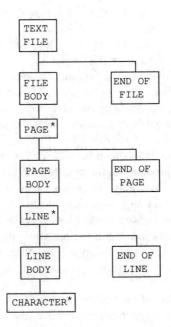

This shows that a text file consists of the body of the file followed by an end-of-file marker. The body of the file consists of an iteration of pages, where each page consists of a page body followed by an end-of-page marker. Each page body consists of an iteration of lines, where each line consists of a line body followed by an end-of-line marker. Each line body consists of a sequence of characters.

This can be used as the description of any text, such as the text which makes up a section of this book. The three end markers, indicating the end of line, end of page and end of file, are not visible when the file is printed or displayed, but are present on the file when it is used by an Ada program. The existence of these markers will have to be taken into account when a program is designed which will use a text file for input or output.

2.11.2 Text file management

The package TEXT_IO contains facilities for the declaration and manipulation of text files, and also GET and PUT procedures which are suitable for the input and output of CHARACTER and STRING values. The additional packages contained within TEXT_IO (the packages INTEGER_IO, FLOAT_IO and ENUMERATION_IO) contain additional GET and PUT procedures for the input and output of additional data types in a text format.

As the facilities for declaring and using text files are contained within the package TEXT_IO, a text file can only be declared and used by the parts of a program where TEXT_IO is in use. The declaration of a text file is very similar to the declaration of structured files introduced in the previous section:

```
with TEXT_IO; use TEXT_IO;

    filein   : TEXT_IO.FILE_TYPE;
    fileout  : TEXT_IO.FILE_TYPE;
```

This program fragment declares two text files, one called filein whose name suggests that it will be used for input and one called fileout which will be used for output. The explicit use of the package name is advocated to make absolutely clear the type of file being declared. The phrase 'TEXT_IO.FILE_TYPE' should be used even when TEXT_IO is the only file package in use and the phrase 'FILE_TYPE' is therefore an unambiguous reference to a text file, as in this example.

As text files are sequential files they can only be used for input or for output at any particular point in a program. The file manipulation subprograms, which were introduced in the previous section for use with sequential files, have corresponding procedures and functions in the package TEXT_IO which can be used with text files. These procedures and functions are as follows:

procedures: OPEN   CREATE   CLOSE   DELETE   RESET

functions: MODE   NAME   IS_OPEN END_OF_FILE

The procedures READ and WRITE have no directly comparable procedures for use with text files; the procedures GET and PUT are used instead. For every GET and PUT procedure which was introduced earlier in this block for the input and output of text information to and from the terminal, there is a corresponding GET procedure which can be used to input information from an external text file and a corresponding PUT procedure to output information to an external text file.

The only difference between the versions of these procedures for input and output to the terminal and for input and output to a text file is the provision of an additional parameter which identifies the external file which is to be used. This parameter is always the first parameter in the parameter list and has the formal name FILE. For example, the effective declaration of the GET and PUT procedures provided in the general package FLOAT_IO, which is contained within TEXT_IO, when configured for input and output of FLOAT values, is as follows:

```
GET( ITEM : out FLOAT );          -- input from terminal

GET( FILE : in  FILE_TYPE;
     ITEM : out FLOAT ):          -- input from file

PUT( ITEM : in  FLOAT;            -- output to terminal
     FORE : in  general_integer;
     AFT  : in  general_integer;
     EXP  : in  general_integer);

PUT( FILE : in  FILE_TYPE;        -- output to file
     ITEM : in  FLOAT;
     FORE : in  general_integer;
     AFT  : in  general_integer;
     EXP  : in  general_integer);
```

There are additional subprograms provided by TEXT_IO which can only be used on text files:

procedures:	SET_LINE_LENGTH	SET_PAGE_LENGTH	NEW_LINE
	NEW-PAGE	SKIP_LINE	SKIP_PAGE
	SET_COL	SET_LINE	

functions:	END_OF_LINE	END_OF_PAGE	LINE_LENGTH		
	PAGE_LENGTH	COL	LINE	PAGE	

These procedures and functions are provided by Ada to control the format of a text file in terms of the file's page and line structure. To specify a value for the number of lines on a page or to specify a value for the number of characters on a line, the package

TEXT_IO provides a new INTEGER data type whose declaration in TEXT_IO is as follows:

```
type    COUNT is range 0 .. { implementation defined };
subtype POSITIVE_COUNT is COUNT range 1 .. COUNT'LAST;
```

The precise value used for '{ implementation defined }' in the declaration of the new INTEGER type COUNT differs from compiler to compiler. The actual value which is used by a compiler can be determined by use of the attribute LAST, as shown in the declaration of the subtype POSITIVE_COUNT.

The procedures SET_LINE_LENGTH and SET_PAGE_LENGTH require an optional file parameter followed by a parameter of type POSITIVE_COUNT. The effect is to specify the number of characters on one line of the file or to specify the number of lines on each page of the file. If a value of 0 is specified then the line length or the page length is *unbounded*, meaning that new lines and new pages are only output when explicitly requested. By default text files are assumed unbounded when opened until these procedures are called.

The functions LINE_LENGTH and PAGE_LENGTH require an optional file parameter and will return a value of type COUNT, which is the current value of the line length or page length of the file. A value of zero indicates that the line or page is unbounded.

The procedures NEW_LINE and NEW_PAGE can take an optional file parameter. The effect is to explicitly force an end-of-line marker or an end-of-page marker to be output to the specified file, which has to be open in OUT_FILE mode. The NEW_LINE procedure can additionally take a second optional parameter with the formal name SPACING of type POSITIVE_COUNT to force the output of more than one new line with a single call.

The procedures SKIP_LINE and SKIP_PAGE require an optional file parameter. The effect is to position the file pointer at the end of the current line or page on the specified file, which has to be open in IN_FILE mode. The SKIP_LINE procedure can additionally take a second optional parameter with the formal name SPACING of type POSITIVE_COUNT, allowing it to skip multiple lines.

The procedures SET_COL and SET_LINE require an optional file parameter and a non-optional POSITIVE_COUNT parameter. The effect is to output sufficient space or new-line characters to the file, if it is open in OUT_FILE mode, until the specified column or line is reached. If the file is open in IN_FILE mode then sufficient characters are input from the file and discarded, until the specified column or line is reached.

The functions END_OF_PAGE and END_OF_LINE require an optional file parameter and return a BOOLEAN value. The value returned is FALSE unless the file pointer is at the end of line or the end of page, in which case TRUE is returned.

The functions COL, LINE and PAGE require an optional file parameter and return a POSITIVE_COUNT value which is the value of the current page, line or column position of the file pointer.

The effective declaration of these subprograms can be found in Appendix C.

2.11.3 Reading and writing text files

To demonstrate the use of text files a program will be developed which will input information from a text file, process it and output the processed information to a second text file. A text file of student records, which may have been produced by another Ada program, or by a program written in another programming language, or even produced by a word processor, is available with the following format:

```
Student Name    Assignments  Exam

Ade Abrahams    85           90
Bessie Bunter   32           40

    ...         ...          ...

Zac Zacharia    68           55
```

The external name of this file is 'oldstu.dat'; it contains a line for each student on a course, starting at line 3 of the file. Each line contains three pieces of information: the student's name, which starts at column 3 of the line and is at most twenty characters in length; an integer assignment score in the range 0 to 100; and an integer exam score in the same range.

It is required to process the file to produce a new output file called 'newstu.dat' which contains the same information in a similar format, with the addition of the student's average score at the end of each line. The average score is determined by a forty-sixty weighing of assignment and exam score and is to be displayed to one decimal place of accuracy. Using the input file shown above the corresponding output file would be as follows:

```
                   STUDENT RESULTS REPORT

Student Name    Assignments  Exams  Average

Ade Abrahams    85           90     88.0

Bessie Bunter   32           40     36.8

    ...         ...          ...    ...

Zac Zacharia    68           55     60.2
```

A suitable design for this program follows:

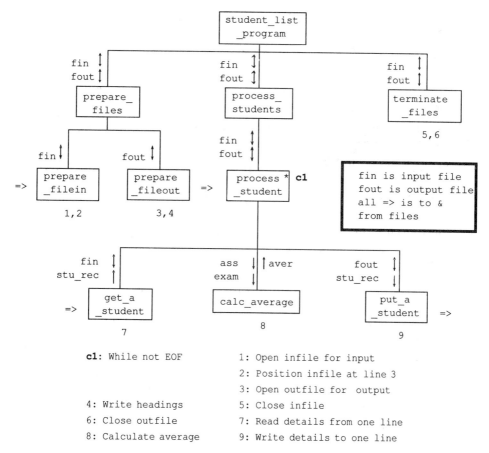

c1: While not EOF

1: Open infile for input
2: Position infile at line 3
3: Open outfile for output

4: Write headings
5: Close infile
6: Close outfile
7: Read details from one line
8: Calculate average
9: Write details to one line

As the design of the program is so straightforward and as the point of the program is to illustrate the use of text files, the program will be implemented as single Ada source file, without the use of packages. The main level of the program will declare the two text files, one for input and one for output, and pass them as in-out parameters to the three main-level procedures. The implementation of the program procedure might be as follows:

```
-- program to input information from a text file,
-- process it and write information to a new text file
-- b2s11p1 see text

with TEXT_IO, int_io, float_inout;
use  TEXT_IO, int_io, float_inout;

procedure b2s11p1 is

    max_stu_name : constant := 20;  -- length of student name
    max_i_score  : constant := 100; -- maximum student score

    filein  : TEXT_IO.FILE_TYPE;
    fileout : TEXT_IO.FILE_TYPE;
```

```
-- subsidiary procedures & function here

begin -- b2s11p1
   prepare_files(    filein, fileout );
   process_students( filein, fileout );
   terminate_files( filein, fileout );
end b2s11p1;
```

The procedure prepare_files and its subsidiary procedures prepare_infile and prepare_outfile can be implemented as follows:

```
procedure prepare_files( filein, fileout : in out
                                   TEXT_IO.FILE_TYPE) is

   procedure prepare_infile( filein : in out
                                   TEXT_IO.FILE_TYPE ) is
   -- procedure to prepare file for input by opening file and
   -- positioning at start of line 3

   begin -- prepare infile
      OPEN( FILE => filein,
            MODE => IN_FILE,
            NAME => "oldstu.dat");

      SET_LINE( filein , 3 );
   end prepare_infile;

   procedure prepare_outfile( fileout : in out
                                   TEXT_IO.FILE_TYPE ) is
   -- procedure to create new file for output and output
   -- headings to the file

   begin -- prepare outfile
      CREATE( FILE => fileout,
              MODE => OUT_FILE,
              NAME => "newstu.dat");
      -- do report heading on line 2
      SET_LINE( fileout, 2 ); SET_COL( fileout, 30 );
      PUT( fileout, "STUDENT RESULTS REPORT ");

      -- do line heading on line 4
      SET_LINE( fileout, 4 );
      SET_COL( fileout, 5 );
      PUT( fileout, "Student Name");
      SET_COL( fileout, 35 );
      PUT( fileout, "Assignments ");
      SET_COL( fileout, 50 );
      PUT( fileout, "Exams ");
      SET_COL( fileout, 65 );
      PUT( fileout, "Average");

      -- move to line 6 for first student line
      SET_LINE( fileout, 6 );
   end prepare_outfile;

begin -- prepare files
   prepare_infile( filein );
```

```
      prepare_outfile( fileout );
   end prepare_files;
```

The procedure prepare_infile, which receives the input file as an in-out parameter, opens the external text file 'oldstu.dat' and then uses the TEXT_IO procedure SET_LINE to move the file pointer to the start of line 3, where the first student data line can be found.

The procedure prepare_outfile, which receives the output file as an in-out parameter, creates the external text file 'newstu.dat' and then uses the procedures SET_LINE, SET_COL and the STRING version of the PUT procedure to output the headings to the file, leaving the file pointer positioned at the start of line 6 ready for the output of the first student detail line.

The procedure terminate_files has the straightforward task of closing both files and can be implemented as follows:

```
procedure terminate_files( filein, fileout : in out
                                         TEXT_IO.FILE_TYPE ) is

-- tidy up by closing open files

begin -- terminate files
   CLOSE( filein );
   CLOSE( fileout );
end terminate_files;
```

The iterative procedure process_students can be implemented using a **while** loop which terminates when the end of the input file is detected. On each iteration of the loop the three subprograms get_a_student, calc_average and put_a_student are called:

```
procedure process_students( filein, fileout : in out
                                      TEXT_IO.FILE_TYPE ) is

-- procedure to process all students by iteratively processing
-- a single student. Requires global constant max_i_score and
-- max_stu_name.

   -- declaration of types to represent a student's details
   subtype scores        is INTEGER range 0 .. max_i_score;
   subtype student_names is STRING( 1 .. max_stu_name );

   type student_records is
   record
     stu_name    : student_names;
     assignment  : scores;
     exam        : scores;
     average     : FLOAT;
   end record;

   -- variable to store a single student's details
   this_student : student_records;

-- process students's subsidiary subprograms here

begin -- process students
   while not( END_OF_FILE( filein )) loop
```

```
    get_a_student( filein,  this_student );
    this_student.average := calc_average( this_student.assignment,
                                          this_student.exam );

    put_a_student( fileout, this_student );
  end loop;
end process_students;
```

The types which are required to represent an individual student's details within the program are declared at this level of the program, as it is only at this level and the levels below it that the precise details are required to be known. This is an example of information hiding; the only parts of the program which know about how a student is represented are those which have a need to know. Just as the program objects which are used to represent objects in the real world are declared at the lowest possible level in a program in order to make them as local as possible, so data types should also be declared to be as local as possible.

The only exception to this rule is the declaration of constants; there should always be declared at the start of a program text in order that they can be easily located and changed should their values have to be modified during maintenance. The procedure get_a_student can be implemented as follows:

```
procedure get_a_student( filein : in out TEXT_IO.FILE_TYPE;
                         a_stu  : out    student_records ) is
-- procedure to input student record from one line of text

begin -- get_a_student
    SET_COL( filein, 3);              -- name commences at col 3
    GET( filein, a_stu.stu_name );    -- get name from cols 3 to 23
    GET( filein, a_stu.assignment ); -- get assignment score
    GET( filein, a_stu.exam      ); -- get exam score
    SKIP_LINE( filein );              -- advance to next line
end get_a_student;
```

The procedure commences by positioning the file pointer at column 3 of a line where the start of the student's name can be found. The STRING version of the GET procedure is used to input the student name. The effect of this procedure is to input from the text file as many characters as the string is capable of holding. The string being used to contain a student's name is 20 characters long and, as the specification states that the maximum length of a student's name is 20 characters, it is long enough to guarantee that the student's name will be input into it.

The procedure continues by the input of the student's assignment score and the student's exam score, using the integer version of the GET procedure. There is no need to position the file pointer at the precise column where these fields can be found on the line using the SET_COL procedure, as the effect of the procedure is to skip over any leading spaces until an integer value is found. Should a non-integer value be found on the file then a DATA_EXCEPTION will be raised. The procedure terminates by advancing the file pointer onto the start of the next line ready for the next student line to be input or the end of file to be detected.

The function calc_average can be implemented in a straightforward manner:

```
function calc_average( assign, exam : scores ) return FLOAT is
-- function to calculate average from assignment & exam values
begin -- calc average
    return ( FLOAT( assign ) * 0.4 +
             FLOAT( exam   ) * 0.6 );
end calc_average;
```

The calculation of the student average is implemented as a distinct function rather than including the calculations within get_a_student or put_a_student, as the calculation is not logically connected with either of those operations. Good design requires that a subprogram should perform one simple logically distinct operation and no more. The calculation is thus implemented separately from the input and output procedures.

The calculation is implemented as a function with two integer subtype parameters returning a FLOAT value, rather than as a procedure with a student record as an input/output parameter for two reasons. First, when a data-flow design indicates that a function is possible, a function should be implemented. Second, subprograms should in general only have as much data flow as is required and no more. If the entire record were passed, then the subprogram would know about the name of the student as well as the three attributes of a student (assignment, exam and average mark) which it has a requirement to know about. Implementing the subprogram in this manner gives it a higher possibility of being able to be reused with no modification, as it is not dependent upon knowledge of the record structure.

Finally, the implementation of the procedure put_a_student would be as follows:

```
procedure put_a_student( fileout : in out TEXT_IO.FILE_TYPE;
                         a_stu    : in      student_records ) is
-- procedure to output student record to one line of text

begin -- put a student
    SET_COL( fileout, 5 ); -- name to start a col 5
    PUT( fileout, a_stu.stu_name );
    SET_COL( fileout, 35 );
    PUT( fileout, a_stu.assignment, WIDTH => 4 );
    SET_COL( fileout, 50 );
    PUT( fileout, a_stu.exam, WIDTH => 4 );
    SET_COL( fileout, 65 );
    PUT( fileout, a_stu.average, FORE => 4, AFT => 1, EXP => 0);
    NEW_LINE( fileout );
end put_a_student;
```

The procedure commences by advancing to column 5 and then outputs the student's name using the STRING version of the PUT procedure. The file pointer is then advanced to the relevant columns and the assignment and exam scores are output using the INTEGER version of the PUT procedure. Likewise, the file pointer is advanced to the required column before the student's average score is output using the FLOAT version of the PUT procedure. The procedure terminates by advancing the file pointer to the next line ready for the next line of student details to be output.

A procedure map of the entire program follows:

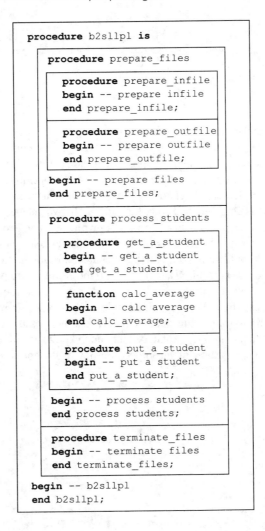

```
procedure b2sllp1 is

    procedure prepare_files

        procedure prepare_infile
        begin -- prepare infile
        end prepare_infile;

        procedure prepare_outfile
        begin -- prepare outfile
        end prepare_outfile;

    begin -- prepare files
    end prepare_files;

    procedure process_students

        procedure get_a_student
        begin -- get_a_student
        end get_a_student;

        function calc_average
        begin -- calc average
        end calc_average;

        procedure put_a_student
        begin -- put a student
        end put_a_student;

    begin -- process students
    end process_students;

    procedure terminate_files
    begin -- terminate files
    end terminate_files;

begin -- b2sllp1
end b2sllp1;
```

EXERCISES

2.11.1 Expand the design and implementation of the student_list program developed in this section so that it will count the number of students processed, calculate the average assignment, exam and total score for the group of students, and display this information at the end of the report.

2.11.2 The Committee Responsible for Ancient Punctuation has commissioned a program which will process a text file, replacing all occurrences of the modern characters 'S' and 's', with the ancient characters 'F' and 'f' correspondingly. Design and implement this program.

2.11.3 Design, implement and test a program which will analyze a text file by counting the number of times each alphabetic character occurs in the file. The program is to treat upper-case and lower-case alphabetic characters as being equivalent. The analysis of the file is to be output to a text file, which will contain the total number of characters in the file and a count for each alphabetic character.

2.11.4 Expand the program developed in Exercise 2.11.3 to include counts of the digit characters ('0'..'9'), common punctuation characters ('.', ',', ';', ':', '?', ' " ') and a separate count of any other characters.

External iterative structures: the direct files

Direct files offer an alternative method of file organization and record access, compared with sequential files. With direct file organization it is possible to access any record in the file, in any sequence. When sequential organization is in use, it is only possible to access the records in the file in the order in which they exist on the file. Direct files also differ from sequential files in that they can be opened in a mode which allows records to be read from or written to; this form of access to records in a file is known as *random* access.

Although it is possible to access a dynamic file in a random manner it is also possible for a dynamic file to be accessed in a sequential manner, commencing at the current position of the file pointer. How the file is accessed will depend upon the requirements of the specification.

Random file access is implemented by use of a *key* value which uniquely identifies a particular record in the file. For random access the key value of the required record has to be specified when the read or write operation is attempted. The key which is used for direct files is the record's *ordinal* position in the file. The ordinal position of a record is the position of the record relative to the start of the file; thus the first record in a dynamic file has an ordinal position of 1 and a key value of 1, the second record has the key value 2, the fifth record the key value 5, the hundredth record the key value 100, etc. If it is required to read the fifth record from a dynamic file then the read operation has to specify that the key of the record which is to be read from the file is 5. If it is required to write the tenth record to a dynamic file then the write operation has to specify that the key of the record to be written to the file is 10.

Files which have a dynamic organization have many advantages over files which have a sequential organization. A dynamic file has all the properties of a sequential file, plus those which are concerned with random access. It does, however, have one major disadvantage: it is not possible for a direct file to have 'holes' in it. If a direct file contains a single stored record whose key value is 100; then all records with key values 1 to 99 are also physically present in the file, although they may not have defined values.

Direct files become most useful when the values of the keys which are used by the file are in a strict ordinal sequence: 1, 2, 3, 4, ... Key sequences which are strictly ordinal are not very common in real-world applications. A third method of file organization known as *indexed* file organization exists where the key values do not have to be strictly ordinal. Indexed files are not defined in the Ada standard, although many compilers include non-standard indexed file facilities.

A second, and minor, disadvantage of direct files is that they require more system resources to implement them. A sequential file can be stored upon a sequential storage medium (such as magnetic tape) or can be stored upon a dynamic medium (such as a magnetic disk). Direct files can only be stored upon a dynamic medium. Although direct files are more expensive to implement than sequential files, for many application the advantages of direct files outweigh the disadvantages.

2.12.1 Creating and maintaining direct files

The general package for the instantiation of direct file input/output packages is known as DIRECT_IO and is used to create new direct input/output packages for use with a particular record type in a manner which is directly comparable to the creation of new sequential input/output packages using SEQUENTIAL_IO. For example:

```
with DIRECT_IO;
package integer_dio is new DIRECT_IO( INTEGER );
-- creation of a package called integer_dio suitable
-- for use with integer values

with DIRECT_IO, daypack;
package day_times_dio is new DIRECT_IO( daypack.day_times );
-- creation of a package called day_times_dio suitable
-- for use with day_time values - see B2S7
```

These packages contain a collection of subprograms for the creation and maintenance of direct files whose records are of the types specified. Many of these subprograms are directly comparable with the subprograms provided for sequential and text files. The following procedures and functions are unchanged from those provided for sequential or text files:

procedures: CLOSE   DELETE

functions: NAME   FORM   IS_OPEN   END_OF_FILE

The following procedures and functions differ from those provided for sequential files, primarily by the addition of a third possible access mode, known as INOUT_FILE:

procedures: CREATE   OPEN   RESET

function: MODE

A direct file open in INOUT_FILE mode can be used at the same point in a program either for input or for output. Direct files can also be opened in one of the modes IN_FILE or OUT_FILE, in which case they can only be read from or written to, respectively. The DIRECT_IO version of the CREATE procedure has the default mode INOUT_FILE; the DIRECT_IO version of the OPEN procedure has no default mode specified.

2.12.2 Using direct files

The direct file packages supply modified READ and WRITE procedures for random reading from and writing to direct files. They also supply unchanged READ and WRITE procedures for sequential reading from and writing to direct files.

The packages also supply a data type for representing the ordinal position of a record in the file and a set of procedures and functions for directly manipulating the file pointer using this type. The data type supplied for representing ordinal positions is a new INTEGER type called COUNT, with a range of values from 0 to a maximum value which differs from compiler to compiler. The package also supplies a subtype of COUNT called POSITIVE_COUNT, whose range of values includes all the values of count apart from 0. The effective declaration of these types in DIRECT_IO is as follows:

```
type      COUNT is range 0 .. {implementa-tion defined };
subtype   POSITIVE_COUNT is COUNT
                    range 1 .. COUNT'LAST;
```

The effective declaration of the new random READ procedure, using the subtype POSITIVE_COUNT to indicate which record is to be read from the file, is as follows:

```
procedure READ   ( FILE  :  in  FILE_TYPE;
                   ITEM  :  out ELEMENT_TYPE;
                   FROM  :  in  POSITIVE_COUNT  );
```

The additional parameter FROM indicates the ordinal position in the file from which the record is to be read. When it is executed, the effect of this procedure is to position the file pointer at the position specified, to transfer the record from that position into ITEM, and then to advance the file pointer to the next record in the file.

There are a number of problems which may occur, preventing the procedure from executing successfully; these will raise the following exceptions:

```
MODE_ERROR   will be raised if the file is in OUT_FILE mode
DATA_ERROR   will be raised if the information read is not
             a value of type ITEM
END_ERROR    will be raised if the position specified is
             beyond the physical end of file
```

The effective declaration of the direct WRITE procedure is as follows:

```
procedure WRITE ( FILE : in    FILE_TYPE;
                  ITEM : in    ELEMENT_TYPE;
                  TO   : in    POSITIVE_COUNT );
```

The additional parameter TO indicates the ordinal position in the file at which the record is to be written. When it is executed, the effect of this procedure is to position the file pointer at the position specified and then to transfer the contents of ITEM to the record at that position. If the position specified is beyond the current end of file then sufficient new uninitialized records are appended to the end of the file to increase its size to that required. The file pointer is then advanced to beyond the end of the record which has just been written.

There are a number of problems which may occur, preventing the procedure from executing successfully; these will raise the following exceptions:

```
MODE_ERROR  will be raised if the file is in IN_FILE mode
USE_ERROR   will be raised if the capacity of the external
            file is exceeded.
```

An additional procedure is provided which can be used to position the file pointer without reading or writing a record. The effective declaration of this procedure in DIRECT_IO is as follows:

```
procedure SET_INDEX( FILE : in    FILE_TYPE;
                     TO   : in    POSITIVE_COUNT );
```

When it is executed, the effect of this procedure is to position the file pointer to the position specified; this point may be beyond the physical end of file, in which case no exception is raised and no records are appended to the file.

Two additional functions are also provided; the first of these can be used to determine the current position of the file pointer. The effective declaration of this procedure in DIRECT_IO is as follows:

```
function INDEX( FILE : in  FILE_TYPE) return POSITIVE_COUNT;
```

The effect of this function is to return the current position of the file pointer; this position may be beyond the physical end of file. No exceptions are associated with this function.

The other additional function can be used to determine the size of a file. The effective declaration of this procedure in DIRECT_IO is as follows:

```
function SIZE ( FILE : in  FILE_TYPE) return COUNT;
```

The effect of this function is to return the size of the file in records; if the file is empty the size returned will be zero. There are no exceptions associated with this function.

2.12.3 Example program specification

To illustrate the use of direct files a program will be developed and implemented which will be used to maintain a series of records concerned with a car fleet. The logical structure of each record in the file will be as follows:

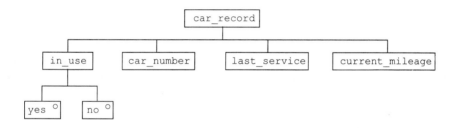

This record structure can be implemented in a package specification file as follows:

```
-- car record package specification file name car_pack.pkg, see text

package car_pack is

    max_car : constant :=   25; -- max no of cars in the fleet
    max_odo : constant := 9999; -- max car odometer reading

    subtype  car_nums        is INTEGER range 1 .. max_car;
    subtype  odometer_reading is INTEGER range 1 .. max_odo;

    type car_record
    is record
        in_use           : BOOLEAN := FALSE; -- flag for file use only
        car_num          : car_nums;          -- car fleet number
        last_service     : odometer_reading; -- mileage at last service
        current_mileage  : odometer_reading;
    end record;
```

The in_use field will be used when records are filed to indicate if the file record is currently in use or not.

The data-flow diagrams for the actions which can be performed with car records follow:

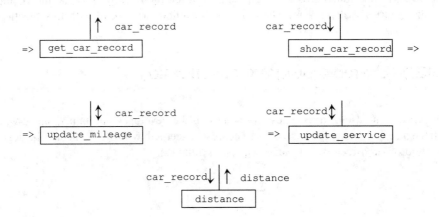

The procedure get_car_record will initialize a car record from the terminal; show_car_record will display a car record on the terminal; update_service will input a new service mileage value from the terminal; and update_mileage will input a new current mileage from the terminal. The function distance will calculate and return the distance travelled since the last service.

Using these data-flow diagrams the car_pack specification file can be completed as shown below:

```
procedure get_car_record( a_car : out car_record );
        -- get car record from the terminal

procedure show_car_record( a_car : in car_record );
        -- show car record on terminal

procedure update_service( a_car : in out car_record );
        -- input new service mileage from terminal

procedure update_mileage( a_car : in out car_record );
        -- input new current mileage from terminal

function distance( a_car : car_record ) return odometer_readings;
        -- calculate and return distance travelled
        -- since last service

end car_pack;
```

The package definition file for this package will have to bring TEXT_IO and int_io into use.

The design of the procedure get_car_record is very straightforward, and could be implemented as follows:

```
-- car pack declaration file, filename car_pac_.pkb

with TEXT_IO, int_io;
use  TEXT_IO, int_io;

package body car_pack is

procedure get_car_record( a_car : out car_record ) is

begin -- get_car_record
   PUT( "Enter car number " );
   GET( a_car.car_num ); SKIP_LINE;
   PUT( "Enter last service " );
   GET( a_car.last_service ); SKIP_LINE;
   PUT( "Enter current mileage " );
   GET( a_car.current_mileage ); SKIP_LINE;
end get_car_record;
```

This implementation assumes that the user will always input a value in the required range; a better implementation would use the safe integer input procedures developed earlier in this block.

The design of the procedure show_car_record will be more complex as it will have to take into account whether or not the record is in use. If the record is in use then the stored details will have to be displayed; if the record is not in use then a suitable message will have to be displayed. The implementation of this procedure could be as follows:

```
procedure show_car_record( a_car : in car_record ) is

begin -- show car record
   PUT("          ");
   PUT( a_car.car_num, WIDTH =>3);
   if ( a_car.in_use ) then
      PUT("          "); PUT( a_car.last_service,    WIDTH => 5);
      PUT("          "); PUT( a_car.current_mileage, WIDTH => 5);
   else
      PUT("      is not in use.");
   end if;
   NEW_LINE;
end show_car_record;
```

The two procedures update_service and update_mileage can be implemented as shown below:

```
procedure update_service( a_car : in out car_record ) is

begin -- update service
   PUT( "Enter new service ");
   GET( a_car.last_service ); SKIP_LINE;
end update_service;


procedure update_mileage( a_car : in out car_record ) is

begin -- update mileage
   PUT( "Enter current mileage ");
   GET( a_car.current_mileage ); SKIP_LINE;
end update_mileage;
```

Again these procedures would be better implemented using the safe integer input procedure to ensure that the user's inputs were within the specified ranges.

Finally, the implementation of the function distance would be as follows:

```
function distance( a_car : car_record ) return odometer_readings is

begin -- distance
   return ( a_car.current_mileage - a_car.last_service );
end distance;
```

This package, which declares car record objects and the actions which can be performed upon them, can be used as the basis of a second package which will provide facilities for manipulating files of such records using direct access techniques. The package declaration file for this second package would be as follows:

```
-- car file declaration package filename car_file.pkg see text

with DIRECT_IO, car_pack;
package car_record_dio is new DIRECT_IO( car_pack.car_record );

with car_record_dio;

package car_file_pack is

   procedure make_new_file(  car_file : in
                                          car_record_dio.FILE_TYPE );
   -- procedure to make new file of unused records

   procedure add_new_record( car_file : in
                                          car_record_dio.FILE_TYPE );
   -- procedure to add new in use record to file
```

```
        procedure update_service( car_file : in
                                       car_record_dio.FILE_TYPE );
        -- procedure to update service mileage of a single record

        procedure update_mileage( car_file : in
                                       car_record_dio.FILE_TYPE );
        -- procedure to update current mileage of single record

        procedure show_a_record ( car_file : in
                                       car_record_dio.FILE_TYPE );
        -- procedure to show a single car record

        procedure show_records  ( car_file : in
                                       car_record_dio.FILE_TYPE );
        -- procedure to show all car records in a file

        procedure remove_record ( car_file : in
                                       car_record_dio.FILE_TYPE );
        -- procedure to mark an in use record as not in use

  end car_file_pack;
```

This package declaration file commences by using the packages DIRECT_IO and car_pack to create a new direct input/output package capable of manipulating files of car records. The direct input/output car_record package (car_record_dio) is then **with**ed before the procedures which are supplied by the package are declared. The package car_record_dio is not brought into use as the advice given in Block 2 Section 10 always to specify the file type is being followed. In this example the package could have been **use**d and the type FILE_TYPE would then have been unambiguous as the car record file package is the only file package in use. Without bringing the package into use the full name of the file type has to be specified, as in 'car_record_dio.FILE_TYPE'.

The first procedure supplied by this package is make_new_file, which requires a car_file of appropriate type and will make or remake the file. It will do this by ensuring that every possible record in the file, one for each possible car, exists and its in_use field is set to indicate that the record is not in use.

The next three procedures, add_new_record, update_service and update_mileage, are concerned with adding a new record to the file, updating the service mileage field of a record on the file, and updating the current mileage field of a record on the file, respectively. They are comparable to the three procedures which perform the same actions on records declared in the car_pack package and will make use of those procedures in their implementation.

The next two procedures, show_a_record and show_records, can be used to show a single record on the file or to show all records on the file, respectively. The final procedure, remove_record, can be used to effectively remove a record from the file by setting its in_use field to the appropriate value.

The heading of the package definition file of this package would be as follows:

```
-- car file definition package, filename car_fil_.pkb

with TEXT_IO, int_io, car_pack, car_record_dio;
use  TEXT_IO, int_io, car_pack, car_record_dio;

package body car_file_pack is
```

The design of the procedure make_new_file, assuming that the file is open, would be as follows:

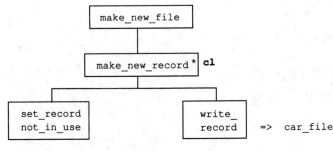

c1: For all possible records.

The data flow information on this structure chart indicates that the output from the module write_record will be to the car_file not to the terminal. The implementation of this design would be as shown below:

```
procedure make_new_file( car_file : in
                         car_record_dio.FILE_TYPE ) is

   new_rec : car_pack.car_record;

begin -- make new file
   for this_car in car_pack.car_nums loop
      new_rec.in_use  := FALSE;
      new_rec.car_num := this_car;
      WRITE( car_file,
             ITEM => new_rec,
             TO => car_record_dio.POSITIVE_COUNT( this_car ));
   end loop;
end make_new_file;
```

The WRITE procedure parameter TO has to be of type POSITIVE_COUNT, which is a distinct INTEGER type, declared within the direct input/output package car_record_dio. The loop parameter this_car is of the INTEGER subtype car_nums, which is declared in car_pack. Type conversion is required to convert the value into the required type before the value can be used as a parameter to the WRITE procedure. The conversion is effected by specifying the full name of the type which the value of this_car is to be converted into. The name of the type is POSITIVE_COUNT which is declared in the package car_record_dio, which defines the expression as follows:

```
car_record_dio.POSITIVE_COUNT( this_car )
```

The effect of the loop is to ensure that every possible car record is written (or rewritten) to the file with its in_use field set to FALSE, indicating that all records on the file are not being used to hold valid car_record details.

The design of the procedure add_new_record would be as shown below:

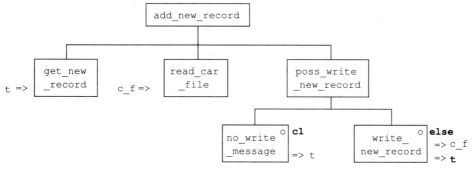

c1: If record already in use.

The implementation of this procedure will implement the component get_new_record as a procedure call to the procedure get_car_record in the package car_pack:

```
procedure add_new_record( car_file : in
                                     car_record_dio.FILE_TYPE ) is

        new_record,                     -- record to be added
        old_record : car_pack.car_record; -- record on file

    begin -- add new record
      get_car_record( new_record ); -- in car_pack
      READ( car_file,
            ITEM => old_record,
            FROM => car_record_dio.POSITIVE_COUNT(new_record.car_num));
      if ( old_record.in_use ) then
        PUT_LINE( "Car already on file, details not changed" );
      else
        new_record.in_use := TRUE;
        WRITE( car_file,
               ITEM => new_record,
               TO   => car_record_dio.POSITIVE_COUNT(new_record.car_num));
        PUT_LINE( "OK, details filed" );
      end if;
    end add_new_record;
```

The design of update_service, which can also be adapted for update_mileage, would be as follows:

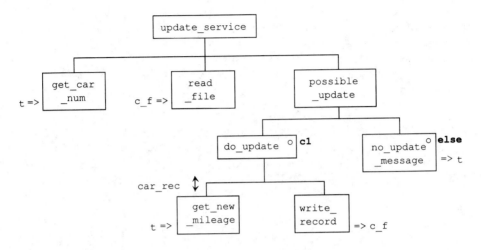

c1: If car record in use.

The implementation of this procedure and the procedure update mileage, using the appropriate procedures from car_pack, could be as follows:

```
procedure update_service( car_file : in
                          car_record_dio.FILE_TYPE ) is

    a_car : car_pack.car_record;

begin -- update service
    PUT( "Enter car number ");
    GET( a_car.car_num ); SKIP_LINE;
    READ( car_file,
          ITEM => a_car,
          FROM => car_record_dio.POSITIVE_COUNT(a_car.car_num));

    if ( a_car.in_use ) then
        update_service( a_car );
        WRITE( car_file,
               ITEM => a_car,
               TO   => car_record_dio.POSITIVE_COUNT(a_car.car_num));
    else
        PUT( "Car not in use, service cannot be updated." );
    end if;
end update_service;
```

```
procedure update_mileage( car_file : in
                          car_record_dio.FILE_TYPE ) is

   a_car : car_pack.car_record;

begin -- update mileage
   PUT( "Enter car number " );
   GET( a_car.car_num ); SKIP_LINE;
   READ( car_file,
         ITEM => a_car,
         FROM => car_record_dio.POSITIVE_COUNT(a_car.car_num));
   if ( a_car.in_use ) then
      update_mileage( a_car ); -- in car_pack
      WRITE( car_file,
            ITEM => a_car,
            TO  => car_record_dio.POSITIVE_COUNT(a_car.car_num));
   else
      PUT( "Car not in use, mileage cannot be changed." );
   end if;
end update_mileage;
```

The design of the procedure show_a_record is straightforward:

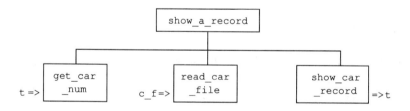

The procedure show_car_record, contained within car_pack, will either display the details of the record if the record is in use, or display a message if the record is not in use. As car records are hidden within the car_pack procedure show_car_record, this procedure does not have to concern itself with these details and consequently is a simple implementation:

```
procedure show_a_record ( car_file : in
                          car_record_dio.FILE_TYPE ) is

   a_car : car_pack.car_record;

begin -- show a record
   PUT( "Enter car number " );
   GET( a_car.car_num ); SKIP_LINE;
   READ( car_file,
```

```
         ITEM => a_car,
         FROM => car_record_dio.POSITIVE_COUNT(a_car.car_num));
   show_car_record( a_car ); -- in car_pack
end show_a_record;
```

In order to show all records, the file pointer has to be reset to the start of file and then all records on the file have to be iteratively passed to the procedure show_car_record. The design of this procedure would be as shown below:

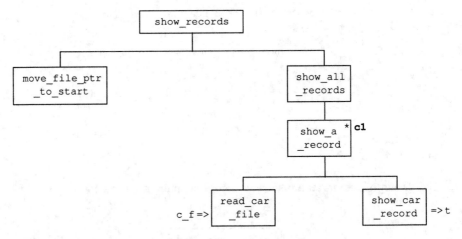

c1: While records remain on the file.

The implementation of this procedure would be as follows:

```
procedure show_records  ( car_file : in
                          car_record_dio.FILE_TYPE ) is

    this_car : car_record;

begin -- show records
    SET_INDEX( car_file, 1 ); -- position file pointer at 1st record

    while not( END_OF_FILE( car_file)) loop
        READ( car_file, this_car );   -- sequential read
        show_car_record( this_car );   -- in car pack
    end loop;
end show_records;
```

This procedure could have been designed and implemented in a similar manner to the procedure make_file, making use of direct file facilities. This implementation uses the SET_INDEX procedure to position the file pointer at the start of file and then uses the sequential facilities to process the file. When the entire contents of a direct file have to be processed from start to end then an implementation which uses sequential facilities should be favoured.

The design of the final procedure remove_record would be as shown below:

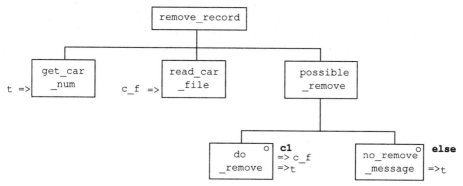

c1: If record in use.

The implementation of this procedure is as follows:

```
procedure remove_record ( car_file : in
                           car_record_dio.FILE_TYPE ) is

    a_car : car_pack.car_record;

begin -- remove record
    PUT( "Enter car number ");
    GET( a_car.car_num ); SKIP_LINE;
    READ( car_file,
          ITEM => a_car,
          FROM => car_record_dio.POSITIVE_COUNT(a_car.car_num));
    if ( a_car.in_use ) then
        a_car.in_use := FALSE;
        WRITE( car_file,
               ITEM => a_car,
               TO   => car_record_dio.POSITIVE_COUNT(a_car.car_num));
        PUT("OK, car removed from file.");
    else
        PUT( "Car not in use, cannot be removed." );
    end if;
end remove_record;
```

The record cannot be physically removed from the file as it is not possible to leave holes in a direct file. Instead the in_use field of the record is set to FALSE, indicating that this record is no longer in use. The intent of this section is to illustrate the use of direct input/output facilities; in a more realistic application the record would have to be shown to the user and confirmation that it is to be removed requested before the remove was effected. When a change is made to the contents of a file, the user interface design should always ask the user for confirmation before the change is effected.

The facilities provided by the car_file_pack can be used by an application program which provides a menu to the user, offering a series of choices each of which will be implemented by a call to one of the procedures within car_file_pack. The design of a similar high-level control structure has already been presented in Block 2 Section 9, the overall structure of this program might be as follows:

```
-- car demo file program b2s12p1 see text

with TEXT_IO, car_file_pack, car_record_dio;
use  TEXT_IO, car_file_pack, car_record_dio;

procedure b2s12p1 is

    car_file : car_record_dio.FILE_TYPE;
    choice   : CHARACTER;

   procedure menu( a_choice : out CHARACTER ) is

   -- procedure to offer choices to user and return validated
   -- choice character in output parameter.

   begin   -- menu

   end menu;

   procedure dispatch( a_car_file : in out car_record_dio.FILE_TYPE
                       a_choice   : in CHARACTER ) is

   -- procedure to dispatch control to one of the procedures
   -- offered by car_file_pack, depending upon the value of
   -- a_choice. File is open and passed onwards as parameter

   begin   -- dispatch

   end dispatch;

begin -- b2s12p1
    CREATE( car_file, MODE => INOUT_FILE, NAME => "cars.dat");
    -- create new car file with name "cars.dat"
    make_new_file( car_file ); -- ensure all records are not in use

    menu(choice)                -- prime the while loop
    while ( choice /= 'x' ) loop
       menu( choice );
       dispatch( car_file, choice );
    end loop;
```

```
        CLOSE( car_file );
    end b2s12p1;
```

The implementation of this application has involved three Ada units stored in five files, two instantiated units (car_file_dio and int_io) and two standard packages (TEXT_IO and DIRECT_IO). If the names of the five files are as follows:

```
        car_pac_.pkg  car pack specification file
        car_pack.pkb  car pack definition  file
        car_fil_.pkg  car file specification file
        car_file.pkb  car file definition  file
        b2s12p1.ada   menu dispatch program
```

then the dependencies between the files and the packages can be visualized as shown below:

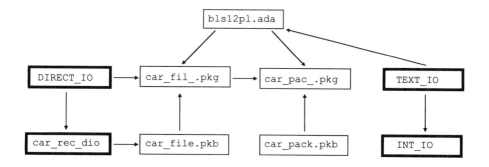

An arrow in this diagram indicates that the compilation of the file or package at the head of the arrow is dependent upon the prior existence of the file or package at the tail of the arrow. These dependencies will dictate the order of compilation, as it is not possible to compile a part of the program until the other parts on which it is dependent have already been compiled and stored in the library. Assuming that int_io has already been created and stored in a program library, this diagram defines a possible order of compilation as:

```
        car_pac_.pkg
        car_pack.pkb
        car_fil_.pkg
        car_file.pkb
        b2s12p1.ada
```

EXERCISES

2.12.1 Complete and implement the menu/dispatch program b2s12p1 as outlined in the text (or adapt it from b2s9p1).

2.12.2   Implement the packages described in the text and test the system using the menu/dispatch program from Exercise 2.12.1.

2.12.3   Implement a procedure called show_services within the package car_file_pack, which will make use of the function distance in car_pack, to display on the terminal a list of vehicles which are due for a service. Include the definition of an INTEGER constant called service_interval within car_pack to indicate the service interval in miles. Amend the menu/dispatch procedure to offer this facility and then test it.

2.12.4   Amend the implementation of add_new_record, using the design below. The basis of the design is to determine if the size of the file indicates that the record requested already exists. If so, the procedure continues as before. If the file is too small records are appended until the file is large enough.

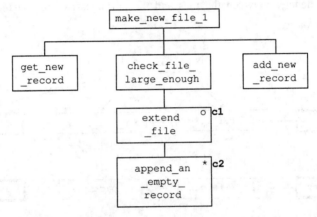

c1: If file not large enough.
c2: While file not large enough.

Hint: Condition 1 can be implemented using the direct_io function SIZE.
     This procedure makes the procedure make_new_file redundant; remove make_new_file and its call in the program procedure b2s12p1. Retest the program to confirm that the implementation is still effective.

2.12.5   Review the user interface of the car file system as developed above. Identify places in the system where the contents of the file are being changed. Amend the user interface design to request confirmation from the user before such changes are effected. Implement the changes by first redesigning the subprograms and then implementing them within the packages.

Block 3
Algorithms and Advanced Data Structures

Section 3.1

Searching algorithms

3.1.1 Standard algorithms

The first part of this block is concerned with *algorithms*. An algorithm is defined as a set of instructions which when followed will achieve some purpose; in other words, an algorithm is a method of doing something. All computer programs are expressions of algorithms: a computer program consists of a sequence of instructions in a computer language which, when executed by the computer, will achieve the program's specification. The algorithm is the method of achieving the specification, the program is an expression of that method.

There are many similar requirements which have to be performed by many different programs, possibly on different data structures. One example of such a requirement is searching a structure, either for the occurrence of a certain value or to locate the lowest (or highest) value in the structure. Another example is sorting a structure to maintain the information in the structure in some defined order. Algorithms to perform tasks such as these are well known, well defined, well documented and readily available. Such algorithms are known as *standard algorithms* and are an essential part of any programmer's toolbox.

A selection of the commonest standard algorithms will be introduced in the first part of this block. They are being introduced for two reasons: first, in order that they can be understood by the reader and added to his or her toolbox of common routines; and second, and more important, in order that they can be used as example algorithms to introduce the techniques of algorithm analysis.

3.1.2 Algorithm analysis

Any algorithm can be analyzed against several criteria; these criteria can then be used to compare two or more algorithms in order to assess which is to be favoured under specified conditions. These criteria could also be used to assess the effects of any attempted optimization of the algorithm. There are many criteria which can be used to assess and analyze algorithms, some of which are the following:

1. Generality: The definition of any algorithm has to specify the input data it will accept and the output data it will produce. An algorithm which can accept a wider range of input data and/or produce a wider range of output data is more general and likely to be a more useful algorithm. It may be usable in a wider range of situations without requiring amendments.
2. Effectiveness: This is concerned with the algorithm fulfilling its specification. The algorithm will have a specification which defines the effects of the algorithm in terms of the transformation of its input data into the output data. An attempt should be made by formal or informal methods to prove or demonstrate that an algorithm is effective.
3. Termination: For an algorithm to be useful it has to terminate at some stage. The design of the algorithm must indicate the conditions under which the algorithm will terminate and attempt to prove that these conditions will be satisfied for all possible sets of input data. Termination is strictly an attribute of effectiveness, but is important enough to be considered separately.
4. Efficiency: The efficiency of an algorithm can be assessed against several subcriteria. Possible criteria include the speed of execution, the size of the algorithm, the amount of storage space required for the algorithm or the amount and complexity of the maintenance which may be required by the algorithm. These criteria can only be assessed when the algorithm is considered *in situ*. For an algorithm concerned with real-time control speed of execution may be an overriding factor. For an algorithm which is to be implemented in an embedded system size considerations may be the most important.
5. Elegance: This is the most subjective aspect of algorithm analysis. An elegant algorithm is one which is both simple and ingenious; of these two factors simplicity is far more important than ingenuity.

These five criteria will be expanded further as they are used to assess the algorithms which are introduced in this block.

3.1.3 Searching algorithms

The commonest search requirement is to establish if a certain value is or is not contained within a data structure. If the value being searched for is contained within the structure then the algorithm should additionally indicate the position in the structure where the value is located.

The data-flow diagram for this version of a search algorithm is as follows:

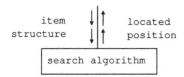

This diagram indicates that the search algorithm will search the *structure*, which is passed as an in-only parameter, for the occurrence of an *item*, which is passed as a second in-only parameter. If the item is found in the structure the BOOLEAN out-only parameter which will be called located will be TRUE and the out-only parameter which will be called position will indicate where in the structure the item is to be found. If the item cannot be found in the structure the out-only parameter located will be FALSE and the value of position will be undefined. These considerations also indicate that the search algorithm is best implemented as a procedure.

The structure which will be used to illustrate the search algorithms presented in this section, and which will also be used to illustrate the sorting algorithms in the next section, will be provided by a package. The structure to be searched or sorted is a list of names, each name being up to twenty characters long.

In addition to providing the structure, the package will also provide utility procedures which can be used with such structures. The first of these, set_up_names, will set the contents of a structure to known values. The second, show_names, will display the contents of the structure. The package will also provide the search procedure declaration. The specification of this package follows:

```
-- search/sort pack data structure specification file
-- filename s_pack_.pkg b3s1 see text
package s_pack is
    max_name_size : constant := 20;
    -- maximum no of characters in a single name

    subtype name_strings is STRING( 1 .. max_name_size );
    -- a string to contain a single name

    type name_lists is array ( NATURAL range < > ) of name_strings;
    -- unconstrained array structure of names

    type name_structs( struct_size : NATURAL ) is
    record
        names  : name_lists( 1 .. struct_size) ;
        in_use : NATURAL;
    end record;
    -- structure which can contain at most struct_size elements
    -- but actually contains the value of in_use

    procedure set_up_names( name_list : in out name_structs );
    -- procedure to set the list of names from an
    -- external file called "names.dat".

    procedure show_names( name_list : in      name_structs );
    -- procedure to display the list of names on the terminal

    procedure search_list( name_list : in  name_structs;
                           a_name    : in  name_strings;
```

```
                    located    : out BOOLEAN;
                    position   : out NATURAL );
        -- procedure to search the structure name_list for occurrence
        -- of the name a_name. If found located is exported TRUE and
        -- position indicates its location. If not found located is
        -- exported FALSE.
    end s_pack;
```

The package commences by declaring a constrained string type called name_strings which will be used to hold an individual name and, following this, an unconstrained array type called name_lists which will be used to hold an iteration of names. The index type of this unconstrained array is declared as a NATURAL INTEGER.

The package implements the list of names with the type name name_structs as a record which has two components. The first component is a constrained instance of the unconstrained array type name_lists called names. The upper bound of the constraint is expressed as a parameter of the record type declaration. Thus if an object of type name_struct is declared using the effective declaration:

```
    demo_names   : name_struct( 15 );
```

this will cause the upper bound of the array contained within the object demo_names to be 15. The other component of the object, the NATURAL variable in_use, will be used to indicate how many of these 15 possible names are actually in use. A parameter used when a record type is declared is known in Ada as a *record discriminant*.

The object demo_names, as declared above, containing ten out of a possible fifteen names, can thus be visualized as follows:

demo_names		names	
	15 - >		
	14 - >		
	13 - >		
	12 - >		
	11 - >		
	10 - >	James	Joyce
	9 - >	Irma	Ironstone
	8 - >	Harry	Houdini
	7 - >	George	Gershwin
	6 - >	Fred	Flintstone
	5 - >	Edna	Everage
	4 - >	Desmond	Dekker
	3 - >	Charlie	Chaplin
in_use	2 - >	Bessie	Bunter
10	1 - >	Ade	Abrahams

This diagram illustrates the structure of the variable object demo_names of type name_structs as declared above. The two components of the object are the array of names constrained to the range 1 .. 15 and a NATURAL object called in_use which currently has the value 10. The value of in_use indicates how many of the names in the array are actually being used at any moment in time. In the diagram ten of a possible fifteen names are in use; these are shown in the diagram as containing values. The remaining five names are not in use; these are shown in the diagram as being empty.

The definition file for this package follows:

```
-- search/sort pack data structure definition file
-- filename s_pack.pkb b3s1 see text

with TEXT_IO; use TEXT_IO;

package body s_pack is

    procedure set_up_names( name_list : in out name_structs ) is

        space      : constant CHARACTER := ' ';   -- ascii space
        name_file  : TEXT_IO.FILE_TYPE; -- text file containing names
        dummy      : NATURAL;           -- required for GET_LINE

    begin -- set up names
        OPEN( name_file, NAME => "names.dat",
                         MODE => IN_FILE );
        name_list.in_use := 0; -- no of names is 0 at this stage

        -- read names from file & store while structure is not
        -- full and names remain on the file
        while ((in_use < name_list.names'LAST) and
               ( not END_OF_FILE( name_file)        ) loop
            in_use := in_use + 1;
            name_list.names( in_use) := ( others => space );
            -- make sure name in structure is empty
            GET_LINE( name_file, name_list.names( in_use ), dummy);
        end loop;
        CLOSE( name_file );
    end set_up_names;

    procedure show_names( name_list : in name_structs ) is

    begin -- show names
```

```
        NEW_LINE(2);
        -- output each name which is in use
        for this_name in 1 .. name_list.in_use loop
           PUT_LINE( name_list.names( this_name ));
        end loop;
        NEW_LINE(2);
     end show_names;

     procedure search_list( name_list : in   name_structs;
                            a_name     : in   name_strings;
                            located    : out  BOOLEAN;
                            position   : out  NATURAL ) is separate;

   end s_pack;
```

The two utility procedures set_up_names and show_names are fully declared in this file. The search procedure is declared as **separate**; the meaning of this declaration will be made clear below.

The procedure set_up_names initializes the names in the structure passed to it by the input of names from an external text file called 'names.dat'. The design of this procedure has to take into account the possibility that the file will come to an end before the structure is completely full and also the possibility that the structure will become full before the file comes to an end.

The procedure show_names displays only those names in the structure which are indicated as being in use. It does this by displaying all names in the list from the start of the list as far as the last name in use. The program structure chart of these procedures is not presented as at this stage in the book they are taken as being obvious.

3.1.4 The sequential search algorithm

The sequential search is the simplest search algorithm to implement. It works by starting at one end of the data structure and traversing the data structure examining each item of the structure to determine if it is the item being searched for. If the item being searched for is located before the end of the structure is encountered the algorithm terminates, setting located to TRUE and setting position to the position of the located item within the structure. If the structure terminates with the item not found the algorithm terminates setting located to FALSE and without setting position to any defined value. The program structure chart for this algorithm follows:

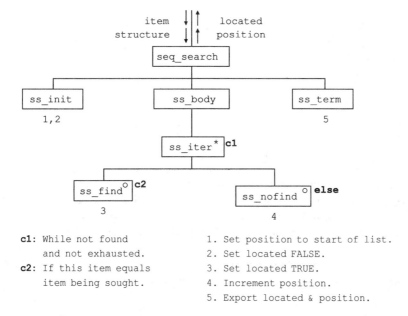

c1: While not found
and not exhausted.

c2: If this item equals
item being sought.

1. Set position to start of list.
2. Set located FALSE.
3. Set located TRUE.
4. Increment position.
5. Export located & position.

The procedure search_list is declared in the package definition file as being **separate**. This is an Ada facility which indicates that the full declaration of the procedure is located in a separate source code file. The advantages of using this facility are fourfold:

1. It reduces the size of the package declaration file, allowing easier editing.
2. It reduces the size of the compilation unit, allowing faster compilation.
3. It reduces recompilation, as a change to the search algorithm will require only the external file to be recompiled and not the whole declaration file.
4. It allows alternative search algorithms to be easily incorporated.

This last point will be expanded upon later in this section.

The text of the file which contains the sequential search algorithm would be as follows:

```
-- external procedure definition file for sequential
-- search algorithm. Filename seq_ser.ads. b3s1 see text

separate (s_pack)

procedure search_list( name_list : in   name_structs;
                       a_name    : in   name_strings;
                       located   : out  BOOLEAN;
                       position  : out  NATURAL ) is

   found     : BOOLEAN := FALSE;
   location  : NATURAL := name_list.names'FIRST;

begin -- search list
   while (( not found) and ( location <= name_list.in_use)) loop
      if ( name_list.names( location) = a_name ) then
         found := TRUE;
```

```
        else
            location := location + 1;
        end if;
    end loop;
    located  := found;
    position := location;
end search_list;
```

The contents of this file are the declaration of the search procedure exactly as it would appear in the search pack declaration file. The procedure is preceded by the reserved word **separate** to indicate that this is a separate definition and the name of the unit (s_pack) from which it is separate. This statement does not require a semicolon to terminate it; the inclusion of a semicolon at this point would cause a compilation error. This file has the recommended file extension .ads to indicate that it is an Ada separate compilation file.

In order to be able to demonstrate the effectiveness of the search algorithm an interactive harness will be required; a suitable harness file might be the following:

```
-- search harness demonstration file
-- filename b3s1p1 see text

with TEXT_IO, int_io, s_pack;
use  TEXT_IO, int_io, s_pack;

procedure b3s1p1 is

    space      : constant CHARACTER := ' ';   -- ascii space
    max_name : constant := 15;
    -- max number of names in this structure

    demo_list : name_structs( struct_size => max_name );
    -- name_struct with named discriminant specification

    to_b_found : name_strings := ( others => space );
    is_found   : BOOLEAN;  -- flag to indicate search success
    dummy      : NATURAL;  -- required for GET_LINE
    is_at      : NATURAL;  -- position within structure

begin -- b3s1p1

    set_up_names( demo_list ); -- initialize structure from file
    show_names(   demo_list ); -- display contents on terminal

    PUT("Enter the name to search for ");
    GET_LINE( to_b_found, dummy ); NEW_LINE;

    search_list( demo_list, to_b_found, is_found, is_at );

    if is_found then
```

```
        PUT ("The name is at position ");
        PUV ( is_at ); NEW_LINE;
    else
        PUT_LINE ("The name is not in the structure. ");
    end if;

end b3s1p1;
```

The harness program declares an object of type name_structs called demo_list with the structure size constrained to the value of the constant max_name (15). This structure is then initialized by the procedure set_up_names, whose execution relies upon the existence of an external file called 'names.dat' containing an indefinite number of names. The contents of the structure are then displayed. Before the list is searched a name to search for is requested from the user. After the structure has been searched, the output-only BOOLEAN object is_found is used to determine if the search was or was not successful. If the name input by the user was found in the structure its position is displayed, otherwise a suitable message is displayed.

In order to execute this file following compilation and linking, a text file called 'names.dat' containing an indefinite number of names is required. This algorithm will be evaluated after an alternative search algorithm has been introduced.

3.1.5 The binary chop algorithm

For structures which are ordered in a way which corresponds to the nature of the item being sought an improved search algorithm known as the *binary chop* can be used. To introduce the binary chop algorithm the task of searching a telephone directory for a known name can be considered.

The sequential search algorithm would commence by examining the first name in the directory and continue by examining every other name in the directory in sequence, until all names have been considered or the name being sought is found.

However, this situation calls for the use of a better search method. The directory can be opened approximately half way through and the name at the top of the left-hand page compared with the name being sought. If the name being sought is alphabetically greater than the name at the top of the page, the right-hand part of the directory can be opened half way through. If the name being sought is alphabetically lower than the name at the top of the page, the left-hand part of the directory can be opened half way through. This process can be continued until the name being sought is found or two adjacent names are found, one of which is lower than the name being sought and the other is greater than the name being sought, which would indicate that the name being sought is not to be found in the directory.

A human searching a telephone directory would have a better algorithm than this for locating a name. Instead of splitting the directory in half each time, he or she could make an estimate of how far away the name is from the name at the top of the page and split the directory by an appropriate amount. This search method is not suitable for implementation as a computer algorithm due to the complexity of instructing the computer to make an estimate.

This improved method of searching for an item can only be used if the structure is organized in a manner corresponding to the nature of the item being sought. A telephone directory is organized alphabetically by name so searching for a name can take advantage of this organization. If a particular phone number was being sought instead of a particular name then the sequential search algorithm would have to be used. A program design for this binary search algorithm would be as follows:

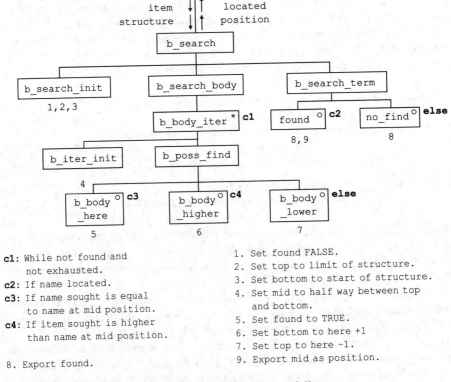

c1: While not found and
not exhausted.
c2: If name located.
c3: If name sought is equal
to name at mid position.
c4: If item sought is higher
than name at mid position.

8. Export found.

1. Set found FALSE.
2. Set top to limit of structure.
3. Set bottom to start of structure.
4. Set mid to half way between top
and bottom.
5. Set found to TRUE.
6. Set bottom to here +1
7. Set top to here −1.
9. Export mid as position.

This design can be implemented in a separate file as follows:

```
-- separate definition file for binary search implementation
-- of search algorithm. Filename bin_ser.ads. b3s1 see text.

separate (s_pack)

procedure search_list( name_list : in   name_structs;
                       a_name     : in   name_strings;
                       located    : out  BOOLEAN;
                       position   : out  NATURAL ) is
```

```
found      : BOOLEAN := FALSE;
top        : NATURAL := name_list.in_use;
           -- initial top of search range is all names in use
bottom     : NATURAL := name_list.names'FIRST;
           -- initial bottom of search range is start of list
mid_name   : NATURAL;

begin -- search list
   while ((not found) and ( top >= bottom )) loop
      mid_name := ( top + bottom ) / 2;
      if ( a_name = name_list.names( mid_name )) then
         found := TRUE;
      elsif ( a_name > name_list.names( mid_name)) then
         bottom := mid_name + 1; -- restrict search to upper half
      else                       -- of range
         top      := mid_name - 1; -- restrict search to lower half
      end if;                      -- of range
   end loop;
   if found then
      located   := TRUE;
      position := mid_name;
   else
      located := FALSE;
   end if;
end search_list;
```

This file can be stored separately from the other search file implementing the sequential search algorithm. The search method which will be used when the harness program is executed is the method implemented by the latest version of the search to be compiled into the program library prior to linking the executable file. A better method of determining which of the two alternative algorithms is to be used by a program will be introduced later in this block.

It is only possible for the two different search algorithms to be interchanged in this way as they both have an identical behaviour. The behaviour is expressed in the number, modes and types of the parameters to the procedure, and the meaning of what is done with these parameters. The files only differ in *how* they do what they do and not in *what* they do. This emphasizes the design principle of separating the what and the how of programs at the package design level.

3.1.6 Compilation considerations

The files and packages in use by this procedure and the dependencies between them can be shown as follows:

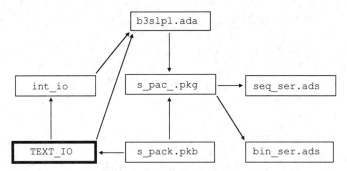

where a unit at the head of an arrow is dependent upon the unit at the tail of the arrow.

3.1.7 Search algorithm analysis

The two search algorithms presented can be evaluated according to the criteria expressed at the start of this section.

The two algorithms have an identical set of parameters. The term used for the number, modes and types of the parameters of a subprogram is the *signature* of the subprogram. As the signatures are identical it might be assumed that the two algorithms have the same degree of *generality*. However, as the name structure which is used by the binary chop algorithm has to be sorted in order for the procedure to be effective, the binary algorithm can be determined to be less general than the sequential algorithm.

There are formal and informal methods which can be used to establish the *effectiveness* of an algorithm. Formal methods rely on attempting to provide a rigorous mathematical proof that the algorithm is effective. These methods are expensive in terms of programmer time and are currently only suitable for algorithms which are important enough to justify the investment required. The details of the techniques of formal algorithm analysis are beyond the scope of this book.

Informal methods stop short of providing a proof but are suitable for general applications. The method advocated here is the provision of a set of *assertions* concerned with the implementation of the algorithm, and the presentation of the assertions and the program code to critical evaluation by other programmers.

An assertion is a statement which, in the context of the algorithm within which it is contained, is always true. The implementation of the binary chop algorithm with assertions added might be as follows:

```
begin -- search list
    -- At this stage search area is entire array &
    -- item has not been found.
    while ((not found) and ( top >= bottom )) loop
        -- At this stage search range is greater than
        -- zero locations & item has not been found.
        mid_name := ( top + bottom ) / 2;
```

```
`-- at this stage mid_name points to middle of search range
    if ( a_name = name_list.names( mid_name )) then
        found := TRUE;
        -- item has been found
    elsif ( a_name > name_list.names( mid_name)) then
        -- if item exists, it must be above mid & below top
        bottom := mid_name + 1; -- restrict search to upper half
        -- bottom now points to bottom of new search range
    else
        -- if item exists it must be below mid & above bottom
        top    := mid_name - 1; -- restrict search to lower half
        -- top now points to top of new search range
    end if;
end loop;
-- at this stage found is TRUE if item has been found
-- otherwise last search range consisted of zero items
-- therefore item could not be found in the structure.

if found then
    located  := TRUE;
    position := mid_name;
    -- position is now equal to location of item in structure
else
    located := FALSE;
end if;
    -- located is now equal to the BOOLEAN result of the search
end search_list;
```

If the program logic consisting of **while** and **if** structures is taken into consideration, the assertions consist of a series of logical arguments which when taken together provide an argument asserting the effectiveness of the algorithm. If the program statements are then related to the assertions it can be concluded that as the assertions argue the effectiveness of the algorithm and the program code is congruent with the assertions then the program code is effective.

This method of establishing the effectiveness of an implementation of an algorithm does not provide a proof. When it is used with formal black-box and white-box testing, and with the critical examination of the assertions and the code, it is a sufficient demonstration of the effectiveness in most cases.

The establishment of the *termination* of an algorithm can be subsumed within the establishment of the effectiveness of the algorithm.

The *efficiency* of these algorithms will be considered in Block 3 Section 3.

The *elegance* of an algorithm is a subjective measure but for searching an ordered structure the binary algorithm is generally held to be more elegant than the sequential algorithm.

EXERCISES

3.1.1 Produce assertions for the sequential search algorithm as implemented in this section.

3.1.2 Design and implement a procedure called search_lowest, which will locate the alphabetically lowest name in a name structure as used in this section.

3.1.3 Devise a black-box test plan for the search requirement, and use it with the harness program to demonstrate that both search algorithms are functionally identical.

3.1.4 When the sequential search algorithm is applied to an ordered list the condition for termination of the search iteration can be expressed as follows:

```
while  ( not found )       and
       ( not exhausted )   and
       ( value to find is less than or equal to the current item )
```

Design and implement this version of the sequential search algorithm and test it using the test plan from Exercise 3.1.3.

Section 3.2

Sorting algorithms

3.2.1 Sorted structures

Many different programs have a requirement to reorder the components of an iterative structure into a defined sequence. Where the components of the structure are records there is the possibility of different possible sequences. For example, a structure may be composed of records containing details of a single person and including the name of the person and the date of birth of the person. In this situation there is the possibility of the components of the sequence being organized in the sequence prescribed by the names of the people in the structure, or being organized by the dates of birth of the people in the structure. The field by which the structure is organized is known as the *key* field.

In addition, the sequence has to be defined as being *ascending* or *descending*, according to the defined key. For example, if the records of the structure illustrated in the previous section are organized by name in ascending order then the name 'Ade Abrahams' will come before the name 'Zac Zacharia'. If the sequence is organized in descending order, then 'Zac' will come before 'Ade'.

The final consideration for sorted structures is the possibility of multiple keys. Using the same example as above, the name field could be divided into two fields, surname and firstname. In this case the usual method of organization would specify that the primary ascending key would be the surname and the secondary ascending key would be firstname. This would ensure that the name 'Bunter Bessie' came before the name 'Bunter Billy' in the sorted sequence. Without specifying a secondary key it could not be guaranteed that 'Bessie' would come before 'Billy'.

It is possible for several different keys to be specified; the order of the keys will define the sequence in which the fields are considered for sequencing the structure. Each multiple key can be separately defined as ascending or descending.

3.2.2 Sorting algorithms

This section will introduce in detail two sorting algorithms which can be used to sort static structures within the computer's main memory: the *selection* sort and the *bubble* sort. There are many other more complex and more efficient sorts which could be used to sort such a structure. The next section will consider a quantitative analysis of the search algorithms introduced in Section 1 and the sort algorithms introduced in the previous section; it will also introduce the basis of the other more complex sort algorithms.

The structure which was used to illustrate search algorithms in the previous section will be used in this section to illustrate sorting algorithms. A sort algorithm expressed as a subprogram should only require the structure to be sorted to be passed to it. As the contents of the structure may have to be changed by the sort process the structure will have to be passed as an in-out parameter. The data-flow diagram of the sort subprogram will be as follows:

This data-flow diagram indicates that the subprogram is best implemented as a procedure. The s_pack package specification file will have to be amended to include the declaration of a sort procedure:

```
-- amendment to s_pack_.pkg to support sorting
procedure sort_names( a_list : in out name_structs );
```

which will also require the package definition file to be amended:

```
-- amendment to s_pack.pkb to support sorting
procedure sort_names( a_list : in out name_structs ) is separate;
```

The procedures set_up_names and show_names will be used by a sort harness program to initialize the list of names from an external file, display the names in the sequence they were read from the file, invoke the sort procedure and then display the list of names to illustrate the effectiveness of the sort. A suitable harness program follows:

```
-- sort demonstration harness file
-- filename b3s2p1.ada see text

with s_pack1, TEXT_IO, int_io;
use  s_pack1, TEXT_IO, int_io;

procedure b3s2p1 is

      max_names : constant := 15;
      -- maximum no of names in a single list

      demo_list  : name_structs( struct_size => max_names);
      -- declare name structure variable for use

begin -- b3s2p1
```

```
-- initialize names from external file
set_up_names( demo_list );

-- display the contents of the structure before sorting
show_list ( demo_list );
-- sort the structure
sort_names( demo_list );
-- display the contents of the structure after sorting
show_list( demo_list );
```

end b3s2p1;

The external file 'names.dat' from which the names list structure will be initialized, will be assumed to contain twelve names in a sequence which will set the variable object demo_list to the following:

demo_list		names	
15 - >			
14 - >			
13 - >			
12 - >	Charles	Chaplin
11 - >	Yvonne	Young
10 - >	Linda	Lovelace
9 - >	Bessie	Bunter
8 - >	Desmond	Dekker
7 - >	Norma	Nugen
6 - >	Esther	Estherson
5 - >	Ade	Abrahams
4 - >	Max	Madden
3 - >	Zac	Zacharia
in_use 2 - >	Fred	Flintstone
12 1 - >	Billie	Bunter

3.2.3 The selection sort algorithm

The selection algorithm proceeds by dividing the structure into a sorted and an unsorted part. Initially the sorted part of the structure consists of zero elements and the unsorted part of the structure consists of all the elements in the structure. If the element with the lowest (or highest) key value is located within the unsorted part of the structure and moved to the first position of the unsorted structure, the sorted part of the structure would have increased by one element and the unsorted part of the structure would have decreased by one element. This process can be repeated until the unsorted part of the structure consists of a single element. At this point the unsorted part is by definition sorted and the whole structure can be regarded as sorted.

In order to implement this sort algorithm, the search-for-lowest algorithm which was mentioned in the last section, and included as Exercise 3.1.2, will have to be implemented. The data-flow diagram for a suitable version of this algorithm follows:

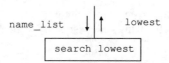

This data-flow diagram indicates that the algorithm search_lowest will search the entire range of the name_list part of a name_structs structure and return an index value which points to the lowest element in the list. The data-flow diagram indicates that it would best be implemented as a function of the type of the structure's index, in this example NATURAL.

The design for this function will be as follows:

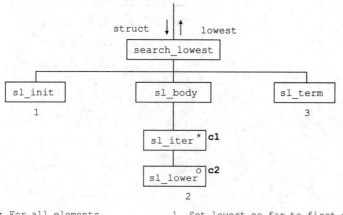

c1: For all elements   1. Set lowest so far to first of list.
    in list.   2. Set lowest so far to this element.
c2: If this element less than 3. Return lowest so far.
    lowest so far.

This design can be implemented as set out below:

```
function search_lowest ( a_list : name_lists ) return NATURAL is
-- function to determine the lowest value in the list
-- supplied and return its index value

    lowest_so_far : NATURAL :=  a_list'FIRST ;
```

```
    -- at this stage lowest so far is the first in the list

begin -- search lowest
    -- consider all remaining names in the list
    for this_name in (a_list'FIRST +1 ) .. a_list'LAST loop
        if ( a_list( this_name ) < a_list(lowest_so_far)) then
            lowest_so_far := this_name;
        end if;
    end loop;
    return lowest_so_far;
end search_lowest;
```

Using this function the design of the selection_search algorithm would be as follows:

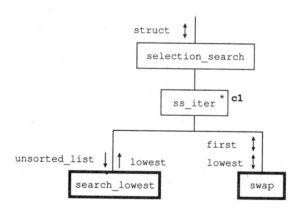

c1: For each possible unsorted list.

Using this design the implementation of the sort procedure would be as set out below:

```
procedure sort_names ( a_list : in out name_structs is

    the_lowest : NATURAL; -- position of the lowest value in the list

begin -- sort_names
    -- move unsorted limit from start to end of list
    for unsorted_limit in
        a_list.names'FIRST .. (a_list.in_use -1) loop
```

```
      -- find lowest name in unsorted part of structure
      the_lowest := search_lowest( a_list.names
                      (unsorted_limit .. a_list.in_use ));
      -- append lowest name to end of sorted list
      swap_names( a_list.names( unsorted_limit),
                    a_list.names( the_lowest));
   end loop;
end sort_names;
```

The procedure contains a definite iteration which commences with the loop parameter at the first element of the list and continues until the loop parameter is one less than the end of the list. This iteration is used to delineate the first element of the unsorted part of the structure. On the first iteration of the loop the entire list is considered to be unsorted; on each succeeding iteration the size of the unsorted list is reduced by one.

Within each iteration the unsorted slice of the array names is passed to the function search_lowest which returns the index value of the alphabetically lowest name in the slice. This name is then swapped with the name at the head of the unsorted list using the procedure swap_names, whose definition would be as follows:

```
procedure swap_names( this_name,
                    that_name : in out name_strings ) is
-- procedure to swap the contents of the two names supplied

   temp_name  : name_strings := this_name;

begin -- swap names
   this_name := that_name;
   that_name := temp_name;
end swap_names;
```

The effectiveness of this algorithm can be demonstrated by considering its application to the initialized structure shown earlier in this section. The state of the structure before the sort will be represented as follows:

	1	2	3	4	5	6	7	8	9	10	11	12
0	Bi B	F F	Z Z	M M	A A	E E	N N	D D	Be B	L L	Y Y	C C

This diagram shows the contents of the elements of the array using initials only (with the exception of *Be*ssie and *Bi*lly Bunter). The value of in_use is 12, indicating that there are twelve names in the list. The double line indicates the extent of the sorted part of the array, which at this stage is zero elements.

The definite loop will iterate, with the value of unsorted_limit changing from 1 to 11. On the first iteration of the loop, the function search_lowest will be called with the slice of the array whose limits are 1 and 12. Search_lowest will return the position of the lowest element in this slice, which is Ade Abrahams at position 5.

The swap procedure will interchange the names at position 1 and 5. The state of the array at the end of the first iteration of the selection algorithm would thus be as follows:

	1	2	3	4	5	6	7	8	9	10	11	12
1	A A	F F	Z Z	M M	Bi B	E E	N N	D D	Be B	L L	Y Y	C C

The lowest element in the structure has been moved to position 1 of the structure, creating a sorted structure of length one element which contains the lowest value in the entire structure. The sorted part of the structure is followed by an unsorted structure of eleven elements.

On the second iteration of the definite loop the value of the loop index unsorted_limit will be 2. This will cause the lowest element in the slice whose range is 2 to 12 to be located (Bessie Bunter) and interchanged with the element at the head of the unsorted structure. The structure will now be ordered as follows:

	1	2	3	4	5	6	7	8	9	10	11	12
2	A A	Be B	Z Z	M M	Bi B	E E	N N	D D	F F	L L	Y Y	C C

The length of the sorted part of the structure has increased to two elements, the first of which, as demonstrated above, is the lowest element in the entire structure, and the second of which is the lowest in the structure excluding the element already positioned. The length of the unsorted part of the structure has now decreased to ten elements.

On the third iteration the lowest element of the unsorted structure will be identified as Billy Bunter in position 9 and will be interchanged with Zac Zacharia at position 3. The state of the structure will now be as shown below:

	1	2	3	4	5	6	7	8	9	10	11	12
3	A A	Be B	Bi B	M M	Z Z	E E	N N	D D	F F	L L	Y Y	C C

The process will continue through eight further iterations, each time locating the lowest element in the unsorted part of the structure and interchanging it with the element at the start of the unsorted part of the structure. The state of the structure after each iteration will be as follows:

	1	2	3	4	5	6	7	8	9	10	11	12
4	A A	Bi B	Be B	C C	Z Z	E E	N N	D D	F F	L L	Y Y	M M

	1	2	3	4	5	6	7	8	9	10	11	12
5	A A	Bi B	Be B	C C	D D	E E	N N	Z Z	F F	L L	Y Y	M M

	1	2	3	4	5	6	7	8	9	10	11	12
6	A A	Bi B	Be B	C C	D D	E E	N N	Z Z	F F	L L	Y Y	M M

On the sixth iteration the lowest element in the range 6 to 12 in the array was searched for. This element was identified as Esther Estherson at the first position in the unsorted range: the swap procedure was called to swap the element at position 6 with the element at position 6! The sort would continue as shown below:

	1	2	3	4	5	6	7	8	9	10	11	12
7	A A	Bi B	Be B	C C	D D	E E	F F	Z Z	N N	L L	Y Y	M M

	1	2	3	4	5	6	7	8	9	10	11	12
8	A A	Bi B	Be B	C C	D D	E E	F F	L L	N N	Z Z	Y Y	M M

	1	2	3	4	5	6	7	8	9	10	11	12
9	A A	Bi B	Be B	C C	D D	E E	F F	L L	M M	Z Z	Y Y	N N

	1	2	3	4	5	6	7	8	9	10	11	12
10	A A	Bi B	Be B	C C	D D	E E	F F	L L	M M	N N	Y Y	Z Z

	1	2	3	4	5	6	7	8	9	10	11	12
11	A A	Bi B	Be B	C C	D D	E E	F F	L L	M M	N N	Y Y	Z Z

At this stage the algorithm terminates. The length of the sorted part of the structure is eleven elements and the length of the unsorted part is a single element which is itself sorted.

In this example the structure was fully sorted after the tenth pass; the remaining pass achieved nothing. If the structure had been fully sorted before the first pass the algorithm would still have proceeded with twelve passes of the structure before concluding. These considerations can be obviated by using a more efficient algorithm.

3.2.4 The bubble sort algorithm

The bubble sort algorithm improves upon the selection sort algorithm by only making as many passes through the structure as are required to ensure it is sorted. It also differs from the selection sort algorithm by interchanging adjacent pairs of records on each pass through the structure. The design of this algorithm follows:

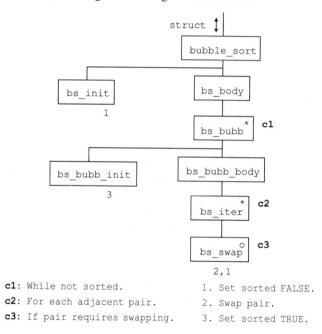

c1: While not sorted.   1. Set sorted FALSE.
c2: For each adjacent pair.   2. Swap pair.
c3: If pair requires swapping. 3. Set sorted TRUE.

This design can be implemented as shown below:

```
procedure sort_names( a_list : in out name_structs ) is

        is_sorted : BOOLEAN := FALSE;

begin -- sort names
    while ( not( is_sorted) ) loop
        is_sorted := TRUE;
        for this_name in 1 .. (a_list.in_use -1) loop
            if ( a_list.names( this_name)  >
                a_list.names( this_name + 1) ) then
                swap_names( a_list.names( this_name ),
                        a_list.names( this_name + 1));
```

```
                is_sorted := FALSE;
          end if;
      end loop;
   end loop;
end sort_names;
```

This implementation requires the swap procedure whose implementation is unchanged from the swap procedure used by the selection sort algorithm. The behaviour of this algorithm can be illustrated by considering the state of the same structure as was used for the selection sort, showing the state of the structure after each pass of the definite inner loop.

The state of the structure before the first pass is as follows:

	1	2	3	4	5	6	7	8	9	10	11	12
0	Bi B	F F	Z Z	M M	A A	E E	N N	D D	Be B	L L	Y Y	C C

During the first pass the first swap would be made when the pair of records at positions 3 and 4 were compared. As the swap is performed within the scope of the **if** the value of the sorted flag will be set to FALSE, indicating that a swap has been performed and preventing the outer indefinite loop from terminating. The state of the structure after this swap has been performed would be as shown below:

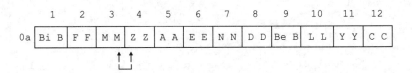

	1	2	3	4	5	6	7	8	9	10	11	12
0a	Bi B	F F	M M	Z Z	A A	E E	N N	D D	Be B	L L	Y Y	C C

The position of the swap has been indicated under the structure. This pass would continue with several more swaps producing a structure in the following state at the end of the first pass:

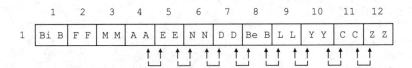

	1	2	3	4	5	6	7	8	9	10	11	12
1	Bi B	F F	M M	A A	E E	N N	D D	Be B	L L	Y Y	C C	Z Z

As a swap was made during this pass a second pass would be made which would leave the structure in the following state:

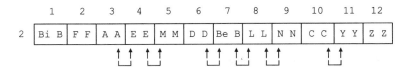

Again, as a swap was made another pass will be required. Following this pass the structure would be in this state:

The algorithm would continue with the following passes:

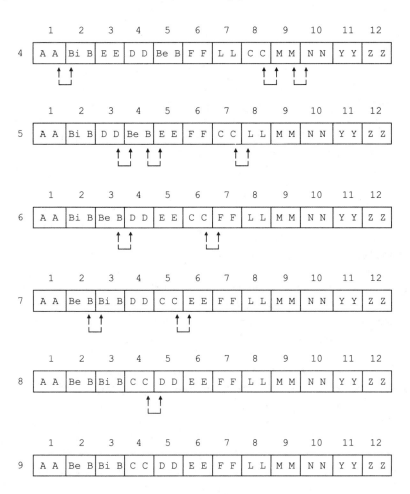

On this ninth pass through the structure no exchanges have been made, thus the structure is known to be sorted and the algorithm can terminate. The reason why this algorithm is known as a bubble sort can be seen if the position of the Charlie Chaplin record is followed through the passes. Starting at position 12 of the structure on the first pass it moves one position upon each iteration until it is located in its final position at the end of the eighth pass.

If the structure were sorted before the first pass the algorithm would require only one pass through the structure. As the structure is sorted no swaps would be made and thus the indefinite loop would terminate following one iteration.

3.2.5 Selection and bubble sorts compared

The selection and bubble sorts can be compared using the criteria established at the start of Block 3 Section 1. Both algorithms have the same degree of *generality*: the signature of both procedures is a structure which can be in any state before the sort is invoked. Both algorithms are totally *effective*, although this has not been sufficiently demonstrated. Both implementations will *terminate*, producing a sorted structure from a structure input in any state. The *efficiency* of the algorithms will be considered in the next section. The *elegance* of the algorithms is again largely subjective; most people favour the bubble sort on the grounds of simplicity.

3.2.6 Multiple key sorts

The records being sorted in this section consisted of a single field of type name_strings. If the structure of the record were made more realistic by dividing the name field into two fields called surname and firstname, the sort might become partially ineffective. If only the surname were specified as the key then the possibility would arise of names which have the same surname being misordered with regard to their firstnames. For example, in the list as considered in this section it would be possible for Billy Bunter to appear in the sorted list before Bessie Bunter.

This does not necessarily mean that the algorithm is ineffective. If the specification for the sort only required the surname to be considered then this ordering of the names would comply with the specification.

If two keys were specified, surname as the primary key and firstname as the secondary key, then there are two possible methods of adapting the implementation of the algorithms. The first of these is to amend the test which determines if a swap is to be made by specifying a comparison involving both keys, as in the following:

```
if (name[this].surname < name[that].surname) then
   swap( name[this], name[that] );
elsif ((name[this].surname = name[that].surname)  and then
       (name[this].firstname < name[that].firstname) )then
       swap( name[this], name[that] );
end if;
```

This approach may be appropriate for a search requiring two keys but would become more and more cumbersome as more and more keys were specified.

A second solution which avoids this problem is to sort the structure by the secondary key before sorting the structure by the primary key. The first sort using the firstname as the key would ensure that Bessie came before Billy, before the second sort using surname as the key commenced. As has been noted, the existing firstname ordering will be preserved by the surname sort, ensuring that the required sequence of both keys is satisfied.

This might imply that two versions of the sort algorithm would be required, one which would sort by surname and one which would sort by firstname. If multiple key sorts were required then this would require multiple versions of the sort algorithm. This problem can be obviated by redesigning the implementation of the sort procedures to make them more general. This redesign and the techniques for implementing it will be introduced in Block 3 Section 4.

EXERCISES

3.2.1 Amend the selection and bubble sort algorithms introduced in this section so that they keep a count of the number of comparisons and the number of swaps while the sorting is taking place. This will require two output-only NATURAL parameters to be added to the signature of the sort procedure:

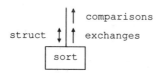

Amend the harness program so that when the structure is sorted the number of comparisons and the number of exchanges is displayed.

Investigate the number of comparisons and exchanges made by each algorithm for structures of different lengths and having different initial organizations. This can be accomplished by having different versions of the 'names.dat' data file available.

3.2.2 The bubble sort as presented in this section can be optimized. Determine the means by which this can be done and design and implement an optimized bubble sort to sort the structure used in this section.

Implement the optimized version as in Exercise 3.2.1 and investigate the degree of optimization.

3.2.3 Reimplement the name_strings declaration in the s_pack package as a record containing a surname and a firstname. Reimplement the package declaration to comply. As a name is read from the external file all characters up to the first space should be placed in the firstname part of the record and all characters succeeding that space in the surname part. You may assume that all names on the data file will comply with this format.

Ensure that the set_up_names and show_names parts of the package are functioning correctly before proceeding to Exercise 3.2.4.

3.2.4 Reimplement the sort algorithms as described in this section using the structure surname as the primary key and the firstname as the secondary key.

Section 3.3

Algorithm analysis

Sections 1 and 2 of this block have reinforced the point previously made that for any requirement there is always more than one effective algorithm. In some cases it is easy to select between different possible algorithms; for example, when searching an ordered structure the binary chop method is clearly preferable to the sequential search method. There are other situations where the choice between different possible algorithms is not as easy to make. For example, under what circumstances is the selection sort algorithm better than the bubble sort algorithm?

An understanding of the dynamic behaviour of these algorithms can lead to an analysis of how well they perform under different circumstances. This is primarily a consideration of the efficiency of an algorithm. These techniques can then be applied to any algorithms to provide some indication of under what circumstances a choice can sensibly be made between them. This section will introduce the techniques of analyzing the dynamic behaviour of algorithms, using the search and sort algorithms introduced in Sections 1 and 2 of this block as examples.

3.3.1 The sequential search algorithm

The behaviour of this algorithm when searching for an item in a structure of n items will be investigated; the changes in the algorithm's behaviour as n increases will then be considered.

The best possible behaviour of this algorithm is for the item being searched for to be located at the start of the structure being searched. When this is the case the main loop of the algorithm will iterate once only.

The worst possible behaviour of this algorithm is for the item being searched for not to be located in the structure being searched. When this is the case the main loop of the algorithm will iterate as many times as there are items in the structure, before it can be concluded that the item being sought is not contained within the structure.

Assuming for a moment that all searches are successful, the average behaviour of this algorithm can be assumed to be when the item being searched for is located half-way through the structure. When this is the case the main loop of the algorithm will iterate n/2 times, where n is the number of items in the structure.

The average overall behaviour of the algorithm when unsuccessful searches are considered can only be stated if the proportions of successful and unsuccessful searches are known. Assuming the proportion of successful searches is Ps and the proportion of unsuccessful searches is Pu, then the average behaviour of this algorithm is

$$\texttt{Ps(n/2) + Pu(n)}$$

These results are summarized in Table 3.3.1.

Table 3.3.1 Sequential search algorithm: number of main-loop iterations required when searching for an item in a structure of n items

best case	1
worst case	n
average case	Ps(n/2) + Pu(n)
average case	n/2
(where Pu = 0)	

The measure being used in this analysis is the number of iterations of the main loop of the algorithm. It was noted in Exercise 3.1.4 that there are variations of the algorithm which can cause the evaluation of the condition which controls the main loop of the algorithm to be simplified and for the contents of the loop to be simplified. This optimization will reduce the time taken for an iteration of the loop but will not allow an absolute timing or even a relative timing to be stated.

All that can be said with any certainty from the analysis above is that in all cases apart from the best-case situation, doubling the size of the structure being searched will double the time taken for the algorithm to execute. A relative statement of this form is the only statement which can be made about an algorithm with this degree of confidence, without extensive investigations.

3.3.2 The binary chop algorithm

The best-case situation for the binary search algorithm is again the possibility of the item being searched for being located on the first iteration of the main loop.

The worst-case situation can be derived from a consideration of the number of iterations required for structures of different sizes. Again, the worst-case situation is where the item being sought does not exist within the structure.

For a structure with one element, one iteration would be required to determine that the item being searched for did not exist within the structure. For a structure with two elements two iterations would be required: the first iteration will determine that the first item examined is not the item required and the second iteration will examine the other item to determine that it is not the item required.

For a structure with four elements a maximum of three iterations would be required. This can be derived from the two-element case. The first iteration will examine the item at position 3 and determine that the item being sought lies above or below position 3. The worst case is for the item to be above position 3, requiring a sub-search of a two-item structure, which will cause a search of two iterations to be required. This makes a total of three iterations to determine that the item does not exist within the structure.

For a structure with eight elements a similar argument will conclude that four iterations will be required. The first will divide the search area approximately in half, requiring a subsearch of a structure with a maximum of four elements, which as shown above will require a maximum of three iterations. Thus a total of four iterations will be required to search unsuccessfully a structure of eight elements.

Continuing this argument, each doubling of the size of the structure will add one to the number of iterations required to search the structure. For a structure of n items the number of iterations required will be equal to $1 + \log_2 n$.

The average-case behaviour of this algorithm for successful searches can be derived from the worst-case behaviour. Each iteration of the algorithm halves the area being searched and focuses on the area where the item being sought may be found. If the item being sought is within the structure being sought then it can be expected to be found towards the end of this process as the search area 'homes in' on the item being sought. Thus the average behaviour of this algorithm approximates to $\log_2 n$.

The average overall behaviour of this algorithm again can only be stated exactly if the proportion of successful and unsuccessful searches is known. If these values are known then the average overall behaviour would be as follows:

$$\text{Ps}(\sim\log_2 n) + \text{Pu}(1 + \log_2 n)$$

which is $\sim\log_2 n$. These results are summarized in Table 3.3.2.

Table 3.3.2 Binary chop algorithm: number of main-loop iterations required when searching for an item in a structure of n items

best case	1
worst case	$\log_2 n$
average case	$\sim\log_2 n$
average case (where Pu = 0)	$\sim\log_2 n$

Table 3.3.2 can be compared with the summary behaviour of the sequential search algorithm. For a structure of n items, apart from the best-case consideration, the binary

chop algorithm will require fewer iterations by a factor of $\log_2 n/n$. As the size of the structure being searched increases, the difference between the two algorithms in the number of iterations required will grow wider. A doubling of the size of the structure will require a doubling of the number of iterations required by the sequential search algorithm, but will only increase the number of iterations required by the binary chop algorithm by 1.

Two other considerations have to be offset against this. First, the body of the loop of the binary chop algorithm is more complex than the body of the loop of the sequential search algorithm. Likewise, the evaluation of the test which controls the iteration is more complex for the binary chop algorithm than for the sequential search algorithm. This increased complexity of the binary chop algorithm will cause it to be less efficient than the sequential search algorithm for very small structures. As the size of structure becomes larger the increased complexity of the binary chop algorithm will be offset by the smaller number of iterations required.

The binary chop algorithm can, however, only be applied to a sorted structure. If the structure has to be maintained in a sorted order, as a part of the system or other program requirements, then the costs of maintaining the structure in a sorted order are not relevant to the costs of searching the structure.

If there is no requirement for the structure to be sorted apart from allowing the search function to be implemented more effectively, then the costs of sorting the structure will have to be included in the considerations of searching costs. To evaluate this the costs of sorting a structure will have to be investigated.

3.3.3 The selection sort algorithm

For the analysis of sort algorithms the best-case, worst-case and average-case situations have to be defined. For this analysis the best-case situation is a structure whose elements are already in order; the worst-case situation is a structure whose elements are in reverse order to the sequence required; for an average case a structure whose elements are in a random order will be considered.

The analysis of the selection sort algorithm will depend upon an analysis of the search_lowest algorithm. This algorithm has a very simple profile; in order to determine the highest element of an unordered structure every element of the structure has to be examined. So for a structure of n items, n iterations of the main loop of the search_lowest algorithm will be required.

In the main part of the selection sort algorithm there will be one fewer iterations of the main loop than the number of elements in the structure. Each iteration of this loop will invoke the search_lowest algorithm. On the first invocation of the search_lowest algorithm the algorithm will be asked to search the entire structure being sorted. On the second invocation of the search_lowest algorithm it will be asked to search one fewer than the number of elements in the structure, on the third two fewer, and so on. On the last invocation of the search_lowest algorithm it will be asked to determine the lowest of a substructure comprising of two elements. Thus on average during the selection search algorithm each invocation of the search_lowest algorithm will be required to search a structure which is approximately n/2 elements in size, where n is the number of elements in the structure being sorted. The search_lowest algorithm will be invoked n-1 times, so the total number of iterations of the loop of the search_lowest algorithm will be n-1(n/2), which is approximately equal to $n^2/2$. This behaviour of the selection sort algorithm is independent of the initial state of the structure being sorted. The algorithm takes no account of when the structure becomes ordered; thus this behaviour holds for the best-case, worst-case and average-case situation.

Before concluding the analysis of the selection sort algorithm the number of comparisons and exchanges required should be noted. The body of the loop which comprises the search_lowest algorithm consists essentially of a comparison; thus the number of comparisons made is equal to the number of iterations as determined above. The body of the loop of the selection sort algorithm consists of an invocation of the search_lowest algorithm, followed by an invocation of the swap algorithm. Thus in addition to the number of comparisons required by the selection algorithm as noted above it also requires n-1 exchanges to be performed.

3.3.4 The bubble sort algorithm

As was noted in Block 3 Section 2, the bubble sort algorithm will terminate when the structure is determined by the algorithm to be sorted; thus the behaviour of this algorithm will be different for the best-case, worst-case and average-case situation.

The analysis of the best-case situation is straightforward. The algorithm will determine on the first iteration of its outermost (**while**) loop that the structure is ordered. This will be determined by the fact that after comparing all adjacent pairs of elements in the structure, using its innermost (**for**) loop, no exchanges were required. The number of adjacent pairs in the structure is one less than the size of the structure, so for the best case the number of comparisons will be n-1 and the number of exchanges will be 0.

For the worst-case situation the analysis is more difficult. The basis of this analysis is to consider the element at the end of the structure; the correct place for this element in an ordered structure will be at the start of the structure. As was noted in the trace of the bubble sort algorithm in Block 3 Section 2, each iteration of the main loop will move the element at the end of the structure one place closer to the position where it is required. Thus to reposition an element from the rear of the structure to the start of the structure n-1 iterations of the main loop will be required. On the last iteration an exchange will be required to position this element at the start of the structure; this exchange will prevent the algorithm from terminating. The next iteration of the main loop will determine that the structure is ordered, thus the total number of iterations of the outer loop will be (n-1) + 1 which is n.

Each iteration of the loop requires all adjacent pairs of elements to be examined using the inner loop; as was noted above this is n-1 comparisons for each iteration of the outer loop. Consequently the total number of comparisons required in the worst-case situation would be n(n-1), which is approximately n^2.

The number of exchanges required can also be determined, assuming a structure containing an odd number of elements. For the worst-case situation the middle element of the structure can be assumed to be in position. The element above the middle element will have to be moved to the position below the middle element which will require two exchanges. Likewise, the element below the middle element will have to be moved to the position above the middle element, which will also require two exchanges. Continuing this argument, the element two positions above the middle element of the structure will have to be interchanged with the element two positions below the middle element of the structure. This will require each element to experience four exchanges.

It has already been noted that the element at the end of the structure will require n-1 exchanges to move it to the start of the structure. The element which was originally at the start of the structure will also require n-1 exchanges to move it to the end of the structure. The element next to the element at the start of the structure will have to be interchanged with the element next to the element at the end of the structure. This will require n-3 exchanges to be performed. Likewise the element next to the element at the end of the structure will also require n-3 exchanges.

For a structure comprising of n elements the number of exchanges required for half the elements in the structure to be positioned can be tabulated as follows:

initial position	start 1	2	3	...	n/2–2	n/2–1	middle n/2
exchanges required	n –1	n –3	n –5	...	4	2	0

The number of exchanges experienced by the elements in the other half of the structure will be equal to the number of exchanges required by the corresponding element in this half of the structure.

Each exchange performed in the algorithm exchanges the position of two adjacent elements, moving each element one position towards the position in which it is required to be for the structure to be ordered. No exchange moves an element away from its final position. Each exchange performed is experienced by two elements in the structure. Thus the total number of exchanges required is equal to half the total number of exchanges experienced by all the elements in the structure.

The total number of exchanges will thus be equal to the sum of the number of exchanges required for each item in the half of the structure as shown in the diagram. If the series of expressions representing the exchanges required is reversed and added to itself term by term the sum will be twice the total number of exchanges required. This sum will be as follows:

original series	$n-1$	$n-3$	$n-5$	...	4	2	0
reversed series	0	2	4	...	$n-5$	$n-3$	$n-1$
original + reversed	$n-1$	$n-1$	$n-1$		$n-1$	$n-1$	$n-1$

Thus as there are n/2 terms in the series the total number of exchanges will be n/2 times (n-1) which is approximately $n^2/2$.

So for the worst-case situation the bubble sort algorithm will make a total of approximately n^2 comparisons and $n^2/2$ exchanges. The average-case behaviour of the bubble sort algorithm can be shown to be approximately equal to the worst-case behaviour. It can be assumed that for a randomized structure every element is on average half the size of the structure away from the position it has to occupy in the ordered structure; this will require n/2 exchanges in order to position it. As the structure comprises n elements the total number of exchanges required will be n(n/2) which is $n^2/2$. If on average there is a fifty-fifty chance of a comparison requiring an exchange then the number of comparisons will be equal to twice the number of exchanges which will be n^2.

3.3.5 Selection and bubble sorts compared

The behaviour of both sorts is summarized in Table 3.3.3. In the best-case situation the bubble sort outperforms the selection sort dramatically. As the situation changes the performance of the selection sort does not change but the performance of the bubble sort declines dramatically, until by the average-case situation the selection sort outperforms the bubble sort.

Table 3.3.3 Selection and bubble sorts: number of main-loop iterations required to sort in items

	SELECTION		BUBBLE	
	comparisons	exchanges	comparisons	exchanges
best case	$n^2/2$	$n-1$	$n-1$	0
average case	$n^2/2$	$n-1$	n^2	$n^2/2$
worst case	$n^2/2$	$n-1$	n^2	$n^2/2$

The advantage of the selection sort becomes clearer when the relative costs of a comparison and an exchange are considered. A comparison of two elements in a structure will be implemented as a relational comparison which will not require large computer resources. An exchange will require much greater resources. Thus the dramatic difference in the number of exchanges confirms the superiority of the selection sort in the average- and worst-case situation.

What can be concluded from the comparison of the selection and bubble sort algorithms is that for nearly ordered structures the bubble sort will outperform the selection sort. As the structure becomes more disordered the selection sort becomes favoured. The degree of disorder which favours the bubble sort can only be determined when the relative costs of a comparison and an exchange are known and the degree of disorder of the structure can be estimated.

It can also be concluded for both these algorithms that as the size of the structure to be sorted increases the number of comparisons and thus the time taken increases in proportion to the square of the number items in the structure.

These costs can be taken into account when the sequential search and the binary chop are compared. If the structure does not have to be sorted for any reason other than to improve the efficiency of the search process, then the costs of sorting the structure have to be taken into account to counterbalance the improved performance of the binary chop. If the search application is time critical then the improved response time of the binary chop has to be evaluated against the time taken to sort the structure or to maintain the structure in an ordered sequence.

If the application is not time-critical then the number of searches which will be required has to be evaluated against the time and resources taken to sort the structure. If only a few searches will be required then the costs of sorting the structure will not be repaid by the improved performance of the binary chop. If a large number of searches will be required then the costs of sorting the structure may be repaid by the improved performance of the searches.

3.3.6 The order of an algorithm

The four algorithms which have been analyzed in this section differ in the amount of resources which they require as the size of the structure they are applied to increases.

The sequential search algorithm was linear. Where n is the size of the structure which is being searched the amount of time required to search the structure, measured as the number of times the loop was iterated, increased in proportion to n.

The binary chop algorithm had a better than linear behaviour. For a structure of size n the amount of time required, measured as the number of times the loop iterated, increased in proportion to $\log_2 n$.

The behaviour of the sort algorithms was worse than linear. For a structure of size n the amount of time required, measured as the number of times the innermost loop of the selection sort algorithm iterated and ignoring the time taken for exchanges, increased in proportion to n^2.

The behaviour of the algorithms is summarized in the form of a graph in Figure

3.3.1. The behaviour of the binary chop algorithm is very acceptable; even for very large structures the amount of time taken to search it will not be too large. The behaviour of the sequential search algorithm is acceptable for large structures, but not for very large structures. The behaviour of the sort algorithms is unacceptable for all but the smallest structures. As the size of the structure being sorted becomes larger the amount of time taken for the sort becomes unacceptably large.

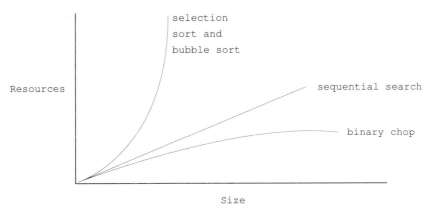

Figure 3.3.1 Approximate comparison of sequential search, binary chop search, selection sort and bubble sort as size of structure increases

Improvements in the efficiency of sort algorithms can be made by sorting half the structure at a time and then merging the two structures together. The total cost of this sort will be made up of the costs of sorting two structures, each of which is half the size of the entire structure, and the cost of merging the two sorted substructures. The merge algorithm which would be required is a linear algorithm. Sorts which operate on this basic method are known as the *shell* sort and the *quick* sort.

EXERCISES

3.3.1 Complete the following table, showing the relative performance of the algorithms. Assume average behaviour in all cases.

size of structure

	32	256	1024	4096	65536	262144
sequential search						
binary chop						
selection sort						
bubble sort						

3.3.2 Using the programs from Exercises 3.1.4 and 3.2.1, attempt to validate experimentally the results from the table in Exercise 3.3.1.

3.3.3 Two other sort algorithms are the shell sort and the quick sort. Locate and implement algorithms for these sorts. Attempt to prove experimentally that they improve upon the performance of the selection and bubble sorts.

3.3.4 Using the divide sort and merge (dsm) description of an improved sort algorithm given above, and assuming that costs of merging two structures each of size n/2 are n comparisons and n exchanges, construct a table similar to the table in Exercise 3.3.1 illustrating the relative costs of the simple bubble and selection sorts compared with the dsm sort for structures of differing lengths. What can be concluded from the table?

Generic searching and sorting

The search and sort algorithms which were introduced in Sections 1 and 2 of this block were initially expressed in very general terms. The implementations of the algorithms in the example programs were, however, very specific. Thus although the algorithm could be used as a description of a method for searching or sorting a list of names or a list of integers or a list of floating-point values or a list of records, the implementation which was produced was only capable of sorting a particular type of list, a list of names.

If it were required to produce a program which had a requirement to search or sort a list composed of a different type of element, then the programs which have already been produced could not be used. The expression of the algorithm in the form of an Ada source file could be adapted with the use of a text editor and resubmitted for recompilation. This would reduce the workload for the programmer, but the programs would still be regarded by Ada as two distinct programs with no similarity between them. It would also be possible for errors to be introduced as the text was edited, which would imply that extensive testing of the adapted implementation would be required.

This duplication of effort can be avoided in Ada programs by the use of *generic* facilities, which can be used to declare a generic subprogram or a generic package. A generic program unit (procedure, function or package) expresses *how* an algorithm can be applied to a particular class of Ada data types; it does not explicitly state *what* the particular type of those objects is. In order to use the generic unit, a specific instance of the unit suitable for a particular instance of the type in use has to be created.

Examples of the use of generic packages have already been extensively used in this book. The packages used for the input and outut of values are examples of generic packages. The package INTEGER_IO contained within TEXT_IO is a generic package which is suitable for the input and output of different types of integer values. In order to use the facilities of INTEGER_IO for a particular type a new instance of the generic package has to be created and brought into use. Thus the declaration

```
package int_io is new TEXT_IO.INTEGER_IO( INTEGER );
```

causes a new instance of the generic package INTEGER_IO which is contained within TEXT_IO, tailored for the input and output of values of the predeclared data type INTEGER. Once created, the new package is placed in an Ada library, from where it can be **with**ed and **use**d by any program which has a requirement for the input or output of integer values. The creation of such an instance of a generic package is known as the *instantiation* of a package.

The advantages which arise from being able to employ predeclared packages such as INTEGER_IO can also be enjoyed by programmer-declared generic packages. For example, the definition and declaration of a generic package called search_pack would express the essence of a version of the search algorithm. Having produced such a generic package, specific instances of the package can be created and used which are suitable for the searching of specific structures. Whenever a program had a requirement to search such a structure a suitable instance of the generic package could be created and used, or if the structure was suitably common an instantiated version of the package could be maintained in the library. As the generic package would have been extensively tested during its development, it could be assumed by the programmer that the search process within the application program would not require further testing.

This section will introduce the facilities available for the creation and use of generic procedures and generic packages by reimplementing generic versions of the search and sort algorithms introduced in Sections 1 and 2 of this block.

3.4.1 Generic procedures

To introduce generic procedures, the swap procedure used in the sorting packages in Block 3 Section 2 will be generically reimplemented. One way of identifying the generic aspect of a unit is to produce two non-generic versions of the unit configured for two different data types. The two versions of the procedure can then be compared to determine what aspects of them are common and what aspects are different. These commonalities and differences can then be used to design the generic unit. Two instances of the swap procedure, one suitable for swapping two INTEGER values and one suitable for swapping two FLOAT values, follow:

```
procedure swap_ints( this_int, that_int : in out INTEGER) is

    temp : INTEGER := this_int;

begin -- swap ints
    this_int := that_int;
    that_int := temp;
end swap_ints;


procedure swap_floats( this_float, that_float : in out FLOAT) is

    temp : FLOAT := this_float;

begin -- swap floats
    this_float := that_float;
```

```
        that_float := temp;
    end swap_floats;
```

Examination of the code of these two procedures will reveal the similarities and the differences between them. Both procedures have two in-out parameters of the type which is to be swapped and both require a local variable of that type to be declared. Both versions of the procedure only require the assignment operation to be performed upon the values being swapped. The only difference between the procedures is in the type of the values being swapped; this indicates that the type of the value to be swapped will be a generic parameter of the generic procedure.

It is now possible to produce the declaration of the generic procedure:

```
generic
    type element is private
    procedure swap( this, that : in out element );
```

This declaration commences with the reserved word **generic**, which indicates to Ada that the declaration of a generic subprogram or a generic package is about to be made. The second part of the declaration, between the reserved word generic and the reserved word **procedure**, **function** or **package**, is used to declare the generic formal parameters of the generic unit. In this example, the type of object which is to be swapped has been identified as the single generic parameter. This type is expressed in a type declaration with the type name element, and is qualified as being **private**. A generic private type can only be assumed to have the assignment and equality operations applied to it within the generic unit. As noted above, only the assignment operation is required within the swap procedure. The heading of the generic procedure completes the declaration of the generic swap procedure. The heading specifies that the procedure is called swap and requires two in-out parameters of generic formal parameter type 'element' to be provided.

Following the declaration of the generic swap procedure the definition of the procedure can be provided. The definition can follow the procedure declaration immediately, or subsequently, or can be defined as being separate. The definition of the generic swap procedure in this example can be expressed as follows:

```
    procedure swap( this, that : in out element) is

        temp : element := this;

    begin -- swap
        this := that;
        that := temp;
    end swap;
```

Having declared the generic procedure, and possibly before it is defined, specific instances of the procedure can be instantiated:

```
procedure swap_ints   is new swap( INTEGER );
procedure swap_floats is new swap( element => FLOAT );
-- assuming s_pack is withed see b3s1 & 2
procedure swap_names  is new swap( s_pack.name_strings );
```

These declarations create new instantiations of the generic procedure swap with the names specified and are capable of swapping values of the actual parameter specified. The first declaration creates a version of the swap procedure called swap_ints, suitable for swapping INTEGER values, the data type for which it is configured is expressed as an actual parameter of the instantiation using positional notation. The second declaration creates a version of the swap procedure called swap_floats suitable for swapping FLOAT values; the data type for which it is configured is expressed as an actual parameter of the instantiation using named notation. The final declaration creates a version of the swap procedure called swap_names suitable for swapping values of type name_strings, where name_strings is a data type declared within s_pack (see Sections 1 and 2 of this block) which is assumed to be in the scope of the declaration.

A test harness program which can be used to demonstrate the effectiveness of these instantiations might be as follows:

```
-- test harness for swap pack demonstration
-- filename b3s4p1.ada, requires s_pack from sections 1 & 2. See text.

with TEXT_IO, int_io, float_inout, s_pack;
use  TEXT_IO, int_io, float_inout;

procedure b3s4p1 is
   -- values to be swapped
   an_int        : INTEGER := 42;
   another_int   : INTEGER := 84;
   a_float       : FLOAT   := 4.2;
   another_float : FLOAT   := 8.4;
   a_name        : s_pack1.name_strings := "forty two       ";
   another_name  : s_pack1.name_strings := "eighty four     ";

   -- declaration of generic procedure
   generic
     type element is private;
     procedure swap( this, that : in out element );

   -- instantiation of new swap procedures
   procedure swap_ints   is new swap( INTEGER );
   procedure swap_floats is new swap( FLOAT   );
   procedure swap_names  is new swap( s_pack1.name_strings );

   -- definition of generic procedure
   procedure swap( this, that : in out element ) is
```

```
         temp : element := this;;

      begin -- swap
         this := that;
         that := temp;
      end swap;

   begin -- b3s4p1
      -- demonstration of INTEGER swap
      PUT( "Integers before "); PUT( an_int ); PUT( "  ");
      PUT( "and "); PUT( another_int ); NEW_LINE;
      swap_ints( an_int, another_int );
      PUT( "Integers after  "); PUT( an_int ); PUT( "  ");
      PUT( "and "); PUT( another_int ); NEW_LINE(2);

      -- demonstration of float swap
      PUT( "Floats before ");
      PUT( a_float, AFT => 1, EXP => 0 ); PUT( "     ");
      PUT( "and "); PUT( another_float,AFT => 1, EXP => 0 ); NEW_LINE;
      swap_floats( a_float, another_float );
      PUT( "Floats after  ");
      PUT( a_float, AFT => 1, EXP => 0 ); PUT( "     ");
      PUT( "and "); PUT( another_float, AFT => 1, EXP =>0 ); NEW_LINE(2);

      -- demonstration of string swap
      PUT( "Strings before "); PUT( a_name ); PUT( "  ");
      PUT( "and "); PUT( another_name ); NEW_LINE;
      swap_names( a_name, another_name );
      PUT( "Strings after  "); PUT( a_name ); PUT( "  ");
      PUT( "and "); PUT( another_name ); NEW_LINE(2);
   end b3s4p1;
```

It would be acceptable to Ada for the three instantiated procedures all to have been called 'swap'. This is an acceptable overloading of the name 'swap' as Ada can determine which of the three swap procedures was intended from the types of the actual parameters specified when the procedure was invoked.

3.4.2 Generic search package

The sequential search procedure which was implemented in Block 3 Section 1 for the searching of a name list can be generically reimplemented as a generic package. The package will be designed to be capable of searching any one-dimensional array, or slice of such an array, for the first occurrence of a specified value.

As with the design of the generic swap procedure, the approach to designing this package is to identify what is common and what is different between two versions of the search algorithm implemented for two different arrays. The commonalities will form the basis of the implementation of the package, while the differences will form the basis of the formal generic parameters.

If an array of characters indexed by integers, whose declaration is

```
min_index : constant := 1;
max_index : constant := 10;

subtype  int_range   is INTEGER range min_index .. max_index;

type     char_arrays is array (  int_range ) of CHARACTER;
```

were to be searched, the declaration of a suitable search procedure would be as follows:

```
-- sequential search algorithm from b1s1, configured for int_arrays

procedure search_list( char_list : in  char_arrays;
                       to_find    : in  CHARACTER;
                       located    : out BOOLEAN;
                       position   : out INTEGER ) is

   found    : BOOLEAN := FALSE;
   location : INTEGER := char_list'FIRST;

begin -- search list
   while (( not found) and ( location <= char_list'LAST)) loop
      if ( char_list( location) = a_char ) then
         found := TRUE;
      else
         location := location + 1;
      end if;
   end loop;

   located  := found;
   position := location;
end search_list;
```

If an array of integers indexed by characters, whose declaration is

```
min_c_ndx : constant := 'A';
max_c_ndx : constant := 'M';

subtype char_range  is CHARACTER range min_c_ndx .. max_c_ndx;

type    int_arrays  is array ( char_range ) of INTEGER;
```

were to be searched, the declaration of a suitable procedure would be as follows:

```
procedure search_int_array( int_array  : in  int_arrays;
                            to_find    : in  INTEGER;
                            located    : out BOOLEAN;
                            position   : out CHARACTER ) is

     found    : BOOLEAN   := FALSE;
     location : CHARACTER := int_array'FIRST;

begin -- search_int_array
   while ( ( not found ) and ( location <= int_array'LAST)) loop
     if int_array( location ) = to_find then
        found := TRUE;
     else
        location := CHARACTER'SUCC( location );
     end if;
   end loop;

   located  := found;
   position := location;
end search_int_array;
```

A comparison of these versions of the sequential search algorithm would reveal the following similarities and differences. Both versions have four parameters. The first is the array to be searched; the second is the item to be searched for and is of the element type of the array; the third is the located flag and is of type BOOLEAN; the fourth is the location in the structure where the element was found and is of the index type of the array.

Within the body of the procedure a local flag of type BOOLEAN is required and an index variable of the index type of the array is required. The index variable is set to the value of the first index value of the array. Subsequently, the index variable is compared with the last index value of the array in order to control the loop. Within the body of the loop the index variable is incremented to index successive elements of the array. Within the procedure the elements of the array are subject to equality testing and assignment operations only.

This identifies three generic parameters of the procedure. The first is the element type of the array. This type will require equality testing and assignment operations only; a suitable generic type for this parameter would be **private**. The second formal generic parameter is the index type of the array. This type will require the FIRST and LAST attributes, and the increment operation; a suitable generic type for this procedure would be a *discrete* type. The array itself is the third parameter which can be declared by reference to the two previous parameters.

The package specification file for a package called generic_search would be as follows:

```
-- generic search package specification file v 1.
-- filename g_s_pal_.pkg. b3s4 see text.

generic
     type element is private;
     type index   is ( < > );
     type g_array is array ( index range < >) of element;

  package g_s_pack is

     procedure g_search_array( an_array : in  g_array;
                               to_find  : in  element;
                               located  : out BOOLEAN;
                               position : out index );
  end g_s_pack;
```

The generic declarations indicate that the package requires three generic parameters. The first of these is a generic **private** type which can be matched upon instantiation by any actual type which has equality and assignment operations available for it. The second type is a discrete type indicated in its formal generic declaration by the box (< >) specifier. It can be matched upon instantiation by any discrete type (see Block 2 Section 8). The third formal generic parameter to the procedure is an array whose elements are of the private type previously declared and whose index type is of the discrete type previously declared. This can be matched upon instantiation by any one-dimensional array which has a corresponding declaration. The package definition file for this package would be as follows:

```
-- g_s_pack definition file. filename g_s_pacl.pkb see text

package body g_s_pack is

  procedure g_search_array( an_array  : in  g_array;
                            to_find   : in  element;
                            located   : out BOOLEAN;
                            position  : out index   ) is

     found    : BOOLEAN    := FALSE;
     location : index      := an_array'FIRST;

  begin -- g_search_array
     while ((not found) and (location <= an_array'LAST)) loop
        if an_array( location ) = to_find then
           found := TRUE;
        else
           location := index'SUCC( location );
        end if;
     end loop;
```

```
      success  := found;
      position := location;
   end g_search_array;
end g_s_pack;
```

The version of the search procedure implemented in this file makes reference only to the generic types and the assumed operations which can be performed upon them. This should ensure that the instantiation of particular instances of this procedure should be capable of searching arrays of different types. The use of the package can be demonstrated in a harness program such as the following:

```
-- generic search demonstration program
-- filename b3s4p2. see text

with TEXT_IO, int_io, g_s_pack;
use  TEXT_IO, int_io;

procedure b3s4p2 is

-- declaration of array types to be searched
min_i_ndx  : constant := 1;
max_i_ndx  : constant := 10;
min_c_ndx  : constant CHARACTER := 'A';
max_c_ndx  : constant CHARACTER := 'M';

type    int_arrays is array ( CHARACTER range < > ) of INTEGER;
type    char_arrays is array ( INTEGER   range < > ) of CHARACTER;

    -- instantiation of new search packages
    package s_int_pack  is new g_s_pack( element => INTEGER,
                                         index   => CHARACTER,
                                         g_array => int_arrays );

    package s_char_pack is new g_s_pack( element => CHARACTER,
                                         index   => INTEGER,
                                         g_array => char_arrays );

    procedure show_int_array( an_int_array : int_arrays ) is
    begin -- show_int_array
       for this_int in an_int_array'RANGE loop
          PUT( this_int); PUT(" contains ");
          PUT( an_int_array( this_int )); NEW_LINE;
       end loop;
       NEW_LINE(2);
    end show_int_array;

    procedure show_char_array( a_char_array : char_arrays ) is
    begin -- show char arrays
```

```
      for this_char in a_char_array'RANGE loop
         PUT( this_char); PUT(" contains ");
         PUT( a_char_array( this_char )); NEW_LINE;
      end loop;
      NEW_LINE(2);
   end show_char_array;

begin -- b3s4p2
  declare
     -- bring packages into use
     use s_int_pack, s_char_pack;
     -- declare & initialize arrays to be searched
     subtype char_range is CHARACTER range min_c_ndx .. max_c_ndx;
     subtype int_range  is INTEGER   range min_i_ndx .. max_i_ndx;

     int_array : int_arrays( char_range )  :=
         ( 19, 30, 74, 12, 34, 45, 67, 89, 34, 56, 21, 45, 23,
     char_array : char_arrays( int_range ) :=
           ( 'a', 'f', 't', 'w', 'y', 'o', 'x', 'l', 'd', 'b' );

     -- declare other variables required
     char_to_find   : CHARACTER;
     int_to_find    : INTEGER;
     char_found_at  : INTEGER;
     int_found_at   : CHARACTER;
     char_is_found  : BOOLEAN;
     int_is_found   : BOOLEAN;

  begin -- declare block
     -- search for an integer
     show_int_array( int_array );
     PUT("Enter integer value to search for ");
     GET( int_to_find ); SKIP_LINE;
     g_search_array( int_array, int_to_find,
                     int_is_found, int_found_at);
     if int_is_found then
        PUT("Found at position "); PUT( int_found_at ); NEW_LINE(2);
     else
        PUT("Not found in array. "); NEW_LINE(2);
     end if;

     -- search for a character
     show_char_array( char_array );
     PUT("Enter character to search for ");
     GET( char_to_find ); SKIP_LINE;
     g_search_array( char_array, char_to_find,
```

```
                        char_is_found, char_found_at);
      if char_is_found then
         PUT("Found at position "); PUT( char_found_at );NEW_LINE(2);
      else
         PUT("Not found in array. "); NEW_LINE(2);
      end if;

   end; -- declare block
end b3s4p2;
```

The package commences by bringing the generic search pack (g_s_pack) into use. Two unconstrained array types are then declared: one is an array of INTEGER with a CHARACTER index; the other is an array of CHARACTER with an INTEGER index. Versions of the search package suitable for use with these arrays are then created. Two utility procedures are then declared to display the contents of each of the two types of array.

The main program procedure commences with a declaration; this is indicated with the use of the reserved word **declare**. A declaration can be made at any point within a subprogram and used to declare constants, types, subtypes, variables, or to bring a package into use. The scope of any objects declared in this way is delineated by the **begin/end** pair accompanying the declaration. The declaration above brings the newly created packages into use and then declares subtypes which will be used in the declaration of constrained array instances of the unconstrained arrays which have been globally declared.

A declaration is necessary at this stage in the program in order to bring the newly created search packages into use. They could not be brought into use at the start of the program as the types for which they are configured did not at that stage exist. They could not have been brought into use after they had been created as a **use** declaration can only appear at the start of a program unit or as a part of a declaration block within a subprogram.

As a declaration was required in order to bring the search packages into use the opportunity was also taken to declare the variable objects which are required for the demonstration within the **declare** scope. The effect of declaring these variables within the **declare** clause is the same as if the objects had been declared in the usual manner as part of the procedure's declarations. The advantage of declaring the variables within the body of the procedure in this way is to ensure that they are clearly associated with the procedure in the program listing. Had they been declared in the normal manner it is possible for the variable declarations to become textually separated from the program code which they are associated with.

The body of the program consists of a demonstration of searching each of the two arrays which have been declared and initialized. In each demonstration the contents of the array are first displayed, following which a value is input from the user, the array is searched using the instantiated versions of the generic search procedure and finally a suitable message is output depending upon the success or otherwise of the search.

3.4.3 Generic procedure parameters

The two show_array procedures which were implemented in the search pack harness program above are very similar. It would seem appropriate to implement them as a procedure within a generic package. This is not, however, possible with the generic mechanisms explained so far as there is no suitable PUT procedure which can be used within a generic package to output their values.

Take the output of the element type in the program above as a specific example. The statement PUT(element) could be included within a generic show_array procedure, but Ada would be unable to resolve the expression. In this program one package was created for arrays whose element type was CHARACTER, and a second package was created for arrays whose element type was INTEGER. It would also be possible for other versions of the generic package to be created whose element type could be any available Ada type. In the context of the generic package definition Ada cannot determine what the actual type of the parameter to the PUT procedure is and thus which version of the PUT procedure to use.

The solution to this problem is to extend the package's generic declarations to include a formal PUT procedure for output of each formal type. Thus when the generic package is used to create specific instances of the package, a suitable actual PUT procedure parameter would have to be supplied. This PUT procedure could then be safely used within the body of the generic procedures. The amendment to the package specification would be as follows:

```
-- generic search package specification file v 2
-- filename g_s_pa2_.pkg. b3s4 see text

generic
   type element is private;
   type index   is ( < > );
   type g_array is array ( index range < >) of element;
   with procedure PUT( an_element : in element);
   with procedure PUT( an_index   : in index );

package g_s_pack2 is
   procedure g_search_array( an_array : in  g_array;
                             to_find  : in  element;
                             located  : out BOOLEAN;
                             position : out index );

   procedure g_show_array( an_array : in g_array );

end g_s_pack2;
```

The package specification file now lists five formal generic parameters which will have to be matched by five suitable actual parameters when an instance of the package is created. The first three parameters have already been introduced in the previous version of this package. The last two formal parameters are procedures with the formal name PUT; this name has been retained and capitalized to emphasize that the intended behaviour of these procedures is compatible with the expected behaviour of the TEXT_IO PUT procedures. The declaration of the formal procedure parameters indicates that they each take a single in-only parameter, of the generic types specified. When an instantiation of this package is made, corresponding actual procedures will have to be supplied.

The package definition file will also have to be amended by the inclusion of a generic procedure called g_show_array, whose declaration might be as follows:

```
-- assumes TEXT_IO is withed but not in use
procedure g_show_array( an_array : in g_array ) is

begin -- g_show_array
   declare
   use TEXT_IO; -- output of strings limited to this proc
   begin -- declare block
      for this_elem in an_array'RANGE loop
         PUT("Location "); PUT( this_elem );
         PUT(" Contains "); PUT( an_array( this_elem ));
         NEW_LINE;
      end loop;
   end; -- declare block
end g_show_array;
```

The procedure commences by bringing TEXT_IO into use using an explicit declaration; this will only be effective if TEXT_IO has been **with**ed at the start of the file. The use of TEXT_IO is limited to this procedure as it is the only procedure in the package which has a requirement for the facilities it provides, particularly the output of strings and use of the NEW_LINE procedure.

Within the procedure the entire contents of the array are output. When the 'PUT (this_elem)' statement is interpreted by Ada, this_elem will be determined to be of the formal generic type index. The appropriate PUT procedure for this type can be determined to be the second formal procedure parameter supplied when the package is instantiated. Likewise, the type of the parameter to the 'PUT(an_array(this_elem))' statement can be determined to be of the formal generic type element, and the corresponding version of the PUT procedure intended is the first formal procedure parameter.

The changes to the part of the harness program which creates the specific search packages from the generic package are the following:

```
-- amended harness program for b3s4p2

procedure put_int( an_int : in INTEGER ) is
-- skin procedure for integer output
begin -- put int
   int_io.PUT( an_int );
```

```
    end put_int;

    package s_int_pack is new g_s_pack( INTEGER, CHARACTER,
                                        int_arrays, put_int,
                                        TEXT_IO.PUT);

    package s_char_pack is new g_s_pack( CHARACTER, INTEGER,
                                        char_arrays, TEXT_IO.PUT,
                                        put_int );
```

These instantiations of the generic sort package supply two additional actual generic parameters. The first of these is a procedure which takes a single input-only parameter of the array element type; the second is a procedure which takes a single input-only parameter of the array index type. The parameters have to specified using positional, not named, notation as two of the parameters have the same formal name. When this is the case named notation cannot be used.

The creation of s_char_pack specifies CHARACTER as the actual element type of the array and correspondingly specifies TEXT_IO.PUT as the actual procedure which can be used for output of this type. INTEGER is specified as the actual index type of the array but the standard integer PUT procedure (int_io.PUT) cannot be specified as the actual procedure parameter.

The reason for this is that Ada specifies that actual and formal procedure parameters have to match in the number, modes and types of the parameters of the actual procedure. The formal procedure declaration specifies a single parameter. The actual procedure declaration of the INTEGER PUT procedure contained within TEXT_IO.INTEGER_IO specifies three parameters: the value to be output; the width of the output field; and the number base to be output in. To make the int_io version of the PUT procedure compatible with the requirements of the formal PUT procedure of the search package the number of parameters has to be reduced from three to one. This is accomplished with the skin procedure put_int, whose sole effect is to implement the reduction in the number of parameters. It is the skin procedure put_int which is specified as the actual parameter when the package is created.

The versions of the show_array procedure which were declared in the previous harness program can be removed from this harness program. The calls of those procedures in the program procedure's body can be replaced with calls of the generically instantiated procedure (g_show_array).

3.4.4 Generic sort procedures

The implementation of a generic sort procedure package suitable for the sorting of arrays of elements will involve similar considerations to the implementation of the search procedure discussed above. The element type, index type and array type will have to be supplied as formal parameters to the package. Two versions of the PUT procedure will also have to be supplied if the show_array generic procedure is to be retained. In addition, a BOOLEAN function to compare two elements will have to be supplied.

The essence of the two sort algorithms introduced in Block 2 Section 2 was to iteratively compare pairs of array elements, deciding on the basis of a relational comparison if the two elements were to be swapped. The formal element parameter of the generic package is private, which implies that a greater than relational operation is not available, unless one is supplied when the package is instantiated. Such an operation can be implemented as a function of type BOOLEAN called "<", which requires two parameters of the element type of the array.

The package specification file of an expanded generic s_pack suitable for sorting an array would consequently be as follows:

```
-- generic search package specification file v 3
-- filename g_s_pack3_.pkg. b3s4 see text

generic
    type element is private;
    type index    is ( < > );
    type g_array is array ( index range < >) of element;
    with procedure PUT ( an_element : in element) is < >;
    with procedure PUT ( an_index   : in index )  is < >;
    with function  "<" ( this, that : element )
                           return BOOLEAN is < >;

package g_s_pack3 is

    procedure g_search_array( an_array : in  g_array;
                                to_find  : in  element;
                                located  : out BOOLEAN;
                                position : out index );

    procedure g_show_array( an_array : in g_array );

    procedure g_sort_array( an_array : in g_array );

end g_s_pack3;
```

The additional function specified as a sixth generic parameter is specified to be a function taking two parameters of type element and returning a BOOLEAN value. The final part of the declaration of the function, the term 'is < >', is optional and can be omitted. Its meaning is that if a function with the same name ("<") and the same signature exists, then it can be used by default if no actual parameter is supplied. This option can also be used in the declaration of a generic procedure parameter, as shown in the declaration of the PUT procedures.

The package definition file will have to have the definition of a sort procedure included within it. The form of a suitable procedure implementing a bubble sort would be as follows:

```
procedure swap( this, that : in out element ) is
-- definition as already given

procedure g_sort_array( an_array : in out g_array ) is

   is_sorted : BOOLEAN := FALSE;

begin -- g sort array
   while ( not ( is_sorted)) loop
      is_sorted := TRUE;
      -- compare all adjacent pairs
      for this_element in an_array'FIRST ..
                        index'PRED( an_array'LAST) loop
         if ( an_array( index'SUCC(this_element) ) <
                     an_array( this_element )) then
            swap( an_array( this_element) ,
               an_array( index'SUCC( this_element)) );
            is_sorted := FALSE;
         end if;
      end loop;
   end loop;
end g_sort_array;
```

This procedure implements the bubble sort algorithm using only those operations which can be assumed to be available for the element type and the index type of the generic array. The element type is only subject to the assignment operation (within swap) and the relational comparison "<" which was specified for operation on this formal type in the package's specification. The index type is a discrete type and objects of this type are only subject to operations which are appropriate for this type; these include the attributes FIRST and LAST and the attribute functions PRED and SUCC.

A harness program to test the above package might be as follows:

```
-- generic sort demonstration program
-- filename b3s4p4.ada see text

with TEXT_IO, int_io, g_s_pack3;
use  TEXT_IO, int_io;

procedure b3s4p4 is

-- declaration of array type to be sorted
   min_c_ndx : constant CHARACTER := 'A';
   max_c_ndx : constant CHARACTER := 'M';

   type int_arrays is array ( CHARACTER range < > ) of INTEGER;

   procedure put_int( an_int : in INTEGER ) is
   -- skin procedure to reduce num of parameters
```

```
    begin -- put int
       int_io.PUT( an_int );
    end put_int;

  package s_int_pack is new g_s_pack3( INTEGER, CHARACTER,
                                       int_arrays, put_int);
begin -- b3s4p4
  declare

    use s_int_pack;
    subtype char_range is CHARACTER range min_c_ndx ..max_c_ndx;

    -- declare & initialize array to be sorted
    int_array : int_arrays( char_range )  :=
        ( 19, 30, 74, 12, 34, 45, 67, 89, 34, 56, 21, 45, 23 );

  begin -- declare block
     g_show_array( int_array );
     g_sort_array( int_array );
     g_show_array( int_array );
  end; -- declare block
end b3s4p4;
```

The bulk of this harness program is similar to the harness program used to illustrate the generic search package. The instantiation of the particular instance of the sort pack specifies only the first four parameters. The fifth parameter, a procedure for the output of the array's index type, has the default option (**is** < >) specified. As a suitable procedure (TE⚡XT_IO.PUT) exists and is in scope no formal parameters need be specified. The sixth parameter, the function parameter, has the default option specified; the predeclared INTEGER relational operator "<" will be used to make the relational comparison which underpins the sort.

The body of the harness program simply displays the contents of an INTEGER array, sorts the array and then displays the contents again to demonstrate the efficacy of the sort. In the example program as implemented above the elements are sorted into descending order.

If the search package were instantiated by specifying the fifth and sixth parameter in the following manner:

```
package s_int_pack is new g_s_pack3( INTEGER, CHARACTER,
                                     int_arrays, put_int,
                                     TEXT_IO.PUT, ">");
```

then the relationship which underpins the sort would be the greater-than relation. This would have the effect of sorting the elements of the array into ascending order.

If a more complex element type were used as the element type of the array, for example a record and array with the declaration

```
type person_recs is
record
  f_name : name_strings;
  s_name : name_strings;
  weight : weights;
  height : heights;
end record;

type person_lists is array ( INTEGER range < > ) of person_recs;
```

which had declared a procedure which would display the information in a single record, such as

```
procedure show_person( a_person: in person_recs );
```

and suitable functions such as

```
function is_lighter( this_person,
                     that_person : person_recs ) return BOOLEAN;

function is_smaller( this_person,
                     that_person : person_recs ) return BOOLEAN;
```

then versions of the generic sort package suitable for sorting by weight or by height could be instantiated as follows:

```
package weight_sort is new g_spack3( person_recs,  -- element type
                                     INTEGER,       -- index type
                                     person_lists,  -- array type
                                     show_person,   -- put element value
                                     put_int,       -- put index  value
                                     is_lighter );  -- sort comparison

package height_sort is new g_spack3( person_recs,  -- element type
                                     INTEGER,       -- index type
                                     person_lists,  -- array type
                                     show_person,   -- put element value
                                     put_int,       -- put index  value
                                     is_smaller );  -- sort comparison
```

Calls of the sort procedure contained within the package weight_sort would sort the list of person records using the is_lighter relationship, producing a list sorted by weight in ascending order. Calls of the sort procedure contained within the package height_sort would sort the list of person records using the is_smaller relationship, producing a list sorted by height in ascending order.

EXERCISES

3.4.1 Implement the generic search package using the sequential search algorithm.

3.4.2 Implement the generic sort package using the selection sort algorithm.

3.4.3 Reimplement the sort package making the ">" function a generic parameter of the sort procedure instead of a generic parameter of the package.

Recursion

Recursion is an iterative programming control technique which is particularly appropriate for manipulating certain advanced data structures which will be introduced shortly. Recursive processes (procedures or functions) are processes which, as part of their execution, invoke a version of themselves. Recursion can also be used where the description of an object involves a reference to the object being described. Recursive processes can be designed by first producing a recursive description of the data structure which the process is to manipulate; the design of the process can then be based upon this description of the structure.

3.5.1 A first example

Tracing an example of a recursive process is the only way to provide an easy explanation of recursion. To do this a procedure called countdown will be implemented. The procedure countdown requires a single in-only INTEGER parameter greater than zero; on execution the procedure will output all the integers from the value of the parameter down to 1. For example, if the procedure countdown were called with a parameter having the value 5, the output would be '5 4 3 2 1'. This requirement could best be implemented using a definite iterative loop of the following form:

```
for num in reverse 1 .. param loop
    PUT( num );
end loop;
```

The procedure will be implemented using recursion in order to allow it to be used as an example of a recursive procedure. The first stage of implementation is to describe the output of the procedure recursively. Using the example above, the output of countdown(5) can be defined as, the output of the integer value 5 followed by the output from countdown(4). The output of countdown(4) can be defined as the output of the integer value 4 followed by the output from countdown(3), and so on.

In general terms the execution of countdown(n) can be defined recursively as the output of the integer value n, followed by the output produced by the execution of countdown(n-1). This description of the output can be expressed in the following Ada procedure:

```
procedure countdown( number : INTEGER) is

-- output the numbers number .. 1 recursively
-- b3s5 incorrect version, see text.

begin -- countdown
   PUT( number );
   countdown( number -1 );
end countdown;
```

The feature of this procedure which makes it recursive is the procedure call to countdown which occurs within the executable statements of the procedure. This implies that in order to perform the procedure countdown the procedure countdown will have to be performed, in order to do which the procedure countdown will have to be performed
. . .

This version of the procedure contains an error. As the procedure is always called recursively from within the procedure there is no limit to the number of calls which could be made. For example, if it were initially called as countdown(3) the execution would be to output the value of the parameter, 3 and then call the procedure with the parameter 'number-1', which is equivalent to 3-1, which is the call of countdown with the value 2. The execution of this call of the procedure will output the number 2 and then call the procedure with the value 2-1, which is a call of countdown with the value 1. The execution of this invocation of the procedure will output the number 1 and then call the procedure with the value 1-1, which is a call of countdown with the value 0. The value 0 will now be output, and the procedure invoked with the value 0-1, which will output the value-1 and invoke the procedure with the value -1-1, which will output the value-2, and so on. The process would continue indefinitely continuing to output negative integers until an attempt were made to evaluate INTEGER'FIRST-1, at which point an exception would be raised. A more likely termination of the program would be for the user to interrupt it before the exception was raised.

The error in this design of the procedure is that the procedure has no terminating condition and enters a process of indefinite recursion. This is similar to an iterative process entering an indefinite iteration. In order to avoid indefinite iteration it is necessary to ensure that within the iterative part of the program a terminating condition will be satisfied preventing any further iteration. Likewise, with recursive processes it is necessary to define a terminating condition which will prevent further recursive calls of the process; it is also necessary to ensure that this condition will at some stage be satisfied.

The general definition of the countdown process has to be expanded to indicate the terminating condition before the procedure can be correctly implemented. In this example the terminating condition can be defined as a call of countdown(0). The output of countdown(0) can be defined as nothing and the execution of countdown(0) will not call any further calls of the countdown procedure. The expanded definition of the countdown process would be as follows: countdown(n) outputs the integer value n and then calls the procedure countdown(n-1), unless the value of n is zero in which case nothing is output. This definition can be implemented as the following Ada procedure:

```
procedure countdown( number : INTEGER) is

-- output the numbers number .. 1 recursively
-- b3s5 corrected version see text

begin -- countdown
   if number > 0 then
      PUT( number );
      countdown( number -1 );
   end if;
end countdown;
```

This version of the procedure will only invoke itself recursively if the value of the parameter is greater than 0. If the value of the parameter is 0 the procedure will terminate without the output of 0 or calling the procedure recursively.

This version of the procedure can be traced as the first version was, with the value 3. The effects of the execution would be to output the value 3, followed by a call of the procedure with the value 2. This invocation would output the value 2 and call the procedure with the value 1. This invocation would output the value 1, followed by a call of the procedure with the value 0. This invocation of the procedure would, as explained above, do nothing, terminating all invocations of the procedure and completing the specified output of the initial call correctly.

3.5.2 A second example

The key phrase in the last paragraph was 'terminating all invocations of the procedure'. The recursive procedure call in the procedure countdown is the last executable statement of the procedure, thus when execution of countdown(0) terminates, control returns to countdown(1). As there are no further executable statements in countdown(1) control returns to countdown(2) and subsequently to countdown(3) where the program terminates. This aspect of the invocation of a recursive procedure can be better explained with a procedure which has actions to be performed following the recursive call of the procedure.

A complementary specification to countdown would be a procedure called countup which has a single integer parameter greater than zero. The output of the procedure will be all the integers from one up to the value of the parameter. So if the procedure were called with the value 5 the output would be '1 2 3 4 5'.

Once again this procedure could best be implemented as a definite loop, but will be implemented recursively to illustrate the processes and use of recursion. The key to implementing the procedure recursively is again to define its output recursively. The output of countup(5) can be defined as the output produced by countup(4) followed by the output of the value 5. In general terms, the output of countup(n) can be defined as the output produced by the execution of countup(n-1) followed by the output of n; unless the value of n is zero in which case nothing is to be output. This will give the following implementation of the procedure:

```
procedure countup( number : INTEGER) is

-- output the numbers 1 .. number recursively
-- b3s5 see text

begin -- countup
    if number > 0 then
        countup( number -1 );
        PUT( number );
    end if;
end countup;
```

In this version of the procedure there is an executable statement following the recursive call of the procedure.

When this procedure is called with the value 3, the sequence of actions will be, first, to call the procedure with the value 'number-1', which is equivalent to a call of the procedure with the value 2. The first action of this invocation of the procedure will be to call the procedure with the value 2-1, which is a call of the procedure with the value 1. The first action of this invocation of the procedure will be to call the procedure with the value 1-1, which is the invocation of the procedure with the value 0. This invocation of the procedure with the value 0 will have no actions as the condition at the start of the procedure will evaluate FALSE and the invocation of the procedure will terminate.

Upon termination of any subprogram program control is returned to the place in the program where control was passed to it. In this example this is the point in the execution of the procedure when the value of the parameter was 1 and the procedure was called recursively with the value 0. The next statement to be executed is the PUT(number) statement which will output the value of number which is 1. There are no further actions to be taken by this invocation of the procedure so it terminates and passes control back to where it was called from. This place is the point in the execution of the procedure when the value of the parameter was 2 and the procedure was called recursively with the value 1. The next statement to be executed is the PUT statement which will output the value 2 and as there are no further actions to be performed the procedure will terminate. Control will be passed back to the point in the procedure where it was called with number equal to 3 which will be output by this invocation of the procedure before it terminates.

This sequence of events can be visualized in a diagram of the recursive transfer of program control to and from invocations of the procedure:

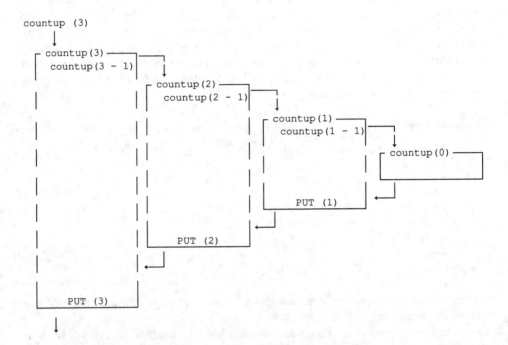

The diagram shows that the initial invocation of countup(3) calls the first recursive invocation of countup with the value of the parameter set to 2. This calls a second recursive invocation with the value 1, which calls a third recursive invocation with the value 0. When the fourth invocation is being executed the other three invocations are suspended, waiting for the invocation to terminate. When the invocation terminates without any output the remaining parts of the third invocation are executed. Following this, remaining parts of second and then the first are executed, before control is passed back to the place in the program where the first invocation was called from.

Each invocation of the procedure is separate from all other invocations of the procedure. The diagram shows that at the maximum recursive level of the execution of countup(3) there are four separate invocations of the procedure. The parameter variable number is a separate variable in all four invocations, having different values in each.

At any point in the execution only one invocation of the procedure is active; the other invocations are inactive but the information required to reactivate them is held on the return stack (stacks will be fully explained in the next section). The information stored in any stack frame would be the name of the subprogram, the position within the subprogram to which control is to be returned, and the value of any local objects.

When the currently executing subprogram terminates this information is used to allow execution to continue from the same point and with the same values reinstated to any local variables. The stack frame when the fourth invocation of the countup procedure executes can be visualized as follows:

```
top of stack ->    | countup,  line 4,  number -> 1 |
                    |--------------------------------|
                    | countup,  line 4,  number -> 2 |
                    |--------------------------------|
                    | countup,  line 4,  number -> 3 |
                    |--------------------------------|
                    | mainprog, line ?,  vars  -> ?  |
```

As control returns from the recursive invocations when they terminate, frames are removed from the top of the stack and used to reinstate the execution of the calling procedure at the point where the procedure was called. The final frame is popped when countup(3) terminates, passing control back to the main program, assuming this is where countup(3) was called from.

The passing of control from the procedure to another invocation of the procedure is known as a *recursive descent*; the consequential passing of control back from the recursively invoked procedure is known as a *recursive ascent*. There is no limit in Ada to the number of frames which can be placed on the stack and thus no limit to the number of levels of recursion which can be invoked. This can lead to the situation of indefinite recursion, where a recursive process continues to descend recursively without ever reaching a terminating condition which would cause a recursive ascent.

3.5.3 A recursive function

Recursion is not limited to procedures; it is also possible for functions to be designed and implemented recursively. To illustrate this, a function called sum_to_n will be implemented, the function is of type POSITIVE and requires a single POSITIVE parameter. When this function is executed, the effect is to compute and return the sum of all the integers between 1 and the value of the parameter. For example, if the function were invoked with the value 5 it would return the value 1 + 2 + 3 + 4 + 5 = 15.

The best method of designing and implementing this function would be to us a definite iteration; a recursive implementation will be used only to illustrate the use of recursive functions. The method of designing a recursive function is to define the actions of the function recursively by saying that the value of sum_to_n(n) is n + the value of sum_to_n(n-1). This is a partial definition; it correctly expresses the recursive method of computing sum_to_n but does not define a terminating condition. As has been emphasized, the terminating condition for a recursive process must be identified before it can be safely implemented. The terminating condition of sum_to_n is the case where it is invoked to compute the sum_to_n value of 1. The recursive definition given above would define this as 1 plus sum_to_n(0); it can be better defined as the simple value 1. The full recursive definition of this function is thus that the value of sum_to_n(n) is n + the value of sum_to_n(n-1), unless the value of n is 1 in which case the value of sum_to_n(1) is 1. Using this definition the function can be implemented as follows:

```
function sum_to_n( number : POSITIVE) return POSITIVE is

-- recursive function to sum all the integers
-- between 1 and number. b3s5 see text

begin -- sum to n
  if number = 1 then
      return 1
  else
      return number + sum_to_n(number - 1)
  end if;
end sum_to_n;
```

The behaviour of this function can be explained by using a diagram of its recursive descent, similar to the diagram used to illustrate the recursive descent of the countup procedure:

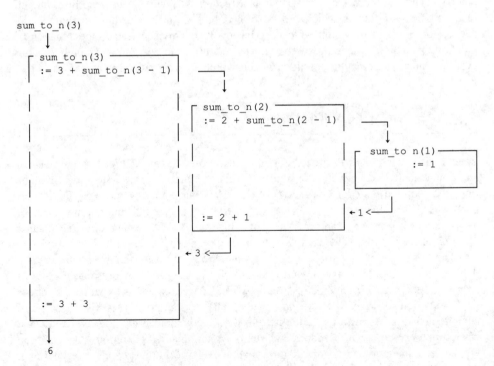

The diagram differs from the countup diagram by indicating the value which is returned from the function when its execution terminates. The execution commences with the request to compute the value of sum_to_n(3), this is computed as '3 + sum_to_n(3-1)' which recursively calls sum_to_n(2). This invocation computes this as '2 + sum_to_n(2-1)' which recursively calls sum_to_n(1). This invocation terminates the recursion, returning the value 1 to the place where it was invoked from. This value is used to evaluate the value of sum_to_n(2) as 2 + 1, completing the execution of sum_to_n(2) and returning the value 3 as the result of sum_to_n(2). This value is used to evaluate sum_to_n(3) as 3 + 3, which is returned as the result of the original call sum_to_n(3).

3.5.4 Recursion and structures

Recursion is a particularly appropriate process to use to manipulate certain data structures. In order to illustrate this, a recursive process to manipulate a simple structure will be designed, implemented and traced. The structure which will be used to illustrate recursive processing of a structure is a STRING. In order to allow recursive string processing to be designed a recursive description of a string will have to be produced.

The recursive description of a STRING commences by describing a STRING as an empty or a non-empty string. An empty string needs no further elaboration; a non-empty string can be described as a character, followed by the rest of the string, which is known as a substring. The substring is itself a string, and can be described as an empty string or a non-empty string. If it is non-empty then it can be described as the character at the start of the substring followed by the substring of the substring. The recursive data-structure diagram of a string would thus be as follows:

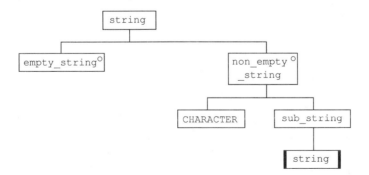

The data-structure diagram of the string includes as part of its description a component which is itself a string; it is thus a recursive description of a string. The recursive nature of the data structure is emphasized by the convention of using recursive component boxes with bold vertical lines.

This diagram identifies the terminating condition which will be required when recursive processes to manipulate strings are designed. Many of these processes will have to traverse the string, terminating when the end of the string is encountered. The end of a string is indicated on the diagram as an empty string. When during the recursive traversal of a string an empty string is encountered, it indicates that all characters in the string have been processed.

The most obvious use of this recursive description is to use it to implement a procedure which will display the string in reverse order. A recursive description of a process to do this would say that, in order to display the contents of a string in reverse order the last character in the string should be displayed, following which the contents of the string apart from the last character should be displayed, unless the string is an empty string in which case nothing should be displayed. A program structure diagram for this procedure would be as follows:

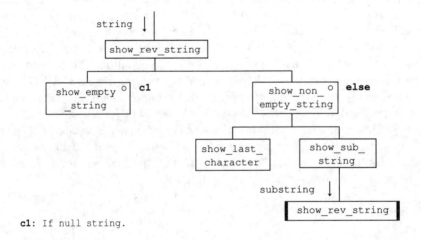

c1: If null string.

The implementation of this procedure would consist of the following statements:

```
procedure rev_string( r_string : in STRING ) is

begin -- rev string
    if ( r_string'LENGTH > 0 ) then
        PUT( r_string(r_string'LAST));
        rev_string( r_string(r_string'FIRST .. (r_string'LAST-1)));
    end if;
end rev_string;
```

If this procedure is initially called with the test string 'a test', upon the first invocation the length of the string will be 6 and the **if** statement will be TRUE. The first of these statement outputs the last character of the string, 't'. The rev_string procedure is then recursively called with a slice of the string which extends from the start of the string to one character less than the end of the string, on this invocation the string 'a tes'.

This string will be processed by the second invocation of rev_string in the same manner as the first. The last character 's' will be output and the string excluding this character ('a te') will be passed on to a third invocation of the procedure.

The third invocation will output the character 'e' and cause a fourth invocation with the string 'a t'. The fourth invocation will output 't' and cause a fifth invocation with the string 'a '. The fifth invocation will output the last character of this string, ' ', a space character, and cause a sixth invocation with the one character string 'a'.

The sixth invocation will output the last character of this string 'a', and cause a seventh invocation with a string which excludes this character. This string is the string '''', which is the null string with a length of 0. This string will cause the **if** statement in the procedure to evaluate as FALSE, and the procedure will terminate without any output.

Upon termination of the seventh invocation control is passed back to the sixth invocation at the point where the seventh invocation was called from. As there are no further executable statements in the procedure the sixth invocation terminates, passing control back to the fifth invocation. The recursive ascent will continue, terminating the fifth, fourth, third, second and finally the first invocation, passing control back to the main program.

The effect of all these calls is to output the sequence of characters 'tset a', which together constitute the original string in reverse order.

A small change in the implementation of the procedure will produce a version of the procedure which will display the string in its normal sequence:

```
procedure show_string( s_string : in STRING ) is

begin -- rev string
   if ( s_string'LENGTH > 0 ) then
      show_string( s_string(s_string'FIRST .. (s_string'LAST-1)));
      PUT( s_string(s_string'LAST));
   end if;
end show_string;
```

The only difference between the two versions of the procedure is in the position of the PUT statement relative to the recursive call of the procedure. The positioning of the PUT statement before the recursive call of rev_string causes the string to be output in reverse order, during the recursive descent. The positioning of the PUT statement after the recursive call in show_string causes the string to be output in normal order during the recursive ascent.

The positioning of the PUT statements in rev_string and show_string is comparable to the positioning of the PUT statement in the procedures countdown and countup used earlier in this section. Countdown and countup differed only in the positioning of the

PUT statement relative to the recursive call of the procedure. The effect of the different positions was to display the list of numbers in ascending or descending order depending upon whether they were displayed during the recursive descent or during the recursive ascent.

The two procedures rev_string and countdown are described as *head-recursive*, while the two procedures show_string and countup are described as *tail-recursive*. The phrases head-recursive and tail-recursive refer to the positioning of executable statements before or after the recursive call of the subprogram of which they are part. It is possible for a subprogram to be both head-recursive and tail-recursive, having executable statements before and after the recursive subprogram call.

3.5.5 Mutual recursion

It is possible for a process to be invoked recursively indirectly. If a process calls a second process non-recursively and this process calls the first process, then the first process has been called by a process which it itself called. The original process which has been called by indirect recursion now has the possibility of recalling the second process recursively. Such a pair of processes are said to be *mutually recursive*.

To illustrate this possibility a program will be presented which will count down and then count up. If this program, called bounce, were invoked as bounce(3) then the output of the program would be '3, 2, 1, 2, 3'. The implementation of this procedure will make use of two mutually recursive procedures, one, called bounce_odd, which will process an odd number and then call the second procedure, called bounce_even, which will process an even number before calling bounce_odd. The implementation of the program is as follows:

```
-- program to illustrate mutual recursion
-- b3s5p5 see text

with int_io; use int_io;

procedure b3s5p5 is

    -- procedure declarations
    procedure bounce_odd(  odd_num  : in POSITIVE );
    procedure bounce_even( even_num : in POSITIVE );

    -- procedure definitions
    procedure bounce_odd( odd_num   : in POSITIVE ) is

    begin -- bounce odd
        if ( odd_num = 1 ) then
            PUT( 1, WIDTH => 4);
```

```
    else
        PUT( odd_num, WIDTH => 4);
        bounce_even( odd_num - 1 );
        PUT( odd_num, WIDTH => 4);
    end if;
end bounce_odd;

procedure bounce_even( even_num : in POSITIVE ) is

begin
    PUT( even_num, WIDTH => 4);
    bounce_odd( even_num -1 );
    PUT( even_num, WIDTH => 4);
end bounce_even;

begin -- b5s5p5
    bounce_odd( 9);
end b3s5p5;
```

The implementation requires the procedures to be declared before they are defined as the definition of bounce_odd requires knowledge of the signature of bounce_even. This can only be accomplished by declaring bounce_even before bounce_odd is defined. The recursive mechanics of the execution of this program will be left as an end-of-section exercise. The only points to note are that the terminating condition is expressed in one procedure, bounce_odd, only and that both procedures are both head- and tail-recursive. This implementation is not totally secure as a call of bounce_odd with an even parameter will cause an exception to be raised.

3.5.6 Recursion and iteration

A recursive design can always be replaced by an iterative design, and an iterative design can always be replaced by a recursive design. The rationale for deciding between recursion and iteration would almost always favour iteration for two reasons.

The first is that iteration is cognitively simple. Iterative situations and processes are met in everyday life; consequently our brains can recognize and apply iteration without too much effort. Recursive situations are very rarely met in everyday life and can cause surprise when they are met.

One of the commonest examples of recursion in everyday life is when two mirrors are set facing each other; walking between these mirrors and looking into one of them you would see a reflection of yourself, and a reflection of yourself from the other mirror. This reflection includes a reflection of the reflection of yourself in the first mirror, which includes a reflection of the reflection of the reflection of yourself in the second mirror ... The effect of this is that when you stand between the mirrors and look into one of them you see an apparently infinite series of reflections of yourself in both mirrors. This situation is recursive and an unusual experience when it is encountered.

The second reason for favouring iteration is that it is less demanding of machine resources. As has been explained above, every level of recursion requires the initialization of a stack frame as the recursive subprogram is called and the restoration from the stack frame when the recursive invocation terminates. This requires the use of large amounts of memory and can slow down program execution dramatically.

There is one major reason for favouring recursion over iteration in some circumstances. Once the cognitive hurdle of recursion as a concept has been overcome, some recursive designs are extremely simple and elegant compared with equivalent iterative designs. In particular, some dynamic data structures, which will be introduced later in this block, have very simple recursive algorithms which can be used to manipulate them, while their equivalent iterative algorithms are complex. Where a recursive process is much more elegant than an equivalent iterative design it is to be favoured for the reasons explained in Block 3 Section 1.

EXERCISES

3.5.1 Produce a recursive descent/ascent diagram modelled upon the diagrams used in this section to illustrate the execution of bounce_odd(3).

3.5.2 If the PUT statement in rev_string and show_string procedures as used in this section is changed to

```
PUT( a_string( a_string'FIRST));
```

what other changes will be required to the procedures? Confirm your answer by implementing the changed procedures.

3.5.3 Design and implement a recursive factorial function, where the factorial of the number n is defined as n * n-1 * n-2 ... * 1.

3.5.4 Design and implement a recursive function called string_rev whose declaration is

```
string_rev( in_string : STRING ) return STRING;
```

The effect of the procedure is to return a string whose contents are the reversed contents of the input string.

Section 3.6

Stacks

3.6.1 Abstract data structures

This section will introduce a new type of data structure. This data structure and other structures which will be introduced in the rest of this block differ from the data structures which were introduced in Block 2 in that Ada itself does not provide the facilities to define and reference them explicitly.

In the case of records, Ada explicitly provided the facilities required to define and reference the record and its component fields. Likewise with arrays and files, Ada explicitly provided the facilities to define the structures and the facilities to reference the elements of their structure.

The data structures which will be defined here are not provided explicitly by Ada. There is no facility in Ada's type definitions to declare objects of these types directly, as there are for records, arrays and files. Likewise, there are no facilities to reference the objects or their elements as there are for the elements of records, arrays or files.

As they are not directly supported by Ada they are known as *abstract data structures*. Abstract data structures are implemented by making use of the simple data structure facilities introduced in Block 2. Although simple structures are used as the basis for implementing the abstract structures, the abstract structures should not be thought of as applications of the simple structures.

In Block 2 the simple data structures allowed the applicability of the predeclared data types provided by Ada to be expanded. An array of records, for example, is used in a different way to the predeclared data objects which comprise the individual record.

In this block the simple data structures will be used in a comparable way to provide the more complex advanced data structures. The advanced data structures which will be developed will allow more efficient and elegant models of the real world to be implemented. As was emphasized in Block 2, the better the model of the real-world objects which is implemented by the program, the more efficient and elegant the program will be.

In order to implement an advanced data structure, a definition of exactly what the structure consists of and exactly what operations can be performed upon it will first have to be produced. The best method for expressing the *what* of a data type is to use an Ada package specification, as explained in Block 2.

3.6.2 The stack defined

The *stack* is an iterative data structure; the elements of the iteration can be of any type required. It is the nature of the iteration and the referencing of the elements of the iteration which determine the stack nature of the structure, not the nature of the elements themselves. This is comparable with arrays; it is the nature of the iteration and the operations which can be performed upon the array which determine the nature of the array, not the elements of the array.

The stack can accept elements and store them on the stack; it can also retrieve elements which have previously been stored on the stack. The action of storing an element on a stack is known as *pushing* an element on to the stack. The action or retrieving an element from the stack is known as *popping* an element from the stack.

The nature of the stack is that elements can only be retrieved from the stack in the reverse sequence to the sequence in which they were stored on the stack. An alternative name for a stack is a last in first out (LIFO) queue.

This does not imply that all pushing operations have to be performed before any popping operations can be performed. The push and pop operations can be performed in any sequence, with the exception that a successful pop can only be applied to a stack which has at least one element stored in it.

The stack differs from the iterative structures which were met in Block 2. The array is an iterative structure which like the stack can either store or retrieve elements at any stage. The sequential file is an iterative structure which can at any stage in the program either store or retrieve records but not both.

The sequential file also differs from the stack and the array in that the elements can only be retrieved in the sequence in which they were originally stored. Elements can be stored in an array and retrieved from an array in any sequence. Elements stored in a stack can only be retrieved in the reverse sequence to the one in which they were stored.

A file differs from an array in that the file can contain an indefinite number of elements, while an array can contain at most the number of elements stated in its declaration. The stack which will be implemented in this section will also have a limit on the number of elements which can be stored in it. In Block 3 Section 10 an alternative implementation of the stack will be introduced which will remove this restriction.

The stack which will be implemented in this section can be in one of three states: a stack can be *empty* if it contains no elements; *full* if it contains the maximum number of elements that it is capable of holding; or *part full* if it contains less than the maximum number of elements and is not empty.

3.6.3 Stack operations

Having defined the nature of the stack, the operations which can be performed on the stack can be defined in terms of the stack. Assuming that a suitable data type for a stack has been declared and a variable of type stack has been declared, there are three operations which can be performed on the stack.

The first of these is to initialize the stack; the effect of this operation is to ensure that the stack becomes an empty stack. The stack need not be empty for this operation to successful; any data which is on the stack when it is initialized is disposed of.

The second operation is to push an element on to the stack. If the stack is not full then this operation will result in the element being stored on the stack. If the stack is full then the element cannot be stored on the stack and an error condition is generated; this error is known as *stack overflow*.

The third operation is to pop an element from the stack. If the stack is not empty then this operation will result in the element at the top of the stack being removed from the stack and made available. If the stack is empty then the stack cannot be popped and an error is generated; this error is known as *stack underflow*.

3.6.4 Stack data-structure implementation

The definition of the stack, as expressed above, has emphasized that the data which are stored on the stack can be of any Ada data type. The explanation of the allowable operations expressed the operations in terms of the stack itself and the elements which can be stored on the stack. This emphasizes the abstract nature of the stack, and implies that the stack is best implemented as a generic package. The generic package will implement the essence of the stack, allowing specific instantiations of the stack to be created which are configured for different actual element types. The generic stack package specification file would be as follows:

```
-- stack pack generic specification file b3s6 see text

generic
   type element is private;
   -- the data type which is to be stored in the stack
package stack_pack is

   type stacks is limited private
   -- details of the implementation are invisible from
   -- outside the package

   -- procedure and function declarations for manipulating stack objects
   -- to be included here

private

   max_stack_size : constant := 5;   -- 5 for test purposes only

   type elem_arrays is array ( INTEGER range < > ) of element;
   -- unconstrained array of elements
```

```
type stacks is
record
    elements     : elem_arrays( 1 .. max_stack_size );
    top_of_stack : POSITIVE := 0;
end record;
    -- stack structure contains at most max_stack_size elements

end stack_pack;
```

The single generic parameter to this package declaration is the element type which the stack will be capable of storing. This parameter is a **generic private** parameter. The effect of the generic private specification is to ensure that the declaration of the package can only employ the assignment and equality operations upon the element objects. This allows the widest possible range of actual parameters to be specified, as assignment and equality are valid for almost all possible Ada data types.

The data type stacks declared in the public part of the package declaration are specified as **limited private**. This ensures that objects of type stacks can be declared by programs which make use of the package but hides the details of the implementation from such programs. The **limited** clause prevents such programs from using even the assignment and equality operations on stack objects. If the stack were declared as **private** rather than as **limited private** then the equality and assignment operations would be available to programs which use the package.

The specification **private** for generic parameters and the specification **private** for types declared in the public part of a package declaration are opposite in their meaning. For a generic parameter the **private** specification limits the use which the package definition can make of the type. The type is private as far as the package itself is concerned. For a **private** package type the **private** specification limits the use which programs using the package can make of the type. The type is private as far as users of the package are concerned.

New versions of the package instantiated to implement stacks capable of storing different types of data element can be created using the normal generic package instantiation syntax. For example:

```
with stack_pack;
   package int_stack_pack is new stack_pack( INTEGER );
   -- package is capable of stacking integer values

with stack_pack, personnel_pack;
   package person_stack_pack is new
                         stack_pack( personnel_pack.person_record);
   -- assuming personnel pack contains a data type called person_record
   -- the new package person_stack is capable of stacking person_records
```

If these new packages are brought into use, then variable stack objects can be declared, as in the following:

```
-- assuming int_stack_pack and person_stack_pack are in withed

an_int_stack : int_stack.stacks;

programmer_stack,
operator_stack    : person_stack_pack.stacks;
```

The precise structure of objects of type stacks is hidden in the private part of the stack_pack declaration and is not visible to a program which uses the package. The declaration of stack objects expressed above declares a logical stack object which has the properties of stacks as expressed in the subprogram declarations contained in the package specification. The actual implementation of the stack is only the concern of the package definition. This example, where stack objects are declared before the structure of these objects has been fully explained, emphasizes this.

As explained above, the stacks which will be implemented in this section will be limited in the number of elements which can be stored upon them. The stack elements will be stored inside the stack objects in an array of such elements. The **private** part of the package specification commences by declaring an unconstrained array data type as an INTEGER indexed array of type element. The stack itself is a record object which contains a constrained instance of this array and a POSITIVE object called top_of_stack.

The index of the array has the bounds 1 .. max_stack_size, the record component top_of_stack has a range whose lower bound is zero. The top_of_stack (tos) is used to indicate which element of the array is currently at the top of the stack. A value of zero for tos indicates that the stack is empty, a value of tos equal to the upper bound of the array indicates that the stack is full, and intermediate values indicate that the stack contains elements but is not yet full.

If a stack is in use whose element type is names, where a name is implemented as a string, and which has been configured to be capable of containing at most five names, then the various states of the stack can be visualized as follows:

empty stack

```
        5 - >   ?
        4 - >   ?
        3 - >   ?
tos     2 - >   ?
 0      1 - >   ?
```

full stack

```
        5 - >  leah
        4 - >  seana
        3 - >  chaim
tos     2 - >  jackob
 5      1 - >  marcia
```

part_full stack

```
        5 - >   ?
        4 - >   ?
        3 - >  chaim
tos     2 - >  jackob
 3      1 - >  marcia
```

The diagrams show objects of type stack, with the array size constrained to five elements each of which is a string. The array is indexed by a subrange integer value and is shown on the right of the diagrams. The top of stack (tos) component is shown on the left of the diagram. In an empty stack the value of tos is zero and the elements of the array have no particular value, shown here as '?'. For a full stack the value of tos is equal to the upper bound of the array index, and all elements of the stack have known values. For a part full stack the tos component indicates the last element placed on the stack, in this example 'chaim' at position 3. All elements up to and including tos have known values; all elements above tos have no particular value.

3.6.5 Stack operations declaration

The declaration of the stack operations can be achieved from a consideration of the operations described above. These can be translated into data-flow diagrams:

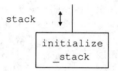

This data-flow diagram indicates that the initialize stack operation can be implemented as a procedure, with a single stack in-out parameter. The effect of the procedure is to initialize the state of the stack to empty.

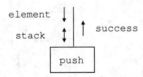

This diagram indicates that the push operation requires an in-only parameter of type element and an in-out parameter of type stack, and has a single out-only parameter indicating the success or failure of the operation. The effect of the procedure when executed, if the stack is not full, is to store the element on the stack and return TRUE in success; if the stack being pushed is full, the element will not be stored and success returned as FALSE, indicating stack overflow.

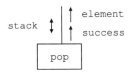

This diagram indicates that the pop stack operation requires an in-out parameter of type stack and has two out-only parameters, one of type element and the other, called success, which indicates the success or failure of the operation. The effect of the procedure, if the stack is not empty, is to export the element at the tos in element and TRUE in success; if the stack is empty, FALSE is returned in success, indicating a stack underflow, and element has no defined value.

These declarations can be included in the stack pack specification file as follows:

```
-- completion of stack pack generic specification file

procedure initialize_stack( new_stack : in out stacks );

-- new_stack is (re)initialized, any data left on the
-- stack is thrown away

procedure push( on_element : in       element;
                a_stack    : in out  stacks;
                success    : out     BOOLEAN);
-- if stack has space element is stored on the stack
-- and success is TRUE. Otherwise success is FALSE.

procedure pop(  off_element : out     element;
                a_stack     : in out stacks;
                success     : out     BOOLEAN);
-- if stack is not empty element on top of stack is
-- returned and success is TRUE. Otherwise success is FALSE.
```

3.6.6 Stack operations definition

The stack initialize procedure can be implemented directly without requiring a design. Its only operation is to set the top of stack pointer (tos) of the stack passed to it to zero. This will indicate that the stack is empty; any data contained in the stack will become inaccessible and be effectively thrown away. The declaration of the data structure in the package specification sets the value of tos to zero which ensures that the stack is in a safe state when it is declared. The initialize procedure need only be called when it is required to reinitialize the stack as the declaration of a stack object initializes it into a safe state.

The pop and push operations will require a program design before they can be implemented. Here is a program design for the push procedure:

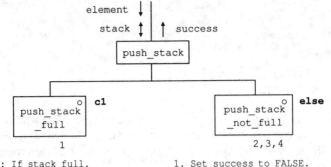

c1: If stack full.   1. Set success to FALSE.
                            2. Increment top of stack.
                            3. Store element at top of stack.
                            4. Set success TRUE.

Here is a program design for the pop stack procedure:

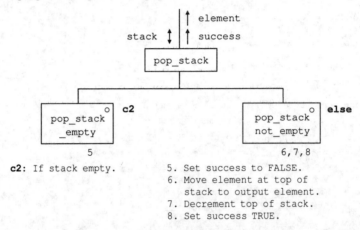

c2: If stack empty.   5. Set success to FALSE.
                            6. Move element at top of
                               stack to output element.
                            7. Decrement top of stack.
                            8. Set success TRUE.

Both of these functions are dependent upon being able to determine the state of the stack. In order to implement this decision a function can be designed and implemented. This function will return a value of an enumerated type called stack_states which is defined as follows:

```
type stack_states is ( empty, part_full, full );
```

Here is a design for this function:

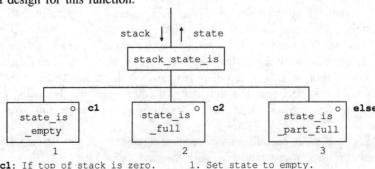

c1: If top of stack is zero.   1. Set state to empty.
c2: If top of stack is equal   2. Set state to full.
    to maximum stack size.   3. Set state to part_full.

The implementation of the generic stack_pack definition file will be as follows:

```
-- stack pack  generic definition file
-- b3s6 see text

package body stack_pack is

   type stack_states is ( empty, part_full, full );
   -- local type to indicate state of stack

   function stack_state_is( a_stack : stacks) return stack_states is
   -- local function to determine and return state of stack

   begin -- stack_state_is
      -- if tos is zero then stack contains no elements
      if a_stack.top_of_stack = 0 then
         return empty;
      -- if tos is equal to size of the array stack is full
      elsif a_stack.top_of_stack = a_stack.elements'LAST then
         return full;
      else -- otherwise stack is not empty and not full
         return part_full;
      end if;
   end stack_state_is;

   procedure initialize_stack( new_stack : in out stacks ) is

   begin -- initialize stack
      -- stack is set empty by setting tos to zero
      new_stack.top_of_stack := 0;
   end initialize_stack;

   procedure push( on_element : in      element;
                   a_stack    : in out  stacks;
                   success    : out     BOOLEAN) is

   begin -- push
      -- if stack is full then element cannot be stored
      if ( stack_state_is( a_stack ) = full ) then
         success := FALSE;
      else -- otherwise element can be stored
         -- increment tos pointer
         a_stack.top_of_stack := a_stack.top_of_stack + 1;
         -- and store element in position indicated
         a_stack.elements( a_stack.top_of_stack ) := on_element;
         success := TRUE;
      end if;
   end push;


   procedure pop(  off_element : out     element;
```

```
                    a_stack        : in out stacks;
                    success        : out     BOOLEAN) is
        begin -- pop
          -- if stack is empty element cannot be popped
          if ( stack_state_is( a_stack ) = empty ) then
             success := FALSE;
          else -- otherwise element can be popped
             -- retrieve element from tos
             off_element := a_stack.elements( a_stack.top_of_stack );
             -- and decrement tos index
             a_stack.top_of_stack := a_stack.top_of_stack -1;
             success := TRUE;
          end if;
        end pop;

     end stack_pack;
```

3.6.7 Stack operations traced

The effect of these operations can best be illustrated by a visualization of a stack as elements are pushed on to and popped off the stack. The stack which will be traced is the name stack which was introduced earlier in this section:

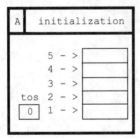
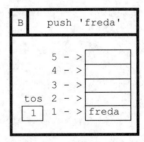

Visualization A shows the state of the stack after initialization; the elements of the array are uninitialized, shown here as empty. The stack index top of stack (tos) is shown as having the value zero indicating that the stack is empty.

Visualization B shows the stack after 'freda' has been pushed on to the stack. First the stack is checked to ensure that it is not full. Following this, tos would have been incremented from 0 to 1, and then the element 'freda' would have been stored in the array element now pointed to by tos (position 1).

Visualization C shows the state of the stack after 'helen' has been pushed on to the stack shown in visualization B. The same sequence of events would have taken place: the stack would have been checked to make sure that it was not full, tos would then have been incremented to 2, and the element 'helen' stored at position 2 of the array.

Visualization D shows the state of the stack after a pop has been performed upon the stack shown in visualization C. First, the stack would have been checked to make sure that it was not empty. As the stack is not empty the element of the array pointed to by tos would have been copied to the output parameter, to export it from the function as the data popped from the stack and finally to decrement tos from 2 to 1.

Visualization D shows that the element of the array where the item which has been popped from has not been explicitly emptied. After 'helen' has been popped from the stack, array position 2 still contains 'helen'. The tos pointer indicates the position in the array which contains the element at the top of the stack; the diagram shows that this is now the name 'freda' at position 1 in the array. Elements in the array above the position indicated by tos are not part of the stack, so 'helen' is not part of the stack.

If another element ('charles') is pushed on to the stack shown in visualization D the stack shown in visualization E1 will be produced. The new element will now overwrite element 2 of the array and tos will indicate that it is the element on the top of the stack.

```
 E1   push 'charles'          E2  pop

         5 - > [       ]            5 - > [       ]
         4 - > [       ]            4 - > [       ]
         3 - > [       ]            3 - > [       ]
   tos   2 - > [charles]      tos   2 - > [ helen ]
   [ 2 ] 1 - > [ freda ]      [ 0 ] 1 - > [ freda ]
```

Alternatively if the stack in visualization D is popped, the stack will be in the situation shown in visualization E2. The element returned by the pop will be 'freda' and the stack pointer tos, having been decremented to zero, will indicate that the stack is empty.

If the stack shown in visualization E2 is popped the pop will fail and the output-only success parameter will return FALSE. The state of the stack is determined using the function stack_state_is; this function will return empty. Within the procedure pop_stack this will cause the procedure to terminate returning success FALSE, indicating an unsuccessful operation.

When the stack is full all the elements of the array will be initialized and tos will have the value 5. If an attempt is made to push an element on to this stack the operation will fail and the success parameter will return FALSE. The sequence of events would be comparable to the sequence of events for the unsuccessful pop traced above. The stack_state_is function would return the value full and this would cause the procedure push_stack to return success as FALSE and off_element uninitialized.

3.6.8 Using the implementation

This implementation of the stack can be verified by reference to a stack's required behaviour, as given above. The operations initialize, push and pop have been implemented, and the states of the stack are implemented, as is the definition of the stack as a limited iteration of an elemental object. Using the formal definition of the stack a black-box test plan can easily be developed. Once the package has been implemented and mounted within a test harness the operations can be demonstrated to be correct.

Having implemented and tested the operations from the formal definition, the actions of initializing, popping and pushing can be incorporated into program designs as elementary operations and used as such in high-level program implementations. A high-level program requiring a stack can implement a stack by bringing the stack pack into use and instantiating a specific version of the stack pack for the element type required.

Such a program can only access the stack by using the functions and procedures which have been included in the stack_pack declaration. A specific implementation of a stack may have a requirement which cannot be met by the declaration of the stack as made available by this package. For example, many applications which use a stack have additional requirements such as establishing the number of elements on the stack, examining the contents of the top of stack without popping the stack, or displaying the contents of the stack without changing the contents of the stack.

There are three design approaches which could be made to implement these additional requirements: expanding the stack pack's declaration; making the high-level program responsible for the actions; and implementing a *skin package* using stack pack. The first of these options should be avoided; the stack declaration as implemented in this section expresses the essential operations which can be applied to a stack and restricting the allowable operations to this smallest possible set produces the most efficient and most general stack package. The second option should also be avoided; a program requiring a stack should be able to regard the stack operations as primitive operations and should not have to concern itself with the precise details of the implementation. The third option is the one which should be used. A skin package would make use of the basic stack package as declared in this section and add additional facilities to those which are provided. For example, the examine_top_of_stack operation could be implemented within the skin package by popping the stack as implemented in this package, to obtain the element at the top of stack. The element would then be immediately pushed back on to the stack to ensure that the stack remains in an unchanged state; the element could then be exported as a copy of the element on the top of stack. This skin package will be implemented as an end-of-section exercise. Skin packages will be introduced more completely in Block 2 Section 10.

3.6.9 Applications of stacks

Applications of stacks tend to be very technical. Many of the commonest examples are taken from system software. System software is the software which implements operating systems, utilities and compilers; the examples here are taken from compilers.

The input to a compiler is a text file. There is a common requirement in a compiler to transform a sequence of digit characters into an integer. The sequence '1234' on a source file can be represented in Ada as a iteration of characters; it is necessary to transform this character sequence into an integer with the value 1234.

The sequence is read from the input file from left to right; the characters in this example arrive in the sequence '1, 2, 3, 4'. There is no way of knowing when the first digit is read that it is to represent the number of thousands in the integer. The sequence could at this stage be '1, 2, 3', in which case the first digit represents the number of hundreds. Alternatively, it could be the sequence '1, 2, 3, 4, 5', in which case the first digit represents the number of ten thousands. What is always the case is that the last digit in the sequence will represent the number of units, the last but one in the sequence, if it exists, will represent the number of tens, and so on.

A solution to this transformation problem is to push each digit character onto a stack as it is read from the input stream. When the last digit has been read and pushed onto the stack, the sequence of digits can then be popped from the stack until the stack is empty. As the digit characters are popped from the stack they can be transformed into integers in the range 0..9, multiplied by a scaling factor and accumulated in an integer value. The scaling factor would start at 1 for the first digit popped off the stack and be multiplied by ten as each succeeding digit is popped.

Another application of stacks is to maintain a list of the procedure and function calls made as an Ada program executes. As a procedure or function call is executed by an Ada program, a 'stack frame' of the local variables and the current execution position in the program is pushed onto a stack, which is known as the 'return stack'. The return stack was introduced in Block 3 Section 5. As each procedure or function comes to an end a stack frame is popped from the return stack and used to determine where in the program control should be returned to.

Suppose, for example, that an Ada program has called from the main program a procedure called high_level, that high_level has in turn called a procedure called mid_level, and that mid_level has in turn called a procedure called low_level which is currently executing. The return stack showing only the names of the procedures would be as follows:

```
top of stack ->   mid_level
                  high_level
                  main_prog
```

When the procedure low_level comes to an end, the stack frame at the top of the stack will be popped and control will be passed to the point within the procedure indicated in this stack frame where control was passed to low_level. This is within the procedure mid_level which, having been popped from the stack and its execution resumed, leaves the tos stack frame as high_level.

When the procedure mid_level comes to an end the process will be repeated, transferring control back to high_level and leaving main_prog as the top of stack. When high_level comes to an end the stack will be popped transferring control back to the main_prog and leaving the stack empty.

EXERCISES

3.6.1 Using an INTEGER stack created from the generic stack_pack presented in this section, implement an interactive harness program which can be used to test the stack operations. The design for such a harness program would be as follows:

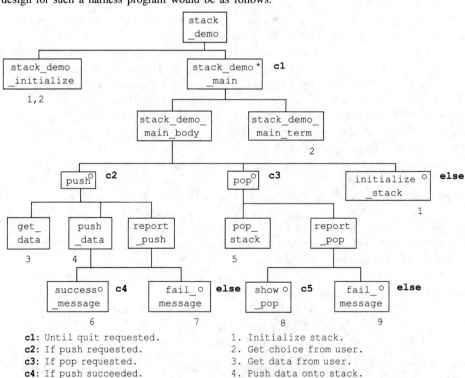

c1: Until quit requested.
c2: If push requested.
c3: If pop requested.
c4: If push succeeded.
c5: If pop succeeded.

1. Initialize stack.
2. Get choice from user.
3. Get data from user.
4. Push data onto stack.
5. Pop data from stack.
6. Display push success message.
7. Display push fail message.
8. Display data popped.
9. Display pop fail message.

3.6.2 Design a test plan to test the stack operations. Use the harness program from Exercise 3.6.1 to verify that the stack has been correctly implemented.

3.6.3 Using a CHARACTER stack instantiated from the generic package presented in this section, implement the string-to-integer application discussed in the section. The high-level design of this program will be as follows:

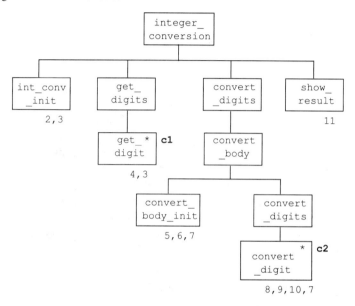

```
c1. While char input is a digit.          2. Initialize stack.
c2. While stack not empty.                 3. Read character.
                                           5. Set result to zero.
4. Push digit.                             7. Pop digit.
6. Set scaling to 1.                       9. Multiply digit by scaling &
8. Convert digit.                             add to result.
10. Multiply scaling by 10.                11. Display result.
```

3.6.4 Implement a skin package which adds an examine_top_of_stack facility to the generic stack_pack. Amend the program implemented in Exercise 3.6.1 to allow this facility to be tested. The skin package should bring the stack pack into use and provide skin procedures which allow access to the existing procedures. It should also supply an additional examine procedure, whose design has been discussed in the text.

Section 3.7

Queues

The second abstract data structure which will be introduced is the *queue*, specifically a first in first out (FIFO) queue. As its name implies, this structure differs from the stack in the way in which elements are retrieved from it. Elements are retrieved from the FIFO queue in the same sequence as they were originally stored within it, while they are retrieved from a stack in the reverse order.

This section will introduce the definition of the queue in the form of an Ada package specification. Two different implementations of the specification will then be developed. This will emphasize again the distinction between the specification, which declares *what* a package will do, and the implementation, which defines *how* the package will implement its specification.

3.7.1 The queue defined

The queue is an iterative data structure; the elements of the iteration can be of any type required. It is the nature of the iteration and the referencing of the elements of the iteration which determine the nature of the queue, not the nature of the elements themselves.

The action of placing an element in a queue is known as a *store* operation, while the action of removing an element from the queue is known as a *retrieve* operation. The store and retrieve operations can be applied to the queue in any sequence. Retrieve operations will only be successful if the queue is in a non-empty state. If a retrieve operation is attempted on an empty queue then an error known as *queue underflow* will occur. Store operations will only be successful if the queue is not in a full state. If a store operation is attempted on a full queue then an error known as *queue overflow* will occur.

A limitation on the size of the queue will be incorporated in the queue implementations introduced in this section. This limitation will be removed in Block 3 Section 10 when an alternative implementation of the queue (and the stack) will be introduced.

3.7.2 Queue operations

The data-flow diagrams for the queue operations will correspond to the data-flow diagrams given in the last section for the stack data structure:

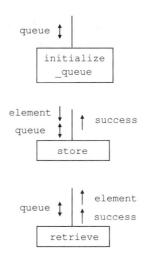

3.7.3 FIFO queue specification

The package specification for a generic queue package called fifo_queue would be as follows:

```
-- fifo queue version 1 generic specification file
-- b3s7 see text

generic
    type element is private;
    -- the data type which is to be stored in the queue

package  fifo_pack is

    type fifo_qs is limited private;
    -- details of the implementation are invisible from
    -- outside the package

    procedure initialize_queue( new_queue : in out fifo_qs );
    -- new_queue is reinitialized, any data left in the
    -- queue is thrown away

    procedure store( on_element : in       element;
                     a_queue    : in out fifo_qs;
                     success    : out      BOOLEAN);
```

```
-- if queue has space element is stored in the queue
-- and success is TRUE. Otherwise success is FALSE.

procedure retrieve( off_element : out     element;
                    a_queue     : in out fifo_qs;
                    success     : out     BOOLEAN);

-- if queue is not empty element on end of queue is
-- returned and success is TRUE. Otherwise success is FALSE.
```

private

```
max_queue_size : constant INTEGER := 5; -- 5 for test purposes only

type elem_arrays is array ( INTEGER range < > ) of element;
-- unconstrained array of elements

type fifo_q is
record
    elements      : elem_arrays( 1 .. max_queue_size );
    end_of_queue : POSITIVE := 0;
end record;
-- fifo_q structure contains at most max_queue_size elements
```

end fifo_pack;

The data structure which is declared in the **private** part of this package specification is similar to the data structure which was declared for a stack in the previous section. The structure is a record which consists of two parts, the first of which is a constrained instance of an unconstrained array type whose element type is the element type which is to be stored in the queue. The index type of the array is INTEGER, with its upper bound constrained to the value of the constant max_queue_size, which in this example has the arbitrary value 5. The second part of the record is an object of the integer subtype POSITIVE called end_of_queue, which will be used to indicate the element of the array which is at the end of the queue. In this implementation the element which is at the front of the queue will always be at position 1 of the array.

If an instance of this package is instantiated to store names comparable with the stack which was used in the previous section is in use, a visualization of the queue would be as follows:

```
+--+----------------------------+
|  |   empty queue              |
|  +----------------------------+
|  |                            |
|  |        5 - >  | ?       |   |
|  |        4 - >  | ?       |   |
|  |        3 - >  | martin  |   |
|  |  eoq   2 - >  | siobhan |   |
|  | +-+    1 - >  | sue     |   |
|  | |3|                         |
|  | +-+                         |
+--+----------------------------+
```

In this visualization the queue contains three names. The name at the front of the queue (position 1) is 'sue'. The name at the end of the queue is 'martin', which is at the position indicated by the value of the end_of_queue (eoq) index.

If the value of eoq becomes zero then this indicates that the queue is empty. If the value of eoq becomes equal to the upper bound of the array then this indicates that the queue is full. Intermediate values indicate the queue is part full.

3.7.4 A first implementation defined

The operations of initializing the queue and of storing an element on the queue do not differ significantly from the operations of initializing a stack and pushing an element on to the stack. The program structure charts which were presented in the previous section for these operations can be used as the designs for the corresponding queue operations. The FIFO queue definition file, excluding the retrieve operation definition, would be as follows:

```
-- fifo queue v 1 generic definition file. b3s7 see text

package body fifo_pack is

   front_of_queue : constant := 1;

   type queue_states is ( empty, part_full, full );
   -- local type to indicate state of queue

   function queue_state_is( a_queue : fifo_qs ) return queue_states is
   -- local function to determine and return state of queue

   begin -- queue_state_is
      -- if eoq is zero then queue contains no elements
      if a_queue.end_of_queue = 0 then
         return empty;
      -- if eoq is equal to size of the queue array queue is full
      elsif a_queue.end_of_queue = a_queue.elements'LAST then
         return full;
      else -- otherwise stack is not empty and not full
         return part_full;
      end if;
   end queue_state_is;

   procedure initialize_queue( new_queue : in out fifo_qs ) is
   begin -- initialize queue
      -- queue is set empty by setting eoq to zero
      new_queue.end_of_queue := 0;
```

```
      end initialize_queue;

      procedure store( on_element : in       element;
                       a_queue    : in out   fifo_qs;
                       success    : out      BOOLEAN) is
      begin -- store
         -- if queue is full then element cannot be stored
         if ( queue_state_is( a_queue ) = full ) then
            success := FALSE;
         else -- otherwise element can be stored
            -- increment eoq pointer
            a_queue.end_of_queue := a_queue.end_of_queue + 1;
            -- and store element in position indicated
            a_queue.elements( a_queue.end_of_queue ) := on_element;
            success := TRUE;
         end if;
      end store;
   end fifo_pack;
```

The operation to retrieve an element from the queue is more complex than the operation to pop an element from the stack. An element is always retrieved from the queue at the front-of-queue position which in this implementation is always position 1 of the array. This can be implemented by setting the output-only parameter which will be used to export the element to the value of the element at position 1 of the array.

The next element to be retrieved from the queue (if any) is now at the next position (position 2) of the array. Before this operation can terminate, this element will have to be moved from position 2 to position 1 of the array. This will ensure that it will become the next element to be retrieved from the queue.

A similar consideration can be applied to the other elements in the queue (if any). Consequently, when an element is retrieved from the queue all remaining elements in the queue will have to be moved down one position in the internal array. When these considerations are taken into account the design of the operation retrieve from queue will be as shown below:

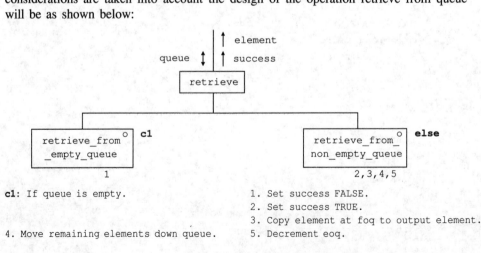

c1: If queue is empty.

1. Set success FALSE.
2. Set success TRUE.
3. Copy element at foq to output element.
4. Move remaining elements down queue.
5. Decrement eoq.

This design can be implemented as follows:

```
procedure retrieve( off_element : out    element;
                    a_queue     : in out fifo_qs;
                    success     : out    BOOLEAN) is

begin -- retrieve
    -- if queue is empty element cannot be popped
    if ( queue_state_is( a_queue ) = empty ) then
       success := FALSE;
    else -- otherwise element can be popped
       success := TRUE;
       -- retrieve element from foq
       off_element := a_queue.elements( front_of_queue );
       -- and decrement foq index
       -- move all remaining elements down
       a_queue.elements( front_of_queue .. (end_of_queue-1))
         := a_queue.elements( (front_of_queue+1) .. end_of_queue)
       a_queue.end_of_queue := a    a_queue.end_of_queue := a -1;
    end if;
end retrieve;
```

3.7.5 A first implementation traced

The effect of these operations can be illustrated by a visualization of a queue as elements are stored on and retrieved from the queue.

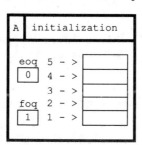

Visualization A shows the state of the queue after initialization; the elements of the array are uninitialized, shown here as empty. The front-of-queue constant (foq) is shown as 1; as it is a constant it will not change as operations are performed upon the queue. The end-of-queue (eoq) index is shown having the value zero, indicating that the queue is empty.

Visualization B shows the state of the queue after 'sue' has been stored in the queue shown in visualization A. First, the queue is checked to ensure that it is not full. Next, the value of eoq is incremented from 0 to 1, and then the element 'sue' is stored in the array element pointed to by eoq.

Visualization C shows the queue after a retrieve operation has been applied to the queue in the state shown in visualization B. First, eoq is checked to make sure that the queue is not empty. Then the element pointed to by foq ('sue') is copied to the output parameter.

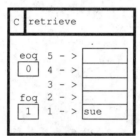

Within the assignment statement the expression 'front_of_queue .. (end_of_queue-1)' evaluates to '1..0', while the expression '(front_of_queue+1) .. end_of_queue' evaluates to '2..1'. Both of these are references to *empty slices*, that is, slices which have a length of zero. The effect of the assignment is that no changes are made to the stack structure. The final statement decrements the eoq from 1 to 0. The queue is then in the state shown in visualization C, the eoq index having the value 0 indicating that the queue is empty.

Visualization D shows the state of the queue after the elements 'maria', 'helen' and 'charles' have been stored in the queue shown in visualization C. These elements occupy positions 1, 2 and 3, respectively. The foq index points to the element which will be retrieved from the queue first, 'maria', which is at position 1 of the array. The eoq index points to the last element which was stored in the queue, 'charles', which is in position 3 of the array.

Visualization E shows the state of the queue after a retrieve opeation has been applied to the queue shown in visualization D. First, the queue is tested to ensure that it is not empty, and then the element at the foq ('maria') is exported.

The expression 'front_of_queue .. (end_of_queue-1)' evaluates to '1..2', and the expression '(front_of_queue+1) .. end_of_queue' evaluates to '2..3'. The effect of the assignment statement is to copy the slice of the array containing 'helen' and 'charles' to positions 1 and 2 of the array. The eoq index would then have been decremented from 3 to 2.

An empty queue would have its eoq index set to 0, which would cause an attempt to retrieve an element from it to fail with a queue underflow error. Likewise, the queue would become full when five elements were stored in it. An attempt to store an element in a queue in this state would fail with a queue overflow error.

The demonstrations of the queue operations given here should give a sufficient understanding of the internal operations of this implementation of a queue for an intuitive feel for the correctness of the implementation to be achieved. This does not constitute a proof of the correctness of the implementation, which is beyond the scope of this book. A more formal demonstration of the correctness of the implementation could be produced by the use of formal testing.

3.7.6 An alternative implementation traced

An alternative possible implementation of the queue data structure will be demonstrated, by tracing a comparable set of operations on visualizations which illustrate the modified data structure which underpins this implementation. The design and implementation of this alternative will be left as an end-of-section exercise.

The data structure which is used for this implementation is more complex than that used for the previous implementation, having four components. The array which is used to store the elements in the queue is identical to that used previously. In addition, there are three record components of the INTEGER subtype POSITIVE, these are called front_of_queue, end_of_queue and size_of_queue. The use of these components will be made clear in the following trace of the storing of names in a queue whose maximum size is five names.

Visualization A shows the queue after it has been initialized. The foq index has been set to 1, the eoq index has been set to the value of the upper bound of the array (5) and the size component has been set to 0, indicating that the queue is empty. The reasons why this is a suitable initialization state will become clear as the rest of the operations are traced.

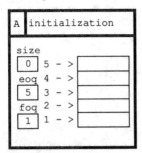

Visualization B shows the state of the queue after 'frank' has been stored in it. The size component has been incremented from 0 to 1, indicating that one element is in the queue. The foq index has not been changed and now correctly points to the element which will be the first to be retrieved from the queue. The eoq index has changed from 5 to 1 and now correctly indicates the last element which was stored in the queue. The operation of changing the eoq index in known as 'an increment across the bounds of the array'; the rules for this incrementation will be made clear later in the trace.

Visualization C shows the state of the queue shown in visualization B after four more store operations, storing 'martha', 'june', 'liam' and 'bob' in the queue. The size of the queue has been incremented four times to the value 5, indicating that five elements are stored in the queue and the queue is now full. The eoq index has also been incremented four times and now has the value 5, indexing the last element stored in the queue ('bob'). The foq index has not changed and still points to the element at the front of the queue ('frank').

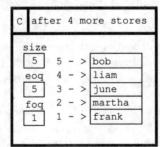

Visualization D shows the state of the queue shown in visualization C after a retrieve operation has been performed. The element pointed to by the foq index ('frank') has been exported by the operation, and the foq index has been incremented from 1 to 2 and now correctly indicates the next element which will be retrieved from the queue ('martha'). The size component has been decremented from 5 to 4, indicating that there are now four elements in the queue.

Visualization E shows the state of the queue shown in visualization D after the element 'yvonne' has been stored in the queue. The eoq index has been incremented across the bound of the array from 5 to 1, and now correctly indicates the last element which was stored in the queue. The size component has been incremented from 4 to 5, the foq index has not changed and still indexes the first element which will be retrieved from the queue.

```
E │ store 'yvonne'              │  F │ after 5 retrieves

   size                            size
   ┌───┐                           ┌───┐
   │ 5 │  5 - > │bob │             │ 0 │  5 - > │bob │
   └───┘        └────┘             └───┘        └────┘
   eoq    4 - > │liam │            eoq    4 - > │liam │
   ┌───┐        └─────┘            ┌───┐        └─────┘
   │ 1 │  3 - > │june │            │ 1 │  3 - > │june │
   └───┘        └─────┘            └───┘        └─────┘
   foq    2 - > │martha│           foq    2 - > │martha│
   ┌───┐        └──────┘           ┌───┐        └──────┘
   │ 2 │  1 - > │yvonne│           │ 2 │  1 - > │yvonne│
   └───┘        └──────┘           └───┘        └──────┘
```

Visualization F shows the state of the queue shown in visualization E after five retrieve operations have been applied to it. Each retrieve operation would have exported the element indexed by the foq component, following which the foq would have been incremented, taking the successive values 3, 4, 5, 1, 2. This would cause the names to be retrieved from the queue in the sequence 'martha', 'june', 'liam', 'bob' and 'yvonne'. After the incrementation of the foq index the size component would have been decremented, taking the successive values 4, 3, 2, 1, 0; the eoq component would not have changed.

The size component now indicates that the queue is empty, preventing a sixth retrieve operation from being successful. A store operation at this stage would cause the eoq index to be incremented and the new name to be stored at position 2; the size component would be 1 and the foq index would remain at 2.

The implementation of these operations requires the eoq and foq indices to be incremented across the bounds of the array. In this example, starting with the value 1, successive incrementations would produce the values 2, 3, 4 and 5. At this stage, a normal incrementation would produce the value 6, which is outside the bounds of the array. Consequently, if the value to be incremented is equal to the upper bound of the array then the increment operation has to be implemented to produce a resulting value of 1. This can best be implemented by a local increment function.

3.7.7 Evaluating the alternatives

As the two alternatives are functionally identical the reasons for choosing one or the other to implement are not immediately clear. For a queue of the size which has been used in the traces in this section there is not a great deal to choose between them. If the size of the queue required increases, the first implementation will become noticeably slower than the second implementation. Every time an element is retrieved from a queue in the first implementation all remaining elements in the queue have to be moved down one position. For a queue which contains a large number of elements or a smaller number of larger elements the time taken for the internal reorganization of the queue may become noticeable. The second implementation does not have this overhead and is consequently more efficient in its operations. It is, however, a little more complex and thus more difficult to understand and maintain. The use of a generic package, however, implies that once a version of the queue has been implemented and tested particular instantiations of the generic package can be assumed to be correct.

3.7.8 Applications of queues

Queues find many applications in many different programs. Whenever a sequence of data items has to be stored and retrieved in the same sequence then a queue structure would be an appropriate choice.

One of the commonest applications of queues is to provide a buffer between a computer and a peripheral device such as a printer. The computer can supply characters to the printer much faster than the printer can accept them. A buffer in the form of a FIFO queue can be used. The computer can fill the buffer by placing characters in the queue until the queue overflow error is encountered. The computer can then leave this process and continue with other processes. The printer can remove characters from the buffer and print them without holding up the computer. When the printer runs out of characters in the queue the queue underflow error will be encountered, and this can be used as a signal that the buffer can now be refilled.

EXERCISES

3.7.1 Refer to Exercise 3.6.1 and develop (or adapt) an interactive harness program which can be used to test the first queue implementation as presented in this section.

3.7.2 Using the queue specification only, develop a black-box test plan. Using the test harness developed in Exercise 3.7.1, subject the first implementation to formal testing.

3.7.3 Design and implement the alternative version of the queue as described in this section.

3.7.4 Subject the queue implementation developed in Exercise 3.7.3 to the test plan developed in Exercise 3.7.2 using the harness developed in Exercise 3.7.1 in order to demonstrate the functional equivalence of the two implementations.

Section 3.8

Dynamic data structures: access types

The implementations of stacks and queues introduced in Sections 6 and 7 of this block have suffered from one restriction: the maximum size of the structure has had to be specified at the design or at the latest at the coding stage. For many applications this is not a problem as the maximum number of data elements can be decided in advance and a structure can be declared capable of holding that amount of information. For some applications, however, the maximum number of data items which will have to be stored cannot be decided in advance. One solution to this problem is to declare a structure capable of holding a large number of data items. It is then hoped that the structure will be large enough to accommodate the largest number of items which may have to be stored when the program is being used.

If such a solution is adopted and the program is used a *large* number of times, a graph of the use of the storage can be produced; this is shown in Figure 3.8.1. The horizontal axis, labelled 'n', represents the number of data items which were actually stored in the structure as the program executed; the vertical axis, labelled 'p', represents the proportion of runs which used this much storage. The curve indicates the proportion of times that a given number of data items were stored in the structure. The vertical line labelled 'm' indicates the maximum number of data items which can be stored, and the vertical line labelled 'a' shows the average number of data items which were stored.

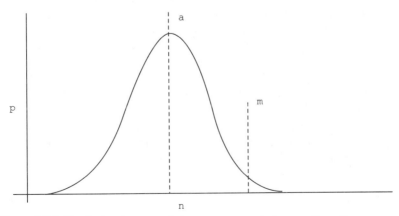

Figure 3.8.1 Graph showing use of storage space against proportion of program runs

The graph shows that very few runs made very little use of the data structure; as the number of items stored increases, so the proportion of runs increases quickly up to point a. As the curve is approximately symmetrical about point a, half of the total number of program runs lie to the left of this line. This indicates that half of the runs of the program used less than half the storage which was reserved for the structure.

To the right of point a the use of the structure decreases very quickly to point m, indicating that very few program runs made maximum use of the structure. The continuation of the graph to the right of point m indicates that a few runs of the program would have required more data items to be stored that the structure had space for; on these runs the stack or queue overflow errors would have been generated.

The graph shows that this method of allocating space for the storage of data suffers from two problems. The first is that many runs of the program do not make good use of the data storage which has been reserved for the data structure thus memory space in the computer is wasted. The second problem is that a few runs of the program are not possible because not enough storage space has been reserved.

There is a method of allocating storage space to a program which overcomes these limitations. Instead of deciding and allocating storage space as the program is designed and encoded, the program can be allowed to allocate storage space as it executes. Whenever during execution of the program the need to store an item of data occurs, the program can request the operating system to allocate sufficient memory for its storage. When the data are no longer required by the program the memory can be released back to the operating system. With this method only as much memory as is actually required to store the data (plus a small overhead) is used. The maximum amount of memory available for storing data is equal to the memory capacity of the computer system. With a computer system which uses paged memory this limit is effectively removed from consideration for most applications.

To use this method a data facility of Ada known as *access types* will have to be introduced. Specific types of this class of types are known as *access data types* and variables of these types are known as *access variables*. These variables do not actually store any information directly but point to a location in the computer's memory where information can be stored. As memory for data storage is required by a program during its execution, memory is allocated and the information is referenced indirectly using the access variable. The memory will be automatically deallocated when the scope of the access type comes to an end or can be deallocated explicitly when the information is no longer required by the program. The Ada concept of an access type is commonly known in other programming environments as a *pointer type*.

Access variables can be used to build structure which can grow and shrink as the program executes; such structures are known as *dynamic structures*. This section will introduce the declaration and use of access types; the next section will use access types to implement a common dynamic structure known as a *linked list*.

3.8.1 Declaring access types and variables

An access data type is declared as a type which can be used to access some other data type. A variable declared as being of this type does not itself contain the data but is capable of indicating where in the computer's memory the data which it is pointing to are located. An example may make this clear.

If a record data type is first declared as follows:

```
type person_records is
record
    f_name : name_strings;
    s_name : name_strings;
    weight : weights := 0.0;
    height : heights := 0;
end record;
```

then an access data type capable of pointing to a record of this data type can be declared:

```
type person_pointers is access person_records;
a_person            : person_pointers;
```

This declaration declares a new data type with the type name 'person_pointers'; the declaration continues with the reserved words **is access** and concludes with the typename of the data object to which it is to point. A variable called a_person is then declared; this object is capable of holding a pointer to an object of type person_record. It itself is not of type person_record and cannot itself store the name or any other information about a person. In order to store such information, an area of computer memory large enough to hold a person record will have to be allocated from available memory and the pointer initialized to point to this area.

This allocation of memory and initialization of the pointer is performed by using the Ada reserved word **new**, which has to precede the type name of the object for which it is to allocate space. The execution of the **new** process results in sufficient memory for an instance of the object type specified being made available and the effective address of this area of memory, known as an *access value*, being returned. This value is then used to initialize an access variable. For example:

```
a_person := new person_record;
```

The effect of this statement which is known as an *allocator statement*, can be visualized using simple diagrams:

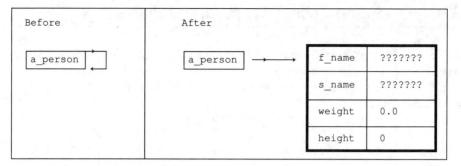

The left-hand diagram shows the pointer variable before execution of the allocator statement. The access variable a_person has upon declaration automatically been given a safe access value. This safe value is **null** and is represented on the diagram as an access variable pointing to itself. The right-hand diagram shows the situation after the allocator statement has been executed. An area of memory capable of holding all the information within a person record has been allocated and the access variable has been initialized to point to it. The fields of the record which is created in this way are uninitialized unless a default value for the field has been specified in the record declaration. This is shown on the diagram: the weight and height fields have been set to their default values of zero, while the f_name and s_name fields are uninitialized and shown on the diagram as '???????'.

It is possible for the contents of an object created by the allocator statement to have a particular value by including an aggregate value for the object in the allocator statement. The aggregate follows the data type name of the object to be created and is separated from it by a single quote character ' '. For example:

```
-- allocator with initial values using named aggregate
a_person := new person_records ' ( f_name => "George   ",
                                    s_name => "Gershwin ",
                                    weight => 56.7,
                                    height => 182 );

-- allocator with initial values using positional aggregate
a_person := new person_records ' ( "Irma     ", "Gershwin ",
                                    52.9, 174 );
```

The effect of these variants of the allocator statement is not only to create a person record object and initialize the pointer to point to it but also to initialize the fields to the values specified, overriding any default values.

3.8.2 Referencing pointer variables

Having declared a pointer and initialized it to point to a record which contains information, there needs to be some way of referencing the information. This is expressed in Ada using the dot notation. For the access variable a_person whose declaration was explained above, the possible references are as follows:

```
a_person           is of type      person_pointers
a_person.f_name    is of type      name_strings
a_person.s_name    is of type      name_strings
a_person.weight    is of type      weights
a_person.height    is of type      heights
```

In addition, the record itself may have to be accessed; this can be done using the reserved word **all**:

```
a_person.all       is of type      person_records
```

The last facility which Ada provides for access variables is to allow them to be given a safe value which can be used to indicate that the access variable does not point to anything. It was mentioned above that this value is **null** and is automatically used as the default value for any access variable which is not given a particular value as it is declared. There are situations in a program which is using access variables where an access variable is not currently being used to point to an object; in these cases the access variable should be explicitly given the value **null**. For example:

```
a_person := null; -- a_person does not point to a record
```

Any attempt to reference an object pointed to by an access variable which has a **null** value will result in a CONSTRAINT_ERROR exception being raised.

3.8.3 Example program

To consolidate the use of pointers a simple program using pointer variables will be developed from the following specification:

A program is required which will input details of two people. Having input the two records it will output them in alphabetical order.

It is assumed that a package called person_pack whose specification is as follows, is available:

```
-- person package specification file b3s8 see text

package pers_pack is

    min_weight   : constant := 0.0;
    max_weight   : constant := 250.0;
    min_height   : constant := 0;
```

```
max_height   : constant := 300;
max_name_len : constant := 15;

subtype weights is FLOAT   range min_weight .. max_weight;
subtype heights is INTEGER range min_height .. max_height;
subtype name_strings is STRING( 1 .. max_name_len );

space        : constant CHARACTER := ' ';   -- ascii space

type person_records is
record
    f_name : name_strings := ( others => space );
    s_name : name_strings := ( others => space );
    weight : weights := 0.0;
    height : heights := 0;
end record;

procedure get_person( a_person : out person_records );
-- procedure to input a person record from terminal

procedure show_person( a_person : in  person_records );
-- procedure to display a person record on terminal

function name_less_than( this_pers,
                         that_pers : person_records )
                         return BOOLEAN;
-- function to alphabetically compare names in record

function name_equal( this_pers,
                     that_pers : person_records )
                     return BOOLEAN;
-- function to alphabetically compare names in record
end pers_pack;
```

The design of this program will be as follows:

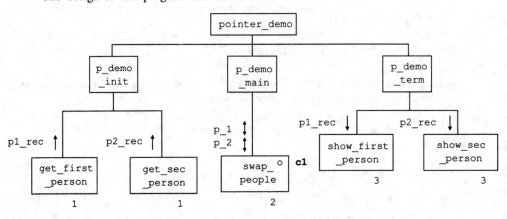

c1: If second name greater than
first name.

1. Set record from keyboard.
2. Swap records.
3. Display record.

where p_1 and p_2 indicate the pointer to the first name and the pointer to the second name, respectively; and p1_rec and p2_rec indicate the record which is pointed to by the pointer.

The implementation of this design would be as shown below:

```
-- program to illustrate the use of pointers. b3s8p1 see text

with pers_pack; use pers_pack;

procedure b3s8p1 is

    -- declaration of access type
    type pers_pointers is access pers_pack.person_records;

    -- declaration of access variables initialized to point to
    -- uninitialized person records.
    person_1 : pers_pointers := new pers_pack.person_records;
    person_2 : pers_pointers := new pers_pack.person_records;

    procedure swap_people( a_person,
                           another_person : in out person_pointers ) is

        temp_person : person_pointers;

    begin -- swap_people
        temp_person    := a_person;
        a_person       := another_person;
        another_person := temp_person;
    end swap_people;

begin -- b3s8p1
    -- input two records from the user
    get_person( person_1.all );
    get_person( person_2.all );

    -- swap records if necessary
    if name_less_than( person_2.all, person_1.all ) then
        swap_people( person_1, person_2 );
    end if;

    show_person( person_1.all);
    show_person( person_2.all);
end b3s8p1;
```

The program commences by declaring an access type which is capable of pointing to objects of type person_records, where person_records is declared inside the package pers_pack. Two variables of this access type are declared and initialized upon declaration to point to uninitialized person records which are created by use of the **new** statements.

The program procedure commences by passing these records to the get_person procedure to be initialized from the terminal. The record which is pointed to by the pointer is passed not the pointer itself. The initialized records are then compared using the name_less_than function and swapped if necessary using the procedure swap_ people. Finally, the contents of the records are displayed using the show_person procedure to confirm that they are in alphabetical sequence.

The swap_people procedure is declared within this program and requires as formal parameters two objects of type pointer to a person record. The effect of the swap_people procedure can best be explained by tracing its behaviour with the aid of diagrams. Assume that the record pointed to by person_1 has been initialized to have its name component contain the value 'freda', and the record pointed to by person_2 has been initialized to have its name component contain the value 'fred', the **if** statement will evaluate as TRUE as 'fred' is less than 'freda' and the swap_people procedure will be called. The formal in-out parameters a_person and another_person will become initialized to the values of the actual parameters person_1 and person_2, respectively. The situation as the procedure is entered can be visualized as follows:

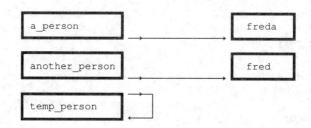

This diagram illustrates that the pointers a_person and another_person point to the records which contain the name components as shown. The local pointer temp_person is also shown, the declaration of this pointer does not assign it a value, and consequently it has the default value **null** which is shown on this diagram as an access variable pointing to itself. The first statement of the procedure is

```
temp_person := a_person;
```

which, following its execution, will result in the following:

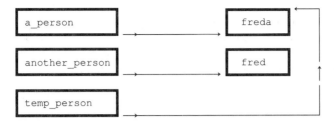

There are now two pointers which point to the same record. The value of the pointer parameter a_person has been copied to the pointer variable temp_person, using the assignment statement. As temp_person now contains the same value as a_person, they must both point to the object to which a_person originally pointed.

The next line of the procedure is

```
a_person := another_person;
```

which will have the effect of causing a_person to point to the same object which another_person points to:

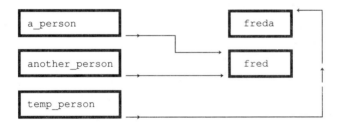

The final line of the procedure is

```
another_person := temp_person
```

which will have the following effect:

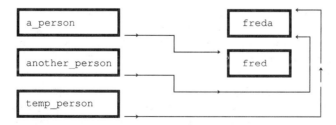

where a_person, which originally pointed to the record which contained 'freda', now points to the record which contains 'fred'; and the pointer another_person, which originally pointed to the record which contained 'fred', now points to the record which contains 'freda'; and temp_person is a local variable of the procedure which will cease to exist when the procedure terminates. As a_person and another_person are in-out parameters, the changes which have been made are exported out of the procedure back to the values of the actual parameters person_1.**all** and person_2.**all**. The effect of the procedure is to interchange the records pointed to by the actual parameters, effectively swapping the records.

3.8.4 Other points

It is possible to use assignment statements with pointers only when the terms on both sides of the assignment statement are of identical types. It is not sufficient for the two sides of the assignment statement to be 'pointers to something'; they have both to be pointers to the same type of thing to be assignment-compatible. If the following declarations are made:

```
type integer_pointers   is access INTEGER;
type character_pointers is access CHARACTER;

integer_pointer   : integer_pointers;
character_pointer : character_pointers;
```

then the following statement would not be allowed:

```
integer_pointer := character_pointer;
```

as the two terms on both sides of the assignment statement are of different types, although they are both access variables. It is not possible to convert the access value to the required access type in an attempt to circumvent this situation.

In the program set out here there is little advantage in using pointers to access the records, as the records are so small, there are so few of them and they are only swapped once. If the records were larger or there were more of them or they were being swapped more often, then the use of pointers may have an advantage. When two records are interchanged, the contents of the records have to be transferred; with large records being swapped a large number of times this can be a considerable contribution towards the total execution time of the program.

When the records are accessed using pointers to swap the records only the values of the pointers have to be swapped. Swapping the values of pointers as opposed to swapping the contents of the records is a much faster operation and can reduce the execution time of the program significantly. The disadvantage of using pointers, besides the complexity of constructing the program, is a small overhead in the total storage space required by the program. In addition to the memory space required to store the records, there is a need to allocate memory space to store the pointers.

When pointers are being used to access data objects, care should be taken to preserve the integrity of the pointers. If the swap_persons procedure as used above were misimplemented as

```
temp_person    := a_person;
another_person := a_person;
a_person       := temp_person;
```

the sequence of events would be, after the first line:

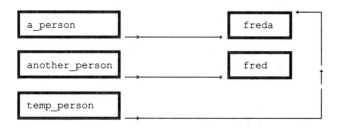

and after the second line:

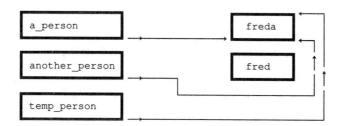

The final line will not change the situation as, as can be seen in the diagram above, a_person and temp_person already have the same value. This must be true as they both point to the same record. The intended effect of the procedure has not been achieved; the pointers have not been interchanged. The record containing the name 'fred' is now inaccessible as there are no access variables which point to it. This will cause the information contained in the record to be lost. Debugging a fault like this can be a very complicated business; the advice is to dry-run all procedures which manipulate pointers using diagrams similar to the ones above to ensure the integrity of the program before it is coded and tested.

   Memory which is allocated to dynamic objects by use of the **new** allocator statement is automatically released back to the operating system when the scope of the access type declaration comes to an end. For most applications this is acceptable as the amount of dynamic memory required during program execution is not excessive. For some applications, however, the memory will have to be explicitly deallocated by the program, releasing the memory back to the operating system as soon as it is no longer required. It is possible for an Ada program to be configured to operate in this manner, but these techniques will not be covered in this book. The part of a computer language run-time system which collects unused dynamic memory and restores it to the operating system is known as the *garbage collector*.

EXERCISES

3.8.1 Using the pers_pack as specified in this section, declare an array of pointers to person records. Initialize the contents of this array and then sort it into alphabetical sequence.

3.8.2 Using your experience from Exercise 3.8.1, implement the generic sort package. The reimplementation should declare a generic element parameter, a generic pointer to the element, an array index parameter and a generic array of pointers:

```
generic
   type element is private;
   type ptr     is access element;
   type index   is ( < > );
   type ptr_arr is array ( index range < > ) of ptr;
   with function "<" ( elem_1, elem_2 : ptr )
                    return BOOLEAN is < > ;
```

3.8.3 Attempt to demonstrate that the sort package implemented in Exercise 3.8.2 is able to sort an array of records faster than the previous versions of the sort package.

Section 3.9

Linked lists

The access data types which were introduced in the last section can be used to implement dynamic structures. In the last section a static access variable was used to point to a dynamically allocated object. If the dynamic object which is pointed to is a record and the record contains a component which is of the access type which points to an object of the record type itself, then this object has the capacity to point onwards to another object of its own type. This second record object also contains an access variable component which can be used to point to a third such object, and so on.

This record structure can thus be used to construct a list comprising an indefinite number of dynamically allocated objects, each of which contains an access variable component which links the objects together. Such a structure is known as a *linked list*. This can be visualized in a diagram. The record components which will form the *nodes* of the list comprise two parts: the *data* part which contains the information stored at the node; and the *pointer* part which can be used to point onwards to the next node of the list:

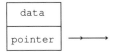

Using a static access variable known as the *base pointer* which is used to point to the first node of the list, a linked list comprising three nodes can be visualized as follows:

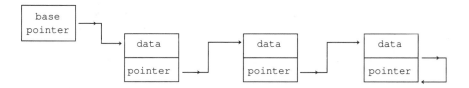

The end of the list is indicated by the fact that the pointer component of the last record has the value **null**. This is shown on the diagram as the pointer pointing to itself.

The only static object which is used to implement the list is the base pointer which is used to point to the first node of the list. When there is a requirement to store another piece of data in the list a record can be dynamically created from memory. The data component of this new record can be set to the value of the data to be stored, and the record can be added to the list by suitable manipulation of the pointers which are used to link the list. Likewise, if it necessary to remove an element from the list, this can be accomplished by suitable manipulation of the pointers isolating the element to be deleted from the list. As records can be added to and removed from the list in any sequence and at any position in the list the size of the list is not constrained to any particular value, allowing structures of indeterminate size to be constructed.

The linked list is a general structure which can be used to implement a number of different structures. If elements are always added to and retrieved from the start of the list then the list will implement the required properties of a stack. If elements are always added to the end of the list and always retrieved from the start of the list then the list will implement the required properties of a LIFO queue. The use of a linked list to implement stacks and queues will be introduced in the next section.

If the information stored in the list is organized according to some property of the information stored, then the list is known as an *ordered linked list*. For example, if the data which is stored in the list consists of person records and they are to be stored within the list in ascending alphabetical sequence defined by the surname and firstname components, a list consisting of two person records might be as follows:

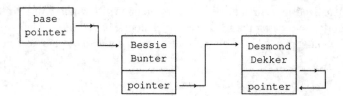

If it is required to insert a record for Charlie Chaplin, it will have to be inserted in the list between the Bessie Bunter record and the Desmond Dekker record, producing a new list:

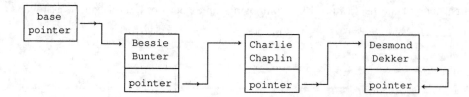

A record for Ade Abrahams would have to be inserted in the list between the base pointer and the Bessie Bunter node. A record for Fred Flintstone would have to be inserted into the list following the Desmond Dekker node and would become the last element of the list.

This section will introduce the declaration of a generic linked list suitable for implementing a general linked list. Only the definition of those parts of the package which are required for the implementation of an ordered linked list will be introduced in this section. Those parts of the package which are required for the implementation of stacks and queues will be introduced in the next section. Skin packages, which can be used to repackage the linked list into stack and queue structures, will also be introduced in the next section.

3.9.1 Generic linked list specification

The generic linked list package will have to have supplied as generic parameters the data type which is to be stored at each node in the linked list and two Boolean comparison functions which can be used by the package definition to maintain an ordered linked list in the required sequence.

The generic parameter declarations and the data structures which will be used to implement the linked list are as follows:

```
-- generic linked list declaration package b3s9 see text
-- filename o_l_list_.pkg


generic
   type element is private;
   with function "<" ( elem_1, elem_2 : element )
                     return BOOLEAN is < >;
   with function equal( elem_1, elem_2 : element )
                     return BOOLEAN;
package link_list is

   type l_lists is limited private;

   -- subprogram declarations here

private

   type list_nodes;

   type e_pointers is access list_nodes;

   type list_nodes is
   record
      data : element;
      next : e_pointers;
```

```
    end record;

    type l_lists is
    record
        front : e_pointers;
    end record;

  end link_list;
```

The generic data type element which will define what objects are to be stored within the list is declared as a generic **private** parameter, allowing only the assignment and equality operations to be used upon objects of this type within the package definition. The comparison function with the formal name "<" requires two such elements to be provided to it and will return TRUE if the key value of the first element is less than the key value of the second element. This generic function parameter has a default value which will allow a pre-existing 'less than' operator to be used if no actual function parameter is supplied upon instantiation. The second function parameter has the formal name 'equal' and will return TRUE if the key components of the two records supplied to it as parameters are equal, or FALSE otherwise. There is no default value specified for this function parameter as it is not possible to redefine the equality operator for generic private types. It is possible to define an equality operator for generic limited private types, but this would also require the assignment operator to be defined.

The data object which will be exported by the package to implement the linked list is called l_lists and is declared in the visible part of the package declaration as being **limited private**. The only actions which can be performed upon such objects outside the package are to declare instances of such objects and supply them as actual parameters to the subprograms contained within the package.

The data objects which will form the nodes of the linked list are declared in the **private** part of the package specification, making them invisible outside the package. The objects have the type name list_nodes and are records which contain a data component of the generic type element and an access component of type e_pointers. The access type e_pointers is declared as capable of pointing to objects of type list_nodes.

It is not possible to declare the record data type list_nodes until the type e_pointers has been declared, as e_pointers is used within the declaration of list_nodes. It is also not possible to declare the type e_pointers until the type list_nodes exists, as e_pointers has to be declared to point to objects of type list_nodes. To resolve this difficulty an *incomplete type declaration* is made. The declaration

```
    type list_nodes;
```

is an example of such a type declaration. It states that a type called list_nodes will be declared but does not supply any details. It allows the access type declaration to be made, following which the full declaration of list_nodes can be made.

Having designed and declared the data types which will be used to implement the linked list, the actions which have to be performed upon the list can be designed and declared. The first of these is a procedure to initialize the list. The initialization operation will initialize a list in any state, producing an empty list. Any data stored in the list prior to initialization will effectively be thrown away. The design and declaration of this procedure would be as follows:

```
procedure initialize( a_list : in out l_lists );
-- procedure to initialize a list throwing away
-- any data already stored
```

There are three places within the list where elements can be added to the list: elements can be added to the head of an unordered list, to the end of an unordered list, or at any position within an ordered list, with the location determined by the generic comparison functions. The data-flow diagrams for these three functions would be as follows:

These data-flow diagrams indicate that the actions are best implemented as procedures declared as shown below:

```
procedure add_head( a_list     : in out l_lists;
                    an_element : in       element);
-- procedure to add an element at the head of a list

procedure add_tail( a_list     : in out l_lists;
                    an_element : in       element);
-- procedure to add an element at the tail of the list

procedure add_in_order( a_list     : in out l_lists;
                        an_element : in       element);
-- procedure to insert element at correct position
-- the list. Sequence defined by the "<" generic parameter
```

Unlike the procedures which were used to push elements on to a stack or to add elements to a LIFO list, introduced earlier in this block, there is no requirement to include an output-only success parameter as the possibility of a linked list becoming full can be discounted.

This is not the case for the equivalent remove procedures as it is possible for an attempt to be made to remove an element from an empty list, or to attempt to remove an identified element from an ordered list where the identified element is not in the list. The data-flow diagrams for these three procedures are the following:

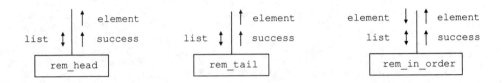

The procedures have the following declarations:

```
procedure rem_head( a_list      : in out l_lists;
                    an_element : out      element;
                    success    : out      BOOLEAN );
-- if list is non empty remove and return element at head of list and
-- set success TRUE else set success FALSE

procedure rem_tail( a_list      : in out l_lists;
                    an_element : out      element;
                    success    : out      BOOLEAN );
-- if list is non empty remove and return element at end of list and
-- set success TRUE else set success FALSE

procedure rem_in_order( a_list        : in out l_lists;
                        in_element  : in      element;
                        success     : out     BOOLEAN;
                        out_element : out     success);
-- if element matching in_element can be found in the list
-- remove from list and export out_element setting success
-- TRUE, else export success FALSE
```

In addition to these procedures which can be used to maintain the list, a further procedure called traverse will be supplied. This procedure will itself require a generic procedure parameter; the parametrized procedure will require a single in-out parameter of the element type. The effect of the traverse procedure will be to visit each node of the list and invoke the generic procedure, supplying the element stored at the node as the parameter to the generic procedure.

An example of the use of this procedure is where a suitable PUT procedure is supplied as the generic procedure. The effect would then be for each element stored in the list to be PUT, allowing the contents of the list to be displayed on the terminal. The data-flow diagram and declaration of this procedure follow:

```
generic
    with procedure do_something( an_element : in out element );
procedure traverse( a_list : in l_lists );
-- procedure to traverse the list applying the do_something
-- procedure to each element in the list
```

3.9.2 Initializing a list: design and implementation

This section will implement only those procedures which are concerned with ordered linked lists: the procedures initialize; add_in_order; rem_in_order and traverse. The remaining procedures will be implemented as end-of-section exercises and used in the next section as the basis of dynamic stack and queue structures. The implementation of the initialize procedure is straightforward; all that is required is to set the value of the access variable contained within the linked list object to **null**:

```
procedure initialize( a_list : in out l_lists ) is

begin
    a_list.front := null;
end initialize;
```

3.9.3 Adding an element: design and implementation

The design for the implementation of the add_in_order procedure will have to take into account the possibility of adding the element at the head of the list or adding the element in the middle of the list. Here is a suitable design:

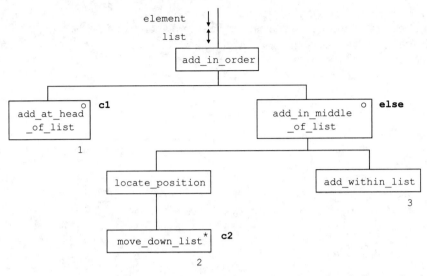

c1: If list is empty or element is less than first node.   1. Store element at head.
c2: While appropriate position not located and not end   2. Move one element along list.
of list.   3. Store element within list.

Here is the implementation of this design:

```
procedure insert_in_order( a_list      : in out l_lists;
                           an_element : in      element) is
   temp_one : e_pointers := new list_node'( data => an_element,
                                            next => null );
   this_one : e_pointers := a_list.front;
begin
   if ( a_list.front = null )              or else
      ( a_list.front.data < an_element ) then
      temp_one.next := a_list.front;
      a_list.front  := temp_one;
   else -- find position to insert
      while ( this_one.next /= null )            and then
            ( this_one.next.data < an_element ) loop
         this_one := this_one.next;
      end loop;
      temp_one.next := this_one.next;
      this_one.next := temp_one;
   end if;
end insert_in_order;
```

3.9.4 Adding an element: traced

This implementation can best be understood by tracing its operation as it executes. It is
assumed that a particular instance of the package has been instantiated suitable for

storing person_records as introduced in the last section. The instantiation of such a package can be accomplished with the following context declarations:

```
with pers_pack, l_lists;
package pers_list is new l_lists( pers_pack.person_records;
                                 pers_pack.name_less_than;
                                 pers_pack.name_is_equal );
```

The generic parameters to the instantiation are the record type supplied by the person package and the 'name_less_than' and 'name_is_equal' functions which are contained within the package. If the new package pers_list is brought into use a linked list object can be created with the following declaration:

```
-- assuming pers_list is withed
person_list : pers_list.l_lists;
```

This object person_list contains a single component of the effective type 'pointer_to_ person_records' which will be used as the static base pointer of the list. The state of the list after this declaration is shown in visualization A:

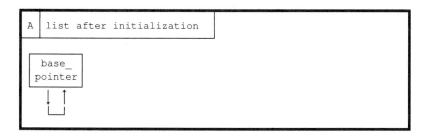

This visualization shows the base pointer pointing to itself, indicating that it contains a **null** value and thus that the list is empty.

If a person record called new_record containing Charlie Chaplin's details is added to the list using the procedure call:

```
pers_list.insert_in_order( person_list, new_record );
```

the sequence of events when the procedure executes is to declare a local pointer object called temp_one and use it to create a dynamic node whose data component is set to the contents of the new_record. A second local node pointer object called this_one is also declared and set to the value of the base pointer. This situation is shown in visualization B.

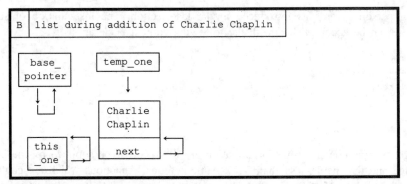

The procedure statements would commence by evaluating the **if** condition. The first term of this condition tests the base pointer to determine if it is a **null** pointer. This test will evaluate as TRUE, which will cause the second term not to be evaluated and the **if** part of the **if** statement to be executed. The effect of the first statement is to assign the value of the base pointer to the next component of the record pointed to by temp_one. The next statement will assign the value of the pointer temp_one to the base_pointer; this will have the effect of causing the base pointer to point to the Charlie Chaplin record. The **else** part of the **if** statement will not be executed and the state of the list as the procedure terminates will be as shown in visualization C.

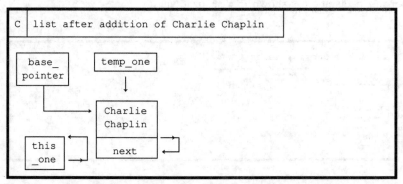

If a record for Bessie Bunter is added to the list shown in visualization C, the state of the list immediately prior to the evaluation of the **if** statement is shown in visualization D.

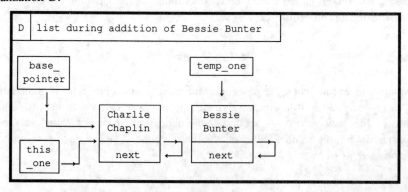

The first term of the **if** statement will this time evaluate as FALSE as the base pointer is not **null**. The second term will be evaluated, causing the generic is_less_than function to be used to compare the new record which is to be stored in the list with the person record pointed to by the base pointer. This is effectively the comparison of Bessie Bunter with Charlie Chaplin, which will evaluate as TRUE. This will cause the statements which form the **if** part of the **if** statement to be executed and the **else** part to be ignored.

The first statement will assign the value of the base pointer to the next component of the record pointed to by temp_one; this will have the effect of causing the next pointer within the Bessie Bunter record to point to the Charlie Chaplin record. The second statement will copy the value of the pointer temp_one to the base pointer, causing the base pointer to point to the Bessie Bunter record. The state of the list as the procure terminates is shown in visualization E:

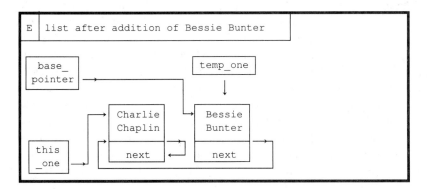

The effect is that the base pointer points to the Bessie Bunter record which points onward to the Charlie Chaplin record, where the list terminates. If a third record for Fred Flintstone is added to the list, the state of the list immediately prior to the evaluation of the **if** statement is shown in visualization F:

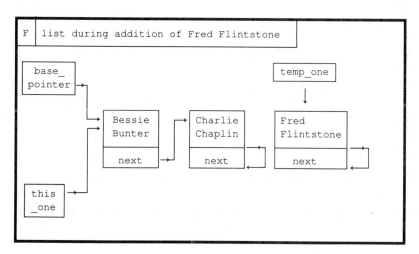

Both terms of the **if** statement will evaluate as FALSE as the base pointer is not **null** and the record to be inserted is not less than the record pointed to by the base pointer. The **else** part of the **if** statement commences with a **while** loop which is controlled by a test which first determines if the node currently pointed to by this_one is the last node in the list and then determines, if it is not the last node in the list, if the name contained in the node beyond the node pointed to by this_one is alphabetically less than the data to be inserted. If either of these conditions is FALSE the new node will be inserted into the list beyond the current node; if both conditions are TRUE the loop will iterate, causing this_one to point to the next node in the list.

In the diagram above, the first evaluation of the loop control statement will be TRUE as the node pointed to by this_one is not the last node in the list and the contents of the new node, 'Fred Flintstone', are not less than the contents of the next node in the list ('Charlie Chaplin'). The effect of the loop body is to cause this_one to point to the next node in the list, the node which contains 'Charlie Chaplin'. The second evaluation of the loop control condition will be FALSE as the node pointed to by this_one is the last node in the list. The loop will terminate and the remaining statements in the **else** part of the **if** statement will be executed. The first of these statements will cause the value of the next pointer in the node pointed to by this_one to be copied to the next pointer in the node pointed to by temp_one. This will cause the node containing Fred Flintstone to have a **null** pointer. The second statement will cause the value of the pointer temp_one to be copied to the next component of the node pointed to by this_one. The effect of this will be to cause the next component of the Charlie Chaplin record to point to the Fred Flintstone record, producing the situation shown in visualization G immediately before the procedure terminates:

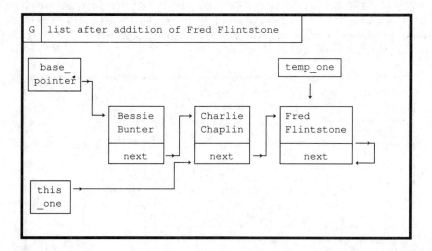

Finally, if a fourth record, 'Desmond Dekker', is added to the list the state of the list immediately before evaluation of the **if** statement is shown in visualization H:

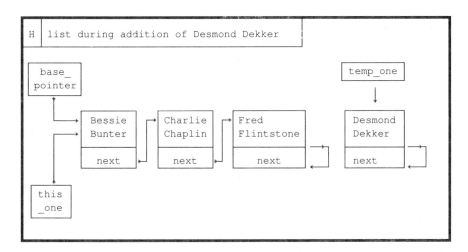

The **if** statement would again evaluate as FALSE and cause the **while** statement contained within the **else** part of the **if** to be evaluated. The first iteration would again evaluate as TRUE as the record pointed to by this_one is not the last record in the list and the name in the next node along the list is less than the new name. The body of the loop would iterate once, causing this_one to point to the node containing 'Charlie Chaplin'.

The second evaluation of the loop condition would evaluate as FALSE. The first term would evaluate as TRUE as the 'Charlie Chaplin' node is not the last in the list, but the second term would evaluate as FALSE as the name in the new node, 'Desmond Dekker', is less than the next name along the list, 'Fred Flintstone'.

The two statements following the **while** loop would then be executed. The first of these would copy the value of the next component of the node pointed to by this_one, the 'Charlie Chaplin' node, to the next pointer component of the new node. This would cause the next pointer component of the 'Desmond Dekker' node to point to the 'Fred Flintstone' node. The second statement would copy the value of the pointer temp_one to the next pointer component of the node pointed to by this_one. This would cause the 'Charlie Chaplin' node to point to the 'Desmond Dekker' node. The state of the list immediately before the procedure terminated is shown in visualization I.

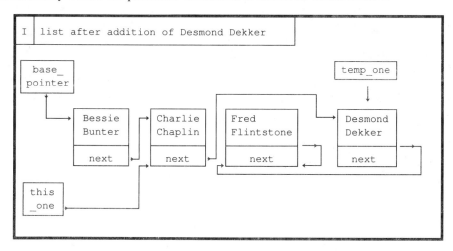

This trace has demonstrated the addition of a node to an empty list, the addition of a node at the head of a non-empty list, the addition of a node at the end of a non-empty list, and the addition of a node in the middle of a non-empty list. Although it does not constitute a proof it is a sufficient test of the algorithm and its implementation.

3.9.5 Removing an element: design and implementation

The rem_in_order algorithm can be designed and implemented as follows:

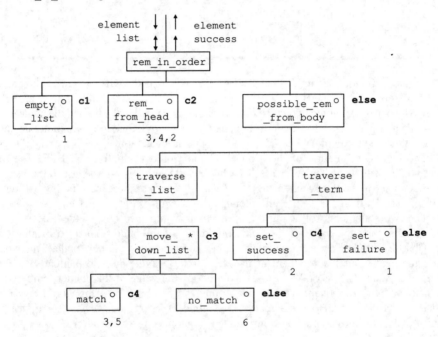

cl: If list is empty.
c2: If first element matches in element.
c3: While not found and list not exhausted.
c4: If element found.

1. Set success FALSE.
2. Set success TRUE.
3. Set out_element to current element.
4. Remove element at head.
5. Remove current element.
6. Move to next node.

```
procedure rem_in_order( a_list      : in out l_lists;
                        in_element  : in     element;
                        success     : out    BOOLEAN;
                        out_element : out    element) is

    this_one : e_pointers := a_list.front;
    is_found : BOOLEAN := FALSE;
    end_list : BOOLEAN := FALSE;

begin -- rem in order
    if ( a_list.front = null ) then
        success := FALSE;
    elsif equal( a_list.front.data, in_element) then
            out_element := a_list.front.data;
            a_list.front := a_list.front.next;
            success := TRUE;
    else
        while (not(is_found) and not(end_list)) loop
            if equal( this_one.next.data, in_element ) then
                out_element := this_one.next.data;
                this_one.next := this_one.next.next;
                is_found := TRUE;
            else
                this_one := this_one.next;
                if ( this_one.next = null ) then
                    end_list := TRUE;
                end if;
            end if;
        end loop;
        success := is_found;
    end if;
end rem_in_order;
```

3.9.6 Removing an element: traced

This procedure can again best be understood by tracing its behaviour as attempts are made to remove elements from different locations in different linked lists. If a list package of the type described above is assumed to be in use the attempt to delete can be made with a procedure call of the following form:

```
-- assuming pers_list is withed, l_lists is declared,
-- rem_person has had name components only set,
```

```
-- in_list is uninitialized BOOLEAN variable and out_person
-- is uninitialized person_record
pers_list.rem_in_order( a_list      => l_lists,
                        in_element  => rem_person,
                        success     => in_list;
                        out_element => out_person );
-- after call in_list is FALSE if name not found on list &
-- out_element is uninitialized; otherwise in_list is TRUE
-- out_element contains copy of data from list and node has been
-- removed from the list.
```

The simplest consideration is an attempt to remove an element from an empty list. In this situation the first **if** test will be TRUE, causing the success parameter to be set FALSE and the procedure to terminate.

The next consideration is an attempt to remove an element from the head of the list. Consider a list of the form shown in visualization J; an attempt will be made to delete the Bessie Bunter record from the list.

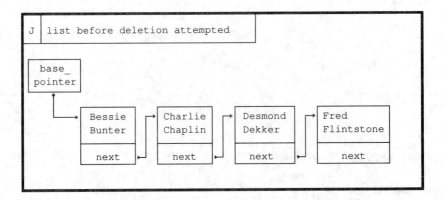

The first **if** condition would evaluate as FALSE as the base pointer is not **null**, causing the **elsif** condition to be evaluated. This condition would evaluate as TRUE as the name of the element to be removed is equal to the name of the first element in the list. This first statement contained in the **elsif** part of the procedure would cause out_element to be set to the data contained in the first node of the list. The second statement would copy the value of the next pointer of the first element of the list to the base pointer. The effect of this is to cause the base pointer to point to the 'Charlie Chaplin' record, isolating the 'Bessie Bunter' record and leaving it to be disposed of by the garbage collector. Finally, the success parameter would be set to TRUE before the procedure terminates.

This procedure would also be effective if 'Bessie Bunter' were the only name in the list. The **elsif** condition would evaluate as TRUE, causing the 'Bessie Bunter' element to be exported and the **null** pointer to be copied from the 'Bessie Bunter' node to the base pointer, causing an empty list to be created.

The removal of the name at the end of the list can be considered by the attempted removal of the 'Fred Flintstone' record. In this case the **if** condition would evaluate as FALSE and the **elsif** would also evaluate FALSE, causing the **else** statements to be executed.

This part of the procedure commences with a **while** loop which terminates when the item being sought is located or the end of the list is encountered. The body of the loop consists of an **if** condition which checks the contents of the record following the record which is pointed to by the pointer this_one. In this trace on the first iteration this_one will point to the 'Bessie Bunter' node and the next node will be the 'Charlie Chaplin' record. As this is not the record to be removed the **else** part of the **if** statement is executed. The first statement causes this_one to point to the next node in the list, the 'Charlie Chaplin' node. A check is then made to ensure that this node is not the last node in the list; as this is not the case the loop will iterate.

On the second iteration the access variable will point to the 'Charlie Chaplin' node and a similar pattern of events will take place. The next node beyond the 'Charlie Chaplin' node is not the node to be removed; the **else** part will cause this_one to point to the 'Desmond Dekker' node and, as this is not the last node in the list, the loop will iterate again.

On this iteration the next node beyond the node pointed to by this_one is the 'Fred Flintstone' node and is the one to be removed. The statements controlled by the **if** statement will be executed. The first of these copies the contents of the 'Fred Flintstone' node to the out_element parameter. The next statement copies the contents of the next node pointer of the 'Fred Flintstone' record to the 'Desmond Dekker' node. As 'Fred Flintstone' is the last node in the list this is a **null** value which causes the 'Desmond Decker' node to terminate the list and leaves the 'Fred Flintstone' node to be collected by the garbage collector. The final statement sets the local BOOLEAN variable is_found to TRUE. This will cause the loop to terminate and the value of is_found will be copied to the success output parameter.

If the trace above was an attempt to remove the 'Desmond Dekker' node then the **if** condition in the **while** loop would have evaluated as TRUE when this_one pointed to the 'Charlie Chaplin' record. The first action of the **if** statements would have been to export the contents of the 'Desmond Dekker' node. The next statement would have copied the value of the next pointer node of the 'Desmond Dekker' node to the next component of the 'Charlie Chaplin' record. This would have caused the 'Charlie Chaplin' record to point to the 'Fred Flintstone' record, isolating the 'Desmond Dekker' node from the list. The success parameter would have been set to TRUE as before.

If the attempt was an attempt to remove a node which did not exist in the list, for example the 'George Gershwin' node, the iteration would have continued until the this_one access variable had pointed to the 'Fred Flintstone' node. This would have caused the inner **if** condition to evaluate as TRUE as the 'Fred Flintstone' node is the last node of the list. The effect of this **if** statement is to set the local BOOLEAN variable end_list to TRUE, which would have terminated the **while** loop. The last statement of the procedure would have assigned the value of is_found to the output success parameter; this value would have been FALSE, causing the failure of the attempt to be communicated back to where the procedure was called from.

3.9.7 List traversal: design and implementation

Finally, the definition of the traverse procedure can be implemented as follows:

```
procedure traverse( a_list : in l_lists ) is

    this_one : e_pointers := a_list.front;

begin
    while ( this_one /= null ) loop
        do_something( this_one.data );
        this_one := this_one.next;
    end loop;
end traverse;
```

When executed, this procedure will iterate through the entire list; on each iteration the local access variable this_one will point to each node of the list. The elemental contents of the node will then be passed as a parameter to the generic do_something procedure. The effect of the traverse procedure is to apply the do_something procedure to every element stored in the list.

The declaration of the generic procedure within the linked list declaration package was as follows:

```
generic
    with procedure do_something( an_element : in out element );
procedure traverse( a_list : in l_lists );
```

An instantiation of the traverse procedure using the pers_pack.show_person procedure as the actual generic procedure parameter, would cause the instantiated traverse procedure to show all the person details on the list. The declaration of the show_person procedure in the person package was as follows:

```
procedure show_person( a_person : in person_records );
```

The formal generic procedure (do_something) specifies an in-out parameter; the actual procedure to be used (show_person) specifies an in-only parameter; Ada will not regard these two procedures as compatible. If it is required to use the show_person procedure as an actual generic parameter in an application the following declarations would be required:

```
-- assuming that pers_list and pers_pack are withed

procedure show_pers ( a_pers : in out pers_pack.person_records ) is
-- skin procedure to convert in parameter to in out parameter
begin -- show pers
   pers_pack.show_person ( a_pers );
end show_pers;

procedure show_people is new
         pers_list.traverse ( do_something => show_pers );
-- instantiation of generic traverse procedure with show_pers as
-- actual generic parameter
```

The execution of the generically instantiated show_people procedure with a person_list object as its actual parameter will cause the element at each node of the list to be displayed using the show_person procedure contained within the pers_pack package.

EXERCISES

3.9.1 Implement the generic linked list package as described in this section. Using the pers_pack package developed in the last section, instantiate a linked list capable of storing person records. (The procedures which are at present undeclared can be included as stubs in the linked list package body.)

3.9.2 Implement a harness program which will instantiate the show_people generic procedure as described in this section and which will offer the user a menu choice which can be used to test the instantiation of the package.

3.9.3 Devise a test plan for the linked list package and, using the instantiation developed in Exercise 3.9.2, subject the linked list implementation to formal testing.

3.9.4 Extend the definition and declaration of the linked list package to implement a procedure called retrieve which will retrieve the contents of an identified node without removing it from the list. Extend the harness program developed in Exercise 3.9.2 to include this facility and test its implementation.

3.9.5 Design and implement the subprograms add_head, add_tail, rem_head and rem_tail which were omitted from the text of this section.

Stacks and queues revisited

The stack and queue structures introduced in Sections 6 and 7 of this block were limited by the number of elements which could be stored. The dynamic linked list introduced in the previous section had no such restriction. This section will repackage the linked list generic package to reimplement the generic stack and queue data structures, thus avoiding the restriction upon the number of elements which can be stored.

The repackaging of the linked list structure will make available to the new packages only those aspects of the linked list package which are required for implementing stacks and queues. The parts of the linked list package which are not required will be hidden by the repackaging. The linked list generic package as implemented in the previous section can be visualized as follows:

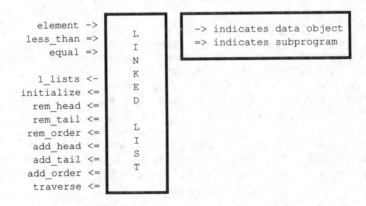

This diagram indicates that the linked list package imports three objects: the elemental type to be stored within the list and two subprograms. It exports nine objects: the data type which implements the linked list and eight subprograms which can be used to operate on linked lists.

3.10.1 Repackaging the linked list

If the operations which are allowed on a linked list are restricted to initialization, adding to the head of a linked list, and removing from the head of a linked list, then the linked list will have the required behaviour of a stack. This can be demonstrated by the considering the addition of a sequence of three integers, 42, 78 and 34, to the head of an initially empty integer linked list. This would produce a linked list in the following state:

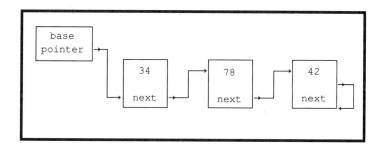

If the three numbers are removed from head of the linked list they will be removed in the sequence 34, 78, 42, which illustrates the required LIFO nature of the stack structure. As the linked list which is being used to implement the stack does not have an effective limit upon its size the number of elements which can be placed on the stack is not constrained.

It would be possible for a programmer to implement a stack data structure by using the linked list package directly and restricting the operations which are applied to the linked list to initialize, add_head and rem_head. This is not an acceptable implementation of a stack for several reasons. The first reason is that there is no guarantee that a programmer (or, more importantly, a maintenance programmer) would restrict the operations to those which are required for implementation of a stack. There would be the possibility that a programmer, in order to fix a bug, might make use of one of the other subprograms; this would then imply that the structure being used was no longer strictly a stack structure.

A second and more important reason for repackaging is to make the dynamic stack compatible with the static stack which has already been introduced. The package specification for the dynamic stack should be functionally identical with the package specification of the non-dynamic stack. This will allow application programs which use the stack to be written without considering if the dynamic or non-dynamic stack is to be used for their implementation, or even allow the actual implementations to be exchanged without changing the application program.

For example, an application using a non-dynamic stack which was encountering problems due to the constrained nature of the implementation could solve the problems by employing a dynamic stack. All that would be required would be a recompilation using the dynamic stack package; no changes would be required to the application program itself.

The repackaging of the stack pack is implemented by use of a *skin package* which makes some facilities of the linked list available and hides others. This is illustrated in the following diagram:

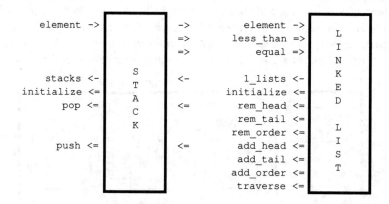

The diagram shows that the stack package imports the elemental type which is to be stacked and exports the data type which will be used to implement the stack; it also exports three subprograms called initialize, pop and push. The diagram also indicates that the stack will be implemented by creating an instantiation of the ordered linked list package suitable for storing the elemental type to be stacked. It will re-export the l_lists data type as the stacks data type, the l_lists initialize procedure as the stacks initialize procedure, the rem_head procedure as the pop procedure, and the add_head procedure as the push procedure.

3.10.2 Dynamic stack and queue implementation

The package specification for the dynamic stack would be as follows:

```
-- dynamic stack pack declaration file as skin package of list_pack
-- conforms to non dynamic stack pack declaration. b3s10 see text
-- filename d_stack_pack_.pkg

with link_list;

generic
    type element is private;
package stack_pack is

    function dummy( elem_1, elem_2 : element ) return BOOLEAN;
```

```
package el_list is new link_list( element, dummy, dummy);
subtype stacks is el_list.l_lists;

procedure initialize_stack( new_stack : in out stacks );

procedure push( on_element  : in      element;
                a_stack     : in out stacks;
                success     : out     BOOLEAN );

procedure pop( off_element : out     element;
               a_stack     : in out stacks;
               success     : out     BOOLEAN );

end stack_pack;
```

This dynamic stack package specification is compatible with the previous static stack package specification in that it requires a private generic parameter, provides the stacks data object and provides three procedures, initialize_stack, push and pop, which can be used with stacks. The procedures provided by this package have identical signatures to the procedures in the non-dynamic package, allowing them to be used interchangeably.

The specification declares the type of the stacks data object as a subtype of an instantiated linked list package data object called l_lists. The linked list package (el_list) which provides this type is an instantiation of the linked list package with its actual generic elemental parameter specified as the formal generic elemental parameter supplied for the instantiation of the stack package. This is shown on the stack package diagram as the element which is being passed to the stack package being passed onwards to the linked list package.

The instantiation of the linked list package also requires two BOOLEAN functions to be specified. These functions are used within the linked list package to implement the ordering of an ordered linked list. The parts of the linked list package which are used by the stack package have no need of these functions as the stack is not ordered. In order to supply suitable functions for instantiation of the linked list package a dummy function with a suitable signature is declared and supplied as an actual parameter for both formal function parameters.

The package definition for this stack specification would be as follows:

```
-- dynamic stack pack definition file as skin package of list_pack
-- conforms to non dynamic stack pack declaration. b3s10 see text
-- filename d_stack_pack.pkb

package body stack_pack is

    function dummy( elem_1, elem_2 : element ) return BOOLEAN is
    begin
        return TRUE;
```

```
    end;

    procedure initialize_stack( new_stack : in out stacks ) is
    begin -- initialize stack
        el_list.initialize( new_stack );
    end initialize_stack;

    procedure push( on_element : in      element;
                    a_stack    : in out stacks;
                    success    : out     BOOLEAN ) is
    begin -- push
        el_list.add_head( a_stack, on_element );
        success := TRUE;
    end push;

    procedure pop(  off_element : out     element;
                    a_stack     : in out stacks;
                    success     : out     BOOLEAN ) is
    begin -- pop
        el_list.rem_head( a_stack, off_element, success );
    end pop;

end stack_pack;
```

The package definition commences with the definition of the dummy BOOLEAN function which is required for the instantiation of the linked_list package el_pack. The function has the required signature to satisfy the requirements of the formal parameter, but has no requirement to perform any actions.

The initialize_stack procedure is a clear example of the re-export of a procedure from the linked list package as a procedure of the stack package. The body of the initialize_stack procedure is implemented as a call to the initialize procedure within the linked list package, with the formal parameter of type stacks supplied to the stack initialize procedure for initialization used as the actual parameter of the linked list initialize procedure. The stacks object is suitable as an actual parameter of the linked list initialize procedure as the stacks type is declared as a subtype of the linked list type l_lists, which is the type specified for the formal linked list initialize procedure. A subtype remains compatible with its base type without requiring type conversion; consequently, the type stacks is compatible with the type l_lists.

The definition of the stack pop procedure is likewise directly implemented as a call to the linked list rem_head procedure, using the formal parameters of the l_list procedure as the actual parameters of the stack pop procedure. This can be shown on a program structure diagram as follows:

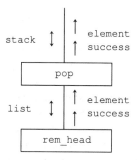

The stacks object is passed onwards to the rem_head procedure where the first element of the list, if any, is removed and exported from the rem_head procedure and is then re-exported from the pop procedure as the element popped from the stack. Likewise, the success out-only parameter which is exported from the rem_head procedure is re-exported from the pop procedure. This out-only parameter will have the value TRUE if it was possible to remove an element from the list, or FALSE otherwise.

The definition of the push procedure is a little more complex. It is effectively impossible to cause the linked list to overflow; consequently, in this implementation it is effectively impossible to cause the stack to overflow. However, to maintain compatibility with the non-dynamic implementation of the stack the success parameter has been retained. In this implementation this parameter is always returned TRUE, indicating that the element was successfully stored on the stack. Only the stacks and the element objects are passed onwards to the add_head linked list procedure. This can be shown on a program structure diagram as follows:

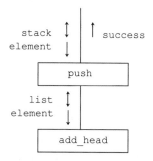

An alternative implementation of the dynamic stack package could be produced by implementing the push procedure as an invocation of the add_tail procedure and implementing the pop procedure as an implementation of the rem_tail procedure. This implementation would have the same LIFO behaviour as the implementation presented, but would be considerably less efficient as it would have to traverse the list on each push or pop process.

A dynamic queue implementation could be provided in a similar manner by implementing the queue store procedure as a call to the add_head linked list procedure and implementing the queue retrieve procedure as a call to the rem_tail procedure. The actual implementation of this package will be left as an end-of-section exercise.

It would be possible to make a more efficient implementation of the dynamic stack or dynamic queue packages by omitting the instantiation of the generic linked list and allowing them to declare and manipulate their own dynamic linked lists directly. Although this would be marginally more efficient, it would in most cases not make a great deal of difference. The advantages of using a core linked list package which can be repackaged to provide an ordered linked list capability, a stack capability and a queue capability will outweigh the costs involved in supporting three separate implementations of list structures.

3.10.3 Error handling

The design decisions taken in Sections 6 and 7 of this block when the static stack and queue packages were designed, concerning the reporting of underflow and overflow conditions, are not the only possible decisions which could have been made. Several other alternative error reporting mechanisms could have been used. The rest of this section will consider possible alternative mechanisms. The mechanisms will be explained with reference to the stack data type, although they are equally applicable to other abstract data types and to other error-reporting situations.

The mechanism which was used earlier in this block was to associate an output-only BOOLEAN parameter with the signature of each subprogram which accessed the stack. The state of this parameter was then used to determine the success or otherwise of the operation. For example, a simple interactive push operation could be implemented as follows:

```
-- error reporting using parameter mechanism
push( a_stack, element, is_stacked );
if ( is_stacked ) then
   PUT("OK, element stored.");
else
   PUT("Stack full, element not stored!");
end if;
```

One alternative possibility would have been to make the stack_state_is function directly visible to the application program; this would also require the stack_states enumerated data type to be made visible. The objects would be made visible to the application program by declaring them in the package specification's public part. The application would then become responsible for determining the state of the stack, before an attempt was made to push or pop elements in the structure. For example:

```
if ( stack_state_is( a_stack ) /= full ) then
   push( a_stack, element );
```

```
    PUT("OK, element stored. ");
else
    PUT("Stack full, element not stored! ");
end if;
```

If this design were implemented then there would be no requirement to communicate success using the parameter mechanism and the success parameter could be removed from the pop and push procedures signatures.

A third possible mechanism is to associate with each stack object a state variable which would be set to indicate the success or otherwise of each operation performed upon the stack. This would require an enumerated type to be declared in the package's public part, an object of this type to be included in the declaration of the stack's structure, and a function which would return the value of this component to be specified. For example, the static stack specification package could be amended as follows:

```
-- amendments to the static stack pack declaration package
-- for alternative error reporting using operation states

    -- stack_states enumerated type no longer required

    type operation_states is ( success, overflow, underflow );

    function last_operation( a_stack : stacks ) return operation_states;

    -- pop & push procedures no longer require success parameter

private

    type    elem_arrays is array ( INTEGER range < > ) of element;

    subtype stack_index_range is INTEGER
                            range 0 .. max_stack_size;
    type stacks
    is record
        elements : elem_arrays( 1 .. max_stack_size);
        tos      : stack_index_range := 0;
        last_op  : operation_states;
    end record;
```

The push and pop procedures would now have a requirement to set the value of the last_op component of the stacks data object to reflect the success or otherwise of each operation. The application program would use this mechanism in the following form:

```
push( a_stack, element );
if ( last_operation( a_stack) = success ) then
    PUT("OK, element stored.");
```

```
else
   PUT("Stack full, element not stored!");
end if;
```

These three mechanisms for determining the success or otherwise of the push and pop operations are largely equivalent. The application program has a mechanism by which it can determine if an operation would be or has been successful. As shown, any of these mechanisms can be used to communicate back to the calling part of the program the result of the operation. The distinctions between them are not too important; all that is required is that the mechanism is described in the package documentation and in the package specification, and that the mechanism is effective. The most important aspect of the design is that the package maintains the integrity of the stack and does not cause any exceptions to be raised.

3.10.4 Exception error handling

There is one other mechanism which could be considered for communicating the success of an operation from the stack package to the application program. This mechanism employs exceptions. The predeclared exceptions introduced in Block 2 could be used; it is also possible for a package to declare its own exceptions and for these to be used. Both of these mechanisms will be expanded.

The use of the predeclared exceptions relies upon a run-time error being generated by the subprogram which operates on the stack and raising a predeclared exception. A static push procedure relying upon predeclared exception handling would be defined as follows:

```
procedure push ( a_stack    : in out stacks;
                 on_element : in      element ) is
-- amended push procedure illustrating predeclared
-- exception error handling

begin -- push
   a_stack.top_of_stack := a_stack.top_of_stack +1;
   a_stack.elements ( a_stack.top_of_stack ) := on_element;
end push;
```

The implementation of this version of the push procedure is much more straightforward as it does not take account of any error possibilities. If an attempt is made to store an element on a full stack an attempt will be made to increment top_of_stack beyond the upper bound of its subtype declaration; at this point a predeclared CONSTRAINT_ ERROR will be raised. As this procedure does not contain an exception handler, the error will be propagated to the place where the push procedure was called from. This part of the program would contain an exception handler to detect and respond to the exception:

```
begin -- of exception handling block
    push( a_stack, element );
    PUT("OK, element stacked.");
exception
    when CONSTRAINT_ERROR =>
            PUT("Stack full, element not stored!");
end; -- of exception handling block
```

One problem with this mechanism is that the CONSTRAINT_ERROR could have been raised by an unrelated fault in the push procedure. This method assumes that the only condition which can cause a CONSTRAINT_ERROR is a stack overflow. For an application of this complexity the assumption is probably correct but cannot always be relied upon.

A better implementation of the exception mechanism would have been to recognize the underflow and overflow situations as exceptions and to declare suitable exceptions in the package specification. One of these exceptions would then be raised under appropriate circumstances. To implement this mechanism the public part static stack package specification would have to be amended to include the declaration of the exceptions, as in the following:

```
-- amendments to static stack pack declaration package to
-- allow error reporting using the exception mechanism

    -- declaration of programmer defined exceptions
    UNDERFLOW : exception;
    OVERFLOW  : exception;
    -- remainder of package specification as before
```

This declares two exception states which are associated with the package; no other changes to the package specification would have to be made apart from removing the success parameter from the push and pop procedures. Notice the style convention whereby exceptions are included in the source file in upper case even though they are programmer-declared not predeclared.

The stack definition file would have to be amended to explicitly raise these exceptions under the appropriate conditions. For example, within the push procedure in this implementation, an attempt to push an element on to a stack which is already full will result in an OVERFLOW exception being raised:

```
procedure push( a_stack    : in out stacks;
                on_element : out     element ) is
-- amended push procedure illustrating user declared
-- exception error handling

begin -- push
```

```
    if ( stack_state_is( a_stack) = full ) then
       raise OVERFLOW;
    else
       a_stack.top_of_stack := a_stack.top_of_stack +1;
       a_stack.elements( a_stack.top_of_stack ) := on_element;
    endif;
end push;
```

The application program which uses the stack package will have to be amended to be able to detect this exception:

```
begin -- of exception handling block
    push( a_stack, element );
    PUT("OK, element stacked ");
exception
    when OVERFLOW =>
            PUT("Stack full, element not stored! ");
end; -- of exception handling block
```

With this implementation it is guaranteed that the OVERFLOW exception will only be raised in the event of an overflow situation being detected during the push operation. Any CONSTRAINT_ERROR exceptions which are generated will not be handled by the OVERFLOW exception handler and will be propagated onwards, allowing them to be detected in the usual manner.

The discussion of the two possible exception mechanisms has clearly indicated that it is preferable for the programmer-declared exception mechanism to be employed rather than predeclared exceptions. The question remains as to whether it is better to report errors using one of the explicit mechanisms described earlier in this section, or to report errors using a user-declared exception. The word 'exception' itself gives a clue to the answer: an exception occurrence is an occurrence which can be foreseen but is regarded as unlikely. Consequently, the exception mechanism should be reserved for error occurrences which are regarded as unlikely and the reporting mechanisms explained above used for error occurrences which are regarded as likely. In this particular situation the overflow and underflow situations would usually not be considered as exceptions. The predeclared exception mechanism should largely be used for reporting unforeseen errors.

One final point concerning user-declared exceptions: a user-declared exception is an object which is usually, but not always, declared within a package. The scope of the visibility of the exception is the package specification and the package declaration. The exception is also visible within the scope of the use of the package in the application program. It is possible for a user-declared exception to be raised within its scope and subsequently propagated beyond its scope. It still exists as an exception outside its scope but its name is no longer visible. An exception propagated beyond its scope in this manner can only be handled as an anonymous exception within a **when others** clause.

To avoid this situation, programs should attempt to provide a handler of some sort for all programmer-declared exceptions which are used within their scope.

EXERCISES

3.10.1   Implement the dynamic stack package as described in the first part of this section. Use the harness program developed in Exercise 3.6.1 and the test plan developed in Exercise 3.6.2 to confirm the equivalence of the two implementations.

3.10.2   Implement the dynamic queue package as suggested in the first part of this section. Use the harness program from Exercise 3.7.1 and the test plan from Exercise 3.7.2 to confirm the equivalence of the two implementations.

3.10.3   Reimplement the static stack package from Block 3 Section 6 to use one of the alternative error-reporting mechanisms. Adapt the harness package from Exercise 3.6.1 and use it to demonstrate the equivalence of the two mechanisms using the test plan from Exercise 3.6.2.

3.10.4   Implement an ordered linked list package as a skin package of the general linked list package developed in the last section. What are the advantages of this implementation?

3.10.5   Reimplement the dynamic stack package using the user-declared exception mechanism. The exceptions should be declared in the general linked list specification initially raised in the general linked list body and propagated through the stack pack body to the application program.

Section 3.11

Binary trees

3.11.1 General trees and binary trees

The final dynamic structure which will be considered in this book is the binary tree. The binary tree data structure is the most general and most useful of a general class of structures known as *trees*. In previous sections the dynamic linked list was introduced and used to implement dynamic stacks and queues. The factor which characterized the linked list as a list was that each element of the list was linked by a pointer to at most one other element. The element at the end of the list had a **null** pointer, so was not linked to any other element, and was used to indicate the end of the list.

The individual elements which comprise a general tree structure are not limited to a single pointer pointing to one further element, but are characterized by being linked to more than one other element. So a general tree could have the following form:

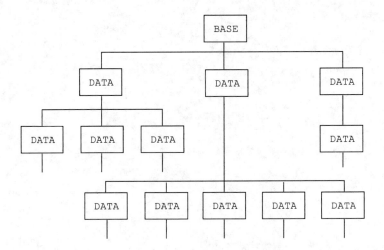

In this general tree each element of the tree is linked to an indeterminate number of other elements of the tree. Such a general irregular structure is difficult to implement and maintain.

A simpler form of the tree structure restricts the number of elements which can be linked to each element of the tree to two. This form of the general tree structure is known as a *binary tree*:

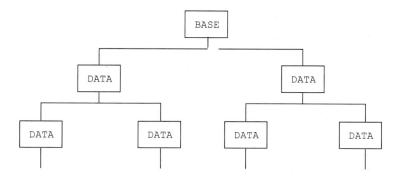

It is possible for any general tree to be implemented as a binary tree, although details of how to do this will not be given in this book.

The base pointer which points to the first item of a tree is known as the *root* of the tree and each element which comprises the tree is known as a *node* of the tree. The pointer within a node of the tree which points to the left subtree is known as the *left pointer* and the pointer which points to the right subtree is known as the *right pointer*. The nodes which exist at the extremities of the tree and which have no subtrees are known as the *leaves* of the tree.

3.11.2 Binary trees defined

The simplest possible binary tree is a tree which has no nodes; this tree is known as an *empty* or *null tree* and is indicated by its root pointer having a **null** value. A non-empty tree can be defined as a sequence of the left subtree (which could be a null tree), the data which is being stored in the node, and the right subtree (which could be a null tree). This can be shown on a recursive data-structure diagram:

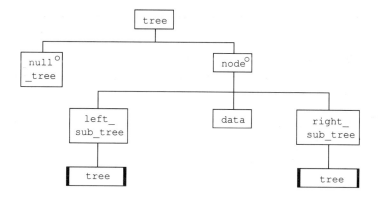

This diagram indicates that a tree is either a null tree or a node. A node is a sequence of the left subtree, the data stored at the node, and the right subtree; the left and right subtrees are themselves trees. The inclusion of a tree as a component of the description of a tree makes this a recursive description. The recursive description of the tree indicates that recursive algorithms can be employed to manipulate the tree.

There is one further aspect of the definition of a binary tree which is not encompassed by the description above. The values of all the data items stored in the left subtree of any node are less than the value of the data item stored at the node. Likewise, the values of all the data items stored in the right subtree of any node are greater than the value of the data item stored at the node.

3.11.3 Adding information to a binary tree

The process of adding information to a binary tree can best be explained by tracing the growth of a binary tree as data are stored in it. If a series of names is to be stored in a tree the tree will grow as follows.

Visualization A shows the tree after the first name 'freda' has been stored in it. The tree consists of a single node containing the data 'freda' and a left and right subtree, both of which are empty. An empty tree is shown on the diagram as a pointer pointing to nothing.

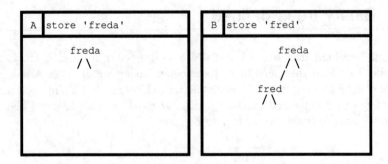

Visualization B shows the tree shown in visualization A after the name 'fred' has been stored in it. The name 'fred' has a lower value than 'freda', so it has been stored in freda's left subtree. It is the only element of this tree and its subtrees are shown as null trees.

Visualization C shows the tree shown in visualization B after the name 'julia' has been stored in it. The name 'julia' has a higher value than the name 'freda', so it is stored in freda's right subtree. It is the only element of this tree and its subtrees are shown as empty trees.

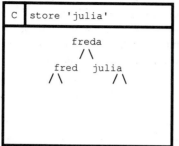

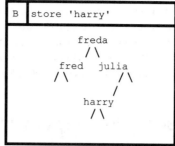

Visualization D shows the tree shown in visualization C after the name 'harry' has been stored in it. The name 'harry' has a higher value than 'freda', so it is stored in freda's right subtree. This subtree is not empty so the value to be stored is compared with the value at the root of this tree. The name 'harry' has a lower value than the name 'julia', so it is stored in julia's left subtree. It is the only element of this tree and its subtrees are shown as null trees.

Visualization E shows the tree shown in visualization D after 'jim' has been stored in it. The name 'jim' is higher than 'freda' so is stored in freda's right subtree which is not empty; 'jim' is less than 'julia' so is stored in julia's left subtree which is not empty; 'jim' is greater than 'harry' so is stored in harry's right subtree which is empty. It is the only element in this tree and its subtrees are shown as null trees.

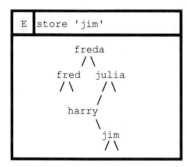

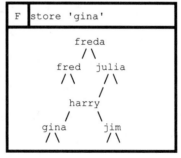

Visualization F shows the tree shown in visualization E after 'gina' has been stored in it. The name 'gina' is greater than 'freda' so is stored in freda's right subtree which is not empty; 'gina' is less than 'julia' so is stored in julia's left subtree which is not empty; 'gina' is less than 'harry' so is stored in harry's left subtree which is empty. It is the only element of this tree and its subtrees are shown as null trees.

The ordered nature of the tree can now be seen; for any node of the tree the names stored in the left subtree are less than the name at the node and all the names in the right subtree are greater than the name at the node. This ordering of the information in the tree will be made use of when the information in a tree is output.

A recursive process for storing information in a tree can now be defined. To store information in a tree start with the root node. If this node is empty, store the information at this node and set the left and right subtrees to null trees. If the node is not empty, compare the information to be stored with the information at the node. If the information to be stored is less than (or equal to) the information at this node store the information in the left subtree. If the information to be stored is greater than the information at this node store the information in the right subtree.

3.11.4 Binary tree implementation

The binary tree is a general structure which can be used to store information of any type. This implies that the tree is best implemented as a generic package which can be instantiated by the provision of the elemental data type to be stored and two BOOLEAN functions. One function will be used to determine the order of two data elements and the other to test two elements for equality.

The generic binary tree, as implemented in this section, will export a procedure which can be used to add a new node to the tree, a procedure which can be used to locate a particular node in the tree, a procedure which can be used to delete a particular node from the tree, and a procedure which can be used to traverse the tree. This can be shown on a package design diagram as follows:

```
                                    ┌─────────┐
                                    │    B    │
             element ->             │    I    │
            less_than =>            │    N    │
                equal =>            │    A    │
                                    │    R    │
               trees <-             │    Y    │
            add_node <=             │         │
         locate_node <=             │    T    │
         delete_node <=             │    R    │
            traverse <=             │    E    │
                                    │    E    │
                                    └─────────┘
```

The package specification for the generic binary tree package, omitting the subprogram declarations, follows:

```
-- generic binary tree declaration package, filename
-- b_tree_.pkg b3s11 see text.

generic
    type element is private;
    with function "<" ( elem_1, elem_2 : element )
         return BOOLEAN is < >;
    with function is_equal( elem_1, elem_2 : element )
```

```
       return BOOLEAN;

package b_tree is

    type trees is private;

    -- subprogram declarations here

private
    type tree_node;

    type trees is access tree_node;

    type tree_node is
    record
      left_tree  : trees;
      data       : element;
      right_tree : trees;
    end record;
end b_tree;
```

The generic declarations and the **private** type declarations included in this specification are comparable with the declarations made to implement the ordered linked list package in Block 3 Section 9. The major difference is in the declaration of the tree_node type which contains within itself two pointers which are capable of pointing to objects of its own type.

The design of a procedure to insert an element into a binary tree is presented below:

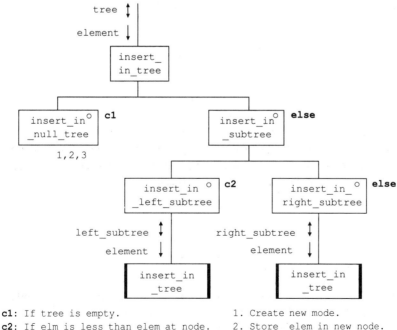

```
c1: If tree is empty.                    1. Create new mode.
c2: If elm is less than elem at node.    2. Store  elem in new node.
                                         3. Set subtrees null.
```

This design indicates that the procedure will require an in-out parameter of type trees and an in-only parameter of the elemental type to be stored. The design assumes that there will never be an attempt to insert an element into a tree when a element with that value already exists in the tree. Using the design above the declaration of this procedure would be as follows:

```
procedure insert_in_tree( root : in out trees;
                          elem : in      element );
-- procedure to insert elem into the tree pointed to by
-- root. Assumes that elem never already exists in tree
-- and that dynamic memory can always be allocated
```

The definition of this procedure in the package body follows:

```
procedure insert_in_tree( root : in out trees;
                          elem : in      element ) is
begin -- insert_in_tree
  if root = null then
    root := new tree_node' ( left_tree  => null,
                             data'       => elem,
                             right_tree => null);
  elsif (elem < root.data) then
     insert_in_tree( root.left_tree,  elem);
  else
     insert_in_tree( root.right_tree, elem);
  end if;
end insert_in_tree;
```

In the traces which will be used to illustrate the operation of this and other subprograms in this section, it is assumed that an instantiation of the binary tree package suitable for the storage of person records (Block 3 Section 8) has been made. This instantiation could be accomplished with the following statement:

```
package pers_tree is new b_tree( element  => pers_pack.person_records,
                                 "<"      => pers_pack.name_less_than,
                                 is_equal => pers_pack.name_equal_to );
```

For the sake of simplicity only the first name of the person record will be considered in the traces, although the functions implemented in the person package make use of both the first and second names when comparisons are being made.

The implementation of the insert_in_tree procedure can be verified by tracing its recursive descent as 'gina' is added to the binary tree shown in visualization E above. The procedure would be called with the following statement:

```
-- pers_tree is variable of type pers_tree.trees
-- pointing to tree shown in visualization E above.
-- new_person is variable of type pers_pack.person_records
-- and has been initialized to contain gina's details
pers_tree.insert_in_tree( pers_tree, new_person );
```

In the diagram of the recursive descent the first call of the procedure is made with the tree's root pointer, which points to the 'freda' node. As 'gina' is greater than 'freda' this causes a second call of the procedure passing the pointer which points to freda's right tree as the parameter, this is identified on the diagram below as R→:

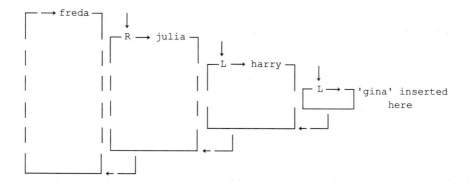

The second invocation invokes a third call to store 'gina' in julia's left subtree. This third invocation compares 'gina' with 'harry' and causes a fourth call to store 'gina' in harry's left subtree. This tree is empty, as indicated by the pointer having a null value, and a new node is created where 'gina' is stored. The fourth invocation's termination causes the recursive ascent through all four invocations to take place, terminating the process.

3.11.5 Searching a binary tree

The second specified subprogram searches a tree to determine if a certain element is or is not stored in the tree. If the element is stored in the tree the entire contents of the element stored at the node and an indication that the search has been successful will be exported from the subprogram. If the name is not stored in the tree then the process should indicate that the search was unsuccessful and the out-only element parameter would have no specified value.

The data-flow diagram of this subprogram would be as follows:

where to_find is the element to be searched for, tree is the tree to be searched, out_elem contains the entire contents of the located element if it can be found, and located is a BOOLEAN flag to indicate if the element was or was not found. The declaration of this procedure in the package specification is presented below:

```
procedure search_tree( root    : in  trees;
                       to_find  : in  element;
                       located  : out BOOLEAN;
                       out_elem : out element );
-- procedure to search binary tree for node matching
-- to_find. If node located, located is TRUE and out_elem
-- is set to contents; otherwise located is FALSE and
-- out_elem is not set.
```

Using the person_tree package whose instantiation was introduced earlier in this section, this procedure could be called in the following form:

```
-- Assuming person_tree is of type pers_tree.tree as
-- in visualization E, name_to_find is of type person_records with
-- name field only set to 'gina'. Is_found is a
-- BOOLEAN variable and ret_record is
-- of type person_records
pers_tree.search_tree( person_tree, name_to_find, is_found, ret_record);
```

After the procedure has completed is_found will be TRUE and ret_record will be set to the complete contents of the 'gina' element stored in the tree.

The program-structure diagram for this procedure would be as follows:

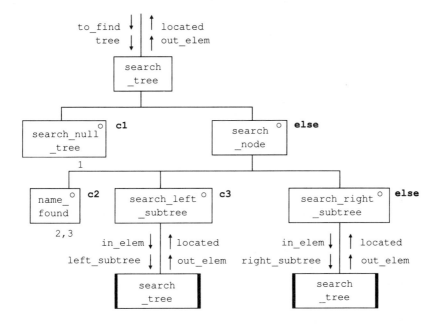

c1: If tree is empty.
c2: If element to locate is equal to element at this node.
c3: If element to locate is less than element at this node.

1. Set located FALSE.
2. Set located TRUE.
3. Set out_element to contents of node.

The design takes advantage of the ordering of the tree; if the tree is not empty and the element to be found is not at the current node then the value of the element to be found is compared with the value of the element at the current node. This comparison will decide if the left or the right subtree is to be searched. The ordering of the tree makes it pointless to search the right subtree if the element to be found is less than the element at the current node, as all the elements in the right subtree are greater than the element at the current node and thus are greater than the value of the element to be found. Likewise, a search of the left subtree can be omitted if the value of the element to be found is greater than the element at the current node.

The process has two conditions which can terminate the recursion. If the element is ever found the recursion is halted and an ascent through any levels of recursive invocations will take place; this termination will return the value TRUE in the BOOLEAN flag and an initialized output record. If the name is not in the tree this situation is detected by a request to search an empty tree; this termination will return the value FALSE in the flag.

The implementation of this function follows:

```
procedure search_tree( root     : in  trees;
                       to_find  : in  element;
                       located  : out BOOLEAN;
                       out_elem : out element ) is
begin -- search_tree
   if root = null then
      located := FALSE;
   else
      if ( is_equal( to_find, root.data )) then
         located := TRUE;
         out_elem := root.data;
      elsif ( to_find < root.data) then
         search_tree( root.left_tree, to_find, located, out_elem );
      else
         search_tree( root.right_tree, to_find, located, out_elem );
      end if;
   end if;
end search_tree;
```

The behaviour of this function can be illustrated as it searches the tree shown in visualization F, first successfully for 'gina', and then unsuccessfully for 'james'. The flow of information within the diagram will illustrate only the value of the pointer shown as before. When an invocation of the procedure terminates, a T indicates that the procedure returned TRUE and an F that it returned FALSE in the BOOLEAN flag. The return of the output record will be omitted from the diagram.

Here is the successful trace:

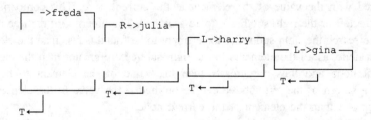

The setting of the flag to TRUE at the fourth level of the recursive descent causes that invocation to initialize the output record to the contents of the 'gina' node. These values are passed back up the recursive ascent and returned from the first level call to the calling part of the program.

The unsuccessful trace for a node containing 'james' is shown below:

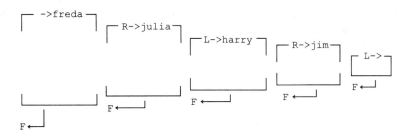

In this diagram the fifth invocation of the procedure has a **null** pointer passed to it, indicating that the search has exhausted the structure without finding the name. This causes the procedure to return the value FALSE in the BOOLEAN flag and terminate without initializing the output parameter. The value FALSE is passed back up the recursive ascent and returned from the first-level call, indicating that the name could not be found. This search of the tree has visited four out of six possible nodes in the tree and concluded that the name does not exist in the structure. An exhaustive search would have had to visit all six nodes to conclude that the name was not in the structure.

3.11.6 Traversing a binary tree

Having stored some information in a binary tree, the information in the entire tree may have to be used. The nature of the ordering within the binary tree allows the information contained within it to be visited in a defined order. It has been shown in the definition of the tree that for any node in the tree all the values of the data stored in the nodes of the left subtree are less than the value of the data at the node and all the values of the data stored in the nodes of the right subtree are higher than the value of the data at the node.

Using this feature of the tree, a process to visit all nodes in tree in order can be expressed by saying: if the tree is null then terminate; else visit all the nodes in the left subtree, followed by the root node, followed by all the nodes in the right subtree. As the information in the left subtree is less than the information at the node and all the information in the right subtree is higher, the nodes in the tree will be visited in order.

The declaration of the traverse procedure in the tree package declaration file specifies a formal generic procedure, which will be applied to each element stored at each node as it is visited during the traversal. This is similar to the traverse linked list procedure introduced in Block 3 Section 9. If a show_person procedure identical to the show_person procedure from that section is specified as the actual generic parameter of the traverse_tree procedure, the effect will be to output all the information stored in the tree in alphabetical order.

A program-structure diagram for the traverse procedure follows:

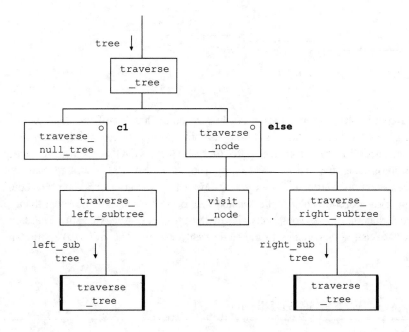

c1: If tree is null.

This procedure can be implemented in the package body as follows:

```
procedure traverse_tree( tree : in trees ) is

begin
    if (tree /= null) then
        traverse_tree( tree.left_tree);
        do_something( tree.data );
        traverse_tree( tree.right_tree);
    end if;
end traverse_tree;
```

This generic procedure can be instantiated within an application program using the person package and the b_tree package as a procedure whose effect would be to output all the personal records in the tree, in the following manner:

```
procedure show_pers( a_person : in out
                     pers_pack.person_record ) is
begin
   pers_pack.show_person( a_person );
end show_pers;

procedure show_tree is new
          pers_tree.traverse_tree( show_pers );
```

The show_person procedure from the person package is first repackaged in order to make its signature compatible with the required signature of the actual parameter of the generic procedure. This repackaged procedure is then supplied as an actual generic procedure to the instantiation of the pers_tree.traverse_tree procedure, creating a new procedure called show_tree.

3.11.7 Traversing a binary tree: traced

The behaviour of show_tree can be illustrated by tracing it as it displays the information stored in the tree shown in visualization F above. The procedure would be called with the following statement:

```
show_tree( pers_tree );
```

In the diagram of the recursive descent of this execution of the procedure the recursive call of the show_tree procedure using the left pointer is shown as L→ and the right invocation as R→. If the pointer being passed is not **null** then the name stored at the node being pointed to is shown, otherwise no name is shown. The output of any names from the invocation of the procedure is shown as =>name. The flow of control arrows has been removed to clarify the diagram.

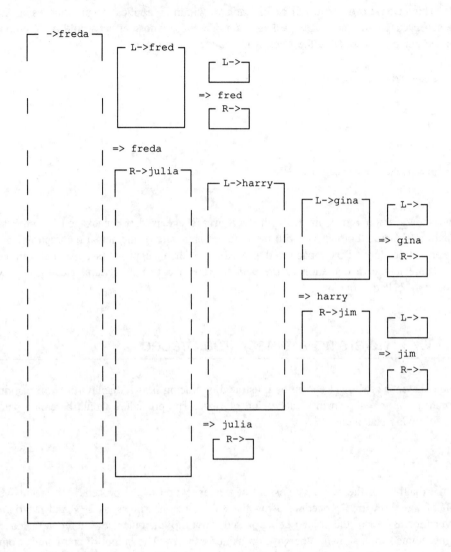

Each invocation of the procedure which has a non-**null** pointer value as a parameter, calls two further invocations of the procedure: one with the node's left pointer as a parameter, and one with then node's right pointer.

The output of this series of recursive descents and ascents is the names which have been stored in the tree in the sequence 'fred', 'freda', 'gina', 'harry', 'jim', 'julia'. The names were originally received by the tree in an unordered sequence; the tree traversal has output them in an ordered sequence.

3.11.8 Deleting information from a binary tree

A further operation required to make use of binary trees is a method of deleting information from the tree. A design for a process to accomplish this operation will be presented with minimal comment. The implementation and verification of this design will be left as an end-of-section exercise.

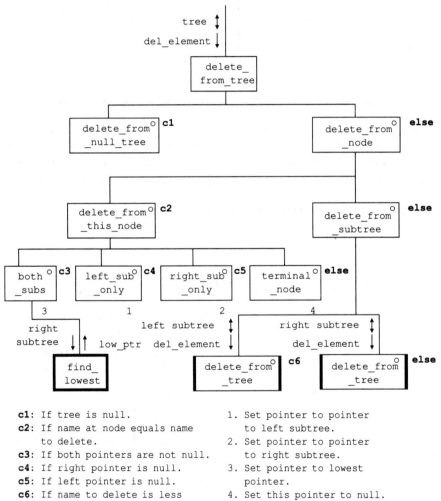

c1: If tree is null.
c2: If name at node equals name
    to delete.
c3: If both pointers are not null.
c4: If right pointer is null.
c5: If left pointer is null.
c6: If name to delete is less
    than name at node.

1. Set pointer to pointer
   to left subtree.
2. Set pointer to pointer
   to right subtree.
3. Set pointer to lowest
   pointer.
4. Set this pointer to null.

Deleting a node which has non-**null** left and right subtrees will require a subsidiary function which will (recursively) locate the highest name from the right subtree of the node which has been identified for deletion. This value will be found in the leftmost position of the subtree. When the node is located the out-only parameter variable is set to point to it and the node will be removed from the tree. The element is then stored in the tree in the place of the deleted element. This can be illustrated by considering the deletion of 'freda' from the tree shown in visualization F.

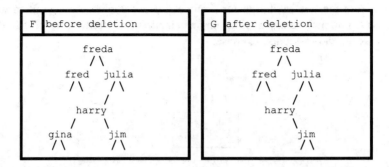

The deletion of 'freda' is accomplished by locating the lowest element in freda's right subtree which is the 'gina' node. This terminal node is removed from the tree and placed in freda's position. The tree shown in visualization G is the result; the integrity of the tree has been maintained with all elements in gina's right subtree greater in value than 'gina'.

The design of the subsidiary find_lowest function follows:

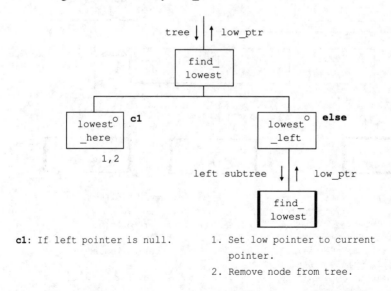

c1: If left pointer is null.   1. Set low pointer to current
                                   pointer.
                                2. Remove node from tree.

The delete_from_tree process has been designed not to signal back to the calling process that the value to be deleted could not be found in the tree. In this case the process will do nothing. If the effect of the procedure was to ensure that the name was not in the tree and the name was not found in the tree then this is the correct action. In other cases a failure to locate the name to be deleted in the tree should be reported back, in which case an out-only data flow could be added to the process. Alternatively, a suitable user-declared exception could be raised to indicate failure.

3.11.9 Balanced trees

The following three trees all contain the same seven elements of character data. They all conform to the definition of a binary tree as given at the start of the chapter. Also, they differ in the shape of the tree.

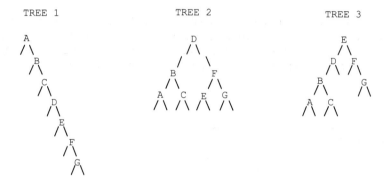

Tree 3 is typical of the shape of a tree which would be produced if the data were received in a random sequence. Tree 1 is a worst-case tree which would be produced if the data were received in alphabetical sequence. Tree 1 is in effect a linked list: for every node in the tree there is only one subtree. Tree 2 is a perfectly balanced symmetrical tree; it is most unlikely to arise by chance as only a few combinations of sequences of input data would produce it. Most trees are of the form of tree 3, that is, neither perfect linked lists nor perfectly balanced trees.

There are advantages in having perfectly balanced trees: the actions of traversing a tree or searching a tree can be performed more efficiently on a perfectly balanced tree. In the examples above, a traversal of tree 1 would require a nine-level recursive descent, tree 3 would require a four-level recursive descent, but tree 2 would only require three levels.

There are processes available which will transform any shape of binary tree into a balanced tree. These processes are complex and are expensive in their use of machine time and resources. Where a tree structure is being used largely for traversal or searching, such a transformation may be worthwhile. Where a tree is expected to have a large number of additions or deletions, transforming the tree into a balanced tree would probably not be worthwhile. The algorithms for balancing a tree will not be presented in this book.

EXERCISES

3.11.1 Implement the delete_from_tree procedure whose design was given in this section.

3.11.2 Implement the generic b_tree package as described in this section. Instantiate a package capable of storing person_records using the person package first used in Block 3 Section 9. Adapt an interactive test harness and use it to test the operation of the tree package.

3.11.3 The tree traversal procedure as implemented in this section traversed the tree in the sequence specified in the tree package's instantiation. Implement a traverse procedure which would traverse the tree in a reverse sequence.

3.11.4 It is often required that, having searched and located a particular node of the tree, a change has to be applied to the information stored there. The best method of implementing this is as a generic procedure called find_and_change which would require a change_something formal procedure parameter. The declaration of this procedure in the binary tree declaration file would be as follows:

```
generic
    change_something( c_elem : in out element );
procedure find_and_change( tree    : in   trees;
                           in_elem : in   element;
                           located : out BOOLEAN );
-- procedure to locate item in_elem in tree, and
-- apply change_something procedure to item stored
-- there. Exports TRUE in located if in_elem is in tree
-- and FALSE otherwise.
```

Implement and test this procedure by instantiating it with a procedure which will allow the weight field of the person record to be changed interactively. Include it within the interactive harness produced in Exercise 3.11.2.

3.11.5 What is the search order of the binary tree? Produce an analysis for the best-case and worst-case situations. Assuming a perfectly balanced binary tree, what is the average-case behaviour?

Section 3.12

Other uses of packages

The package facilities which have been introduced in this book have concentrated upon using packages to implement abstract data types. This is not the only use which can be made of Ada's package facilities. Three other common uses of packages are: to provide a set of related constants; to provide a set of related subprograms; and to implement a model of a machine. The first two alternative uses of packages are very straightforward, the third is more complex. This section will introduce each in turn.

3.12.1 Using a package to provide constants

Many application programs are written within a particular sphere of activity which has a set of constants common to many different programs. For example, a team of programmers may specialize in the writing of scientific software. Many programs written by this team may have a requirement to access such universal scientific constants as the speed of light, the mass of an electron, and the acceleration due to gravity. It is more convenient for the production of such programs if these constants are declared in a package which can be used by all programs being written, rather than having to be redeclared in every program. The package specification file for such a program might be as follows:

```
-- package declaration file to provide a set of scientific
-- constants. b3s12 see text.

package scientific_constants is

    speed_of_light              : constant FLOAT := 3.0E8;
                                        -- metres per second
    c : FLOAT renames speed_of_light;

    mass_of_an_electron         : constant FLOAT := 9.1E-28;
                                        -- grams
    e : FLOAT renames mass_of_an_electron;
```

```
     acceleration_due_to_gravity : constant      := 9.8E0;
                                           -- metres per second squared
     G : FLOAT renames acceleration_due_to_gravity;


     -- other common constants similarly declared

  end scientific_constants;
```

This package specification contains only the declaration of constants of type FLOAT and their associated values. As it does not contain any subprogram declarations there is no requirement for a package body to accompany it. Each constant which is declared in the file has a long meaningful name associated with it in the usual manner. Each constant also has a conventional symbolic name provided as an alternative. This alternative is achieved by the use of a **renames** declaration. A **renames** declaration provides an alternative name for a program object. In the example above the constant value of the speed of light can be referenced in a program which uses this package by either of the identifiers 'speed_of_light' or 'c'. The programmer could chose which name to use on the basis of meaningfulness. In some circumstances the long name would be appropriate, in other circumstances the short name would be appropriate.

The **renames** facility is not limited to constants; it is also possible for a **renames** declaration to be used to rename a variable, a subprogram, a package or an exception. The scope of the **renames** declaration is the usual scope of a declaration. In the example above, the **renames** declaration has the entire scope of the usage of the package. If a **renames** declaration were made as part of a subprogram's declarations then the scope of the rename would be limited to the subprogram.

A **renames** declaration can be used to provide a convenient alternative name for an object, as used above. It can also be used to provide an alternative name for an object when two objects would otherwise have the same name; a **renames** declaration can be used to disambiguate the two names. It can also be used for convenience to allow the use of a shorter name for an object which has a long name. For example, a complex record declaration may have a record declaration within it and be accessed by an access variable; the full name of an object may thus be

```
  access_var.main_record.sub_record.field_name
```

A **renames** declaration could be used to provide a shorter, more acceptable and meaningful name for the same object. It can be used in the following form:

```
  simple_ref : simple_type renames complex_ref;
```

A commercial programming environment may have a similar requirement to provide a set of related constants. For example, a team of programmers writing financial software may make extensive use of the following constants:

```
-- package declaration file to provide a set of financial
-- constants. b3s12 see text.

package financial_constants is

    value_added_tax : constant FLOAT := 0.175;
    vat             : FLOAT renames value_added_tax;

    basic_tax_rate  : constant FLOAT := 0.25;

    --    other common constants similarly declared

end financial_constants;
```

The use of a package for constants of this nature may not be the most appropriate implementation decision. A dependency diagram of a program using this package may look like this:

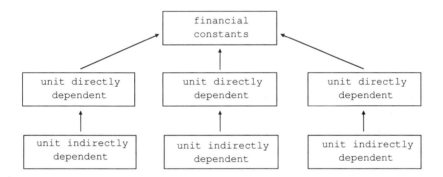

A constant such as the rate of VAT or the basic tax rate is not an absolute constant in the same way as the speed of light is constant. It is very unlikely that the value of the speed of light will ever change, but it is likely that at some time the rate of VAT will change (indeed, during the final production of this book the rate of VAT was changed from 15% to 17.5%). When this happens the value of the constant in the package specification will have to be changed. This change will make the package specification obsolete and will cause it to have to be recompiled. This recompilation will cause units directly dependent upon it to become obsolete and require recompilation. Likewise, indirectly dependent units will also become obsolete. The effect of a minor change to the value of one of the constants in the constants package will have the effect of causing the entire system to require recompilation. This will reduce the advantage which accrued from declaring the constants in a package specification.

An alternative decision is to implement the 'constants' as parameterless functions of the required type, and to return the 'constant' values within the associated package body. For example:

```
-- package specification file to provide a set of financial
-- constants. b3s12 see text.

package financial_constants is

    function value_added_tax return FLOAT;
    -- function to return current value of VAT

    function vat              return FLOAT renames value_added_tax;

    function basic_tax_rate   return FLOAT;
    -- function to return current basic tax rate

    -- other common constants similarly declared as functions

end financial_constants;
```

This package will require a package definition:

```
-- package definition file to provide a set of financial
-- constants. b3s12 see text.

package body financial_constants is

    function value_added_tax return FLOAT is
    begin
        return 0.175;
    end value_added_tax;

    function basic_tax_rate   return FLOAT is
    begin
        return 0.25;
    end basic_tax_rate;

    -- other function body definitions

end financial_constants;
```

The reference to a parameterless function can be made at any place in a program where a reference to a constant could be used. Both are objects which require no parameters and evaluate to a value of the required type. The differences between the two implementations can be made clear from a dependency diagram:

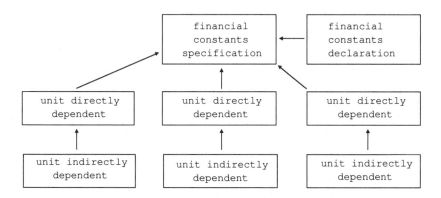

Any changes to the value of the 'constants' can now be implemented by changing the values in the package body. As this file has no dependent units, no other file need be recompiled as a consequence of its being changed. This mechanism will allow constants of this nature to be implemented in a more convenient manner than implementing them as absolute constants.

3.12.2 Using a package to provide subprograms

A second use of Ada's constant facilities is in the provision of a package which provides a set of related subprograms. The commonest example of such a package is a mathematics package which provides a set of functions which can be used to implement mathematical operations which are not predeclared by the Ada standard. A part of a suitable package declaration file might be the following:

```
package MATH_LIB is

    function sqrt ( a_float : FLOAT) return FLOAT;
    -- Square root.

    function log  ( a_float : FLOAT) return FLOAT;
    -- natural logarithm - log base e

    function log10( a_float : FLOAT) return FLOAT;
    -- Common logarithm - log base 10

    -- other mathematical & trigonometrical
    -- function declarations here
```

Packages such as this are usually provided by the compiler manufacturer and provide a clear example of the distinction between the *what* and the *how* of package implementations. The user of such a package only requires a knowledge of the signature and the meaning of a returned value. A user of the package has no requirement to know anything about the definition of these functions. The actual definition of these functions will most probably not be an Ada package definition file but an interface to operating system run-time routines or a machine-code implementation of algorithms to calculate the required values.

Other packages supplied by a compiler manufacturer may provide a set of graphical routines, statistical routines, operating system facilities, specialized input/output interfaces (e.g., mouse support), and the like. Such facilities should be used with some care as they are specific to a particular compiler manufacturer and will have implications for the portability of programs which rely upon the facilities provided. With this reservation such packages should be used, as they can simplify program development and prevent a programmer from having to reinvent the wheel.

3.12.3 Using a package to implement a machine

Superficially this use of package facilities is very similar to the use of package facilities to provide an abstract data type. Packages which implement a machine have one important difference: such packages are said to have a 'memory' which causes them to be classed as *memory packages*. Within such a package a model of a physical or logical system is implemented; this model is not exported from the package as a data type but is maintained entirely within the package. The state of the machine can be changed from outside the package using a defined interface and such changes are permanently recorded within the package as a change to the internal state of the machine.

An abstract data type package provides a model of a physical or logical system in the form of a data type which is exported from the package. The state of this data type can be changed by supplying it as a parameter to a subprogram which is provided by the package. The changes to the data object are re-exported within the object.

An example memory package specification

The use of a memory package will be introduced by implementing a package which models a physical machine, a canned drinks dispenser. This should not be taken to imply that only physical machines can be implemented in this manner. There are a number of 'abstract machines' (for example, a state transition parser) which are also suitable for implementation within Ada as a memory package.

The scenario for this specification is the implementation of software which will control a soft drinks dispenser as illustrated below:

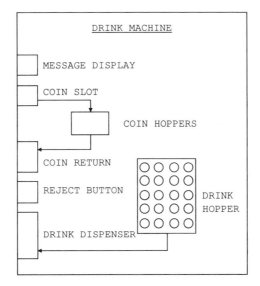

Here is a summary of the specification of the machine:

> The machine will be operated by the user entering coins into the coin slot. The value of the coins input will be displayed on the message display. When a sufficient value has been input by the user a can of drink will be dispensed from the drink hopper and the change due will be dispensed from the coin return. If it is not possible for the machine to make the change required, no drink will be dispensed and the value of the coins input by the user will be returned.
>
> At any stage during the input of coins before a sufficient value has been input the user can press the reject button and have the value of the coins already input returned.
>
> If the drinks hopper ever becomes empty or any other fault occurs in the machine, the value of any coins input by the user should be returned and the machine should shut down with a suitable message on the display.
>
> It is intended that this machine will be used in different countries and the software should be engineered appropriately.

It is intended that the software will be interfaced to the machine when the physical design of the machine is complete. In the interim any physical parts of the machine should be modelled by input from or output to the terminal.

The package which implements the machine will hide the details of the modelling of the physical components of the machine (the drink hopper, the coin hopper and the message display) inside the package definition. The state of these objects will be maintained solely within the package definition. For example, when a can is dispensed from the hopper, the number of cans remaining in the hopper will be reduced by one and this will be a permanent change in the state of the drink hopper object. This is the precise meaning of describing the package as having a 'memory'.

The package specification will provide suitable interfaces to perform actions upon the machine's components. For example, the specification will provide an action called dispense_can which will make sure that change is available and if so dispense a can and the appropriate change. If the change required cannot be provided by the machine then this action will return the value of the coins input.

Design and implementation

The first stage in the development of this software is to design the data types and data objects which will be used to represent the state of the internal mechanisms of the machine. The modelling of the drink hopper can be very simply implemented:

```
-- machine package definition drink hopper modelling

max_drink_stack : constant := 6; -- test value only
-- maximum number of cans in the hopper

subtype drink_hoppers is INTEGER range 0 .. max_drink_stack;
-- subrange type for cans in hopper

drink_hopper : drink_hoppers;
-- variable to represent no of cans actually in hopper
```

The modelling of the coin hopper can be implemented as follows:

```
-- machine package definition. coin hopper modelling

max_coin_stack  : constant := 50;
-- maximum number of any coin which can be accepted

type    coins is ( one_p, two_p, five_p, ten_p,
                   twenty_p, fifty_p, hundred_p );
-- different denominations of coins available

package coins_io is new TEXT_IO.ENUMERATION_IO( coins );
-- coins io facilities

subtype coin_stacks    is INTEGER range 0 .. max_coin_stack;
-- subrange type for num of coins in a coin stack

type    coin_hoppers is array (coins) of coin_stacks;
-- hopper containing stack for each coin denomination

coin_denoms : array (coins) of POSITIVE
              := ( 1, 2, 5, 10, 20, 50, 100 );
-- value of each type of coin

coin_hopper : coin_hoppers;
-- the actual coin hopper
```

These two objects, the coin_hopper and the drink_hopper, as well as the types which support them are declared within the package definition and as such are not visible outside the definition. Even the package specification does not know about them and cannot access them directly.

The package specification will have to provide the high-level actions which are available to the user. A suitable specification might be the following:

```
-- package specification to implement a dispensing machine
-- Scenario is that the machine can accept coins from the user
-- and will dispense a can of drink and the correct change if
-- the correct coins are inserted. b3s12 see text.

package drink_machine is

    -- cost of a single can
    can_cost : constant := 30;

    -- value of coins input
    subtype coin_values is NATURAL;

    MACHINE_FAULT  : exception;
    REJECT_PRESSED : exception;

    procedure accept_coin( value  : in out coin_values);
    -- procedure to accept a coin from the user, updating value,
    -- which is displayed on the message display

    procedure dispense_can( value : in coin_values );
    -- procedure to dispense a single can of drink and change
    -- due if can be made otherwise returns value in coins

    procedure give_change( value : in coin_values );
    -- procedure to dispense value from the hopper, should
    -- only be called if it can be guaranteed that change
    -- can be made

    procedure shut_down;
    -- message to say that the machine is empty

end drink_machine;
```

A design decision has been taken that the action of a user pressing the reject button on the machine will be treated as an exception; this is not necessarily the best decision as such an action would not be regarded as exceptional. This decision has been taken in this implementation to reinforce the use of programmer-declared exception handling, which was introduced in Block 2 Section 10.

The decision to implement a machine_fault exception is a valid design decision. It is hoped that the machine will be regularly serviced and restocked. If the machine ever runs out of cans or if an error ever occurs such as a jammed dispenser, it is hoped that the machine will be able to detect the error and *raise* this exception causing the machine to shut down in a controlled manner.

The specification of the individual subprograms has been largely taken from the machine specification. Using these subprogram specifications the application program which will control the machine's operations can be designed:

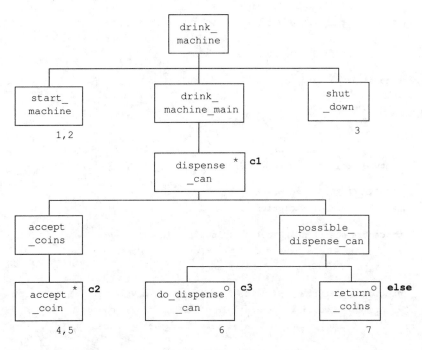

c1: While not machine error
c2: While value less than cost
    and not reject pressed
    and not machine fault
c3: If reject not pressed
    and not machine fault
    and change can be made

1. Fill drink hopper.
2. Fill change hoppers.
3. Display shut down message.
4. Accept coin.
5. Show value.
6. Dispense can and make change.
7. Return coins.

This design can be implemented as follows:

```
with drink_machine;
use  drink_machine;

procedure b3s12p1 is
    money_in      : coin_values := 0;
```

```
begin
   while ( TRUE ) loop
   begin -- exception handler block
      money_in := 0;
      while ( money_in < can_cost ) loop
         accept_coin( money_in );
      end loop;
      dispense_can( money_in ) ;
   exception
      when REJECT_PRESSED =>
            give_change( money_in );
   end -- exception block;
   end loop;
   exception;
      when MACHINE_FAULT =>
         shut_down;
end b3s12p1;
```

This implementation uses the exception-handling mechanism to cause an exit from the main loop. The loop control condition is the BOOLEAN constant TRUE, which implies that the loop will iterate forever. If a reject_pressed exception is raised it is handled within the scope of the loop, causing any money already in the machine to be returned to the user. As this exception handler is declared within the scope of the loop, after the handler has executed the loop will reiterate. If a machine_fault exception is raised within the loop a suitable exception handler will be found outside the loop, this exception handler will cause the shut_down procedure to be invoked, following which the program will terminate. The only way in which the main loop can terminate is thus upon the occurrence of a machine error.

The model of the drink machine can be completed by implementing the subprogram definitions which were specified in the package specification. The procedure accept_coin will for the moment simulate the input of a coin into the coin slot by an interactive selection from the terminal. The implementation of the interactive parts of this procedure will not be explained in detail:

```
procedure accept_coin( value  : in out coin_values) is

   choice     : CHARACTER := ' ';
   min_choice : constant CHARACTER := 'A';
   max_choice : CHARACTER := min_choice;
   this_coin  : coins;

begin -- accept coin
   -- display prompts
   NEW_LINE(2);
   PUT_LINE("Please insert coin, or press reject ");
```

```
  NEW_LINE;
  for this_coin in coins'FIRST .. coins'LAST loop
      PUT( max_choice ); PUT("    ");
      coins_io.PUT( this_coin, SET => lower_case );
      NEW_LINE;
      max_choice := CHARACTER'SUCC(max_choice);
  end loop;
  PUT( max_choice ); PUT("    ");
  PUT("reject "); NEW_LINE(2);

  -- get user's input
  while ( (choice < min_choice) or (choice > max_choice)) loop
      PUT("Enter choice "); GET( choice ); SKIP_LINE;
      if ((choice < min_choice) or ( choice > max_choice)) then
         PUT_LINE("Enter value in range please.");
      end if;
  end loop;

  -- process user's choice
  if ( choice = max_choice ) then
      PUT_LINE("Reject button pressed !");
      raise REJECT_PRESSED;
  else -- accept the coin
      this_coin := coins'VAL( CHARACTER'POS( choice )
                            - CHARACTER'POS(min_choice)    );
      coin_hopper( this_coin ) := coin_hopper( this_coin ) + 1;
      value := value + coin_denoms( this_coin );
      show_value( value );
  end if;
end accept_coin;
```

The basic design of the procedure is to display a menu to the user, automatically adjusting it to the number of possible coins specified in the declaration of the enumerated type coins. The last possible coin is followed by an option to press the reject button. The validated user's input is then obtained. If the user pressed the reject button the REJECT_PRESSED exception is raised, otherwise the coin is accepted.

The user's character input is first converted into a coins enumeration value using suitable attribute functions. This enumeration value is then used to increment the number of coins stored in the appropriate coin hopper and the value of the coins input is incremented with the coins' denominations. The references to the coin_hopper and coin_denoms program objects at this point of the program are global references. These objects are declared within the scope of the package body and are not passed to the procedure as parameters.

The use of a global reference in this situation is acceptable for the following reasons. First, it is the only mechanism by which the package can be given a memory.

Second, the scope of the objects is strictly limited; outside the procedure they are restricted to the scope of the package body. Third, it reflects the real-world perception of the machine; the coin hoppers are not visible outside the machine, so restricting their visibility to the part of the program which models the physical machine is congruent with the real-world perception of the coin hopper which is not visible outside the machine.

The procedure also has a requirement to display the total value of the coins input on the machine's message display. This is accomplished by the procedure show_value, which in this simulation will display the value on the terminal screen. The implementation of this procedure will not be presented.

The dispense_can procedure can be implemented as follows:

```
procedure dispense_can( value : in coin_values ) is
begin
    if ( can_give_change( value - can_cost)) then
        drink_hopper := drink_hopper -1;
        PUT_LINE("A can has just been dispensed !!");
        NEW_LINE;
        give_change( value - can_cost );
    else
        show_message("Use exact change please !");
        give_change( value );
    end if;
    check_can_hopper;
end dispense_can;
```

The procedure commences by ensuring that it is possible to dispense the correct change to the user by calling the BOOLEAN function can_give_change. This function will return the value TRUE if it is possible to supply the required change from the coin_hopper, or FALSE otherwise. The implementation of the can_give_change function will be given shortly. If it is possible to dispense a can it is simulated by decrementing the drink_hopper by 1; this is again an allowable global reference. A message is then displayed on the terminal to simulate the can being dispensed, and procedure give_change is called to dispense the change required.

If it is not possible to dispense a can, a suitable message is simulated on the machine's message, display using the procedure show_message and the value of the coins input is returned using the procedure give_change. Before the procedure terminates the drink hopper is checked to ensure that it is not empty. The implementation of the check_can_hopper procedure would be as follows:

```
procedure check_can_hopper is
begin
    if drink_hopper = 0 then
        raise MACHINE_FAULT;
```

```
      end if;
   end check_can_hopper;
```

Once again this procedure makes a global reference to the drink_hopper object; should it ever indicate that the drink hopper is empty a MACHINE_FAULT is raised which will have the effect of shutting the machine down. The implementation of the function can_give_change follows:

```
function can_give_change( value : coin_values ) return BOOLEAN is

   rem_value   : coin_values  := value; -- remaining value
   temp_hopper : coin_hoppers := coin_hopper;

begin  -- can give change
   for this_coin in reverse coins'FIRST .. coins'LAST loop
      while (   (rem_value >= coin_denoms(this_coin)) and
                (temp_hopper( this_coin ) > 0))        loop
         rem_value := rem_value - coin_denoms( this_coin );
         temp_hopper( this_coin ) := temp_hopper( this_coin ) -1;
      end loop;
   end loop;
   if rem_value > 0 then
      return FALSE;
   else
      return TRUE;
   end if;
end can_give_change;
```

This function commences by making a local copy of the coin hopper. It is not acceptable for the function to operate upon the actual coin hopper as the state of the actual coin hopper should only be change when a coin is input or output. The basis of the function is to iterate through all hoppers from the largest to the smallest denomination, removing coins from each hopper until the hopper is empty or the value to be returned is less than the value of the coin. If at the end of this process the remaining value to be returned is zero then it is possible to return the value required from the unchanged actual coin hopper and the function returns TRUE. If the remaining value is not zero then it indicates that it would not be possible to return the correct change and the function returns FALSE.

The implementation of the give_change procedure is similar to the can_give_change function but operates upon the actual coin_hopper rather than on a copy. The return of a coin to the user in this simulation is implemented by a suitable message on the terminal; the detailed implementation of this procedure will not be presented. The shut_down procedure can be implemented in this simulation by simply sending a message to the machine's display:

```
procedure shut_down is
begin
    show_message("This machine is empty !");
end shut_down;
```

The initialization of the machine can be accomplished by including an executable component in the package body. This executable component will be executed every time the package is brought into use and will simulate the actions which are to be performed on the machine every time it is serviced and resupplied. In this example program it will be used to initialize the drinks machine by filling its drink hopper and placing some change in all the coin hoppers, apart from the highest denomination. A suitable executable package body routine would be as follows:

```
begin -- of procedure body executable routine
    -- fill drink can hopper
    drink_hopper := max_drink_stack;
    -- fill coin hoppers apart from last one
    for this_coin in coins'FIRST .. coins'PRED(coins'LAST) loop
        coin_hopper( this_coin ) := 5;
    end loop;
    -- empty last coin hopper
    coin_hopper( coins'LAST ) := 0;
end drink_machine;
```

This completes the simulation of the drink machine. The parallels between the physical machine and the model presented in this package should be clear. The high-level interface to the machine is presented in the package specification file which provides facilities which a user of the machine can manipulate: entering a coin, receiving a dispensed can, receiving returned coins. The high-level control of the machine is implemented in the application program which can only control the machine through the facilities in the package declaration.

The package definition implements the low-level machine facilities which are hidden from the user: the drink hopper, the coin hopper and the message display. As these are hidden aspects of the machine they are declared and hidden within the package body where the variable objects which represent them are manipulated globally by the subprograms declared in the package.

If a real machine were being engineered then only the package definition file would have to be changed. The parts of the machine which at the moment are implemented by terminal simulation (the acceptance of a coin, the dispensing of cans and return of coins) would be replaced by the specific program code which could be used actually to perform these actions.

Ada is commonly used for the development of software which is used to control physical machines; such software is known as *embedded software*. The use of memory packages which restrict the physical implementation of the machine to the package body assist in the processes of developing such software. By providing a logical interface to the machine in the package specification and constraining the actual details to the package body, it is possible to develop and test the high-level software before the machine has been actually constructed. The use of memory packages also reduces the complexity of the high-level software as the precise details of the machine are hidden inside the package body.

EXERCISES

3.12.1 Implement the missing parts of the package declaration file and then construct the machine simulation.

3.12.2 Devise a test plan for the machine and use it to verify the machine's simulation.

3.12.3 The American version of the machine will accept 5, 10, 25, 50 and 100 cent coins; a can of drink will cost 65 cents. Adapt and retest the machine to this specification.

3.12.4 The drinks machine as presented in this section contains a fault; when coins are accepted from the user no check is made to ensure that the appropriate coin hopper is not full. Suggest at least two methods by which the machine could cope with this situation, evaluate the alternatives and implement one of them.

3.12.5 A revised version of the machine will hold a range of different drinks at different prices. Implement this machine.

Appendices

Appendix A

Solutions to selected exercises

Ideally this appendix should contain solutions to all the exercises suggested in the text. However, this would make what is already a long book much too long. Consequently, only a selection of the solutions are presented here.

The solutions are presented as Ada program listings, with the designs implicit. Again, it would be preferable to present the designs and the listings, but the designs have had to be omitted for reasons of space.

It must be emphasized that the solutions presented are not the only ones possible. For any exercise there are a large number of possible solutions; the solutions presented here can best be used as a bench-mark against which other solutions can be compared.

A complete set of solutions and the programs used in the text are available to academic institutions. For details please contact:

FINTAN@UK.AC.SOUTHBANK-POLY.VAX

filename b1s2e2.lis

```
0001   -- filename b2s2e2 - solution to b1s2 exercise 2 - see text
0002   -- program to illustrate (shortened) VAX Ada eror messages
0003   -- corrected version
0004
0005   with TEXT_IO; use TEXT_IO;
0006
0007   procedure b1s2e2 is -- semicolon removed
0008
0009      msg1 : constant STRING := "Data design + ";
0010      -- constant & STRING reversed, double quotes
0011
0012   begin -- b1s2e2
0013         -- b1s2e2 should be a comment
0014      PUT( msg1 );
0015           -- quotes removed
0016      PUT( "+ program design ");
0017      PUT( " = programming.");
```

```
0018  end b1s2e2;
0019  --  correct procedure name appended
0020
```

filename b1s2e3.lis

```
0001  -- filename b1s2e3 - solution to b1s3 exercise 3 - see text
0002
0003  with TEXT_IO; use TEXT_IO;
0004
0005  procedure b1s2e3 is
0006
0007     msg1 : constant STRING := "Ada error messages ";
0008     msg2 : constant STRING := "are not always very helpful";
0009          -- added closing terminating double quote
0010     num_err : constant STRING := " five ";
0011
0012  begin -- b1s2e3
0013     PUT_LINE( msg1 ); PUT_LINE(msg2 );
0014                     -- semicolon between statements
0015     PUT( "This program contains at least" );
0016          -- added closing double quote
0017     PUT( num_err) ; PUT_LINE( " errors. ");
0018          -- only one string per PUT or PUT_LINE
0019     PUT( "and is only 16 lines long. ");
0020  end b1s2e3;
0021       -- comment removed
0022
0023
0024
```

filename b1s3e1.lis

```
0001  -- filename b1s3q1  - solution to b1s3 exercise 1 - see text
0002
0003
0004  with TEXT_IO;
0005  package int_io is new TEXT_IO.INTEGER_IO( INTEGER );
0006
0007  with TEXT_IO,int_io; use TEXT_IO,int_io;
0008
0009  procedure b1s3e1 is
0010
0011     big,                      -- num to subtract from
```

```
0012    little,                 -- num to subtract
0013    difference,             -- result of subtraction
0014    first_num,              -- first num to multiply
0015    second_num,             -- second num to multiply
0016    product,                -- result of multiplication
0017    divisor,                -- num to divide
0018    dividend,               -- num to divide by
0019    divided    : INTEGER;   -- result of division
0020
0021
0022    begin -- of b1s3e1
0023       -- subtraction
0024       NEW_LINE;
0025       PUT ( "Please enter num to subtract from ");
0026       GET ( big ); SKIP_LINE;
0027       PUT ( "Please enter num to subtract      ");
0028       GET ( little ); SKIP_LINE;
0029       difference := big - little;
0030       PUT("The result is "); PUT( difference );
0031       NEW_LINE;
0032
0033       -- multiplication
0034       NEW_LINE;
0035       PUT ( "Please enter first  num to multiply ");
0036       GET ( first_num ); SKIP_LINE;
0037       PUT ( "Please enter second num to multiply ");
0038       GET ( second_num ); SKIP_LINE;
0039       product := first_num * second_num;
0040       PUT("The result is "); PUT( product );
0041       NEW_LINE;
0042
0043       -- divide
0044       NEW_LINE;
0045       PUT ( "Please enter num to be divided ");
0046       GET ( divisor ); SKIP_LINE;
0047       PUT ( "Please enter num to divide by ");
0048       GET ( dividend ); SKIP_LINE;        i
0049       divided := divisor / dividend;
0050       PUT("The result is "); PUT( divided );
0051       NEW_LINE;
0052
0053    end b1s3e1;
0054
```

filename b1s3e3.lis

```
0001   -- filename b1s3e3 - solution to b1s3 exercise 3 - see text
0002
0003   with TEXT_IO, int_io;
0004   use  TEXT_IO, int_io; -- context clause required
0005
0006   procedure b1s3e3 is
0007
0008      num1,      -- comma not semicolon
0009      num2  : INTEGER ; -- colon not semicolon
0010
0011   begin -- b1s3e3
0012      num1 := 42; -- := not =
0013      num2 := 56; -- := not =
0014      PUT("The result of multiplying 42 by 56 is ");
0015      PUT( num1 * num2 ); -- include within put statement
0016      NEW_LINE;
0017   end b1s3e3; -- correct name
0018
0019
```

filename b1s3e4.lis

```
0001   -- filename b1s3e4.ans - solution to b1s3 exercise 4 - see text
0002   -- program to input length & height of a rectangle
0003   -- and display the area
0004
0005   with TEXT_IO, int_io;
0006   use  TEXT_IO, int_io; -- context clause required
0007
0008   procedure b1s3e4 is
0009
0010      lenf,              -- length of rectangle
0011                         -- use 'lenf' as LENGTH is predeclared
0012      height,            -- height of rectangle
0013      area   : INTEGER; -- area of rectangle
0014
0015   begin -- b1s3e4
0016      NEW_LINE;
0017      PUT("Please enter length ");
0018      GET( lenf ); SKIP_LINE;
0019      PUT("Please enter height ");
0020      GET( height ); SKIP_LINE;
0021
```

```
0022      area := lenf * height;
0023      NEW_LINE;
0024      PUT("The area is ");
0025      PUT( area );
0026      SKIP_LINE;
0027   end b1s3e4;
0028
```

filename b1s4e1.lis

```
0001   -- filename b1s4e1 - solution to b1s4 exercise 1 - see text
0002
0003   with TEXT_IO, int_io;
0004   use  TEXT_IO, int_io;
0005
0006   procedure b1s4e1 is
0007
0008        zero     : constant INTEGER := 0;
0009        minus_one : constant INTEGER := -1;
0010        an_int   : INTEGER;          -- value input by user
0011
0012   begin -- b1s4e1
0013      -- get number
0014      PUT( "Please enter an integer value ");
0015      GET( an_int); SKIP_LINE;
0016
0017      -- poss convert
0018      if (an_int < zero) then
0019         an_int := an_int * minus_one;
0020      end if;
0021
0022      -- show number
0023      PUT( "The absolute value is ");
0024      PUT( an_int ); NEW_LINE;
0025   end b1s4e1;
0026
```

filename b1s4e2.lis

```
0001   -- filename b1s4e2.ans - solution to b1s4 exercise 2 - see text
0002
0003   with TEXT_IO, int_io;
```

```
0004  use  TEXT_IO, int_io;
0005
0006  procedure b1s4e2 is
0007
0008     min_width : constant INTEGER := 3;
0009                    -- minimum width for lower cost carpet
0010     lo_cost   : constant INTEGER := 7; -- lower  carpet cost
0011     hi_cost   : constant INTEGER := 9; -- higher carpet cost
0012
0013     lenf,             -- length of room
0014     width,            -- width of room
0015     area,             -- area of room
0016     cost    : INTEGER; -- cost of carpet
0017
0018  begin -- b1s4e2
0019     -- get length & width
0020     PUT( "Please enter length of room ");
0021     GET( lenf ); SKIP_LINE;
0022
0023     PUT( "Please enter width  of room ");
0024     GET( width ); SKIP_LINE;
0025
0026     -- calculate area & cost
0027     area := lenf * width;
0028
0029     if width < min_width then
0030        cost := area * hi_cost;
0031     else
0032        cost := area * lo_cost;
0033     end if;
0034
0035     -- show area & cost
0036     PUT( "The area of the room is ");
0037     PUT( area ); NEW_LINE;
0038
0039     PUT( "The cost of the carpet is ");
0040     PUT( cost ); NEW_LINE;
0041
0042  end b1s4e2;
0043
```

filename b1s4e5.lis

test_1	test_2	test_3	s_1	s_2	s_3	s_4
				Statement executed		
F	F	F				*
F	F	T			*	
F	T	F		*		
F	T	T		*		
T	F	F	*			
T	F	T	*			
T	T	F	*			
T	T	T	*			

test_1	test_2	test_3	s_1	s_2	s_3	s_4
				Statement executed		
F	F	F				*
F	F	T			*	
F	T	F				*
F	T	T			*	
T	F	F		*		
T	F	T		*		
T	T	F	*			
T	T	T	*			

filename b1s5e2.lis

```
0001  -- filename b1s5e2.ans - solution to b1s2 exercise 2 see text
0002
0003  with TEXT_IO, int_io, float_inout;
0004  use  TEXT_IO, int_io, float_inout;
0005
0006  procedure b1s5e2 is
0007
0008     table_range : constant INTEGER := 5;    -- range of table
0009     vat_rate    : constant FLOAT := 0.175; -- rate of VAT.
0010
0011     table_centre,                          -- centre value of table
0012     lo_table,                              -- start of table
```

```
0013    hi_table : INTEGER;                    -- end of table
0014
0015    single_cost,                           -- cost of single item
0016    multiple_cost,                         -- cost without vat
0017    vat_cost        : FLOAT;               -- cost with vat
0018
0019  begin -- b1s5e2
0020     -- show title
0021     PUT_LINE( "            READY RECKONER ");
0022     NEW_LINE;
0023
0024     -- get single cost
0025     PUT( "Please enter the cost of a single item ");
0026     GET( single_cost ); NEW_LINE(2);
0027
0028     -- get centre value
0029     PUT( "Please enter centre of table ");
0030     GET( table_centre ); NEW_LINE(2);
0031
0032     -- show vat rate
0033     PUT( "The VAT rate is ");
0034     PUT( ( vat_rate * 100.0), FORE=>3, AFT=>2, EXP=>0 );
0035     PUT( "%"); NEW_LINE(2);
0036
0037     -- show table header
0038     PUT( "     No of items         cost         cost with vat ");
0039     NEW_LINE(2);
0040
0041     -- calculate bounds
0042     lo_table := table_centre - table_range;
0043     hi_table := table_centre + table_range;
0044
0045     -- show table
0046     for num_items in INTEGER range lo_table .. hi_table loop
0047        multiple_cost := FLOAT( num_items) * single_cost;
0048        vat_cost      := multiple_cost + ( multiple_cost * vat_rate );
0049        PUT( num_items, WIDTH => 16);
0050        PUT( multiple_cost, FORE => 9, AFT => 2, EXP =>0);
0051        PUT( vat_cost, FORE => 9, AFT => 2, EXP => 0);
0052        NEW_LINE;
0053     end loop;
0054
0055  end b1s5e2;
0056
```

filename b1s6e4.lis

```
0001  -- filename b1s6e4 - solution to b1s6 exercise 4
0002
0003  with TEXT_IO, int_io, float_inout;
0004  use  TEXT_IO, int_io, float_inout;
0005
0006  procedure b1s6e4 is
0007
0008     min_year        : constant INTEGER := 1988;
0009     max_year        : constant INTEGER := 1999;
0010
0011     initial_value,            -- initial value of investment
0012     doubled_value,            -- doubled value of investment
0013     current_value : FLOAT;  -- current value of investment
0014
0015     original_year,            -- year of investment
0016     current_year,             -- current year
0017     years_taken   : INTEGER; -- years taken to double
0018
0019     interest_rate : INTEGER; -- interest rate as %
0020
0021  begin -- b1s6e4
0022     -- get inputs from user
0023     PUT("Please enter original investment ");
0024     GET( initial_value ); SKIP_LINE;
0025     PUT("Please enter investment rate     ");
0026     GET( interest_rate );
0027
0028     -- prime loop to fail
0029     original_year := max_year +1;
0030     while ((original_year < min_year) or (original_year > max_year)) loop
0031        PUT("Please enter calendar year      ");
0032        GET( original_year );
0033        if ((original_year < min_year) or (original_year > max_year)) then
0034           PUT("Valid years are in the range ");
0035           PUT( min_year, WIDTH => 4); PUT(" to ");
0036           PUT( max_year, WIDTH => 4); PUT_LINE(".");
0037        end if;
0038     end loop;
0039
0040     -- get ready for main loop
0041     current_value := initial_value;
0042     doubled_value := initial_value * 2.0;
0043     current_year  := original_year;
0044
0045     -- loop
0046     while ( current_value <= doubled_value ) loop
```

```
0047        current_value := current_value +
0048                      current_value * ( FLOAT( interest_rate) / 100.0 );
0049        current_year  := current_year +1;
0050     end loop;
0051
0052     years_taken := current_year - original_year;
0053     PUT("The investment will take "); PUT( years_taken );
0054     PUT_LINE(" years to double. ");
0055     PUT("It will be worth "); PUT( current_value, AFT => 2, EXP => 0);
0056     PUT(" in "); PUT( current_year, WIDTH =>4); PUT_LINE(".");
0057
0058  end b1s6e4;
0059
```

filename b1s7e3.lis

```
0001  -- filename b1s7e3.ans - solution to b1s7 exercise 3 - see text
0002
0003  with TEXT_IO, float_inout;
0004  use  TEXT_IO, float_inout;
0005
0006  procedure b1s7e3 is
0007
0008     far_zero     : constant FLOAT := 32.0;      -- farenheit zero value
0009     cels_to_far : constant FLOAT := 9.0/5.0;  -- c to f conversion factor
0010     far_to_cels : constant FLOAT := 5.0/9.0;  -- f to c conversion factor
0011
0012     direction : CHARACTER;  -- direction of the conversion
0013     in_temp   : FLOAT;      -- value to be converted
0014     out_temp  : FLOAT;      -- converted value
0015
0016     procedure get_dir_and_temp is
0017     -- procedure to get direction and input temperature from user
0018     -- implemented as two subprocedures
0019
0020        procedure get_dir is
0021        -- procedure to get validated direction from user
0022
0023        begin -- get_dir
0024           -- prime loop to fail
0025           direction := 'Q';
0026           while ((direction /= 'C') and ( direction /= 'F')) loop
0027              -- issue prompt
0028              PUT_LINE ("Please enter 'C' for celsius to farenheit ");
0029              PUT ("or 'F' for farenheit to celsius conversion ");
```

```
0030                    -- obtain input
0031                    GET ( direction ); SKIP_LINE;
0032                    -- convert to upper case
0033                    if ( direction = 'c') then direction := 'C'; end if;
0034                    if ( direction = 'f') then direction := 'F'; end if;
0035                    -- issue error message
0036                    if ((direction /= 'C') and ( direction /= 'F')) then
0037                        PUT_LINE("Enter 'C' or 'F' only ");
0038                    end if;
0039                end loop;
0040            end get_dir;
0041
0042        procedure get_temp is
0043        -- procedure to get in temperature value from user
0044
0045        begin -- get temp;
0046            PUT("Enter temperature to be converted ");
0047            GET( in_temp ); SKIP_LINE;
0048        end get_temp;
0049
0050        begin -- get dir and temp
0051            get_dir;
0052            get_temp;
0053        end get_dir_and_temp;
0054
0055    procedure perform_conversion is
0056
0057    begin -- perform conversion
0058        if ( direction = 'C') then
0059            out_temp := (in_temp * cels_to_far ) + far_zero;
0060        else
0061            out_temp := (in_temp - far_zero ) * far_to_cels;
0062        end if;
0063    end perform_conversion;
0064
0065    procedure show_conversion is
0066    -- procedure to show the result of the conversion
0067
0068    begin -- show conversion
0069        PUT("Converted temperature is          ");
0070        PUT( out_temp, FORE => 4, AFT =>2, EXP => 0 );
0071    end show_conversion;
0072
0073 begin -- b1s7e3
0074    get_dir_and_temp;
0075    perform_conversion;
0076    show_conversion;
0077 end b1s7e3;
0078
```

filename b1s11e6.lis

```
0001  -- filename b1s11e6.ans - solution to b1s11 exercise 6 - see text
0002
0003  with TEXT_IO, int_io, float_inout;
0004  use  TEXT_IO, int_io, float_inout;
0005
0006  procedure b1s11e6 is
0007
0008      num_of_stu       : INTEGER;
0009      min_so_far       : INTEGER;
0010      max_so_far       : INTEGER;
0011      the_total_score  : INTEGER;
0012      the_first_score  : INTEGER;
0013
0014      procedure get_single_score( a_score : out INTEGER ) is
0015      -- procedure to get a single score from the user
0016
0017          local_score : INTEGER; -- local input variable
0018
0019      begin -- get single score
0020          PUT( "Enter score (or -1 to finish) ");
0021          GET( local_score ); SKIP_LINE;
0022          a_score := local_score; -- export value input by user
0023      end get_single_score;
0024
0025      procedure do_all_students( total_score : out INTEGER;
0026                                 num_stu     : out INTEGER;
0027                                 max_score   : out INTEGER;
0028                                 min_score   : out INTEGER;
0029                                 first_score : in  INTEGER ) is
0030
0031          local_total   : INTEGER := 0;            -- local total score
0032          local_num_stu : INTEGER := 0;            -- local num of students
0033          local_max     : INTEGER := first_score; -- local max score
0034          local_min     : INTEGER := first_score; -- local min score
0035          this_score    : INTEGER := first_score; -- current input score
0036      -- note local variables are required as parameter variables are
0037      -- output only; and can only be used on lhs of an assignment. Thus
0038      -- cannot be used in the form 'var := var + value', as they appear
0039      -- on the rhs. Possible solution is to declare them as in out vars;
0040      -- Better solution is to declare as output only & use local vars to
0041      -- accumulate values then export through parameter vars
0042
0043      begin -- do all students
0044          -- initialization of local variables done in declaration
0045
```

```
0046            -- iterate for all students (if any )
0047            while this_score > -1 loop
0048                local_num_stu := local_num_stu + 1;
0049                local_total   := local_total   + this_score;
0050
0051                if this_score > local_max then
0052                    local_max := this_score;
0053                end if;
0054
0055                if this_score < local_min then
0056                    local_min := this_score;
0057                end if;
0058                get_single_score( this_score );
0059            end loop;
0060
0061            -- initialize output paramaters
0062            total_score := local_total;
0063            num_stu     := local_num_stu;
0064            max_score   := local_max;
0065            min_score   := local_min;
0066        end do_all_students;
0067
0068
0069        procedure do_summary( grand_total   : in INTEGER; -- the total score
0070                              total_num_stu : in INTEGER; -- the num of stu
0071                              the_min_score : in INTEGER;
0072                              the_max_score : in INTEGER) is
0073
0074            average_score : FLOAT; -- average score var declared at this level
0075                                   -- as it is only concerned with the summary
0076        begin -- do summary
0077            NEW_LINE(2);
0078
0079            PUT("No of students is "); PUT( total_num_stu, WIDTH => 4); NEW_LINE;
0080
0081            if (total_num_stu > 0) then
0082                average_score := FLOAT( grand_total) / FLOAT( total_num_stu);
0083                PUT("Highest score is "); PUT( the_max_score, WIDTH => 8); NEW_LINE;
0084                PUT("Lowest  score is "); PUT( the_min_score, WIDTH => 8); NEW_LINE;
0085                PUT("Average score is ");
0086                PUT( average_score, FORE => 4, AFT => 2, EXP => 0); NEW_LINE;
0087            end if;
0088        end do_summary;
0089
0090    begin -- b1s11e6
0091        get_single_score( the_first_score );
0092        do_all_students( the_total_score, num_of_stu,
```

```
0093                        max_so_far, min_so_far, the_first_score );
0094    do_summary( the_total_score, num_of_stu, min_so_far, max_so_far );
0095 end b1s11e6;
0096
```

filename b1s12e1.lis

```
0001 -- filename b1s12e1.ans. Program to calculate sales persons' payments
0002 -- used to illustrate general function. See text.
0003
0004 with TEXT_IO, int_io, float_inout;
0005 use  TEXT_IO, int_io, float_inout;
0006
0007 procedure b1s12e1 is
0008
0009    -- global constants
0010    basic_pay          : constant FLOAT := 10.00;
0011                       -- rate of pay for basic hours
0012    overtime_pay       : constant FLOAT := 15.00;
0013                       -- rate of pay for overtime hours
0014    basic_pay_limit    : constant FLOAT := 40.00;
0015                       -- num of basic hours
0016
0017    basic_commission   : constant FLOAT := 0.05;
0018                       -- commission rate for basic sales
0019    excess_commission  : constant FLOAT := 0.75;
0020                       -- commission rate for xs sales
0021    basic_sales_limit  : constant FLOAT := 1000.00;
0022                       -- value of basic sales
0023
0024    basic_miles        : constant FLOAT := 0.50;
0025                       -- mileage rate for basic miles
0026    excess_miles       : constant FLOAT := 0.40;
0027                       -- mileage rate for xs miles
0028    basic_miles_limit  : constant FLOAT := 500.00;
0029                       -- value of basic miles
0030
0031
0032    -- program variables
0033    hours_worked,              -- no of hours worked
0034    sales_made,                -- value of sales made
0035    miles_travelled,           -- no of miles travelled
0036    pay,
0037    commission,
0038    car_expenses    : FLOAT;
```

```
0039
0040        procedure get_details( hours_in,
0041                               sales_in,
0042                               miles_in : out FLOAT) is
0043
0044        -- procedure to display program title and input three values
0045
0046        begin -- get details
0047           -- display program heading
0048           PUT_LINE( "     SALES PERSON DETAILS ");
0049           NEW_LINE(2);
0050
0051           -- input hours
0052           PUT( "Please enter hours worked   ");
0053           GET( hours_in); SKIP_LINE;
0054
0055           -- input sales
0056          PUT( "Please enter value of sales ");
0057           GET( sales_in ); SKIP_LINE;
0058
0059           -- input mileage
0060           PUT( "Please enter mileage        ");
0061           GET( miles_in ); SKIP_LINE;
0062
0063           NEW_LINE(2);
0064        end get_details;
0065
0066
0067        procedure do_calcs( hours, sales, miles   : in  FLOAT;
0068                            paid,  comm, car_exp : out FLOAT ) is
0069
0070        -- procedure to calculate pay due, commision due and car expenses
0071        -- due from input values of hours worked, sales made & miles travelled
0072        -- using three subsidiary functions
0073
0074           function general_calc( input_value,
0075                                  input_limit,
0076                                  basic_factor,
0077                                  excess_factor : FLOAT ) return FLOAT is
0078
0079
0080        -- function to calculate general expenses using rule that if input
0081        -- value is less than or equal to input limit value is input value
0082        -- times basic factor. Otherwise value is input limit times basic
0083        -- factor plus amount of input value over input limit times
0084        -- excess factor.
0085
0086           out_value : FLOAT; -- function variable
```

```
0087
0088        begin -- general_calc
0089           if ( input_value <= input_limit ) then
0090              out_value := input_value * basic_factor;
0091           else
0092              out_value := (( input_limit * basic_factor )
0093                        + (( input_value - input_limit) * excess_factor));
0094           end if;
0095           return out_value;
0096        end general_calc;
0097
0098    begin -- do_calcs
0099        paid    := general_calc ( hours, basic_pay_limit,
0100                                   basic_pay, overtime_pay );
0101        comm    := general_calc ( sales, basic_sales_limit,
0102                                   basic_commission, excess_commission );
0103        car_exp := general_calc ( miles, basic_miles_limit,
0104                                   basic_miles, excess_miles );
0105    end do_calcs;
0106
0107    procedure show_results( pay_out,
0108                            comm_out,
0109                          car_exp_out  : in FLOAT ) is
0110
0111
0112    -- procedure to display value of three parameters followed
0113    -- by their total.
0114
0115        the_total : FLOAT; -- total value of params
0116
0117    begin -- show_results
0118        the_total := pay_out + comm_out + car_exp_out;
0119
0120        -- display params
0121        PUT( "Salary     # ");
0122        PUT( pay_out, FORE =>4, AFT=>2, EXP =>0);
0123        NEW_LINE;
0124        PUT( "Commission # ");
0125        PUT( comm_out, FORE =>4, AFT=>2, EXP =>0);
0126        NEW_LINE;
0127        PUT( "Mileage    # ");
0128        PUT( car_exp_out, FORE =>4, AFT=>2, EXP =>0);
0129        NEW_LINE(2);
0130
0131        -- display total
0132        PUT( "Total      # ");
0133        PUT( the_total, FORE =>4, AFT=>2, EXP =>0);
0134        NEW_LINE;
```

```
0135      end show_results;
0136
0137  begin -- b1s12e1
0138      get_details( hours_worked, sales_made, miles_travelled );
0139      do_calcs( hours_worked, sales_made, miles_travelled,
0140                pay, commission, car_expenses);
0141      show_results( pay, commission, car_expenses);
0142  end b1s12e1;
0143
```

filename b2s1e5.lis

```
0001  -- filename b2s1e5 contains solutions of e2 e3 e4
0002
0003  with TEXT_IO, float_inout, int_io;
0004  use  TEXT_IO, float_inout, int_io;
0005
0006  procedure b2s1e5 is
0007      -- variables for e2
0008          a : INTEGER := 15;
0009          b : INTEGER := 3;
0010          f : INTEGER;
0011      -- variables for e3
0012          pi : FLOAT := 3.142;
0013          c  : FLOAT := 456.789;
0014
0015
0016  begin -- b2s1e5
0017      -- solution of 2.1.2 n
0018      f := a ** b;
0019      PUT("The result of a ** b, with a as ");
0020      PUT( a, WIDTH => 4); PUT(" and b as ");
0021      PUT( b, WIDTH => 4); PUT("is ");
0022      PUT( f ); NEW_LINE(2);
0023
0024      -- solution to 2.1.3 g
0025      PUT("The output of PUT( c, FORE => 1, AFT => 3, EXP =>0 ) is ");
0026      PUT( c, FORE => 1, AFT => 3, EXP => 0);
0027      NEW_LINE(2);
0028
0029      -- solution to 2.1.4 b
0030      PUT("The result of multiplying ");
0031      PUT( pi, FORE =>4, AFT => 4, EXP =>0 ); PUT(" by ");
0032      PUT( a, WIDTH =>4); PUT(" is ");
0033      c := pi * FLOAT( a);
```

```
0034     PUT( c, AFT => 4, EXP => 0);
0035
0036  end b2s1e5;
0037
```

filename b2s2e4.lis

```
0001  -- filename b2s2e4.ans - safe integer input procedure
0002  -- note not totally secure (why??)
0003
0004  with TEXT_IO, int_io;
0005  use  TEXT_IO, int_io;
0006
0007  procedure b2s2e4 is
0008
0009     min_grungit  : constant := 12;
0010     max_grungit  : constant := 42;
0011
0012     subtype grungit_sizes is INTEGER range min_grungit .. max_grungit;
0013
0014     grungit_size : grungit_sizes; -- variable declaration
0015     an_int       : INTEGER;
0016
0017     procedure safe_get_int( the_value        : out INTEGER;
0018                             min_val, max_val : in  INTEGER;
0019                                     prompt : in  STRING
0020                        := "This is the default prompt " ) is
0021
0022        value_in   : INTEGER := max_val + 1;
0023
0024     begin -- safe get int
0025        while ( ( value_in < min_val ) or
0026               ( value_in > max_val ) loop
0027        begin -- explicit loop block
0028           PUT( prompt );
0029           GET( value_in );
0030           -- DATA_ERROR exception will be raised if input not valid integer
0031           if ( (value_in < min_val) or (value_in > max_val)) then
0032              raise DATA_ERROR;
0033           end if;
0034           -- this point can only be reached if a valid input was provided
0035           SKIP_LINE;
0036        exception
0037           when DATA_ERROR =>
```

```
0038                    PUT_LINE("Invalid value. Please input value between ");
0039                    PUT( min_val ); PUT( " and "); PUT( max_val );
0040                    value_in := max_val +1;
0041                    NEW_LINE; SKIP_LINE;
0042            end; -- explicit loop block
0043            end loop;
0044            the_value := value_in;
0045        end safe_get_int;
0046
0047    begin -- safe int demo
0048        PUT_LINE("Starting test of safe integer input ");
0049        NEW_LINE;
0050
0051        safe_get_int( grungit_size, min_grungit, max_grungit,
0052                        "Please enter a gungit size ");
0053
0054        PUT("The grungit size entered is ");
0055        PUT( grungit_size ); NEW_LINE;
0056
0057        NEW_LINE(2);
0058        PUT_LINE("Starting test with default prompt ");
0059        NEW_LINE;
0060
0061        safe_get_int( an_int, 100, 200 );
0062        PUT("The value entered is ");
0063        PUT( an_int ); NEW_LINE;
0064    end b2s2e4;
0065
```

filename b2s3e9.lis

```
0001    -- filename b2s3e9.ans - see text
0002
0003    with TEXT_IO, int_io;
0004    use  TEXT_IO, int_io;
0005
0006    procedure b2s3e9 is
0007
0008        max_str_length : constant NATURAL := 40;
0009        subtype encrypt_strings is STRING( 1 .. max_str_length );
0010
0011        in_str, out_str  : encrypt_strings;
0012
0013        num_char_entered : NATURAL;
```

```
0014        shift_value      : INTEGER;
0015
0016        function encrypt( str_in : STRING;
0017                          shift  : INTEGER ) return STRING is
0018        -- encrypt a string by encrypting each character of the string
0019
0020           local_string : STRING( str_in'RANGE);
0021
0022           function encrypt( char_in : CHARACTER;
0023                             shift   : INTEGER ) return CHARACTER is
0024           -- encrypt a character by obtaining its ascii value,
0025           -- adding the shift to it and then converting back
0026           -- to a character. Not totally secure as it may
0027           -- shift into a non printing character
0028
0029           begin -- encrypt character
0030              return CHARACTER'VAL( CHARACTER'POS( char_in ) + shift );
0031           end encrypt;
0032
0033        begin -- encrypt string
0034           for this_char in str_in'RANGE loop
0035              local_string( this_char ) := encrypt( str_in(this_char), shift);
0036           end loop;
0037           return local_string;
0038        end encrypt;
0039
0040   begin -- b2s3e9
0041      PUT_LINE("       ENCRYPTION DEMO ");
0042      NEW_LINE(2);
0043
0044      PUT("Please enter the string to be encrypted ");
0045      GET_LINE( in_str, num_char_entered );
0046      PUT("Please enter the shift value              ");
0047      GET( shift_value ); SKIP_LINE;
0048
0049      out_str( 1 .. num_char_entered ) :=
0050         encrypt( in_str( 1 .. num_char_entered), shift_value );
0051
0052      NEW_LINE(2);
0053      PUT("The converted string is ");
0054      PUT_LINE( out_str( 1 .. num_char_entered));
0055   end b2s3e9;
0056
```

filename b2s4e5.lis

```
-- filename b2s4e5.ans - see text
-- contains solution to exercises 4 & 5
```

Exercise 2.4.4

Black-box diagram

```
sex        ->
car_age    ->              -> BOOLEAN
ins_group  ->
```

Range diagrams

```
sex                'f'         'm'
                    ^           ^

                    a           b

car_age         0------5---------- ?
                       ^^
                       cd
ins_group       0------3---------- ?
                       ^^
                       ef
```

Test cases
(a) sex = 'f'
(b) sex = 'm'
(c) car_age = 4
(d) car_age = 5
(e) insurance_group = 3
(f) insurance_group = 4

Test log

Test No	sex	car_age	ins_group	sex = 'f'	c_a < 5	i_g <=3	c_a < 5 or i_g <= 3	sex and (c_a or i_g)
1	f	4	3	T	T	T	T	T
2	f	4	4	T	T	F	T	T
3	f	5	3	T	F	T	T	T
4	f	5	4	T	F	F	F	F
5	m	4	3	F	T	T	T	F
6	m	4	4	F	T	F	T	F
7	m	5	3	F	F	T	T	F
8	m	5	4	F	F	F	F	F

Exercise 2.4.5

Equivalent expression

not(sex = 'm' or (car_age >= 5 and insurance_group > 3))

Test No	sex	c_a	i_g	sex = 'm'	c_a >= 5	i_g >3	c_a >= 5 and i_g < 3	sex = 'm' or (c_a & i_g)	not(sex or (c_a & i_g))
1	f	4	3	F	F	F	F	F	T
2	f	4	4	F	F	T	F	F	T
3	f	5	3	F	T	F	F	F	T
4	f	5	4	F	T	T	F	T	F
5	m	4	3	T	F	F	F	T	F
6	m	4	4	T	F	T	F	T	F
7	m	5	3	T	T	F	F	T	F
8	m	5	4	T	T	T	T	T	F

filename b2s5e2.lis

```
0001  -- filename b2s5e2.ans - see text
0002  -- other enumeration demonstrations
0003
0004  with TEXT_IO, INT_IO;
0005  use  TEXT_IO, INT_IO;
0006
0007  procedure b2s5e2 is
0008
0009     type    week_days    is ( Mon, Tue, Wed, Thu, Fri, Sat, Sun );
0010     subtype work_days    is week_days range Mon .. Fri;
0011     subtype weekend_days is week_days range Sat .. Sun;
0012
0013     type    rainbow_colours is ( red, orange, yellow, green,
0014                                  blue, indigo, violet );
0015
0016     a_day    : week_days;
0017     rest_day : weekend_days;
0018
0019     package week_day_inout is new ENUMERATION_IO( week_days );
0020     package rainbow_inout  is new ENUMERATION_IO( rainbow_colours);
0021
0022     use week_day_inout, rainbow_inout;
0023
0024     function next_day( this_day : week_days ) return week_days is
0025
0026     begin -- next day
0027        if this_day = sun then
0028        -- relational comparison of an enumerated type
0029           return Mon;
0030        else
0031           return week_days'SUCC( this_day );
0032           -- attribute of an enumerated type
0033        end if;
0034     end next_day;
0035
0036  begin -- b2s5e2
0037     PUT_LINE("    Enumeration demonstrations ");
0038     NEW_LINE(2);
0039
0040     -- use of enumerated types for loop control
0041     PUT("The colours of the rainbow are ");
0042     for this_colour in rainbow_colours loop
0043        PUT( this_colour, SET => LOWER_CASE );
0044        if ( this_colour < rainbow_colours'LAST ) then
0045           PUT(", ");
0046        else
```

```
0047              PUT_LINE (".");
0048           end if;
0049       end loop;
0050
0051       -- function call using enumerated type
0052       NEW_LINE( 2 );
0053       PUT("The day following Mon is "); PUT( next_day( Mon )); NEW_LINE;
0054       PUT("The day following Sun is "); PUT( next_day( Sun )); NEW_LINE;
0055
0056       -- pos attribute applied to enumerated type
0057       NEW_LINE(2);
0058       PUT("Wed is day number "); PUT( week_days'POS( Wed )); NEW_LINE;
0059
0060       -- val attribute applied to an enumerated type
0061       PUT("Day number 5   is "); PUT( week_days'VAL( 5 )); NEW_LINE;
0062
0063       -- pos of a subtype
0064       rest_day := Sat;
0065       NEW_LINE(2);
0066       PUT("The pos of "); PUT( rest_day, WIDTH => 4);
0067       PUT(" is "); PUT( weekend_days'POS( rest_day));
0068
0069       NEW_LINE(2);
0070   end b2s5e2;
0071
```

filename b2s6e2.lis

```
0001   -- filename b2s6e2.ans - see text
0002
0003   with TEXT_IO, int_io, float_inout;
0004   use  TEXT_IO, int_io, float_inout;
0005
0006   procedure b2s6e2 is
0007
0008       max_title_len : constant := 4;
0009       max_name_len  : constant := 15;
0010       max_phone_len : constant := 8;
0011       min_age       : constant := 16;
0012       max_age       : constant := 80;
0013       min_weight    : constant := 0.00;
0014       max_weight    : constant := 250.00;
0015
0016       subtype title_strings is STRING( 1 .. max_title_len );
0017       subtype name_strings  is STRING( 1 .. max_name_len );
0018       subtype phone_strings is STRING( 1 .. max_phone_len );
0019
```

```
0020      type    sexes is (male, female );
0021      subtype person_ages    is INTEGER range min_age .. max_age;
0022      subtype person_weights is FLOAT   range min_weight .. max_weight;
0023
0024      package sex_io is new TEXT_IO.ENUMERATION_IO( sexes );
0025      use sex_io;
0026
0027      type person_names is
0028      record
0029         title : title_strings;
0030         fname : name_strings;
0031         sname : name_strings;
0032      end record;
0033
0034      type person_records is
0035      record
0036         name   : person_names;
0037         phone  : phone_strings;
0038         sex    : sexes;
0039         age    : person_ages;
0040         weight : person_weights;
0041      end record;
0042
0043      standard_male : constant person_records
0044      -- initialization using named notation
0045         := ( name   => (title => "Mr. ",
0046              fname => "Fred          ",
0047              sname => "Bloggs        "),
0048              phone => "123 4567",
0049              sex   => male,
0050              age   => 21,
0051              weight => 52.0 );
0052
0053      customer : person_records;
0054
0055      procedure show_person( a_person : in person_records ) is
0056
0057      begin
0058         PUT("Title  "); PUT( a_person.name.title ); NEW_LINE;
0059         PUT("Fname  "); PUT( a_person.name.fname ); NEW_LINE;
0060         PUT("Sname  "); PUT( a_person.name.sname ); NEW_LINE;
0061         PUT("Phone  "); PUT( a_person.phone ); NEW_LINE;
0062         PUT("Sex    "); PUT( a_person.sex, SET => LOWER_CASE ); NEW_LINE;
0063         PUT("Age    "); PUT( a_person.age, WIDTH => 4 ); NEW_LINE;
0064         PUT("Weight "); PUT( a_person.weight, FORE => 4, AFT => 2, EXP => 0);
0065         NEW_LINE(2);
0066      end show_person;
0067
0068 begin -- b2s6e2
```

```
0069    show_person( standard_male );
0070
0071    -- initialization using positional notation
0072    customer := (("Ms. ", "Freda          ","Bloggs         "),
0073               "876 5432", female, 21, 46.00 );
0074
0075    show_person( customer );
0076 end b2s6e2;
0077
```

filename b2s7e4.lis

```
0001  -- filename b2s7e4.ans
0002  -- requires date_pack - see text
0003
0004  with TEXT_IO, int_io, date_pack;
0005  use  TEXT_IO, int_io, date_pack;
0006
0007  procedure b2s7e4 is
0008
0009    test_day   : days;
0010    test_month : months;
0011    test_year  : years;
0012    test_date  : dates;
0013    good_date  : BOOLEAN;
0014
0015  begin -- b2s7e4
0016    PUT_LINE("   Date pack test harness ");
0017    NEW_LINE(2);
0018
0019    --test set_date (invalid date 29/02/1980)
0020    set_date( 29, 2, 1981, good_date, test_date );
0021    if good_date then
0022       PUT_LINE("Failed set date test ");
0023    else
0024       PUT_LINE("Passed set date test ");
0025    end if;
0026    NEW_LINE(2);
0027
0028    -- test set date ( valid date 28/02/1992 )
0029    set_date( 28, 2, 1992, good_date, test_date );
0030    if good_date then
0031       PUT_LINE("Passed set date test (28/02/1992) date set to :- ");
0032       put_date( test_date ); NEW_LINE;
0033    else
```

```
0034       PUT_LINE("Failed set date test ");
0035    end if;
0036    NEW_LINE(2);
0037
0038    -- test extract parts
0039    PUT_LINE("Testing extract parts with ");
0040    put_date( test_date); NEW_LINE;
0041    extract_parts( test_date, test_day, test_month, test_year );
0042    PUT("Day   part is   "); PUT( test_day );   NEW_LINE;
0043    PUT("Month part is   "); PUT( test_month );NEW_LINE;
0044    PUT("Year  part is   "); PUT( test_year ); NEW_LINE(2);
0045
0046    -- test get date
0047    PUT_LINE("Testing get date ");
0048    GET_DATE( test_date, "Enter test date ");
0049    PUT("The date entered is "); PUT_DATE( test_date ); NEW_LINE(2);
0050 end b2s7e4;
```

filename date_pack_.pkg

```
0001 -- filename date_pack_.pkg : date package specification file
0002 -- required for b2s7e4 see text
0003 -- minimal implementation
0004
0005 package date_pack is
0006
0007     min_day        : constant := 1;
0008     max_day        : constant := 31;
0009     min_month      : constant := 1;
0010     max_month      : constant := 12;
0011     min_year       : constant := 1900;
0012     max_year       : constant := 2050;
0013
0014     subtype days   is INTEGER range min_day   .. max_day;
0015     subtype months is INTEGER range min_month .. max_month;
0016     subtype years  is INTEGER range min_year  .. max_year;
0017                        -- should be large enough !
0018
0019     type dates is private;
0020
0021    procedure get_date( a_date : out dates;
0022                        prompt : STRING := "Enter date " );
0023    -- procedure to set the date from the terminal in format dd/mm/yyyy
0024
0025    procedure put_date( a_date : in dates );
0026    -- procedure to display date on terminal in format dd/mm/yyyy
0027
```

```
0028        procedure set_date( dd    : in  days;
0029                            mm    : in  months;
0030                            yy    : in  years;
0031                            valid : out BOOLEAN;
0032                            date  : out dates );
0033     -- procedure to set a date from its component parts
0034
0035        procedure extract_parts( date : in  dates;
0036                            dd    : out days;
0037                            mm    : out months;
0038                            yy    : out years );
0039     -- procedure to extract component parts from date object
0040
0041 private
0042          type dates is
0043          record
0044            day   : days;
0045            month : months;
0046            year  : years;
0047          end record;
0048
0049 end date_pack;
0050
```

filename date_pack.pkg

```
0001 -- filename date_pack.pkb : date package definition file
0002 -- required for b2s7e4 see text
0003 -- minimal implementation
0004
0005 with TEXT_IO, int_io;
0006 use  TEXT_IO, int_io;
0007
0008 package body date_pack is
0009
0010 procedure get_date( a_date : out dates;
0011                     prompt : STRING := "Enter date " ) is
0012 -- procedure to set the date from the terminal in format dd/mm/yyyy
0013 -- minimal implementation!
0014
0015     local_input : STRING( 1 .. 10); -- 10 char in dd/mm/yyyy
0016     num_char_in : NATURAL;
0017     local_day   : INTEGER;
0018     local_month : INTEGER;
0019     local_year  : INTEGER;
0020     good_date   : BOOLEAN := FALSE;
```

```
0021
0022    begin -- get date
0023
0024        while not good_date loop
0025            PUT( prompt );
0026            GET_LINE( local_input, num_char_in );
0027            -- start by testing format
0028            if ( num_char_in    /= 10) or else
0029                (local_input(3) /= '/') or else
0030                (local_input(6) /= '/') then
0031                    PUT_LINE("Please enter date in format dd/mm/yyyy.");
0032            else
0033                good_date := TRUE;
0034            end if;
0035
0036            -- format ok - test values
0037            -- extract dd mm yyyy as integer values
0038            if good_date then
0039                local_day   := INTEGER'VALUE( local_input(1..2));
0040                local_month := INTEGER'VALUE( local_input(4..5));
0041                local_year  := INTEGER'VALUE( local_input(7..10));
0042
0043                -- test giving best possible error message
0044                -- easier to assume date good at this point
0045
0046                if (local_month < min_month) or (local_month >max_month) then
0047                    PUT_LINE("Month must be in range 1 to 12.");
0048                    good_date := FALSE;
0049                elsif (local_year < min_year) or (local_year > max_year) then
0050                    PUT("Year must be in range "); PUT( min_year, WIDTH=>5);
0051                    PUT(" to "); PUT( max_year, WIDTH =>5); PUT_LINE(".");
0052                    good_date := FALSE;
0053                else
0054                    -- prime 0 day to fail & give appropriate error message
0055                    if local_day < 1 then local_day := max_day +1; end if;
0056                        case local_month is
0057                            -- 30 days have september, april, june & november
0058                            when 9 | 4 | 6 | 11 =>
0059                                if local_day > 30 then
0060                                    PUT("Day must be in range 1 to 30 for month ");
0061                                    PUT( local_month ); PUT_LINE(".");
0062                                    good_date := FALSE;
0063                                end if;
0064                            -- febuary !!!
0065                            when 2 =>
0066                                if ((local_year rem 4) = 0) then -- leap year
0067                                    if local_day > 29 then
0068                                        PUT("Day must be in range 1 to 29 for month ");
```

```
0069                              PUT( local_month ); PUT_LINE(" in a leap year.");
0070                                  good_date := FALSE;
0071                          end if;
0072                      else
0073                          if local_day > 28 then
0074                              PUT("Day must be in range 1 to 28 for month ");
0075                              PUT( local_month ); PUT_LINE(" in a non leap year.");
0076                              good_date := FALSE;
0077                              end if;
0078                      end if;
0079                  -- all the rest
0080                  when others =>
0081                      if local_day > 31 then
0082                          PUT("Day must be in range 1 to 31 for month ");
0083                          PUT( local_month ); PUT_LINE(".");
0084                          good_date := FALSE;
0085                      end if;
0086              end case;
0087          end if;
0088        end if;
0089      end loop;
0090
0091      -- date is good so export
0092      a_date.day   := local_day;
0093      a_date.month := local_month;
0094      a_date.year  := local_year;
0095  end get_date;
0096
0097  procedure put_date( a_date : in dates ) is
0098  -- procedure to display date on terminal in format dd/mm/yyyy
0099
0100  begin
0101      if a_date.day < 10 then
0102          PUT('0'); PUT(a_date.day, WIDTH =>1);
0103      else
0104          PUT( a_date.day, WIDTH =>2);
0105      end if;
0106      PUT('/');
0107
0108      if a_date.month < 10 then
0109          PUT('0'); PUT(a_date.month, WIDTH =>1);
0110      else
0111          PUT( a_date.month, WIDTH =>2);
0112      end if;
0113      PUT('/');
0114      PUT( a_date.year, WIDTH =>4);
0115  end put_date;
0116
```

```
0117   procedure set_date( dd    : in  days;
0118                       mm    : in  months;
0119                       yy    : in  years;
0120                       valid : out BOOLEAN;
0121                       date  : out dates ) is
0122      -- procedure to set a date from its component parts
0123      good_date : BOOLEAN := TRUE;
0124
0125   begin -- set date
0126      if ( mm < min_month ) or ( mm > max_month) then
0127         good_date := FALSE;
0128      elsif ( yy < min_year ) or ( yy > max_year ) then
0129         good_date := FALSE;
0130      else
0131         case mm is
0132            when 9 | 4 | 6 | 11 =>
0133               if ( dd < min_day ) or ( dd > 30 ) then
0134                  good_date := FALSE;
0135               end if;
0136            when 2 =>
0137               if ( (yy rem 4) = 0 ) then
0138                  if ( dd < min_day) or ( dd > 29 ) then
0139                     good_date := FALSE;
0140                  end if;
0141               elsif ( dd < min_day) or ( dd > 28 ) then
0142                  good_date := FALSE;
0143               end if;
0144            when others =>
0145               if ( dd < min_day ) or ( dd > 30 ) then
0146                  good_date := FALSE;
0147               end if;
0148         end case;
0149      end if;
0150
0151      if good_date then
0152         date.day   := dd;
0153         date.month := mm;
0154         date.year  := yy;
0155      end if;
0156
0157      valid := good_date;
0158   end set_date;
0159
0160   procedure extract_parts( date : in  dates;
0161                            dd   : out days;
0162                            mm   : out months;
0163                            yy   : out years ) is
0164   -- procedure to extract component parts from date object
```

```
0165  begin
0166     dd := date.day;
0167     mm := date.month;
0168     yy := date.year;
0169  end extract_parts;
0170
0171  end date_pack;
0172
```

filename b2s8e5.lis

```
0001  -- filename b2s8e5.ans
0002  -- requires rain_pack, months_io
0003
0004  with TEXT_IO, float_inout, rain_pack, months_io;
0005  use  TEXT_IO, float_inout, rain_pack, months_io;
0006
0007  procedure b2s8e5 is
0008
0009     test_year_rain   : year_rainfalls;
0010     average_rainfall : rainfalls;
0011     wettest          : months;
0012     driest           : months;
0013
0014  begin -- b2s8e5
0015     PUT_LINE(" Rainpack demonstration file ");
0016     NEW_LINE(2);
0017
0018     get_rainfalls( test_year_rain );
0019     NEW_LINE(2);
0020
0021     put_rainfalls( test_year_rain );
0022
0023     average_rainfall := calc_average ( test_year_rain );
0024     wettest          := wettest_month( test_year_rain );
0025     driest           := driest_month( test_year_rain );
0026
0027     NEW_LINE(2);
0028     PUT("The average rainfall is ");
0029     PUT( average_rainfall, FORE => 3, AFT => 1, EXP => 0); NEW_LINE;
0030     PUT("The wettest month is ");
0031     PUT( wettest, SET => LOWER_CASE ); NEW_LINE;
0032     PUT("The driest month  is ");
0033     PUT( driest, SET => LOWER_CASE ); NEW_LINE;
0034
```

```
0035  end b2s8e5;
0036
```

filename rain_pack_.pkg

```
0001  -- filename rain_pack_.pkg - rain pack specification file
0002  -- required for b2s8e5 - see text
0003
0004  package rain_pack is
0005
0006      type months is ( january, february, march, april, may, june, july,
0007                       august, september, october, november, december );
0008
0009      max_monthly_rainfall : constant := 100.0;
0010      subtype rainfalls is FLOAT range 0.0 .. max_monthly_rainfall;
0011
0012      type year_rainfalls is array ( months ) of rainfalls;
0013
0014      procedure get_rainfalls( year_rain : out year_rainfalls );
0015
0016      procedure put_rainfalls( year_rain : in  year_rainfalls );
0017
0018      function  calc_average  ( year_rain : in year_rainfalls ) return rainfalls;
0019
0020      function  wettest_month ( year_rain : in year_rainfalls ) return months;
0021
0022      function  driest_month  ( year_rain : in year_rainfalls ) return months;
0023
0024  end rain_pack;
0025
```

filename rain_pack.pkb

```
0001  -- filename rain_pack.pkb - rain pack declaration file
0002  -- required for b2s8e5 - see text
0003  -- note instantiates months_io so must be compiled before b2s8e5.ans
0004
0005  with TEXT_IO, rain_pack;
0006      package months_io is new TEXT_IO.ENUMERATION_IO( rain_pack.months );
0007
0008  with TEXT_IO, float_inout, months_io;
0009  use  TEXT_IO, float_inout, months_io;
0010
0011  package body rain_pack is
0012
```

```
0013    procedure get_rainfalls( year_rain : out year_rainfalls ) is
0014    -- minimal implementation with no input checking
0015
0016    begin -- get_rainfalls
0017       for this_month in months loop
0018          PUT("Please enter the rainfall for ");
0019          PUT( this_month, SET => LOWER_CASE, WIDTH => 10 );
0020          GET( year_rain( this_month)); SKIP_LINE;
0021       end loop;
0022    end get_rainfalls;
0023
0024    procedure put_rainfalls( year_rain : in  year_rainfalls ) is
0025
0026    begin -- put_rainfalls
0027       for this_month in months loop
0028          PUT( this_month, SET => LOWER_CASE, WIDTH =>10 );
0029          PUT( year_rain( this_month), FORE =>4, AFT=>1, EXP=>0);
0030          NEW_LINE;
0031       end loop;
0032    end put_rainfalls;
0033
0034    function calc_average ( year_rain : year_rainfalls ) return rainfalls is
0035
0036       total_rainfall   : FLOAT := 0.0;
0037       average_rainfall : rainfalls;
0038
0039    begin -- calc_average
0040       for this_month in months loop
0041          total_rainfall := total_rainfall + year_rain( this_month);
0042       end loop;
0043
0044       -- note average calculated using enumeration attributes, there will
0045       -- never be other than 12 months - but the principle applies
0046       average_rainfall := total_rainfall /
0047                             FLOAT( months'POS( months'LAST) +1);
0048       return( average_rainfall);
0049    end calc_average;
0050
0051
0052    function wettest_month ( year_rain : year_rainfalls ) return months is
0053
0054       wettest_so_far : months := months'FIRST;
0055
0056    begin -- wettest_month
0057       for this_month in months loop
0058          if year_rain( this_month ) > year_rain( wettest_so_far ) then
0059             wettest_so_far := this_month;
0060          end if;
```

```
0061        end loop;
0062        return( wettest_so_far );
0063     end wettest_month;
0064
0065     function driest_month ( year_rain : year_rainfalls ) return months is
0066
0067        driest_so_far : months := months'FIRST;
0068
0069     begin -- driest_month
0070        for this_month in months loop
0071           if year_rain( this_month ) < year_rain( driest_so_far ) then
0072              driest_so_far := this_month;
0073           end if;
0074        end loop;
0075        return( driest_so_far );
0076     end driest_month;
0077
0078  end rain_pack;
0079
```

filename b2s9e3.lis

```
0001  -- filename b2s9e3.ans - see text
0002  -- requires theatre package
0003
0004  -- minimal demo - show bookings, make booking
0005  --
0006
0007  with theatre; use theatre;
0008
0009  procedure b2s9e3 is
0010
0011     demo_bookings : day_bookings := clear_bookings;
0012
0013  begin -- b2s9e3
0014     PUT_LINE(" Theatre package demonstration ");
0015     NEW_LINE(2);
0016
0017     show_day_bookings( demo_bookings );
0018     make_booking( demo_bookings );
0019     show_day_bookings( demo_bookings );
0020     make_booking( demo_bookings );
0021
0022  end b2s9e3;
0023
```

filename theatre_.pkg

```
0001   -- filename theatre_.pkg - theatre package specification file
0002   -- required for exercise b2s9e3 see text
0003
0004   package theatre is
0005
0006      type day_bookings is private;
0007
0008      function clear_bookings return day_bookings;
0009      -- procedure to set all bookings to vacant
0010
0011      procedure show_day_bookings( bookings : in day_bookings );
0012      -- procedure to display a booking map on the terminal display
0013
0014      procedure make_booking( bookings : in out day_bookings );
0015      -- procedure to make a booking by interactive terminal dialogue
0016
0017   private
0018      -- the seat row index
0019      min_row : constant CHARACTER := 'A';
0020      max_row : constant CHARACTER := 'Z';
0021      subtype seat_row_range is CHARACTER range min_row .. max_row;
0022
0023      -- the seat index
0024      min_seat        : constant := 1;
0025      max_seat        : constant := 20;
0026      aisle_position : constant := 10;
0027      subtype seat_range is INTEGER range min_seat .. max_seat;
0028
0029      type bookings is ( vacant, booked );
0030
0031      type rows is array ( seat_range ) of bookings;
0032
0033      type day_bookings is array ( seat_row_range ) of rows;
0034
0035   end theatre;
0036
```

filename theatre.pkb

```
0001   -- filename theatre.pkb - theatre package specification file
0002   -- required for exercise b2s9e3 see text
0003
0004   with TEXT_IO, int_io;
0005   use  TEXT_IO, int_io;
```

```
0006
0007  package body theatre is
0008
0009      function clear_bookings return day_bookings is
0010      -- procedure to set all bookings to vacant by
0011      -- an array aggregrate
0012
0013          bookings : day_bookings
0014                      := (others => (others => vacant));
0015
0016      begin -- clear bookings
0017          return bookings;
0018      end clear_bookings;
0019
0020      procedure show_day_bookings( bookings : in day_bookings ) is
0021      -- procedure to display a booking map on the terminal display
0022      -- by a double iteration through the array
0023
0024
0025      begin -- show day bookings
0026          -- show the header
0027          PUT_LINE("         THEATRE BOOKINGS "); NEW_LINE;
0028          PUT("      ");
0029          for this_seat in seat_range loop
0030              if this_seat = aisle_position then
0031                  PUT("    ");
0032              end if;
0033              PUT( this_seat, WIDTH =>3);
0034          end loop;
0035          NEW_LINE(2);
0036
0037          -- show the bookings
0038          for this_row in seat_row_range loop
0039              -- show the seat letter
0040              PUT( this_row ); PUT("    ");
0041              for this_seat in seat_range loop
0042                  if this_seat = aisle_position then
0043                      PUT("    ");
0044                  end if;
0045                  if bookings( this_row )( this_seat ) = vacant then
0046                      PUT("   ");
0047                  else
0048                      PUT(" X ");
0049                  end if;
0050              end loop;
0051              NEW_LINE;
0052          end loop;
0053      end show_day_bookings;
```

```
0054
0055
0056
0057     procedure make_booking( bookings : in out day_bookings ) is
0058     -- procedure to make a booking by interactive terminal dialogue
0059     -- uses unsafe terminal input better to use safe input procedures
0060
0061         seat_required : seat_range;
0062         row_required  : seat_row_range;
0063
0064     begin -- make booking
0065         NEW_LINE(2);
0066         PUT_LINE("    Make a booking"); NEW_LINE;
0067         PUT("Please enter row  required ");
0068         GET( row_required ); SKIP_LINE;
0069         PUT("Please enter seat required ");
0070         GET( seat_required ); SKIP_LINE;
0071
0072         if bookings( row_required)( seat_required) = vacant then
0073             bookings( row_required)( seat_required) := booked;
0074             PUT_LINE("O.K. - seat has been booked.");
0075         else
0076             PUT_LINE("Sorry - seat already booked. ");
0077         end if;
0078     end make_booking;
0079
0080
0081  end theatre;
0082
```

filename b2s10e5.lis

```
0001  -- filename b2s10e5.ans
0002  -- subsumes exercises 2, 3 and 4 - see text.
0003
0004  -- the following two lines only need to be compiled once
0005  -- insert comments if bin_p_io is already in library
0006
0007  with bin_pack, SEQUENTIAL_IO;
0008  package bin_p_io is new SEQUENTIAL_IO( bin_pack.bin_records );
0009
0010  with TEXT_IO, bin_pack, bin_p_io;
0011  use  TEXT_IO, bin_pack, bin_p_io;
0012
0013  procedure b2s10e5 is
```

```
0014
0015    space                     : constant CHARACTER := ' ';
0016    max_fname_len             : constant := 20;
0017    type file_name_strings is STRING( 1 .. max_fname_len );
0018
0019    procedure write_bin_file is
0020    -- procedure to write exactly 20 records to a bin file
0021    -- test version 3 records only
0022
0023       num_records_to_write : constant INTEGER := 3; -- test value
0024       out_bin_file         : bin_p_io.FILE_TYPE;
0025       a_bin                : bin_records;
0026       file_name            : file_name-strings  := ( others => space );
0027       f_name_len           : NATURAL;
0028
0029    begin -- write bin file
0030       NEW_LINE; PUT_LINE("Write bin records "); NEW_LINE;
0031       PUT("Please enter the file name ");
0032       GET_LINE( file_name, f_name_len );
0033
0034       -- attempt to create the file: no exception handler!
0035       CREATE( out_bin_file, MODE => OUT_FILE,
0036                             NAME => file_name( 1 .. f_name_len));
0037
0038       for this_bin in 1 .. num_records_to_write loop
0039          get_bin_details( a_bin );
0040          WRITE( out_bin_file, a_bin );
0041       end loop;
0042
0043       CLOSE( out_bin_file );
0044    end write_bin_file;
0045
0046
0047    procedure open_bin_file( a_bin_file : in out bin_p_io.FILE_TYPE ) is
0048    -- procedure to safely open a file by interactive user dialogue
0049
0050       file_is_open         : BOOLEAN := FALSE;
0051       file_name            : file_name_strings;
0052       f_name_len           : NATURAL;
0053
0054    begin -- open bin file
0055       while not file_is_open loop
0056          begin -- explicit exception block
0057             file_name := ( others => space );
0058             PUT("Please enter the file name ");
0059             GET_LINE( file_name, f_name_len );
0060
0061             OPEN( a_bin_file, MODE => IN_FILE,
```

```
0062                                    NAME => file_name( 1 .. f_name_len));
0063
0064              -- this point can only be reached if the file was opened
0065              file_is_open := TRUE;
0066           exception
0067              when bin_p_io.STATUS_ERROR |
0068                   bin_p_io.NAME_ERROR   =>
0069                PUT("The file "); PUT( file_name( 1 .. f_name_len));
0070                PUT_LINE(" could not be opened.");
0071                NEW_LINE;
0072           end; -- explicit exception block
0073        end loop;
0074     end open_bin_file;
0075
0076     procedure read_bin_file is
0077
0078        in_bin_file   : bin_p_io.FILE_TYPE;
0079        in_bin_record : bin_records;
0080
0081     begin -- read bin file
0082        NEW_LINE; PUT("Read bin file" ); NEW_LINE;
0083        open_bin_file( in_bin_file );
0084
0085        while (not (END_OF_FILE( in_bin_file))) loop
0086           READ( in_bin_file, in_bin_record );
0087           show_bin_details( in_bin_record );
0088        end loop;
0089     end read_bin_file;
0090
0091  begin -- b2s10e5
0092     write_bin_file;
0093     read_bin_file;
0094  end b2s10e5;
0095
```

filename bin_pack_.pkg

```
0001  -- filename bin_pack_.pkg, package specification file for warehouse specification.
0002  -- required by b2s10e1 - see text.
0003
0004  package bin_pack is
0005
0006     min_bin : constant CHARACTER := 'A';
0007     max_bin : constant CHARACTER := 'Z';
0008     min_bin_num : constant INTEGER := 1;
0009     max_bin_num : constant INTEGER := 120;
```

```
0010        max_bin_str : constant INTEGER := 25;
0011
0012      subtype bin_letters is CHARACTER range min_bin .. max_bin;
0013      subtype bin_numbers is INTEGER   range min_bin_num .. max_bin_num;
0014      subtype bin_strings is STRING( 1 .. max_bin_str );
0015
0016      type bin_records is record
0017          bin_letter   : bin_letters;
0018          bin_number   : bin_numbers;
0019          bin_contents : bin_strings;
0020      end record;
0021
0022      procedure get_bin_details( a_bin : out bin_records );
0023
0024      procedure show_bin_details( a_bin : in  bin_records );
0025
0026  end bin_pack;
0027
```

filename bin_pack.pkb

```
0001  -- filename bin_pack.pkb, package definition file for warehouse specification.
0002  -- required by b2s10e1 - see text.
0003
0004  with TEXT_IO, int_io;
0005  use  TEXT_IO, int_io;
0006
0007  package body bin_pack is
0008
0009      procedure get_bin_details( a_bin : out bin_records ) is
0010
0011          space : constant CHARACTER := ' ';
0012          temp_bin_contents : bin_strings := ( others => space );
0013          dummy : NATURAL;
0014
0015      begin -- get bin details
0016          PUT("Please enter the bin letter  ");
0017          GET( a_bin.bin_letter ); SKIP_LINE;
0018          PUT("Please enter the bin number  ");
0019          GET( a_bin.bin_number ); SKIP_LINE;
0020          PUT("Please enter the bin contents ");
0021          GET_LINE( temp_bin_contents, dummy );
0022          a_bin.bin_contents := temp_bin_contents;
0023      end get_bin_details;
0024
0025      procedure show_bin_details( a_bin : in  bin_records ) is
```

```
0026
0027    begin -- show bin details
0028       PUT("Bin letter   ");
0029       PUT( a_bin.bin_letter ); NEW_LINE;
0030       PUT("Bin number   ");
0031       PUT( a_bin.bin_number ); NEW_LINE;
0032       PUT("Bin contents ");
0033       PUT_LINE( a_bin.bin_contents );
0034    end show_bin_details;
0035
0036 end bin_pack;
0037
```

filename b2s11e2.lis

```
0001 -- filename b2s11e2.ans - see text
0002
0003 with TEXT_IO;
0004 use  TEXT_IO;
0005
0006 procedure b2s11e2 is
0007
0008    max_line_len     : constant := 132;
0009    max_filename_len : constant := 20;
0010    space            : constant CHARACTER := ' ';
0011    subtype filename_strings is STRING( 1 .. max_filename_len );
0012
0013    modern_file,
0014    ancient_file : TEXT_IO.FILE_TYPE;
0015
0016    procedure open_input_file( infile : in out TEXT_IO.FILE_TYPE ) is
0017    -- procedure to input a filename from the user
0018    -- and open the file for input
0019
0020       in_file_name  : filename_strings := ( others => space);
0021       file_name_len : NATURAL;
0022       is_good_name  : BOOLEAN := FALSE;
0023
0024    begin -- open input file
0025       while not is_good_name loop
0026       begin -- exception block
0027          PUT("Please enter input filename ");
0028          GET_LINE( in_file_name, file_name_len );
0029          OPEN( FILE => infile,
0030                NAME => in_file_name( 1 .. file_name_len),
```

```
0031                    MODE => IN_FILE );
0032               -- this point can only be reached if file is opened
0033               is_good_name := TRUE;
0034           exception
0035               when STATUS_ERROR | NAME_ERROR =>
0036                   PUT_LINE("The file could not be opened!");
0037                   PUT_LINE("Please try again.");
0038                   in_file_name := (others => space );
0039           end; -- exception block
0040           end loop;
0041       end open_input_file;
0042
0043       procedure open_output_file( outfile : in out TEXT_IO.FILE_TYPE ) is
0044       -- procedure to input a filename from the user
0045       -- and create the file for output
0046
0047           out_file_name : filename_strings := ( others => space);
0048           file_name_len : NATURAL;
0049           is_good_name  : BOOLEAN := FALSE;
0050
0051       begin -- open output file
0052           while not is_good_name loop
0053           begin -- exception block
0054              PUT("Please enter output filename ");
0055              GET_LINE( out_file_name, file_name_len );
0056              CREATE( FILE => outfile,
0057                      NAME => out_file_name( 1 .. file_name_len),
0058                      MODE => OUT_FILE );
0059              -- this point can only be reached if file is created
0060              is_good_name := TRUE;
0061           exception
0062              when STATUS_ERROR | NAME_ERROR =>
0063                  PUT_LINE("The file could not be created!");
0064                  PUT_LINE("Please try again.");
0065                  out_file_name := (others => space );
0066           end; -- exception block
0067           end loop;
0068       end open_output_file;
0069
0070       procedure crap( infile, outfile : in TEXT_IO.FILE_TYPE ) is
0071
0072           subtype file_line is STRING( 1 .. max_line_len );
0073
0074           small_f : constant CHARACTER := 'f';
0075           big_f   : constant CHARACTER := 'F';
0076
0077           small_s : constant CHARACTER := 's';
0078           big_s   : constant CHARACTER := 'S';
```

```
0079
0080          this_line : file_line;
0081          line_lenf : NATURAL;
0082
0083      begin -- crap
0084          while not (END_OF_FILE( infile )) loop
0085              GET_LINE( infile, this_line, line_lenf );
0086              for this_char in 1 .. line_lenf loop
0087                  if this_line( this_char ) = small_s then
0088                      this_line( this_char ) := small_f;
0089                  end if;
0090                  if this_line( this_char ) = big_s then
0091                      this_line( this_char ) := big_f;
0092                  end if;
0093              end loop;
0094              PUT_LINE( outfile, this_line( 1 .. line_lenf));
0095          end loop;
0096      end crap;
0097
0098
0099
0100  begin -- b2s11e2
0101      open_input_file( modern_file );
0102      open_output_file( ancient_file );
0103
0104      crap( modern_file, ancient_file );
0105
0106      CLOSE( modern_file );
0107      CLOSE( ancient_file );
0108
0109  end b2s11e2;
0110
```

filename b2s12e4.lis

```
0001  -- filename b2s12e4.ans -- summary of solution to exercise 4
0002  -- the amended procedures to make_new_file and add_new_record only
0003
0004      procedure make_new_file( car_file : in car_record_dio.FILE_TYPE ) is
0005
0006      begin -- make new file
0007          null; -- no action needs to be taken
0008      end make_new_file;
0009
0010      procedure add_new_record( car_file : in  car_record_dio.FILE_TYPE ) is
```

```
0011
0012        new_record,                        -- record to be added
0013        old_record   : car_pack.car_record; -- record on file
0014        dummy_record : car_pack.car_record := ( FALSE, 1, 1, 1);
0015        current_size : NATURAL;
0016
0017     begin -- add new record
0018        get_car_record( new_record ); -- in car_pack
0019        current_size := NATURAL(SIZE( car_file )); -- number of records in file
0020        if new_record.car_num > current_size then -- file is not big enough
0021           -- initialize and write the new records
0022           for this_car in current_size + 1 .. new_record.car_num loop
0023              dummy_record.car_num := this_car;
0024              WRITE( car_file,
0025                    ITEM => dummy_record,
0026                    To   => car_record_dio.POSITIVE_COUNT(dummy_record.car_num));
0027           end loop;
0028        end if;
0029        READ( car_file,
0030             ITEM => old_record,
0031             FROM => car_record_dio.POSITIVE_COUNT(new_record.car_num));
0032        if ( old_record.in_use ) then
0033           PUT_LINE( "Car already on file, details not changed" );
0034        else
0035           new_record.in_use := TRUE;
0036           WRITE( car_file,
0037                 ITEM => new_record,
0038                 TO   => car_record_dio.POSITIVE_COUNT(new_record.car_num));
0039           PUT_LINE( "OK, details filed" );
0040        end if;
0041     end add_new_record;
0042
```

filename b3s1e2.lis

```
0001  -- filename b3s1e3.ans - see text
0002  -- requires search_pack
0003
0004  -- procedure search lowest implemented here, possibly
0005  -- better to implement it in the package after development
0006
0007  with search_pack, TEXT_IO, int_io;
0008  use  search_pack, TEXT_IO, int_io;
0009
0010  procedure b3s1e2 is
0011
```

```
0012        max_names : constant := 15;
0013        -- maximum no of names in a single list
0014
0015        demo_list  : name_struct( struct_size => max_names);
0016        -- declare name structure variable for use
0017
0018        lowest_position : NATURAL;
0019        -- the position of the lowest name in the list
0020
0021     function find_lowest_name( search_list : name_struct ) return NATURAL is
0022     -- function will search the name_struct passed to it and return the
0023     -- position of the alphabetically lowest name in the list.
0024
0025        lowest_so_far : NATURAL := 1; -- first name in list
0026
0027     begin -- find_lowest_name
0028        for this_name in 2 .. search_list.in_use loop
0029            if search_list.names( this_name ) <
0030                search_list.names( lowest_so_far) then
0031                lowest_so_far := this_name;
0032            end if;
0033        end loop;
0034        return lowest_so_far;
0035     end find_lowest_name;
0036
0037 begin -- b3s1e2
0038    PUT_LINE("   Search lowest demonstration ");
0039    NEW_LINE(2);
0040
0041    set_up_names( demo_list );
0042    -- display the contents of the structure
0043    show_list ( demo_list );
0044
0045    lowest_position := find_lowest_name( demo_List );
0046
0047    PUT("Alphabetically lowest name is at position ");
0048    PUT( lowest_position ); NEW_LINE;
0049
0050 end
```

filename b3s2e1.lis

```
0001 -- filename b3s2e1.ans - see text
0002 -- requires s_pack1a
0003
```

```
0004  with s_pack1a, TEXT_IO, int_io;
0005  use  s_pack1a, TEXT_IO, int_io;
0006
0007  procedure b3s2e1 is
0008
0009      max_names : constant := 15;
0010      -- maximum no of names in a single list
0011
0012      demo_list  : name_structs( struct_size => max_names);
0013      -- declare name structure variable for use
0014
0015      num_comps,
0016      num_swaps  : NATURAL := 0;
0017
0018  begin -- b3s2e1
0019     PUT_LINE(" Search algorithm comparisons ");
0020     NEW_LINE(2);
0021
0022     set_up_names( demo_list );
0023     -- display the contents of the structure
0024     show_list ( demo_list );
0025
0026     sort_names( demo_list, num_comps, num_swaps );
0027
0028     show_list( demo_list );
0029     PUT("Number of comparisons "); PUT( num_comps );
0030     PUT("Number of swaps  ");      PUT( num_swaps );
0031     NEW_LINE;
0032  end b3s2e1;
0033
```

filename se1_ser1.ads

```
0001  -- alternate separate definition file for selection sort algorithm,
0002  -- filename sel_ser1.ads. Required for b3s2e1 - see text
0003  -- note requires amendments to be made to s_pack, producing s_pack1
0004  -- to allow the search algorithms to export the number of comparisons
0005  -- and the number of swaps
0006
0007  separate ( s_pack1 )
0008
0009  procedure sort_names( name_list : in out name_structs;
0010                        num_comps : out    NATURAL;
0011                        num_swaps : out    NATURAL ) is
0012
0013     the_lowest  : NATURAL;
```

```
0014     local_comps : NATURAL := 0;
0015     local_swaps : NATURAL := 0;
0016
0017     procedure swap_names( this_name , that_name : in out name_strings ) is
0018     -- procedure to swap the contents of the two names supplied
0019
0020        temp_name  : name_strings;
0021
0022     begin -- swap names
0023        temp_name := this_name;
0024        this_name := that_name;
0025        that_name := temp_name;
0026     end swap_names;
0027
0028     function search_lowest( a_list : name_lists ) return NATURAL is
0029     -- function to determine the lowest value in the list
0030     -- supplied and return its subscript value
0031
0032        lowest_so_far : NATURAL :=  a_list'FIRST ;
0033        -- at this stage lowest so far is the first in the list
0034
0035     begin -- search lowest
0036        for this_name in (a_list'FIRST +1 ) .. a_list'LAST loop
0037          if ( a_list( this_name ) < a_list(lowest_so_far)) then
0038             lowest_so_far := this_name;
0039          end if;
0040        end loop;
0041        return lowest_so_far;
0042     end search_lowest;
0043
0044 begin -- sort names
0045     for unsorted_limit in name_list.names'FIRST ..
0046                            (name_list.in_use -1) loop
0047        the_lowest := search_lowest( name_list.names ( unsorted_limit ..
0048                                          name_list.in_use ));
0049        -- count the number of swaps made
0050        local_comps := local_comps + ( name_list.in_use - unsorted_limit );
0051        swap_names( name_list.names( unsorted_limit),
0052                   name_list.names( the_lowest ) );
0053        -- count a swap
0054        local_swaps := local_swaps + 1;
0055     end loop;
0056
0057     -- export the swaps and comparisons
0058     num_comps := local_comps;
0059     num_swaps := local_swaps;
0060 end sort_names;
0061
```

filename b3s5e4.lis

```
0001  -- filename b3s5e4.ans - see text
0002
0003  with TEXT_IO, int_io;
0004  use   TEXT_IO, int_io;
0005
0006  procedure b3s5e4 is
0007
0008     fore_string : STRING( 1 .. 26 ) := "abcdefghijklmnopqrstuvwxyz";
0009     back_string : STRING( 1 .. 26 );
0010
0011     function rev_string( in_string : STRING ) return STRING is
0012     -- recursive function to reverse and return the string passed
0013
0014        out_string : STRING( in_string'RANGE);
0015
0016     begin -- revstring
0017        if ( in_string'LENGTH ) = 0 then
0018           return "";
0019        else
0020           out_string := in_string(in_string'LAST) &
0021                            rev_string( in_string(in_string'FIRST ..
0022                                           (in_string'LAST -1)));
0023           return out_string;
0024        end if;
0025     end rev_string;
0026
0027  begin -- b3s5e4
0028     PUT("Forward  string "); PUT( fore_string); NEW_LINE;
0029     back_string := rev_string( fore_string );
0030     PUT("Backward string "); PUT( back_string); NEW_LINE;
0031  end b3s5e4;
0032
0033
```

filename b3s6e3.lis

```
0001  -- filename b3s6e3.ans - see text
0002  -- requires stack_pack
0003
0004  with stack_pack;
0005     package char_stack is new stack_pack( element => CHARACTER );
0006
0007  with TEXT_IO, int_io, char_stack;
0008  use   TEXT_IO, int_io, char_stack;
0009
```

```
0010    procedure b3s6e3 is
0011
0012        a_char       : CHARACTER;
0013        an_int       : INTEGER;
0014        a_char_stack : char_stack.stacks;
0015        is_stacked   : BOOLEAN := TRUE;
0016        is_popped    : BOOLEAN := TRUE;
0017        scaling      : INTEGER := 1;
0018        popped_value : INTEGER := 0;
0019
0020        subtype digit_chars is CHARACTER range '0' .. '9';
0021
0022    begin -- b3s6e3
0023        PUT_LINE("    Character stack demonstration ");
0024        NEW_LINE(2);
0025
0026        initialize_stack( a_char_stack );
0027        PUT("Please enter an integer ");
0028        GET( a_char );
0029
0030        while  (a_char in digit_chars ) and
0031                is_stacked                 loop
0032            push( a_char, a_char_stack, is_stacked );
0033            GET( a_char );
0034        end loop;
0035        SKIP_LINE;
0036
0037        pop( a_char, a_char_stack, is_popped );
0038        while is_popped loop
0039            popped_value :=   popped_value
0040                        + ( CHARACTER'POS( a_char ) - CHARACTER'POS('0'))
0041                        * scaling;
0042            scaling := scaling * 10;
0043            pop( a_char, a_char_stack, is_popped );
0044        end loop;
0045
0046        PUT("The value is ");
0047        PUT( popped_value ); NEW_LINE;
0048
0049    end b3s6e3;
0050
```

filename fifo_1_pack_.pkg

```
0001    -- filename fifo_1_pack_.pkg - generic fifo queue declaration v2
0002    -- (subprogram interface identical to fifo_pack_.pkg)
0003    -- b3s7e1 - see text
```

```
0004
0005  generic
0006     type element is private;
0007     -- the data type which is to be stored in the stack
0008  package  fifo_1_pack is
0009
0010     type fifo_qs is limited private;
0011     -- details of the implementation are invisible from
0012     -- outside the package
0013
0014     procedure initialize_queue( new_queue : in out fifo_qs );
0015     -- new_queue is reinitialized, any data left on the
0016     -- queue is thrown away
0017
0018     procedure store( on_element : in      element;
0019                      a_queue    : in out  fifo_qs;
0020                      success    : out     BOOLEAN);
0021     -- if queue has space element is stored on the queue
0022     -- and success is TRUE. Otherwise success is FALSE.
0023
0024     procedure retrieve( off_element : out     element;
0025                         a_queue     : in out fifo_qs;
0026                         success     : out     BOOLEAN);
0027     -- if queue is not empty element on top of queue is
0028     -- returned and success is TRUE. Otherwise success is FALSE.
0029  ·
0030  private
0031
0032     max_queue_size : constant := 5; -- 5 for test purposes only
0033
0034     type    queue_index_range is new INTEGER range  0 .. max_queue_size ;
0035     subtype queue_indexes      is      queue_index_range
0036                                          range  1 .. max_queue_size ;
0037     -- queue will contain queue_indexes (1 .. ~) elements. index_range
0038     -- type will be used to store size of queue therefore has to have
0039     -- capability of representing empty (0) in addition to all possible
0040     -- positions within the array
0041
0042     type elem_arrays is array ( queue_indexes ) of element;
0044     type fifo_qs is
0043     record
0044        elements        : elem_arrays;
0045        front_of_queue : queue_indexes     := 1;
0046        end_of_queue   : queue_indexes     := max_queue_size;
0047        size_of_queue  : queue_index_range := 0;
0048     end record;
0049
0050  end fifo_1_pack;
```

filename fifo_1_pack.pkb

```
0001    -- filename fifo_1_pack.pkb - generic fifo queue definition file v.2
0002    -- b3s7e1 - see text
0003
0004    package  body fifo_1_pack is
0005
0006       type queue_state is ( empty, part_full, full );
0007       -- local type to indicate state of queue
0008
0009       function queue_state_is( a_queue : fifo_qs ) return queue_state is
0010       -- local function to determine and return state of queue
0011
0012       begin -- queue_state_is
0013          -- if size component is zero then queue contains no elements
0014          if a_queue.size_of_queue = 0 then
0015             return empty;
0016          -- if size compoenent is equal to max size of the queue, queue is full
0017          elsif a_queue.size_of_queue = max_queue_size then
0018             return full;
0019          else -- otherwise queue is not empty and not full
0020             return part_full;
0021          end if;
0022       end queue_state_is;
0023
0024       function increment_queue_index( an_index : queue_indexes )
0025                                       return queue_indexes is
0026       begin -- increment queue index
0027          if an_index = max_queue_size then
0028             return 1;
0029          else
0030             return an_index + 1;
0031          end if;
0032       end increment_queue_index;
0033
0034       procedure initialize_queue( new_queue : in out fifo_qs ) is
0035
0036       begin -- initialize queue
0037          -- queue is set empty by setting components appropriately
0038          new_queue.front_of_queue := 1;
0039          new_queue.end_of_queue   := max_queue_size;
0040          new_queue.size_of_queue  := 0;
0041       end initialize_queue;
0042
0043       procedure store( on_element : in      element;
0044                        a_queue    : in out  fifo_qs;
0045                        success    : out     BOOLEAN) is
0046
```

```
0047      begin -- store
0048         -- if queue is full then element cannot be stored
0049         if ( queue_state_is( a_queue ) = full ) then
0050            success := FALSE;
0051         else -- otherwise element can be stored
0052            success := TRUE;
0053            -- increment tos pointer
0054            a_queue.end_of_queue := increment_queue_index( a_queue.end_of_queue );
0055            a_queue.elements( a_queue.end_of_queue ) := on_element;
0056            a_queue.size_of_queue := a_queue.size_of_queue + 1;
0057         end if;
0058      end store;
0059
0060      procedure retrieve( off_element : out     element;
0061                          a_queue     : in out fifo_qs;
0062                          success     : out     BOOLEAN) is
0063
0064      begin -- retrieve
0065         -- if queue is empty element cannot be retrieved
0066         if ( queue_state_is( a_queue ) = empty ) then
0067            success := FALSE;
0068         else -- otherwise element can be retrieved
0069            success := TRUE;
0070            -- retrieve element from foq
0071            off_element := a_queue.elements( a_queue.front_of_queue );
0072            a_queue.front_of_queue := increment_queue_index( a_queue.front_of_queue);
0073            a_queue.size_of_queue := a_queue.size_of_queue - 1;
0074         end if;
0075      end retrieve;
0076
0077   end fifo_1_pack;
0078
```

filename b3s8e1.lis

```
0001   -- filename b3s8e1.ans - see text
0002   -- requires pers_pack
0003
0004   with TEXT_IO, pers_pack;
0005   use  TEXT_IO, pers_pack;
0006
0007   procedure b3s8e1 is
0008
0009      type person_pointers is access pers_pack.person_record;
0010      max_people : constant := 4; -- four for test purposes only
0011
```

```
0012    type person_pointers_arrays is array ( NATURAL range <> )
0013        of person_pointers;
0014
0015    demo_array : person_pointers_arrays( 1 .. max_people );
0016
0017
0018    procedure initialize_array( people_pointers :
0019                                    in out person_pointers_arrays ) is
0020    -- procedure to initialize the array of pointers by
0021    -- allocating space for each record, initializing the
0022    -- pointer to point to the record then using get_person to
0023    -- input details from the terminal
0024    begin -- initialize array
0025        for this_person in people_pointers'RANGE loop
0026            -- allocate space and initialize pointer
0027            people_pointers( this_person ) := new pers_pack.person_record;
0028            get_person( people_pointers( this_person ).all );
0029        end loop;
0030    end initialize_array;
0031
0032    procedure display_array( people_pointers :
0033                                    in person_pointers_arrays ) is
0034    -- procedure to display the contents of all the records pointed to
0035    -- by the array on the terminal
0036    begin -- display array
0037        for this_person in people_pointers'RANGE loop
0038            show_person( people_pointers( this_person ).all );
0039        end loop;
0040    end display_array;
0041
0042    procedure swap_people( a_person,
0043                                another_person : in out person_pointers) is
0044    -- procedure to swap the contents of two records by swapping thier
0045    -- pointers.
0046
0047        temp_person : person_pointers;
0048
0049    begin -- swap_people
0050        temp_person    := a_person;
0051        a_person       := another_person;
0052        another_person := temp_person;
0053    end swap_people;
0054
0055    procedure sort_array( people_pointers :
0056                                in out person_pointers_arrays ) is
0057    -- procedure to sort the records pointed to by the array
0058    -- by ascending name, using an insertion sort
0059
```

```
0060          lowest_so_far : NATURAL;
0061
0062      begin -- sort array
0063          for sorted_limit in people_pointers'FIRST ..
0064                              (people_pointers'LAST -1) loop
0065              lowest_so_far := sorted_limit;
0066              for find_lowest in (sorted_limit +1) ..
0067                              people_pointers'LAST loop
0068                  if name_less_than( people_pointers( find_lowest).all,
0069                              people_pointers( lowest_so_far ).all) then
0070                      swap_people( people_pointers( find_lowest),
0071                              people_pointers( lowest_so_far ));
0072                  end if;
0073              end loop;
0074          end loop;
0075      end sort_array;
0076
0077
0078  begin -- b3s8e1
0079      PUT_LINE("    Person pointers sorting demonstration ");
0080      NEW_LINE(2);
0081
0082      -- get records from the user
0083      initialize_array( demo_array );
0084      NEW_LINE(2);
0085
0086      display_array( demo_array );
0087      NEW_LINE(2);
0088
0089      sort_array( demo_array );
0090
0091      display_array( demo_array );
0092      NEW_LINE(2);
0093
0094  end b3s8e1;
0095
0096
```

filename pers_pack_.pkg

```
0001  -- filename pers_pack_.pkg - person package declaration file
0002  -- required for b3s8 and subsequent sections - see text
0003
0004  package pers_pack is
0005
0006      subtype heights is INTEGER range 0    .. 300;
```

```
0007      subtype weights is FLOAT   range 0.0 .. 250.0;
0008
0009      subtype name_strings is STRING( 1 .. 10 );
0010
0011      type person_record is
0012      record
0013         f_name : name_strings := ( others => ' ');
0014         s_name : name_strings := ( others => ' ');
0015         weight : weights := 0.0;
0016         height : heights := 0;
0017      end record;
0018
0019      procedure get_person( a_person : out person_record );
0020      -- procedure to input a person record from the terminal
0021
0022      procedure show_person( a_person : in person_record );
0023      -- procedure to output a person record on the terminal
0024
0025      function name_less_than( pers_1, pers_2 : person_record ) return BOOLEAN;
0026      function name_equal_to( pers_1, pers_2 : person_record ) return BOOLEAN;
0027      -- functions to implement relational comparisons of person records,
0028      -- comparisons based upon the name components only
0029
0030   end pers_pack;
0031
```

filename pers_pack.pkb

```
0001   -- filename pers_pack.pkb - person package definition file
0002   -- b3s8 see text
0003
0004   with TEXT_IO, int_io, float_inout;
0005   use  TEXT_IO, int_io, float_inout;
0006
0007   package body pers_pack is
0008
0009      procedure get_person( a_person : out person_record ) is
0010
0011         this_per : person_record;
0012         dummy    : NATURAL;
0013
0014      begin -- get person
0015         PUT(" Enter firstname ");
0016         GET_LINE( this_per.f_name, dummy );
0017         PUT(" Enter surname   ");
0018         GET_LINE( this_per.s_name, dummy );
```

```
0019        PUT(" Enter weight      ");
0020        GET( this_per.weight ); SKIP_LINE;
0021        PUT(" Enter height      ");
0022        GET( this_per.height ); SKIP_LINE;
0023        NEW_LINE(2);
0024        a_person := this_per;
0025      end get_person;
0026
0027      procedure show_person( a_person : in person_record ) is
0028
0029      begin -- show person
0030        PUT("Firstname " & a_person.f_name );
0031        PUT(" Surname  " & a_person.s_name );
0032        PUT(" Weight   "); PUT( a_person.weight, FORE =>4, AFT => 1, EXP=> 0);
0033        PUT(" Height   "); PUT( a_person.height, WIDTH => 4);
0034        NEW_LINE;
0035      end show_person;
0036
0037      function name_less_than( pers_1, pers_2 : person_record )
0038                              return BOOLEAN is
0039      begin -- name less than
0040        if ( pers_1.s_name = pers_2.s_name ) then
0041          return ( pers_1.f_name < pers_2.f_name );
0042        else
0043          return ( pers_1.s_name < pers_2.s_name );
0044        end if;
0045      end name_less_than;
0046
0047      function name_equal_to( pers_1, pers_2 : person_record )
0048                              return BOOLEAN is
0049      begin -- name equal to
0050        return ( ( pers_1.s_name = pers_2.s_name) and then
0051                 ( pers_1.f_name = pers_2.f_name) );
0052      end name_equal_to;
0053
0054  end pers_pack;
0055
```

filename b3s9e2.lis

```
0001  -- filename b3s9e2.ans - see text
0002  -- requires link_list and pers_pack
0003
0004  with TEXT_IO, link_list, pers_pack;
0005  use  TEXT_IO, pers_pack;
```

```
0006
0007   procedure b3s9e2 is
0008
0009      package pers_list_pack is new link_list( pers_pack.person_record,
0010                                               "<" => name_less_than,
0011                                               equal => name_equal_to);
0012      use pers_list_pack;
0013
0014      person_list : pers_list_pack.l_list;
0015
0016      menu_choice   : CHARACTER := ' ';
0017
0018
0019      function menu return CHARACTER is
0020
0021         menu_char    : CHARACTER := 'x';
0022         valid_choice : BOOLEAN := FALSE;
0023
0024         procedure show_menu is
0025         begin -- show menu
0026            PUT_LINE("Integer stack demonstration menu ");
0027            NEW_LINE;
0028            PUT_LINE("   a    store person");
0029            PUT_LINE("   b    remove person");
0030            PUT_LINE("   c    display people");
0031            PUT_LINE("   d    (re)initialize list ");
0032            PUT_LINE("   e    exit program ");
0033            NEW_LINE;
0034         end show_menu;
0035
0036      begin -- menu
0037         show_menu;
0038         while not valid_choice loop
0039            PUT("Enter choice ");
0040            GET( menu_char ); SKIP_LINE;
0041
0042            valid_choice := ( menu_char in 'a' .. 'e') or
0043                            ( menu_char in 'A' .. 'E');
0044
0045            if not valid_choice then
0046               PUT_LINE("Enter 'a', 'b', 'c', 'd' or 'e' only!");
0047            end if;
0048         end loop;
0049         return menu_char;
0050      end menu;
0051
0052
0053      procedure store_person( pers_list : in out pers_list_pack.l_list ) is
```

```
0054
0055          a_pers : person_record;
0056
0057      begin -- store_person
0058         NEW_LINE(2);
0059         get_person( a_pers );
0060         insert_in_order( pers_list, a_pers );
0061         PUT_LINE("O.K. person stored ");
0062         NEW_LINE(2);
0063      end store_person;
0064
0065      procedure remove_person( pers_list : in out pers_list_pack.l_list ) is
0066
0067          person_to_remove : person_record;
0068          is_removed       : BOOLEAN;
0069          removed_person   : person_record;
0070      begin -- remove person
0071         PUT_LINE("Please enter details of person to remove ");
0072         PUT_LINE("(only the name fields need to be entered.");
0073         get_person( person_to_remove );
0074         rem_in_order( pers_list, person_to_remove,
0075                       is_removed, removed_person );
0076         if is_removed then
0077            PUT_LINE("O.K. person removed, full details are ");
0078            show_person( removed_person );
0079         else
0080            PUT_LINE("Person not found in list!");
0081         end if;
0082         NEW_LINE(2);
0083      end remove_person;
0084
0085
0086      procedure show_a_person( a_person : in out person_record ) is
0087      -- repackaging of show_person from person pack. Repackaging
0088      -- required as the modes do not match. The generic procedure
0089      -- do_something from l_list requires an in out parameter, the
0090      -- show_person procedure from pers_pack requires an in only parameter
0091
0092      begin -- show_a_person
0093         pers_pack.show_person( a_person ); -- make it explicit
0094      end show_a_person;
0095
0096      -- instantiation of generic traversal procedure to show people
0097      procedure put_people is new
0098              pers_list_pack.traverse( do_something => show_a_person );
0099
0100      procedure show_people( pers_list : in pers_list_pack.l_list ) is
0101      begin -- show_people
```

```
0102        NEW_LINE(2);
0103        put_people( pers_list );
0104        NEW_LINE(2);
0105     end show_people;
0106
0107     procedure initialize_person_list ( pers_list :
0108                                    in out pers_list_pack.l_list ) is
0109     begin
0110        initialize( pers_list );
0111     end initialize_person_list;
0112
0113 begin -- b3s9e2
0114    menu_choice := menu;
0115    while ((menu_choice /= 'e') and
0116           (menu_choice /= 'E')) loop
0117       case menu_choice is
0118          when 'a'|'A' => store_person( person_list);
0119          when 'b'|'B' => remove_person( person_list );
0120          when 'c'|'C' => show_people( person_list );
0121          when 'd'|'D' => initialize_person_list( person_list );
0122          when 'e'|'E' => NEW_LINE;
0123                         PUT_LINE(" have a nice day !");
0124          when others => null;
0125       end case;
0126       menu_choice := menu;
0127    end loop;
0128 end b3s9e2;
0129
```

filename l_list_.pkg

```
0001 -- filename l_list_.pkg - generic linked list package declaration
0002 -- b3s9 see text
0003
0004 generic
0005    type element is private;
0006    with function "<" ( elem_1, elem_2 : element )
0007                       return BOOLEAN is <>;
0008    with function equal( elem_1, elem_2 : element )
0009                       return BOOLEAN;
0010 package link_list is
0011
0012    type l_list is private;
0013
0014    procedure initialize( a_list : in out l_list );
0015    -- procedure to (re)initialize a list throwing away
```

```
0016      -- any data stored in the list
0017
0018      procedure add_head( a_list      : in out l_list;
0019                          an_element : in element);
0020      -- procedure to add an element at the head of a list
0021
0022      procedure add_tail( a_list      : in out l_list;
0023                          an_element : in element);
0024      -- procedure to add an element at the tail of the list
0025
0026      procedure rem_head( a_list      : in out l_list;
0027                          an_element : out element;
0028                          success    : out BOOLEAN );
0029      -- procedure to remove and return the element
0030      -- at the head of list
0031
0032      procedure rem_tail( a_list      : in out l_list;
0033                          an_element : out element;
0034                          success    : out BOOLEAN );
0035      -- procedure to remove and return the element
0036      -- at the end of list
0037
0038      procedure insert_in_order( a_list : in out l_list;
0039                                 an_element : in element);
0040      -- procedure to insert element at correct position
0041      -- the list. Sequence determined by the "<" generic param
0042
0043      procedure rem_in_order( a_list      : in out l_list;
0044                              in_element : in       element;
0045                              success    : out      BOOLEAN;
0046                              out_element : out      element);
0047      -- procedure to remove and return an identified element from
0048      -- the list. Element identified by the "=" generic param
0049
0050      generic
0051         with procedure do_something( an_element : in out element );
0052      procedure traverse( a_list : l_list );
0053      -- procedure to traverse the list applying the do_something
0054      -- procedure to each element in the list
0055
0056   private
0057
0058      type list_node;
0059
0060      type e_pointers is access list_node;
0061
0062      type list_node is
0063      record
```

```
0064          data : element;
0065          next : e_pointers := null;
0066       end record;
0067
0068       type l_list is
0069       record
0070          front : e_pointers;
0071       end record;
0072
0073  end link_list;
0074
```

filename 1_list.pkb

```
0001  -- generic linked list definition package
0002  -- b3s9 - see text
0003
0004  package body link_list is
0005
0006     procedure initialize( a_list : in out l_list ) is
0007     begin -- initialize
0008        a_list.front := null;
0009     end initialize;
0010
0011     procedure add_head( a_list    : in out l_list;
0012                         an_element : in element) is
0013
0014        this_one : e_pointers := new list_node;
0015
0016     begin -- add head
0017        this_one.next := a_list.front;
0018        this_one.data := an_element;
0019        a_list.front  := this_one;
0020     end add_head;
0021
0022     procedure add_tail( a_list    : in out l_list;
0023                         an_element : in element) is
0024
0025        this_one : e_pointers := a_list.front;
0026
0027     begin -- add tail
0028        if a_list.front = null then
0029           a_list.front      := new list_node;
0030           a_list.front.data := an_element;
0031        else -- list contains at least one element
0032           -- traverse to end of list
0033           while ( this_one.next /= null ) loop
```

```
0034                 this_one := this_one.next;
0035             end loop;
0036             this_one.next      := new list_node;
0037             this_one.next.data := an_element;
0038         end if;
0039     end add_tail;
0040
0041     procedure rem_head( a_list    : in out l_list;
0042                         an_element : out element;
0043                         success    : out BOOLEAN ) is
0044
0045     begin -- rem head
0046         if ( a_list.front = null ) then
0047             success := FALSE;
0048         else
0049             an_element   := a_list.front.data;
0050             a_list.front := a_list.front.next;
0051             success      := TRUE;
0052         end if;
0053     end rem_head;
0054
0055     procedure rem_tail( a_list    : in out l_list;
0056                         an_element : out element;
0057                         success    : out BOOLEAN ) is
0058
0059         this_one : e_pointers := a_list.front;
0060
0061     begin -- rem tail
0062         if ( a_list.front = null ) then
0063         -- no elements in the list
0064             success := FALSE;
0065         else
0066             success := TRUE;
0067             if ( a_list.front.next = null ) then
0068                 -- only one element in the list
0069                 an_element   := a_list.front.data;
0070                 a_list.front := null;
0071             else
0072                 while ( this_one.next.next /= null ) loop
0073                     this_one := this_one.next;
0074                 end loop;
0075                 an_element   := this_one.data;
0076                 this_one.next := null;
0077             end if;
0078         end if;
0079     end rem_tail;
0080
0081     procedure insert_in_order( a_list : in out l_list;
```

```
0082                             an_element : in element) is
0083
0084        temp_one : e_pointers := new list_node'( data => an_element,
0085                                                 next => null );
0086        this_one : e_pointers := a_list.front;
0087
0088     begin -- insert in order
0089        if ( a_list.front = null )  or else -- empty list
0090           ( an_element < a_list.front.data ) then
0091           -- insert as first in list
0092           temp_one.next := a_list.front;
0093           a_list.front  := temp_one;
0094        else -- insert in middle of list
0095           while ( this_one.next /= null ) and then
0096                 ( this_one.next.data < an_element ) loop
0097              this_one := this_one.next;
0098           end loop;
0099           temp_one.next := this_one.next;
0100           this_one.next := temp_one;
0101        end if;
0102     end insert_in_order;
0103
0104     procedure rem_in_order( a_list      : in out l_list;
0105                             in_element  : in      element;
0106                             success     : out     BOOLEAN;
0107                             out_element : out     element) is
0108
0109        this_one : e_pointers := a_list.front;
0110        is_found : BOOLEAN := FALSE;
0111        end_list : BOOLEAN := FALSE;
0112
0113     begin -- rem in order
0114        if ( a_list.front = null )  then
0115           success := FALSE;
0116        elsif equal( a_list.front.data, in_element) then
0117           -- remove from head of list
0118           out_element := a_list.front.data;
0119           a_list.front := a_list.front.next;
0120           success := TRUE;
0121        else
0122           while (not(is_found) and not(end_list)) loop
0123              if equal( this_one.next.data, in_element) then
0124                 is_found := TRUE;
0125                 out_element := this_one.next.data;
0126                 this_one.next := this_one.next.next;
0127              else
0128                 this_one := this_one.next;
0129                 if (this_one.next = null) then
```

```
0130                          end_list := TRUE;
0131                      end if;
0132                  end if;
0133              end loop;
0134              success := is_found;
0135          end if;
0136      end rem_in_order;
0137
0138      procedure traverse( a_list : l_list ) is
0139
0140          this_one : e_pointers := a_list.front;
0141
0142      begin -- traverse
0143          while ( this_one /= null ) loop
0144              do_something( this_one.data );
0145              this_one := this_one.next;
0146          end loop;
0147      end traverse;
0148
0149 end link_list;
0150
```

filename b3s10e2.lis

```
0001 -- filename b3s10e2.ans
0002 -- queue demonstration program
0003 -- b3s10e2 solution see text
0004
0005 with d_queue_pack;
0006     package int_queue  is new d_queue_pack( INTEGER );
0007
0008 with TEXT_IO, int_io, int_queue;
0009 use  TEXT_IO, int_io, int_queue;
0010
0011 procedure b3s10e2 is
0012
0013    menu_choice   : CHARACTER;
0014    an_int_queue  : queues;
0015
0016    function menu return CHARACTER is
0017
0018        the_choice : CHARACTER := ' ';
0019
0020    begin -- menu
0021        PUT(" queue demo menu "); NEW_LINE(2);
```

```
0022            PUT_LINE(" a  . . . store    integer ");
0023            PUT_LINE(" b  . . . retrieve integer ");
0024            PUT_LINE(" c  . . . initialize integer queue ");
0025            PUT_LINE(" d  . . . exit ");
0026            NEW_LINE(2);
0027
0028            while ( the_choice not in 'a' .. 'd' ) loop
0029               PUT("Please enter choice ");
0030               GET( the_choice ); NEW_LINE;
0031            end loop;
0032
0033            return the_choice;
0034      end menu;
0035
0036      procedure store_int(  the_int_queue : in out queues ) is
0037
0038         an_int    : INTEGER;
0039         is_stored : BOOLEAN;
0040
0041      begin -- store int
0042         PUT("Enter integer to be stored ");
0043         GET( an_int ); SKIP_LINE;
0044
0045         int_queue.store( an_int, the_int_queue, is_stored );
0046
0047         if is_stored then
0048            PUT_LINE("OK stored in queue ");
0049         else
0050            PUT_LINE("store overflow - not stored ");
0051         end if;
0052         NEW_LINE(2);
0053      end store_int;
0054
0055      procedure retrieve_int( an_int_queue : in out  queues ) is
0056
0057         an_int       : INTEGER;
0058         is_retrieved : BOOLEAN;
0059
0060      begin -- retrieve int
0061         int_queue.retrieve( an_int, an_int_queue, is_retrieved );
0062
0063         if is_retrieved then
0064            PUT("Retrieved "); PUT( an_int ); NEW_LINE;
0065         else
0066            PUT_LINE(" queue underflow !! ");
0067         end if;
0068      end retrieve_int;
0069
```

```
0070  begin -- b3s10e2
0071     menu_choice := menu;
0072     while (menu_choice /= 'd') loop
0073        case menu_choice is
0074           when 'a' => store_int( an_int_queue  );
0075           when 'b' => retrieve_int(  an_int_queue  );
0076           when 'c' => initialize_queue( new_queue => an_int_queue );
0077           when 'd' => NEW_LINE;
0078                       PUT_LINE(" have a nice day !");
0079           when others => null;
0080         end case;
0081         menu_choice := menu;
0082     end loop;
0083  end b3s10e2;
0084
0085
```

filename d_stack_pack_.pkg

```
0001  -- filename d_stack_pack_.pkg - dynamic stack pack declaration file
0002  -- skin package for list_pack
0003  -- conforms to non dynamic stack pack declaration
0004
0005  with link_list;
0006
0007  generic
0008     type element is private;
0009  package d_stack_pack is
0010
0011     function dummy( el_1, el_2 : element ) return BOOLEAN;
0012     -- dummy function required for package instantiation
0013
0014     package el_list is new link_list( element, dummy, dummy);
0015     -- instantiation of linked list package
0016
0017     subtype stacks is el_list.l_list;
0018     -- repackaging of linked list as stacks type
0019
0020     procedure initialize_stack( new_stack : in out stacks );
0021     -- procedure to (re)initialize the stack
0022
0023     procedure push( on_element : in      element;
0024                     a_stack    : in out stacks;
0025                     success    : out     BOOLEAN );
0026     -- procedure to push element onto the stack, although success will
0027     -- always return TRUE in this implementation; parameter has been
```

```
0028        -- retained to allow compatibility with non dynamic stack pack
0029
0030    procedure pop( off_element : out     element;
0031                   a_stack      : in out stacks;
0032                   success      : out     BOOLEAN );
0033    -- procedure to pop element of stack returning element and success
0034    -- TRUE if successful. Success is FALSE and element is undefined
0035    -- if unsuccessful
0036
0037 end d_stack_pack;
0038
```

filename d_stack_pack.pkb

```
0001 -- filename d_stack_pack.pkb - dynamic stack pack definition file
0002 -- skin package for list_pack
0003 -- conforms to non dynamic stack pack declaration
0004
0005 package body d_stack_pack is
0006
0007    function dummy( el_1, el_2 : element ) return BOOLEAN is
0008    begin -- dummy
0009       return TRUE;
0010    end;
0011
0012    procedure initialize_stack( new_stack : in out stacks ) is
0013    begin -- initialize stack
0014       el_list.initialize( new_stack );
0015    end initialize_stack;
0016
0017    procedure push( on_element : in     element;
0018                    a_stack      : in out stacks;
0019                    success      : out     BOOLEAN ) is
0020
0021    begin -- push
0022       el_list.add_head( a_stack, on_element );
0023       success := TRUE;
0024    end push;
0025
0026    procedure pop( off_element : out     element;
0027                   a_stack      : in out stacks;
0028                   success      : out     BOOLEAN ) is
0029    begin -- pop
0030       el_list.rem_head( a_stack, off_element, success );
0031    end pop;
0032
0033 end d_stack_pack;
```

```
0033  end d_stack_pack;
0034
```

filename b3s11e1.lis

```
0001  -- filename b3s11e1.ans - see text
0002  -- requires pres_pack and b_tree
0003
0004  with TEXT_IO, pers_pack, b_tree;
0005  use  TEXT_IO, pers_pack;
0006
0007  procedure b3s11e1 is
0008
0009     package pers_tree_pack is new b_tree( person_record,
0010                                           "<" => name_less_than,
0011                                           is_equal => name_equal_to);
0012     use pers_tree_pack;
0013
0014     pers_tree : pers_tree_pack.trees;
0015
0016     menu_choice   : CHARACTER := ' ';
0017
0018
0019     function menu return CHARACTER is
0020
0021        menu_char   : CHARACTER := 'x';
0022        valid_choice : BOOLEAN := FALSE;
0023
0024        procedure show_menu is
0025        begin -- show menu
0026           PUT_LINE("Integer stack demonstration menu ");
0027           NEW_LINE;
0028           PUT_LINE("   a   store person");
0029           PUT_LINE("   b   search for person");
0030           PUT_LINE("   c   display people");
0031           PUT_LINE("   d   exit program ");
0032           NEW_LINE;
0033        end show_menu;
0034
0035     begin -- menu
0036        show_menu;
0037        while not valid_choice loop
0038           PUT("Enter choice ");
0039           GET( menu_char ); SKIP_LINE;
0040
0041           valid_choice := ( menu_char in 'a' .. 'd') or
0042                           ( menu_char in 'A' .. 'D');
```

```
0043
0044          if not valid_choice then
0045              PUT_LINE("Enter 'a', 'b', 'c' or 'd' only!");
0046          end if;
0047        end loop;
0048        return menu_char;
0049    end menu;
0050
0051
0052    procedure store_person( pers_tree : in out pers_tree_pack.trees ) is
0053
0054        a_pers : person_record;
0055
0056    begin -- store_person
0057        NEW_LINE(2);
0058        get_person( a_pers );
0059        insert_in_tree( pers_tree, a_pers );
0060        PUT_LINE("O.K. person stored ");
0061        NEW_LINE(2);
0062    end store_person;
0063
0064    procedure search_person( pers_tree : in pers_tree_pack.trees ) is
0065
0066        pers_in  : person_record;
0067        is_found : BOOLEAN;
0068        pers_out : person_record;
0069
0070    begin -- search_person
0071        NEW_LINE(2);
0072        PUT_LINE("Please enter person to search for ");
0073        PUT_LINE("(only name parts need be entered).");
0074        get_person( pers_in );
0075        pers_tree_pack.search_tree( pers_tree, pers_in,
0076                                   is_found, pers_out );
0077        if is_found then
0078            show_person( pers_out );
0079        else
0080            PUT("Person not stored in tree!");
0081        end if;
0082        NEW_LINE(2);
0083    end search_person;
0084
0085    procedure show_a_person( a_person : in out person_record ) is
0086    -- repackaging of show_person from person pack. Repackaging
0087    -- required as the modes do not match. The generic procedure
0088    -- do_something from b_tree requires an in out parameter, the
0089    -- show_person procedure from pers_pack requires an in parameter
0090
```

```
0091    begin -- show_a_person
0092       pers_pack.show_person( a_person ); -- make it explicit
0093    end show_a_person;
0094
0095    -- instantiation of generic traversal procedure to show people
0096    procedure put_people is new
0097             pers_tree_pack.traverse_tree( do_something => show_a_person );
0098
0099    procedure show_people( pers_tree : in pers_tree_pack.trees ) is
0100    begin -- show_people
0101       NEW_LINE(2);
0102       put_people( pers_tree );
0103       NEW_LINE(2);
0104    end show_people;
0105
0106
0107 begin -- b3s11e1
0108    menu_choice := menu;
0109    while ((menu_choice /= 'd') and
0110           (menu_choice /= 'D')) loop
0111       case menu_choice is
0112          when 'a'|'A' => store_person( pers_tree );
0113          when 'b'|'B' => search_person( pers_tree  );
0114          when 'c'|'C' => show_people( pers_tree );
0115          when 'd'|'D' => NEW_LINE;
0116                         PUT_LINE(" have a nice day !");
0117          when others => null;
0118       end case;
0119       menu_choice := menu;
0120    end loop;
0121 end b3s11e1;
0122
```

filename b_tree_.pkg

```
0001    -- filename b_tree_.pkg generic binary tree package declaration
0002    -- b3s11 see text.
0003
0004    generic
0005       type element is private;
0006       with function "<" ( elem_1, elem_2 : element )
0007             return BOOLEAN is <>;
0008       with function is_equal ( elem_1, elem_2 : element )
0009             return BOOLEAN;
0010    package b_tree is
0011
```

```
0012        type trees is private;
0013
0014        procedure insert_in_tree( tree : in out trees;
0015                                  elem : in      element );
0016    -- procedure to insert elem into the tree pointed to by
0017    -- tree. Assumes that elem never already exists in tree
0018    -- and that dynamic memory can always be allocated
0019
0020        procedure search_tree( tree     : in   trees;
0021                               to_find  : in   element;
0022                               located  : out  BOOLEAN;
0023                               out_elem : out  element );
0024    -- procedure to search binary tree for node matching to_find
0025    -- if found located is TRUE and out_elem set to contents
0026    -- otherwise located is FALSE and out_elem is not set
0027
0028    generic
0029        with procedure do_something( an_elem : in out element );
0030        procedure traverse_tree( tree : in trees );
0031
0032 private
0033        type tree_node;
0034
0035        type trees is access tree_node;
0036
0037        type tree_node is
0038        record
0039            left_tree  : trees;
0040            data       : element;
0041            right_tree : trees;
0042        end record;
0043    end b_tree;
0044
```

filename b_tree.pkb

```
0001    -- filename b_tree_.pkb generic binary tree package definition
0002    -- b3s11 see text.
0003
0004 package body b_tree is
0005
0006        procedure insert_in_tree( tree : in out trees;
0007                                  elem : in      element ) is
0008    -- procedure to insert elem into the tree pointed to by
0009    -- tree. Assumes that elem never already exists in tree
0010    -- and that dynamic memory can always be allocated
0011
```

```
0012        begin -- insert_in_tree
0013          if tree = null then
0014            tree := new tree_node' ( left_tree  => null,
0015                                      data       => elem,
0016                                      right_tree => null);
0017          elsif (elem < tree.data) then
0018              insert_in_tree( tree.left_tree,  elem);
0019          else
0020              insert_in_tree( tree.right_tree, elem);
0021          end if;
0022        end insert_in_tree;
0023
0024        procedure search_tree( tree    : in  trees;
0025                               to_find: in element;
0026                               located  : out BOOLEAN;
0027                               out_elem : out element ) is
0028        begin -- search_tree
0029          if tree = null then
0030              located := FALSE;
0031          else
0032              if ( is_equal( to_find, tree.data )) then
0033                  located := TRUE;
0034                  out_elem := tree.data;
0035              elsif ( to_find < tree.data) then
0036                  search_tree( tree.left_tree, to_find, located, out_elem );
0037              else
0038                  search_tree( tree.right_tree, to_find, located, out_elem );
0039              end if;
0040          end if;
0041        end search_tree;
0042
0043        procedure traverse_tree( tree : in trees ) is
0044        begin -- traverse tree
0045          if (tree /= null) then
0046              traverse_tree( tree.left_tree);
0047              do_something( tree.data );
0048              traverse_tree( tree.right_tree);
0049          end if;
0050        end traverse_tree;
0051  end b_tree;
```

filename b3s12e3.lis

```
0001  -- filename b3s12e3.ans
0002  -- solution for b3s12e3 see text
0003  -- the following changes would have to be made to the
```

```
0004   -- drink_machine.pkb file to convert it for America
0005
0006      -- different denominations of coins
0007      -- type    coins is ( nickle, dime, quarter,
0008      --                       half_dollar, dollar )
0009
0010      -- coin values
0011      -- coin_denoms : array (coins) of POSITIVE
0012      --               := ( 5, 10, 25, 50, 100 );
0013
0014
```

Appendix B

The predeclared environment

The Ada standard mandates several packages and compilation units which must or may be provided by the compiler manufacturer. The four major units are STANDARD, TEXT_IO, SEQUENTIAL_IO and DIRECT_IO; a full listing of these units is included in this Appendix.

Other units which comprise the predeclared environment are the following:

the package CALENDAR
– for dealing with dates and times
the package SYSTEM
– containing the actual values of MAX_INT, etc.
the optional package MACHINE_CODE
– to allow machine code to be included in Áda listings
the generic procedure UNCHECKED_DEALLOCATION
– for programmer-controlled garbage collection
the generic function UNCHECKED_CONVERSION
– for illicit conversions between types!
the package IO_EXCEPTIONS
– defines exceptions used in all input/output
– see Appendix C
the package LOW_LEVEL_IO
– to allow actual physical input/output devices to be controlled

The package STANDARD

```
package STANDARD is

    -- the predeclared type BOOLEAN and its operators
    type BOOLEAN is ( FALSE, TRUE );

    function "="    ( LEFT, RIGHT : BOOLEAN ) return BOOLEAN;
    function "/="   ( LEFT, RIGHT : BOOLEAN ) return BOOLEAN;
    function "<"    ( LEFT, RIGHT : BOOLEAN ) return BOOLEAN;
    function "<="   ( LEFT, RIGHT : BOOLEAN ) return BOOLEAN;
    function ">"    ( LEFT, RIGHT : BOOLEAN ) return BOOLEAN;
```

```
function ">=" ( LEFT, RIGHT : BOOLEAN ) return BOOLEAN;

function "and" ( LEFT, RIGHT : BOOLEAN ) return BOOLEAN;
function "or"  ( LEFT, RIGHT : BOOLEAN ) return BOOLEAN;
function "xor" ( LEFT, RIGHT : BOOLEAN ) return BOOLEAN;

function "not" ( RIGHT : BOOLEAN ) return BOOLEAN;

-- the universal type universal_integer is predefined
-- the predeclared type INTEGER and its operators is

type INTEGER is { implementation_defined };
-- the actual definition of INTEGER differs from compiler to compiler

function "="  ( LEFT, RIGHT : INTEGER ) return BOOLEAN;
function "/=" ( LEFT, RIGHT : INTEGER ) return BOOLEAN;
function "<"  ( LEFT, RIGHT : INTEGER ) return BOOLEAN;
function "<=" ( LEFT, RIGHT : INTEGER ) return BOOLEAN;
function ">"  ( LEFT, RIGHT : INTEGER ) return BOOLEAN;
function ">=" ( LEFT, RIGHT : INTEGER ) return BOOLEAN;

function "+"   ( RIGHT : INTEGER ) return INTEGER;
function "-"   ( RIGHT : INTEGER ) return INTEGER;
function "abs" ( RIGHT : INTEGER ) return INTEGER;

function "+"   ( LEFT, RIGHT : INTEGER ) return INTEGER;
function "-"   ( LEFT, RIGHT : INTEGER ) return INTEGER;
function "*"   ( LEFT, RIGHT : INTEGER ) return INTEGER;
function "/"   ( LEFT, RIGHT : INTEGER ) return INTEGER;
function "rem" ( LEFT, RIGHT : INTEGER ) return INTEGER;
function "mod" ( LEFT, RIGHT : INTEGER ) return INTEGER;
function "**"  ( LEFT, RIGHT : INTEGER ) return INTEGER;

-- the universal type universal_real is predefined
-- the predeclared type FLOAT and its operators is

type FLOAT is implementation_defined;

function "="  ( LEFT, RIGHT : FLOAT ) return BOOLEAN;
function "/=" ( LEFT, RIGHT : FLOAT ) return BOOLEAN;
function "<"  ( LEFT, RIGHT : FLOAT ) return BOOLEAN;
function "<=" ( LEFT, RIGHT : FLOAT ) return BOOLEAN;

function ">"  ( LEFT, RIGHT : FLOAT ) return BOOLEAN;
function ">=" ( LEFT, RIGHT : FLOAT ) return BOOLEAN;

function "+"   ( RIGHT : FLOAT ) return FLOAT;
function "-"   ( RIGHT : FLOAT ) return FLOAT;
function "abs" ( RIGHT : FLOAT ) return FLOAT;

function "+"   ( LEFT, RIGHT : FLOAT ) return FLOAT;
function "-"   ( LEFT, RIGHT : FLOAT ) return FLOAT;
function "*"   ( LEFT, RIGHT : FLOAT ) return FLOAT;
```

```
function "/"   ( LEFT, RIGHT : FLOAT ) return FLOAT;
function "rem" ( LEFT, RIGHT : FLOAT ) return FLOAT;
function "mod" ( LEFT, RIGHT : FLOAT ) return FLOAT;
function "**"  ( LEFT : FLOAT; RIGHT INTEGER ) return FLOAT;

-- the following operators are predefined for universal types

function "*" ( LEFT : universal_integer; RIGHT : universal_real )
                                         return universal_real;
function "*" ( LEFT : universal_real; RIGHT : universal_integer )
                                         return universal_real;
function "/" ( LEFT : universal_real; RIGHT : universal_integer )
                                         return universal_real;

-- the type universal_fixed is predefined
-- the only operators declared for this type are
function "*" ( LEFT : any_fixed_point_type; RIGHT any_fixed_point_type )
                                            return universal_fixed;

function "/" ( LEFT : any_fixed_point_type; RIGHT any_fixed_point_type )
                                            return universal_fixed;

-- The following characters form the standard ASCII character set
-- Character literals corresponding to control characters are not
-- identifiers; they are shown without quotes in this definition.

type CHARACTER is
    ( nul,   soh,   stx,   etx,   eot,   enq,   ack,   bel,
      bs,    ht,    lf,    vt,    ff,    cr,    so,    si,
      dle,   dc1,   dc2,   dc3,   dc4,   nak,   syn,   etb,
      can,   em,    sub,   esc,   fs,    gs,    rs,    us,
      ' ',   '!',   '"',   '#',   '$',   '%',   '&',   ''',
      '(',   ')',   '*',   '+',   ',',   '-',   '.',   '/',
      '0',   '1',   '2',   '3',   '4',   '5',   '6',   '7',
      '8',   '9',   ':',   ';',   '<',   '=',   '>',   '?',
      '@',   'A',   'B',   'C',   'D',   'E',   'F',   'G',
      'H',   'I',   'J',   'K',   'L',   'M',   'N',   'O',
      'P',   'Q',   'R',   'S',   'T',   'U',   'V',   'W',
      'X',   'Y',   'Z',   '[',   '\',   ']',   '^',   '_',
      ''',   'a',   'b',   'c',   'd',   'e',   'f',   'g',
      'h',   'i',   'j',   'k',   'l',   'm',   'n',   'o',
      'p',   'q',   'r',   's',   't',   'u',   'v',   'w',
      'x',   'y',   'z',   '{',   '|',   '}',   '~',   del );

for CHARACTER use -- 128 ASCII character set without holes
    ( 0, 1, 2, 3, 4, 5, . . . ... 125, 126, 127 );

-- The predefined operators for the type CHARACTER are the
-- same as for any enumeration type

package ASCII is -- a package of character constants
        -- Control characters:
```

```
    NUL : constant CHARACTER :=  nul     SOH : constant CHARACTER :=  soh
    STX : constant CHARACTER :=  stx     ETX : constant CHARACTER :=  etx
    EOT : constant CHARACTER :=  eot     ENQ : constant CHARACTER :=  enq
    ACK : constant CHARACTER :=  ack     BEL : constant CHARACTER :=  ack
    BS  : constant CHARACTER :=  bs      HT  : constant CHARACTER :=  ht
    LF  : constant CHARACTER :=  lf      VT  : constant CHARACTER :=  vt
    FF  : constant CHARACTER :=  ff      CR  : constant CHARACTER :=  cr
    SO  : constant CHARACTER :=  so      SI  : constant CHARACTER :=  si
    DLE : constant CHARACTER :=  dle     DC1 : constant CHARACTER :=  dc1
    DC2 : constant CHARACTER :=  dc2     DC3 : constant CHARACTER :=  dc3
    DC4 : constant CHARACTER :=  dc4     NAK : constant CHARACTER :=  nak
    SYN : constant CHARACTER :=  syn     ETB : constant CHARACTER :=  etb
    CAN : constant CHARACTER :=  can     EM  : constant CHARACTER :=  em
    SUB : constant CHARACTER :=  sub     ESC : constant CHARACTER :=  esc
    FS  : constant CHARACTER :=  fs      GS  : constant CHARACTER :=  gs
    RS  : constant CHARACTER :=  rs      US  : constant CHARACTER :=  us
    DEL : constant CHARACTER :=  del

    -- Other constants:
    EXCLAM     : constant CHARACTER := '!';
    QUOTATION  : constant CHARACTER := '!';
    SHARP      : constant CHARACTER := '#';
    DOLLAR     : constant CHARACTER := '$';
    PERCENT    : constant CHARACTER := '%';
    AMPERSAND  : constant CHARACTER := '&';
    COLON      : constant CHARACTER := ':';
    SEMICOLON  : constant CHARACTER := ';';
    QUERY      : constant CHARACTER := '?';
    AT_SIGN    : constant CHARACTER := '@';
    L_BRACKET  : constant CHARACTER := '(';
    BACK_SLASH : constant CHARACTER := '\';
    R_BRACKET  : constant CHARACTER := ')';
    CIRCUMFLEX : constant CHARACTER := '^';
    UNDERLINE  : constant CHARACTER := '_';
    GRAVE      : constant CHARACTER := '''';
    L_BRACE    : constant CHARACTER := '{';
    BAR        : constant CHARACTER := '|';
    R_BRACE    : constant CHARACTER := '}';
    TILADE     : constant CHARACTER := '~';

    -- Lower case characters
    LC_A : constant CHARACTER := 'a';
    . . .
    LC_Z : constant CHARACTER := 'z';
end ASCII;

-- Predefined subtypes

subtype NATURAL  is INTEGER range  0 .. INTEGER'LAST;
```

```
subtype POSITIVE is INTEGER range  1 .. INTEGER'LAST;

-- Predefined STRING type

type STRING is array( POSITIVE range <> ) of CHARACTER;

function "="   ( LEFT, RIGHT : STRING ) return BOOLEAN;
function "/="  ( LEFT, RIGHT : STRING ) return BOOLEAN;
function "<"   ( LEFT, RIGHT : STRING ) return BOOLEAN;
function "<="  ( LEFT, RIGHT : STRING ) return BOOLEAN;
function ">"   ( LEFT, RIGHT : STRING ) return BOOLEAN;
function ">="  ( LEFT, RIGHT : STRING ) return BOOLEAN;

function "&"   ( LEFT : STRING     : RIGHT STRING )     return STRING;
function "&"   ( LEFT : CHARACTER   : RIGHT STRING )     return STRING;
function "&"   ( LEFT : STRING     : RIGHT CHARACTER ) return STRING;
function "&"   ( LEFT : CHARACTER  : RIGHT STRING )     return STRING;

type DURATION is delta implementation_defined
                range implementation_defined;
-- the predefined operators for the type DURATION are the same as
-- for any fixed point type.

-- The predefined exceptions

CONSTRAINT_ERROR : exception;
NUMERIC_ERROR    : exception;
PROGRAM_ERROR    : exception;
STORAGE_ERROR    : exception;
TASKING_ERROR    : exception;

end STANDARD;
```

The package TEXT_IO

```
with IO_EXCEPTIONS;

package TEXT_IO is

   type FILE_type is limited private;
   type FILE_MODE is (IN_FILE, OUT_FILE);
   type COUNT is range 0 .. INTEGER'LAST;
   -- the value of INTEGER'LAST is implementation defined

   subtype POSITIVE_COUNT is COUNT range 1 .. COUNT'LAST;

   UNBOUNDED : constant COUNT := 0; -- line and page length

   subtype FIELD       is INTEGER range 0 .. INTEGER'LAST;
   subtype NUMBER_BASE is INTEGER range 2 .. 16;

   type type_SET is (LOWER_CASE, UPPER_CASE);
```

```
-- file management
procedure CREATE(FILE : in out FILE_TYPE;
                 MODE : in FILE_MODE := OUT_FILE;
                 NAME : in STRING := "";
                 FORM : in STRING := "");

procedure OPEN(FILE : in out FILE_TYPE;
              MODE : in FILE_MODE;
              NAME : in STRING;
              FORM : in STRING := "");

procedure CLOSE(FILE :  in out FILE_TYPE);

procedure DELETE(FILE : in out FILE_TYPE);

procedure RESET(FILE : in out FILE_TYPE; MODE : in FILE_MODE);
procedure RESET(FILE : in out FILE_TYPE);

function MODE(FILE : in FILE_TYPE) return FILE_MODE;
function NAME(FILE : in FILE_TYPE) return STRING;

function FORM(FILE : in FILE_TYPE) return STRING;

function IS_OPEN(FILE : in FILE_TYPE) return BOOLEAN;

-- Control of default input and output files

procedure SET_INPUT(FILE : in FILE_TYPE);
procedure SET_OUTPUT(FILE : in FILE_TYPE);

function STANDARD_INPUT return FILE_TYPE;
function STANDARD_OUTPUT return FILE_TYPE;

function CURRENT_INPUT return FILE_TYPE;
function CURRENT_OUTPUT return FILE_TYPE;

-- Specification of line and page lengths
procedure SET_LINE_LENGTH(FILE : in FILE_TYPE; TO : in COUNT);
procedure SET_LINE_LENGTH(TO    : in COUNT);

procedure SET_PAGE_LENGTH(FILE : in FILE_TYPE; TO : in COUNT);
procedure SET_PAGE_LENGTH(TO    : in COUNT);

function LINE_LENGTH(FILE : in FILE_TYPE) return COUNT;
function LINE_LENGTH return COUNT;

function PAGE_LENGTH(FILE : in FILE_TYPE) return COUNT;
function PAGE_LENGTH return COUNT;

-- Column, Line, and Page Control
procedure NEW_LINE(FILE    : in FILE_TYPE;
                   SPACING : in POSITIVE_COUNT := 1);
```

```
procedure NEW_LINE(SPACING : in POSITIVE_COUNT := 1);

procedure SKIP_LINE(FILE    : in FILE_TYPE;
                    SPACING : in POSITIVE_COUNT := 1);
procedure SKIP_LINE(SPACING : in POSITIVE_COUNT := 1);

function END_OF_LINE(FILE : in FILE_TYPE) return BOOLEAN;
function END_OF_LINE return BOOLEAN;

procedure NEW_PAGE(FILE : in FILE_TYPE);
procedure NEW_PAGE;

procedure SKIP_PAGE(FILE: in FILE_TYPE);
procedure SKIP_PAGE;

function END_OF_PAGE(FILE : in FILE_TYPE) return BOOLEAN;
function END_OF_PAGE return BOOLEAN;

function END_OF_FILE(FILE : in FILE_TYPE) return BOOLEAN;
function END_OF_FILE return BOOLEAN;

procedure SET_COL(FILE : in FILE_TYPE; TO : in POSITIVE_COUNT);
procedure SET_COL(TO   : in POSITIVE_COUNT);

procedure SET_LINE(FILE : in FILE_TYPE; TO : in POSITIVE_COUNT);
procedure SET_LINE(TO   : in POSITIVE_COUNT);

function COL(FILE : in FILE_TYPE) return POSITIVE_COUNT;
function COL return POSITIVE_COUNT;

function LINE(FILE : in FILE_TYPE) return POSITIVE_COUNT;
function LINE return POSITIVE_COUNT;

function PAGE(FILE : in FILE_TYPE) return POSITIVE_COUNT;
function PAGE return POSITIVE_COUNT;

-- Character Input-Output
procedure GET(FILE : in FILE_TYPE; ITEM : out CHARACTER);
procedure GET(ITEM : out CHARACTER);

procedure PUT(FILE : in FILE_TYPE; ITEM : in CHARACTER);
procedure PUT(ITEM : in CHARACTER);

-- String Input-Output
procedure GET(FILE : in FILE_TYPE; ITEM : out STRING);
procedure GET(ITEM : out STRING);

procedure PUT(FILE : in FILE_TYPE; ITEM : in STRING);
```

```ada
procedure PUT(ITEM : in STRING);

procedure GET_LINE(FILE : in FILE_TYPE; ITEM : out STRING;
                                        LAST : out NATURAL);
procedure GET_LINE(ITEM : out STRING;   LAST : out NATURAL);

procedure PUT_LINE(FILE : in FILE_TYPE; ITEM : in STRING);
procedure PUT_LINE(ITEM : in STRING);

-- Generic package for Input-Output of Integer types
generic
   type NUM is range <>;
package INTEGER_IO is

   DEFAULT_WIDTH : FIELD := NUM'WIDTH;
   DEFAULT_BASE  : NUMBER_BASE := 10;

   procedure GET(FILE : in FILE_TYPE; ITEM : out NUM;
                                     WIDTH : in FIELD := 0);
   procedure GET(ITEM : out NUM; WIDTH : in FIELD := 0);

   procedure PUT(FILE  : in FILE_TYPE;
                 ITEM  : in NUM;
                 WIDTH : in FIELD := DEFAULT_WIDTH;
                 BASE  : in NUMBER_BASE := DEFAULT_BASE);
   procedure PUT(ITEM  : in NUM;
                 WIDTH : in FIELD := DEFAULT_WIDTH;
                 BASE  : in NUMBER_BASE := DEFAULT_BASE);

   procedure GET(FROM : in STRING; ITEM : out NUM; LAST : out POSITIVE);
   procedure PUT(TO   : out STRING;
                 ITEM : in NUM;
                 BASE : in NUMBER_BASE := DEFAULT_BASE);

end INTEGER_IO;

-- Generic package for Input-Output of Real types
generic
   type NUM is digits <>;
package FLOAT_IO is
   DEFAULT_FORE : FIELD := 2;
   DEFAULT_AFT  : FIELD := NUM'DIGITS-1;
   DEFAULT_EXP  : FIELD := 3;

   procedure GET(FILE : in FILE_TYPE; ITEM : out NUM;
                                     WIDTH : in FIELD := 0);
   procedure GET(ITEM : out NUM; WIDTH : in FIELD := 0);

   procedure PUT(FILE : in FILE_TYPE;
                 ITEM : in NUM;
                 FORE : in FIELD := DEFAULT_FORE;
```

```
                      AFT  : in FIELD := DEFAULT_AFT;
                      EXP  : in FIELD := DEFAULT_EXP);
   procedure PUT(ITEM : in NUM;
                      FORE : in FIELD := DEFAULT_FORE;
                      AFT  : in FIELD := DEFAULT_AFT;
                      EXP  : in FIELD := DEFAULT_EXP);

   procedure GET(FROM : in STRING; ITEM : out NUM; LAST : out POSITIVE);
   procedure PUT(TO   : out STRING;
                      ITEM : in NUM;
                      AFT  : in FIELD := DEFAULT_AFT;
                      EXP  : in INTEGER := DEFAULT_EXP);

end FLOAT_IO;

-- Generic package for Input-Output of Enumeration types
generic
     type ENUM is (<>);
package ENUMERATION_IO is
   DEFAULT_WIDTH   : FIELD := 0;
   DEFAULT_SETTING : TYPE_SET := UPPER_CASE;
   procedure GET(FILE : in FILE_TYPE; ITEM : out ENUM);
   procedure GET(ITEM : out ENUM);

   procedure PUT(FILE  : in FILE_TYPE;
                      ITEM  : in ENUM;
                      WIDTH : in FIELD := DEFAULT_WIDTH;
                      SET   : in TYPE_SET := DEFAULT_SETTING);
   procedure PUT(ITEM  : in ENUM;
                      WIDTH : in FIELD := DEFAULT_WIDTH;
                      SET   : in type_SET := DEFAULT_SETTING);

   procedure GET(FROM : in STRING; ITEM : out ENUM;
                                   LAST : out POSITIVE);
   procedure PUT(TO   : out STRING;
                      ITEM : in ENUM;
                      SET  : in type_SET := DEFAULT_SETTING);

end ENUMERATION_IO;

-- exceptions

STATUS_ERROR    : exception renames IO_EXCEPTIONS.STATUS_ERROR;
MODE_ERROR      : exception renames IO_EXCEPTIONS.MODE_ERROR;
NAME_ERROR      : exception renames IO_EXCEPTIONS.NAME_ERROR;
USE_ERROR       : exception renames IO_EXCEPTIONS.USE_ERROR;
DEVICE_ERROR    : exception renames IO_EXCEPTIONS.DEVICE_ERROR;
END_ERROR       : exception renames IO_EXCEPTIONS.END_ERROR;
DATA_ERROR      : exception renames IO_EXCEPTIONS.DATA_ERROR;
LAYOUT_ERROR    : exception renames IO_EXCEPTIONS.LAYOUT_ERROR;

private
```

```
      -- private declaration are implementation specific

  end TEXT_IO;
```

The package SEQUENTIAL_IO

```
with IO_EXCEPTIONS;
generic
   type ELEMENT_TYPE is private;
package SEQUENTIAL_IO is

   type FILE_TYPE is limited private;

   type FILE_MODE is (IN_FILE, OUT_FILE);

   procedure CREATE( FILE  : in FILE_TYPE;
                     MODE  : in FILE_MODE := OUT_FILE;
                     NAME  : in STRING := "";
                     FORM  : in STRING := "");

   procedure OPEN(   FILE  : in FILE_TYPE;
                     MODE  : in FILE_MODE;
                     NAME  : in STRING := "";
                     FORM  : in STRING := "");

   procedure CLOSE ( FILE : in out FILE_TYPE );
   procedure DELETE( FILE : in out FILE_TYPE );
   procedure RESET ( FILE : in out FILE_TYPE; MODE : in FILE_MODE);
   procedure RESET ( FILE : in out FILE_TYPE );

   function MODE(    FILE : in FILE_TYPE ) return FILE_MODE;
   function NAME(    FILE : in FILE_TYPE ) return STRING;
   function FORM(    FILE : in FILE_TYPE ) return STRING;
   function IS_OPEN( FILE : in FILE_TYPE ) return BOOLEAN;

   procedure READ(  FILE : in FILE_TYPE; ITEM : out ELEMENT_TYPE );
   procedure WRITE( FILE : in FILE_TYPE; ITEM : in  ELEMENT_TYPE );

   function END_OF_FILE( FILE : in FILE_TYPE ) return BOOLEAN;

   -- exceptions

   STATUS_ERROR  : exception renames IO_EXCEPTIONS.STATUS_ERROR;
   MODE_ERROR    : exception renames IO_EXCEPTIONS.MODE_ERROR;
   NAME_ERROR    : exception renames IO_EXCEPTIONS.NAME_ERROR;
   USE_ERROR     : exception renames IO_EXCEPTIONS.USE_ERROR;
   DEVICE_ERROR  : exception renames IO_EXCEPTIONS.DEVICE_ERROR;
   END_ERROR     : exception renames IO_EXCEPTIONS.END_ERROR;
   DATA_ERROR    : exception renames IO_EXCEPTIONS.DATA_ERROR;

private
```

```
   -- private declarations are implementation specific
end SEQUENTIAL_IO;
```

The package DIRECT_IO

```
with IO_EXCEPTIONS;
generic
   type ELEMENT_TYPE is private;
package DIRECT_IO is

   type FILE_TYPE is limited private;

   type FILE_MODE is (IN_FILE, INOUT_FILE, OUT_FILE);

   type    COUNT          is       range 0 .. { implementation_defined };
   subtype POSITIVE_COUNT is COUNT range 1 .. COUNT'LAST;

   procedure CREATE( FILE : in FILE_TYPE;
                     MODE : in FILE_MODE := INOUT_FILE;
                     NAME : in STRING := "";
                     FORM : in STRING := "");

   procedure OPEN(   FILE : in FILE_TYPE;
                     MODE : in FILE_MODE;
                     NAME : in STRING := "";
                     FORM : in STRING := "");

   procedure CLOSE ( FILE : in out FILE_TYPE );
   procedure DELETE( FILE : in out FILE_TYPE );
   procedure RESET ( FILE : in out FILE_TYPE; MODE : in FILE_MODE);
   procedure RESET ( FILE : in out FILE_TYPE );

   function MODE(   FILE : in FILE_TYPE ) return FILE_MODE;
   function NAME(   FILE : in FILE_TYPE ) return STRING;
   function FORM(   FILE : in FILE_TYPE ) return STRING;
   function IS_OPEN( FILE : in FILE_TYPE ) return BOOLEAN;

   procedure READ( FILE : in  FILE_TYPE;
                   ITEM : out ELEMENT_TYPE );
   procedure READ( FILE : in  FILE_TYPE;
                   ITEM : out ELEMENT_TYPE;
                   FROM : in  POSITIVE_COUNT);

   procedure WRITE( FILE : in  FILE_TYPE;
                    ITEM : in  ELEMENT_TYPE );
   procedure WRITE( FILE : in  FILE_TYPE;
                    ITEM : in  ELEMENT_TYPE;
                    TO   : in  POSITIVE_COUNT );

   procedure SET_INDEX( FILE : in FILE_TYPE;
```

```
                        TO   : in POSITIVE_COUNT );

   function INDEX( FILE : in FILE_TYPE ) return POSITIVE_COUNT;
   function SIZE(  FILE : in FILE_TYPE ) return COUNT;

   function END_OF_FILE( FILE : in FILE_TYPE ) return BOOLEAN;

   -- exceptions

   STATUS_ERROR    : exception renames IO_EXCEPTIONS.STATUS_ERROR;
   MODE_ERROR      : exception renames IO_EXCEPTIONS.MODE_ERROR;
   NAME_ERROR      : exception renames IO_EXCEPTIONS.NAME_ERROR;
   USE_ERROR       : exception renames IO_EXCEPTIONS.USE_ERROR;
   DEVICE_ERROR    : exception renames IO_EXCEPTIONS.DEVICE_ERROR;
   END_ERROR       : exception renames IO_EXCEPTIONS.END_ERROR;
   DATA_ERROR      : exception renames IO_EXCEPTIONS.DATA_ERROR;

private
   -- private declarations are implementation specific
end DIRECT_IO;
```

An Ada style guide

The following style guide provides an overview of common Ada syntax and recommended layout conventions. It is intended as an *aide-mémoire* which could be used while a program is being developed. It is not intended to be a complete formal description of the Ada language.

Filenames

Main program files should be named using the name of the main procedure, with the extension '.ada'. (e.g., 'a_prog.ada').

Package declaration files should be named using the name of the package, followed by an underscore, with the extension '.pkg'. (e.g., 'a_pack_.pkg').

Package definition files should be named using the name of the package; with the extension '.pkb'. (e.g., 'a_pack.pkb').

Separate subprogram files should be named using the name of the subprogram, with the extension '.ads'. (e.g., 'sub_prog.ads').

Declarations

Constants

```
const_name    : constant type := value;
named_number  : constant      := value;
```

Numeric types

```
type integer_type  is new   INTEGER    range lo_value .. hi_value;
type floating_type is digits num_digits range lo_value .. hi_value;
type fixed_type    is delta  accuracy   range lo_value .. hi_value;
```

Subtypes

```
subtype subtype_name is base_type range value .. value;
```

Enumerated types

```
type type_name is ( enumeration_literal, . . ., enumeration_literal );
```

Records

```
type record_type is
record
   field_name : field_type := default_value;
   field_name : field_type := default_value;
end record;
```

Constrained arrays

```
type array_type_name is array  ( index_range ) of element_type;
```

Unconstrained arrays

```
type array_type_name is array ( index_type range <> ) of element_type;
```

Access types

```
type access_type is access referenced_type;
```

Private types

```
type type_name is private;          -- equality and assignment only
type type_name is limited private;   -- no operations allowed
```

Exception declaration

```
exception_name : exception;
```

Renames declaration

```
new_name renames old_name;
```

Variable declaration

```
variable_name : variable_type := initial_value;

record_var    : record_type   := ( positional_values );
record_var    : record_type   := ( field_name => field_value;
                                    field_name => field_value);

array_var     : array_type    := ( positional_values );
array_var     : array_type    := ( index_range   => value;
                                    value | value => value;
                                    others        => value;
array_var     : unconstrained_array_type( index_range );
```

Subprograms

Procedure declaration

```
procedure procedure_name ( formal_parameters );
```

Function declaration

```
function function_name ( formal_parameters ) return return_type;
```

Generic subprogram

```
generic
   generic_formal_parameters;
subprogram_declaration;
```

Separate subprogram declaration

```
subprogram_declaration is separate;
```

Procedure definition

```
procedure procedure_name ( formal_parameters ) is
   declarations;
begin -- procedure name
```

```
      statements;
   end procedure_name;
```

Function definition

```
   function  function_name  ( formal_parameters ) return return_type is
      declarations;
   begin -- function_name
      statements;
      return value;
      (statements;)
   end function_name;
```

Generic subprogram instantiation

```
   subprog_name is new generic_subprog_name( generic_actual_parameters);
```

Separate subprogram definition

```
   separate pack_name -- note no ';'
   subprogram definition;
```

Packages

Generic instantiation

```
   package pack_name is new g_pack_name( generic_actual_parameters);
```

Package declaration

```
   context_clause;

   generic
      generic_actual_parameters;
   package pack_name is
      declarations;
   private
      private_declarations;
   end pack_name;
```

Package definition

```
context_clause;

package body pack_name is
   declarations;
   definitions;
begin -- pack name
   package's executable statements
end pack_name;
```

Generic formal parameters

```
type parameter_name is private;
type parameter_name is limited private;
type parameter_name is range  <>;
type parameter_name is digits <>;
type parameter_name is delta  <>;
type parameter_name is <>;
with subprogram_parameter is <>;
```

Statements

Block statement

```
block_name:
begin
   statements;
   declare
      declarations;
   begin -- declaration scope
      statements;
   end -- declaration scope
   statements;
exception
   when exception_name => exception_handler;
   when others          => exception_handler;
end block;
```

if statement

```
if condition then    if condition then    if condition then
   statements;           statements;          statements;
end if;              else                 elsif condition then
                        statements;          statements;
                     end if;              end if;
```

case statement

```
case selector is
   when value            => statements;
   when value .. value   => statements;
   when value | value    => statements;
   when others           => statements;
end case;
```

Definite loop

```
for loop_index in index_type range low .. high loop
   statements;
end loop;

for loop_index in reverse index_type range low .. high loop
   statements;
end loop;
```

Indefinite iteration

```
loop              loop                while condition loop
   statements;       statements;         statements;
   exit;             exit when condition;  end loop;
   statements;       statements;
end loop;         end loop;
```

raise statement

```
raise exception_name;
```

Predeclared exceptions

Declared in STANDARD

CONSTRAINT ERROR: most commonly raised by an attempt to assign a value to an object outside its allowable range.

NUMERIC ERROR: uncommon error raised when accuracy cannot be guaranteed.

PROGRAM ERROR: uncommon error, most probably raised in simple programs by a function reaching its **end** without encountering a **return**.

STORAGE ERROR: uncommon error, most probably raised when dynamic memory cannot be allocated.

TASKING ERROR: uncommon error concerned with multi-tasking which is not considered in this book.

Declared in IO_EXCEPTIONS

DATA ERROR: raised during input operations if the input obtained cannot be interpreted to represent a value of the specified type.

DEVICE ERROR: raised when an operation cannot be completed due to a hardware fault.

END ERROR: raised by an attempt to read beyond the end of a file.

LAYOUT ERROR: raised when an attempt is made to extend a text file beyond limits implicit in declaration of COUNT type.

MODE ERROR: raised by an attempt to apply an operation to a file when the file is in an inappropriate mode.

NAME ERROR: raised when a CREATE or OPEN procedure call specifies an illegal external filename.

STATUS ERROR: raised by an attempt to apply an operation to an unopened file, or an attempt to open an already opened file.

USE ERROR: raised by an attempt to apply an inappropriate operation to a file (distinct from a MODE ERROR).

Common attributes

O'DIGITS   value of type universal_integer indicating the number of significant digits in the subtype's declaration.

O'FIRST   where O is a scalar type or subtype the value is of the same type as O and indicates the lower bound of the subtype's declaration.
where O is an array type, subtype or object; the value is of the same type as the array's index type and indicates the lower bound of the index.

O'FIRST(N)   where O is a multi-dimensional array type, subtype or object; the value is equivalent to O'FIRST for the dimension indicated by N.

O'FORE   value of type universal_integer indicating the number of digits in the integer part of the decimal representation of any value of the type.

O'IMAGE(o)   where O is a discrete type or subtype, the value is of type STRING and contains the character representation of the value o.

O'LAST   where O is a scalar type or subtype, the value is of the same type as O and indicates the upper bound of the subtype's declaration.
where O is an array type, subtype or object; the value is of the same type as the array's index type and indicates the upper bound of the index.

O'LAST(N)   where O is a multiple dimension array type, subtype or object; the value is equivalent to O'LAST for the dimension indicated by N.

O'LENGTH   where O is an array type, subtype or object; the value is of type universal_integer and indicates the number of elements in the array.

O'LENGTH(N)   where O is a multi-dimensional array type, subtype or object; the value is equivalent to O'LENGTH for the dimension indicated by N.

O'POS(o)   where O is a discrete type or subtype, the value is of type universal_integer and indicates the position of o in the base type's declaration.

O'PRED(o)   where O is a discrete type or subtype, the value is of the base type and has the value of the predecessor of o in the base type's declaration. A CONSTRAINT_ERROR will be raised if o has the value of the base type's FIRST value.

O'RANGE   where O is an array type, subtype or object; the value is the index range of the array (effectively O'FIRST .. O'LAST).

O'RANGE(N)   where O is a multi-dimensional array type, subtype or object; the value is equivalent to O'RANGE for the dimension indicated by N.

O'SUCC(o)   where O is a discrete type or subtype, the value is of the base type and has the value of the successor of o in the base type's declaration. A CONSTRAINT_ERROR will be raised if o has the value of the base type's LAST value.

O'VAL(o)   where O is a discrete type or subtype, the value returned is of the base type of O, o can be of any integer type. The value returned is the value indexed by o in the base type's declaration. A CONSTRAINT_ERROR will be raised if the value of o is outside the appropriate bounds.

O'VALUE(o)   where O is a discrete type or subtype and o is a STRING, the value returned is of O's base type and has a value indicated by the sequence of characters in the string. A CONSTRAINT_ERROR will be raised if the IMAGE of the string does not indicate an appropriate value.

Appendix D

ASCII chart

32 \<space\>	33 !	34 "	35 #
36 $	37 %	38 &	39 '
40 (	41)	42 *	43 +
44 ,	45 -	46 .	47 /
48 0	49 1	50 2	51 3
52 4	53 5	54 6	55 7
56 8	57 9	58 :	59 ;
60 \<	61 =	62 \>	63 ?
64 @	65 A	66 B	67 C
68 D	69 E	70 F	71 G
72 H	73 I	74 J	75 K
76 L	77 M	78 N	79 O
80 P	81 Q	82 R	83 S
84 T	85 U	86 V	87 W
88 X	89 Y	90 Z	91 [
92 \	93]	94 ^	95 _
96 `	97 a	98 b	99 c
100 d	101 e	102 f	103 g
104 h	105 i	106 j	107 k
108 l	109 m	110 n	111 o
112 p	113 q	114 r	115 s
116 t	117 u	118 v	119 w
120 x	121 y	122 z	123 {
124 |	125 }	126 ~	

Index

0854

F